TURNER PUBLISHING COMPANY
412 Broadway • P.O. Box 3101
Paducah, Kentucky 42002-3101
(502) 443-0121

Copyright © 1998 Col. Edward T. Imparato
Publishing Rights: Turner Publishing Company

This book or any part thereof may not be reproduced without the written consent of the author and publisher.

Turner Publishing Company Staff:
Editor: Herbert C. Banks II
Designer: Shelley R. Davidson

Library of Congress Catalog Card No.
98-60808
ISBN 978-1-63026-949-4

Additional copies may be purchased directly from the publisher. Limited Edition.

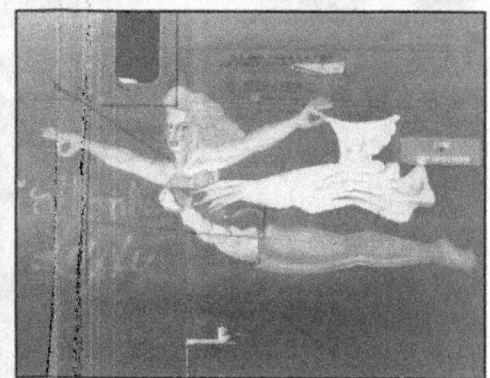

Table of Contents

	Foreword	4
	Preface	7
	Acknowledgement	9
	Introduction	10
	In the Beginning	14
Chapter I:	Overview of the Troop Carrier War 1941 - 1942	15
Chapter II:	1942 - 1943	45
Chapter III:	1943	58
Chapter IV:	1944 - 1945	84
Chapter V:	1945	100
Chapter VI:	Final Phase	122
Appendix 'A':	Charter Roster - 374th Troop Carrier Group	123
Appendix 'B':	Commendation - 13 January 1943	128
Appendix 'C':	Prentiss Letter - 24 September 1943	129
Appendix 'D':	6th Troop Carrier	130
Appendix 'E':	21st Troop Carrier	131
Appendix 'F':	22d Troop Carrier	132
Appendix 'G':	33d Troop Carrier	133
Appendix 'H':	374th Troop Carrier Group	134
Appendix 'I':	54th Troop Carrier Wing	135
Appendix 'J':	Fifth Air Force	136
Appendix 'K':	Battles and Campaigns	137
Appendix 'L':	Operations	138
Appendix 'M':	Cartoon	139
Appendix 'N':	Aircraft Losses	140
Appendix 'O':	Photos of Awards	148
Appendix 'P':	"Distinguished Unit Badge" Article	152
Appendix 'Q':	Awards and Decorations	153
Appendix 'R':	Enlisted Men, Warrant Officers and Flight Officers Receiving Direct Commissions	165
Appendix 'S':	Return of Personnel to the United States	166
Appendix 'T':	Personnel Transferred to 54th Troop Carrier Wing	180
Appendix 'U':	Officer Staffing	181
Appendix 'V':	"WW II plane found in New Guinea" Article	185
Appendix 'W':	Unit Citation - 2 August 1945	186
Appendix 'X':	Battle Participation Credit - Luzon Campaign	187
Appendix 'Y':	Battle Participation Credit - Bismarck Archipelago Campaign	188
Appendix 'Z':	Deceased, Missing In Action and Missing Personnel	189
Appendix 'AA':	"Whole Divisions Moved by Air In Rout of Japs" Article	191
Appendix 'BB':	"G.I. Diary"	192
Appendix 'CC':	"Life In Nadzab"	195
Appendix 'DD':	"Skytrains"	196
Appendix 'EE':	Commendation - 18 February 1944	197
Appendix 'FF':	Synopsis "Into Darkness: A Pilot's Journey Through Headhunter Territory"	198
Appendix 'GG':	Synopsis "Rescue From Shangri-La"	199
Appendix 'HH':	Synopsis "MacArthur - Melbourne To Tokyo"	201
Appendix "II":	Final Roster	202

FOREWORD

To the best of our present knowledge, the concept of airborne operations in wartime began during WWI when then senior officer of the American wartime air service, General Billy Mitchell, suggested to General Pershing that his heavy bombers be used to drop supplies and paratroopers to the advancing Allied Armies and even dropping paratroopers behind enemy lines.

General Pershing, at that time, had not yet accepted airplanes and air warfare as a viable or useful adjunct to the Army and Navy operations. Mitchell's suggestions were summarily dismissed initially by General Pershing. This was the spring of 1918.

The French had experimented some with dropping supplies and even suggested using two-man paratroop teams behind German lines to cut critical German communication lines. In due course Pershing relented and asked Mitchell to develop a plan for the use of airborne supplies and paratroopers on the western front during the planned spring offensive of 1919. (The war ended before the plan could be tested.) General Mitchell assigned the task of developing the plans to his operations officer Maj. Lewis H. Brereton. The same Lewis H. Brereton who as a Major General commanded MacArthur's air arm in the Philippines in the early phase of the WWII Japanese attack on the Philippines.

The early concept envisioned by Billy Mitchell of vertical envelopment of enemy forces gave the military forces a new dimension. The full potential of this new concept was not realized at the time, mainly because it was not tested in war. This new concept, as with many other tactical and strategic possibilities that were developing from experiences in WWI, lay fallow after the end of WWI.

Germany, the defeated enemy of the allied powers and undoubtedly the most aggressive and intelligent military strategists in the world, were stripped of the ability to develop anything militarily by the terms of the armistice after their defeat by the Allied Armies.

In all allied countries and especially in the United States, military budgets were stripped to the bone because the nations of the world and its people felt in their hearts that we had just fought the war to end all wars. There was little development in military technology anywhere. Military minds were inhibited by slim budgets and lack of support on the part of powerful elements in the civilian economy, religious and cultural groups and liberal forces looking for ways to make life more comfortable, more interesting, more joyous for all. There was little resources left for the slimmed down military establishment.

Mitchell in his constant striving for achieving acceptance of the Air Force as a legitimate, viable and necessary arm of U.S. military forces, acquired more enemies than friends when he pressed his airborne plans with too much vigor and persistence in the face of an Army and Navy which remained unconvinced of the vertical envelopment theory, and reduced budgets so restricted them that they could not fully carry out their own maintenance and development of new programs.

Mitchell put to rest for all time the real value of the Air Force in any future war by his miraculous, magnificent and successful demonstration by aerial bombing of naval vessels.

In 1920 Mitchell felt ships at sea could be destroyed by aerial bombardment. So sure of his ability to destroy any vessel at sea from the air that he announced to Congress that the Air Corp "could destroy, put out of commission, sink any battleship in existence, or any that could be built." This declaration resulted in an interesting controversy between the Army Air Corp and the Navy. After this statement by Mitchell, the Secretary of the Navy became so incensed that he announced these things could not be done and that he was willing to stand on the bridge of any ship while the Air Corp bombed it.

Congress was impressed by Mitchell's prediction and with initiatives introduced in Congress by Senator New and Mr. Anthony of the House of Representatives, Congress passed a resolution authorizing the President of the United States to designate warships to be used as targets for the experiments.

The German prizes of war were about to be turned over to the United States, under treaty arrangement, to be destroyed. What an ideal situation for the demonstration and tests. The vessels had to be destroyed under armistice terms to prevent any of the German vessels from augmenting the allied navies and at the same time the allied powers could learn all the lessons possible from the tests and comply with the treaty terms at the same time.

Forced to action by the joint resolution of Congress, the Navy Department drew up plans to provide submarines, destroyers, a cruiser, the Frankfort and the German dreadnaught, the battleship Ostfriesland. This battleship was reputed to be the best battleship in the world. Designed under special orders from German Admiral Von Terpitz, the underwater construction was considered the best known and is still the general pattern today for battleship substructures.

Three possible sites for the ship stations were selected and it was necessary to select a site that provided a depth of at least one hundred fathoms. The sites that provided the required depth were Cape Cod where the one-hundred fathom curve began at 10 miles from shore, the Cape Hatteras site one-hundred fathom curve was at 20 miles off shore and the deep fathom curve off Chesapeake Bay was at 75 miles off shore.

The naval officers were confident that the Air Force would fail and their air attacks would prove ineffective. At the same time it was the desire of the Navy to demonstrate the expected failure to Congress. On this assumption the Navy selected the Chesapeake location for the test. The proximity of the Chesapeake location to Washington, D.C., they reasoned, would attract many Congressmen to view the tests.

The 100 fathom depth was necessary to insure the complete sinking of the vessels in deep water as stipulated in the international agreement and to insure the vessels did not become hazards to sea navigation.

The Chesapeake site selected by the Navy was not to the Air Force liking because of the distance the airplanes had to fly to the site over water, bomb their targets in a number of passes and then return to their staging air field at Langley Field.

The Air Force accepted the Navy's conditions on the strength they forced the tests in the first place and therefore accepted the conditions as they were offered. Mitchell felt the conditions were about as hard as could be drawn for what was in fact a very difficult experiment.

Bombers and expert crews were flown into Langley from all parts of the U.S. In all, thirty bombers assembled at Langley and were assigned to units for each mission.

Three heavy bombers - one Handley-Page and two Caponis - came from Texas. Martin bombers came from the Martin aircraft facility at Cleveland, Ohio. The assembled aircraft were assigned to a provisional organization the "First Provisional Air Brigade." This unit contained all the elements necessary for the operation of a large Air Force. There was pursuit aviation to protect the bombers, light bombers consisting of DeHaviland airplanes were designed to attack torpedo craft, transports, and light vessels, in case anti-aircraft artillery from the big ships caused any serious concern. The heavy bombers, the Martins, had a cruising range of 550 miles and carried 2 to 3 thousand pounds of bombs.

While awaiting the arrival of the warships the Air Brigade conducted training exercises over a whole series of possible ship maneuvers and alignments to try to insure their capability under any number of difficult situations. Test runs were made on targets towed by tugs just a few miles off shore. The tow-lines were 1000 feet long. Using sand bags as bombs the crews became so accurate in bomb drops that the tugs shortened their tow lines on the targets to 300 feet. On ship wrecks offshore live bombs were used and again the airplane crew marksmanship proved phenomenally accurate. Confidence grew and soon Mitchell pronounced the Air Force ready for the demonstration.

The risks involved were great not only for General Mitchell but for the Air Force as a whole. Success, of course, would advance the time table for progress in development of airborne tactics and techniques for air war operations. It would also allow for the development of new weapons of destruction, larger and more destructive bombs, time release explosives for altitude explosion and underwater explosives, dive bombing and its accuracy and over the shoulder bombing which incidentally was developed under General Curtis LaMay during World War II. The art of war is not an art by a linear process of development based on the degree of input. In other words, the more effort of input of brains, money and need the greater the success in development. In developing an idea such as that expounded on by Mitchell on vertical envelopment the more effort applied can produce untold new results and better results exponentially.

General Mitchell continued his testing and training until the big ships arrived at the designated sites. In establishing his aerial armada at Langley Field, Mitchell assembled all the greatest pilots in the Air Forces available to him. All the pilots had three to five years experience as pilots and had considerable training as bombardiers, pilots and aerial gunners. The principal aircraft to be used as bombers was the Martin, the latest aircraft developed by the Air Force and just coming off the production line at the Martin aircraft plant at Cleveland. The Martin's range and bomb carrying capacity was just what the Air Force needed at this time. The Martin's range was 550 miles and a bomb carrying capacity of one 3000-pound bomb or three 1000-pound bombs. After familiarization flights and many test runs and bombing exercises the pilots felt they had the aircraft that would do the job at the demonstrations.

Finally everything was in readiness. The target warships were in place and the Air Force was alerted to stand by for the first attack. The Air Force now had the opportunity to prove its claims to being able to destroy from the air any sea-going vessel of any configuration including the latest type battleships. If these demonstrations were successful it would mean eventually that aircraft would be able to control all traffic during war - on the land and on the sea and in the air. Army and Navy tactics would have to be modified and adjusted to the new threat from the air and new more advanced tactics would have to be developed to avoid the devastation that aerial assault could cause. The whole structure of war would have to be rethought. Never again would trench warfare be a part of the ground forces military tactics but "mobility" would be a new word in all military plans. Battle fields would no longer be measured in feet, yards, miles, cities or sections of an enemy country but the whole of an enemy country would become the battlefield. Distances and space measured only by the range of bombers and fighters to escort them.

The Atlantic fleet consisting of eight battleships, several cruisers, many destroyers and auxiliary vessels, hospital ships and tenders moved into Chesapeake Bay to observe the bombing tests. Many considered the trials to be useless. In the Navy view it was impossible to sink or seriously injure a battleship. The men of the First Provisional Air Brigade, on the other hand, felt success would vindicate them in their quest for recognition.

The first attack was made by the Naval Air Service on a submarine by three flying boats, flying in a V formation. Each airplane carried three 180-pound bombs. The center of impact of the volley struck the submarine squarely in the center and it split in two and sank.

A few days later the Army Air Service was given as a target the "ex German torpedo Destroyer G-102." This attack was made by an assortment of aircraft types simulating an actual enemy attack at sea. Pursuit aircraft, DH light bombers, and Martin heavy bombers were used for the attack on the G-102 to demonstrate to the observers the many different ways an enemy ship could be attacked. The attacking force did such a remarkable job that after the Martin bombers dropped their load of 180-pound bombs on the destroyer it broke in two and sank.

The third exercise of the test was designed to prove the ability of aerial bombs to damage a cruiser heavily protected with side-armor, deck-armor, watertight compartments and bulkheads. The cruiser Frankfurt, with every perfection of a modern vessel of that class and a beautiful ship, was selected for this test. This test was intended to prove the effectiveness of varying size bombs beginning the exercise with the smaller 100-pound bombs and with each phase increasing the bomb size to the 300 pounder. However, the test was stopped early to inspect the damage from the lighter bombs which were not intended to sink the vessel. After the inspection the signal was given to continue to bombing with 600-pound bombs. Initially it was not intended to sink the Frankfurt but the stream of bombers with the 600-pound bombs could not be stopped and the cruiser, mortally damaged, turned over on its side and sank.

Finally the bombing demonstration of the Ostfriesland was set to begin. This was the real test. Failure here would minimize the early successes and set back aerial bombing of sea craft for a long time. The same system of bombing was to be used on this test beginning with the lighter 100-pound bombs then hold for checking and assessing damage then proceeding with heavier bombs. Air Force expectations were high. "We felt with confidence," Mitchell said, "our 1000-pound bombs would kill the Ostfriesland." The demonstration was stopped after the 1000-pound bombs had been dropped due to weather. The battleship was severely damaged, listing and taking on water at the conclusion of the day's activity.

On the following day, each Martin bomber was equipped with 2000-pound bombs. During the night the Ostfriesland was down some by the stern, drawing about forty feet of water. She had sunk considerably as a result of the prior day's attack. Captain Lawson lead the attack with seven airplanes flying in a line of attack with their 2000-pound bombs. All bombs hit the target with direct hits or close enough to the sides of the battleship to cause serious damage. In a minute the Ostfriesland was on its side, in two minutes she was sliding down by the stern and turning over, in three minutes she was bottoms up, in a few minutes more she was touching bottom with only the stern showing above the water in her perpendicular position.

Now, what effect did the long dissertation about bombers and battleships have on the 374th Troop Carrier Group in WWII? Well! Really many lessons were learned by these tests and demonstrations. It certainly proved that even with opposition and lack of funds some progress can be made by having a good strategy, vision, and strong determination. It also focused on the difficulty in the military forces structure to introduce, sell and successfully prove a new theory or technology. The diverse forces at work within the military and political structure really inhibits progress, stifles initiative and imagination and overall slows the desired aim of all military leaders to make the services better, more efficient, more powerful and permit a more effective and cost conscious allocation of tax dollars for the benefit of the country in time of peace.

The Mitchell era showed the world the great versatility of air power. Only lack of funds and internal bickering within the services can slow down progress. However, this is not the case in a war setting. At war a commander does what he can do or must do to win an advantage over the enemy. He is obligated to use all his initiative, his imagination and all the tools at his disposal to get the job done. And it was this great wide open challenge that made the 374th T.C.G. the most highly praised, the most highly decorated and certainly one of the most important contributors to MacArthur's charge to Tokyo.

Billy Mitchell was instrumental in building mightily the image of the Air Force and the variety of types of missions the Air Force was capable of performing in time of war. Almost nothing, however, was accomplished in the specialty of air transport. From the time of the dramatic bombing demonstration conducted in the early 1920's until early in 1940 nothing of significance occurred in the field of air transport capability. That is, nothing happened until 1939 when Germany, at war with Greece, used paratroopers to capture the island of Crete. The U.S. Army high command immediately saw the value of large scale paratroop operations and set up a training school for paratroopers at Lawson Field, Ft. Benning, Georgia, under command of Col. Bill Lee. The Army Air Corp assigned support responsibility to the 3rd Transport Squadron from Duncan Field, San Antonio, Texas.

There were no essential preliminary instructions issued to the 3rd Transport Squadron except to make contact with Col. Lee at Ft. Benning and assist the 501st Parachute Battalion in developing plans and procedures for the best use of aircraft in paratroop and supply and equipment drop from aircraft in flight and to provide for safe exit procedure from the aircraft of individual and in a stream of paratroopers leaving the aircraft.

Much was learned from the German experience in Crete, and it was now our job to learn by analyzing the German operation and try to find a way to do it better.

The new association of airborne forces and the great mobility of the airplane provided a wide ranging vision of new and unusual strategic concepts involving great mobility of forces over a wide ranging area of conflict with the technological advances in communication and vertical envelopment of paratroopers and their means of survival behind enemy lines. If one new military tactic had to be singled out as the newest and best use of available resources in WWII, it would have to be this concept of mobility and stealth provided by the Air Force/Army Airborne marriage and the use of vertical envelopment. This technology was extensively used in the Pacific War. More detailed explanations of vertical envelopment will be offered later in the text when individual squadron operations and the feats of daring they performed are explained.

Needless to say it was this vertical envelopment tactic in close support of MacArthur's Armies as they advanced steadily on the march to Tokyo, that enabled MacArthur to employ a variety of airborne principals and maneuvers, especially the by-pass technique he used to perfection. The close support of his advancing armies provided by all the Troop Carrier Groups under his command enabled him to advance more rapidly with never a setback because he could always count on troop carriers to provide his ground forces with continuous mobility, adequate supplies of ammunition, supplies, rotational personnel, evacuation of ill and wounded, food and fuel. In a sense it was not necessary to halt an advance to replace battle weary troops. MacArthur's general movement forward simply used another battalion, regiment, division or army to maintain momentum, leaving the latest engagement to work itself out while he bypassed the conflict cutting off all supply support to the Japanese where their only choice was surrender or go bush and starve to death. The structure of the terrain, the high impenetrable mountains and harsh jungle on the left and the sea on the right, enabled MacArthur to limit the mobility of the Japanese while his own mobility improved.

A solid mesh of geography, MacArthur's brilliant strategy, air superiority, air bombardment successes on key targets, and strong naval support on MacArthur's right flank and the unbelievable dedicated, consistent and reliable troop carrier support, gave MacArthur the magic formula under his leadership to advance over 6500 miles of territory with less loss of life than in any war in history.

Prior to WWII, military transport operations were limited to carrying personnel and supplies to locations where they were needed. With the onset of WWII in the Pacific Theater, the 374th with its four squadrons was called upon to respond to some very unusual operations never before attempted by an Air Force unit. Here are some of the unusual missions and accompanying hazards the 374th encountered. Parachute drops of both paratroopers and their supplies, glider towed support of paratroop operations, precision airborne drops of supplies, ammunition and food without parachutes (using carefully protected cases for sensitive items such as eggs) from very low altitudes of 50 to 100 feet; cutting large items in two or more pieces so they could be loaded through a cargo door then reassembled after landing at a forward airdrome, air evacuation of ill and wounded soldiers and airmen, carrying mules and other animals over high altitude mountain ranges, dropping pathfinders behind Japanese lines; glider snatch operations from a 5500 foot plateau (never attempted before or since), carrying a C-47 wing under the belly of a C-47 because it was too large to get into the cabin of the airplane, carrying a complete radio station 1500 miles by cutting the tower into small enough pieces to fit into a C-47 then rewelded at destination, carrying PSP (pierced steel planking) to establish suitable air fields out of the jungle for sustained operations in support of group military operations. All these and more will be revealed and described as the story of the 374th unfolds.

The seeds that were sown at Chesapeake by Mitchell was the tree that most great leaders in WWII called the third military force - "the Air Force and vertical envelopment." MacArthur was generous in his praise of the Air Force's roll in the southwest Pacific which was his area of responsibility. He singled out the great work done by the bombers and fighters but reserved special praise for the troop carriers which made the tactical movements of bypass operations possible and extremely successful. Not to mention the great savings in time and equipment and supplies. But one of the greatest assets of his vertical envelopment strategy was in the savings of life. It was reported that MacArthur's personnel losses, injured, missing, killed and taken prisoner during his charge from Melbourne to Tokyo were less than the manpower losses on Okinawa alone.

PREFACE

This history of the 374th Troop Carrier Group written and is now published as a result of hundreds of requests from members of the group. Their feeling toward their World War II organization was one of loyalty, love, and a strong desire to have their accomplishments recorded for history and posterity. Most men and women who performed deeds of valor in war were not writers. It was necessary for others to record their great deeds in combat operations.

Most of the material in this book is supported by solid evidence of facts. The prime source of the raw material emanated from official documents, on-the-spot writing by individual officers, and men who had the ability to write short articles and essays of events in which they were a part. Further, official orders and detail records at the squadron level provided precise times and places of events for accuracy of information. Occasional newspaper articles written by seasoned war correspondents provided background information and scenes and events by trained and qualified observers for national and international distribution.

Every effort was made to check and recheck information which was not officially documented by military authorities. The resources of many of the officers and men of the 374th still living were tapped to their limits. Literally hundreds of telephone calls were made to likely sources of information through contacts emanating from the numerous squadron, group and wing reunions held periodically since WWII.

The general quality of historical material being published today is suspect. Many writers who delve into the near and distant past try to find substance for their own writing from published articles, biographies and published history, are simply compounding the errors that creep into biographies and histories today. And then there are the glaring errors that some of the so-called historians today find it so convenient to rewrite history to satisfy their social and political agenda.

One of England's great writers of history, poetry and also an art critic wrote in his classic tome *"The Stones of Venice"* which was published in 1856, that all history written by so-call historians, biographers and general writing professionals should be scrutinized carefully to discover if the writer used basic raw material from the time of the actual events being written about. In his book he writes: "The only history worth reading is that written at the time of which it treats, the history of what was done and seen, heard out of the mouths of the men who did and saw." This terse formulation of a truth by John Ruskin should alert all who read history, or who write it, to be careful of the honesty of all the source material and to be aware of individual bias everyone possesses from the people who are making the history and explaining it to journalists and other writers and the bias of the writers themselves in interpreting the facts as he hears them from the root sources. Ruskin was a true classicist as all his beautiful writing will attest.

The early Greek and Roman historians were classicist in spirit, in mind and in body. They sought to adhere to the Greek and Roman principals of classicism. Their writing reflects the rigid rules of classicism which are represented by their objectivity and their adherence to these principals, formality, balance, simplicity, dignity and restraint. Their adherence to these principals tended to help them avoid the bias or prejudice which somehow develops in all of us.

Being fully aware of all of the above, I do represent myself as a neoclassicist. I have tried to adhere to the classicist model of a good historian in the writing of this book. The time frame of the 374th history covers the period of over 50 years ago with occasional before and after facts and stories which have added depth and substance which may have contributed to an action which eventually occurred in the period December 7, 1941 to September 2, 1945.

The 6th Troop Carrier Squadron is a good example of this unusual possibility. The 6th was the only part of the 374th TCG which was already an active troop carrier squadron before December 7, 1941. The remaining three squadrons were activated after the beginning of WWII. The 33rd Squadron being activated in early 1942 in the United States, the 21st and 22nd Squadrons were activated in Australia in early 1942.

For the most part, the individuals who had a story to tell are identified and their stories essentially unedited are included in this volume to maintain as much of the flavor and aura of the times as possible.

This is part of our effort to comply with Ruskin's edict that the only true history is that which is written by the men and women who were there, saw and heard the words being spoken or actually recorded the words that made the history.

The crash of the Flying Dutchman into the mountains of New Guinea shortly after its arrival in our theater is a good example of this. Most of the crew survived the crash but died awaiting rescue. Two groups set out to find help and few survived. It was not until months later that New Guinea natives discovered the wreckage and guided search parties to the plane. The story of this great saga is beautifully described by Australian official and historian Robert Piper in his book *"The Hidden Chapters"*; untold stories of Australians at war in the Pacific. With Piper's permission we have included his complete chapter titled "Courage on an Aircraft Door" on this tragedy in this book.

Col. Edward T. Imparato, Commanding Officer.

Piper writes about this episode in New Guinea as follows: "Of all the stories of tragedy and survival in the Southwest Pacific during WWII, that of the C-47 transport named the "Flying Dutchman", serial number 41-18564, is one of the most remarkable. It was a story of courage and hopelessness and a reminder of how unforgiving the mountainous jungles of Papua New Guinea are."

The most dangerous enemy in the New Guinea campaigns of WWII was not the Japanese; it was the New Guinea jungle with its towering mountains, deep impenetrable jungle growth, earth that was mostly mud and swamp, the terrible heat in the day time and freezing cold in the mountains at night. The incessant rain in torrents and floods making water passage or crossing of rivers impossible. And then the diseases, the bugs, the mosquitoes, the gnats, the slithering animals, poison snakes of every description and the huge Monitor Lizards that could fell a man with one swipe of its tail.

The mountains of New Guinea crest up to 16,000 feet and flying in the afternoon when the rains came after the drifting lowering cumulus clouds cover the mountains the clouds suddenly covering even the lower barrier mountains to the high passes, their soft fleecy appearance disguising the fact that the clouds are mere cover for solid rock centers. This is the devils work. Nothing could be more beautiful than a rolling raising cumulus cloud. Most pilots "for the love of flying" would want to take a chance. Most of the troop carrier losses in New Guinea were not due to enemy action, but to the hard center candy clouds of mountainous New Guinea. If the crash didn't kill you, the jungle would.

An associate of mine, Colonel Robert Barr Smith, made a profound judgement in New Guinea. He said, "there is no good place to fight a war. But certainly two of the worse places on earth are the Burma Jungle and New Guinea. And New Guinea is at the top of the list." He got it right.

The color, aura, smells and sounds of our New Guinea adventure can be found scattered in the text. Look for the descriptive poetry of Sgt. Robert Patrick; the chronologies and site reports by Master Sgt. now Col. Glenn D. McMurray. Glenn's descriptive prose reflects the changing mood and landscape as the war progressed toward Japan.

Major J. H. Paul, an Air Force pilot of long flying experience, makes his appearance in this volume with a number of his inimitable poems about flying in New Guinea. Major Paul, a pilot we knew before WWII on the transport circuit in the U.S., would rather write poetry than fly, but no one could tell a pilot's story better.

Corporal Hal J. Roche's 1000 word article on our first look at the Philippines after its recapture by General Douglas MacArthur's forces, gives our 374th Group a new environment in which to operate; one free of the great hazzards of New Guinea and with a touch of civilization including attractive Philippine young women.

The final important mission was assigned to the 374th Troop Carrier Group when on the 20th of August, 1945, we were ordered to fly General MacArthur's negotiating team to Tokyo before the Japanese surrender, to test the Emperor's resolve to end the war. MacArthur told his staff, we later discovered, that this flight was one of the biggest gambles in history.

As 374th Group Commander I have written a book about MacArthur and this important flight. The book *"MacArthur - Melbourne to Tokyo"* was published by White Mane Publishing Co., Shippensburg, Pa., 1997.

George Wamsley, one of the commanders of our 33rd Transport Squadron, provides a sparkling rendition of his tongue-in-cheek description of his flight over the vast Pacific Ocean when his squadron was ordered to Australia in late 1942.

Pilots of the 374th Troop Carrier Group - Edward Imparato shaking hands with Major Langbartel, commanding officer of the 22nd Troop Carrier Squadron.

ACKNOWLEDGMENT

Any attempt to acknowledge all the individuals who made a significant contribution to the production of this work would require another book as an appendix. Because that is not possible I will, of necessity, confine my acknowledgment to those individuals with whom I have had personal contact by letter or telephone and those individuals whose written stories or comment are included in the book.

The assembly of all the material necessary to provide a complete story was truly a labor of love. When the word went out that a history of the 374th was in the works, calls and letters came pouring in from all over the U.S. The response was ignited by the word of mouth and notices recorded in the Air Force reunion circuit. As a result many stories and special events have now been reported that otherwise would not ever have seen the light of day and much vital history would have lain fallow for all time.

The 374th Troop Carrier Group, unique in its origin, development and maturity, provides an unusual longitudinal study of what can be accomplished when the need exists, the determination and the cause is right and just and the men and women are ready to accept the challenge. This was our point of origin. Never in my 25 years in close association with the Army and Air Force have I seen another unit fuse and bond together for the duration as well, as completely, as the 374th. From its inception in early 1942 the neucleous unit of the 21st grew rapidly and provided mother-like support to the forming 22nd Squadron. The two original squadrons fused in their unmatched assault for General MacArthur on the first offensive actions of WWII with the Kokoda and the Buna, Gona vertical envelopment strategy. It was not possible to find a line between the 21st and 22nd Squadrons. They bonded as one to accomplish the mission and this bonding continued in like fashion with the arrival of the 6th Troop Carrier Squadron in October 1942 and the 33rd Troop Carrier Squadron in November. The espirit of the five elements of the 374th firmed into a solid unit of cooperation and dedication to the goals established by MacArthur and General George C. Kenney, the Far East Air Force Commander. The total amalgamation of the 374th was the result of the terrible tradegies endured in the large loss of life during the Kokoda, Buna, Gona and Wau campaigns. The Nadzab campaign was the ultimate result of our prior experience with the earlier assaults when the total group effort resulted in new records for the movement of supplies, equipment, ammunition and personnel without loss of aircraft or personnel.

The measured flow of personnel rotating to the U.S. and the influx of new pilots and men to fill their shoes was easily accommodated as the new arrivals adapted to the seasoned noteworthy and oldest and most highly regarded Troop Carrier Group in the theater.

Certain individuals made body and soul efforts to see this project through and they deserve very special thanks and recognition. My typist Ellen Schaefer, whose special secretarial skills helped me through tangled dialogue and a maze of lists to be sure of maximum accuracy. My wife Jean, whose patience and willingness to read and reread some of my confusing and complicated prose. The council and reviews by James DeGarmo, a seasoned WWII veteran, FBI agent and college professor, my undying gratitude. Lastly the skilled writer JoAnn Warden, whose final polish of the manuscript made it so much more readable and understandable to the uninitiated in WWII prose, battles, airplanes and strategy. To George Wamsley, my former 33rd Squadron Commander who at age 81 is still the most active and effective source of material for this book. Finally Ned Farr, whose extensive knowledge of troop carrier aircraft and the technology of vertical envelopment kept me on line in writing about the technical aspects of troop carrier operations.

The individuals who made major contribution to this history in submitting material which is included in the book, or individuals who made a major effort to research and provide me with source material I could not otherwise have had, are included in the acknowledgment. Those singled out for recognition are as follows:

Lucas J. Ashcroft
David Aisenson, Radio Operator, 6th Squadron
Charles R. Baer
Mel Clack
John A. Crandell
James M. Coutts
Janice DeMeza
Philip M. Eckberg
W. J. C. Fahey
William Gerry
Ernest C. Ford
Roger J. Gerling
Jay Hackman, 22nd Squadron
Major Hackett, 22nd Squadron
William Horn, Silent Wings
Jean C. Imparato
Clarence A. Lakin
Bob Livingstone
Russell E. Means
Joe McIlvain
Bruce McLean
Glenn D. McMurray
Blesch Malmstone
Robert S. Monson
S.A.E. Ted Newton, Wing Commander, RAF
John E. Olson - Reporter
George M. Pearce, Jr.
Perry H. Penn
Robert and Misako Piper
William Samuels
Ellen and Dick Schaefer
Ralph R. Simons, Radio Operator, 22nd Squadron
David C. Vaughter
JoAnn G. Warden
Wilbur H. Weedin
Herman C. Wood - Secretary, Sgt. Pilot's Assn.
Keith P. Yeisley
Colonel Charles H. Young, Author "Into The Valley".

INTRODUCTION

HEADQUARTERS
374TH TROOP CARRIER GROUP

APO 713 Unit #1,
20 September 44.

SUBJECT: Letter of Welcome from the Commanding Officer.

TO: All Personnel of the 374th Troop Carrier Group.

You are now a member of the 374th Troop Carrier Group, the oldest Troop Carrier Group in this theater. I wish to take this opportunity to welcome you to our organization.

The 374th has a long record of achievement, one of which you can justly be proud. The Group will be equally proud of you as you do your part to maintain the high standards of efficiency and devotion to duty which are characteristic of this organization.

In order to fully appreciate the accomplishments of the 374th you need to know a little of its history. Following is a condensed version of the Group history which I believe will help you to understand why the 374th Troop Carrier Group is what it is today, the best Troop Carrier Group in the United States Army Air Forces.

Although the 374th Troop Carrier Group as such was not activated until 21 November, 1942, elements of what later became the 374th began operations in Australia early in January 1942. The forerunner of the 374th, designated as the Air Transport Command, was activated on 28 January 1942, at Amberley Field, Queensland, Australia. Upon activation, the organization had only 14 officers and 19 enlisted men. For more than two months after it was activated, the Air Transport Command had only eight enlisted personnel available for maintenance. Working on a 24 hour basis, however, each man putting in an average of 17 and 18 hours a day, all six available aircraft were kept flying.

During the latter part of January and the early part of February, 1942, equipment was flown to bases in Java by Air Transport Command aircraft. Late in February, when the Netherlands East Indies were falling before the onslaught of superior Japanese forces, Air Transport Command aircraft participated in the evacuation of military and civilian personnel. Between January and July, 1942, the Air Transport Command flew more than 5,000,000 miles rushing supplies to strategic points on the Southwest Pacific front.

The Air Transport Command, Archerfield, Brisbane, was redesignated the 21st Transport Squadron and assigned to Headquarters, Air Transport Command, Melbourne, Victoria, on 3 April, 1942. The same order activated the 22nd Transport Squadron and based them at Essendon Airdrome, Melbourne. The strength of the 21st and 22nd Squadrons was soon increased with the addition of veteran bombardment and pursuit pilots from the Philippine and Java Campaigns and a cadre of enlisted men from the United States.

On 22 May 1942, the 21st Transport Squadron made its first operational flight in New Guinea, carrying troops and supplies to Wau and Bulolo, Allied mountain airdromes, previously used only for very light aircraft. The 21st and 22nd Squadrons continued to operate several planes between Port Moresby and Wau at intervals despite intense Japanese activity and fighter cover consisting of only five or six P-39's. When the Japanese landed troops at Buna in July, 21st Squadron planes landed Australian reinforcements and supplies at Kokoda. During the fighting for that mountain airdrome the planes often circled the field without knowing whether or not it was in friendly or enemy hands. In August 1942, during the Australian retreat which ended in an Allied offensive in Iorabaiwa Ridge, 30 air miles from Port Moresby, 21st and 22nd Squadron planes dropped tons of supplies and equipment to the Australian troops. Without these supplies the Jap offensive might not have been stopped.

On 26 July 1942, the 21st and 22nd Transport Squadrons were redesignated the 21st and 22nd Troop Carrier Squadrons. The first large troop movement by these Squadrons was started in September, 1942, when three regiments of the Buna-busting 32nd (U.S.) Division were flown, with all of their equipment, from Brisbane and Townsville on the Australian mainland to New Guinea.

During the middle of October 1942, a very concentrated movement was made from Milne Bay and Port Moresby for the final Allied drive on Buna. The 6th Squadron arrived during the movement, three of its ships making trips the day after its arrival. During the Buna Campaign a continual flow of men and supplies was maintained by Group aircraft. The 33rd Squadron arrived in November of 1942 and just in time for the final Allied assault on Buna. Fighter cover was very slight during the Buna Campaign and several of our transports were shot down by Japanese aircraft.

On the 12th of November, 1942, the 374th Troop Carrier Group was activated with Lieutenant Colonel Erickson S. Nichols as its Commanding Officer. The 6th, 21st, 22nd, and 33rd Squadrons were assigned to the newly formed Group.

By the end of February 1943, the Group was operating in its entirety from Port Moresby under the immediate jurisdiction of the Advance Echelon, Fifth Air Force. Early days in New Guinea were attended by many discomforts. From November 1942, to the middle of February 1943, night raids by enemy bombers were all too frequent. It was not until the middle of March 1943 that the customary diet of bully beef was varied with an occasional meal of fresh meat.

When the air strip at Wau was threatened by a new Japanese offensive late in January 1943, aircraft of the 374th flew in men and supplies which stopped the Japs just short of their goal. Several planes received bullet holes when they landed as fighting was in progress on the field.

The task of the 374th after the middle of February 1943, was to move personnel and supplies in three principle directions: first, to Dobodura where a large base was being constructed; second, to Wau and Bulolo where Allied Forces advancing on Lae and Salamaua had their rear bases; and third, to the patrols skirting Lae and Salamaua by dropping supplied.

During the Lae Campaign which started in September of 1943, aircraft of the 374th played a leading part. In fact flights of our C-47s were the first planes to land at Nadzab and Lae Airdromes. On 1 October 1943 the Group was given respite from combat flying and was transferred back to the mainland. The 21st Squadron was assigned to Brisbane and the 6th, 22nd and 33rd Squadrons and Group Headquarters were assigned to Townsville. The movement was entirely by air and was completed by 7 October 1943. There, the Group was placed under the operational control of the Directorate of Air Transport, Allied Air Forces.

Immediately upon its arrival on the mainland of Australia, the Group settled down to the accomplishment of its mission of maintaining an uninterrupted flow of men, supplies, and equipment to units in Australia and in the New Guinea area.

In April of 1944 the 33rd Squadron moved back to Port Moresby after a six months stay at Townsville. The 33rd still continued under the operational control of D.A.T. Late in August 1944, the 6th Squadron, 21st Squadron, and Group Headquarters moved to Nadzab and were placed under operational control of the 54th Troop Carrier Wing. At the same time the 22nd Squadron moved to Finschhafen where the squadron operated under the control of D.A.T.

During its long service in the Southwest Pacific the 374th Troop Carrier Group has received two Presidential Citations. Personnel of the Group have received numerous awards such as the Distinguished Flying Cross with Oak Leaf Clusters, Air Medal with Oak Leaf Clusters, the Silver Star, the Legion of Merit, the Soldier's Medal, and the Purple heart.

/s/ Edward T. Imparato
EDWARD T. IMPARATO,
Lt. Col., Air Corps,
Commanding.

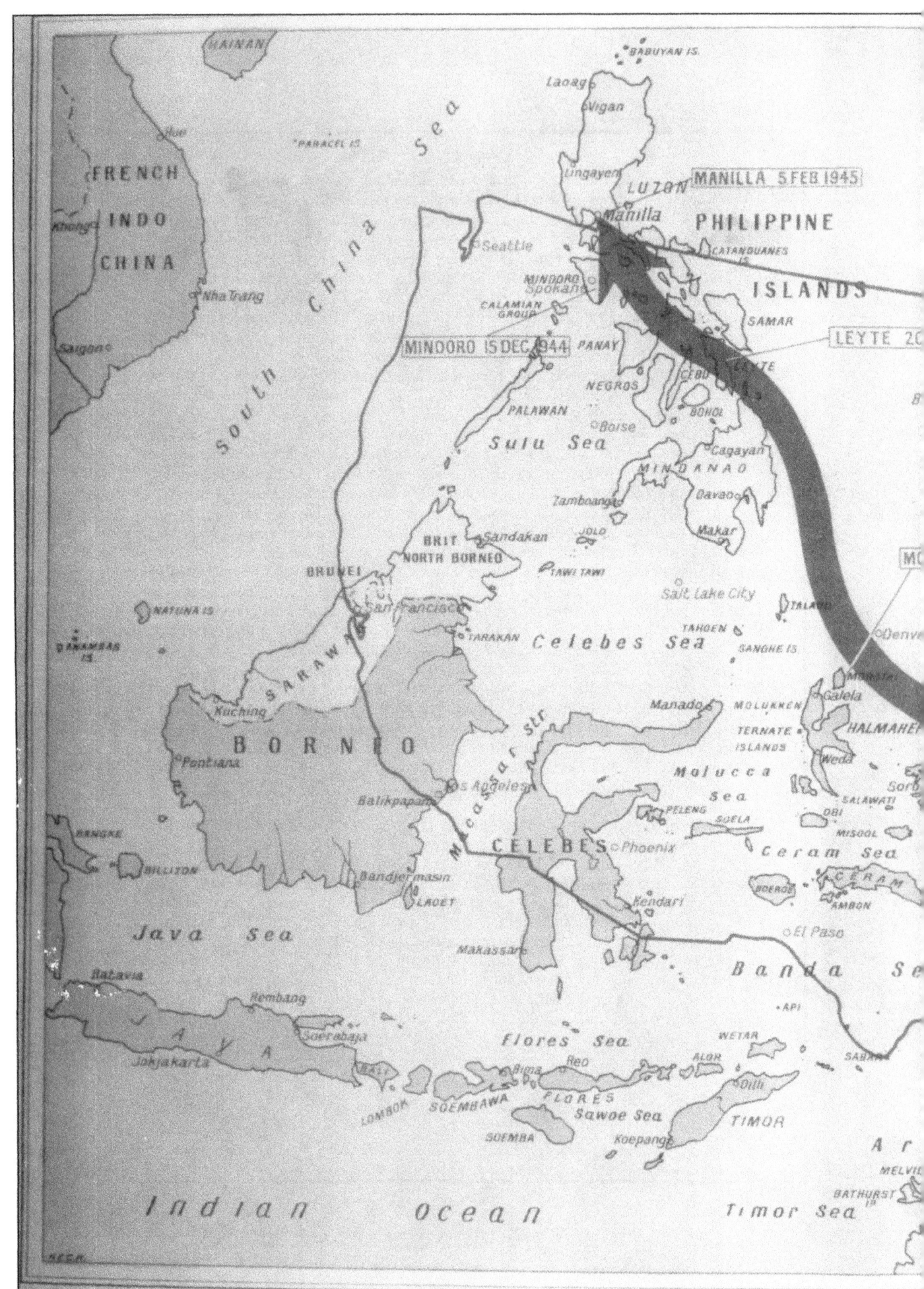

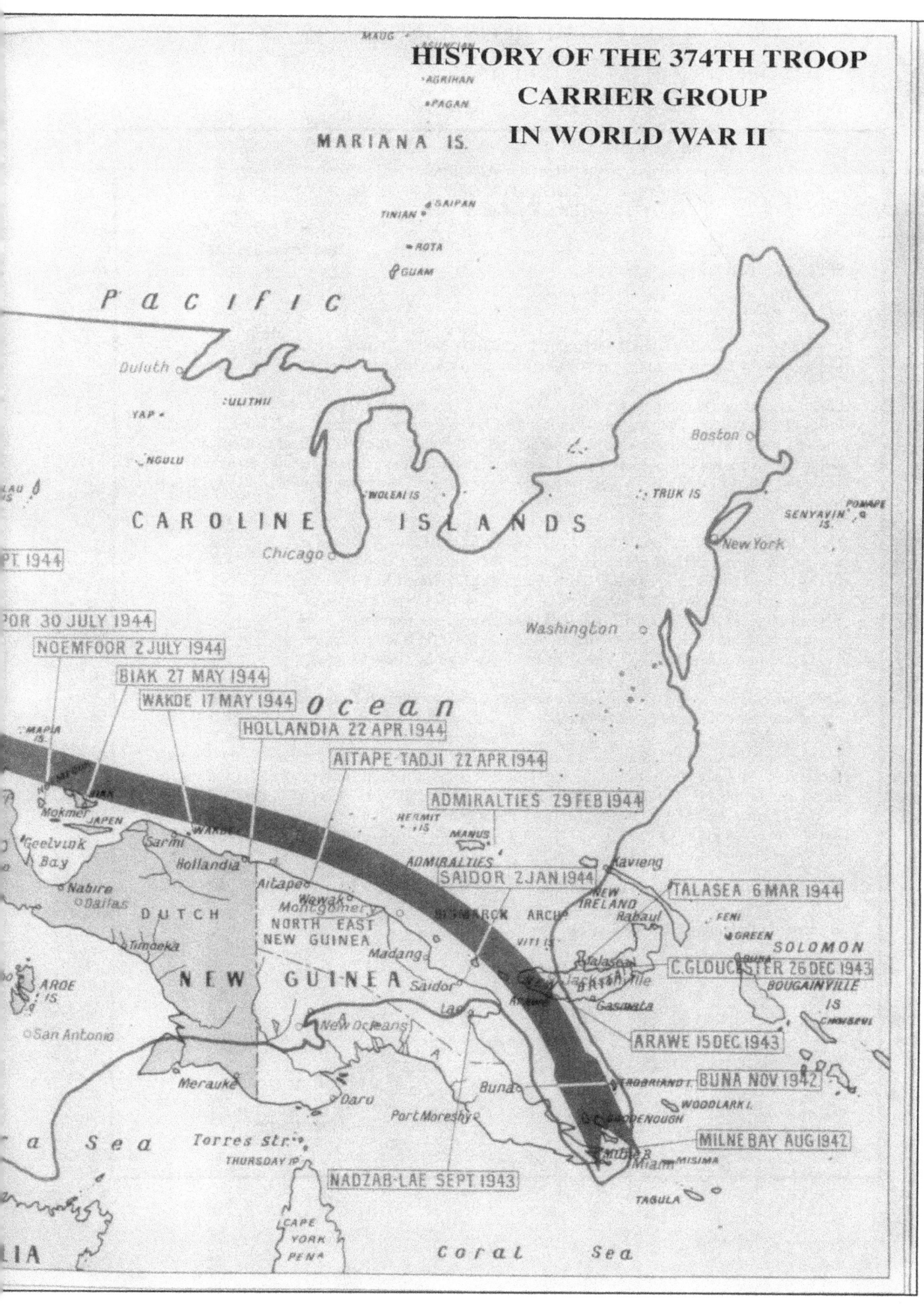

IN THE BEGINNING

HEADQUARTERS
OGDEN AIR DEPOT
Hill Field, Ogden, Utah

December 18, 1941.

SPECIAL ORDERS)
:
NO.   125)

1. Under the provisions of AR 95-70, Private LEROY M. NORGAN, 6563656, 8TH Transport Squadron, Air Corps, is rated Air Mechanic, First Class.

Pursuant to authority contained in Radio, W.D., dated December 17, 1941 and ASC-T-253, ASC, Wright Field, Dayton, Ohio, dated December 18,1941, the following officers and enlisted men are relieved from their presentassignment and duty at Hill Field, Ogden, Utah, and will proceed, by rail,from this station to Hamilton Field, California, reporting thereat, not laterthan December 21, 1941, to Lieut. Colonel J. B. Jordan, Air Corps LiaisonOfficer, San Francisco Port of Embarkation for instructions as to furthermode of travel to final destination:

First Lieutenant FRED M. ADAMS, 0-361754, Air Corps, Pilot
Second Lieutenant CHARLES R. BAER, 0-403051, Air Corps, Copilot
PFC AM 1cl LEROY M. NORGAN, 6563656, 8th T.S., Crew Chief
First Lieutenant EDWARD T. IMPARATO, 0-376554, Air Corps, Pilot
Second Lieut. ROBERT J. GERLING, 0-429400, Air Corps, Copilot
Corporal AM 2nd Cl. RAMON C. SELL, 6936286, 8th T.S., Radio Operator
PFC Spec 5th Cl. EARL T. WHITMORE, 6936286, 8th T.S., Crew Chief

The Quartermaster Corps will furnish the necessary transportation for enlisted men. Enlisted men are transferred w/o loss of grade or rating.

It being impracticable for the government to furnish cooking facilities for rations, the Finance Department will pay in advance to the above-named enlisted men the monetary travel allowances prescribed in Table II, AR 35-4520, as amended by Circular 50, W.D., March 26, 1941, at the rate of Three Dollars ($3.00) per day for four (4) men for one (1) day for rations. Procurement authority for enlisted men FD 1401 P 3-06 A 0410-2 and QM 1600 P 61-07 A 0525-2 and for officers FD 1402 P 1-06 and P 15-06 A 0410-2.

The travel directed is necessary in the military service.

By order of Colonel BERMAN:

                    s/ ARTHUR E HOLT
                    t/ ARTHUR E. HOLT,
                        1st Lieut., A.C.,
OFFICIAL: Adjutant.
    s/ ARTHUR E. HOLT   A TRUE COPY:
    t/ ARTHUR E. HOLT,   s/ James W. Ingram
        1st Lt, A.C.,   t/ JAMES W. INGRAM,
        Adjutant.   1st Lt, AC, Adj,
                                           21st Troop Carrier Sq.

CHAPTER I

OVERVIEW OF TROOP CARRIERS WAR

1941 - 1942

The destiny of eight men took a dramatic turn in mid December, 1941. Eleven days after war was declared against Japan on December 7, 1941, the eight men, four officers and four enlisted men of the U.S. Army Air Force out of Hill Field, Ogden, Utah, stood on the railroad platform at Ogden on December 18, 1941, for a distant and yet secret destination. Orders indicated the Far East - specific location secret. Their instructions - to serve as a highly trained and experienced nucleus to form a full service air transport operation at destination. The men, 1st Lt. Fred M. Adams, pilot; 2nd Lt. Charles R. Baer, co-pilot; 1st Lt. Edward T. Imparato, pilot; 2nd Lt. Robert J. Gerling, co-pilot; Pvt. 1st Class Clarence G. Higgins, radio operator; Pvt. 1st Class Leroy M. Norgan, crew chief; Corporal 2nd Class Ramon C. Sell, radio operator; and Pvt. 1st Class Spec. 5th Class, crew chief.

The immediate destination was San Francisco. The instructions: report to Lt. Colonel J. B. Jordan, Air Corp Liaison Officer, San Francisco Port of Embarkation.

First indications were that we would be assigned two B-17s with full crews to fly to Hawaii and await further instructions. These indications were soon changed to board the USS President Coolidge as soon as it was loaded and depart San Francisco. Incidentally this ship, the USS President Coolidge, was the same ship that carried MacArthur to the Philippines in 1937. Further orders would be issued after departure from the port of San Francisco.

The team of eight boarded the Coolidge on January 12, 1942, for an unknown destination. The Coolidge was filled to the gunwale with men, material, supplies, food, weapons, a few P-40 fighters and aircraft parts for the fighters. There was engineering equipment and supplies for building bridges, airfields and revetments and for small buildings and enough canvas to shelter an army. The holds were filled to capacity and sealed to present discovery of items classified secret and top-secret and the officers and crew of the Coolidge were tight-lipped about everything aboard.

As soon as the Coolidge passed under the Golden Gate Bridge with everyone on deck to view the magnificent structure, some for the last time, many eyes glistened from moist eyes. There must have been thoughts of home and leaving loved ones, as treasured young memories pored from the hearts of many as they realized the heartbreak they were being asked to endure for their country for many months, perhaps years.

Many stayed on deck for a long long time looking back at the bridge, the shoreline of the magnificent and beautiful harbor, and the harbor traffic which accompanied the Coolidge, almost to the edge of this great harbor, as they turned back to dock at San Francisco.

When we cleared the entrance to the harbor, most returned to their cabins with sadness in their hearts.

We were soon on the open sea and then the inevitable zigzagging began. First to the right 30 degrees, then to the left 60 degrees, then right 60 degrees, all the way to our destination. The zigzagging was necessary, of course, to provide less of a target to Japanese subs which just might be lurking on our route.

As darkness closed in on us, mournful thoughts and expressions of sorrow crossed many a lip as each mile from home tightened the gut a little more. The anguish was deeply felt by many young soldiers who had never been away from home before and it was not unusual to hear a whimper now and then and watch someone dabbing his eyes to catch the flow of tears.

As time passed, the men seemed to settle down to a daily routine. All aboard were required to keep themselves clean, keep their clothes clean, clean up their quarters, be ready for inspection which occurred every other day. Everyone eventually learned to accept the inevitable - we were going to war and it was not going to be nice.

Aboard ship the wheels of progress, organization and administration burst into full flower. Messages from Washington and Air Force Headquarters began arriving daily directed to the senior air officer aboard. Capt. John D. Howe, as the senior officer and troop commander organized a small staff and began issuing instructions to all elements of the military on board. There were signal people, a military post office department detachment, engineers, administrative personnel and intelligence department experts. There were pilots and crew members and there were air depot personnel. The senior officers of each unit were receiving instructions from their US-based Headquarters on action to be initiated in preparation for our assembly at our unknown destination. Washington certainly knew where we were headed, but for reasons unknown did not let us know.

Our initial objective we thought was Hawaii, but after five days at sea we did not seek port there. Our second guess was the Philippines. However, the daily shipboard newsletter gave strong indications that the Philippines would not be our target because the invasion of Luzon by the Japanese was proving successful for them and plans were underway by MacArthur to evacuate the Luzon area and Manila and retreat to Corregidor. For a period of two weeks there was no new word or even rumor of our destination.

In the meantime our eight-man contingent began to grow from the assignment of six new officers fresh out of flying school. The six pilots were unknown to us at the time of their assignment. The new members of our contingent were 2nd Lt. Bernard Cederholm, 2nd Lt. Arthur D. Thomas; 2nd Lt. Victor A. Yuska; 2nd Lt. Willard R. Stearns; 2nd Lt. Uriah F. Corkrum; and 2nd

21st TCS Officers group picture.

Lt. Melvin C. Lewis. Our small team of eight had miraculously grown to ten pilots. This small group formed the early staffing for our Air Transport Operation. 1st Lt. Adams, the senior officer of our group, was appointed Squadron Adjunct; Imparato, Engineering and Maintenance Officer; Baer, Supply Officer; Arthur Thomas, Operations Officer,; Robert Gerling, Assistant Operations Officer. All the remainder of the group were initially assigned as pilots as primary duty.

The days were getting warmer so we reasoned we were heading further south from the Hawaii and Philippine track. Then suddenly on the 2nd of February, 1942, land appeared. We were approaching Melbourne, Australia.

We were received at the port by the Australians with great joy and I am sure, with great relief. The port of Melbourne was open to us with brass bands and jubilation.

The Australians were short of transportation and fuel and as a consequence, the 2000 soldiers from the Coolidge, after being restrained aboard ship for 22 days, were now required to march the five miles to our assigned bivouac at Camp Darley. Darley, a military installation just outside the city limits of Melbourne, was an adequate bivouac and served us well during our four days stay there. It was here that we were introduced to the Australian standard dinner fare - mutton. It was mutton for breakfast, mutton for lunch and mutton for dinner the first few days at Darley.

The group of 14 officers and men received official orders from Headquarters, United States Army Forces in Australia issued February 6, 1942, for transfer of our 14-man contingent from Camp Darley, Melbourne, Victoria, to Archer Field, Brisbane, Australia, for assignment to the Transport Command. Travel was by train from Melbourne to Brisbane via Sydney. The group arrived at Brisbane the following day.

To our surprise on arriving at Brisbane we discovered a group of ten pilots and fifteen airmen and three transport aircraft already assigned to the transport command. Originally scheduled for the Philippines on a freighter, the men and aircraft were directed to Brisbane when it became certain that the Philippines were being overrun by the advancing Japanese. This new group composed of fighter and bomber pilots landed at Brisbane on December 22, 1941.

This change of fate that coalesced the three separate skills of transport pilots, fighter pilots and bomber pilots into a tightly knit, cohesive unit at Brisbane resulted ultimately into one of the finest troop carrier groups ever to be assembled under the wings of the Air Force and the Fifth Air Force of WWII.

1st Lt. Edgar Wade Hampton, former aide to Major General Brereton who was so recently criticized - falsely, for having lost so many of his bombers and fighters on the ground in the Philippines, took command of the forming unit of the Air Transport Command at Amberly Aerodrome, Brisbane until the arrival of the contingent from Melbourne then transferred the assembled unit to Archer Field.

The letter activating the ATC (Air Transport Command) ordered "All United States transport planes in Australia and all combat airplanes flyable but unfit for combat be converted to transport aircraft and to be part of the Air Transport Command[1]."

Upon activation, the original Troop Carrier Command had 14 officers and 19 airmen all assigned under verbal orders of the Commanding Officer, Brisbane. Only two of the 14 officers, Adams and Imparato, were fully qualified troop carrier pilots. The remaining 12 had to be retrained for transport operations in transport aircraft. Of the 19 airmen, 12 were qualified aircrew members.

Within 30 days of our arrival at Archer Field, The ATC organization was redesignated the 21st Troop Carrier Squadron. Lt. Hampton was moved up to ATC headquarters and Captain Paul I. (Pappy) Gunn, former managing director of the Philippine Airlines, succeeded Hampton in command of the 21st Troop Carrier Squadron.

The first significant missions for the fledgling 21st Troop Carrier Squadron occurred in late January, 1942, through mid February, 1942, when P-40 mechanics and equipment were flown by Troop Carriers to bases in Java. In late February, 1942, when the Netherlands East Indies was falling before the onslaught of superior Japanese forces, Troop Carrier aircraft participated in the evacuation of military and civilian personnel. Also during February, 1942, civilians serving in the Broome - Wyndham area of Western Australia were evacuated to Perth, Western Australia, some 900 miles south of Broome. These missions, an estimated 90% of all 374th Troop Carrier group missions during WWII, were considered combat missions.[2]

Two aircraft were lost during this hectic period. Pilots flew in all kinds of weather and often without adequate maps. Time was of the essence. One pilot returning from Java, found Darwin to be "zero-zero", and was forced to set down on an emergency strip for light planes at Bathurst Island, 60 miles north of Darwin. Landing in a cross-wind, the plane damaged its left wing tip and aileron. The craft was destroyed by Zeros before repairs could be effected.

The second transport became lost and made a crash landing near Wyndham after running out of gasoline. It was en route from Perth to Broome. Personnel escaped uninjured and were picked up two days later by an Australian flying boat.

In March 1942, Lt. Col. Erickson S. Nichols was named commanding officer of the Troop Carriers, which in turn were placed under the Directorate of Allied Air Transport. Col. Nichols is the brother of the famous and illustrious aviatrix Ruth Nichols who established many flying records for women in the 1920s and 1930s. Group Capt. Harold Gatty, R.A.A.F., of Post and Gatty fame, became director of the D.A.T.

The problem of securing sufficient planes was acute. Somehow Col. Nichols and Lt. Hampton scraped together enough old planes, with a few replacements, to equip a squadron (a Troop Carrier Squadron normally had 13 C-47 planes). Col. Nichols first squadron, the 21st, was assembled using 14 different types of transport planes.

"If we had to make a repair," Col. Nichols said, "we would wed a DC-2 wing to a DC-3 plane; an engine from one type to another - anything to keep them flying. If an air speed indicator or some instrument went out, well, we'd just stamp it 'N.I.S.' (Not In Stock) and the pilot would fly without it."

Between January and July of 1942 the Troop Carriers flew more than 5,000,000 miles, rushing equipment and supplies to strategic points on the Southwest Pacific front. During the period of March 10th to March 22nd, planes transported the entire 102nd Coast Artillery (Anti-Aircraft) Battalion, with complete equipment, from Brisbane to Darwin, a distance of 1800 miles.

---

[1] The ATC - the original name for the transport operation in Australia did not have the same function as the Air Transport Command as we know it now. The name of our ATC was soon changed to "Troop Carrier." The function of Troop Carrier is to fly men, supplies and equipment from forward bases into actual front line fields with supplies, drop supplies to infantry engaged in battle, and carry paratroopers. ATC generally flies supplies from rear bases to behind the line depots. Another essential difference is that troop carrier planes are part of a tactical organization, the third arm of General C. Kenney's Far East Air Forces and used under combat conditions.

[2] A combat mission was defined at the time as any flight which entered a preselected line into or bordering on Japanese territory or subject to enemy attack due to the flight's proximity to enemy forces, by sea, by land or from the air.

The battalion was moved in small balanced units with guns and ammunition ready for instant action. This battery, set up in the previously unprotected Darwin area, provided a very effective surprise for Japanese planes in subsequent raids. Wounded and evacuee personnel were flown to Brisbane from Darwin on the return flights.

This was the first time in air history that a fully equipped battalion had been moved by air - a feat which was to be duplicated later in every theater of operations where the Allies were fighting. The movement of men and supplies by air often spelled the difference between victory and defeat on the battlefield.

For more than two months the Troop Carriers had only eight enlisted personnel available to maintain all the aircraft. Working on a 24-hour basis, however, with each man putting in an average of 17 or 18 hours a day, all available planes were kept flying. During March one aircraft, C-53 No. 42-20070, VHCWA, flew a record total of 272 hours, carrying more than 300 tons of supplies a distance of 2000 miles. This record was unsurpassed for a long while, and when surpassed, was broken by another Troop Carrier plane, a C-47, in the Southwest Pacific area.

Late in March planes and pilots of the Netherlands East Indies Airlines, K.N.I.L.M., joined the American unit on a contract basis. The planes were purchased from K.N.I.L.M. and turned over to the Troop Carrier Command, which had been expanded considerably in pilot officer and enlisted strength by assignment from casual units.

The Dutch had flown whatever ships they could salvage from Java to Australia. The flying experience of the Dutch pilots was more than worth the price of the planes. Troop Carrier Command was well aware of this and scheduled these pilots on many important missions.

The Troop Carrier Command, Archer Field, Brisbane, was redesignated as the 21st Transport Squadron on April 3, 1942. The 22nd Transport Squadron was activated at the same time at Essendon Airdrome, Melbourne, Victoria, Australia. Ten pilots and 10 enlisted men were transferred to the 22nd Squadron from the 21st Squadron. Veteran bomber and fighter pilots from the Philippines and Java campaigns, and a cadre of enlisted men from the United States completed the strength of the 22nd Squadron. Several K.N.I.L.M. planes (Dutch ships), including L-4's, C-56's, DC-5's, DC-2's, DC-3's and B-17C's, were assigned to the 22nd.

MACARTHUR AND THE 374TH TROOP CARRIER GROUP

MARCH 1942

The 21st Troop Carrier Squadron's affiliation with and association with General Douglas MacArthur began in March, 1942. MacArthur had been ordered out of the Philippines in mid-March 1942 by President Roosevelt after a great deal of bickering between Washington and the General over whether he would obey the legitimate orders from the President or stay and fight with his men in the Philippines. MacArthur wanted to stay and fight, even considered resigning from the Army rather than defy his President, but finally good sense prevailed and he made preparation for leaving Corregidor with his family and key personnel, including his Chief of Staff, General Richard Sutherland. After a very difficult 600-mile journey in a PT boat, commanded by Lt. John B. Bulkeley U.S. Navy, the group managed to reach Del Monte Air Field on the north coast of Mindanao, the very large southernmost island of the Philippines. There, after recovering from the extremely hazardous trip from Corregidor, with the constant threat from Japanese aircraft and submarines, they rested while awaiting the arrival of two B-17s from Australia to fly them to Australia. On

The cleanup gang at Archer Field in Brisbane, early 1942.

their arrival at DelMonte, the B-17s looked like sick ducks. The dilapidated B-17s, needing maintenance, but flyable, were in command of Lt. Frank Bostrom. Frank had a crippled airplane but was determined to get MacArthur to Australia. They departed Del Monte Air Field as soon as minor repair was accomplished. Flying was not the choice of travel for either General MacArthur or his wife Jean in those early days of World War II. The flight to Darwin, the nearest usable airfield on the northwest corner of Australia, had been under constant air attack from Japanese bombers. The island of Timor just off the coast of northwest Australia was believed to be occupied by Japanese troops and aircraft and a great potential hazard to the flight.

As he approached Darwin, Frank Bostrom radioed Darwin tower for landing instruction and was advised that an air raid was in progress and to use the alternate airfield at Batchlor, a short distance from Darwin. Frank was under considerable pressure to touch down because one of his four engines was failing and the very heavy load he was carrying could not maintain safe flight with only three engines. The landing was safely made, certainly due to the great flying skill of Frank Bostrom. The passengers were stiff, tired, hungry, and disgruntled. On deplaning, Frank approached MacArthur and told him the B-17 could go no farther, it would need an engine change and that would take at least one week. The engine replacement would have to come by air from Brisbane or Melbourne. MacArthur seemed relieved and made a passing comment to the effect that he had enough flying for a while. MacArthur then inquired about facilities for transportation to Melbourne and was informed that via airplane was the only way to go. Mrs. MacArthur was tired, grumpy, unhappy, and very much concerned about Arthur Junior who was not well. It was a difficult trip for him. She more than the General, disliked flying at this stage in their lives, and after seven days of an excruciating existence - first with three days of high speed PT boat maneuvering through a sea of wind, rain and bouncing, rolling ocean, then the very uncomfortable airplane ride in a converted B-17 without comfortable accommodation. She was distressed and was heard making a statement heard all over Australia. "Never again will anyone get me into an airplane."

MacArthur, in an effort to accommodate Mrs. MacArthur, inquired about road or rail facilities and asked to be taken to the rail station. He was informed that the nearest railhead was at Alice Springs, nearly 1,200 miles away.

It was at that point that the 21st Transport Squadron was called upon to pick up General MacArthur and his entourage at Batchlor and fly them to Alice Springs where MacArthur boarded the train and then made a triumphant arrival at Melbourne a few days later.

On March 4th the 21st Squadron Maintenance Officer, Lt. Edward T. Imparato, was sent to Melbourne from Archer Field in

Wise, Henry, McCollough, Stover, Moore, and Vandiver; the first group of 21st TCS pilots to be rotated back to the United States.

Brisbane to receive twelve Lockheed Loadstars evacuated from and purchased from the Dutch East Indies and Singapore Airlines. The airplanes were in excellent condition. Our mission stated Imparato was to thoroughly inspect the aircraft and accept them for the U.S. Army Air Corps. After a satisfactory result on inspection, we proceeded to have the teams of pilots and mechanics checked out in the airplane, after which the airplanes were dispatched to Archer Field for immediate use in our Australia transport operation. Our stay at Melbourne was from the 4th to the 24th of March, 1942.

While at Melbourne, we had the opportunity to meet General MacArthur. It was this meeting that began the long, gratifying and rewarding adventure serving MacArthur and his Headquarters. This association lasted through the final wartime mission of the special flight to Atsugi, Japan, and MacArthur's arrival there on August 30, 1945.

General MacArthur was appointed Commander of all Allied Forces in the southwest Pacific area after his arrival at Melbourne. The discomfort, fear and uncertainty about our ability to stop the advance of the Japanese Forces into Australia ended for us and I know for many others when MacArthur arrived and assumed command. On our arrival at Melbourne, February 2, 1942, after the long zigzag sea trip on the USS Coolidge from San Francisco, after departing San Francisco in mid-January, we found a conglomerate of high-ranking officers - all evacuees from the many hot spots around the South Pacific. They came from Hawaii, the Philippines, Java, Singapore, China and India. There did not seem to be any organization or direction in the feverish activity that was generated by the threat from the advancing Japanese forces. There was no equipment to fight with, no airplanes to get what equipment could be commandeered to places where it was needed.

The first month in Australia was sheer chaos. We visited the headquarters of the Army and Air Force Command in Melbourne and could feel the confusion. We found civilians from the Java Airline sitting in positions of authority directing Air Corps activities, issuing orders and directives that made no sense to us. We were sent to Australia as part of a ten-officer group to organize a transport operation. We were trained and ready to perform but found no airplanes, or supplies or facilities from which to begin our organization.

The Aussies had begun to panic. The Australian Chief of Staff made plans to establish a defensive line from Brisbane to Darwin ready to concede almost one half of the Australian continent to the advancing Japanese. At that time in early February and March of 1942, the last blocking action was an attempt to halt the Japanese advance at Kokoda Pass deep in the Owen Stanley mountain range of New Guinea. Failing this, Port Moresby was doomed and the undefended north coast of Australia would be an easy target for the Japanese.

MacArthur's arrival at Melbourne could not have been at a better time. The day after his arrival he made a hasty trip to Canberra, the Australian capital, to confer with the Prime Minister. As a result of that meeting, the two principals decided on an immediate reversal of the Australian strategy. MacArthur stated at that time:

> "The Aussie concept was purely one of passive defense, and I felt it would result only in eventual defeat. Even if so restrictive a scheme were tactically successful, its result would be to trap us indefinitely on an island continent ringed by conquered territories and hostile ocean, bereft of all hope of every assuming the offensive.
>
> "I decided to abandon the plan completely, to move a thousand miles forward into eastern Papua, and to stop the Japanese on the rough mountains of the Owen Stanley range of New Guinea - to make the fight for Australia beyond its own borders. If successful, this would save Australia from invasion and give me an opportunity to pass from defense to offense, to seize the initiative, move forward, and attack.
>
> "This decision gave the Australians an exhilarating lift, and they prepared to support me with almost fanatical zeal. As a matter of fact, throughout the war, the most complete cooperation existed not only with the Australians but with the other nationalities under my command - Dutch, British, and New Zealanders."

General MacArthur's arrival at Melbourne gave the theater a whole new sense of purpose. The negative attitudes turned to optimism. The confusion settled to less panic and more progress toward constructive accomplishments. Shortly, even the attitudes of the military, both American and Australian, turned to attack rather than defense. We were sure now that the Japanese could be stopped in their attempt to invade Australia. It was not long before the aura of MacArthur's presence inspired all of us to do more, to do better to win this war.

MacArthur's presence at Melbourne did much to change attitudes. He seemed to know instantly and instinctively what to do and how to do it. Here are his own views on what had to be done.

> "The immediate and imperative problem which confronted me was the defense of Australia itself. Its actual military situation had become almost desperate. Its forces were weak to an extreme, and Japanese invasion was momentarily expected. The bulk of Australia's ground troops were in the Middle East, while the United States had only one division present, and that but partially trained. Its Air Force was equipped with almost obsolete planes and was lacking not only in engines and spare parts, but in personnel. Its Navy had no carriers or battleships. The outlook was bleak."

Shortly after we arrived back at Archer Field at Brisbane, I was sent on a trip to Darwin with personnel of both Australian and American military forces and air freight. The pilot was Pappy Gunn - the Pappy Gunn of renown - former President of Philippine Airlines and a mechanical genius. The Pappy Gunn about whom General Kenney later wrote a book. Pappy was our second Squadron Commander at the 21st, having joined us at Archer Field in early February 1942. He was evacuated from the Philippines and had to leave his family behind. Pappy was a pilot of unusual skill and daring. He could jump into the cockpit of almost any airplane without prior briefing and instructioned test flight and do well with it. On this particular flight I don't believe we got over 50 feet off the ground for the whole 1,500 mile trip both ways. I cannot remember how many families of kangaroos we scattered while flying over the great outback.

On the return flight we stayed overnight at Daly Waters, an Australian advance air force base and Australian airline stop. At this site, during the night, I experienced the most astonishing and unusual sounds. Needless to say, I did not sleep well that night. The sound resembled a low roaring rumble associated with a steady, wood-sawing noise. It was very loud. I would judge at about 90 decibels. At breakfast the following morning, in discussions with the Aussies, I was told the noise came from millions of termites doing their own thing, chewing on the wood structure in which we lived. The termites were large, about the size of a wasp - not the size of a small ant as in America. Further, this seemed to confirm the fact that the tremendous twelve-foot anthills in Australia are actually termite mounds!

During the months of February, March and April 1942, landings at Darwin were always questionable and hazardous due to the fact that Japanese air raids were a daily event. It was necessary to call the Darwin Airport control tower when 100 to 150 miles out to ascertain whether an air raid was underway or expected by our arrival time in about 20 minutes. The tower would advise us of recommended options of using either Darwin or Batchlor Air Fields. Batchlor airport was about 40 miles from Darwin. We were without fighter protection on these flights and, at this distance from our departure point of Cloncurry, about 400 miles away from Daly Waters, an alternate airport if both Batchlor and Darwin were unusable.

These approaches to Darwin area were always harrowing experiences. Our pilots always flew unarmed transports. Our only protection, when it was available, was top cover fighter support. Our crews were armed only with a .45 pistol and ammunition belt and that was all. The pistol was mainly intended for use in the event of bailout over jungle or enemy territory. It would afford us a measure of protection from man or beast. It could be used also for shooting game for food or if it came to that - oneself - to end it all.

On return from our Darwin flight, the squadron resumed its routine duties. Services generally improved and the structural changes under more competent leadership served us well. More and more aircraft joined our squadron and at its peak we had 25 aircraft - 18 were different types of airplanes. The largest was a converted B-24; the smallest, an Australian Gypsy Moth which was used for training and joyriding. The maintenance problems were horrendous, the mechanics, young and not fully trained, and the supply of maintenance parts and tools almost nonexistent. It was not an easy job for the maintenance officer.

From April through the latter part of 1942, the 21st Transport Squadron acted as MacArthur's personal Air Force. Most of our missions were directed by General Headquarters and, as necessary, to fly the General and his staff wherever they needed to go. These flights included those into Port Moresby, New Guinea, and as far into the front line combat operations as the needs of the ground force troop required. At this early stage all the front line troops were Australian infantry defending Port Moresby. Our airborne supply to the Aussies in the Owen Stanley range at Kokoda assisted in preventing the Japanese from capturing Port Moresby. The loss of Moresby would have made MacArthur's plan of advance almost impossible this early in his "Return to the Philippines" strategy. A major beachhead assault to recapture Moresby (on the southern coast of New Guinea), if lost, would have been very difficult, if not impossible.

In the opinion of many, the one mission which successfully turned the tide of battle against the Japanese and prepared the U.S. and Australian forces for the march to Tokyo was the behind-the-Japanese-line air landing of two regimental combat teams of the 32nd Infantry Division, at Buna and Gona on the north coast of New Guinea over the Owen Stanley mountain range. The carrying forces were all the airplanes which were in commission from the 21st and 22nd Troop Carrier Squadrons. Our group, the 374th, received its first of three Presidential Unit Citations for this mission. The citation reads as follows:

WAR DEPARTMENT
General Orders, Washington, January 14, 1943.
No. 3
EXTRACT
Section
* * *

Citation of Unit in United States Forces in Southwest Pacific — III
* * *

III — Citation of unit in United States Forces in Southwest Pacific — As authorized by Executive Order 9075 (Sec. III Bull. 11, W.D., 1942), a citation in the name of the President of the United States, as public evidence of deserved honor and distinction, is awarded to the following named unit. The citation reads as follows:

The 374th Troop Carrier Group, United States Army, is cited for out standing performance of duty in action during the period September 19, 1942 to December 22, 1942. This unit was charged during this period with transportation by air of the troop equipment and supplies to the forward areas in Papua and the evacuation of casualties to the rear areas and although attacked by enemy aircraft, the group efficiently and successfully accomplished its assigned mission. Utilizing various types of unarmed aircraft an

Archer Field Maintenance Crew in Brisbane, 1942.

2nd Lt. James W. Ingram at Archer Field, May 1942.

S/S. Lester M. Brady, Assistant Line Chief, April 1942.

1st Lt. Fred G. Henry, best pilot in the 21st Squadron, April 1942.

Cpl. Ned Allen of the Royal Australian A.F.

Engine dolly being hauled to a job, April 1942.

Capt. Edward Imparato getting some training in celestial navigation, March 1942.

average of 100 tons of supplies a day was flown to the troops and casualties were evacuated daily. Several thousand troops, including artillery, were quickly transported to battle areas by this means. The high degree of technical ability, the devotion to duty, and the excellent morale of the group as a whole made possible this outstanding contribution to the success of the campaign in this area.

By order of the Secretary of War:
G. C. Marshall

Chief of Staff
    Official: J. A. Ulio,
                      Major General
                      The Adjutant General

A TRUE EXACT COPY

John D. Pearson
Major, Air Corps

After the Buna campaign, Imparato was ordered to the 374th Group Headquarters at Port Moresby for duty as director of engineering and maintenance for all the group's aircraft and facilities as well as duty as a combat pilot.

The success of the Buna campaign gave the army some time to regroup, rest, and await reinforcements from the United States. MacArthur continued his efforts to coordinate and integrate the joint Australian and American ground forces. However, the air war escalated with the arrival of bomber and fighter units from America. The U.S. Navy in the Pacific, struggling to recover from the devastation that was called the "Day of Infamy" by President Roosevelt - the Japanese attack on Pearl Harbor - began to provide major support on MacArthur's right flank. The very significant carrier-based air support and the navy and marine successful assault on Guadalcanal, cleared the way for the concerted army, air force and navy combined strategy for the eventual assault on the Philippines, Okinawa, and the planned massive beachhead assault on the Japanese mainland.

The 374th Troop Carrier Group had no direct contact with MacArthur through the Markham Valley paratroop operation at Nadzab, New Guinea. This operation resulted in the capture of the airfield at Nadzab and Lae, New Guinea. Lae was the Japanese army and air force stronghold for their planned assault on Port Moresby and eventually on Australia. With their loss of this strategic position, it should have appeared inevitable to the Japanese, that their planned strategy for the New Guinea operation was in jeopardy. Their extended lines of communication and supply were under constant attack from the U.S. Navy on the east and north and the U.S. Army and Air Forces from the south.

MacArthur's army forces methodically and forcefully kept heavy pressure on the Japanese forces from the ground to take, in a steady advance, Salamaua, Lae, Finschhafen, Sador, Madang and Wewak. All these enemy strong points were captured with minimum losses primarily because of MacArthur's bypass technique. Rather than confront the enemy in frontal attacks, the bypass operation caused them to wither on the vine for lack of food, arms, water and reinforcements from their New Guinea central command.

The 374th Troop Carrier Group was pleased to see the fall of Lae because it was from this base and airfield that the Japanese made the air and ground attack on Wau, nearly captured Wau and nearly destroyed the 374th. It was during this operation that the 374th suffered its greatest losses in damaged and downed aircraft. The Wau support operation very nearly turned into a disaster for the 374th and it was this operation as much as any other action which resulted in our group being awarded the second of its three Presidential Unit Citations.

WAR DEPARTMENT
Washington, May 6, 1943.
General Orders
No. 21- EXTRACT -Section
* * *
Citation of units in the United States Forces in the SouthwestPacific Area

* * *

IV - - Citation of units in the United States Forces in Southwest Pacific Area. — As authorized by Executive Order No. 9075 (sec III, Bull. 11, W.D., 1942), citation in the name of the President of the United States, as public evidence of deserved honor and distinction, was awarded to the following named forces. The citation is as follows:

The Papuan Forces, United States Army, Southwest Pacific Area, are cited for outstanding performance of duty in action during the period July 23, 1942, to January 23, 1943. When a bold and aggressive enemy invaded Papua in strength, the combined action of ground and air units of these forces in association with Allied units, checked the hostile advance, drove the enemy back to the seacoast and in a series of actions against a highly organized defensive zone, utterly destroyed him. Ground combat forces, operating over roadless jungle-covered mountains and swamps, demonstrated their courage and resourcefulness in closing with an enemy who took every advantage of the nearly impassable terrain. Air forces, by repeatedly attacking the enemy ground forces and installations, by destroying his convoys attempting reinforcement and supply, an by transporting grounds forces and supplies to areas for which land routes were nonexistent and sea routes slow and hazardous, made possible the success of the ground operations. Service units, operating far forward of their normal positions and at times in advance of ground combat elements, built landing fields in the jungle, established and operated supply points, and provided for the hospitalization and evacuation of the wounded and sick. The courage, spirit, and devotion to duty of all elements of the command made possible the complete victory attained.

By order of the Secretary of War:
G. C. MARSHALL,
Chief of Staff.
Official:
J. A. ULIO,
Major General,
The Adjutant General.

A TRUE EXTRACT COPY:

/s/ John D. Pearson
JOHN D. PEARSON,
Major, Air Corps.

The success of the Markham Valley airborne operation relieved the pressure on the Allied Forces' campaign to rid New Guinea of Japanese forces.

On May 22, 1942, the 21st Transport Squadron, led by Capt. (now Col.) E. W. Hampton, made its first operational flight in New Guinea, carrying Australian Commando troops and supplies to Wau and Bulolo, Allied mountain airdromes previously used only by very light aircraft. Wau airdrome, at an altitude of 3300 feet, was very rough and had an uphill incline of one foot in twelve with a crescent of 7000-feet mountains at its far end. Bulolo, also very rough, was approximately 2500 feet long, usually quite soft and very wet.

Despite intense Japanese fighter plane activity, the 21st Squadron continued to operate at intervals several planes between Port Moresby and Wau, our fighter cover consisting of only five of six P-39's. When the Japanese landed troops at Buna in July, 21st Squadron planes landed Australian reinforcements and supplies at Kokoda, a small, unkempt, civilian mountain airstrip which was never meant for Troop Carrier planes. In the fighting for that mountain airdrome, our planes often circled the field without knowing whether it was in friendly or enemy hands.

During the Australian retreat from Kokoda, which ended in an Allied offensive at Iorabaiwa Ridge, 30 air miles from Port Moresby, and during the fight to drive the Japs back across the Owen Stanley mountains, troop carrier planes dropped tons of supplies and equipment to the Australian troops, thus taking adequate care of a supply problem which otherwise would have prolonged the fighting for months.

An extract from "The War in New Guinea" (a Port Moresby daily newspaper) describes the conditions under which the ground soldiers were fighting when troop carrier planes were dropping supplies and bringing reinforcements to them:

> "To combat the Japanese, soldiers climbed slippery, precipitous mountain tracks on hands and knees - forced their way through dense jungle - waded knee-deep in mud - desperately weary, tried to sleep on sodden ground under constant tropical downpour.
>
> "At one stage those in contact with the enemy lit no fires, had no warm food, nor took off a single piece of clothing for four weeks. When finally able to have a spell their socks, and in some cases their boots, had to be cut from their feet - water-sodden skin was torn away with socks - feet left raw.
>
> "Many wounded men walked for days to medical aid; those who couldn't walk were carried on rough bush stretchers by native Fuzzy Wuzzies[3]. Sometimes it took ten natives to carry one wounded soldier over this difficult terrain. Complete lack of roads was the most difficult problem in the campaign; without roads it appeared impossible to supply our troops...."

Since there are no roadways in the skies, Troop Carriers became the "forty-and-eight" freight car of the skyways and the "Biscuit Bomber" of this war.

Living and flying conditions were almost as difficult for air ground crews and pilots. Terminal weather forecasts were found to be fairly accurate when available, but for the most part pilots took off for airdromes such as Wau, Bulolo, and Bena Bena with no accurate information on the weather, trusting to luck, flying skill, and personal knowledge of New Guinea weather habits and terrain to get them to their landing strips and dropping targets.

Decisions on weather in New Guinea are still left to the pilot, for the most part, since the weather changes so rapidly that only pilots who have just returned from a particular area are capable to reporting on and predicting the weather. Pilots were constantly confronted with ground fogs, heavy rain, thick stratus and cumulonimbus clouds previously unreported.

Australian War correspondent George Johnston's vivid description of flying conditions is again applicable:

At Archer Field, Brisbane, Australia; (back) Thomas, Baer, Stover, Mihalos, (front) Grimes, Murry F. Crossette - Wright Aero Co., and Imparato.

"Within a month the fresh-faced kids from Maine and Florida, from Oklahoma and Texas, from Nebraska and Michigan, had lines carved round their eyes, and the set of their jaws had stiffened. Most of them had accumulated between 180 and 200 hours of flying time in combat areas. That was quite a bit different from flying training school. The fact that their planes were virtually unarmed - what are two Tommy guns and a pilot's .45 against the cannon and machine guns of a Zero? - added to the fun.

"We had seen them, day after day, as briefly seen specks scooting through the gaps in the giant jungle trees. Occasionally when we were in an area cleared out of the jungle for use as a dropping ground, we would see them come banking in with motors throttled back, great wings almost scraping the trees. As they circled, you could see the men in the open doors frantically hurling and kicking out the boxes. The black specks streamed down.

"There was a bit of anxiety after it was discovered that mortars dropped in specially padded boxes gave trouble when they were used in action. The troops found out about it the hard way. Several Australian mortar crews were blown to pieces when the bomb exploded inside the mortar. But mistakes had to be made in an organization that was groping its way along the tough road toward perfection. When a mistake was discovered, it was never repeated....

"There were only two kinds of flying conditions for the young American pilots: 'lousy' or 'goddam lousy'. There is only one negotiable air pass through the peaks of the Owen Stanley range - a narrow, twisting gap at a height of between 5000 and 7000 feet. The high peaks are hidden in clouds, and mist and rain hang over the pass and trail, away down to the foothills. The pilots on the coastal air strips would look savagely up toward where the great purple range was smothered in cloud and mutter, 'Those clouds are full of rocks today!'"[4]

"I flew several times across the range in these transports. But I can't remember any trip when my stomach didn't feel as if it were doing slow rolls or when the hair at the nape of my neck was not bristling with fear. I never could get accustomed to driving through a gray rain cloud, seeing a vaguely darker shape ahead, realizing sickeningly that it was the side of a mountain wall just as the plane lurched violently and nearly rolled over as it turned to get out of trouble.

"Once, with another Australian war correspondent, I was leaving the front-line positions near Buna to bring some dispatches back to Port Moresby. Clouds were down over the entire range. There was a dogfight between Zeros and P-40's in full swing over Buna as we circled endlessly to gain sufficient height to cross the summit. Each agonizing circle took us almost into the middle of the whirl of Japanese and American fighters. Eventually we popped out of the cloud, came into sunshine above a rolling cumulus through which the high purple peaks protruded majestically. My colleague and I breathed profound sighs.

"Then my friend pointed behind. The blood was draining out of his face. I looked. A little black fighter had poked out of the cloud about a mile behind and was diving in our direction. The American sergeant shifted his gum to the side of his mouth and braced himself against the doorway with his Tommy gun poking out into the air.

"'I think it's a P-40,' I said, without even convincing myself.

"Everybody was uneasy until the plane swept past. It was a Kittyhawk. Nobody said anything for a while. I spoke first.

"'As a matter of fact I didn't think it was a P-40. I thought it was a Zero."

"My shirt was drenched with sweat.

"The men who flew the transports crossed the range six, eight or ten times a day, and for some of them it was a job that lasted without a break for five months. That took guts and stamina and morale and will power and all the other things that are easy to write about. Yet the main topic of conversation among these kids was how much stuff they could get through to the troops.

"In that period there was one airfield at Port Moresby - the transportation field - that must have been almost the busiest airfield in the world. Four hundred

---

[3]Fuzzy Wuzzies - Name given friendly New Guinea natives who assisted allied forces in manual duties during the New Guinea fighting.
[4]Author's note: This pass is the original "Hump" and where the expression "Flying over the Hump" originated.

Maj. Fred Adams and the 21st Troop Carrier Squadron at Archer Field in Brisbane, Australia, 1942.

takeoffs between dawn and sundown were everyday stuff. When we were back at Moresby we practically lived there.

"They were up at 4 a.m. every day, in the air by 'first light' and flying right through until dusk if the weather was even reasonable - 'reasonable', that is, by Papuan standards.

"Once a Jap sniper, by a lucky fluke, brought down a Douglas with a single shot from his rifle. The plane burned before the bully beef could be saved and a company of Australian infantry went hungry that night. That was the narrow margin between adequate supply and starvation. If the planes failed to get through the troops couldn't fight. No air transportation - no campaign...."

On September 8, 1942, Allied General Headquarters realized that it was impossible to march sufficient troops over the ranges to drive the Japs from Papua. Other means of transport were investigated. The ranges were explored for routes, upon which roads were to have been built, but without success. Plans to march troops up the coast from Milne Bay, where they could be brought by ship, were not practical because of the impassable swamp country. Transporting of troops by air to the north coast was reckoned as limited, as landing fields were soft with incessant rain and heavy aircraft bogged easily.

General Kenney said it could be done. Capt. Norman Wilde, liaison officer of the A.N.G.A.U. (Australia and New Guinea Administrative Unit) Forces with Troop Carrier, explored the country in a small plane. He found suitable landing spots near Wanegela, Pongani, Popondetta, and Dobodura. Working right under the nose of the enemy, Capt. Wilde recruited natives to hew rough landing strips from the kunai grass.

Between September 18 and 25, the 21st and 22nd Troop Carrier Squadrons transported 4000 fully equipped men of the American 32nd Infantry Division from Brisbane and Townsville to Port Moresby, and then flew them into action against the Japanese, landing on these native-hewn strips. From here the troops marched into battle at Buna.

This was the utilization of air movement as advocated by General Kenney. It was the first time in air history that such a large number of fully-equipped troops were transported by air and flown into battle. It changed the course of the entire battle for New Guinea.

Maj. Frank C. Church, former A-3 of the 54th Wing who participated in the flights with the 32nd Division, declared the landing fields looked like "postage stamps".

"We thought we never would get in and once in thought we never would get out," he said. "We made our landings almost straight down and our take-off almost straight up. We were lucky to get off, as the fields were muddy beneath the grass. We had to use full power to make it."

To effect this first mass transportation of troops and their supplies, Col. Hampton commandeered every type of plane possible, including some bombers which were undergoing repairs. An average day's haul was 500,000 pounds, with 700,000 pounds being a record day.

Maj. Ray Vandiver, of The Dalles, Oregon, Operations Officer, said,

"We would land a planeload of soldiers and pick up a planeload of wounded to bring back for hospitalization. The planes were never empty and were busy day and night, being refueled and rechecked.

"Literally everything that an entire army division would need was flown by the Troop Carriers - malaria pills, jeeps, road tractors, ammunition, guns, food, and hospital units - in the ferrying operation. Those troops knew they would go into action as soon as they landed. They had practiced setting up their guns fast in order to be ready. When they did land, the Japs were waiting for them with snipers, or in Zeros, which swept down to strafe the field.

"One time the troops shot down two Zeros a few moments after landing and setting up their anti-aircraft guns. On the ground you talked in a whisper to keep the enemy from hearing you. Whenever the bushes rattled, they were sprayed with machine-gun fire."

In the meanwhile, the 21st and 22nd Transport Squadrons were redesignated Troop Carrier squadrons by a general order. Word was received that more Troop Carrier squadrons were on their way. In the Middle of October, 1942, the air echelon of the 6th Troop Carrier Squadron, commanded by Capt. John H. Lackey (now Col.) arrived in New Guinea. It was the first complete Troop Carrier squadron to fly the Pacific Ocean. Its ground echelon, commanded by Capt. Frank W. Smith (now Maj.) joined it on December 13, 1942. Six airplanes of the 33rd Troop Carrier Squadron, commanded by Capt. Eugene Jackson (now Maj.), were delayed for a month in New Caledonia, to ferry personnel and supplies to Guadalcanal.

The battle for possession of the Solomon Islands, on which Guadalcanal is located, was in full swing at that time. The 33rd

Squadron's planes aided mostly in the evacuation of wounded and in leading fighter planes over long water hops. (Fighter planes do not have navigators and may easily become lost in bad weather.)

The remaining airplanes of the 33rd Squadron proceeded to Cairns, Northern Queensland, and operated from there to New Guinea until December 10, when they went to New Guinea permanently. Its ground echelon joined it in Port Moresby on December 28, 1942.

All the Troop Carrier squadrons - 6th, 21st, 22nd, and 33rd - were assigned to the 374th Troop Carrier Group, Lt. Col. Nichols commanding. When Lt. Col. Nichols (now full colonel) returned to the U.S. on December 17, 1942, Col. Paul H. Prentiss (now brigadier general), assumed command. It was from the 374th Troop Carrier Group that the actual 54th Troop Carrier Wing was formed.

As the year 1942 ended, the 374th had two full squadrons, the 6th and 33rd, operating in New Guinea as well as air echelons of the 21st and 22nd Squadrons. The 374th had successfully carried into the front lines more than 40,000,000 pounds of airborne supplies with a loss of 15 planes.

The assault on Wau by the Japanese continued in force. In this new offensive their purpose was intended to dislodge the Aussies from Wau.

George Johnston vividly describes this attack and the Troop Carrier work:

"Down the green slopes of the Bulolo Valley came the full-scale Japanese attack against the important gold-fields airport of Wau. The small Australian garrison, outnumbered five to one, was pushed back almost to the outskirts of the landing field. It was then, when it seemed impossible that the vital little tropic town could be held, that the "bully-beef" bombers were again rushed in to save the day. They rushed to and fro across the great jagged peaks of the Owen Stanleys, bringing everything else needed to stem the waves of Japanese troops that swarmed across the low rounded hills of the mountain valley. They came under a patrolling top cover of P-38's and P-40's in which every pilot's finger was itching on the gun button.

"Once the Japs decided to smash the resistance and fracture our aerial supply by launching a fierce 'blitz' on Wau airfield with scores of Zeros and dive bombers. The sky was black with aircraft and pocked with the gray and white puffs of bursts from anti-aircraft guns. Plane after plane came crashing down, trailing black smoke and red flame. A Douglas transport on the field was disintegrated. Another Douglas raced up the valley with two Zeros chasing it, guns and cannons blazing. But out of the sun came the P-38's, and the Zeros went smashing straight into the great green mountain wall, belching oily smoke into the sky as they hit. Altogether 40 Japanese planes were destroyed in that wild melee. The rest were driven off. Natives on the Wau drome bent their backs to their shovels as they filled in the bomb craters. Within an hour the Douglas transports were streaming in again.

"Twenty-four hours after the beginning of the Japanese attack on the Wau airfield the enemy was in full retreat, leaving a thousand enemy dead.

"The victory was won by Australian artillery and infantry of the 17th Brigade, but without the eleventh-hour support of the American transport planes it would have been a disastrous defeat. Often the Americans who manned the transports grabbed their revolvers and Tommy guns and sprinted down to the front line 500 yards away, to empty magazines at the Japs in the few minutes they had to spare while their planes were being emptied of supplies and loaded up with wounded."

General Prentiss, who with Col. Hampton was awarded the Silver Star for searching for a lost plane far behind the enemy lines, supplied the cold statistics which made this spontaneous air movement unprecedented in the history of air warfare.

"Landing at Wau airdrome, which rises one foot in every twelve with a crescent of mountains at its far end that makes it impossible to 'go around' at the last moment, 40 airplanes made 66 trips on January 30. The next day 35 airplanes made 71 trips; on February 1, 40 airplanes landed 53 plane loads of over 6000 pounds each. This made a total of 1,140,000 pounds of personnel and equipment flown into Wau in three days, with a loss of only three aircraft. Co-ordination with fighter cover, the efforts of all Troop Carrier personnel in furnishing aircraft at a moments notice, and the skill and devotion to duty of the flying personnel made this swift victory possible."

NEW MEMBERS OF THE CATERPILLARS CLUB

JUNE 1942

On the long uneventful flight from Archer Field to Darwin in June of 1942, the two pilots were serenely drifting along to their destination without concern for the war raging around them. They didn't even feel too much concern that the approach to Darwin would be a problem. They had made the flight many times before. Pilot 2nd Lt. Charles R. Baer (later Capt. Baer of Pan Am Airlines) and co-pilot 2nd Lt. Grimes (one of the discovers of Hidden Valley) were now considered veterans of the Pacific War. The landing at Darwin was without incident. There was no Japanese air raid to contend with on this day and a fast turn around for a return

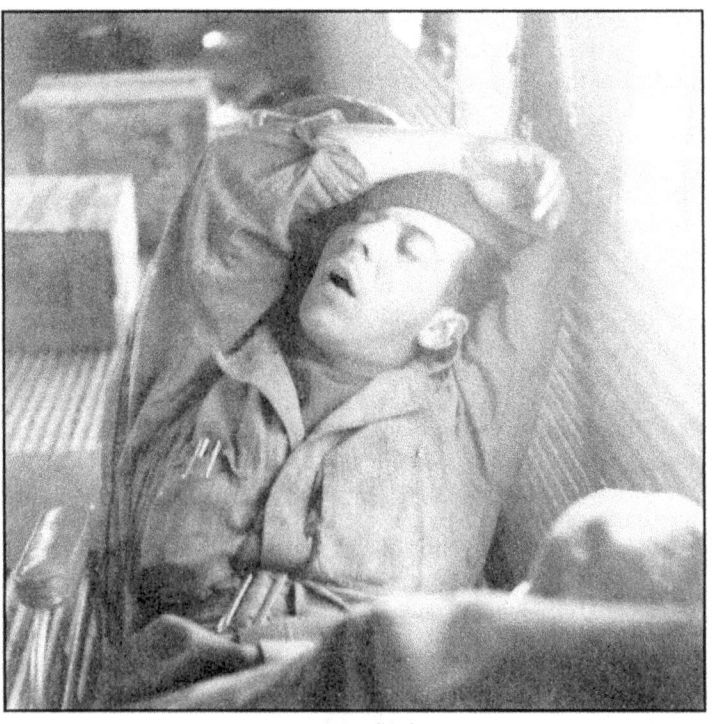

A crew chief.

Chick Bair and Mel Lewis with Australian beauties in Brisbane, 1942.

Yuska – 21st T.C. Squadron.

Roger Gerling at Archer Field in Brisbane, Australia, 1942.

Imparato, Pitaro, and Corkrun at Archer Field, 1942.

Schuster and Imparato.

Key 21st Squadron Personnel, Archer Field, 1942.

> ### SONG OF THE TROOP CARRIERS
>
> When the last bloody sword has been broken;
> When the saga of war has been told;
> When the last of the heroes is cited,
> I shall tell you a tale of the bold.
> I shall sing you a song of the transports,
> The sturdiest ships in the sky!
> I shall sing you a song of the warriors
> Who asked nothing more than to fly.
> Unarmored, unarmed, overladen,
> Their mighty grey wings took the air,
> Through storms - the unknown - through the moon's hush
> With freight that must always get there.
> Hugging the hills and the valleys;
> Vaulting the cliffs and the trees;
> Dodging the weather - the Zeros;
> Honor the youngest of these!
> Aching to fight, but quite helpless;
> Yearning for speed that's not there.
> Clumsy with freight - out of balance;
> Chained to the flight of despair!
> You can't slug it out with a Mitsu.
> You can't run - you haven't the speed.
> So - it's hide in the trees or the weather,
> But take it through - stick to the creed!
> The wounded aboard are your charges,
> You're shackled to rudder and wheel.
> No 'chutes and no belts and no life-rafts;
> You'll slam them to hell, if you fail!
> Or - the engines on board, for a "Lightning"
> Are grounding a fighter, tonight;
> While a dozen or twenty-odd Zeros
> Will live, till she's back in the fight.
> "Take it through! Take it through!" is your war-cry;
> To hell with the flak in your way!
> To hell with the Nips and the weather!
> Your number was called yesterday.
> You're living because you've been lucky.
> Or possibly - could it be so? -
> Some bright angel rides there beside you.
> Ride her, boy! Win, place, or show!
> This is the song of the transports,
> Weary from many a mile;
> A song of the pilots who ride them
> Down into hell with a smile!
>   MAJOR J. H. PAUL, U.S.A.

to Cloncurry was arranged. The 2000 mile round trip - Cloncurry to Cloncurry - with the stop at Darwin was tiring. They were happy to hit the sack late that evening on arrival back at Cloncurry. The last leg of the flight from Cloncurry to Archer Field at Brisbane with a refueling stop at Charleville would be a snap so they decided on a late rising and ate breakfast before their departure for Charleville.

The next day, June 17, 1942, the crew departed Cloncurry at noon for the short 600 mile flight to Charleville. The flight was concluded without incident. At the refueling stop at Charleville the crew picked up sandwiches and coffee and reentered the aircraft for the short 450 mile flight to Archer Field, their home port. It was to be a three hour flight. Take off was made at 6:00 p.m. with estimated time of arrival at Archer, 9:00 p.m. The weather was clear en route. One hour after takeoff from Charleville, dusk began to settle over the land as the sun gradually sank below the horizon in the west.

The flight proceeded as planned until one hour out of Archer Field an explosion of the left engine engulfed the total engine and its nacelle in a burst of menacing red-orange flame threatening to explode the fuel tanks which were directly behind the engines.

Pilot Baer ordered in a clear precise tone to his copilot, "Pull the left fire extinguisher actuator and feather the left prop!"

Copilot Grimes replied, "Yes sir!"

The fire extinguisher did not reduce the flame and the prop would not feather.

Pilot Baer to crew, "Don parachutes and prepare for further instructions." One minute later, "All bail out quickly!"

Copilot Grimes left his seat and went to the cargo door with the rest of the crew. The crew chief released the cargo door and the bail out proceeded. The cabin was in complete darkness except for the menacing flashes from the engine fire.

Pilot Baer put the aircraft on autopilot and left his seat to turn to the rear and the cargo door for his bail out. It appeared to him that all the crew had cleared the aircraft and he would be the last man out. This is normal procedure. As Baer descended in his parachute he could see the airplane in stable flight and it appeared to him the fire seemed to be fading. The airplane was soon out of his sight and Baer suddenly found himself enmeshed in the canopy of low level trees and heavy brush. He sprained his ankle on landing unable to judge his descent precisely due to the darkness.

Meanwhile back in the airplane at time of bail out, Grimes, while racing to the cabin door, fell headlong into the rear of the cabin and lay there as all others had cleared the aircraft. Grimes head cleared, but felt the airplane was in a steep dive and would soon crash. He ran to the cockpit to orient himself and found the fire was out and the airplane flying straight and level on autopilot. Some altitude had been lost but otherwise the aircraft appeared flyable. Grimes debated whether to remain with the airplane or bail out. His decision to remain with the airplane was the result of clear thinking in a stressful situation. The loss of altitude was minimal, the empty aircraft was able to maintain altitude on one engine with no difficulty and he was less than an hour out of home base. Grimes continued the flight to Archer and landed safely only 30 minutes short of the scheduled arrival time. The remainder of the crew parachuted to safety and except for sprains and bruises, found support from farmers in the parachuted area for a safe return to Archer.

All the crew who bailed out of their C-49 received the Caterpillar emblem and are life members of the Caterpillar Club as their reward for a successful jump from a crippled airplane. Grimes received a letter of commendation for his superb, clear thinking, high risk performance and for saving a much needed airplane.

6TH TROOP CARRIER SQUADRON

JUNE 1942 - JANUARY 1943

Dick Vaughter

The origin and first mass flight of the 6th Troop Carrier Squadron, June, 1942 to January, 1943, as described by Sgt. Dick Vaughter, Pilot. Dick was soon commissioned and was reported to have flown the greatest number of hours in one month in combat.

> "The 6th Transport Squadron was transferred from Middletown Air Depot to Camp Williams, Wisconsin, June, 1942. Camp Williams to Selfridge Field, Michigan, in August, 1942 as part of the 63rd Transport Group, which then became the 63rd Troop Carrier Group. Other squadrons in that group were the 3rd, 9th and 52nd.

"In September the 6th was separated from the group, transferred to Dodd Field, San Antonio, Texas, then to McCellan Field, Sacramento, California, for replacement aircraft, then to Hamilton Field, California for final overseas assignment.

"Still as an independent squadron without a group or wing assignment, the 6th Troop Carrier Squadron departed Hamilton Field as the first mass flight of C-47s across the Pacific. Takeoffs began at midnight, 1 October, 1942, following at three minute intervals until all 13 aircraft were airborne. As was custom for war time, all running lights were extinguished except for the low-power blue formation lights which could only be seen for a short distance above and aft.

"All aircraft were equipped with the usual 800 gallon wing tanks, plus two 400 gallon fuselage tanks mounted just aft of the cockpit. The flight crews were briefed to use low RPM 1620 and manifold pressure estimated to produce approximately 130 MPH. Captain John Lackey, our squadron commander, suggested that we find smooth power settings that would enable us to get the plane "on the step" as close to the desired 130 MPH as possible and maintain that situation to the point of no return for fuel evaluation. We (in Norma) were the number 12 ship for takeoff. Our fuel situation at the point of no return was excellent and we were in clear daylight conditions, so decided to let our speed build as the aircraft lightened in weight. Throughout the dark and early morning hours we saw no other aircraft. Finally we spotted the first ahead of us as we descended toward the island of Oahu. The aircraft ahead started an identifying 360 degree turn and broke radio silence by calling Hickam Tower. It was our lead ship 'Linda Ann'. We had passed the other ten aircraft, which departed Hamilton Field ahead of us and landed number two behind 'Linda Ann'.

"Our time en route was 13 hours and 45 minutes, fastest by over half an hour. When our fuel tanks were checked for amount remaining, we had approximately 590 gallons. Our power/speed management proved much better than forecast. One other thing that might have helped our performance was our reverting to basic dead reckoning navigation after our brand new (out of navigation school) navigator began en route heading changes of 25 degrees and 35 degrees. Our weather/wind briefing had forecast light winds, so we went to forecast headings and only made heading changes of 5 degrees or less when recommended by the navigator. This made our course more direct than if we had followed the big heading changes called for while the navigator was getting settled down and gaining expertise in the use of the sextant and celestial navigation.

"The auxiliary fuel tanks were removed at Hickam. Our itinerary on departure was Canton Island, Christmas Island, Samoa, Fiji, New Caledonia, Brisbane and Townsville, Australia, ending at Jackson Strip, Port Moresby, New Guinea.

"Our first night in New Guinea was memorable. We listened to the Tokyo Rose radio broadcast (with good American swing music) and received her "Welcome to the arrival 6th Troop Carrier Squadron at Jackson Strip." It was hard for us to believe that the Japanese spy chain would be so up-to-date on the movements of a single troop carrier squadron. Rose promised, and delivered, an air raid on Jackson later that night which killed three men; fortunately, none of ours.

"We learned quickly that we had much to learn about aerial supply drops. Lt. Lattier and I in "Norma" suffered the first damage when our rear cargo door was fouled and blown off its mounts by the out-going cargo and wind blast. The door struck the horizontal stabilizer and cut a 12" deep hole. We were able to return to base for repairs.

"Less than a month later, the squadron had two similar incidents involving door loss and elevator damage or fouling. Then on 5 November 1942, we lost our first aircraft, "Maxine", complete with crew as a cargo chute deployed and passed over the horizontal stabilizer while the cargo box of ammo passed under the stabilizer. The immediate nose over caused the aircraft to dive into the mountain jungle below. Witnessed by Staff Sgt. Pilot George Beaver.

"Hard lesson learned: remove the rear and front cargo doors; drop from at least 300 feet instead of 10 to 20 feet; use a longer static line on parachute drops."

6TH TROOP CARRIER SQUADRON

1942 - 1943

Ernest C. Ford

Lieutenant Ernest C. Ford reports on early 6th Troop Carrier Squadron activities.

"Little has been published of the airmanship, courage and hardships endured by the 6th Troop Carrier Squadron in New Guinea in 1942 and the early months of 1943. Alexander The Great in 323 BC may have had such a squadron in mind when he penned:

'God and soldier we adore,
In time of danger and not before.
The danger passed and the wrong
Is righted, God is forgotten and
The soldier is slighted.'

"It is time the 6th record became a matter of public knowledge.

"The 6th Transport Squadron was activated at Middletown Air Depot, Olmsted Field, Middletown,

Perry Penn at Archer Field with a C-47 aircraft, 1942.

Pennsylvania on 14 October 1939. They were the second Air Transport Squadron to be formed in the United States Army Air Corps. They were the first Troop Carrier to fly to Australia, departing Hamilton Field, California on 2 October 1942. The 6th was the first Troop Carrier Squadron to be permanently stationed in New Guinea. The 21st and the 22nd were activated in Australia in the spring of 1942, and were stationed in Australia. They would fly up to Jackson Airdrome, Port Moresby; refuel, go on a mission; refuel and return to the mainland.

"The 6th arrived at Jackson Airdrome on 13 October 1942, the 33rd arrived on 10 December 1942, the 22nd on 14 February 1943, and the 21st on 18 February 1943. 5th Air Force was activated on 4 September 1942, the 374th Troop Carrier Group was formed on 12 November 1942, and the 54th Troop Carrier Wing was activated on 20 May 1943.

"Rather than spending time describing camp life - mosquitoes, monsoons, the weather, bombing and strafing raids - I'll write a few words about flying with the 6th Troop Carrier Squadron in the early days of the war in New Guinea.

"When the 6th Troop Carrier Squadron departed Hamilton Field, California, they were flying 13 new C-47A aircraft each with a crew of five; pilot, co-pilot, navigator, crew chief and radio operator. Our squadron commander was Captain John H. Lackey, Jr. The first pilots were: one captain, three first lieutenants, seven second lieutenants and two staff sergeant pilots. The two staff sergeant pilots remained first pilots for their tour of duty. Flying from the States as co-pilots were three second lieutenants and ten staff sergeant pilots. All of the staff sergeant pilots received battle field commissions as second lieutenants on 8 April 1943, and were promoted to first lieutenants on 4 September 1943, all on the same order.

"The night the 6th arrived at Jackson Airdrome, Port Moresby, Papua, New Guinea, we were briefed. "While you're in New Guinea wear your dog-tags and a C-ration can opener around your neck, carry your steel helmet with mosquito head net attached, loaded 45 with a live bullet in the chamber and with at least three full clips of ammo, Bolo knife, full water canton, mirror and compass, Atabrine and salt pills with you at all times, no exceptions. The extra shell in the chamber is for use in the event of capture either by the Japs or headhunters, for neither take prisoners. One tortures, interrogates then kills; the cannibals will also eat you.

"There are no maps of New Guinea; the Australian infantry briefing officer sketched out on the ground the eastern end of the island. For the year we spent in New Guinea, the second largest island in the world, we had no maps. We were then briefed that if Jackson Field fell the Allies would abandon all of New Guinea and the northern half of Australia. The reason was that there were not enough ground troops and air support to defend such a large area. 'There are enemy troops within five miles of this airdrome. The Allies are holding on to Moresby by the skin of our teeth. If the enemy captures Jackson Airdrome we go. Until the situations becomes more stable or we leave New Guinea take everything with you on each mission, for you may not be landing back here.'

"We were then instructed on how to walk out of New Guinea jungle. If you look at a map, your first thought is, it cannot be done. Here is how we were to do it. 'If the field is captured you are to fly as far up the coast to the west as fuel will permit. Then land on the beach with the wheels either down or up. Take all your survival equipment, water, C-rations, compass and mirror both hanging around your neck, 45s and all the ammunition you can carry. Leave the nice hard beach by the water and walk in the sand next to the trees. For if the Japs fighters catch you walking on the beach you'll be strafed and killed before you can make it to the trees. While next to trees if you should hear a plane take cover in the trees. If it is a friendly aircraft, signal with your mirror. If it is an enemy aircraft, do not shoot at it for it will return and strafe the entire area and all the crew will be lost. That goes for firing at a strafer when in a slit trench in the camp area.

"'Continue walking west up the coast until you arrive at the Fly River which is a very wide, deep and fast moving river. Walk inland up this side of the river for at least a fortnight, yes, fourteen days. Then find a log and make a paddle. Get on the log and paddle for all your worth for the other side and hope that before you reach the ocean you're on the other side of the river. Do not go swimming for either a man-eating crocodile or shark will have a meal!

"'Continue to walk up the beach next to the trees until you see small off-shore islands on your left. Then signal with your mirror to the natives on the island. They will row over and you will be able to go from island to island for the hundred miles between New Guinea and Australia. Walk down the east coast of Australia until you join up with friendly troops.'

"We were then told about our mission. 'Your job is to stop the enemy!!' That caught all of our attention. 'If you can carry Aussie and Yank soldiers, supplies, equipment and evacuate the wounded when and where we need them, in the quantity required all without air cover we can stop and turn the Japs around. The only escort you will have is one 'Wirraway' aircraft, you Yanks call it an AT-6, it has two 30 caliber machine guns. The plan is for the AT-6 to fly 5,000 feet above your squadron leader. When the AT-6 pilot spots enemy aircraft the 'Wirraway' will go into a vertical dive for the trees. All aircraft are to break formation, scatter and fly as close to the trees as you dare and zig-zag to the coast. If you fly in a straight line it is easy for the fighters to line up on you. Stay over the forest and away from the open spaces for it is easier to be spotted from the air. If the prop hits the very tops of the tree, it will only nick the blades and put leaves in the oil coolers. Buzzing is legal only to keep away from the enemy. Do not make steep banks when flying at tree top level for if a wing goes into the trees the aircraft will cartwheel and that will be the end of one aircraft. You will hear Tokyo Rose, she plays the latest American Hit Parade music from the States and some of the best propaganda you'll ever hear. She will announce your arrival in the morning,' and she did.

"The first week we flew in New Guinea was to drop (free fall) supplies and equipment to the ground troops in small clearings between the trees. For this period the T-6 was grounded and we were on our own. Yes, we could see the Jap fighters and bombers from where we were flying just above tree tops. Our first combat loss was on the third day after our arrival. An enemy fighter caught one of the our C-47s in a clear area while dropping supplies. Over the next 13 months, the 6th Troop Carrier Squadron lost five aircraft and crews in combat.

"On 3 November 1942, the 6th Troop Carrier Squadron was the first squadron to land at Kokoda Strip on the north side of the Owen Stanley Mountains. It was the first time for the squadron to land at a field (other than at Jackson or Wards Airdromes) behind enemy lines less than 24 hours after the field had been captured. Kokoda Airstrip was a bombed-out mined, dirt, grass and rock strip. It was at 1,260 foot elevation, 1,500 feet long from trees to trees. The landing strip was located on the north side of the Owen Stanley Mountains up to the side of a 13,440 foot mountain peak. Troops were flown in with their gear, supplies and equipment. On the return flight, the 6th Troop Carrier Squadron air-evacuated the first wounded patients by air in the New Guinea Campaign. Only four P-39 fighter aircraft flew escort on this mission; that was all the fighters available. At that time Kokoda Airstrip was only 20 air miles from Poppendetta, a Jap fighter base. I guess that is why they told us we were expendable, the mission of the 6th was to support the infantry and it was a must that we supported all their needs. In those days on the north side of the mountains no traffic patterns were over 200 feet above touch down.

"On 24 January we made our first landing at Wau, New Guinea. This is a strip that books and a movie could be written about. With an up hill runway slope of 12% and a 700 foot usable dirt landing area it had the added attraction of a village of cannibals at the upper end of the strip. There were no go arounds at this strip. The hillside was littered with aircraft that had tried to make another try at it. To add to the excitement the enemy were hitting the field with mortar and heavy rifle fire. It was a miracle that any aircraft was ever able to land at Wau in peace time let alone during a raging ground battle.

"On 6 February 1943 the war for Wau heated up. Bombers were added to the enemy's determination to capture this important piece of real estate. Jap bombers dropped bombs as four transports landed. This was in addition to the mortar thumping in the runway and the enemy infantry ground fire. It was just like a John Wayne movie, and ten times as scary. An Aussie Wirraway landed and as the crew were abandoning their aircraft it was hit by a bomb and destroyed. One of the four C-47s from another squadron was shot down on takeoff by enemy infantry ground troops that were trying to capture the air field.

"As pilot of one of the four Goonie Birds on the ground I was recommended for the Silver Star for saving the three loaded aircraft, twelve crew members, eighty-seven Australia infantry troops and their equipment. For some strange, unexplainable reason the award was never received. However, the award of the decoration was published in 1943 by *American Heroes Of The War In The Air*, Volume One, by Howard Mingoes, Lanciar Publishers, Inc., New York, on page 293, under The Fight For Island Air Bases,: 'Staff Sgt. Ernest C. Ford, Air Corps, U.S. Army, Manzanola,

Lt. Bill Sterns laughs at his own joke; Brisbane, Australia, 1942.

Colo. Silver Star'. Between the period of January to May, 1943, as first pilot, I made twenty-four landings at Wau Airstrip.

"By this time in the war the 6th was landing at all the forward strips on both sides of where the ground fighting was taking place. Many of the supplies were delivered by air, either free fall or by parachutes. Everything the Army required to fight a war on the ground was flown in and out by C-47s. They flew out thousands of wounded and never with a medical corpsman aboard. Some of the patients did die en route back to Wards Airdrome.

"On 15 August 1943, the squadron was briefed that we would be flying to Tsilli Tsili airstrip in the Markham Valley area behind Lae. This would be the first time any aircraft had landed at this field, so we were to watch out for holes in the stubble grass and dirt landing strip. The enemy had fighter bases closer to the field than the Allies. I was flying Tail-End-Charlie. As we joined up into formation climbing out from Wards, two other C-47s from the group closed in, one on either wing. Whenever the squadrons flew group or wing formation, we were briefed to close in all gaps for better fighter protection. Both our top and close fighter cover on this mission were P-39s.

"As we in the second flight of troop carrier aircraft were just entering the traffic pattern to land, Japanese fighters attacked from above and behind. The 6th was in a right echelon when one of their Zeros came in from high and behind and on one pass shot down both my wingmen. No. 3 went into a graveyard spiral, crashed and burned near the edge of the grass airstrip. The right wingman was last seen heading for the mountains on fire and smoking. The Zero did a sharp 180 and came back head on for me. By this time I was just above the trees at full throttle. Then came his tracers. How they missed only God knows. Not one bullet touched "Irene". We skidded, banked and reduced airspeed, too low and slow for the Zero to line us up in his gun sight. What evasive tactics can one do?

"From the first firing of his machine guns that got both my wingmen until the last pass at me, it could not have been over six or seven minutes by the clock. But in my memory it was an eternity. I can still see the tracers and the Jap fighter pilot's big flying goggles as

Roger Gerling, Perry Penn, and Mel Lewis.

he pulled up to avoid a midair collision. He was not a Kamikaze pilot, one of the "Divine Wind Boys", for he did not ram me head on. Our closure speed was as high as 550-560 mph and on the low side of 220 mph. In WWII that was fast, that is if one aircraft was a transport and the other a fighter.

"Most fighter pilots arrange their ammo belts so that one to five or one to seven rounds are tracers. The tracers are so the pilot will be able to see where he is shooting and correct accordingly. In my case I was sure he was aiming for my No. 1 engine. After many changes of heading, airspeed, skids and banks, here came two of our P-39s and that is all that saved us. Our escape literally defied all odds. You do not have time to think. If you want to stay alive, it's all by reflexes. This all took place over the grass field where we were to land. Either we had no ground ack-ack or they were afraid that they would hit our aircraft.

"All airborne C-47s were clearing the area, cutting a crooked zig-zag path through the tall Kunai grass for the mountains and Wau and then back to Wards. A fierce air battle was going on all around us with fighters, bombers and transports being shot down. We could see that several of our fighters were shot down as the enemy had many more aircraft than we had. When we were well out of the area we climbed over the mountains, in and around the clouds and returned to Moresby. Each C-47 came back to base on his own without fighter escort.

"The 6th Troop Carrier Squadron spent 354 days in combat before being rotated out of the combat zone back to Australia. The squadron's flight crews had been awarded The Distinguished Unit Citation Device with two Oak Leaf Clusters, 245 Distinguished Flying Crosses, and 163 Air Medals including Oak Leaf Clusters.

"By the end of World War II there were 19 troop carrier squadrons in the Pacific Theater. No troop carrier squadron in the Pacific during all of WWII came close to being awarded this many decorations. And this was only the first tour of combat for the 6th TCS during the war. On this one tour of duty during WWII the 6th was awarded 408 flight decorations. In only 354 days of combat (or about 35% of total days of fighting) the 6th was awarded 15% of all the DFCs that the other 18 troop carrier squadrons combined received for the 1001 days of fighting in World War II.

Not a bad record for a squadron that had more enlisted pilots than officer pilots.

"Weather was one of the big enemies to flying in New Guinea. When flying was called off as being below minimums, group operations of the 374th Troop Carrier Group would call some of the eager, capable first pilots and ask if they wished to fly. In the 6th, Sgt. Dick Vaughter and I were always eager, ready and waiting to fly. That is why we flew the most missions of any crew members in the 54th Troop Carrier Wing. We always delivered the urgently needed troops, supplies and equipment and returned the wounded without one single accident. When I flew my last combat mission in New Guinea, my record was 364 as a C-47 troop carrier pilot. I received six Distinguished Flying Crosses and two Air Medals. Returning to the United States, I went on Bond Tours where I was billed as having the most combat missions of any pilot in the United States Army Air Force. Vaughter was always only a few combat missions behind."

Whole Divisions Moved by Air In Route of Japs

By H. E. Patterson
(Accredited War Correspondent)
WITH THE TROOP CARRIER COMMAND,
SOUTHWEST PACIFIC

—America has created two machines without which the allies would not be able to run this war - one is the jeep and the other is the Douglas C-47 airplane.

The man who made that flat declaration is Lt. Col. Edward T. Imparato, executive officer of the first Troop Carrier Command unit organized in the Southwest Pacific, the gang who flew 5,000,000 miles carrying troops and supplies in the first six months of the war, the gang whose exploits make even the most fantastic Hollywood air war pictures look silly.

Back in 1942, a year before we finally captured Salamaua, this outfit flew 200 Australian Commando troops into an old gold strip at Wau. The commandos were to try to capture, or at least harass the Japs at Salamaua. The strip at Wau is short, 3,300 feet, and runs uphill with a 7,000-foot mountain at the end of it.

DOES JOB IN HURRY

"We flew in, six ships at a time, landed on the strip, slowed down just enough for the troops to leap out, turned around and took off without a stop," said Captain Harvey Rehrer of Reading, Pa., one of the squadron leaders. "The landing was very tricky. You are climbing when you land. One of the boys cracked up because he could not figure the approach right."

Back in March, 1942, when the Japs were bombing Darwin, the Troop Carrier unit flew an entire battalion of anti-aircraft troops, complete with their guns and ammunition, 1,800 miles across Australia to Darwin.

"We loaded them so that each plane carried a gun, ammunition and crew, ready to jump out, set up and start shooting," said Colonel Imparato. "The Japs had a big surprise the day when they came over."

WHOLE DIVISION BY AIR

In September, 1942, the unit moved an entire division of men from Australia and landed them southeast of Buna. They were landed on a strip surrounded by impassable jungle, were supplied by air all the time they were driving the Japs back from their big push on Port Moresby - and were moved out again by C-47s in January, 1943.

The saving of the Wau airdrome back in January, 1943, was one of the unit's proudest - and most rugged - operations.

"The Japs made a push from Salamaua and Lae to capture the strip at Wau and we flew in 700 troops a day for four days to stop the drive," sand Captain James Watson, of Dallas, Texas.

"To make our approach up the valley we had to fly over the Jap lines, over ack-ack and mortar fire. The Japs killed a number of troops at one end of the runway while one of our ships was turning around and getting off again.

WIND IS SMALL WORRY

"Snipers were shooting at us as we made our turn and we had to take off and fly out over the Jap lines again. But the takeoff was down hill and we got away from there fast. We paid no attention to wind direction, just banged in, dropped the troops, spun around and gunned out again."

Back in October, 1942, part of the outfit flew supplies to our troops on Guadalcanal, landed at Henderson Field when the Japs were only 1,000 yards away.

"Jap snipers used to kill our men while they were putting gas into the ship," said Lieut. Burl Ashley, of Tetark Falls, Ohio. "We flew in ammunition and took out wounded. We always carry stretchers in the airplane and in all our operations where we carry in supplies we haul out wounded. A man can be shot in New Guinea and in a few hours be resting in a general hospital in Australia."

THIS IS A REST

The unit has now been pulled out of front line action and are now "resting" - hauling supplies and men along an 1,800 mile airline from Australia to New Guinea. They are flying C-47 airplanes with 5,000 pound payloads in all kinds of weather.

All C-47 airplanes used in this theater now are flown to Australia from the west coast of America.

"There were 13 planes that took off," said Captain Conrad Rowland of Ezel, Ky., who made such a flight. "We flew down here in six hops and never lost a plane. When we landed in Australia we had flown more than 7,000 miles over open ocean in 54 hours flying time."

This is the gang that flew two and a half ton trucks into Wau - they even hauled mules.

THEY FLY EVERYTHING

"I think that mule hauling deal was an experiment to determine if we could haul whole artillery units," said Major George Foster, of Wellesley, Mass. "We rigged up special stalls and catwalks and put three mules in the C-47. They took off and flew around a couple of times to see if it could be done. We have hauled about everything else you can mention."

They mentioned a few: planes loaded with bread, with bombs, with grenades, with troops, lumber, pipe, bulldozers, caterpillar tractors. They even hauled a complete radio station up to Darwin in the early days of the fighting - cut the big radio tower in sections and loaded it in.

"You know that steel runway at Doboura - we hauled every one of those mats across the mountains," said Capt. Robert G. Whittington of Dallas. "We lugged 7,000,000 pounds of steel mats over to Doboura for the runways."

The mats are eight by two and a half feet and weight 69 pounds. They carried 80 mats per trip.

- Wings For Invasion -

33RD TROOP CARRIER SQUADRON

EARLY HISTORY

THE PACIFIC OCEAN SAGA OF GEORGE WAMSLEY

The organization, early development and overseas saga of the 33rd is best told by its future commander and talented writer, George Walter Wamsley, Jr. In his book *"American Fly Boy"* he recounts his personal experiences from childhood and his developing interest in flying from an early age. His formative years were during the great depression where dollars were hard to find but he scrounged and worked hard to find a few dollars to satisfy his love of flying.

It was the late 1930's and the war in Europe was heating up. The U.S. Government sent out a call for men to qualify for flying instruction. The College Pilot Training Program known as CPT began at selected colleges and universities nationwide in 1938. The response from second year students was encouraging. The CPT program expanded at a rapid pace. It was with this CPT program that George Wamsley found his niche and eased his way to a second lieutenant commission in the U.S. Army Air Corp. From primary trainers to advanced trainers, George graduated to qualify as a C-47 pilot.

The U.S. Army Air Force Troop Carrier Command established in early 1942, took over command responsibility for assembling, indoctrinating and training all officers assigned to troop carrier duty. The breakdown of the command into wings, groups and squadrons established the command structure. A wing consisted of two or more groups; a group, two or more squadrons and squadrons normally consisting of 13 to 18 aircraft, 50 to 80 pilots and up to 300 airmen. Thus from this structure the 33rd Troop Carrier received its number and key staff to organize an effectively trained and manned fighting unit. This was accomplished in mid 1942. It was at this period that the 374th Troop Carrier Group received its designation and record as the first troop carrier group to be organized overseas. Only two squadrons were initially assigned to the 374th Troop Carrier Group. The squadrons were the 21st Troop Carrier Squadron and the 22nd Troop Carrier Squadron which were organized primarily from casual pilots and crews arriving in the southwest Pacific theater unassigned and evacuees from Java and the Philippines. The first aircraft assigned were those aircraft commandeered by U. S. forces from a number of sources in the theater which could be used as transport aircraft.

Out of Florence, South Carolina, in mid-summer the 33rd received its designation as the 33rd Troop Carrier Squadron and was ordered to Sacramento, California. After a short training cycle and the installation of cabin fuel cells at Sacramento, the squadron was ordered to Hamilton Field to await further orders. There was no doubt in the minds of the crews that the added fuel cells portended long overseas flights but the destination was still unknown. The addition of drift meters reaffirmed the crews' suspicions. Drift meters are essential for over water flights because no land checkpoints or radio aids are available for many hundreds of miles and wind shifts and wind speeds over open water can greatly alter an aircrafts tract over a period of time.

At the preflight briefing at Hamilton Field prior to departure for Hawaii and Hickam Field the briefing officer, a young 2nd Lt., gave the crews what little information he was privy to regarding the first leg of the flight to Hickam. With tongue in cheek, George Wamsley recounts the briefing officer's comments:

> "It didn't seem like adequate information, but we were too dumb to ask any intelligent questions. He did give us this information and these instructions:

"'You will be landing at Hickam Field, which is just across the bay from Honolulu, if you find it. Hickam tower frequency is such and such. Go around Diamond Head and up Waikiki Beach a mile or so. Hickam will be off to your left at about ten or eleven o'clock, across the bay. The distance from Hamilton to Hickam is right at 2,400 miles.

"'You will be flying individually, not as a formation. Takeoff will be at twenty- to thirty-minute intervals. You will each be assigned an altitude at which to fly and each will have different power settings so we can determine which is the most efficient. <u>If you get there give us a call and we'll know your settings were okay</u>. Hey, that's a joke. Don't look so pale.

"'The Coast Guard reports no serious weather conditions, but they don't know beyond 500 miles. There is a radio beam out of Hilo that you might be able to receive an hour or so before you reach the island of Oahu.

"'Maintain Radio Silence.

"'Here is a list of power settings for each plane and an approximate takeoff time. It will be dark for takeoff, but you will gain *x* number of hours of daylight, so you'll have plenty of light left for landing at Hickam. Hickam will brief you on the balance of your flight to Australia.

"'Incidentally, the magnetic compass heading to Hickam is such and such, but remember the direction will change some as you go along.'

"So this was it, I guess we were about to make a little history. Naturally we had to feel excitement, but I recall being calm, confident, relaxed, and ready, not cocky or macho. New adventures were almost a daily occurrence, so why not feel at ease about this one? Here we were heading out on an unknown mission to a faraway part of the world that we barely knew existed, over a body of water so large we couldn't imagine it. I guess we had to be adaptable. I don't recall ever having any written orders sending me away. We had no navigator. Probably no sense or we wouldn't be doing this, but we adapted. There was evidently a list of crews for the thirteen airplanes, which I first saw in 1988, forty-six years later. These thirteen planes and crews were each a story by themselves, though the memory does get foggy as to specifics.

"This I clearly remember: the way it felt to taxi that C-47 out toward the end of a big, long runway and knowing that it would be a long, long flight over a lot of water before the landing gear touched back down on Mother Earth. I feel it now but can't describe it. So what! There was work to be done.

"We didn't have preflight written checklists in those days, but my hand touched every control or gauge that had to be working properly, to be sure all was in order. Because of the extreme overweight, I wanted as much runway as possible so I got as far as possible to the starting end. I think the tail wheel must have hung off the runway. After a final check and a good listen to the sweet-sounding engines, I released the brakes and pushed the throttles just a little more than maximum forward. The roll began. I could feel the overload, but the roll accelerated very nicely. The speed indicator rose just like during any other takeoff, and lo and behold, by the time we were halfway down the runway, the speed was over normal takeoff. I pulled

Port Moresby, New Guinea Hotel, 1942.

the tail down a little, the wheels gently left the ground, and we gained some altitude. That plane, with that wing and with those engines, was so good that it didn't even know it was being abused. It just purred along over the bay, over the lights of San Francisco, and over the Golden Gate on the way to the other side of the Pacific ocean.

"My assigned altitude was 8,000 feet, so in my naïveté I thought that meant 8,000 feet. There were some clouds and some thunder heads that could have been avoided by going left or right a few miles or up or down some, but that nice young second lieutenant said 8,000 feet, so that's what we maintained.

"My assigned power settings, both boost and RPMs, were about as low as you could use and still stay in the air; but again, that's what the man said and that's what he got. Had I known enough to go up to 9,000 feet and then gradually descend to 8,000 feet, we could have picked up a few miles per hour air speed and maintained that for a long time. Nothing said this maneuver couldn't be done several times on a single flight, but that we didn't know. A day or two later, as we became veterans at this, we learned that and many other fine points of properly handling a flying machine.

"We didn't see any other airplane, hear any radio chatter, or even see any ships afloat. That is, except when Shea came in with, 'Hey, look down below. That's a battleship.' I knew his voice very well, but he must have been some distance away, because we didn't see anything. And it wasn't a battleship, probably a destroyer. Our battleships were all in the far Pacific or sunk in Pearl Harbor.

"The first time we had any idea of about where on the line to Hickam we really were was when we intersected the beam from Hilo. Our radio operator, Ben King, had picked up Hilo's A-quadrant signal some time back, but that didn't tell us much. In Morse code the A-quadrant is a dot-dash, dot-dash. On these old-fashioned radio ranges they could direct those quadrants covering one-quarter or a circle outward from the range station. The N-quadrant is a dash-dot, dash-dot. By slightly overlapping those two signals the sound would be a steady sound; hence it was referred to as the beam. That would give us a position on a line

Edward Imparato and Perry Penn eating bananas at Archer Field, 1942.

out from Hilo but it didn't say whether you were too close to the big island of Hawaii or too close to Alaska or right on your planned route to Hickam. At least it was comforting because we knew that we were about three-quarters of the way there. Not long after that, three fighter planes from Hickam came out to look us over. That should have been their procedure a few months earlier: December 7, 1941, to be exact.

"The atmosphere in the cockpit changed considerably. It wasn't so lonely anymore Ben King didn't usually talk much, but he started talking, obviously relieved. Thompson, the crew chief, wasn't much for talk either, but he started talking, obviously relieved. Bryce Smith, the copilot, seldom talked, but he started talking, obviously relieved. The pilot joined in the babble. He was also relieved. He had just taken his first leak since San Francisco. Through the relief tube. Right into the Pacific Ocean. That was real relief.

"After an elapsed time of fifteen hours and forty-five minutes we finally touched down at Hickam Field. We had fifteen minutes of fuel left over. Today the FAA would frown at that small amount of margin as being inadequate. But that fifteen minutes of fuel was okay by me.

"Somewhere along the line, four of the eight extra fuel tanks in the cabin were removed. It was probably done at Hickam. I don't recall any more flights of over nine or ten hours.

HICKAM TO CHRISTMAS ISLAND

"I had never heard of Christmas Island when somebody said, 'That's where you are headed on the next leg of your journey.' Christmas Island was apparently located southwest of Hawaii. As small as it was, there was no point in giving us a map of the island, because if you can find the island you can see the strip, since they are almost the same size. The somebody gave us the longitude, the latitude, and the nautical miles as well as the magnetic heading. We logged nine hours on that leg; thus I presumed it was about 1,500 miles from Hickam. Simple to get there, I guess. Just head out in the proper direction, fly nine hours, and if you see an island, land on it. There aren't any other islands for many miles, so you don't get any alternative.

The drift meter got plenty of use that day,. The main worry was wind direction. That included all directions: front, back, left, and right, because it would move us off the intended track. In this area there was no information about current weather conditions. Old mariners' maps didn't record anything about prevailing winds, and the ocean currents data didn't help us much.

THE RICKENBACKER INCIDENT

"Capt. Eddie Rickenbacker was heading over to the southwest Pacific on official War Department business. (He should have hitched a ride with one of us.) He had a B-17, a four-engine bomber, with a crew of eight or ten military. One crewman was a full-fledged navigator who, so the story goes, stumbled while boarding their plane at Hickam and dropped his sextant on the concrete. He picked it up and climbed aboard. Capt. Bill Cherry, the pilot, the rest of his crew, Rickenbacker, and his aide climbed in, and they took off for Palmyra Island, which would be some 200 or 300 miles west and north of our destination that day, Christmas Island. They didn't navigate by drift meter and luck. They had a trained navigator using an expensive sextant that could read the stars, the moon, and the sun. By having an accurate twenty-four-hour watch set on Greenwich time, charts, azimuths, horizons, and a compass, and perhaps even having been a Nobel candidate in math, theoretically the navigator could place the B-17 accurately over any spot on earth at that particular moment. But something didn't work. They were lost out over that ocean that day. I don't laugh. It wasn't funny, but it was so incongruous that equipped as they were, they were lost. I didn't think we were lost, yet, but we still had some miles to go to our planned destination with only a drift meter to keep us going in the proper direction.

"Our radio operator, Ben, had picked up a plain English radio transmission on one of his available frequencies, but not on the universal emergency frequency, 550. It went something like this: 'To anyone receiving this message. This is U.S. Army B-17 #___ heading for Palmyra. We have exceeded our ETA (estimated time of arrival) and have begun circular search procedure. (That means starting in small circles and gradually increasing radius.) We have less than four hours of fuel.' The signal came in quite strong, but over water this did not necessarily mean it was real close. We had a radio direction finder that had been installed at Sacramento, but it only pointed toward the transmission on 550. And it would only receive for forty or fifty miles. But for some reason the B-17 never did transmit on the 550 wavelength. We heard a later transmission with information that they had less than two hours of fuel and that the VIP on board was Rickenbacker.

"By then we had used up some of our time and a lot of our fuel zigzagging back and forth and shooting off in various directions every time we saw some imaginary object in the sky or on the water. Some others of our squadron were doing the same type search, but even though we could communicate with them, we couldn't tell our relative locations, because we were just scattered somewhere over that big patch of water. Some of our planes searched an extra day or two out of Christmas Island, some did the same out of Canton Island, and some went on to Fiji. As I recall, it was by pilot option what we chose to do. Our plane searched until dark one day, all of the following day, and two or three hours at first light the next day out of Canton Island.

"Rickenbacker and a couple of members of that B-17 crew were rescued three weeks after ditching in the ocean.

"Near the end of hostilities I was at Bergstrom Air Force Base in Texas when Captain Cherry, the pilot of Rickenbacker's B-17 and one of the very few survivors of three weeks in their life raft, came by. I think he was a colonel by then. We talked at length about the situations that could have conceivably contributed to his being unable to hit Palmyra back then. He was quite sure, as was the investigating team, that some damage had been done to the navigator's sextant when he dropped it at Hickam, so that he was taking incorrect position shots. That, or course, resulted in his track being to either the left or the right of the intended heading. Cherry didn't have any idea where they went into the water or which direction it was from Palmyra. They know now where they were finally found but had no idea from which direction they had come. If memory serves me, he also said that during those twenty or thirty days they were in the water they saw not one vessel or aircraft. They should have had a drift meter. I rubbed it in!

"During the early 1960s, when I lived in Scottsdale, Captain Rickenbacker, then president of Eastern Airlines, came to Phoenix to promote his airline. At a press lunch reception for him I was asked by the chairman to sit at Rickenbacker's table. Captain Rickenbacker had always made it known that he wanted to shake the hand of anyone who had worked on his rescue. Well, we didn't rescue him, but we tried hard and sure risked our own lives; thus I always thought we qualified for that handshake. After some chamber-of-commerce-type remarks about Phoenix and about Eastern Airlines, the chairman said, 'Captain Rickenbacker, everyone knows about your terrible accident in the pacific Ocean way back in 1942. Several planes and many naval vessels searched for survivors, but after a few days they abandoned the search and gave you and your crew up for dead. Everyone knows that two or three of you survived, under extremely adverse conditions. The story of you catching a lone sea gull that landed on your head and helped you to survive is a classic. We also know that you publicly stated on numerous occasions that you wanted to shake the hand of every person who had searched for you. We are pleased to introduce you to one of the military pilots who spent time doing just that in that big Pacific Ocean, almost twenty years ago. Meet George Wamsley.'

"Rickenbacker was a crotchety old guy and getting mighty old by that time. Tough, too. He looked me straight in the eye, no trace of a smile. 'You looked in the wrong place!' he practically shouted. There wasn't a sound. My heart sank to my shoes. My face turned red in embarrassment. Then he put on a big grin, shook my hand, patted me on the back, and said, 'Thanks, buddy.'"

From Christmas Island Wamsley and crew flew to Canton Island, a seven hour flight without incident. George was disappointed when they got to the halfway point. He said he had heard so much about the Equator and was excited about possibly seeing it. He searched almost as diligently for the Equator as he and his crew searched for Rickenbacker but he never found it.

The next flight took the crew to Fiji Island. The flight to Fiji was a 1,400 mile, nine hour flight.

The fifth leg of the ocean saga placed the crew at the French Colony of New Caledonia and its main city, Plainer des gaiacs (PDG). It was at this point in "MacArthur's War" that the Coral Sea naval battle just concluded with the U.S. achieving a smashing victory. On Wamsley's arrival at PDG he found six other 33rd Squadron C-47s which had just been commandeered by Admiral Bull Halsey. Bull Halsey needed airborne support to help clean up his logistical problems after the Coral Sea battle. The date was October 25, 1942.

"This might be a good time to clarify the scenario: Before we got anywhere near PDG, the marines, who had landed on Guadalcanal a few weeks earlier, were having one helluva time. The navy that put them there was hard put to resupply them with a fraction of the equipment that the marines needed. The Japanese controlled all of Guadalcanal except Henderson Field (airstrip), and some days they controlled that. Our navy had lost many vessels to a vastly superior Japanese navy force but didn't even think of pulling back. Our forces outscored the Japanese but were running out of firepower. (You heard about Iron Bottom Bay that was at Guadalcanal.)

"The luxury liner *President Coolidge* had been pressed into military service and was bringing a load of supplies, ammunition, equipment, and a complete hospital to Espíritu Santo in the New Hebrides, about 450 miles from PDG. The *President Coolidge* pulled into the friendly harbor of Espíritu Santo on October 26, 1942. Unfortunately, as the ship entered the harbor, it hit two U.S. mines and began to sink (Ira Wolfert, eyewitness). Surprisingly, only 5 lives were lost, because of the proximity to shore. The vessel sank rapidly and actually rolled over as it went down into the coral reefs. Salvage effort, for the cargo, that is, began immediately. I don't know just what percentage of the cargo was retrieved, but there were piles of equipment, crates and boxes scattered for two or three hundred yards along the shoreline. 5 lives were lost; 5,435 saved ('Wreck of the *Coolidge*' by David Doubilet. *National Geographic*, April 1988). The *Coolidge* sank on the second day we were at PDG, but we didn't know about it until four or five days later when we were dispatched to Espíritu Santo.

"Because of these existing conditions, Admiral Halsey, new on the job, thought our C-47s could ferry some of the most critical items from Espíritu Santo to Guadalcanal by air. The navy had no air transport, and their water transport was cut to ribbons. Halsey's title was Commander, South Pacific, and that included all branches of the military. He had been in command for probably ten days now. (MacArthur was Commander, Southwest Pacific, and the command boundary passed between New Caledonia and Australia.)

"U.S. Navy and Marine fighter planes were doing extremely well, victory wise. But Admiral Halsey was in Nouméa, quite nervous. General Vandegrift, Marines, was on Guadalcanal, and very nervous. Both commanders were vitally concerned with the lack of transport and supplies: the Thirty-third had six planes in Brisbane and seven planes in PDG.

"Regardless of bad weather we went back and forth the estimated 200 miles from PDG to Tontouta (Nouméa) for two days, hauling supplies needed by the new temporary theater command headquarters at Nouméa. Then the next day we all were to go to Espíritu Santo, three or three and a half hours away. It was time for the mandatory 100-hour check on our airplanes, so we did it after dark. Since we had no mechanics or ground crew, we just did it ourselves: pilot, copilot, crew chief, radioman, using the book of instructions in the 'glove compartment." One item that was to be checked, along with many, many others, was the trim tab. That was done by turning the trim tab control, located by the pilot's right knee, to one extreme position. We were on the ground then getting out of the aircraft and by flashlight visually checking that the trim unit actually had moved completely into the maximum position. Then whoever was doing that had to climb back into the cockpit and turn the tab control to the opposite extreme position and then climb back out and by flashlight verify that the trim unit had gone into the opposite position from the previous check. All was well. This was sort of like doing a lube job for your car, changing the engine oil, and getting your car checked over for a long trip. We fueled up and were ready to go bright and early the next morning.

"We had not heard of a pretakeoff written checklist, whereby one pilot in the cockpit calls out the item to be checked and the other looks at that item, touches it, and verifies it by saying, 'Check.' What we did in those days was just a cursory look-see. If the important things like fuel, RPM, oil pressure, flaps, and alternator looked okay, we'd presume we were prepared for takeoff. We didn't bother to notice that one trim tab control was in extreme left position.

"With throttle, boost, and RPM pushed forward, the plane started down the narrow runway. The aircraft seemed to pull left a little, so I pushed in some more left engine throttle. As we gained speed, the plane seemed to still pull left, so I braked the right gear some and pulled right throttle back a little. We had no cargo, so the acceleration was quite rapid. I rolled in a little right rudder and that seemed to help, so I rolled in some more. It helped some more, but by now we were getting quite close to the left side of the runway and going pretty fast, too. As we approached flying speed the plane was almost hopping. Just off the left of the runway was a construction trench about six feet deep and beyond that some torpedo bombers.

"I hollered to Smitty, 'Help with right rudder!' He thought I didn't mean it, that it was just a turbulent takeoff. I rolled in some more right rudder trim and gave more left engine throttle and more right aileron as the plane became airborne just over the trench and was fast approaching the parked torpedo bombers. One more turn on the right rudder trim tab and everything began to smooth out, except it wasn't certain we would

Mel Lewis and Edward Imparato.

clear the bombers. I was prepared to say, 'oh, shit!,' which is the standard pilot report just before he goes in. We cleared the first bomber by the grace of God, with inches to spare. However, our plane was flying and we were gaining altitude. I looked down at the trim tab and it was exactly on zero, where it should have been before takeoff. Obviously, one of us had failed to return the tab to zero position last night during the 100-hour check. That was as close to a deadly accident without having one as I can imagine.

"Not much was said in the cabin for about the first hour out over water. Finally, Smitty, said, 'George, do you still have those two Saint Christopher medals?'[5] I thought he wanted one. That he had seen the light. That he was convinced they worked. Then he added, 'I think you'd better get out the other one. The one in your pocket must be worn out!'

"Guadalcanal! Just the spoken word would conjure up visions of disaster. We actually knew very little about the place, but during the past few days rumors had become fact that the entire action was taking a turn for the worse. The marines had an almost impossible job of holding the portion of the island that they had taken at great cost. The opposing navies seemed to be moving for a decisive kill, which could go either way. The ground reinforcements had been aboard the *Coolidge* and were now ashore at Espíritu Santo, but there was no way to get all of them and their equipment to Guadalcanal because of the major sea battles going on just offshore. Seven C-47s that could haul

---

[5]Saint Christopher Medal - a small usually metal object bearing an emblem representing the patron saint of travelers for people of the Catholic religion; abolished from sainthood by Pope Paul VI in 1969.

Fred Adams.

only half-loads weren't going to make more difference than a drop in the bucket, but we were gung-ho to do whatever might help. We headed out for Espíritu Santo to do something. The code name of Espíritu Santo was Buttons.

"It was three and a half hours over water to Buttons. The navy guys at the airfield sure didn't know what to do with us. They knew we were available to haul whatever we could pile aboard from the merchandise on the beach, but no one was really in charge to make decisions and give orders. Their shore hands were few in number and worn out from round-the-clock emergency duty. At least Buttons had fuel.

"I asked one of the navy officers, 'How do we find Henderson Field?'

"'Oh, you head out about this direction.' he said as he indicated a somewhat northwesterly direction with his hand. 'About 150 miles out you will see San Cristobal. Stay along the north side of that island. When you run out of island hold your heading for about 150 miles till you hit the tip of Guadalcanal. Stay on the north side for about 200 miles, and you will see Henderson Field (code: Cactus) cut out of the palm trees. They don't have much of a radio tower at the field, but call them on frequency *xxx*. Be sure to ask them for the condition of the field, because sometimes they don't own it. When they give you the condition of the field, if it's green, it's controlled by marines and you can land. If it's yellow, they are sharing with Japs or maybe soon will be. They may suggest something, but you will have to be the judge of what to do next. There is no alternative airfield except back here. You will have to get there before dark. Good luck.' He didn't mention accommodations.

"'What if the condition is red?' I asked.

"'Guess you'll have to come back here. We don't have many lights, but if it's stormy we'll turn on an antiaircraft searchlight. Those lights can penetrate 20,000 feet through clouds.' I didn't think that bit through very well.

"Henderson had no fuel. Let's see. Four hours or more up there, an hour or so hanging around wondering what to do. Then four or more hours back here to begin looking for that searchlight beam. Thanks to the confusion, there wasn't time to worry!

"We did not fly in formation on the way from PDG to Buttons. We got strung out on purpose, because we were 100 percent vulnerable to enemy fighter planes that might be in the same area. Guess the thought was it was better to lose one plane than six or seven. But we didn't spend much time fretting about that. At Buttons it took some time to get a plane loaded, pointed toward Cactus, fueled, and off the ground. Thus we got strung out more. Besides, I'm sure the marines at Cactus didn't want more than one or two strange planes on their runway at the same time. That's in case we made it that far.

"November 1942 was a busy flying time, according to my Form 5 flying record. Back and forth between the islands of New Hebrides and the Solomons, mostly over water. The work was totally exhausting; I remember that part. But it couldn't have been any worse than what those guys on the ground were experiencing. The only days my Form 5 doesn't show some time logged are the tenth and seventeenth. Maybe they were Sundays.

"On November 8 the navy guys at Buttons said things were pretty tight at Cactus, but we should take a load anyway. They said Cactus wouldn't let us stay overnight, as they didn't want any planes on the strip. The navy guys also promised to have the searchlight on and to have a few vehicles with lights along the sides of the runway back here, at Buttons, in case we returned during the night.

"Hensman took off about an hour ahead of me. We would both be returning to Buttons about midnight, we thought. The formalities of landing at Cactus had been modified some. The marines had cleared out most of the Japanese between the strip and the water, but not all. There was no conversation with the ground. If there was heavy activity in the immediate area they would call us as soon as they saw us and tell us to beat it. Meaning, go away.

"When we got there, we made a straight-in approach from the water and touched down on the very first part of the strip, the marines waved us to come to one end, and that we did. Hensman had been there, unloaded, and taken off toward the water. He was shot down by ground fire about the time he reached the shoreline and crashed into the water. I remember it as being only a mile or maybe two miles from shore at most. There were no survivors. We lost four good people: S. Sgt. Pilot Ray Hensman, S. Sgt, Pilot Robert Dillman, T. Sgt. Albert Kirsch, and Corp. Jim Lamar.

"By the time we were unloaded, it was almost getting dark. One of the marines on the unloading detail told me Hensman had made a gradual right turn just after takeoff and suggested I not make a right turn until after we got over the water. I did him one better. After a maximum climb takeoff, I edged off toward the left and got as high as I could as fast as I could. We saw no indication we were being shot at, so after a few minutes we headed into heavy rain in the direction of Buttons. It was dark. The rain was steady, but the air was not rough. The windshield leaked, so our pant legs got wet, but that didn't bother us at all. That searchlight was a real worry, though. We had no idea whether we were being blown to the left or to the right; thus when we were about one hour out, we decided to go down low over the water in hope of seeing waves or land. Occasional breaks in the clouds gave us an occasional peek at the water, but we couldn't see it plain enough through our drift meter to determine any amount of wind effect. As we continued to use up our estimated time to the island, I kept feeding in just a little bit of right correction. There was a small mountain, about 3,000 feet high, on the north end of the island and that was on the left. As we were about 400 to 500 feet above sea level, the danger of getting close to that mountain became more and more apparent. No panic, yet, but plenty uncomfortable.

"The rain became less severe, but we were still over water and we estimated our time was running out. It ran out. Still over water. Still no searchlight. I decided to overrun the same heading before admitting we were lost. As we edged close to the twenty minutes remaining, allocated by guess, we were all four with our noses forward and eyeballs looking harder than we had ever looked before. We had about two hours of fuel left and no place to go except to that searchlight. At ETA, plus twenty minutes, we started our search pattern of circling left with gradually increasing circles. We were hoping to see any shoreline for a more favorable place to ditch if necessary or the light beam or anything except the 3,000 foot high mountain. Before we completed the first circle at about 500 feet altitude, there, just outside the window by my left elbow, was that beautiful searchlight. It could hardly be seen in the rain, and I bet only shone through about 1,000 feet of clouds instead of 20,000, as the guy had told me. But the field was also about twenty minutes or about fifty miles farther than planned and definitely off to the left some distance. It was a pretty sight at just about midnight. Chalk up another for Saint Christopher.

"Other members of our squadron in New Guinea weren't so lucky. On November 10, 1942, my good friend George Vandevort was taking a load of infantry from Port Moresby to Wanogela Mission across the Owen Stanley Range near Buna' on the north side of New Guinea. He was in a mountain pass partially obscured by clouds when he ran into a mountain. Only the radio operator, Sergeant Kirschner, miraculously survived after spending thirty-eight days in the jungle. That made three planes and six men lost only twenty days after leaving the United States.

"On another trip into Henderson Field during this very critical time for both the navy in the waters off the Solomons and the marines on land on Guadalcanal, a new service was inaugurated by the Thirty-third gooney birds. Apparently, on the twelfth and thirteenth of November (from my Form 5 again) a single trip from Tontouta, to Buttons, to Cactus, to Roses (Efate), to Tontouta was required. Seventeen hours of flying time was too, too much. It's hard to recall just how tired, how weary, how beat a person could get under these circumstances, but the mission was very important and ended okay. We must have lived through it, because the Form 5 said we went back to Buttons on the Fourteenth.

"On that trip to Guadalcanal, we again arrived shortly before dark. My preference would have scheduled arrival time earlier in daylight, but the pace of battle in that area was still at its height. Planes from floating bases would go there to crash-land (not to fuel, because there was no fuel there). Japanese fighters and bombers were irregularly able to do damage to the strip, and the continuing naval battles were sometimes close to Guadalcanal and sometimes some distance away. The Japanese were pouring a lot of power into this fracas from their major base at Rabaul. So many ships from both sides had been sunk or put out of commission that no one could tell who might be the ultimate victor. The Japanese navy was larger, but ours was better.

"Anyway, when we arrived and were unloaded, the marines pointed out a sight I shall never forget. Just off the strip, barely protected under some trees, was a line of wounded marines futilely awaiting evacuation to ships offshore that had some medical facilities aboard. Those ships were so loaded with casualties they just couldn't receive any more wounded. Besides, vessels capable of moving them from shore to ships were unavailable. Someone knew of a new tent hospital that was up, or partially up, at Efate (code name: Roses). I had never been there but knew where it was, about an hour southwest of Buttons. Buttons had only a dispensary. Roses had a strip with lights, fuel, and a field hospital under construction. It didn't take long to decide we should load some of those wounded and head for Roses. Because we still had four 100-gallon fuel tanks in the cabin, it was plain we couldn't load very many stretcher cases. The marine corpsman in charge of those horribly wounded men supervised getting a few stretcher cases aboard and also some that were able to sit. I saw and heard one stretcher case say just before they were to put him aboard, 'Hey, I'll sit, That'll make room for about six more.' He had a shoulder, part of his neck and part of his upper arm blown off and was bandaged only with stripped clothing. There were no bandages. I wonder if he even had painkillers. Almost all the medicines and hospital supplies en route to Guadalcanal had been lost on the *Coolidge*. The corpsmen finally boarded all they could pack in, I'd guess about twenty-eight or thirty people. Probably eight were on stretchers. Not a moan or a groan was heard during loading. There were likely many sounds before the six-hour flight to Roses was completed. Those guys were tough. And great. I love the marines. Even today. Forth-eight years later, I weep when I think of those helpless wounded, so many of them.

"It was four days before we got back to Guadalcanal. That was because we were not permitted to use the airstrip. If conditions were any tighter during those three days, it's hard to imagine how they could have been. How could there by any more crucial events than during the past two weeks? Historians agree that the month of November 1942 was the period when our navy in the Solomons began to get the upper hand. There was more Japanese tonnage on the bottom at Iron Bottom Bay than there was American.

"I was back into Guadalcanal on November 18. This was probably the time Gen. Alexander Vandegrift, commanding officer of the marines, hitched a ride in. They, the marines, didn't yet have their air transport in the area, if they had it at all. Later, they had the Marine Air Transport Command. Since they widely used C-47s, one would have to presume the general liked what he saw in our small effort. But he never did write any letter about it.

"I'd prefer to recall that the general told me that things were beginning to look a little brighter and that our side would soon begin to push back the Japanese area and line of control, but I can't stretch the truth quite that far. However, in the following week or so we seemed to pick up more rumors that the battle for the Solomons was about over. We also heard rumors, or started some, that significant reinforcements would be coming into Tontouta and that this might be an auspicious time for our five crews to head out for Australia and on to New Guinea to join the rest of our squadron.

"Because we had no written orders keeping us in the Solomon area, we surely didn't need any definite orders, verbal or written, in order to sneak off to Brisbane. That's what we decided we would do just as soon as we were sure that several contingents of reinforcements had arrived at Tontouta.

"We could truly say we had worked alongside such heroes as Halsey, Vandegrift, General Holcomb, and pilots such as Pappy Boyington, Joe Foss, and Indian Joe Bauer (who was shot down and killed in aerial combat over Henderson Field on November 14, 1942.

"Several years later the world learned that part of the success of our outnumbered and outgunned navy over the Japanese navy in the Solomon area was again due to the ingenuity and expertise of the U.S. troops fighting vigorously in defense of our country. Some intelligence people in a radio facility somewhere had, for the first time, broken a major Japanese secret code and were intercepting the operational orders regarding the deployment of their vessels and ground forces. Our commanders were then able to meet most of their new landing forces with well-placed and organized troops of our own. The Japanese would try a new location, and by golly, the marines would be there waiting for them. The same things were happening to their naval forces. The Japanese interpreted this strong defense to mean that the marine forces were much larger and better equipped than they really were. Thanks to the guys who came up with ULTRA, the code breaker.

"Just before the end of November a sizable contingent of reinforcements began arriving at Tontouta. That was our agreed upon sign to get out of this hellhole. We fueled up and refused to let anyone put supplies aboard. We came from wherever we were to PDG. The next morning, bright and early, we took off singly and headed for Brisbane.

"The contingent that arrived at Tontouta brought a big bunch of new people. New faces were everywhere in that limited space. There is a saying, 'imagine my surprise.' Imagine mine when I heard one of them holler out, 'Hey, George, is that you?' It came from Alan Fryberger, the piano-playing genius of Charlo, Montana. He claimed he was a propeller specialist. Baloney. Those ground grippers just needed music for fun and formality, so within the membership of the authorized Tables of Organization they inserted enough qualified musicians whose secondary duty was 'Band.' A year or two later, I saw Alan again, performing in his secondary duty in a fine, large military jazz band. Several of his mates were, or had been before the war, professional musicians with name bands. They made up a fine military band and gave much pleasure to those who heard them.

"We presumed the actual line of demarcation between the South Pacific Command under Admiral Halsey and Southwest Pacific Command under General MacArthur would be the halfway line between New Caledonia and Australia. Since we estimated a six-and-a-half-hour flight to Brisbane, that line should be three and a quarter hours out of PDG. When we reached the halfway point and had not been shot down for being AWOL or some other criminal act, we set up a joint holler: 'So long, Solomons; hello, Brisbane!' We presumed we'd get billeted in a nice metropolitan hotel, with baths and food from a menu and handshakes of congratulation from dignitaries for a piece of a job well done. Nope. We landed at Amberly Field and were told to go right on to Archer Field and then on to Port Moresby tomorrow morning, November 28, 1942. So much for the bright lights of a big city outside the combat zone."

On arrival at Archer Field the group of six aircraft that did yeoman duty at Guadalcanal were instructed to report to its 33rd Squadron commanding officer at Townsville, Australia. This action finally completed the circle and the 33rd Squadron flight echelon was together again. It was two months later before the ground support group finally joined the flight echelon.

HEADQUARTERS ECW/res
ADVANCE ECHELON
FIFTH AIR FORCE
APO 929

29 November, 1942.

SUBJECT: Commendation.
TO: Commanding Officer, Air Carrier Service, Maple.

1. The undersigned commends the excellent work performed by the troop carrier personnel at Maple. The extraordinary devotion to duty by the operating crews of the airplanes is in my opinion an outstanding performance

in the current Buna campaign. These crews have operated through all kinds of weather and in the face of enemy opposition. The skill of these crews in operating from emergency strips in the Buna area indicates the high degree of flying proficiency.

/s/ Ennis C. Whitehead
/t/ ENNIS C. WHITEHEAD,
Brigadier General, AUS,
Deputy Air Force Commander

THE FLYING DUTCHMAN

NOVEMBER 10, 1942

The Japanese were not our only enemy in New Guinea. There were other elements at work to destroy us in our fast-forward pursuit of victory. The animals, the insects, the disease, the terrible heat and the mountains - always the mountains which claimed so many.

Final and accurate statistics of loss of life by the Air Force in combat missions over New Guinea are not available. Three years of combat flying in New Guinea reveal, in estimate, that as many losses occurred due to the unforgiving jungle mountains and weather as resulted from actual aerial combat by fighters, bombers and transport aircraft.

The threat of the ever present jungle was always on the minds of our pilots. Every effort was made to equip all combat aircraft with survival gear to insure a measure of safety if forced down in the jungle or if it was necessary to bail out of a severely damaged aircraft.

Search and rescue teams were always on the ready - prepared to seek out aircraft that did not return to base when expected. If the downed aircraft or crew who bailed out were not found within three days the chance for discovery would be almost zero. The jungle would have swallowed the sight of the crash by the fast growing brush, vines and trees. The massive jungle growth of the rain forest conceals everything on the ground. The ground is in perpetual twilight. Only an occasional small clearing or rock outcropping would expose a crash site or a downed airman. The huge, thick canopy of the rain forest in New Guinea is so dense that sunlight never reaches the earth and the rains come every day.

It was this type of saga that was experienced by the crew and passengers of the "Flying Dutchman." The aircraft and crew were assigned to the 33rd Squadron.

The most complete description of the horrible ordeal suffered by the survivors of the crash is best described by Robert Piper in his book *"The Hidden Chapters"* Chapter 12, *"Courage on an aircraft door."* Author, historian, former RAAF Historical Officer in Canberra and award winning writer for the quality and depth of his works.

"There can be nothing so agonizing as to wait for help that never comes.

"Eight injured Americans, stranded with the wreckage of their crashed plane on an unknown Papuan mountain-top at 9000 feet, had no way of knowing whether rescue was coming or not. They could only sit tight. Those waiting were never to know, but six of their party had walked to safety through the jungle - although it had taken them a month. Search parties trying to retrace their steps were forced to give up, beaten by cold, a lack of food and near-impenetrable mountains and undergrowth. Those back at the crash site kept a diary, scribbled on the back of a door of their wrecked plane. Its simple words were not to come to light for almost 20 years, but every word of that unknown writer spells courage.

"Of all the stories of tragedy and survival in the South West Pacific during World War II, that of the C-47 transport plane named the Flying Dutchman, serial number 41-18564, is one of the most remarkable. It was a story of courage and hopelessness and a reminder of how unforgiving the mountainous jungles of Papua New Guinea are.

"Seven injured Americans stranded at 9000 feet in the wreckage of the Flying Dutchman were to wait for months for help that never came. The healthy who survived the crash unscathed set out in two parties of four in different directions on perilous treks to safety that took them over a month.

"Australians who tried to retrace the steps of the survivors in an attempt to find the wreck and rescue those left behind, faced bitter cold and extreme conditions before being forced to abandon their search. A reward was offered to local mountain people if they could find the missing plane. More than two months after it had disappeared, Papuan searchers finally located the missing American aircraft high on a peak in the Owen Stanley ranges.

"Of the crash survivors, only one was still alive, Captain Theodore W. Barron, the padre, who was blind from malnutrition and so light that he "felt like a baby" when the native men moved him. A bare semi-circle on the ground outside the plane indicated he had been tearing up mountain moss for sustenance and moisture. The Papuans cooked a banana and tried to feed Barron but he was past help, after 60-odd days with little or no food, and he died in their arms. They left his body beside the others but retrieved his Bible, which he had overwritten with a diary of his last days, as proof of their discovery.

"There was another diary that they left behind - but the natives were not to be blamed for not noticing it. This diary was penned simply on the inside of a door of the wrecked plane. The remarkable document spanned the days of the men's hopeless wait. Its unknown author or authors lay dead nearby.

"Captain Barron and his assistant Corporal Peterson were last-minute passengers, the decision being made on the flip of a coin, with two Corporals, Fernow and Pemberton, being off-loaded to allow them aboard. Little did the latter two then realise that giving up their seats at the last moment saved their lives. Another American C-47 transport, Eightball, which left immediately after the Flying Dutchman on the same route, completed the flight safely. The fateful flight, one of thousands over the Owen Stanley ranges during World War II, started from Wards Strip, just outside Port Moresby at 1 p.m. on 10 November 1942.

"The destination was Pongani, on the north coast. In addition to the crew of three was army chaplain Barron, his assistant, and 18 other U.S. soldiers due to join the Allied advance on Buna. The solders were all members of the U.S. Army's 32nd Division, 126th Regiment, better known by the name of Red Arrows.

"Piloting the aircraft was Lieutenant George Vandervort, a pre-war private aviator who at one stage had owned his own aircraft. Because of his Dutch background it was he who had given the aircraft the name Flying Dutchman.

"Sergeant Ed Holleman, who later led a group out to safety, takes up the story:

"*'We had been flying for almost half an hour when suddenly the plane was caught in a downdraft and fell. Someone who was looking out of a window said: 'Boy, that was close! We clipped the tops off some trees.'*

"*'The next moment we crashed. I remember spinning out of my seat, a fire was burning fiercely and ammunition was exploding all over the place. Seven-*

Roger Gerling in New Guinea, 1942.

teen of us got clear through the door, walked and slid down a steep slope to a more level spot. It was raining and all immediately began to shiver from the cold.

"'Several hours later, when the flames died down, we were able to return to the plane. It was lying on the mountainside but was being held fairly level by the stumps of trees cut down as it crashed. The front was destroyed back to the wings and only a third of the rear was still intact.

"'The next morning we found all the supplies had perished in the fire but in the back compartment were three rifles, six K rations, one and a half gallons of tomato juice, a first aid kit, two balloons, a box kite and some flares. At night, if a plane was heard, I would climb up on top of the fuselage and strike a flare. It seemed to light up the sky so much that we felt they couldn't help but see it, but so far as I know no one ever did.

"'During the day we kept the entire fuselage, which was a camouflage colour, covered with maps found in the aircraft. It was hoped in this way we would be spotted.

"'The first attempt to launch a balloon above the treetops was unsuccessful. However, a second was a little luckier. It started rising in the sky, drawing with it the aerial which could be used as an anchor. It had just cleared the treetops when a plane exactly like ours appeared out of the mists as if by magic, flew directly over us only to be swallowed up a moment later in the low clouds. Our last hope of attracting attention had disappeared when the balloon sank back into the jungle.

"'While searching around the wreckage one day we ventured further in front of it than usual when we suddenly came upon the body of the engineer, Sergeant Pitch, who had been catapulted there in the accident. Beside him, was the instrument panel with an unbroken compass.'

"Sergeant Steven J. Pitch was buried and the compass removed. The compass was later to save Sergeant Holleman's life and that of three others when they trekked to safety on a month-long walk through the jungle. Two parties of four decided to set out for help. Eight injured men were to remain. One had died, with the fittest of those, Private Patton, tending them and carrying water.

"The first party departed two days after the November 12 crash to the base of the mountain and generally in an easterly direction. On the fifth day of their journey they came to a narrow gorge, scattered with boulders, on the Moni River. The sides of the ravine were too steep to traverse on foot, so each man secured himself to a log and attempted to ride the rapids down the fast-flowing river.

"Privates Frank Thomas and Duane Butler, said the other two Privates, Carlos Failing and Gerald Grove, disappeared out of sight downstream and presumably drowned where a waterfall in the river dropped about eight feet. The pair reported they had stopped and searched for the others for two days without success.

"Thomas and Butler then proceeded towards Safia, being guided from village to village, where an emergency food store near the small airfield was used for a week while they regained strength. Local natives then directed them towards Abau on the south coast, the men eventually arriving after 32 days.

"It was here, at Abau Island in Cloudy Bay, at the government administrative headquarters for the area, that Thomas and Butler were met and interviewed by the Australia New Guinea Administrative Unit's Warrant Officer David Marsh. Marsh, now a retired post-war New Guinea District commissioner living in Sydney, still has his original notes from the 1942 interrogation.

"Thomas and Butler were then moved to Port Moresby, by light aircraft, where they entered hospital on 14 December and were treated for burns and exposure. Unknown to them, survivors back at the Flying Dutchman lingered on.

"The second group left the crash site on 16 November and consisted of Sergeants George B. Kershner and Ed Holleman, and Privates Floyd August and John Mobley. For the first 10 days they scarcely saw the sun, except on one occasion when they passed through a silent, eerie field of moss. Direction was maintained with the retrieved aircraft compass. Luckily, Holleman remembered the plane's approximate heading and applied the reverse as best as possible.

"On the 10th day the four struck a defined trail and from here were assisted by a native constable and friendly villagers. Eventually, after a month in the jungle, they arrived at Kokobagu Plantation, near Rigo. Here they were met by Australians, Warrant Officer Ed Hicks and medical orderly Ron Davies. The survivors were fed, showered, given fresh clothes and their injuries treated.

"A scribbled note earlier sent forward with local natives by Sergeant Holleman, had been received by Ed Hicks at Rigo, who had recognised the name and moved up to Kokobagu to assist the Americans. By an amazing coincidence Hicks and Holleman had been on patrol together a month earlier, with a combined Australian and American Army party, in the same area and seeking a walking route over the mountains. It was the skills that Holleman quickly learnt on the first trek that enabled him to bring his party of four to safety on the second.

Ed Imparato, Maintenance Officer with an exploded oil tank.

"Meanwhile, a rescue attempt quickly got under way with David Marsh, Lt. Arthur "Paddy" Ethell (ANGAU) and an American, Private Scheer, being flown into the halfway point at Safia. By Christmas Day this group was well upstream, sleeping in caves at night where possible, and rationed to half a tin of meat and four ounces of rice a day.

"Ethell had a radio and antenna which could be carried aloft with an inflatable balloon. The equipment was tested once and proved unsuccessful. Had it functioned, air supply drops could have been arranged. On Sunday 28 December David Marsh celebrated his 21st birthday. He remembers being tired, hungry and cold. The rescue party's movement was being hampered by the thin air which quickly sapped their energy. Where steep areas could not be traversed in the river a stout stick, attached to a rope in its centre, was thrown until it caught between two boulders on the other side of the ravine. Then it was a case of going up, hand over hand.

"On the afternoon of 31 December they stumbled across an exciting discovery. There, sitting neatly on top of a large boulder, was a set of U.S. Army leggings.

"On New Year's Day 1943 the party turned left and headed south-west towards the crest of Mount Obree at 10,200 feet. They thought that from the heights something might more easily be seen and also believed, mistakenly, on advice given by Thomas and Butler, that the plane lay in that direction.

"They also encountered the same moss forest that the Holleman party had struck on the second day of their walkout.

"None of the rescue party had coats of wet weather clothes and each only had half a blanket to ward off the chilly nights. Food that evening consisted or army hard tack biscuits ground and mixed with malt powder. Everybody, including the carriers, were now beginning to suffer intensely. Ice was found in a water bucket the next morning.

"That day, bitterly disappointed, they were forced to withdraw before they too became casualties. At that stage the would-be rescuers were not to know that if they had turned right at the "leggings" discovery the party might well have found the elusive Flying Dutchman. So close and yet so far.

"In May 1944 aerial reconnaissance commenced a search to relocate the crash site. An aircraft was made available from the American 33rd Troop Carrier Squadron, the same unit as the Flying Dutchman, and flown by Captain Ridley and Lieutenant Bill "The Falcon" Biggers. Also on board was Private Bates of the U.S. Graves Commission, an American Army photographer and Warrant Officer Charles White (ANGAU) accompanied by two village constables from the Mount Brown area, south of Mount Obree. Despite good flying weather and carefully scrutiny of the approximate crash site area, nothing was seen. However, at the end of the same month a village constable from Mount Brown reported a crashed aircraft with bodies, which one of his local villagers said he had seen in September the previous year.

"A special team sent by ANGAU, and led by Warrant Officer Charles White, accompanied by Cadet Officer Jeffries, came across the aircraft after an epic walk in from the Rigo side, via Mount Brown. The remains of those at the crash site, as well as many personal items, including notes left by the passengers, were recovered and returned to the U.S. that same year.

"In 1961 the crash site was again in the international news when it was sighted by light planes searching for a latter-day missing aircraft flown by Captain G. Wallace, a civil Piaggio (VH-PAU), which was subsequently never found.

"Cadet Patrol Officer John Absolom with U.S. Army men, Lieutenant R. Wheeler and Sergeant J. Paolillo, were directed towards the site which was found with some difficulty. The last three days required cutting a path through the dense jungle.

"During this visit Sergeant Paolillo noted a legible diary written with a graphite pen on the aircraft's interior tailcone door. The diary door was subsequently retrieved on a second trip there by Absolom, brought into Port Moresby and exhibited at the Cultural Museum.

"This tragic diary, exactly as written, is as follows:
Crashed 1.30 Tues. 10 Nov. 1942
Tues. 10 - 17 men alive
Wed. 11 - 16 men alive
Thurs. 12 - 4 men started for help
Fri. 13
Sat. 14 - Tried to put up balloon
Sun. 15 - Cracker and cheese
Mon. 16 - 4 men started for help - due south - leaves 8 men left
Tues. 17 - Small piece of cheese
Wed. 18 - Chocolate bar
Thurs. 19 - Found one chocolate bar
Fri. 20 - 1/3 can tomato juice
Sat. 21 - 1/3 can tomato juice
Sun. 22 - Drank last 1/3 can of tomato juice
Mon. 23 - Last cigarette - even butts
Tues. 24 - First day - no rain
Wed. 25 - 2nd day - no rain
Thanksgiving Thurs. 26. Rain today also clear in morning
Fri. 27 - Buckets full water this morning - still got our chin up
Sat. 28 - Clearest day we have had
Sun. 29 - Nice clear day. Boy we're getting weak still have our hope
Mon. 30 - Still going strong on imaginary meals
December Tues. 1 - My! My! Summer is here - went to Spring today
Wed. 2 - Just slid by but Boy it rained
Thurs. 3 - Kinda cold and cloudy today - still plenty hungry. Boy a big would do good
Fri. 4 - Same old thing - clear this morn
Sat. 5 - Boy nothing happened just waiting
Sun. 6 - Had service today. Still lots of hope
Mon. 7 - Year ago today the war started - Boy, we didn't think of this then
Wed. 9 - Cloudy, God is looking out for our water supply
Thurs. 10 - Just thirty days to go. We can take it but would be nice if someone came
Fri. 11 - Cold rainy today, We would like to start out before Christmas
Sat. 12 - Fairly nice day - still plenty of water
Sun. 13 - Beautiful morning everyone has high hopes

Crandell, Franklin, Eckberg, McCullock, and Imparato.

Mon. 14 - Waiting
Tues. 15 - Waiting
Wed. 16 - New water place today
Thurs. 17 - Running out of imaginary meals. Boys shouldn't be long in coming now, 6 more shopping days.
Fri. 18 - Nice and warm this morning. Rained in the afternoon
Sat. 19 - Pretty cold last night. Cold this morning too. Water pretty low. Five more days to Xmas
Sun. 20
Mon. 21 - Plenty of water
Tues. 22 - Rained all three days
Wed. 23 - Thinking about home and Christmas. Still hoping
Thurs. 24 - Tonite is Christmas eve. God make them happy at home
Fri. 25 - Christmas Day
Sat. 26
Sun. 27
Mon. 28 - Rain every day
Tues. 29
Wed. 30 - Johnnie died today
Thurs 31
Fri. - New Year's Day
Pat
Mart
Ted (on lower left door)

"Four survivors, two from each party, were in recent years traced by the author to their current addresses in the U.S. One of them, ex Sergeant Ed Holleman and his wife Gert, of Hudsonville in Michigan, advised they were anxious to contact the Australians who had assisted and treated Ed on his party's arrival near Rigo.

"The medical orderly Ron Davies and former Warrant Officer Ed Hicks were also located, living in retirement close to Melbourne and Sydney respectively. However, fate once more took a hand. A letter sent by Davies was returned four weeks later advising that Ed Holleman had died in his sleep without warning.

"In 1980 the author, through the U.S. embassy in Canberra, advised their Air Force Museum of the existence of the diary door and its historic background. It was subsequently generously donated by the Papua New Guinea Government to the Americans, who returned a perfect facsimile in its stead the same year.

"An appropriate display is now in both countries as an unforgettable reminder of tragedy, courage and survival in the jungles of New Guinea during World War II.

"John Absolom, the cadet Patrol Officer who recovered the Flying Dutchman diary door in 1961, disappeared in 1972 on a solo boating trip off New Guinea.

"Those aboard the Flying Dutchman on her last flight were:

Crew: Lieutenant George W. Vandervort (Portsmouth, Ohio) pilot - killed; Corporal George R. Kershner (Dayton, Ohio) radio - survived (with party two); Sergeant Steven J. Pitch (Etna, Pa.) Engineer - killed.

Killed at time of crash: Sergeant James Verstey (Grand Rapids, Michigan); Private Vernon Moak (East Grant's Pass, Oregon); Private Charles Raddatiz (Lincoln, Nebraska); Private Charles Stokes (Petersburg, Nebraska); Private Margarito Padilla (Trujillo, New Mexico) - died first night.

Left behind with the aircraft and died: Captain Theodore W. Barron (Wenatchee, Washington) chaplain; Corporal Lawrence Peterson (Chicago, Illinois) chaplain's assistant; Private Theodore Romero (Brush, Colorado); Private William Smith (Shaw, Colorado); Private John Bellus (Omaha, Nebraska); Private Martin Brandon (Hart, Michigan); Private Antonio Montez (La Union, New Mexico); Private Marvin Patton (Dayton, Washington).

Party One: Private Duane Butler (Homer, Michigan) - survived; Private Frank Thomas (Petersburg, Nebraska) - survived; Private Carlos Failing (Big Rapids, Michigan) - killed on walkout; Private Gerald Grove (Scranton, Iowa) - killed on walkout.

Party Two: Sergeant Ed Holleman (Hudsonville, Michigan) - survived; Private Floyd August (Dorchester, Nebraska) - survived; Private John Mobley (Oakland, California) - survived; George Kershner (listed under crew)."

HEADQUARTERS ECW/res
ADVANCE ECHELON
FIFTH AIR FORCE
APO 929

7 November, 1942.
SUBJECT: Commendation.
TO: Commanding Officer, Air Carrier Service, Maple.

1. The message quoted below has been received from the Commander-in-Chief, SWPA:

NOVEMBER 3RD, 1942.
"TO: COMMANDER ALLIED AIR FORCES
FROM :   CHQ, SWPA
NR :   NONE THIRD

PLEASE EXPRESS TO ALL RANKS OF THE AIR CORPS CONCERNED MY ADMIRATION FOR THE MAGNIFICENT PART THEY HAVE PLAYED IN THE CAMPAIGN WHICH HAS RESULTED IN THE CAPTURE OF KOKODA
     MacARTHUR

1. The splendid work by all ranks is a tremendous source of pride to me, and I desire to congratulate and thank all for their whole-hearted effort in consummating a job which merits the commendation of the Commander-in-Chief.

/s/ Ennis C. Whitehead
/t/ ENNIS C. WHITEHEAD,
Brigadier General, AUS,
Deputy Air Force Commander

LATE 1942

The two original squadrons of the newly formed 374th Troop Carrier Group formed the nucleus of the 374th operating staff. The 21st and 22nd Troop Carrier Squadrons lost operations personnel, maintenance personnel, intelligence personnel and administrative personnel. Col. Paul P. Prentice, newly arrived in the theater, assumed command of the 374th. Lt. Col. Edgar Wade Hampton, former commander of the 21st Troop Carrier Squadron, was named executive officer of the 374th Troop Carrier Group. The 6th Squadron, newly arrived in the southwest Pacific theater, was assigned to the group on November 12, 1942. The 33rd Troop Carrier Squadron, after struggling and straggling across the Pacific with detached aircraft doing yeomen service en route to Australia at New Caledonia, Guadalcanal, North Solomons, Bismark Archipelago and the western Pacific theater, finally arrived in Australia as a full squadron, November 19, 1942 and was assigned to the 374th Troop Carrier Group. The four independent troop carrier squadrons were finally coalesced into the full combat ready and surprisingly effective 374th Troop Carrier Group.

OPERATIONS OR JUST DOING THE JOB

By M/SGT. Glenn D. McMurray
from the book Moresby to Manila Via troop Carrier

The mechanics of how a job is done - its difficulties - is an integral part of any story. In New Guinea the difficulties were numerous, the mechanics of the job exacting. The fact that the job was done so magnificently is a tribute to the pilots and ground crews.

All take-offs were made during the hours of daylight. This was done because of lack of accurate weather data prior to dawn, and because adequate fighter escort, or "cover", was virtually an impossibility during the night hours. Personnel and maintenance problems were also causes. Group operations controlled all flights. Special consideration was often given to the request of experienced pilots to fly after operations in general had been called off because of weather. These extra flights paid off in thousands of pounds of freight transported to areas in need of it.

Since attack by enemy aircraft was probable and expected during flights across the Owen Stanley Range, pilots made maximum use of all types of camouflage. They flew as low as possible, and chose, when practicable, terrain which harmonized with the camouflage of the aircraft. They avoided presenting silhouettes and used maximum cloud cover. The radio operator monitored the air constantly for information on local enemy activity. When the position of a hostile or unidentified aircraft was broadcast, it was immediately charted on a grid map. Visual watch for enemy planes was also maintained, and all unidentified aircraft were considered hostile.

When approaching fields, pilots let down as fast as possible until they reached tree-top level. Turns were made as close to the field as flying safety permitted One plane at Popondetta made his approach a bit too high and wide and received a Jap shell in his fuselage.

Weather over the Owen Stanleys was almost as serious a hazard as hostile aircraft. Vertical cloud development began rather abruptly and often "built up" before a plane faster than it could climb. Haze, fog, and rain were expected at all times. On trips to the Philippines from Biak tropical storms appeared like magic. Fronts, which would ordinarily have postponed flying even in the early days of 1943, now were navigated as routine. The old saying was, "You have to get through and to do it you must know your weather."

The pilots did know their weather and the planes did get through. On flights to Wau, Bulolo, Mindoro, Luzon, and other airfields in the Philippines, transports were protected by fighter escort varying in numbers according to the size of the formation. Transports usually flew in a formation of nine or twelve planes. They were protected by twelve of fifteen "close cover" fighters. The transports flew in tight, stepped-up javelin formation. The "close cover" fighters swept back and forth above the formation. The "top cover" P-38's patrolled several thousand feet higher. Fighter co-operation in advising the transports of actual or suspected pres-ence of enemy aircraft, and in protecting them against enemy attack, was excellent. Loss of one transport occurred when the pilot broke formation and thus lost the benefit of fighter cover, which acted to protect the formation as a whole. "Top cover" fighters gave valuable information on weather conditions at and near the target area. Information as to whether it was advisable for transports to go under or over cloud formations was particularly valuable especially in dropping areas.

During the early operations in New Guinea, C-53's carried loads of 6000 to 6500 pounds with 500 gallons of gasoline. This weight proved impracticable for dropping missions, since the planes often had to side-slip at low speeds to arrive low enough over the dropping area. Heavy loads also were a handicap to the pilot when he found it necessary to dive or climb quickly. Cargo carried in Troop Carriers included troops, foodstuffs, jeeps and trailers, antiaircraft and field guns, ammunition, bombs, belly tanks for fighter planes, aircraft engines, steel runways, building material, motor-vehicle and aircraft gasoline, tar and pitch, and every other type of article conceivable for setting up and operating a base. During the Bismarck Sea battle, where the Jap navy suffered terrific losses, Troop Carriers ferried loads of bombs and ammunition to advanced landing fields to enable fighters and bombers to operate more effectively.

The "miracle" of airborne loads is shown in the creation of a new airfield or air base. First the airborne engineers would be blown in on a rough field. Then would come their airborne trucks, bulldozers, graders, concrete mixers, gravel sorters and other road building machinery, all brought in by Troop Carriers.

Townsville, Australia, 1942.

With these a strip would be prepared, upon which Troop Carriers could land safely with lumber, generators, squadron equipment, operations personnel, office supplies and food. Then an operations office would be set up. Soon supply buildings appeared; mess halls erected, transit camps built; all through airborne supplies. Thus a base is born to grow fat as the fires of battle warm it and to die as its airborne mother - the Troop Carriers - leave it to follow the Gods of War.

Dropping supplies was one of the more important functions of Troop Carriers and was the salvation of many isolated infantry units. It was conceived by the Australian New Guinea Administration Unit after they learned that native carriers alone were unable to supply Australian troops in forward areas. Dropping targets were located, when possible, in natural open areas which planes could reach with the least amount of danger. In many instances, however, military necessity called for dropping in clearings on mountain sides or in native villages at the bottom of valleys. The dropping areas were usually about 50 yards by 25 yards. Approaches to these areas, such as between the Iorabaiwa Ridge and Kokoda, were quite difficult. Many times, s in the Philippines, planes flew low over enemy territory to reach the target and were subject to intense small-arms and machine-gun fire. In one spot, at Menauri, it was necessary to drop over a 3900-foot ridge into a valley, while flying at 100 miles an hour, wheels down, throttle all the way back, and side-slip from one side of the gorge to the other at tree-top level. In pulling out of drop areas like this, it was necessary to climb to 4200 feet within a very short distance. This called for maximum power and expert timing, for slight miscalculations resulted in fatal crashes.

In ordinary droppings, the plane was brought over the target at approximately 120 miles an hour at a height of 200 or 300 feet. When approaching the target, a crew of three of four men, who had placed a portion of the load in the doorway, pushed it out of the door upon a signal from the pilot. The pilot continued in level flight, or preferably nosed slightly downward, to guard against the bundle hitting the tail section of the plane. Wheels were immediately pulled up (if down) and necessary power applied to gain proper altitude. Care was taken not to pile the supplied too high in the doorway. Bundles on top of a high pile have farther to fall and might hit a tail section. Light bundles were placed at the bottom of the pile so that they would clear the tail section more quickly. In dropping bundles by parachute from a height of 300 feet or less, wind drift was taken into consideration. Unless this was done, many of the parachutes would drift into the bush and sometimes into gorges, from where it was extremely difficult to recover them. A high percentage of the supplies dropped by air was recoverable by ground troops.

21st TC Squadron Gypsy Moth - a tragic accident with the loss of 2nd Lt. Drver and a passenger.

Port Moresby, 1942.

The Billet at Brisbane, 1942.

CHAPTER II

1942 - 1943

The 21st and 22nd Troop Carrier Squadrons were formed essentially from stray officers and men headed elsewhere. There were casuals without assignment orders, escapees from the Philippines, Java and other parts of the Far East and fighter and bomber pilots without aircraft to fly in their own specialty. They were all dedicated men far from home eager to join any organization and do a job they felt qualified to do. The assignment of the unassigned group soon filled the available slots in the two squadrons. From the time of their assignment to the 21st and 22nd squadrons starting in January, 1942, through June, 1942, they easily qualified in the variety of transport aircraft available and were flying missions in combat, learning transport and airborne operations as they gained experience under qualified transport pilots. The men of the original core of 14 which left the U.S. on January 12, had gradually grown to two fully manned and trained troop carrier squadrons of 50 pilots and 400 airmen each by August, 1942. It was time now for the real test of their ability, skill, dedication and fortitude.

A very critical and insidious factor which was ever present in the minds of our transport pilots was the inherent dangers occasioned by the very nature of their flying missions. This entailed flying long missions into the very heart of Japanese territory and territory over which the Japanese held air superiority. This was the case early in 1942 through the middle of 1943. Flights such as those into Darwin, Australia where daily flights with a number of aircraft were involved with the 21st Squadron flying out of Brisbane's Archer Field and the 22nd Squadron flying out of Townsville. The distance to Darwin is 2,000 miles from Brisbane. The overnight layover was at Cloncurry, Queensland, 1,000 miles from Brisbane and 1,000 miles from Darwin. All through 1942 and into mid 1943, Darwin was raided by an assortment of Japanese heavy and light bombers and occasionally zero fighters. There was no radio communication available with Darwin until the pilot was about 100 miles out from his destination at which time the pilot would contact Darwin tower for instruction for his approach and landing instructions there. The 22nd Squadron out of Townsville had the same problem. Australian territory a few hundred miles inland from the coastal regions is mostly barren desert land with few settlements in the so called outback. There is no safe haven for an aircraft in trouble in the 1,000 mile stretch from Cloncurry to Darwin. A forced landing in this desert region from whatever cause would result in a disaster unless spotted by search aircraft almost immediately. The desert is cruel here. There is no water and no vegetation. The point of no return for an aircraft of the C-47 type, which was our primary aircraft, would be 500 miles from Cloncurry. A mechanical problem beyond this point would require a continuation of the flight to Darwin. In the event an air raid was in progress at Darwin, the pilot would have to make a decision whether to hold his position and wait out the air raid or head for Daly Waters the only alternate airport available. Daly Waters is 350 miles southeast of Darwin. Depending on the pilot's position on the Cloncurry to Darwin leg, the pilot would immediately have to calculate his remaining fuel to insure reaching Daly Waters or continuing on to Darwin chancing arriving at Darwin after the air raid, or crash landing in the vicinity of the Darwin complex to insure survival of the crew.

These "what if" questions are constantly in the minds of experienced pilots. What would I do if I had engine failure? What would I do if I lost both engines? What would I do if I ran out of fuel? What would I do if an engine caught fire? What would I do if an enemy aircraft attacked my aircraft. All these problems faced the pilots of the 374th during WW II. Some under the most trying conditions of time, weather, terrain, enemy action and mechanical problems. 99% made the right decision and survived.

Similar circumstances faced the pilots on the 700 mile over water flights to Port Moresby from Townsville. However, on the long over water flights, a new and threatening factor of unexplained origin faced the flight crews. This new danger usually struck at the half-way point of the flight - the point of no return. At this time both the aircraft and the crews were violently attacked by the vicious but mythical gremlins. The gremlins had some effect on some pilots and crew members. There was a great deal of conversation about them.

One added factor of concern for flight crews flying in New Guinea was the jungle. Most of New Guinea is mountainous with high soaring peaks to 16,000 feet and dense impenetrable jungle. A forced landing in the jungle or mountainous region was almost as bad as being shot down and killed. The chances of survival are slim. The jungle growth can swallow an airplane in three days and it may never be found. There is an occasional newspaper article reporting the discovery of an aircraft in relatively good condition deep in the jungle uncovered by scientists on exploratory missions even to this day - 50 years after the loss of the aircraft in combat. A pilot who must bail out of a damaged fighter over the jungle may survive the parachute landing then face impenetrable jungle with it's difficult terrain, snakes, Monitor lizards 10 feet long, lack of food (New Guinea is a protein deficient country), daily rain in torrents, mosquitoes, extreme cold at night, a million different insects, tropical disease and above all hostile, head-hunting cannibals who resent intrusion into their territory. The challenge is formidable.

A noted historian has stated, "there is no good place to fight a war but certainly two of the world's worst areas for a war are India Burma China area (the CBI) and New Guinea. And New Guinea takes the prize for being the worst due in part because a crash or bail out in Burma was survivable due to it's more highly populated country and the less treacherous and forbidding geography and no great concern over hostile indigenous tribes.

How the 21st and 22nd Squadrons of the group were assembled and trained was established earlier in the text. For the record, here we will show the official Air Force listing of each squadron and the group as the listing appears in the Air Force Official Register.

COMMANDING OFFICERS

GROUP HEADQUARTERS

Lt. Colonel Erickson S. Nichols was the first Group Commander, assuming command on 12 November, 1942, the date of activation of the Group, and relinquishing command on 14 December, 1942, when he was returned to the United States. From 14 December, 1942, to 17 December, 1942, Major E. W. Hampton was nominal Group Commander. On 17 December, 1942, Colonel Paul H. Prentiss was assigned to the Group and assumed command. On 22 May, 1943, Colonel Prentiss having assumed command of the 54th Troop Carrier Wing, Major Fred M. Adams assumed command of the Group. Upon the return of Lt. Colonel

From left: Pappy Sexton, Line Chief of the 33rd Sqadron; John Booth, Douglas Aircraft Factory representative; Doggie Payton, Crew Chief of the 33rd Squadron; Major Edward T. Imparato, Pilot of the 374th TCG; Captain Charles R. Baer, Co-Pilot of the 21st TC Squadron; and Ed Shine, Radio Operator of the 6th TC Squadron; standing in front of a C-47 Jayhawk aircraft.

Hampton from the United States on 12 July, 1943, he became the Commanding Officer of the Group. On 2 August, 1943, Lt. Col. Hampton was transferred to the 54th Troop Carrier Wing, whereupon Major Fred M. Adams again assumed command of the Group. On 3 August, 1943, Major Adams was promoted to the rank of Lt. Colonel.

COMMANDING OFFICERS

6TH TROOP CARRIER SQUADRON

On 14 October, 1939, the date of activation of the squadron, Major John R. Dunn assumed command. On 4 November, 1939, Major Dunn was relieved of command and succeeded by Major George J. Cressey. On 28 March, 1940, Major Cressey was relieved of command, Captain John J. Keough assuming command. On 10 June, 1940, Captain Keough was succeeded in command by 1st Lt. Hamish McClelland. On 17 February, 1942, the 315th Transport Group was activated and on the same date Captain Hamish McClelland was transferred to become commanding officer of the group, 1st Lt. John H. Lackey, Jr., assuming command. From 23 September, 1942, to 1 December, 1942, while the air echelon and ground echelon were separated, Captain Frank W. Smith acted as commanding officer of the ground echelon. On 22 May, 1943, Major John H. Lackey, Jr., was transferred to the 54th Troop Carrier Wing, Captain William D. Wells assuming command. On 3 December, 1943, Major William D. Wells was ordered to return to the United States, and Captain William A. Peterson assumed command.

COMMANDING OFFICERS

21ST TROOP CARRIER SQUADRON

On 3 April, 1942, at the time Air Transport Command, Archer Field, Brisbane, was re-designated 21st Transport Squadron, Major Edgar W. Hampton was Commanding Officer, retaining command until 12 October, 1942, when Major Fred M. Adams assumed command. When Major Adams assumed command of the 374th Group on 23 May, 1943, Captain Philip N. Eckberg assumed command of the squadron. Upon Major Eckberg's receipt of orders returning him to the United states, Major Myron J. Grimes assumed command of the squadron, on 23 September, 1943.

COMMANDING OFFICERS

22ND TROOP CARRIER SQUADRON

On 3 April, 1942, the date of activation of the squadron, 1st Lt. Francis R. Feeney assumed command of the squadron. Upon the assignment of Captain Raymond T. Swenson to the squadron on 2 May, 1942, he superseded Lt. Feeney as commanding officer. Upon the assignment of Major William L. Bradford to the squadron on 21 May, 1942, he superseded Captain Swenson as squadron commander. Upon the transfer of Major Bradford from the squadron on 22 July, 1942, Major Francis R. Feeney assumed command, retaining command until 6 April, 1943, when he was transferred to Group Headquarters; on the same date Captain Pearre D. Jacques assumed command. On April 30, 1943, Major Pearre D. Jacques received orders returning him to the United States, whereupon Captain Fred G. Henry assumed command. On 30 May, 1943, Major Fred G. Henry received orders returning hm to the United States, whereupon Captain Perry H. Penn assumed command. When Major Perry H. Penn received orders on 26 September, 1943, returning him to the United States, Major Robert C. Beebe, having been transferred from Group Headquarters, assumed command of the squadron.

COMMANDING OFFICERS

33RD TROOP CARRIER SQUADRON

1st Lieutenant Elmer F. Estrumse, having been transferred to the 33rd Transport Squadron from the 6th Transport Squadron, on 17 February, 1942, assumed command thereof. On 1 September, 1942, upon Captain Estrumse's transfer to Group Headquarters,

315th Troop Carrier Group, 1st Lt. Campbell M. Smith assumed command of the squadron. Upon the departure of the air echelon of the squadron for Hamilton Field, California, on 30 September, 1942, Captain George C. Kimball became acting commanding officer of the ground echelon. Captain Kimball was succeeded by Captain Robert L. Ward as commanding officer of the ground echelon on 7 October, 1942. On 11 October, 1942, Captain Eugene E. Jackson joined the squadron, assuming command the same date. Upon the arrival of the ground echelon to join the air echelon at Port Moresby, New Guinea, on 28 December, 1942, Captain Jackson took over complete command. Upon the transfer of Major Eugene R. Jackson to Group Headquarters on 15 October, 1943, Captain George W. Wamsley, Jr., assumed command of the squadron.

HISTORY - THE 6TH TROOP CARRIER SQUADRON

The 6th Transport Squadron was activated pursuant to letter from the Adjutant General's Office, dated 14 October, 1939, at Middletown Air Depot, Olmsted Field, Middletown, Penna., with Major John R. Dunn as commanding officer. Among the first officers to be assigned to the squadron on 20 November, 1939, was 2nd Lt. John H. Lackey, Jr. The squadron was originally a unit of the 10th Transport Group, but it was under the operational control of the Middletown Air Depot and the 50th Transport Wing. Later the squadron was assigned to the 63rd Transport Group.

Approximately six months after its activation, aircraft were assigned to the squadron. On April 3, 1940, two C-33s and four C-39s were delivered and began to be employed in the transportation of cargo to all parts of the United States, with station at Middletown, Penna.

On 1 December, 1940, the squadron was designated the parent organization to furnish a cadre of officers and enlisted men for the 12th Transport Squadron of the 60th Group, and for Headquarters and Headquarters Squadron of the 61st Transport Group.

On 1 February, 1941, an unknown number of officers and enlisted men were transferred from the Sixth and designated as cadres for the 10th and 12th Transport Squadrons. There were also additional transfers of officers and enlisted men from the squadron to the 60th and 61st Groups.

On 5 November, 1941, six C-53s were assigned to the squadron, bringing the strength in aircraft to a total of twelve.

On 24 November, 1941, the squadron conducted its own maneuvers in the Middletown area consisting of a march to bivouac with simulated chemical gas and strafing attack. The morale of the men was very high and the maneuver was considered successful.

On 17 February, 1942, the 315th Transport Group was activated with headquarters at Middletown Air Depot, with three newly activated squadrons, the 33rd, 34th and 35th. At this time, Captain Hamish McClelland was transferred to the 315th Group, assuming command thereof, 1st Lt. John H. Lackey, Jr. assuming command of the Sixth. 1st Lt. Elmer F. Estrumse was relieved from assignment to the Sixth to become commanding officer of the 33rd Squadron. Six officers and 64 enlisted men were also transferred forming cadres for the 34th and 35th Squadrons.

On 23 May, 1942, the 6th Squadron moved to Camp Williams, Camp Douglas, Wisconsin, to join its parent organization, the 63rd Transport Group. On 2 July, 1942, it was redesignated the 6th Troop Carrier Squadron. The squadron operated as a unit of this group until the departure of the air echelon on 5 August, 1942 for Selfridge Field, Michigan. On September 12, 1942, the air echelon moved to Pope Field, Ft. Bragg, N.C., and on 16 September, 1942, to Dodd Field, Texas. The ground echelon departed Camp Williams for Dodd Field 16 September, 1942, arriving there two days later.

On 23 September, 1942, the air echelon consisting of a full contingent of C-47s with 16 officers, 15 Staff Sergeant Pilots and 60 other enlisted men under the command of Captain John H. Lackey, Jr., departed Dodd Field for the Sacramento Air Depot where they received transition training for overseas duty. The ground echelon was placed under the command of Captain Frank W. Smith. It departed Dodd Field on 7 October, 1942, arriving at Camp Stoneman, California, on 11 October, 1942.

The air echelon went from Sacramento Air Depot to Hamilton Field, California, from which point it departed the United States on 2 October, 1942, in its 13 C-47s, being the first transport squadron to fly the Pacific. It arrived at Port Moresby, New Guinea, 13 October, 1942.

The ground echelon departed from San Francisco, California, on 26 October, 1942, with a strength of 11 officers and 155 enlisted men, stopping at Hawaii for 6 days; it arrived at Townsville, Queensland, Australia, on 24 November, 1942. There it remained at Camp Cluden until 1 December, 1942, when it was flown in squadron planes to its permanent station at Ward's Drome, Port Moresby, New Guinea, pursuant to Movement Order No. 41, Headquarters, Air Service Command, Fifth Air Force, dated 6 November, 1942. The movement was completed by 13 December, 1942.

Pursuant to par. 2, General Order No. 32, Headquarters, Fifth Air Force, APO 923, dated 12 November, 1942, the 6th Troop Carrier Squadron had been assigned to the newly designated 374th Troop Carrier Group.

HISTORY - THE 21ST AND 22ND TROOP CARRIER SQUADRONS

Air transport activities in the southwest Pacific had their inception in early January of 1942 when 10 officers and 15 enlisted men of the 7th Bomb Group and 35th Pursuit Group began, under verbal orders, to fly cargo in two old B-18s, an old C-39 from the Philippines, and five new C-53s which were "found" aboard a ship in the first convoy which had started for the Philippines, but which docked at Brisbane, Australia, under changed orders, on 22 December, 1941. These first air transport pilots received their transport transition training under A.N.A. airlines pilots during January 1942.

The forerunner of the 374th Troop Carrier Group, designated as the Air Transport Command, was activated on 28 January, 1942, at Amberley Airdrome, Queensland, Australia, by authority of Letter, Office of the Air Officer, Base Section No. 3, dated 28 January, 1942. This Letter named 1st Lt. Edgar W. Hampton as commanding officer, and ordered that "all United States transport airplanes now in Australia and all combat airplanes flyable but unfit for combat will be part of the Air Transport Command." Upon activation, the organization had 14 officers and 19 enlisted men, all assigned under verbal orders of the commanding officer, Base Section No. 3. None of the officers was thoroughly trained to fly transport type aircraft and 75 percent of the enlisted men were only semi-skilled as air crew members.

On 4 February, 1942, Air Transport Command headquarters was moved from Amberley Airdrome to Archer Field, Brisbane, and Captain Paul I. Gunn, former Manager of Operations of the Philippine Airlines, was placed in command. A complement of 10 officers and 10 enlisted men, all thoroughly trained in transport flying and operations, joined the organization on 8 February, 1942.

At Archer Field personnel were quartered in barracks and at first were messed with an Australian unit. During May 1942, cooks having been assigned to the organization, a mess hall was set up. Food was satisfactory and for recreation the men had a day room set up in one of the barracks, equipped with a piano, radio and reading material.

During the latter part of January and the early part of February, 1942, F-40 mechanics and equipment were flown to bases in Java by Air Transport Command aircraft. Late in February, when the Netherlands East Indies was falling before the onslaught of superior Japanese forces, Air Transport Command aircraft participated in the evacuation of military and civilian personnel. Also, during February, the Broome-Wyndham area in Western Australia was evacuated by A.T.C. planes which flew evacuees to Perth, Western Australia, and to Brisbane, Queensland. Two C-53s were lost during this hectic period, during which the pilots had to fly in all kinds of bad weather without adequate maps. One C-53, returning from Java, found Darwin to be Zero-Zero and was forced to land on an emergency strip for light planes on Bathurst Island, 60 miles north of Darwin. Landing in a crosswind, the plane damaged its left wing tip and aileron. The craft was destroyed by Japanese Zeros before repairs could be effected. The second C-53 became lost and made a crash landing near Wyndham after running out of gasoline. It was en route from Perth to Broome. Personnel escaped safely and were picked up two days later by an Australian flying boat.

The function of the Director of Air Transport was handled by A-3, Air Force, during this early period, per verbal orders of the Commanding General, U.S.A.F.I.A. They were relieved of this duty in March, 1942, by Lieutenant Colonel Erickson S. Nichols. Group Captain Harold Gatty, of Post and Gatty fame, became Director of the Directorate of Allied Air Transport, and Lieutenant Colonel Nichols became Commanding Officer of the Air Transport Command.

Between January and July, 1942, the Air Transport Command flew more than 5,000,000 miles in rushing equipment and supplies to strategic points on the southwest Pacific front. During the period of 10 March to 22 March, 1942, A.T.C. planes transported the entire 102nd Coast Artillery (anti-aircraft) Battalion, (U.S.) With complete equipment from Brisbane to Batchlor Field at Darwin, a distance of 1800 miles. The Battalion was moved in small balanced units with guns and ammunition ready for instant action. This battery, set up in the previously unprotected Darwin area, provided a very effective surprise for Japanese planes in subsequent raids. Wounded and evacuated personnel were flown to Brisbane on the return flights.

For more than two months after it was activated, the Air Transport Command had only eight enlisted personnel available for maintenance. Working on a 24-hour basis, however, each man putting in an average of 17 and 18 hours a day, all six available planes were kept flying. During March, one aircraft, a C-53, No. 41-20070, flew a record total of 272 hours, carrying more than 300 tons of supplies a distance of 2,000 miles. Late in March, 1942, planes and pilots of the Netherlands East Indies Airlines, K.N.I.L.M., joined the American Unit on a contract basis. These planes were purchased from the K.N.I.L.M., and turned over to the Air Transport Command, which had expanded considerably in pilot officers and enlisted strength by assignment from casual units.

The Air Transport Command, Archer Field, Brisbane, was redesignated the 21st Transport Squadron and assigned to Headquarters, Air Transport Command, Melbourne, Victoria, on 3 April 1942. The same order activated the 22nd Transport Squadron with 5089 Headquar ters, U.S.A.F.I.A., based at Essendon Airdrome, Melbourne. Ten pilots and 19 enlisted men were transferred to the 22nd Squadron from the 21st Squadron. Veteran bombardment and pursuit pilots from the Philippines and Java campaign and a cadre of enlisted men from the United States brought the strength of the 22nd up to 19 officers and 196 enlisted men by the end of May, 1942. Several K.N.I.L.M. planes, including L-14s, C-56s, DC-5s, DC-2s and DC-3s, were assigned to the 22nd. Personnel of the 21st Squadron, previously assigned only by verbal orders, were officially relieved from assignment to the Air Transport Command, Archer Field, and re-assigned to the 21st Transport Squadron per Special Order No. 89, paragraph No. 1, Headquarters, U.S.A.F.I.A., Melbourne, Victoria, dated 13 April, 1942.

The 22nd Squadron had the advantage of excellent camp and messing facilities at Essendon Airdrome. Personnel lived in barracks; shower buildings were supplied with hot and cold running water. The officers dined at their club and the enlisted men messed in two mess halls. Excellent food was enjoyed by all. Although there was some athletic equipment, no organized recreation was provided. Churches in Melbourne provided the men their spiritual needs.

On 22 May, 1942, the 21st Transport Squadron, led by Captain E. W. Hampton, made its first operational flight in New Guinea, carrying troops and supplies to Wau and Bulolo, allied mountain airdromes previously used only by very light aircraft. Wau Airdrome, at an altitude of 3,300 feet, was very rough and had an uphill incline of one foot in 12 with a crescent of 7,000 feet mountains at its far end. Bulolo, also very rough, was approximately 2,000 feet long, slightly down-grade and very wet. No aircraft were damaged in these landings. The 21st and 22nd Squadrons continued to operate several planes between Port Moresby and Wau at intervals, despite intense Japanese activity and fighter cover consisting of only five or six F-39s. When the Japanese landed troops at Buna in July, 21st Squadron planes landed Australian reinforcements and supplies at Kokoda and during the fighting for that mountain airdrome, the planes often circled the field without knowing whether it was in friendly or enemy hands. In August, 1942, during the Australian retreat which ended in an allied offensive at Iorabaiwa Ridge, 30 air miles from Port Moresby and during the fight back across the Owen Stanley, 21st and 22nd Squadron planes dropped tons of supplies and equipment to the Australian troops, thus taking adequate care of a supply problem which otherwise would have prolonged the fighting for months. By the recommendation of General Scanlon, in charge of the Allied Air Force in New Guinea, 1st Lts. Fred G. Henry and James A. McCullough and 2nd Lt. Talmadge E. Walker, of the 21st Squadron, were awarded the Purple Heart for outstanding flying in the area.

The 21st Transport Squadron was redesignated the 21st Troop Carrier Squadron and the 22nd Transport Squadron redesignated the 22nd Troop Carrier Squadron per General Order No 20, paragraph No. 1, Headquarters, U.S.A.A.S., S.W.P.A. dated 26 July, 1942. Headquarters, Air Transport Command was redesignated Air Carrier Service, per General Order No. 10, paragraph No. 1, Headquarters, Air Service Command, Fifth Air Force, APO 923, dated 21 October, 1942, and Lieutenant Colonel Erickson S. Nichols assumed command.

The first large troop movement conducted by the Group started in September, 1942, when the 126th, 127th, and 128th Infantry Regiments of the 32nd (U.S.) Division, together with their equipment, were flown from the mainland to New Guinea. For this movement, all available transports, civilian airlines planes and several new B-17Es were utilized. One Ferry pilot, a Mr. Burke, made three landings at 7-Mile Drome in one 24-hour period. He took off from the mainland about 3 A.M. and 3 P.M., thereby landing at 7-Mile Drome just after daylight and just before dark, returning immediately to the mainland.

During the middle of October, 1942, a very concentrated movement was made from Milne Bay and Port Moresby to Wanagela Mission for the start of the final allied drive on Buna. Captain Charles A. Gibson loaded from Milne Bay and Lieutenant Marvin M. Scott supervised loading from Port Moresby. All available U.S. and RAAF transport aircraft, together with civilian airlines planes were utilized in the movement. Both Australian and American troops were moved; infantry, anti-aircraft and engineer troops, together with many native bearers were transported. The 6th Squadron arrived during the movement, three of its ships making trips the day after its arrival. An average of about 1000 men and equipment, were moved daily, the movement of approximately 3,600 men and equipment being accomplished in three days. The supply of those units then added to the work of the Group to maintain their effectiveness in combat. The order of the day was, supplies in - sick and wounded out.

During the latter part of October, 1942, a C-49 was assigned as a Red Cross ship to evacuate wounded from areas where it could land. S/Sgt Pilot Neil O. Maxwell of the 22nd Squadron was its pilot until about the middle of November, 1942, when Lt. Ronald E. Notestine was sent to relieve him. Over 50 men were brought to hospitals by this ship during that period, and thousands of pounds of dressings and medicines were delivered to aid stations along the Kokoda Trail.

Early in November, 1942, Kokoda fell to the Australians and our planes flew over the Owen Stanleys with ever increasing numbers of men, jeeps, trailers, small bull-dozers, road graders, steam rollers, runway matting, fuel and many other items needed for combat use.

Also in November, 1942, a large scale movement of troops and supplies to the Buna area was initiated. An average of 1500 men and equipment were transported from Ward"s and Jackson Dromes daily.

In all three movements only one ship was lost. During the movements every ship available was used, including C-56s, C-60s, DC-2s, DC-3s, DC-5s, C-39s, C-49s, C-53s and the new C-47s which had arrived with the 6th and 33rd Squadrons.

Pursuant to orders, the 22nd Squadron changed its station from Essendon Drome, Melbourne, Victoria, to Garbutt Field, Townsville, Queensland. The movement was commenced September 17, 1942 and completed 11 October, 1942. It was accomplished by rail in two echelons. Several of the barracks in the transient camp area, know as Project No 2, Garbutt Field Area, were set aside for the use of the squadron. The officers and enlisted men dined in the same mess hall; the consensus of opinion was that good food was served. Showers were equipped only with cold running water. Drinking water required chlorination inasmuch as Army authorities had condemned the Townsville supply of water as unfit for drinking purposes. There was no organized participation in athletics, although softball games between officers and enlisted men were quite frequent. A small chapel at the edge of the post and churches in Townsville provided means of worship.

In pursuance to Movement Order No. 25, Base Section 3, dated 29 January, 1943, the 21st and 22nd Squadrons changed their stations from Archer Field, Brisbane, and Garbutt Field, Townsville, respectively, to Ward's Drome, Port Moresby, New Guinea. The air echelon of the 21st Squadron left Brisbane on 18 February, 1943, by plane arriving at Ward's Drome, Port Moresby, New Guinea, the same day. The ground echelon left Brisbane, Queensland, by boat, arriving at Port Moresby, New Guinea, via Milne Bay on 6 March, 1943. The air echelon of the 22nd Squadron left Townsville on 24 January, 1943, arriving at Ward's Drome, Port Moresby, New Guinea, the same date. The first part of the ground echelon left Townsville by air on 24 January, 1943, arriving at Ward's Drome, Port Moresby, New Guinea, the same date. The remaining personnel left Townsville by boat 10 February, 1943, arriving at Port Moresby, 14 February, 1943.

Pursuant to par 2, General Order No. 32, Headquarters, Fifth Air Force, APO 923, dated 12 November, 1942, the 21st and 22nd Squadrons had been assigned to the newly designated 374th Troop Carrier Group.

HISTORY - THE 33RD TROOP CARRIER SQUADRON

On 17 February, 1942, per General Order No. 7, Middletown Air Depot, dated 14 February, 1942, the 33rd Transport Squadron was activated and became a unit of the 315th Transport Group. The original cadre was selected from the 2nd Transport Squadron. First Lieutenant Elmer F. Estrumse was transferred to the 33rd from the 6th Transport Squadron and assumed command. Shortly after its activation, the squadron began to operate with at least 3 C-39s hauling cargo from Middletown, Pa., to widely scattered points in the United States as well as Newfoundland, Haiti, Cuba and other foreign points.

On 17 June, 1942, the squadron changed its station to Bowman Field, Kentucky. Its personnel was increased from a cadre to approximately half its T/O strength. The squadron continued to haul cargo to diverse points from Bowman Field. While at Bow-

Left to right: Maj. Hellweg, Lt. McCullen, Capt. Feigus, Lt.Col Imparato, Capt. Scott, Sgt. Appling, Capt. Leiberman, Capt. Simpson, Sgt. Ressenger, Sgt. Rife, Sgt. Deshazer, Sgt. Boulden, Sgt. Sevic, Sgt. Hammond, and Sgt. Dewitt.

The boys at play in Townsville, Australia.

Catcher and pitcher of the 374th's baseball team.

Sgt. Larry Horst and Capt. Sam Ketchman.

man Field, the squadron instituted an extensive training program for both flying and ground personnel.

During early July, 1942, the 33rd Transport Squadron was redesignated the 33rd Troop Carrier Squadron, pursuant to War Department letter.

On 3 August, 1942, per Special Order No. 80, Headquarters, 315th Troop Carrier Group, the squadron changed its station from Bowman Field, Ky., to the Army Air Base, Florence, South Carolina. The movement was completed on 5 August, 1942. An intensive overseas training program was immediately undertaken. Flying personnel engaged in night flying and dropped paratroops in southern maneuvers. The ground personnel was given infantry and commando training. The personnel of the squadron was increased above T/O strength but was reduced to approximately 90% T/O strength prior to its departure overseas. While at Florence, S.C., the plane strength of the squadron was increased until it reached 13 in number.

On 30 September, 1942, per secret order, 72 officers and enlisted men formed an air echelon and departed for Hamilton Field, California for overseas transition training. The ground echelon departed Florence, S.C., by rail on 20 October, 1942, arriving at Camp Stoneman, Pittsburg, California, 27 October, 1942. On 18 October, 1942, the air echelon, under the command of Captain Eugene E. Jackson, departed Hamilton Field with 13 planes, per Operations Order No. 97, Air Transport Command, Headquarters, Pacific Wing, dated 17 October, 1942. Upon their arrival at Canton Island, the evening of 21 October, 1942, 10 planes and crews assisted in the search for Captain Eddie Rickenbacker and his companions for two days.

The air echelon arrived at New Caledonia, 25 October, 1942. Seven of the squadron's planes and crews were delayed there until 29 November, 1942, by the Island Command, VOCO, General Harmon, and ferried personnel and supplies to Guadalcanal and New Hebrides Islands, using Tontuta as a base. Wounded personnel were returned from Guadalcanal. Here the squadron sustained its first casualties in the southwest Pacific area. On 8 November, 1942, a C-47 with S/Sgt Pilot Ray V. Hensman at the controls, was seen to burst into flame after take-off, as it passed over the northerly end of Henderson Field, then in the hands of the Japanese. It had apparently been struck by enemy ground fire. On 22 November, 1942, another plane was totally demolished in a crash after taking off at New Hebrides with a load of hand grenades. The crew was seriously injured but there were no fatalities. On 29 November, 1942, the five remaining planes departed Tontuta, arriving at Cairns, Queensland, on 30 November, 1942, joining the air echelon at Ward's Drome, Port Moresby, New Guinea, on 2 December, 1942.

The remaining planes continued on to Brisbane, Queensland, thence to Cairns, Queensland, VOCO Lt. Colonel Nichols, and operated from there and New Guinea until 10 December, 1942, when TWX instructions from Lt. Colonel Nichols sent them to their permanent station in New Guinea. On 5 November, 1942, 33rd Squadron planes had participated in their first New Guinea mission.

The ground echelon of the 33rd Squadron left the United States by water on 2 November, 1942. It arrived at Auckland, New Zealand, on 22 November, 1942, remaining there four days. On Thanksgiving Day, 26 November, 1942, it departed Auckland, arriving at Camp Doomben, Brisbane, Queensland, 1 December, 1942. On 21 December, 1942, the ground echelon departed Brisbane by water en route Port Moresby, New Guinea. Christmas Day, 25 December, 1942, was spent aboard the transport in the Townsville, Queensland harbor. On 28 December, 1942, it arrived at Port Moresby, where it joined the air echelon, establishing its permanent camp site at Ward's Drome. Authority for the movement to New Guinea was Movement Orders No. 44, Headquarters, Air Service Command, APO 923, dated 16 November, 1942.

Pursuant to paragraph 2, General Orders No. 32, Headquarters, Fifth Air Force, APO 923, dated 12 November, 1942, the 33rd Troop Carrier Squadron had been assigned to the newly designated 374th Troop Carrier Group.

Activation and Development of the 374th Troop Carrier Group

The Air Carrier Service was redesignated the 374th Troop Carrier Group and the 6th Troop Carrier Squadron, 21st Troop Carrier Squadron, 22nd Troop Carrier Squadron and the 33rd Troop Carrier Squadron were assigned to the 374th Troop Carrier Group, per General Order No. 32, Headquarters, Fifth Air Force, APO 923, dated 12 November, 1942. Lieutenant Colonel E. S. Nichols was designated as commanding officer. On 15 November, 1942, Major E. W. Hampton was appointed commanding officer of the advance echelon of the Group at Port Moresby, New Guinea. On 14 December, 1942, Lt. Colonel Nichols was ordered to return to the United States and was relieved from command of the group. Major Hampton assuming temporary command. On 17 December, 1942, Colonel Paul H. Prentiss was assigned to the Group and assumed command.

Group Headquarters was first stationed at Brisbane. On 12 November, 1942, the strength of Group Headquarters was 17 officers and 82 enlisted men, most of whom were on DS at various control stations throughout Australia and Papua. During November and December, 1942, while a nucleus of Group Headquarters personnel was being moved to its new station at Port Moresby, the greater part of these officers and enlisted men on DS were transferred to Directorate of Air Transport. After the original cadre of 5 officers and 3 enlisted men arrived in New Guinea, a small number of enlisted men from reorganized Fighter Control units were assigned to Headquarters bringing its strength up to approximately 50% of its T/O strength by 1 February, 1943.

Before the ground echelons of the 22nd and 33rd Squadrons arrived in New Guinea, personnel of group headquarters, the 21st, 22nd and 33rd Squadrons already in New Guinea lived in a tent area at Arcadia, operated by the 8th Service Group. Food and messing facilities have been reliably described as horrible. The 6th Squadron took over the camp area of the 220th Service Squad-

George Wamsley, Gerald Wentworth, Bob Carlson, and Arthur Merman of the 33rd TC Squadron.

ron (later designated the 478th Service Squadron) upon the arrival of its ground echelon in December, 1942. Prior to that time the air echelon was billeted and messed with the 220th Service Squadron.

By the end of February, 1943, the Group was operating in its entirety from Ward's and Jackson Dromes, Port Moresby, New Guinea, under the immediate jurisdiction of the Advance Echelon, Fifth Air Force, APO 929, commanded by Brigadier General Ennis C. Whitehead. Early days in New Guinea were attended by many discomforts. From November 1942 to the middle of February, 1943, night raids by enemy bombers were all too frequent. It was not until the middle of March, 1943, that the personnel of the group were able to vary their customary diet of bully beef with an occasional meal of fresh meat, when supplementary rations became available.

Group Headquarters and the four squadrons had set up camp sites at the southeasterly end of Ward's Drome. Personnel lived in tents for the most part without flooring. Electricity was obtained by means of generators set up and maintained by the squadrons, and water was piped from the Laloki River. In early days, before showers were set up, personnel traveled to Port Moresby in trucks to obtain shower baths. The 33rd and 22nd Squadrons had projectors and showed nightly movies on outside screens. A large outdoor stage was constructed by group headquarters during the latter part of May, 1943; latest run motion pictures were among those shown. In July, 1943, Joe Lewis, the popular night club entertained appeared in person at the Group Theater. He was followed shortly thereafter by Little Jack Little and Ray Bolger. Edwin McArthur and Lansing Hatfield also appeared 15 August, 1943. During its stay in New Guinea there was little or no organized group recreation. However, the squadrons had softball and volleyball teams entered in Port Moresby Area Leagues.

The 317th Troop Carrier Group arrived in the southwest Pacific area During January, 1943. Its 39th, 40th, 41st and 46th Squadrons each operated 13 new C-47s. They flew in New Guinea along with the four squadrons of the 374th during the battle for the Wau strip in January and February, 1943, when the Japs were driven from the area by air-transported Australian troops. In February, the 317th returned to the mainland of Australia after exchanging its new C-47s for the older ships of the 374th.

Significantly, the reward for the Group's efforts was that for the first time, the advance of the Japanese in the Southwest Pacific Theater had been stopped by airborne troops. Whether the battles of the Coral Sea and Bismarck Sea could have been won by the Allies without an allied foothold in southern New Guinea is now a moot question. Suffice it to say, the 374th had done its part.

Major Wentworth, Major Snow, and Captain Glotzback.

In recognition for its services during these crucial months the group received a citation under the provisions of par III, War Department, General Order No. 3, dated 15 January, 1943. The citation reads as follows:

"The 374th Troop Carrier Group, United States Army, is cited for outstanding performance of duty in action during the period September 19, 1942 to December 22, 1942. This unit was charged during this period with transportation by air of troop equipment and supplies to the forward areas in Papua and the evacuation of casualties to the rear areas and although attacked by enemy aircraft the group efficiently and successfully accomplished its assigned mission. Utilizing various types of unarmed aircraft an average of 100 tons of supplies a day was flown to the troops and casualties were evacuated daily. Several thousand troops, including artillery, were quickly transported to battle areas by this means. The high degree of technical ability, the devotion to duty, and the excellent morale of the group as a whole made possible this outstanding contribution to the success of the campaign in this area."

As a unit of the Papuan Forces during the period 23 July, 1942, to 23 January, 1943, the Group was included in the citation awarded under par. IV, War Department General Order No. 21, dated 6 May, 1943. The citation reads as follows:

"The Papuan Forces, United States Army, Southwest Pacific Area, are cited for outstanding performance of duty in action during the period July 23, 1942, to January 23, 1943. When a bold and aggressive enemy invaded Papua in strength, the combined action of ground and air units of these forces, in association with Allied units checked the hostile advance, drove the enemy back to the seacoast, and in a series of actions against a highly organized defensive zone, utterly destroyed him. Ground combat forces, operating over roadless jungle-covered mountains and swamps, demonstrated their courage and resourcefulness in closing with an enemy who took every advantage of the nearly impassable terrain. Air forces, by repeatedly attacking the enemy ground forces and installations, by destroying his convoys attempting reinforcement and supply, and by transporting ground forces and supplies to areas for which land routes were nonexistent and sea routes slow and hazardous, made possible the success of the ground operations. Service units, operating far forward of their normal positions and at times in advance of ground combat elements, built landing fields in the jungle, established and operated supply points, and provided for the hospitalization and evacuation of the wounded and sick. The courage, spirit, and devotion to duty of all elements of the command made possible the complete victory attained."

Under the provisions of paragraph 3b., Operations Memorandum, Hq., Advance Echelon, Fifth Air Force, dated 22 March, 1943, the Commanding Officer, 374th Troop Carrier Group, was designated as Base Commander of Ward's Drome and was accordingly vested with the responsibility of conducting Base Operations. This complex and highly important function was performed by the Group until 30 September, 1943. It might appropriately be said that operations on Ward's Drome and the Group's New Guinea operations went hand in hand despite the fact that the 21st Squadron operated off Jackson Drome for several months, because of overcrowded conditions at Ward's Drome.

It might be well at this point to relate briefly the origin and expansion of Ward's Drome. In August, 1942, Ward's Drome was a dummy strip in a tree covered flat, built to deceive the enemy and draw bombs from 7-Mile (Jackson) Drome. However, during the first of September, 1942, the original strip of the drome was cut through the trees to make a landing field for RAAF Beaufighters and Beaufort Bombers. This strip was gradually improved until by the middle of October, 1942, it was ready for use by transports. From this single strip the movement of troops in the first part of November, 1942, was accomplished, planes landing one way and taking off the other. Gasoline service in these early days was from 50-gallon drums and trucks pumped by small power pumps, but in spite of this the planes averaged less than 12 minutes on the ground during flying hours. No stops were made for lunch, sandwiches and coffee being handed the crews during that period. The spirit of the day was to get as much done as was humanly possible. This beginning of transport operations on Ward's Drome was the start of what was to be the most rapid growth of an air terminal in the area.

The completion of the second strip in March, 1943, made Ward's Drome the most active airfield in the Southwest Pacific Theater with over 300 planes operating off the drome. Transport history was made on Ward's Drome and the Japs will long remember it as the base from which the airborne drive to Tokyo was begun.

The task of the 374th in New Guinea after the middle of February, 1943, was to move personnel and supplies in three principal directions; first, to Dobodura, where a large base was being constructed and the gains of the Buna-Gona campaign were being consolidated; second, to Wau and Bulolo, where Allied Forces advancing on Lae and Salamaua had their rear bases; third, to the patrols skirting Lae and Salamaua, by dropping supplies. The four squadrons participated equally in their tasks, under the supervision of Group Operations at Ward's Drome. The group's planes were based at Ward's and Jackson Drome. This three-pronged operational program continued to be the daily order of flight, with occasional trips to Bena Bena, Mt. Hagen and other points until July, 1943.

Personnel of the Group witnessed a last display of enemy air power in New Guinea, on 12 April, 1943. Shortly before noon, approximately 100 enemy bombers and fighters flew over 14-mile Drome and Ward's Drome dropping sticks of bombs on both strips. Five of the group's planes based at Ward's Drome were damaged and immediately repaired; others were sprayed with shrapnel. Although scores of group personnel were in the immediate vicinity at the time the bombs exploded and although several of our ships were landing at the time of the raid, not a single casualty was sustained. Group activities continued as usual.

Troop Carrier activities began to expand by leaps and bounds. Headquarters and Headquarters Squadron, 54th Troop Carrier Wing was activated 13 March, 1943, as of 1 March, 1943, under General Order No. 49, Colonel Paul H. Prentiss was relieved from assignment to the Group on 22 May, 1943, and assigned to the 54th Troop Carrier Wing per paragraph 11, Special Order No. 140, Advance Echelon, Fifth Air Force, dated 20 May, 1943. Major Fred M. Adams, assumed command of the group.

During the month of July, 1943, the flying echelon of the 375th Troop Carrier Group arrived in New Guinea. Personnel of its four Squadrons and headquarters were billeted and rationed with the various squadrons of the 374th Group; pilots received their New Guinea transition training under the supervision of the pilots of respective squadrons to which they were attached. In August, 1943,

At desk: Capt. Hal B. Simpson and Capt. Pete Rennels at Townsville, 1943.

the flying echelon of the 65th and 66th Troop Carrier Squadrons of the 403rd Troop Carrier Group arrived in New Guinea; they were billeted and rationed with the 21st and 22nd Squadrons and likewise received their transition training at the hands of the 21st and 22nd pilots. Late in September, 1943, group headquarters and the flying echelon of the four squadrons of the 433rd Troop Carrier Group arrived in New Guinea. They too, were billeted and rationed with the 374th Group and received transition training under the supervision of our pilots.

From the 29th of August to 5 September, 1943, 6 ships and crews under the command of Captain Harvey E. Rehrer were stationed at Tsilli Tsilli, hauling men and supplies to Bena Bena, Garoke, Amami and other points, then strategically important.

As a prelude to highly important operations, on September 2, 1943, with Major Perry H. Penn in command, 36 planes and crews selected from the four squadrons, relieved a similar number of planes and crews of the 375th Troop Carrier Group at Dobodura, and hauled personnel and supplies to Tsilli Tsilli until 5 September, 1943, when they returned to their proper stations.

5 September, 1943, marked the opening of the campaign against Lae. Following a weather reconnaissance by Captain Arthur D. Thomas, of the 21st Squadron, in the B-25 weather ship, 36 planes of the 317th Troop Carrier Group, 36 planes of the 375th Troop Carrier Group and 10 planes of the 65th and 66th Squadrons of the 403rd Troop Carrier Group loaded with American paratroops and a battery of Australian Artillery paratroops, stood poised for flight at Ward's and Jackson Dromes. With Colonel Paul H. Prentiss, Commanding Officer of the 54th Troop Carrier Wing in command of the lead plane of the lead element, and Major John H. Lackey, Jr., Deputy Wing Commander, piloting the lead plane of the second element, the transports took off and under cover of a smoke screen laid down by A-20s, dropped their human cargo around the Nadzab Drome. Significantly enough, the Allied Nations had, for the first time in the Southwest Pacific Area, made use of paratroops to capture an enemy-held objective.

Grass, set ablaze by the paratroops at the captured Nadzab Drome, was still burning when 12 Group ships, led by Lt. Colonel Fred M. Adams, and carrying engineers' equipment for drome repairs and artillery for drome security, were landed on 6 September, 1943, at the strip.

A composite squadron of 12 planes and crews and a complement of ground personnel selected from the 21st and 33rd Squadrons was taken to Tsilli Tsilli on 6 September, 1943, by Lieutenant Colonel Adams. Upon Lt. Colonel Adams' departure three days later, Captain Arthur D. Thomas of the 21st Squadron assumed command, assisted by Captain Gene R. Glotzback of the 33rd Squadron. Between 6 September and 13 September, the planes shuttled back and forth to Nadzab, carrying Australian troops, supplies and organizational equipment, making a total of 303 trips. One plane alone made a record total of 8 trips in one day.

On 16 September, 1943, a formation of 13 group planes, carrying Australian commando troops, landed at Leron, an improvised landing field south of the Kaiapit strip. The following day, the highly strategic Kaiapit drome was captured by Allied troops. One plane was lost in landing at the strip during the operation.

Immediately following the capture of the Lae drome on 16 September, 1943, our transports began to haul a steady stream of men and supplies into Lae. In fact our C-47s were among the first planes to land at the Lae drome. From that time until the end of September, 1943, our transport activities continued upon an ever-increasing scale.

Troop Movement Directive No. 116, Headquarters, Fifth Air Force, dated 20 September 1943, as amended by Troop Movement Directive No. 116/1, Headquarters, Fifth Air Force, dated 30 September, 1943, and letter AG 370.5, dated 26 September, 1943, Headquarters, Advance Echelon, Fifth Air Force, ordered Headquarters, 6th, 22nd and 33rd Squadrons to Townsville and the 21st Squadron to Brisbane. The group was placed under the administrative control of the Fifth Air Force and the operational control of Directorate of Air Transport, Allied Air Forces. In effect, the movement resulted in an exchange of station and operations between the 374th and the 317th Groups. Each group carried with it only its own planes, files and individual personnel equipment.

The movement began on 28 September, 1943, with the 21st Squadron taking its assigned station at Archer Field, Brisbane, Queensland. The movement of the 21st Squadron was completed on 30 September, 1943; total weight of personnel (249 officers and enlisted men) and individual equipment moved by 15 plane loads was 32,744 lbs. The 6th Squadron commenced its movement to Garbutt Field, Townsville, Queensland, 1 October, 1943. The movement was completed 2 October, 1943; total weight of personnel (251 officers and enlisted men) and individual equipment moved by 18 plane loads was 90,000 lbs. The 22nd Squadron began its movement to Garbutt Field, 2 October, 1943, completing it 4 October, 1943. Total weight of personnel (242 officers and enlisted men) and individual equipment moved by 17 plane loads was 83,000 lbs. On 5 October, 1943, the 33rd Squadron moved personnel (244 officers and enlisted men) and individual equipment of a total of 58,106 lbs. to Garbutt Field, in 14 planes. Between 5 October, 1943, and 7 October, 1943, Group Headquarters personnel (90 officers and enlisted men) of a total weight of 27,505 lbs., were moved to Garbutt Field in 6 planes. The completion of the movement of the group showed 70 plane loads, hauling 1076 personnel and equipment of a total weight of 341,355 lbs. The move was accomplished without a mishap.

Immediately upon its arrival on the mainland of Australia, the group settled down to the accomplishment of its mission of maintaining an uninterrupted flow of men, supplies and equipment to units in Australia and in the New Guinea area. Operations were stepped up with a correspondingly heavy load being shouldered by group personnel. During October, November and December, 1943, the four squadrons operated on a normal six squadron basis, keeping approximately 55 planes flying each day. Compiled statistics for these months reveal record breaking performances. In addition, the group operated three leave ships daily between Mackay, Queensland, and Port Moresby, New Guinea.

For its own personnel the group at first sent one leave ship per week to Sydney and return; in December, 1943, two leave ships per week began to be dispatched to Sydney for 374th leave personnel.

The 6th, 22nd and 33rd Squadrons are quartered in barracks and tents at Project No., 2, Garbutt Field. Cold running water is available in limited quantities and drinking water requires chlorination. The 22nd and 33rd Squadrons conduct a consolidated mess while the 6th Squadron and Group Headquarters mess together. The purchase of supplementary rations has materially raised the quality and quantity of food served. The squadrons have embarked upon an active special services program. Group baseball and basketball teams are entered in local leagues. Horseshoe pitching has become a current popular pastime. For the evening's entertainment, the 45th Service Group conducts nightly movies in the camp area. In addition, enlisted personnel of group units stationed at Garbutt Field have been holding at least one party each month. Officers of the group have their own Club at 7 Oxford Street, Hyde Park, Townsville, Queensland. Enlisted personnel of the group have the use of a group day room; however, they have no clubs of their own. Living conditions can be described as fair. The post is over-run with ants, horses, cows and dogs. At Archer Field the 21st Squadron is housed in barracks. Both officers and enlisted men are living under crowded conditions; a new orderly room and officer's barracks are in the course of construction. The squadron operates its own officer's and enlisted men's mess halls and conducts a Branch Port Exchange in its camp area under the supervision of the Base Section 3 Port Exchange. An Officers' Club and an excellent Non-commissioned Officers' Club are conducted within walking distance of the camp area.

Inasmuch as the 317th Troop Carrier Group had during the first nine months of the year 1943 conducted its operations on a scale similar to that of the 374th during the last three months of 1943, comparative figures are revealing. During July, 1943, its most successful month, the 317th Group carried a total of 7,731,087 lbs. of freight and personnel. During the month of October, 1943, the 374th hauled a total weight of 8,577,581 lbs.; in November, 1943, it hauled a total weight of 8,360,492 lbs.; during December, 1943, it hauled a total weight of 10,661,142 lbs..

Since returning to Australia the planes of the four squadrons have been shuttling back and forth on the mainland between their respective stations and Horn Island to the north, and Sydney to the south. Almost daily trips were taken to Port Moresby, Fall River, Lae, Nadzab, Gusan, Finschhafen, Dobodura, Goodenough Island, Trobriand Islands, and Woodlark Island. Group planes and pilots also from time to time engaged in test dropping of paratroops at Cairns, Queensland, Australia.

In accomplishing its mission during the last three months of the year 1943, the group has not come through unscathed. The season's inclement weather took its toll in men and equipment. On 19 October, 1943, the 6th Squadron lost a plane and crew at Cloncurry, Queensland. On 16 November, 1943, a plane and crew of the 21st Squadron was lost at Springsure, Queensland. On 21 November, 1943, a 21st Squadron plane and crew disappeared in the vicinity of Rockhampton, Queensland. On 19 December, 1943, the group suffered its worse disaster since activation when a 22nd Squadron plane with its crew and 27 passengers exploded in mid-air near Rockhampton, Queensland, killing all aboard.

The year 1943 ended on a favorable note. In the Southwest Pacific Theater of operations, the balance sheet showed that Australia had in all probability been saved; wide gains were made in New Guinea; New Britain had been breached. Personnel of the 374th Group had worked ceaselessly and endured much for its part in those achievements.

Air Raids

More than 100 air raids were conducted by the Japanese over the Port Moresby area, and some personnel of the units which later became a part of the 374th Troop Carrier Group, were probably present during every raid. Considering the intensity of the raids, it is remarkable that no casualties were sustained by these units during the raids.

In the early months of the struggle in New Guinea when the enemy possessed air superiority, the raids were methodical. In most cases, day raids occurred between 1100 and 1200 hours, generally about 1130.

At first, and until the middle of July, 1942, after the bombing raids, the fighters came down and strafed the fields, often rolling their wheels on the runways, but with the arrival of more allied fighter planes and anti-aircraft units, low level dive bombing and strafing by fighters ceased. The last large day raid prior to that of 12 April, 1943, occurred on 7 September, 1942, when 24 bombers came over. One of the most disastrous raids was that of 17 August, 1942, when four group aircraft were hit; two C-56s and one DC-5 were completely destroyed and one DC-3 was put out of commission for about two months.

The night raids usually occurred just after dark and just before daylight, and generally consisted of two to six planes, with the strips as targets. The raids were nearly nightly during August and September, 1942, tapering off to occasional raids during October and November, 1942. The damage was usually light, being mostly off the runways. In a vain attempt to destroy the morale of the troops, the Japanese often broadcast the time of the next day's raid and would come over at the appointed time. After December, 1942, the raids were mainly nuisance raids of one or two planes, mostly at night, varying greatly from day to day as to time. On a moonlit night one could usually plan on spending most of it in a slit trench.

Apparently the Japanese had seen the handwriting on the wall, when on 12 April, 1942, they sent over 46 bombers and 60 zeros only to be repulsed with heavy losses. Five of our aircraft were damaged but were rebuilt. Very little other damage was done. It was a thrilling aerial spectacle.

At first there was little or no effective warning system of portending raids, the enemy often being overhead before they were detected. However, from January, 1943, until the group left New Guinea, the detector and warning systems on the island were very effective allowing as a rule at least 20 minutes' time to prepare for a raid. A 'yellow alert' signified unidentified aircraft approaching whereas a 'red alert' signified that enemy aircraft were approaching. Needless to say, yellow alerts were exceedingly numerous.

The following is an unofficial record of enemy air activity in the Port Moresby Area from 15 July, 1942, to 1 October, 1943:

Date	# of Enemy Planes (Daylight Raids)	# of Enemy Planes (Night Raids)
1942		
20 July	27 Bombers	
24 July	25 Bombers	
25 July	3 Zeros (Strafing attack)	
26 July	5 Zeros (Strafing attack)	
27 July		1 Flying Boat
28 July		3 Flying Boats
29 July	12 Bombers	
30 July		3 Bombers
1 August		4 Bombers
17 August	23 Bombers	
6 September	24 Planes	
7 September	24 Bombers	
17 September		3 Flying Boats
19 September		3 Flying Boats
21 September	27 Planes	
23 September		2 Flying Boats
24 September		3 Flying Boats
20 October		1 Bomber
22 October		2 Flying Boats
25 October		2 Bombers
29 October		2 Bombers
1 November		3 Bombers
24 November		2 Bombers
25 November		2 Bombers
27 November		3 Bombers
1942		
29 November		1 Zero, 4 Bombers
13 December		1 Bomber
14 December		1 Bomber
16 December		2 Bombers
17 December		1 Bomber
1943		
14 January		1 Bomber
15 January		2 Bombers
23 January		3 Bombers
24 January		6 Bombers
25 January		3 Bombers
26 January		3 Bombers
27 January		(Unknown)
31 January		(Unknown)
12 February		(Unknown)
21 February		3 Bombers
12 April	46 Bombers, 60 Zeros	
13 May		3 Bombers
15 May		6 Bombers
24 May		(Unknown)
13 June		2 Bombers (3 passes)
17 June		4 Bombers
20 September		1 Bomber

Chief of Maintenance Captain Mile Soular and his team.

Life in Port Moresby

By M/Sgt. Glenn D. McMurray
from the book Moresby to Manila Via Troop Carrier

Port Moresby in 1942 wasn't a Paris or even a Lae. It was nothing more than a small seaport where occasional shipping anchored to drop off a few supplies to the gold miners at Wau or to let the tourists buy a few trinkets to prove they had seen the wilds of New Guinea.

When the Yanks decided to build a Port Moresby into an island fortress there was no force that could stop them. The Japs attempted, but found out it was useless. Even the elements, rain, fog and intense heat, failed to stop them.

In late 1942 the lifebuoy of transports began to move in supplies, equipment and men to build up Port Moresby as a base. Hills rarely trodden by native feet began to flatten out into airstrips. Roads were built and bridges were made. Nothing was spared. Thousands of men came pouring in to build this tremendous base. Trucks, jeeps, and heavy equipment moved over the dirt roads until the surface became a powder. Then came the oil highways. There is no place where the Yanks have seen such an elaborate highway set-up in such a remote spot. There were four and five lane roads to taxi all aircraft which might possibly drop in on their way to bomb the Japs.

Late in December 1942 Port Moresby announced the arrival of Brigadier General Paul H. Prentiss, then a colonel. A Troop Carrier sympathizer from the start, General Prentiss eagerly set about building up an organization which was to break the hump over the Owen Stanleys to Nadzab, Lae, Hollandia, Biak, Palau, Leyte, Luzon and soon we hope to Tokyo.

Going was rough at Port Moresby for several months. Supplies and equipment to make life easier were not to be had. You ate in the open and liked it. Every kind of dehydrated food was put before you. This went on for weeks, but it did not stop tactical operations. This progress that was made was nothing short of a miracle.

The camp area of the 374th Troop Carrier Squadron was well placed in more ways than one. First, it was on a hill overlooking both Ward's and Jackson's dromes. Second, it was located on the site of an old ack-ack outfit and ammo dump, always a target for the Japs. Third, a tremendous gas dump was within a stone's throw. Now, had the Japs been good shots, there would have been no cause for alarm, but being such miserable shots, their bombs were liable to hi anywhere from one-half to two miles from the strips.

The Yank who comes overseas now and sees all the comforts, thinks that it has always been that way. Little does he know!

The 374th Troop Carrier Group rapidly grew too big for her boots, and plans were laid for the activation of a Troop Carrier Wing. It was a surprise to many, but to those who knew the ropes it was the natural result of much planning - planning which left room for expansion on a tremendous scale, which is now self-evident. With a small staff of officers and a handful of enlisted men, General Prentiss undertook the real man-sized job of putting the Wing on a "paying basis". A building was erected beside the 374th Troop Carrier Group Headquarters on the hill, and then personnel began to be drawn in to take over Wing Headquarters.

At the beginning, most of the men came from the 374th Group. Later personnel came in from all groups along with overages from other commands and a few replacements from the States.

By July or August 1943 a new camp was constructed for the Wing Headquarters and Headquarters Squadron across the road from the 374th Group area. This time, however, it was located between two hills and it was not possible to see out as it had been in the old area. However, it was a nice clean area, and very comfortable and cool at night.

Up until this time nothing has been said about the air raids. Well, after July there were not many. Prior to that there were plenty of them, especially during 1942 and the first three or four months of 1943 when three or four raids on a moonlight night were expected. Yes, moonlight, and as regular as the clock. When the moon was full, it was time to look out. Say 2300 hours, or perhaps 0200 and 0400. There was a honey of a raid during April. Over 100 planes raided Moresby. That was really a sight. No one who saw it will forget that raid. Accounts of it are written and told over and over again.

Aussies! Goodness, the island was overrun with them. It was to be expected, since New Guinea really was their charge and they would take over after we left. They always had something to sell you - plexiglass bracelets, rings and all sorts of things. They usually wanted a fortune for them too. If they weren't selling something they were mooching "cigs". Our Yanks lived like kings in comparison. It seemed to cause a little discontent, but no trouble came from it.

Those who pass through Moresby now say it is a ghost town. The strip that was rushed to completion to accommodate the B-29 is now used as a transient strip. It never felt the weight of a B-29. Ward's drome finally was turned over to the Aussies for their use. The Yanks moved out, lock, stock and barrel. In some respects it is even cleaner than when the Yanks went in.

On a wing and a prayer – C-47 left wing flown to Advance Base Bena Bena by C-47 aircraft, spare left wing is strapped to the belly of C-47.

Yes, Port Moresby was a hole. It housed thousands of troops and had an almost equal number of diseases. Atabrine arrived and saved the day from Malaria. It was hot - beastly hot. Then it would rain, floods of the wet stuff. Then the dust would blow. There were hills to climb until your back and legs were almost broken. We will not forget her. Her ports and dromes opened the drive to Tokyo. She stretched her legs and found them strong. She bore a powerful, rightful force up and over its gravest dangers, and now she is ready to rest. Her job for the present is done. What Port Moresby will do in the future is anyone's guess, but on the whole the Yanks will tell you in one voice, "Give 'er back to the natives and let me go on to Tokyo and home!"

The year 1942/1943 brought a number of changes to the 374th Troop Carrier Group. There was loss of life by valiant crews due to enemy action in combat and a series of isolated air crashes and ground accidents in war related duties.

The group as a whole matured in 1943. It became the most effective, fully trained combat ready organization under General George Kenney's Far East Air Forces. There was no airborne mission it could not perform. It even devised and developed new ways and better ways to do the airborne jobs.

It was during this period that the C-47 "Gooney Bird" received recognition by military leaders world wide as the most versatile, most effective and most reliable weapon so far in WWII. More detailed explanations on the reasons for the accolades will be pointed out in the narrative in this chapter. Two of the unusual and striking new techniques employed by troop carrier are pointed out here and explained in detail later.

Phyco, the group's mascot who flew along on many missions.

First, a C-47 with a damaged left wing at a forward mountain airdrome would have been left to die through cannibalization of the airplane for parts. However, the critical need for aircraft demanded action and imagination to salvage the aircraft if possible. A replacement left wing was available from another unrepairable C-47 damaged by enemy action. The available wing was at Port Moresby, the damaged wing was at outpost Bena Bena 250 miles away. A C-47 wing is too large to fit into a C-47 or any other Air Force aircraft. The solution: strap the replacement wing to the belly of a C-47 and fly it in to Bena Bena.

A cartoon by John Hix depicting the flight appeared in the Spartanburg, South Carolina Herald, November 1, 1943. The title: "3 Wings and A Prayer." (See Appendix 'M')

The second unique use of the C-47 was its use as a bomber which is detailed later.

A third unbelievable first-time use of the C-47 is described in the chapter on the Shangri La rescue.

C-47s delivering supplies to Army troops in New Guinea, early 1943.

Brig. General Warren Carter, CG 54th Troop Carrier Wing.

CHAPTER III

1943

ORDER OF THE DAY
On Completion Of
RECAPTURE OF BUNA-GONA AREA
By
Lieutenant-General E. F. HERRING
C.B.E., D.S.O., M.C., E.D.
G.O.C., NEW GUINEA FORCE
Headquarters
New Guinea Force,
22 January, 1943.

The campaign we have been engaged in for the recapture of the BUNA-GONA area is now virtually at a close. I desire to express to all Australian and
American alike who have taken part in this long and tedious campaign my heart-felt congratulations and my appreciation of all you have done.

I would thank the Air Forces for their magnificent work, for the shattering blows they have delivered to the air forces of the enemy and his ships, which have tried so often and so vainly to reinforce and supply him. <u>To the air transport service which made this campaign a feasible operation, for your untiring efforts in all weathers, I thank you.</u>[1]

E. R. HERRING,
Lieutenant-General,
G.O.C. New Guinea Force

THE WAR OPERATION

JANUARY - FEBRUARY, 1943

Perhaps the most significant operation of WW II for the 374th Troop Carrier Group was the battle to hold the Wau Airfield. The period covered by this operation was January and February, 1943. The 374th was finally fully manned and operational and it was the only troop carrier unit in operation in the Pacific War. The assault on Wau by the Japanese was launched from Lae only 20 miles from Wau and included Japanese ground forces and massive air support operations. The Japanese forces hauled their military hardware over mountain and dell and thick rain forest jungle. Their equipment consisted of small arms, machine guns, grenade launchers, small artillery, ground clearing equipment and vehicles. The trek over the 20-mile route was not easy for them but they did penetrate to the very edge of the Wau air strip.

In the meantime the 374th flying all their aircraft fully loaded with Aussie troops and their equipment, weapons and tons of ammunition through the full span of daylight and returning to Port Moresby with wounded personnel. Some of our aircraft made four and five round trips a day. There was no rest for air crews or ground crews or administrative personnel.

The capture of Wau by the Japanese was essential to their plan to clear the way for their continued successes in the New Guinea campaign. Unless Wau was neutralized on their right flank, their stronghold at Lae would be in jeopardy and it might well interfere with the logistical support to the Lae forces which were being supplied by both air and sea support elements.

The 374th part of this saving operation was under grave stress. The air cover support consisted usually of four P-40s for high cover and four P-40s for low altitude cover. The cover was provided over the full 200 miles of the trip track. The flow of C-47 aircraft into and out of Wau formed a continuous stream of supply support to the Aussies in their valiant effort to hold Wau.

In this all out effort by the Aussies and the 374th and the fighters, it was inevitable that gaps in fighter support would form and Japanese Zeros would, with their high maneuverability and speed, penetrate our unarmed transports stream and cause havoc with our aircraft and crews.

The operation though ultimately successful took a heavy toll in aircraft losses and personnel killed and wounded in action. It did constitute the most severe strain on the 374th resources in WW II. The operation did also produce the greatest number of combat awards for a single operation of any other battle of WW II in the Pacific. The awards were Silver Star, Legion of Merit, Distinguished Flying Crosses and air medals. The 374th Group received the second of its three Presidential Unit Citation Awards for their part in the Wau operation.

There was general media coverage for the Wau operation because it was one of the turning points in the Pacific War. One article covering this operation is included in this book but it falls to our talented 33rd Squadron Commander George Wamsley who writes about the Wau saga in his book *"American Fly Boy."* His eye-witness account and his day-to-day participation cannot be equaled by any roving war correspondent. George Wamsley's story follows.

"The last major air assault by the Japanese in New Guinea was made on Milne Bay - the eastern tip of New Guinea. There were sixty to eighty bombers escorted by about 100 Japanese Zeros. Our fighters were up in strength and hit them head-on as the formation approached Milne Bay harbor. So many of their bombers were shot down on the initial attack that the remaining bombers did not complete their runs but turned tail and headed back to Rabaul. Sitting on the ground beside my C-47 I saw with my own eyes at least thirty enemy bombers go down. I believe we lost only four fighters. Can you imagine that? Score: thirty to four. I remember thinking I'd bet the folks back home would not believe the figures if they made the papers. That was not an uncommon ratio. Our guys were good. And the Japanese were beginning to realize it. But they were pushing hard on many fronts. They wanted Port Moresby.

"Milne Bay was one prong in their thrust. Another was the Wau/Bulolo area just a few miles inland from Lae. Wau seemed an unlikely spot to fight for. The town had fewer than 100 natives. There was no road to anywhere except a dirt trail back toward Lae. It was on the Japanese side of the mountains, and there was no way to punch a road over to our side. The airstrip was good for only the lightest of planes and of course the C-47s.

" The Wau Strip has been described as one of the world's oddest. It had mountains on three sides, so

---

[1] This was primarily a 374th Troop Carrier Group operation

once you decided to land, you landed. There was no going around for another look. The strip was about 3,000 feet long, and the front end was 300 feet lower in elevation than the back end. So it was easy to land after the first time: Just cross the stream and drive the gear into the ground, When the plane slows down, which it will real fast, gun it so you can taxi to the upper end. Turn sideways, put the brakes on, and let the guys (mostly Aussies) open the door and jump to the ground ready to fight.

"Lots of times we didn't even stop the engines,. When the crew chief closed the door, we goosed the engines, turned downhill, and headed for home. Regular pilots don't believe it, but I have pictures.

THE SCHWENSEN INCIDENT

"In January of 1943, the Japanese were reinforcing their ground troops approaching Wau by bringing in supplies and personnel over a mountain trail on foot. We had been bringing in additional Aussie troops regularly during the month, because the Japanese were getting close to the Wau airstrip and our side was not about to give them any more ground. On February 6, the Japanese were in control of one side of the creek at the foot of the airstrip and the Aussies had control of the other side and the 500 to 600 yards up to and including the airstrip.

"I left Port Moresby at about 10::00 a.m. with a load of ammunition and hand grenades and a one-star Australian brigadier. I was leading a three-plane flight with Schwensen on my left wing. The general had asked if he could hop a ride to run up and see how his boys were doing. I agreed and he stood between me and the copilot for quite awhile and then went back to look out the side windows. The only place he had to sit was on the wooden boxes containing the ammo and the grenades. Those boxes had no covers - they were just open boxes.

"It was much smarter to go toward Wau at a rather low altitude, staying out of the high mountains on our side until we came to a pass that we could take and still remain at a level below the mountaintops. If you didn't know the right pass to enter by sight, you'd get partway into a wrong pass and then run out of space, requiring a quick turnaround. That turnaround was easy enough for a single plane if you saw the end of the pass coming toward you but there wasn't really enough room to turn around a formation.

"Japanese fighter and bomber planes had been making sporadic small-volume attacks on Wau and Bulolo for some time, but not every day,. Those distractions were frequent enough that we had learned to approach Wau as low as possible in order to avoid giving enemy fighters an easy shot at us. A three-plane formation could slip out the end of the pass, lower gear, spread out, and hit the end of the runway with as little exposure as possible. Three planes were about all the strip could handle at one time anyway. It was our planes the Japanese were after, because we were carrying either more troops or supplies.

"Just before we reached the opening into the small Wau valley, two Japanese Zeros came out of the clouds directly in front of me. Our fighter cover was four P-40s low and four high. They would sweep back and

C-60 waiting for unloading.

forth with the lead pair moving off to the side while the trailing pair was directly overhead and slightly behind. Our four low-cover group was just making a pass overhead when I saw the two Zeros directly in front and pointed straight at us and not very far away. They were firing. We could see the tracers going by. I didn't have much leeway to go down any lower but took every inch available - right then. The nose went down and the tail went up until we were practically in the creek. The creek was narrow, but we were not a very good target. I looked over to see Schwensen, who had been six or ten feet off my left wing when the Zeros showed up, but he wasn't in sight. The other C-47 who was on my right was turning off to the right, and he appeared to be about ten feet above tree level also.

"The lead P-40 plane passing overhead was past the line of the Zeros and didn't get a shot off on this pass. His wingman, Danacher, I think, was trailing just enough that with instant reaction he was able to get off a short burst of about forty rounds. He knocked down one Zero. I stayed creek-high, passed the end of the airstrip, and went on toward Bulolo. Must have stayed quite low, because I recall on some sharp turns I'd watch the wing tip to make sure it didn't touch water. My copilot, Sergeant Johnson, was looking out the windows the best he could and hollering an excited blow-by-blow report on the dogfight going on

"About that time, the brigadier nudged between the crew chief and radio operator, who were leaning over the pilot seats trying to see whatever they could, and asked, 'Will we be landing pretty soon? It's awfully rough in the back end, and those crates are flying all over the cabin." He didn't feel too well. I had forgotten about him being aboard. When I finally saw those cases scattered all over the cabin I realized he must have had a pretty rough ride back there. We got downstream, probably five miles, got behind a ridge and over the mountains, and headed home without delivering our load.

"I think six Japanese planes were shot down and we lost one P-40 and one C-47. We assumed that the second Zero got Schwensen.

"On October 8, 1988, forty-six years later, an Associated Press dispatch[2] from Port Moresby told of the finding of the wreckage of Schwensen's plane buried in a hillside about two miles from Wau. In the dispatch the plane was properly identified, the crew was properly named, and the circumstances of the finding were explained. A team of specialists in recovery and identification procedures was immediately sent from Hawaii to map the crash site and determine the feasibility of recovery. They traveled from Lae to Wau by jeep and then to the crash area by helicopter They spent four miserable days during heavy rain on a steep mountainside using shovels, brooms, and hand brushes, locating recovering, and mapping each fragment found.

"The remains of the five crew members were returned to the U.S. Army Central Identification Laboratory in Hawaii for identification. That lab does extensive analysis and reporting on such casualties. These men performed a very unpleasant task in a very conscientious manner. The final report on each individual was sixty to eighty pages on the various stages of the process. Data was recorded, signed over, forwarded on, followed up, analyzed, summarized, and closed out by the proper authorities. Many signatures by high-ranking people and several committees' reports resulted in positive identification of each individual. Seems like a lot of effort, but any surviving kin must be completely satisfied that those remains of so long ago are really those of the lost family member.

"The locating of next of kin or other surviving family members was not easy. I felt our Thirty-third Squadron people would be a good source of that information, so I got in touch with Arizona's fine congressman, John McCain, and he immediately gave me the number of the man in charge in Washington who handled that problem. That person, a Mr. Manning, wanted all the help he could get but hesitated about giving us a free hand to handle the situation. After all, it was his job and sometimes the next of kin have other axes to grind with the government or the military and need special treatment.

"Within two weeks of the news item, I had received eight or ten phone calls from our squadron people from all parts of the United States. (We don't have very many members left.) So we set about finding remaining family members. I acted as the clearinghouse. Between us and Manning, we located one 94-year-old mother and at least one family member for each of the casualties.

"These were the crewmen:

"Schwensen: Lieutenant, pilot, Kansas. His wife had remarried (and has grandkids). One brother lives in California, and another lives in Texas. Two other brothers were killed in WW II in the European theater.

"Sherman: Lieutenant, copilot, New York City. One brother lives in Pennsylvania.

"Erickson: Corporal, radio operator, Minnesota. One brother lives in Minnesota.

"Fawn: Private, crew chief, Ohio. His mother was still alive in Ohio at the time of the burial ceremonies; she died a short time after the funeral. Six brothers and sisters living. Four brothers and sisters deceased.

"Piekutowski: Private, first class, assistant crew chief, Michigan. One brother lives in South Dakota. One sister lives in Wisconsin.

"The positive identification took almost a full year to accomplish, and by then all relatives were located and notified.

"Newspaper stories and TV interviews in the home states of the victims gave the incident wide coverage. After all, it was a long time between the deaths and the burials. Lieutenant Sherman was buried in Arlington with full military honors. The three enlisted men were also buried in Arlington, but in a single casket. Their remains were so intermingled in the rear of the airplane that individual caskets didn't seem proper. Lieutenant Schwensen was buried beside his brothers at the Fort Leavenworth, Kansas, military cemetery in an elaborate ceremony. The funeral included an old C-47 flying over the parade route and a missing man flyby with some modern jet aircraft.

"I made quite a few new friends among those families. Two different ones wanted nothing to do except close the book on their 'presumed dead' family member. I was trying to make up an album about each individual and needed old pictures and news reports. After letters and phone calls and boxes of See's chocolates, everyone responded as best they could. I took the album to our latest squadron reunion, in Wichita, Kansas, and it was well received. I recently talked to an officer from the U.S. air base in Frankfurt, Germany, who had seen the coverage of the events in his base newspaper. He said, 'You guys were great. You were pioneers and heroes, and you made some history. The air force is proud of you.'

"About this time, February, 1943, we were sending twelve planes in a single formation with lots of fighter cover on every mission. The squadron CO occasionally wanted to lead the flight. Okay, rank has its privileges. On this particular flight, as we approached the area to go through the mountains, he turned into a dead-end canyon, which the rest of us knew about. There was strict radio silence, because we were close to the Japanese air base at Salamaua, thus we couldn't warn him. The rest of us knew that there would be no way to turn that formation around at the altitude we were entering. So we all moved up a little higher and higher, where there would be more room to maneuver when turning back. The CO found himself quite alone. There was no danger being low down in the canyon for a single plane, but when he saw his eleven other planes quite a bit higher and falling back, he asked over the radio, 'What's going on here?' A voice came back that some of us recognized as Glotzbach; he was singing a hymn. 'Where he leads me, I will follow - unless it's into a dead-end canyon.' Our CO was mortified.

"We had now lost, out of the original thirteen planes and fifty-two crewmen, five planes and sixteen crewmen. We had been out of the U.S.A. for only 109 days. The places we were hauling to principally at this time included: Wau, Bulolo, Pongani, Gona, Milne Bay, Kokoda, Dobodura, Popondetta, and Thirty Mile I'm sure there were others."

---

²See Appendix 'V'

HEADQUARTERS
ADVANCED ECHELON
FIFTH AIR FORCE
APO 929

31 January, 1943

SUBJECT: Commendation
TO: Commanding officer, 374th Troop Carrier Group, APO 929.

1. All of our Armed Forces in the Southwest Pacific are grateful for the fine piece of work which the 374th Troop Carrier Group performed on January 29, 30 and 31st, 1943. Only the efficiency of your organization and the bravery and the skill of your flying personnel in moving combat troops, artillery, ammunition and food saved the valuable airdrome area of the Bulolo Valley from capture by the enemy. History is replete with historical illustrations of dramatic arrival of reinforcements on the field of battle. The operations of your group into Wau carrying men and guns while enemy mortar fire and small arms fire was reaching the landing strip adds another epic illustration in the history of the war. Your group has again proven the great striking power of a properly organized and coordinated Troop Carrier Effort.

1. It is requested that the above be brought to the attention of every organization in your group.

/s/ Ennis C. Whitehead
/t/ ENNIS C. WHITEHEAD,
Brigadier General, AUS.
Deputy Air Force Commander.

1st Ind.

Headquarters, 374th Troop Carrier Group, APO 929, 3 February, 1943.
To : Commanding Officer, 22nd Troop Carrier Squadron, APO 929.

1. May I add my commendation and thanks to those of General WHITEHEAD.

2. The work that the flying crews have accomplished is evident to all and theirs is the greater risk; nevertheless their aircraft could not fly with out proper maintenance. The high standard of maintenance is the result of conscientious and careful work under far from ideal conditions. I wish to bring out that the above commendation is to each and every one in this organization who have teamed together to help carry on.

/s/ Paul H. Prentiss
/t/ PAUL H. PRENTISS,
Colonel, Air Corps,
Commanding.

13TH FEBRUARY WARDS TO BENA BENA

WING DAMAGE AT BENA BENA 27 JANUARY 1943

The need to conserve manpower resources in the southwest Pacific War was paralleled by the necessity to protect and conserve material resources. The supply lines were long. Most of the needs of the fighting forces came from the United States and the first priority for the available assets to carry on a war was to the war in Europe. From the earliest engagement of MacArthur in the Philippines to the beginning of the Allied offensive action against Japan initiated from Australia and Port Moresby in new Guinea, conservation of limited resources was essential to provide even limited offensive action. At this early stage in the Pacific War, aircraft were most critical to protect the limited ground actions our manpower could sustain. Japan, until mid 1943, had overwhelming control of the air. The extent to which our Air Force went to keep them flying, may best be explained by the following official report:

One aircraft of the 6th Troop Carrier Squadron, while on a supply mission to outpost Bena Bena, was severely damaged on landing there. Observers reported that the pilot of the aircraft appeared to be experiencing difficulty with his approach to the airfield due to violent up and down drafts and strong cross winds. The aircraft, a C-47, stalled in on landing, (the aircraft falling off on the left wing from 25 feet altitude). Severe damage was suffered by the aircraft as the left wing struck the ground and the aircraft ground looped. The left wing was beyond repair. The aircraft was taxied to the edge of the airfield which was rimmed with brush and a low tree line. The damaged wing was removed and the airplane completely camouflaged to conceal it from the Japanese who were making frequent observation sorties over Bena Bena.

General George C. Kenney, commander Far East Air Forces in his book "*General Kenney Reports*", Duell Stoan and Pearce, described Bena Bena as "A plateau up in the middle of New Guinea, inhabited by partially reformed cannibals discovered there by explorers and gold seekers. We didn't know how many of the natives were for us and how many were for the Japanese."

The treacherous air strip at 5100 feet altitude and a short 1500 foot runway with a 10% grade and a hump in the middle made every landing a potential disaster.

A substitute left C-47 wing was found at the aircraft graveyard at Port Moresby. But how to get the wing to Bena Bena? The wing was too large to get into the cabin of a C-47 or any other aircraft. There was no road to Bena Bena nor river to float the wing to Bena Bena nor railroad flat car to rail it there.

The pilots, engineers and mechanics of the 33rd Squadron put their ingenuity and imagination to work and decided the only solution, albeit a risky one, was to strap the substitute wing under the belly of a C-47, streamline it to the best of their ability, especially the butt end which was two feet thick, to reduce drag as much as possible then try to find a pilot daring enough to attempt to fly it to Bena Bena. All the pilots of the 33rd Troop Carrier Squadron plus pilots from the 6th, 21st and 22nd who were aware of the venture, volunteered. The task, however, fell to the 374th Troop Carrier Group chief engineer and maintenance officer.

The engineering and maintenance work on fashioning the fairing and structural design to sustain the wing under the belly of the carrying C-47 was accomplished at Wards Air Field, Port Moresby, New Guinea by the 478th Service Squadron, the affiliated organization that provided major repair and maintenance for the 374th Troop Carrier Group.

The engineers and design technicians could not assure the safety of the sub-structure. The steel cables and fittings used to attach the wing to the belly of the C-47 appeared strong enough to take the stress of air speeds of up to 125 miles per hour. The proof would be in the flying. There was fear in some quarters that the

33rd TC Squadron Orderly Room Members. Maj. Gerorge Wamsley on left.

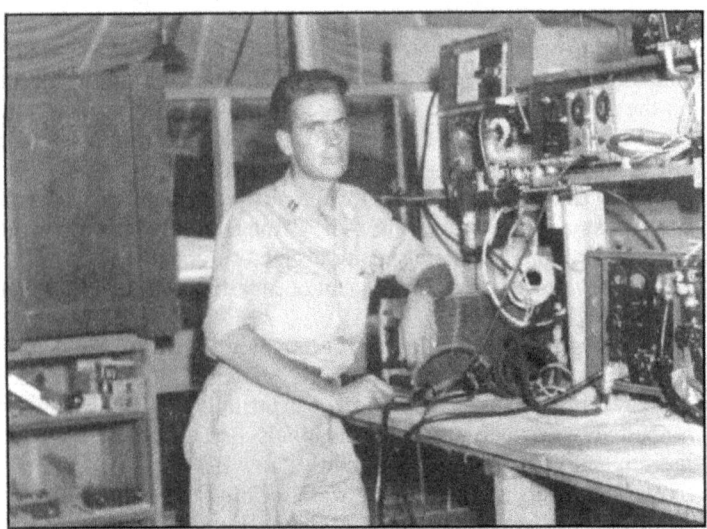
Captain Henry G. Coile.

force of the wind at 125 MPH would cause the attached wing with its protruding wing butt, to tear loose and seriously damage the airplane to the extent that it would be necessary to abandon the aircraft. It was also feared that such severe vibrations would set in to require abandoning the aircraft. In all, the number of hazardous possibilities could render the aircraft so severely damaged aerodynamically, that a safe landing at the treacherous air strip at Bena Bena could not be made. When all the work was completed the take off was set.

The take off from Ward strip at Port Moresby was made at 9 a.m., 13 February, 1943. Take off was smooth and normal. The external burden required a longer take-off roll and a more labored climb out. There was no noticeable aerodynamically observable flying characteristic changes. The wheels were retracted and the slow climb to 7000 feet was effected without difficulty.

The two and one half hour flight to Bena Bena was uneventful. Air speed was set at 120 MPH.

The approach to the Bena Bena air strip was made with cautious concern. The 5100 feet altitude and added drag from the under belly carrying wing, required a higher landing speed than normal.

The nature of the plateau strip setting in the only position possible required that the approach leg pass over the deep cut on the plateau's edge, a drop of 300 feet, at the beginning of the runway. A go-around was not feasible because high hills extended over the far end of the runway. All landings were made toward the hills and take offs away from the hills. Severe wind shifts and violent up and down drafts with cross winds were expected and we were prepared for this danger on the final approach leg of the landing pattern.

The landing was made without incident. The replacement wing was removed from the carrying aircraft within one hour. Thirty natives carried the replacement wing to the waiting damaged bird and within 24 hours it was on its way to Port Moresby and returned to active service.

Troop carrier operations expanded rapidly during the early 1943 period. Three new Troop Carrier Groups arrived in the theater; the 317th Troop Carrier Group commanded by Col. Samuel V. Payne; the 375th Troop commanded by Col. Joel G. Pitts and the 433rd Troop Carrier Group commanded by Lt. Col. Cecil B. Guile.

In October the Troop Carrier mass was augmented by the fully manned and troop carrier trained 2nd Combat Cargo Group. This Group was fully equipped with combat ready C-46 Curtis Commandos. Its commander was Col. William J. Bell a West Pointer who switched to the Air Force and qualified as a pilot through Randolph and Kelly Field - West Point of the Air.

Because General Douglas MacArthur was the Supreme Commander of Allied Forces in the southwest Pacific, it is well to reflect on the similarity of his experience in preparation for his unit in World War I.

MacArthur was assigned as Chief of Staff of the 42nd Division. The 42nd Division called the rainbow division because in assembling manpower, personnel were drawn from 20 different states.

Prior to being ordered to France, he used great care in the selection and training of his men - both officers and enlisted. Training continued at a rapid pace until orders arrived for boarding ship for France. The 42nd Division was the first Division to be shipped overseas because it was the only fully manned and trained unit in the U. S. Army.

On arriving in France, the division continued training under MacArthur, now a full Colonel. On arrival in France the training continued under MacArthur's tutelage and there was a great deal of joint training with the French because the rainbow division was assigned to the French 10th Corp.

General Pershing as the Commander of the American Expedition Forces, kept pressing Washington for more divisions. Soon they began arriving in France, but as skeleton forces lacking training and with only a few trained officers, Pershing proceeded to strip MacArthur of his carefully trained and skilled officers and men to build the new divisions into viable fighting units. All the protests by MacArthur were to no avail, he simply had to find new officers and men of quality to rebuild his rainbow division.

There is a great deal of similarity in the account of the staffing of the 54th Troop Carrier Wing and MacArthur's experience with his rainbow division.

The influx of Troop Carrier Groups into the theater demanded a method of control, supervision and coordination for the massive tasks being assigned the troop carrier operations in the theater. There was need for retraining troop carriers for paratroop operations required as isolated paratroop missions, pathfinder missions and large scale combat parachute drops of division and smaller size such as the paradrop at Markham Valley with a regimental combat team and the paradrop at Noemfoor. These were followed by the Rock Force Assault the paradrop on Corregidor in the recapture of the Philippines and isolated parachute personnel drops at the universities and hospitals at Manila (where it was suspected prisoners were being held by the Japanese) and finally glider tow operations. Additionally a daily requirement was to satisfy MacArthur's ground forces in their advance up the coast of New Guinea with food, ammo, equipment and supplies. Where airfields were available a steady stream of supplies, equipment, guns, ammunitions and personnel were delivered to ground forces all over the theater of operations. And each day the line of communications seemed to grow longer as the Army and Navy advances toward Tokyo traveled further and further form their bases of supply in Australia, Port Moresby and isolated sea ports where freighters dropped their massive tunnage from the U.S. to be transported to the troops in battle, mostly by air.

The 54th Troop Carrier Wing was born under General Order No. 49, dated March 13, 1943. It was not until May that it actually took form and started to function. Headquarters personnel were drawn almost entirely from the 374th Troop Carrier Group. (See Appendix 'T')

Col. Paul H. Prentiss, former 374th Troop Carrier Group Commander, became wing commander on May 20, 1943. Col. John H. Lackey, former Sixth Squadron commander, became chief of staff on May 25, and later deputy commander when Col. Edgar W. Hampton returned from temporary duty in the States and assumed the position of chief of staff.

Assistant chief of staff positions were as follows: A-1 and Adjutant, Maj. Frank W. Smith, former commander of the Sixth Squadron ground echelon; Assistant A-1, Capt. Lacy W. White, former 374th Group adjutant; A-2, Lt. Col. John F. Jacobs, assisted by Maj. William H. Quinn of the 33rd Troop Carrier Squadron; A-3, Lt. Col. A. J. Beck, former 374th Group operations officer; Assistant A-3's, Maj. Leonidas Baker of the 22nd Squadron, Maj. Blesch Malmstone of the Sixth Troop Carrier Squadron, and Capt. James N. LaRoche, 33rd Troop Carrier Squadron; A-4, Lt. Col. William P. Jennings, former 374th Group intelligence officer; Assistant A-4's, Maj. Harry M. Hayes and Capt. Morris I. Sherman as maintenance officers.

Special staff officers were Capt. Curtis King of he 374th Group headquarters, statistical; Capt. Richard Krolik, 33rd Troop Carrier Squadron, special services; and Maj. Earl L. Youngren, Signal Corps, signal officer.

With the establishment of the Wing Headquarters there was a corresponding shift of personnel within the 374th Group. Lt. Col. Fred M. Adams, former 21st Squadron commander, was announced as group commander.

Maj. John D. Pearson, former assistant group adjutant, became group adjutant and personnel officer. Other changes found: Col. Edward T. Imparato, former group materiel officer, as group executive officer; Maj. Lamont N. Rennels of the 33rd Squadron, group intelligence officer; Maj. George M. Foster, former assistant group operations officer, as group operations officer; Maj. Philip Cartwright, former 33rd Squadron operations officer, as assistant group operations officer, and Maj. A. J. Graves, of the 33rd Squadron, group supply officer.

The late Raymond Clapper, noted news analyst, described accurately Troop Carrier operating difficulties at the time the Wing was formed. Clapper wrote:

"To a considerable degree this has been a battle for airfields out here. It has been a matter of taking airfields from the Japs or cutting out our own fields inland at points where we need fighter bases. The key to much of the war out here is the struggle to push our fighter planes forward to cover all kinds of operations, whether landings, ship movements or flights of transport planes.

"It is impossible to get men and supplies over the mountains by ground, and until recently it was too hazardous to use shipping. As a result, Troop Carrier planes opened up airfields in the interior at spots inaccessible except by air. Scouts get the natives to mow down a strip of waist-high kunai grass. Then a transport plane lands with engineers. They even have baby bulldozers which are small enough to get through airplane doors. They have carried 2_ ton trucks, bombs, jeeps, sawmills, gasoline and steel matting for runways."

Interior airfields had been created, and more were to be created as the Australians and Americans pressed towards Salamaua and Lae after the defeat of the Japs at Buna and Wau. Our overall job was to move personnel and supplies in three chief directions:

1. To Dobodura where a large base was being constructed and the gains of the Buna - Gona campaign were being consolidated.

2. To Wau and Bulolo where Allied Forces advancing on Lae and Salamaua had their rear bases.

3. To the patrols skirting Lae and Salamaua by dropping supplies as close to their position as possible.

From the early part of 1943 to July this work was done by the 374th Group, which later was joined by the 375th Troop Carrier Group, the 65th and 66th Troop Carrier Squadrons of the 403rd Group of the 13th Air Force and finally the 433rd Group. In August two squadrons of the 317th Group, the 41st and 46th, joined the Wing and were followed by the entire 317th Group in October. At this time the 374th Group left New Guinea to take over the functions of the 317th Group on the mainland of Australia.

The first objective which the Troop Carriers had to supply was the Allied drive on Mubo and from there across Komiatum Ridge to Salamaua. This campaign was called the Battle of the Ridges and was fought in the most difficult terrain where air drops and native carriers were the only means of supply. Dropping supplies in such terrain was a difficult problem which was overcome by the tenacity of the Troop Carrier pilots.

The Australian Government describes the campaign in its official publication:

"The Battle of the Ridges was a vital part of a master plan worked out by Major General S. G. Savige, whose enlarged command replaced, on 23 April, Kanga Force, which was commanded by Brigadier General M. J. Moten. His plan embraced four phases:

"1. Seizing Bobdubi Ridge by 15th Brigade Group to dominate the Japanese supply line to Mubo.

"2. Landing American troops at Nassau Bay and pushing them inland and along the coast to place guns within range of Salamaua.

"3. Destruction of the Japanese forces in the Mubo area by 17th Brigade, under whose command a battalion of U.S. troops was placed to assist.

"4. Driving the Japanese back from Komiatum to Salamaua.

"Subsequent fighting was to be a 'blind' to an Australian landing near Lae, from which Salamaua was to be the magnet to draw and drain the Japanese manpower.

"How well this ruse succeeded is now history. The Jap fell right into the Salamaua trap. He continually fed troops from his big garrison at Lae into the

William Randall Crecelius, killed in action - 1943.

Pictured: (back) Hal Simpson, Dusty Rhodes, Sam Ketchman, Robert Beede, (front) Charles Hellweg Surgeon, and Fred Adams, 1943.

Salamaua area - which was our 'killing pen.' But it was in the mud and mists of Lababia, Observation Hill, Mubo, Bobdubi Ridge and Komiatum, that the foundations of victory were laid.

"Mubo was an important outpost of Salamaua, for it controlled the comparatively good track which goes to Komiatum and thence across the river flats to Salamaua. The native village of Mubo itself, together with its small civil airstrip, is at the bottom of a gorge through which flows the Bitoi River. The approaches to Mubo are overlooked on the east by the great jungle-clad spur known as Lababia Ridge, on the western slopes of which is Vickers Ridge, which overlooks Mubo itself. The Guadasgasal Saddle area controls the approaches to Lababia Spur. To the northwest Mubo is dominated by Observation and Garrison Hills, and to the northeast by Bitoi Ridge.

"It was on the Mubo bottleneck that the men of 17th Australian Brigade fought for the ridges - for the law of jungle warfare is, 'He who holds the ridges, holds the country.' They came creeping inexorably through the jungle, over the tough Crystal Creek trail from Wau. They seldom saw their enemy in the blank, green wall of the jungle; they waited for his first burst of fire to reveal his presence. Hide and seek. Kill and go. See and never be seen. Those were the rules of the fighting on the razorbacks and in the dank, twilit rain forests where visibility was reduced to a few feet.

"An immense effort now became necessary to maintain supplies from Kanga Headquarters main base at Wau. This main base was supplied wholly by Troop Carriers. Beyond this jeep-head a native carrier line had to be organized to transport forward food and ammunition, and to bring back the sick and wounded.

"In their labors along these trails - particularly along the Crystal Creek trail to Mubo - the New Guinea native carriers worked as magnificently as had their Papuan brothers on the Kokoda Track. Troop Carrier planes dropped necessary supplies which often meant the difference between defeat and victory.

"Carriers and troops moved at times for hours up to their knees in gluey mud. Under the rain-clouds at high altitudes men were never dry. They slept, marched, fed, sweated and squirmed their way along the trail in almost continual dampness; but always the vital life-line of supplies kept up with them. Food and ammunition dumps, fed by Troop Carriers alone, grew, mushroom-like, at the staging camps along the trail - at Ballams, Summit and Skindewai. This was the foundation for the long Battle of the Ridges."

EARLY, 1943

During March and April, large amounts of supplies were transported by Troop Carriers into the supply depots at Wau and Bulolo. Flights to these airstrips were decreased as the Allied drive pushed back the Japs closer to Nadzab and Lae - the springing-off places for the future push up the Markham-Ramu Valley.

By May new supply dumps were needed nearer the fighting fronts. In July, when the Australians and Americans pushed closer to their objectives, a new strip was opened at Bena Bena. Thousands of tons of materiel were poured into this field.

In May also, another strip, Tsilli Tsilli, was opened west of Salamaua. It proved to be of great value. Finally Dobodura, just west of Tsilli Tsilli, was opened. This base became the largest and most important one until the Allied drive up the Markham Valley and along the Huon Peninsula. From July to September millions of pounds of critical items were flown from Port Moresby over the "Hump" to "Dobo" for front-line troops.

While the Troop Carriers in New Guinea were transporting the men and supplies over the dangerous mountains, the 317th Troop Carrier Group, which left New Guinea for Australia after the battle of Wau in February, 1943, was holding up its part on the other end of the supply line.

This Group's job was to get the supplies to New Guinea as well as the outer defense perimeter of northern Australia. Thousands of trips were made across the 700-mile stretch of the Coral Sea to New Guinea without the loss of a single airplane. Food and other supplies were ferried across the northern end of Australia in huge quantities to the outer defense posts of Darwin, Fenton (a bomb base), Horn Island, Groote Island and Merauke in Dutch New Guinea.

Flying difficulties were as dangerous for this group as for its sister groups in New Guinea. Up-to-date maps, latest weather and natural-hazard information, and radio ranges - four necessities to efficient and safe operation for any organization - virtually did not exist in Australia at that time.

Flights across the northern Australia territory were made by contact flying. This type of flying often became an impossibility as ground fog, forest fires, and the natural camouflage around the airfields hampered pilots in recognizing landmarks. Yet thousands of tons of material were transported with the loss of only a few airplanes.[3]

Pilots and navigators gathered valuable flight information on these trips. This information was correlated and published in a book form, containing information on: radio ranges; routes; natural hazards such as newly discovered mountains and rivers; lengths of runways; emergency landing fields; and typical weather condi-

---

[3] A related story concerning downed aircraft is recorded in a book written by Edward T. Imparato. *Into Darkness: A Pilot's Journey Through Headhunter Territory*© 1995 published by Howell Press, Inc., 1147 River Road, Suite 21, Charlottesville, Virginia 22901. See Appendix 'FF'

tions of the various localities throughout the Northern Territory, Western Australia, Queensland and New South Wales. This was the first time that such information was gathered for airline use, and it has proved to be priceless for future air operations in Australia.

MT. HAGEN AND KEROWAGI OR FRESH VEGETABLES

By M/Sgt. Glenn D. McMurray
from the book Moresby to Manila Via Troop Carrier

Stepping through the mirror in *Alice in Wonderland* has nothing on flying over dense jungle and suddenly landing in a beautiful valley 160 miles northwest of Nadzab, nestled 5500 feet above sea level on the other side of the Kubor mountain range. It is the home of Mt. Hagen and Kerowagi. Col. Don W. Smith was one of the fortunate ones to step through the mirror.

Sweeping through a ground fog, Col. Smith, the pilot, saw acres and acres of beautiful flowers and hundreds and hundreds of large native gardens. Rows of sweet corn poked their heads into the rising sun. Everything seemed unreal as the morning fog quickly dissipated under the warmth of a friendly sun.

The landing strip appeared - a great, green runway of carefully tended grass. It was so beautiful that one hesitated to land for fear of spoiling it. Natives could be seen working with crude instruments hacking away at the Kunai grass. The edges of the runway were as carefully trimmed as that of any gold course.

No wonder this is called the "Garden Spot of New Guinea". Troop Carriers were lucky that this garden spot was near their camp sites. Working in conjunction with the officials of the Australian New Guinea Administration, the Wing was able to procure luscious native-garden sweet corn, large ripe tomatoes, leafy heads of lettuce, giant yams, and great red bananas. These additions to the regular army issue gave us meals long to be remembered by all units stationed in the Markham-Ramu Valley.

Col. Smith, who was the first pilot to fly a jeep to Mt. Hagen, describes what happened when he landed:

"The natives rushed towards the plane and then stopped suddenly at a respectful distance away. You could see that they wanted to come closer. They edged forward slowly, and then came on with a rush when they saw we wanted to be friendly.

"Our men started to unload a jeep - the first the natives had ever seen. Suddenly the natives began to snap their fingers in high excitement and the noise of the hundreds of fingers snapping at the same time gave forth a sort of rhythmic music. I learned that this was their way of expressing surprise.

"One native suddenly broke away from the group and walked to me. He touched my leg. An Australian standing nearby said, 'He only wants to know whether you are afraid of him. He can tell by the goose pimples on your leg and by its tension.' I immediately relaxed and the native laughed and yelled in glee. When the jeep was driven off, you could see their amazement. They really treated the jeep like a god. (When I came back on a second trip some time later they had carefully hacked out a beautiful jeep road, planted hedges on both sides of it and made sure that the road remained in good condition.)

"But the biggest surprise came when an air evacuation nurse who accompanied us on the trip stepped from the plane. The Marys - name given to female natives - rushed her immediately. They touched her hair, clothes and face. They even tried to take off some of her face powder and taste it. Soon the nurse disappeared. I learned later that she had been escorted to a special shack where she was to stay for the night.

"The next morning the native women awoke her, gave her breakfast in bed. She then was escorted to a bathhouse where the Marys threw water on her and gave her a thorough Turkish-style bath. When the nurse started to dress, she discovered all her clothes missing. The Marys had taken them and washed them while she was being given a bath. The result was we had to remain until the nurse's clothes dried.

The climate at this spot is as fine as anywhere in the world - cool nights, no mosquitoes and little disease. The natives are exceptionally clean, live in native huts which have wooden floors. They are exceptionally intelligent.

"One could not help thinking that this valley could be a wonderful resort - terrain for a fine golf course, ideal weather, just the right spot for a quiet vacation.

"As we left, one of the men took out his camera. The natives ran away. The Australian told us to wait a minute. Soon they reappeared, dressed in their finest - all trinkets, feathers, gadgets, etc. - and posed for the picture. They love to have their picture taken and go to any extreme to please the photographer."

Troop Carriers, after they left Nadzab for more forward bases, learned quickly at their dinner table what the "Garden Spot of New Guinea" meant besides beauty.

HEADQUARTERS FWS/gdm
54TH TROOP CARRIER WING
OFFICE OF THE WING COMMANDER
APO 929

19 August, 1943.
SUBJECT: Commendation.
TO: Commanding Officer, 374th Tr Carrier Gp, & 375th Tr Carr Gp; 65th Tr Carr Sq. & 66th Tr Carrier Sq.

1. The following radiogram, received at this headquarters, is quoted for the information of all concerned:
GENERAL BLAMEY AND GENERAL HERRING EXTEND THEIR HEARTIEST CONGRATULATIONS ON THE MAGNIFICENT VICTORY ACHIEVED LAST NIGHT AND TODAY PD WITHOUT THE MANY WEEKS OF TROOP CARRIER HAUL TO A FORWARD AIRDROME AND THE INTENSIVE TRAINING AND FINE SPIRIT OF YOUR ORGANIZATIONS CMA THE SUCCESS OF THIS DECISIVE OPERATION WOULD NOT HAVE BEEN POSSIBLE PD I WANT TO ADD MY PERSONAL SINCERE CONGRATULATIONS TO ALL THREE COMMANDS PD
MAJOR GENERAL ENNIS C. WHITEHEAD

1. The contents of this letter will be disseminated to all members of this command and will be posted on Bulletin Board for one (1) week.
By order of Colonel PRENTISS
FRANK W. SMITH
Captain, Air Corps,
Adjutant.

SEPTEMBER, 1943

On September 3, 1943, all units of the Wing were alerted for a co-ordinated air attack on Nadzab. This was to be the first paratroop combat mission ever staged in the southwest Pacific. Led by General Prentiss, Wing commander, 86 Troop Carrier planes dropped 1500 men and officers of the 503rd Parachute Infantry Regiment with full equipment in the target area at Nadzab on September 5, 1943.

Later in the day an Australian artillery battery with its weapons was dropped in the same target area. American paratroops and

Natives gather on arrival of the C-47 at Mt. Hagen, New Guinea - 1943.

Australian artillerymen jumped from a lower altitude than ever attempted before in battle.

Medium and heavy bombers flew over the target first, protected from above by a blanket of fighters. Two planes swept low, laying a smoke screen, and then scores of giant transport planes came in. Suddenly a myriad of parachutes dotted the sky, billowing earthwards . . . and the affair was completed in a little over a minute from the time the first troops jumped until the last man landed. Some of the Australians were jumping for the first time without any previous training - a valiant feat that ranks with any exploit of the war.

The suddenness and boldness of the action bewildered the enemy. Once again Nippon was caught napping.

As soon as the airstrip at Nadzab was ready - that was within three hours - a message went out, "You can bring in the planes." Soon a steady stream of Troop Carriers from Tsilli Tsilli, bringing men of the 7th Australian Division, materiel and equipment, landed. In the first 20 days of September, after the airstrip had been hacked out of kunai grass. More than 2000 plane loads were put down there. Hour after hour the transports landed at the rate of one a minute. The 7th Division pushed towards Lae.

This rapid deployment of men and arms did not give the Japs a chance to regroup and counter-attack. Again the utilization of mass troop and supply movement by Troop Carriers proved its value.

On September 6, at 6:30 a.m. - in the largest amphibious operation up to that time - Australians of the 9th division landed in force at Huon Gulf, northeast of Lae. The Japs were taken by complete surprise. A ring around the Lae-Salamaua area was completed, trapping the remnants of four Jap divisions.

The two-pronged advance on Lae proceeded according to plan. The synchronized campaign against Salamaua was now shown to be actually a feint attack, not to be pressed home until the right moment. This was designed to fool the Japanese into believing that the main fighting was to be centered at Salamaua. Reinforcements were rushed in by the Japs to stem the expected attack. Thus the enemy was taken completely by surprise when the Allies descended in force on Lae. It was a shrewd, successful and magnificent bluff.

On September 16, Lae fell, and four days later Lt. Col. A. J. Beck, Assistant A-3, landed to inspect it. The next day Col. Hampton, Wing chief of staff, led a five-ship formation into the field. The planes carried important radio equipment and personnel, needed to set up Australian fighter radar units.

Lae is at the mouth of the Markham River, which flows down in a valley of the same name from the headwaters of the Ramu River. The Ramu-Markham, a continuous valley, was of the utmost importance to the Japanese. It was the first place the enemy had occupied in New Guinea and the last place he wanted to lose. It was the stepping stone to the proposed recapture of Wau and occupation of Port Moresby. With the capture of Lae - a deepwater port - and Nadzab, an ideal air operations field, the Allies obliterated this plan.

But the Japs had no intention of giving up this valley without a fight. They considered it one of the richest prizes in the war. Jap troops came down over the Bogadjim road from Madang, another Jap stronghold. These troops crossed the foreboding Finisterre Mountains and infiltrated into the valley. They were in strength and were supported by air power from the strongholds of Wewak and Finschhafen.

An advance Jap detail was observed reconnoitering Kaiapit. An emergency call was sent to the Troop Carriers on September 17. A special flight of 13 ships, led by Maj. Frank Church, then commanding officer of the Sixth Squadron, carried infantry of the Australian 7th Division and their equipment to a rough field at Leron, 13 miles east of Kaiapit. Two ships were damaged in the landing, one being completely washed out. The Australians walked to Kaiapit and captured it on September 21. Two days later 45 planes landed there with full supply loads. This capture saved the Markham-Ramu Valley from complete Jap occupation.

On September 30, another new strip was opened up by the Troop Carriers 10 miles northwest of Kaiapit. It was named Sagerak. More than 55 plane loads landed there the next day. It became at that time the last outpost from which the Australians went out on patrols. This campaign - the Markham-Ramu Valley Campaign - was unique in that for the first time a great military force was entirely transported, serviced and maintained by air.

In one hop, men were brought across the mountains and swamps that would have taken weary weeks and months on foot. From the forward airstrips roads were cut through dense bush, new landing grounds found and formed, and men were able to advance farther through the jungle in the Upper Ramu Valley.

GENERAL HEADQUARTERS
SOUTHWEST PACIFIC AREA
ADVANCE ECHELON, APO 500
18 September, 1943.

GENERAL ORDERS)
              :
NO..................37)

Section

Congratulatory Message from Prime Minister John Curtin of Australia.......I

1. The Commander-in-chief takes great pride and pleasure in publishing to the command the following congratulatory message from Prime Minister John Curtin of Australia conveying the thanks and admiration of the Government and People of Australia on the occasion of the capture of Lae on 16 September:

"This splendid feat of arms following so closely the successes at Salamaua and the Solomons Islands marks another notable stage of the Pacific War. I convey to you, to your commanders and to all officers and men of the land, naval and air forces the thanks and admiration of the Government and People of Australia. They have demonstrated superiority over a tenacious foe. The invincible comradeship in arms and the achievements of the forces of our two countries constitute a happy portent of greater things to come."

By command of General MacARTHUR:
    R. K. SUTHERLAND,
    Major General, United States Army,
    Chief of Staff.

OFFICIAL:
/s/ B. M. Fitch,
/t/ B. M. FITCH
Colonel, Adjutant General's Department,
Adjutant General.

HEADQUARTERS
54TH TROOP CARRIER WING
APO 929

24 September, 1943.

TO THE OFFICERS AND MEN OF THE 374TH TROOP CARRIER GROUP:

It is with real regret that I realize that the close association with you over a period of almost a year in New Guinea is about to terminate. It has been an honor and a pleasure to have commanded such an organization.

I believe I am correct in saying that the personnel of your group have received more decorations than any other organization of similar size in our services and it is rightly so as the records of deeds done will testify. You can leave here for your new assignment knowing that your work was well done, and that you have brought comfort, supplies, and aid to thousands of our own troops and to those of our Allies and much discomfort to our enemies.

I feel sure that you will continue your brilliant record and hope that the relief from the strain of combat flying and air raids and with some of the conforts of civilization available, that those of you who are war weary will soon regain your former good health.

The friendships and assoiations made here will always be a pleasurable recollection and I hope that those of you who fly up here from time to time will make it a point to come by and see us and give us all the good news from down below.

So long, good luck, and happy landings,

    s/Paul H. Prentiss
    t/PAUL H. PRENTISS
    Colonel, Air Corps,
    Commanding.

A CERTIFIED TRUE COPY:

    s/John D. Pearson
    t/JOHN D. PEARSON
    Major, Air Corps,
    Adjutant,
    374th Tr Carrier Gp.

Late 1943

Using Nadzab as its main jumping-off field, operations in October were devoted to building up the bases in the Markham-Ramu Valley.

Another landing field in the "Valley" was opened at Gusap on the first of October. This became another of the more important bases, a location where large stockpiles were readied for transmission farther up the valley. Eight days later Dumpu, a field west of Gusap, was opened. More than four and a half million pounds of freight went to these two new fields from Nadzab, now the largest Troop Carrier base.

An article by F. B. Peterson in the Brisbane *Telegraph* (Australia) summed up the Troop Carrier work in this valley. On October 30, he wrote:

"Every single item of equipment carried by air for the famous A.I.F. force fighting in the Markham-Ramu Valley and up in the rugged Finisterre Mountains was weighed in advance to prepare one of the most amazing loading schedules ever compiled by the Army.

"Supply Experts even weighted single rounds of ammunition and put on the scales ammunition boxes made in different parts of Australia to test any variation in the weight of wood used in box construction.

"This is the first time an Australian division has ever been supplied and maintained entirely by air. It is stated to be the first occasion in any war theater that an air supply job of this magnitude has been carried out.

"There is no special magic in the airplane as a load-carrier. In fact the freight-carrying transport is subject to many strict limitations not encountered in land or sea transportation. The Douglas transport (C-47's), which daily roar up the New Guinea valleys to the supply point of this Australian force, can carry the same load as a large truck. And that is a small vehicle compared with the giant six-wheelers which rumble over the roads in New Guinea's rear areas every day.

"An amazing fact about this big operation 'up the valley' is that every single item of food and equipment, from the inevitable tin of bully beef to the bulky field gun, has been flown in. The airplane has done the job which in a normal operation would be handled by land, sea and air transport. The transports have even 'carried the carriers' - large numbers of jeeps that handle the trail haulage, and natives who comprise the daily food and ammunition trains up into the hills. The experts who planned every phase of this big air supply project were faced with the task of carrying out the same work, with limited plane loads a day, as a division operating in the Western Desert employing hundreds of freight-carrying trucks.

"This meant the compilation of a huge 'ready reckoner' which filled 75 pages of foolscap length and

Mt. Hagan, 1943.

twice foolscap width. This blueprint is regarded as the air supply 'bible' in New Guinea. British armies all over the world are watching the air supply experience with the greatest interest. Copies of the load tables have been sent to the British War Office.

"Achievement of the objective would never have been possible without the enthusiastic co-operation of the American Troop Carrier organization, and Australian supply officers pay the highest tribute to the keenness of the pilots and crews who, particularly in the early days of the campaign, worked 'like beavers'. In the first 20 days the transports made 2000 takeoffs and landings at Nadzab. The American crews saw that the men and the equipment were delivered at the right spot at the right time.

"The supply experts operate on the formula that for every man in the field so many pounds of food, ammunition, clothing, equipment and medical stores are required every day. The forecast, made weeks before the move into the valley was undertaken, has worked out 'almost to the ounce'. These soldiers are being fed on a ration scale which comprises 36 items. Even the 'hard' scale has 16 items. So smoothly has the supply schedule been worked out that the troops have never missed a meal, even when the advance was being made at a breakneck pace in the first days out from Kaiapit.

"When troops reached advance positions at the end of a long day's hike the planes sometimes resorted to dropping to keep up supplies. At some stages the troops even enjoyed the luxury, for this part of the world, of fresh meat and bread. At no stage had they to fall back on operational rations. Just behind the front lines they were able to get new uniforms and boots, gaiters, mosquito nets, ground sheets, and water bottles and all the 'mod. cons.' of a rear area quartermaster store."

The next important chapter in the Wing's history was its part in the battle of Finschhafen. The need for Troop Carrier in this battle, especially to evacuate wounded, is amply described in the official Australian booklet, *Action in New Guinea*:

"Straight from success at Lae a force from the 9th Australian Division moved by sea to invade the Huon Peninsula on September 22. After 10 days of some of the hardest, bitterest fighting in New Guinea, 'guts and bayonets' drove the Japanese from Finschhafen and the heights surrounding it. Caked with mud, gaunt, begrimed and desperate from lack of sleep, the troops finally drove the enemy out of its strongholds. For several days food ran short because of the difficulty of getting supplies forward over land routes; every hardship was suffered from shattering gunfire to sheer physical exhaustion.

"In this engagement the enemy fought with frenzied determination and incredible savagery. Practically every inch of the way meant bloody hand-to-hand fighting until at last the defeated Jap left in a hurry, leaving meals half eaten, card games unfinished."

It was on December 7, that the strip at Finschhafen was finally finished and Troop Carrier planes started to land. And by December 13, loads averaging 1,745,000 pounds daily were being flown from Nadzab to the completed strip.

Fighting continued with exceptional bitterness in the Finschhafen area for the next month as the Australians pushed the enemy back from the peninsula. This established a strong force as a flank cover for the U.S. landings to be made in New Britain.

As the year 1943 came to a close, the Allies had made tremendous forward steps in driving the Jap from his former strongholds. The opening of the Markham-Ramu Valley, with its forward bases, allowed the Allies to batter the up-to-now inaccessible Jap air bases of Alexishafen, Madang, New Hanover and Wewak. The enemy base of Wewak had been hit on August 18, catching the Jap unawares and destroying 120 planes on the ground. This broke the back of the Jap air power in New Guinea. Because of these heavy air attacks in 1943, the Japs husbanded their air strength at rear airdromes.

Not only was Jap air power severely curtailed, but his shipping became a prime target. Efforts to reinforce Wewak or New Hanover resulted in high shipping losses, as fighters and medium bombers, flying from forward bases in the Markham Valley, caught the helpless convoys at sea. The increased range of the fighters and bombers was made possible only by supplies flown into advanced bases by Troop Carriers.

This withdrawal of air power from this forward airdrome allowed the Allies to build up their supply depots without too much interference from Jap bombing. It also prevented him from giving his troops close air support.

The battle for Noemfoor Island was similar to that for Biak - with the Japs dug in and resisting fiercely. This island became an important fighter base, from which our own and the Aussie planes struck at Jap strongholds in the Halmaheras.

The mobility of Troop Carrier squadrons in this war of movement in the southwest Pacific was aptly demonstrated.

September was the first month in the last ten that Troop Carrier planes did not extend their zone of operations. But prospects for future extension loomed bright when on September 15, the Allies landed on Morotai Island, the northernmost of the Halmahera Group, approximately 390 miles southwest of Davao in the Philippines. U.S. troops quickly occupied the only strip on the island, but found it useless for heavy operations. A new strip was constructed by a crack Australian engineering unit several miles from the original Jap strip of Pitoe, but it was not completed until October 6, when the first Troop Carriers landed. A shallow beach and thick mud made it extremely difficult to land supplies from vessels. Movement of critical items, even anti-aircraft shells, by air became necessary. Morotai Island was extremely valuable to the Allies for it was like a dagger pointed at the heart of the Jap's Halmahera bases and his Philippine shipping.

Four days after D-day an operational freight team of the 21st Service Group - the freight forwarding organization for the Wing -

landed at Morotai. The function of this organization was to set up operations to move and unload cargo landed at the strip. Trained like infantry, this operational team completed its mission and had freight operations running smoothly when the strip was opened.

The usefulness of Nadzab as a Troop Carrier base was over by September. It was too far away from the center of operations. In October the Wing headquarters, the 375th Group, the 374th Group and the 433rd Group moved to Biak, Dutch New Guinea. Here was an ideal base for the last phase of our main plan - the landing in the Philippines. The 317th Group remained at Hollandia.

Since the surrender of our troops at Corregidor, General MacArthur publicly stated he had one objective - retaking the Philippines. Early campaigns at Buna, Wau, Salamaua and Lae were designed to keep the enemy off our backs and provide us with bases in New Guinea from which to drive the enemy before us.

As the campaign in the Solomons progressed, it became more and more evident that we did not have to stop and kill every Jap who stood before us. We could just as effectively knock him out by isolating him from the battleground. Our landings at Hollandia, Wakde, Biak, Sansapor and Morotai were made primarily for the purpose of obtaining air bases from which we could strike at the enemy's lines of supply, thereby rendering his troops at by-passed bases ineffective as fighting units.

Thousands of Japanese at Rabaul, Bougainville, Kavieng, Wewak, Manokwari and the Halmaheras were left sitting on their haunches in the steaming jungles. This was isolation by air power - an isolation in which the Troop Carriers played a vital part. So successful was the application of air power and so successful was the strategy of the Navy, that sooner than expected U.S. troops swarmed ashore on October 20, on the landing beaches of Tacloban and Dulag in the Philippines. The Jap had not expected a landing here and had deployed his forces in other strategic locations. Before he could regroup, we had established our beachheads.

Within a short time the troops had captured the airdrome at Tacloban and the strips at Dulag and Burauen although plans called for Troop Carriers to land on the 25th, it was not until October 31, that a flight of 18 planes, led by Col. Joel G. Pitts of the 375th Group, landed at Tacloban. The flight was made via Angaur and Peleliu Islands of the Palau Group. Fighter escort was provided from Palau to Leyte. The cargo of the Troop Carrier planes was personnel of a Fighter Group badly needed at Leyte to defend that island against increasing enemy air opposition. A freight operational team of the 21st Service Group also landed with the planes. This team set up the same organization for handling freight as it did at Morotai Island. But the gluey mud and the ever-present rain, which made airfields literally sink and roads disappear, hampered operations. Added to this were the continual attacks by Jap airplanes.

To offset the latter, Troop Carriers were called to transport more and more fighter groups to Leyte until the airstrips became the "busiest in the world", in the number of take-offs and landings of all types of planes. It was another Tadji - only triple the size.

November found our infantry troops battering their way through Leyte, while Troop Carriers landed there every day with more fighter and bomber personnel and needed priority cargoes.

Between November 11 and December 11, dropping missions were made for the Sixth Army on both Leyte and Samar Islands. Two aircraft were lost, three crew members killed in action and one wounded. But the supplies were brought to the men who needed them - thousands of pounds of quartermaster items, ordnance equipment, medical supplies, signal items and hand grenades.

GENERAL STATISTICAL DATA ON OPERATIONS, MATERIAL, COMMUNICATIONS, INTELLIGENCE, MEDICAL AND RECREATION OF REAL SIGNIFICANCE

In the early days of the Air Transport Command, loading charts were unavailable, and often, after becoming available were ignored for the simple expediency of transporting as much freight as possible as quickly as possible, with the limited amount of air cargo space available. It was more the rule than the exception for a plane to take off with several thousand pounds over-load. This was especially true in operational areas, although not as often at Brisbane and Melbourne bases. C-39s with full gasoline tanks often took off with cargo weighing 5,000 to 6,000 pounds. Pay load of a C-39 fully serviced with 700 gallons of gasoline is 2,100 pounds. Fully serviced C-53s often transported pay loads of 6,500 to 7,500 pounds. Loading charts placed the proper pay load at 5,000 pounds with full service of 822 gallons of gasoline. Lt. Colonel Nicholas introduced in April, 1942, loading charts based upon A.A.F. Technical Orders, which were strictly complied with. The C-39 plane which crashed at Alice Springs on 25 May, 1942, upon investigation, disclosed an overload of 2,762 pounds. On 30 May, 1942, Lt. Col. Nicholas issued a strict warning against overloading by pilots. Pilots who overloaded their planes were immediately brought to account. Length of flights were cut, allowing a reasonable pay load with less gasoline. For instance, instead of Air Transport planes flying from Brisbane to Cloncurry (925) miles) and from Cloncurry to Batchelor (900 miles), the trip was reduced to four hops, viz., Brisbane to Charleville (432 miles), Charleville to Cloncurry (560 miles), Cloncurry to Daly Waters (565 miles), and Daly Waters to Batchelor (325 miles).

Authority for directing the hauling of freight and passengers was reposed in the Director, Directorate of Allied Air Transport. Freight would be hauled to the hangars maintained by Air Transport Command and later the 21st and 22nd Squadrons. Our ships would then haul the passengers and freight to duly designated points. Normally, freight was loaded by enlisted personnel assigned to Headquarters, Air Transport Command (later Air Carrier Service). Likewise, control officers were provided by the 21st and 22nd Squadrons under Headquarters, Air Transport Command.

Mt. Hagan, 1943.

New Guinea

Weights and Gasoline Service

During early operations in New Guinea, C-53s carried loads of 6,000 to 6,500 pounds with 500 gallons of gasoline. This weight proved impracticable on dropping missions, especially since the planes often had to be sideslipped at low speeds in order to arrive over some of the dropping areas low enough to drop the supplies effectively and efficiently. Heavy loads were a handicap to the pilot who found it necessary to dive and climb around clouds while attempting to find his way into landing fields in the mountains. C-53 and C-49 weights were reduced to 5,000 pounds with 500 to 550 gallons of gasoline; weights for C-50s were reduced to 4,000 pounds with 500 gallons of gasoline; weights for C-60s were reduced to 3,500 pounds and 400 to 550 gallons of gasoline. The normal load for a C-47 was 5,000 pounds with 700 gallons of gasoline. The large safety margin of gasoline, even on fairly short trips, was found to be desirable in New Guinea's unpredictable weather, which often forced a pilot to keep his ship aloft for several hours.

Responsibility for Loading

In early days in New Guinea, loading of planes was the responsibility of an Australian unit under Lt. Whiston and later under a Captain Lownie. Later, and until August, 1943, each organization which had previously obtained an authorization from A-3, Advance Echelon, Fifth Air Force, to ship its men and equipment, was charged with the responsibility of loading the airplanes designated for that purpose by Group (later 54th Wing) operations. Personnel and supplies to and from Australia were loaded by personnel of Director of Air Transport. In August, 1943, increased Troop Carrier activities between Port Moresby and forward areas made this method impracticable. Loading of United States Army equipment was taken over by First Air Freight Forwarding Squadron under the Fifth Air Service Command. Loading of Australian equipment was done by an Australian unit stationed at Ward's Drome.

Transport Control

Transport control in New Guinea had its inception on 15 July, 1942, when Headquarters, Air Transport Command, assigned Lt. Charles F. Franklin to his new station at 7-Mile (later Jackson) Drome. Lt. Franklin was relieved by Captain Charles A. Gibson on 12 August, 1942. Late in August, 1942, transport activities were transferred to 3-Mile (Kila) Drome. On 7 September, 1942, 1st Lt. Steinkurchner and Marvin M. Scott were sent to Port Moresby to take over field operations. About the middle of September, operations were returned to 7-Mile (Jackson) Drome, where they continued until the latter part of October, 1942, when they were transferred to the newly constructed Ward's Drome.

During this period in 1942 when group planes operated both from bases on the mainland and in New Guinea, the planes and their crews came under a dual operational control. When they were physically on the mainland, they came under the operational control of the Directorate of Allied Air Transport. When physically present in New Guinea, they came under the direct operational control of A-3, Advance Echelon, Fifth Air Force. This control was made complete in November, 1942, when Brigadier General Ennis C. Whitehead, by VOCO, ordered the planes to remain permanently in New Guinea, under his operational control.

Australian Mainland (1943 -   )

Immediately upon its return to Australia in September and October, 1943, the group came under the operational control of the Directorate of Air Transport, Allied Air Forces. Loading of all cargo and personnel is supervised and accomplished by that headquarters. The normal pay load is still 5,000 pounds and 700 gallons gasoline.

Cargo Hauled by the Group

Prior to December, 1942, no compiled monthly records of cargo hauled by group ships were kept. It is unfortunate that the achievements of the 21st and 22nd Squadrons during the first nine months of 1942 are not available as they contributed in a large measure to the success of the East Indies and Papuan Campaigns during these months by their ceaseless stream of supplies.

As of 31 January, 1943, the Group's best month in terms of weight carried was April, 1943, when the four squadrons hauled 12,678,077 pounds of cargo over the Owen Stanleys. The best daily record was achieved on 22 June, 1943, when 38 group ships hauled 744,025 pounds to Dobodura.

The following facts and figures compiled by Captain Harold B. Simpson, Group Statistical Officer, from Headquarters, Advance Echelon, Fifth Air Force files, in September, 1943, affords an analysis of the Group's New Guinea achievements:

Total Weight Carried	102,694,608 pounds
Hours Flown	38,938 Hours
Miles Traveled	4,949,750 Miles
Number of Personnel Moved	51,840 Men
Number of Sick and Wounded Evacuated	19,287 Men
Cargo Dropped	7,000,000 Pounds

Type of Cargo	Breakdown on Cargo Carried Weight
Personnel	10,368,050
Artillery	1,224,000
Small Arms	4,805,000
'E' Rations	10,328,000
'N' Rations	3,064,000
Motor Transportation	630,000
Gas and Oil	9,498,000
Signal Equipment	550,000
Medical Supplies	221,000
Engineering Equipment	4,894,000
Q.M. Supplies	10,346,000
Aircraft Engines	58,000
Mail	27,500
Unit Equipment and Supplies	46,710,100

New Guinea native carrying jungle forest food, 1943.

Units Totally or Partially Moved By the 374th Troop Carrier Group

32ND Infantry Div.	8th Bomb Squadron
41st Infantry Div.	5th Bomber Command
43rd Engineers	94th Anti-Aircraft
48th Service Sq.	96th Engineers
30th Sq. (R.A.A.F.)	46th Service Gp.
49th Fighter Group	61st Service Sq.
5th Fighter Command	13th Bomb Sq.
7th Fighter Sq.	90th Bomb Sq.
8th Fighter Sq.	89th Bomb Sq.
9th Fighter Sq.	440th Signal Battalion
3rd Bomb Gp. Hq.	49th Service Sq
27th Air Depot Gp.	

Various components of the New Guinea Forces
Various Components of the Australian Army

Note: Above statistics include New Guinea operations from October, 1942 to October, 1943.

Flying

Take-offs and Landings (Australia - 1942)

Air Transport Command aircraft, flying on a self-established operational schedule, as a rule, took off about an hour before dawn on flights such as those to Darwin. Discounting delay because of engine trouble, this put the plane into Batchelor Field just after sundown. In the early days this was a good policy at Darwin, as it was later at Port Moresby, because of Japanese aerial activity in the area. Aircraft sometimes took off for Cloncurry, Queensland, on the return trip the same night, either spending the night at Cloncurry or continuing on to Brisbane. Usually, take-offs for Batchelor Field were about two hours before dawn the following day, the aircraft arriving in Brisbane about 1430. This schedule gave time for maintenance work, thus making it possible for the plane to return to Batchelor or go elsewhere the next morning.

Only local weather conditions influenced take-offs from any field in most instances in these early days of transport flying, since weather reports were either unavailable or entirely unreliable. With the establishment of more weather stations, better communications facilities, and competent operations sections at airdromes along the eastern coast of Australia, take-offs from fields in this area became increasingly supervised. In these early days in Australia, Troop Carrier pilots were quite frequently compelled to make landings on short, muddy and very rough fields.

New Guinea Take-offs and Landings

All take-offs in New Guinea (since activation of the 374th Group) were effected during the hours of daylight. This was partly true because of lack of accurate weather data prior to dawn and partly because fighter escort or "cover" was virtually an impossibility during hours of darkness. Personnel and maintenance problems were also important factors.

Group Operations controlled the take-off of each individual plane or flight. Special consideration was often given to highly experienced pilots who expressed a willingness and eagerness to take-off on an additional flight after flying in general had been canceled because of weather. This concession to experienced pilots paid dividends in terms of thousands of pounds of extra freight hauled without a single mishap resulting. Experienced pilots sometimes completed two or three missions after the majority of aircraft were grounded.

The USS West Point enroute from San Francisco to Milne Bay, New Guinea.

Landings at advanced airdromes in New Guinea were, as a rule, quite hazardous. Heavily loaded planes had to be landed on short fields that were often wet, muddy, slippery, and very rough. Some of the strips were on inclines. That of Wau, for instance rose one foot in twelve with a crescent of mountains at its far end which made it impossible to "go around" at the last moment. The approach and landing at Bulolo was slightly downhill, the drome itself being short, rough and wet. The Bena Bena strip, perched on the top of a sharp ridge, was sway-backed. Wau's parking area was at 3,300 feet and Bena Bena's at 5,000 feet. Altitude of these fields called for added caution in making landings and take-offs because of the thinner air and increased power requirements. Most landings in New Guinea were subject to cross winds and down winds, which were often quite violent.

Flying Over the Owen Stanley Mountain Range

Since attack by enemy aircraft was probable and expected during operational flights across the Owen Stanley mountain range, pilots made maximum use of natural camouflage by flying as low as possible and choosing, when practicable, terrain which harmonized with the aircraft camouflage. They avoided presenting silhouettes against the sky and made maximum use of cloud cover. The pilot, co-pilot and radio operator maintained constant watch visually and on the radio for information on local enemy activity. The position of unidentified or hostile aircraft mentioned on the radio was noted immediately by use of grid maps. The pilot, co-pilot and engineer, the latter watching out the dome, also kept constant visual watch for enemy aircraft. All unidentified planes were considered hostile and necessary evasive action was taken.

When letting down after crossing the range, as in the Buna area for instance, pilots lost altitude as fast as practicable until they reached tree-top level. Approaches to fields such as Dobodura No. 4 were seldom made at altitudes of more than 300 feet above the tree tops. During the fighting in the Buna area, transports were seldom more than 50 feet above the tree-tops, even when making steep turns. Turns were made as close to the field as flying safety would allow. (One plane, at Popondetta, made his approach too high and wide and got a Japanese anti-aircraft shell in his fuselage. Luckily it did not explode. Another pilot flew too high above the terrain and was attached by Japanese dive bombers. They were carrying their bombs, which slowed them down considerably, and he, luckily too, managed enough speed to get away with only a few machine gun bullets in his airplane.)

Weather over the Owen Stanleys was almost as serious a hazard as hostile aircraft to pilots on operational missions. Vertical cloud development began rather abruptly and clouds often built up in front of a plane faster than the plane could climb. Haze, fog and rain were expected at all times.

FIGHTER PROTECTION IN NEW GUINEA

On flights to Wau, Bulolo and Bena Bena and to dropping areas in the vicinity of those mountain airdromes, transports were protected by a fighter escort varying in size according to the number of transports. Transports proceeding to these areas usually were in flights of nine or twelve aircraft and were protected by 12 to 15 "close cover" fighters and from four to eight "top cover" fighters. The transports flew in tight, stepped up Javelin formation and the "close cover", P-39s and P-40s, swept back and forth just above them. The top cover, usually P-38s, patrolled several thousand feet above.

Fighter cooperation in advising the transports of actual or suspected presence of enemy aircraft and in actually protecting them during attempted enemy attack was excellent. (Loss of one transport due to enemy action occurred because the transport pilot broke formation and thus did not have the benefit of the fighter cover which had its hands full in caring for the main flight.) Fighters, especially the "top cover", give valuable information to the transports in regard to weather conditions at and near the target area. Their information as to whether it was advisable for the transports to go under or over cloud formations in the area was particularly valuable.

During transport operations in the Buna - Dobodura area a constant fighter patrol was kept up. There was no actual escort, except in cases of emergency, for the transports took off and flew individually. Constant watch and the taking of immediate evasive action kept transport losses in this area to a minimum.

SOME REMINISCENCE AND THE TECHNOLOGY OF AIR DROP OF SUPPLIES IN NEW GUINEA

HISTORY

Free dropping of material and supplies from aircraft to units in isolated mountain areas was conceived and begun of necessity after the Japanese landing at Buna in July, 1942, when it was seen that native carriers could not adequately supply Australian troops in the fighting areas. The idea was the brain child of an Australian ANGAU Lieutenant, and the pilots of the 21st Troop Carrier Squadron, who also cooperated in dropping tests and convinced higher military authorities of the feasibility of dropping.

DROPPING STRIPS

Dropping strips were located, when possible, in naturally open areas which the planes could reach with the least amount of effort. For instance on flat topped kunai grass ridges. In most cases, however, military necessity called for clearing of trees on mountain sides or in native villages at the bottom of valleys. These open areas usually were about 50 yards by 25 yards. Approach to those used during the fighting between Iorabaiwa Ridge and Kokoda as a rule were quite difficult. At Menauri, considered the most difficult of all, it was necessary to drop over a 3,900 foot ridge into the valley at 100 miles per hour, with wheels down and throttles all the way back and then side slip from one side of the gorge to the other at tree-top level in order to come over the 1,000 foot target low enough and slow enough to drop effectively. Pulling out of dropping areas such as this where it was necessary to climb to 4,200 feet within a very short distance, called for maximum power and expert timing on the part of the pilot. Slight miscalculations have resulted in damaged wing-tips, ailerons, elevators, and rudders and an occasional hole in the wing. (A fatal crash occurred at Menauri and another at Skindaiwa.)

DROPPING THE LOAD

The aircraft was brought over the area at approximately 120 miles per hour (less, if possible and practicable) at a height of 200 to 300 feet. Dropping from this height had been proven to give the best results in recovery. When approaching the target the pilot flashed his "caution" light which was normally used as a preparatory signal for paratroop jumps. A crew of three of four men, who carried a portion of the load to the open doorway, then pushed and kicked the supplies out the door when the pilot turned on his alarm bell. The pilot continued to hold his plane in level flight or, preferably, nosed slightly downward as a safety precaution against the possibility of a bundle hitting his tail section. Wheels were immediately pulled up (if down) and necessary power applied to climb away safely. (The prop pitch was left in climbing rpm at all times during dropping missions.) Crews then began carrying bundles to the rear again for the next drop. Care was taken not to pile the bundles too high at the doorway because bundles on top of a high pile had farther to fall and often hit the tail section. Light bundles were placed on the bottom of the pile so they would clear the tail section more quickly.

Dropping of supplies was made easier and safer for the dropping crews by the use of a new all-metal slide which fitted flush with the bottom of the open doorway and flush against the opposite wall of the airplane about three feet from the floor. A removable stop was inserted at the lower end and the supplies piled up in the slide. Upon the signal from the pilot, the stop was removed and the supplies slid easily out of the doorway in a compact group. There were no instances of supplies hitting the tail section when the slide was used. The slide also obviated the necessity for tying in the dropping crews, as usually was done when a slide was not in use.

Pilots had very little to worry about wind drifts when dropping ordinary supplies, which were wrapped loosely in heavy burlap, because the plane was so close to the trees that the dead weight was little affected by wind during its comparatively short fall. In dropping parachutes, which were turned loose usually at a height of 300 feet and seldom less than 200 feet, however, wind drift had to be taken into consideration. Unless this was done, moreover, a great portion of the chutes would drift into the bush and sometimes down into deep gorges where it might take a day to find them and return them to the dropping area.

Before taking off on a drop mission in a C-47, the paratroop door was removed and the rest of the large cargo door securely roped or wired to the opposite side of the fuselage to prevent it from being blown out and damaging the empennage. When using aircraft with passenger type doors only, the door was removed before take-off.

A highly successful experiment made by the 374th Troop Carrier Group was the installation of a trap door in the floor of the C-47 for dropping purposes. This allowed dropping from the pseudo-bomb-bay and the door as well.

PERCENTAGE OF MATERIAL AND SUPPLIES RECOVERED BY GROUND TROOPS

A percentage of 85 to 90 percent of supplies dropped from the air usually was recovered by ground troops. Of this amount recovered, approximately 60 to 65 percent was in excellent condition. Canned goods usually took a pretty rough beating, according to ground troops who said they got pretty tired or eating jam mixed with biscuits, beans, bully beef and an occasional .45 caliber slug.

Dropping of mortar shells and fuses was discontinued after it was discovered that the impact over-sensitized the charge.

ACCIDENTS

One Australian soldier was killed at Menauri when a tin of Bully Beef careened off the top of a native hut and hit him on the head while he was standing at the edge of the clearing. Several other Australian soldiers were seriously injured by dropping supplies.

WEATHER REPORTING

Weather reports were unreliable during the early days of intensive flying by units that are now a part of the 374th Group. Pilots were compelled to depend entirely upon their own judgment as to probable weather conditions, especially on the runs across the continent, such s between Brisbane and Darwin, Melbourne and Darwin via Adelaide, Oodnadatta, Alice Springs and Daly Waters. In these regions, up until September, 1942, weather reporting was done by Australian postmasters, a slow and highly unreliable method. Weather reports for trips over this area improved somewhat during the later stages of operations on the mainland (September to December 1942) but only insofar as weather in the immediate vicinity of the destination and refueling airdromes were concerned. Reports for flights along the eastern coast of Australia were fairly accurate. Between such points as Darwin and Perth, weather reporting is still highly unsatisfactory as it is done by postmasters.

In the middle of July, 1942, the 15th Weather Squadron began to operate on the mainland, with headquarters at Essendon Drome, Melbourne, Victoria. In November, 1942, the headquarters was moved to Garbutt Field, Townsville, Queensland. In conjunction with RAAF weather units and the AACS and Australian communication units, weather reporting and forecasting on the mainland and later in New Guinea was placed on a more reliable and scientific basis.

After October, 1942, the 15th Weather Squadron and RAAF began furnishing reliable weather reports in New Guinea. Wherever forecasting stations were set up, Army Airways Communication System would send and receive forecasts and reports. However, at reporting stations, reports would be sent via signal corps or other methods of communications.

Terminal weather advice in New Guinea, until May or June, 1943, was found to be fairly accurate when available, but for the most part pilots took off for airdromes such as Wau, Bulolo, and Bena Bena with no accurate information on the weather, trusting to luck, flying skill, and a personal knowledge of New Guinea weather habits and terrain to get them to their landing strips and dropping targets. Decisions on weather are still left up to the pilot for the most part, since the weather changes so rapidly that only pilots who have just returned from an area are capable of reporting on the weather. Pilots when in New Guinea are constantly confronted with ground fogs, heavy rain, thick stratus and cumulonimbus clouds previously unreported.

In July, 1943, the group began to send a Troop Carrier pilot as an observer on a B-25 which took off at 0500 and flew the complete route of Troop Carrier operations for the day. Reports were radioed back. If, for any reason, the ship did not take off, or reports were not received, the operations officer would be compelled to rely on fighter pilots' reports, just as they did from October, 1942, until July, 1943.

Since its return to the mainland, the Group has found weather reporting in Australia and in New Guinea to be on a reliably scientific basis.

ENGINEERING AND MAINTENANCE

THE 21ST AND 22ND SQUADRONS

Never was so much done with so little. In these words can be summed up the achievement of the engineering echelon of the 374th Troop Carrier Group in the Southwest Pacific Area. It is a saga of men who kept 'em flying with hands and grit alone.

When air Transport Command began it operations in Australia, the latter part of January, 1942, the only tools available were those which the maintenance crews assigned from bombardment units brought along in their kits. Practically all American tools and spare parts had originally been diverted to Java and destroyed prior to evacuation by American forces. Spare parts for the planes, if available at all, were purchased from Australian National Airline. In February, 1942, only eight ground crew mechanics were maintaining eight airplanes. This crew worked 15 and 16 hours a day, 7 days a week, for about two months until more men were attached from other units as more planes were added. From then on the organization began to work on a 24-hour basis, in two shifts of 12 hours each.

To make possible a 24-hour working schedule, a string of six power and light outlets had to be installed at Archer Field. The electrical system and hangar lighting was altered so as to accommodate a 110 volt system to make possible the use of U.S. equipment such as electric drills and soldering irons. The organization also acquired two gasoline driven generators for night maintenance of any ships out of reach of the power and light outlets.

Spare parts being virtually unobtainable, repair rather than replacement of a defective part was the rule. Any part needing welding was given to the 8th Materiel Squadron (U.S.) for repair, then reinstalled. In one instance, the entire hydraulic panel of a C-39 had to be removed as it was clogged with muck. This turned out to be a 12 hour job for two men inasmuch as the reservoir,

New Guinea native in hunting pose.

pressure regulator, and pressure relief valve had to be dismantled, cleaned and overhauled. Another tribute to the engineering section in those early days was its installation of two strange engines in a C-45 Beechcraft to replace two worn out engines.

When a wing was needed for a B-17 at Archer Field, a wing was removed from a B-17 and used as a pattern so that brackets could be made to fit it to the belly of a C-39. Captain Harold G. Slingsby then took the C-39 to Darwin and brought back the badly needed wing, a dangerous undertaking for which Captain Slingsby was awarded the Distinguished Flying Cross.

Late in March, 1942, eleven Lockheed Lodestars and one Martin B-19 were purchased from the Netherlands East Indies Government for $1,030,000 and were assigned to the newly activated 21st and 22nd Squadrons. At the time of delivery, engine time as well as airplane time were unknown quantities. No spare parts for Lockheeds where available in the theater. To add to the gargantuan problems already confronting "the line", the instrument readings on the planes were in liters for volume and kilometers for air speed; all instructions were in Dutch script. The aid of a Dutch civilian employee of the Qantas Airways was solicited. It was our misfortune that he was unfamiliar with the particular Dutch dialect used in connection with our ships. The trial and error method was the only solution; the mechanics and pilots learned only by doing and experimenting. As new engines for these planes were unprocurable, it was necessary to substitute and improvise in order to keep these "crates" in commission. Improvised tools had to be used to remove blower gear; valve grinding gear was made on the lathe and grinding compound was borrowed.

In May, 1942, ten additional planes were procured from the Dutch. They consisted of two DC-2s, two DC-3s, three DC-5s and three Lockheed 14s. Of the ten, three had 10 hours left and seven needed engine changes. Also, there were four new engines for the DC-3s and 48 cases of spares at Sydney which were obtained along with the ten aircraft. (Memo from Lt. Col. Nicholas, dated 13 May 1942.)

A letter, dated 22 October, 1942, written by Corporal Ned Allen, (RAAF), who supervised the engine overhaul department, having been loaned to the 21st Squadron, details several of the early "miracles" accomplished. In one instance, a Lodestar arrived at sundown, one engine consuming six gallons of oil an hour. The worst cylinders were removed, and the valves were ground, some rings were fitted, the cylinders were reinstalled and the aircraft was flying again by sunrise. Then also, there was the instance in which three cylinders were removed from a Douglas plane, three different types cylinders (the only ones available) were installed - pistons rings were installed and the aircraft completed 250 more flying hours. In another instance, a C-39 arrived showing excessive oil consumption. Only 27 piston rings were procurable because of the acute shortage in this theater; they were fitted along with 27 old rings which were replaced. This aircraft was then able to complete 300 more flying hours. When a DC-2 arrived with broken hold-down cylinder studs, the engine was removed, the nose section and front crank-case were partially removed; the old broken studs were removed, drilled out and replaced. All parts were reassembled, the engine replaced and the plane was flying in record time. On a number of occasions, after newly major overhauled engines were installed in the planes, it was found that maximum rpm and manifold pressure could not be obtained. This would require that the engine, all accessories and the blower section be removed, the two position blower clutch overhauled; then the motor would be reassembled and the engine replaced.

As a matter of fact, the repair department became so widely known for its efficiency that it was quite common for other organizations to send their planes to Archer Field for overhauls.

In the first few months of operations it was impossible to comply with existing Technical Orders as there were none available to us. For proper inspection of aircraft, past experience was the only guidepost. Typical of the difficulties that were confronted were those in connection with compass checking. As there were no straight roads, railroads or other check points on the ground by which compasses could be checked, it became necessary to inquire of the Australians how they had checked theirs. Their system of using a master compass and lining up the aircraft on a particular bearing, proved to be too impractical for the 21st Squadron, as it took too long and was not accurate enough. A solution to the problem was the construction of a "compass rose" large enough so that aircraft could be taxied around to each point and checked without killing the engines. It was not long until this "compass rose" began to be used by all airlines and RAAF personnel who knew of its existence.

In the electrical and instruments sections, lack of equipment called for improvisation and inventive ingenuity. Most generator troubles having been due to a faulty generator control panel, a test stand was devised upon which the control panel could be mounted and checked under conditions simulating normal plane operation. This test stand was constructed by utilizing a small gasoline engine which was removed from a field energizer not in use. The voltmeter and ammeter were obtained from Technical Supply. The gasoline engine was fitted with a ten inch pulley and drove a standard aviation generator on which a three and one half inch v-type pulley was fitted. The latter pulley could easily be removed making it possible to attach it on any specified type of generator used in conjunction with the particular control panel being tested.

In some cases the points on units were so badly burned as to render them unworkable. No new points being available, the only alternative was to make them. This was accomplished by soldering part of a three pence coin in place and then dressing and polishing them to proper specifications.

Much difficulty was experienced in obtaining twelve volt starter motors and meshing solenoids. To overcome this difficulty it was necessary to rewind and repair the armatures and field coils, as well as to move the commutators around. Some armatures had been reworked so often that it was necessary to fit brushes longer than standard in order to secure good commutations.

All the Dutch aircraft were equipped with direct drive starters, which were not standard with the Army Air Corps. Brushes for this starter having been unavailable it was necessary to manufacture them from carbon blocks to which the old leads were fas-

Sgt. Sam Frank and Capt. George Foster in Port Moresby, New Guinea.

tened by drilling through the brush and leads and securing the leads with a piece of silver solder.

The inadvisability of the direct drive starters in combat was proven conclusively by our pilots on a number of occasions when they landed in New Guinea at forward strips and cut off the motor. In some cases the starter would not function. A picturesque means of starting the engine was the placing of a boot over one prop tip and tying a three foot length of shock cord and a rope to it; then two or three men would heave with all their might.

Meshing solenoids were repaired by the purchase locally of Number 18 magnet wire which was used to rewind the coils of faulty solenoids. The average unit had a lift of pull of 17 pounds which was slightly above required specifications.

Since the DC-2 type aircraft (formerly KNILM Airliners) did not use standard air corps fuses, and since what supply we had had been captured by the Japanese, it became necessary to improvise fuses. To repair the fuse, the burned out fuse lining was removed and replaced with fuse wire of a specified carrying and fusing capacity. In some cases, several strands of wire had to be wound together and checked on a ohmmeter to determine correct size.

The source of most electrical and ignition trouble was found to be in broken conduit and harness. The harness and conduit having been subjected to oil, heat and vibration caused the wire to short circuit and ground out. Cannon plugs were also damaged in the same manner. None of these items having been available at the time, they were taken from wrecked planes wherever they would be found. Often it was necessary to completely rewire and revise the parts so obtained in order to render them serviceable for the particular job for which they were needed. In one instance, it was necessary to rewire the ignition and electrical distributing system on a DC-2 completely. No new harness and very little new wire having been available, the job was satisfactorily completed by re-working and wiring the harness with material obtained from five wrecked planes of various types in the field "graveyard". In such cases, special care was exercised in removing the salvaged parts and if found unsuitable for the particular job were tagged and stored for future use. This wise practice made it possible in many instances to place a plane in service that might otherwise have been grounded for lack of such an item. When no conduit was obtainable it was found necessary to repair breaks by chemically cleaning one-half inch on each side of the break, tinning it, then wrapping with very fine brass safety wire and soldering.

Batteries were also highly critical items. It became necessary on occasions to extract good cells from previously condemned batteries and exchange them for dead cells in batteries in service. The tools used were a blow torch, a soldering iron and a brace and bit.

The instrument section was more often than not compelled to devise, modify and improvise. On one occasion an E-4 tachometer generator was used in place of a model 724-C by changing the resistance and remagnetizing the magnets. A C-4 hydraulic gauge was used to replace a model 3 _ AD-4201 type by building an auxiliary panel and using adapters on the connections plus a length of weatherhead tubing. There were many other substitutions, modifications and adaptations. A C-5 flight indicator was used in a panel built for a C-3 type by cutting off self-locking nuts and changing the fittings. A C-7 was used in a C-3 type panel by removing the caging knob and taping gear in the "uncage" position. Electric Tachometers were calibrated by using dry cell batteries connected in series with a rheostat and voltmeter. Lack of proper replacements was of course the principal difficulty encountered. This was over come by changing the wiring and adding resistance in some cases; in other cases the difficulty was solved by altering the instrument panel. In one case two serviceable instruments were taken apart and a good one assembled from the two, the other then being sent in for repair.

In April, 1942, the 21st Squadron was faced with one of the most serious maintenance problems of its early career. Day by day, the supply of spark plugs was being depleted until an inventory disclosed a stock of only 225 spark plugs for ten aircraft. Chances of obtaining replacements from Air Corps supply were slim as the demand was far in excess of the supply. A spark plug overhaul department was organized for the purpose of reconditioning old plugs without outside help. Within two weeks after opening the department, 300 plugs were on hand over and above what was being used on the aircraft. These were ferreted out of every nook and cranny of the hangars and supply rooms. One enlisted man was sent to a civilian spark plug overhaul depot to gain what knowledge they had to offer regarding spark plug performances and problems in tropical climate. With that information, he was sent to various U.S. Air Corps fields in Australia where he picked up further information on Depot methods in overhauling used spark plugs. As the department progressed, a monthly report was made to keep an accurate check on what types were needed and what plugs were most needed. As of the latter months of 1942, the squadron was using approximately 1200 plugs every month, all this made possible by the conservation policy of the early months and the gradual increase until in October, 1942, the squadron had on hand over 3,000 spark plugs of the required type. The reputation of the squadron spark plug department had become so well established that civilian, non-combatant and combat squadrons knew and took advantage of the fact that the 21st Squadron could, at Archer Field, supply their ships with new or reconditioned spark plugs of guaranteed dependability.

During the last months of 1942, replacements for the C-49 engines, the R-1820-71 type were not available in Australia. On several ships 1820-65 engines were substituted. This entailed the following changes: (1) Blast tubes to magnets had to be manufactured; (2) Prop feathering oil lines had to be manufactured; (3) Primer line had to be lengthened; (4) Fuel feed line from fuel pump to carburetor had to be heated and rebent to permit installation; (5) Prop blade settings had to be changed; (6) Four or five other minor changes. On several other planes, 1820-89 engines were substituted. Cowling pads had to be fitted and manufactured to get a proper fit of the cowling. In addition, prop feathering lines had to be manufactured.

The paint and fabric shop was started with several men with experience and a number who taught themselves. Fabric needles were improvised by grinding down a welding rod to the desired size, sanding and drilling a small hole in the end and hammering it out flat.

The 22nd Squadron likewise started at scratch upon its activation on 3 April, 1942, with station at Essendon Aerodrome, Melbourne, Victoria. The squadron's first planes were the Dutch planes which had been used in the evacuation of Java. Two of these planes were shot full of holes, blood stains on the interior still showing mute but eloquent evidence of their past history. Under present conditions these aircraft would have been salvaged. The only skilled mechanics were pursuit plane mechanics and one heavy bombardment mechanic, all veterans from the Philippines and Java. The rest of the "line" consisted of basic soldiers fresh from the United States with little over one month in the Army. But there were no tools! The glorious pages of history of the Army Air Corps were further embellished by the resourcefulness of these unsung heroes. They made, begged and "borrowed" some of their tools; others they purchased with their own funds at the 5 and 10 cent stores in Melbourne. It is said that the first tool box consisted of a mallet, screw driver, adjustable wrench and a roll of bailing wire. All tools previously sent from the United States had arrived in Java. During the evacuation, all available boat and plane space was used to evacuate personnel. The tools were placed in vehicles, gasoline poured on and burnt up.

When generators and starters were burnt out, or controls went out, these unskilled mechanics referred to above did their own repair work in Australian work shops. A number of these men showed so much promise that they were sent to Australian schools.

All maintenance work at Essendon Drome was done on the field; however, a portable hangar was available for windy and rainy weather. Major overhauling was done by A.N.A.

During its early days the 22nd Squadron was beset by the same problems as the 21st, and solved them in much the same manner. Spare parts were found in salvaged dumps and were improvised and modified until they fitted our ships.

In August, 1942, one of the 22nd Squadron's ships returning from Batchlor Field to Essendon stopped at a small service and radio station in the desert. In taking off it was discovered that the booster coil in the right engine was out. The crew borrowed a Model T. Ford at the radio station and hooked the coil up between the battery and magnet. After the engine started they had to remove the wires and replace the cowling while the engine was running - very dangerous, to say the least.

When six of the squadron's planes were struck by bombs at Jackson Drome, Port Moresby, New Guinea, on 17 August, 1942, three were total losses; the remaining three, consisting of a C-39 and two C-53s, were patched with dope and fabric and within four or five days were flown back to the mainland for major repair work.

In September, 1942, a prop was badly needed to make a C-56 flyable. A different type was obtained from the Navy and was installed after the engineering section had manufactured its own jigs, clamps and cowl flaps.

At Garbutt Field major overhauling was done by the depot and the 2nd Service Squadron. In November, 1942, the proper type engine having been unavailable for a C-39, a different model engine was obtained from the depot and installed after modifications were made. Incidentally, the first tools ever requisitioned and received by the 22nd Squadron came from the 2nd Service Squadron.

Another instance of the resourcefulness of the "grease monkeys" occurred at Garbutt Field as a result of an acute shortage of filters. Kotex was considered a fairly satisfactory substitute - but Kotex also was very scarce in Australia - in fact it is reliably reported that one of the men, without attempting to be fresh or facetious, approached a female acquaintance of his, and made an urgent request for her assistant in that dilemma.

For one week during December, 1942, 22nd Squadron crews were stationed at Dobodura frequently being caught at work on their planes while the strip was being strafed. They slept beneath their planes and messed with an engineering unit which was located in the jungle about 100 yards from the strip. Most of them contracted malaria on that assignment. While at Port Moresby in the latter months of 1942 and January of 1943, the crews slept in or beneath the aircraft and ate one meal a day at Arcadia. In these early days in New Guinea, the crews always worked at night by flashlight and jeep and beep lights because the ships had to be flown during the day.

In November, 1942, a Lockheed C-56 was grounded because of one bad prop; none was available in this theater. A wire was sent to the United States for a new prop. The prop arrived seven months later and was turned over to the 27th Air Depot Group. Hope had long before been lost for its delivery, the aircraft having been turned over to the 33rd Troop Carrier Squadron in the interim.

When the advance detail of the squadron ground echelon arrived, shortage of transportation became critical. Requisitions could not be filled. The story can now be told, albeit with tongue in cheek. The 32nd Division was on its return journey to the mainland. Part of their cargo was a number of assorted vehicles, including jeeps and command cars wich had been written off as lost in combat. Barter became the order of the day. B-4 bags, leather flying jackets and liquor were traded for vehicles. One transaction, as reported by reliable authority, was four jeeps and two command cars for two B-4 bags, four leather flying jackets, and two navigator's brief cases. In those early days badly needed parts were obtained with the assistance of a bottle of liquor. Our engineering sections would trade with other units on a mutual trade basis.

During the months of August and September 1942 and until the arrival of the air echelon of the 6th Squadron at Port Moresby on 13 October, 1942, crews were sent to New Guinea from the mainland by the 21st and 22nd Squadrons and these crews performed maintenance on their aircraft until 100 hour inspections were due, at which time plane and crew were returned to their squadrons. Replacement crews and planes were then sent to New Guinea to continue operations under great handicaps. Since planes were flown continuously during the day, maintenance was carried on after flying was discontinued generally by flashlight after dark. In tribute to the unstinting devotion of the crews, it is a matter of record that only rarely was any plane out of service during flying hours.

Upon the arrival of the air echelon of the 6th Squadron at Port Moresby on 13 October, 1942, it brought with it a detachment of the 220th Service Squadron to perform as ground crew members for the 6th Squadron aircraft. Disregarding hours, this detachment worked day and night to keep the group's planes in New Guinea flying. When the 6th Squadron established its camp site at the northerly side of Wards Drome, the 220th detachment set up its messing facilities for themselves and the 6th Squadron and carried on in that capacity until the 6th Squadron's ground echelon arrived in December, 1942, whereupon the 6th Squadron set up its own messing facilities. The 220th was then attached to the 6th Squadron for rations until January, 1943, when it set up its own camp area and mess hall adjacent to the 6th Squadron. During this period the 220th Service Squadron had been redesignated the 27th Service Squadron, and later the 478th Service Squadron.

While the group was stationed in New Guinea, the 478th Squadron did most of the sheet metal work required on the planes and performed 3rd and 4th echelon maintenance at times. Whenever a group ship was badly damaged it would be turned over to the 478th for repair.

In December, 1942, Group Engineering actually started to function with Major Edward T. Imparato at the head of the Section. The Section acted in a supervisory capacity and made the technical inspections.

The squadrons performed all maintenance in the open and did their own 1st, 2nd and some 3rd echelon maintenance, overhauling their own engine accessories and doing much of their own sheet metal work, at times in the shops of the 478th Squadron. Engines, new and overhauled, were drawn from the 27th Air Depot Group through the 478th. Special tools were made in the shops of the 8th Service Group. Sheet metal sections manufactured many of their own tools such as jigs, clamps and cowl flaps.

If an aircraft was severely damaged, it was the task of the 478th Squadron to salvage it. However, the squadrons always being in need of various critical items would unofficially dispatch crews to the scene before the crews of the 478th arrived. The crews would engage in good natured rivalry in bartering for the much needed equipment as they stripped the plane. A typical example of the speed with which these crews would get to the scene of a crash was the incident of the crash of a 375th Group plane at Jackson Drome in August, 1943. The ship had crashed at approximately 0700 and had to be salvaged. One engine was still serviceable. The 22nd Squadron had a plane out of commission because it lacked an engine. The crew had removed the engine from the crashed ship, installed the engine in its own ship and had the ship in the air by 1600 the same day.

During January, February and March, 1943, the crews made a practice of prowling through dumps and salvage yards in the vicinity of Port Moresby to salvage batteries and other items from damaged planes.

Until February, 1943, planes were refueled by means of hand-driven pumps attached to 50 gallon drums. Later trucks were acquired saving much needed time and man power.

When on April 12, 1943, five of the group's ships were damaged on the ground as a result of enemy bombing activity, three of the damaged planes were repaired the same day, one within a week, and the fifth within two weeks.

During the first six months of 1943, the C-34 and C-35 spark plugs required by the C-47 engines were unprocurable in the Southwest Pacific Area. This necessitated the use of LS-85 and LS-87 type plugs which were highly unsatisfactory as they would burn up the leads in the harnesses; the ignition harnesses would have to be restrung and copper ferrell had to be improvised from copper tubing.

In May, 1943, the 22nd Squadron took an engine out of a hydraulic test stand and a generator from an energizer and set up a power system for its tent shops. In July, 1943, M/Sgts. John Warren, Glenn F. Greening, T/Sgt. William P. Boddie and others in the 22nd Engineering Department developed a process for pickling blower sections of airplane engines, consisting of a pressure tank to force anticorrosion compound into the blower section of the engine. This process is now followed as standard procedure by Fifth Air Force units.

Also in July, 1943, Lt. Rexford W. Echard, 6th Squadron Engineering Officer, devised an ignition harness tester, plans of which were submitted to Wright Field, Dayton, Ohio.

The following critical items were usually stripped from salvaged planes: wheel assemblies, instruments (flight and engine), check valves, electrical leads, hydraulic lines, fuel lines, cockpit windows, wing tips, and all engine accessories.

ENGINEERING AND MAINTENANCE (OCTOBER 1943 -)

Upon the arrival of the 6th, 22nd and 33rd Squadrons at Garbutt Field in October, 1943, their engineering sections were set up at the large hangar on the field. Technical Supply was for the first time consolidated. The squadrons maintain a sheet metal section in a small building near the hangar; the same building houses a group welding shop. For the use of the welding department, T/Sgt. Philip J. Staun put together a carbide acetylene generator. Upon replacing the 317th Group an electrically powered air compressor was inherited and installed in the sheet metal and welding shop; overhead lines were constructed running into each sheet metal department and the welding section. A do-all, lathe and drill press were also "inherited" from the 317th and immediately utilized.

The personnel of the group's electrical departments were called upon to install a complicated wiring system for the welding and sheet metal shop, since the hand powered tools received from the states require 110 volts while the Australian equipment in the shop requires 220 volts and in some cases 450 volts.

Supplies and spare parts have been obtained by the three squadrons at A.P.O. 922, from the 4th Air Depot Group. In December, 1943, the group for the first time was able to requisition a few automatic pilots to replace those which had been disabled.

The 21st Squadron has since the first part of October accomplished its maintenance work at Archer Field. Most of the work is done in the open. A hangar which houses Technical Supply is also used by the Sheet Metal Department, the Welding and Electrical Departments and the Propeller Shop.

At Lea New Guinea, 1944.

Since the return of the group to the mainland, after its ships have accumulated 1,000 flying hours, they are sent to Essendon Airdrome for overhaul by A.N.A. The group has also maintained its own test pilot at Essendon Airdrome. Occasionally, major overhauls have been performed by A.N.A. at Mascot Field, Sydney, Australia, and the 4th Air Depot Group, APO 922.

COMMUNICATIONS

When the Army Air Forces first arrived in the Southwest Pacific Area, there were only Australian Radio facilities on the Australian mainland; these stations were operated either by RAAF or the Aeradio. In the main, the facilities afforded were adequate unless a pilot was unfortunate enough to stray far from the established routes in the Northern Territory of Western Australia.

Serious problems were encountered by Air Transport Command and later by the 21st and 22nd Squadron, when early in 1942, a number of aircraft were purchased from the Netherlands East Indies Airlines and the Dutch Army. These planes were equipped with Dutch radio equipment or American equipment adapted for use by the Dutch. Great confusion existed from the start as all markings and instructions which were only occasionally available were in Dutch. Wiring diagrams and spare parts generally were not available and maintenance had to be accomplished by trial and error. After three to 4 months use, U.S. Army Signal Corps receiving sets were installed in these aircraft. The transmitters, being satisfactory, were retained. During these early days, it was not uncommon for either the receiving or transmitting equipment on a plane to be "out"; on occasions there was a dearth of trained radio operators. The planes flew nonetheless.

A case in point was a C-40 acquired from the Dutch and late in 1942 assigned to the 6th Squadron. It was operated on a daily run from Port Moresby to Milne Bay. The radio mechanics had never been able to place the radio equipment in operating order because wiring diagrams were missing, among other reasons. However, the ship was operated for several months until it was sent to Townsville for overhaul and the installation of American radio equipment.

Competent radio mechanics were unavailable in the early months of 1942. As a matter of fact, the 22nd Squadron had only one trained radio mechanic servicing its planes until September, 1942, when another mechanic with no Army Service School training, was assigned to the communications section. When ever sets of the 22nd Squadron went bad and could not be repaired in the Squadron, they were taken to the Air Depot or the Amalgamated Wireless of Australia, Pty Ltd, and as a rule the defects were immediately remedied.

From the radio mechanic's standpoint the widely assorted planes assigned to the 21st and 22nd Squadrons also represented a wide selection of G.I. and commercial type radio equipment. In the first days of the Squadrons there was little or no maintenance or test equipment or technical manuals to work with. Maintenance was often miraculously accomplished to a satisfactory degree only by good luck, perseverance and sleepless nights.

During July, 1942, while the 22nd Squadron was stationed at Essendon Airdrome, a case of sabotage of radio equipment was discovered. The equipment had been tested the previous day and found to be in proper order. The next day it would not function. When torn down, it was discovered that a fuse had been removed from the transmitter and in the compartment was found excelsior and other waste scraps. An immediate extensive investigation was instituted.

After the 22nd Squadron moved to Garbutt Field in October, 1942, several C-60's were assigned to the squadron. They were good aircraft and had excellent radio equipment but they came without technical orders, technical manuals or the necessary maintenance parts. Although they were equipped with a powerful type of transmitter, the frequencies of the crystals were not correct for this area, nor was the transmitter flexible enough in design for military use. The C-60s had a new type of command set which is now in common use. The only difficulty experienced with these sets was the habit of the springs burning off the banana plugs making the set or part of the set inoperative. The interphone amplifier was also a source of trouble. Moisture got into the set causing mildew of the cotton insulation of the wiring, the insulation then falling away, resulting in a short circuit.

Technical Orders on radio equipment were all but non-existent until October and November, 1942, when they began to trickle in. However, upon the acquisition of C-47s by the squadrons, complete Radio G Files accompanied each aircraft.

During 1942, Radio Navigation Range Facilities in Australia were all operated by Australian Airways Radio Ranges. In December, 1942, 5th Army Airways Communication System began to set up its own radio stations in Australia and New Guinea. As a rule 5th AACS operated in the same sectors as R.A.A.F. and Aeradio. Although AACS set up radio ranges in Australia immediately upon its arrival in the Southwest Pacific in December, 1942, it was not until April, 1943, that ranges could be used in New Guinea; then they were used only in emergencies upon request inasmuch as the Japanese could also utilize them.

In December, 1942, because of a dearth of point to point radio communications between New Guinea and the mainland, a circuit was established by the group between Port Moresby and Townsville, the Port Moresby Station being operated by the 6th Squadron and the Townsville Station by the 22nd Squadron. The circuit was used primarily for PXing our aircraft movements between the mainland and New Guinea and for group administrative traffic to the squadrons. The circuit operated very successfully. (When the 22nd Squadron moved to New Guinea in February, 1943, the Townsville Station was taken over by the 317th Troop Carrier Group.)

Until January, 1943, radio repair facilities in New Guinea were meager. Aside from squadron repair units there were only one or two Signal Corps units servicing the entire island and they were overworked and under-staffed.

When the ground echelons of the squadrons arrived in New Guinea, they preceded their radio repair equipment. For a time there were no spare parts and repairs were effected through improvisations, ingenuity and perseverance. Installations were of necessity very primitive during the early days in New Guinea. For example, the radio repair shop of the 6th Squadron originally consisted of a pyramidal tent pitched on the bare ground. The work bench consisted of a packing crate and the only tools available were those in the kits on the planes. Reports and paper work when prepared at all were typed on a signal corps typewriter using all capital letters.

(The 6th and 33rd Squadrons arrived in the Southwest Pacific with C-47s; the 21st and 22nd Squadrons began acquiring C-47s in January and February, 1943; after February, 1943, the group used C-47s only and in May, 1943, began to acquire C-47As. The C-47 is equipped with an excellent type of Automatic Radio Compass. The radio equipment on the whole is very satisfactory. The old SCR183 command set with which it is equipped has been outmoded for a number of years. One persistent source of trouble encountered was caused by acid or water getting into the compass loop housing. This caused rust and corrosion to set up in the loop motor and autosyn transmitter; as a consequence, the radio transmitter became inoperative.)

The problems of the radio repair departments was considerably alleviated during the middle of 1943 when a regulation required that each squadron be equipped with two complete spare sets of any radio equipment then in the planes.

The first Group Communications Officer was 1st Lieutenant Blair D. Baylor. He was succeeded by 2nd Lieutenant David T. McCartney during the first week in January, 1943, after Group Headquarters had moved to New Guinea. The first work undertaken was the installation, operation, and maintenance of the "Dexter" switchboard, which provided Group Headquarters and the 33rd Squadron with telephone communications. By the first week of March, 1943, a switchboard was set up in the Operations grass shack at Wards Drome, making direct communication with Headquarters, Advance Echelon Fifth Air Force, Fifth Bomber Command and Fifth Fighter Command for the first time possible. The Group Message Center was also operated by the Communications Section.

The 33rd Squadron constructed and equipped a ground radio station at Wards Drome the latter part of January, 1943. This station was able to receive and transmit and was a material asset to the group's operations and activities.

On 4 February, 1943, Lt. McCartney having been hospitalized, 2nd Lt. Stanley F. Horr, succeeded him as Group Communications Officer. 1st Lt. Alexander Lieberman took over Group Communications vice Lt. Horr on 28 February 1943. On 8 March, 1943, Captain Pearre D. Jacques was assigned as Group Communications Officer vice Lt. Lieberman who was appointed Assistant Communications Officer. On 2 May, 1943, Captain Alexander Lieberman resumed the same duty vice Major Pearre D. Jacques, returned to the United States. On 8 June, 1943, Captain Lieberman, having been hospitalized, 1st Lt. Stanley F. Horr became Group Communications Officer. On 22 June, 1943, Captain Emmett E. Rhoades, having joined Group Headquarters, became Group Communications Officer vice Lt. Horr.

In June, 1943, Group Communications installed and maintained a teletypewriter in the newly constructed Operations Building at Wards Drome. The teletypewriter was directly connected wit Headquarters, 54th Troop Carrier Wing.

While in New Guinea our planes maintained contact with the 33rd Troop Carrier Squadron ground station. Each plane was assigned a call number; daily letters of the day, changed every eight hours, were used. All communication between planes and stations was by code; clear communications were prohibited except on take-off, landing and in emergences. The C-47s have always been equipped with I.F.F. sets but have never received Rebecca-Eureka equipment.

Since the return of the group to the mainland in October, 1943, the 33rd Squadron set up and maintained, in the Project No. 2, Garbutt Field Camp area, a ground radio station. Radio contact continued to be maintained by our planes with 5th AACS and Aeradio stations as well as the 33rd Station. A teletypewriter is main tained at Group Operations connected with the 33rd Ground Station.

Major J.D. Pearson, 1943.

All group ships en route to Garbutt Field radio their ETAs 30 minutes out. Pilots are also required to radio the fact of RON whenever they are detained for any reason.

The group also operates a daily weather ship, a C-47 going north every morning, weather permitting, radioing the weather in to the 33rd station or AACS which in turn teletype it to Group or Base Operations respectively.

Since the return of the group to the mainland in October, 1943, a radio station has been operated at Mackay, Queensland. Originally a small air to ground, point to point station was received from the 317th Troop Carrier Group. Because of its apparent inadequacy, 5th AACS furnished equipment during the latter part of January, 1944, which, since installation, has permitted a hookup with AACS stations. A detachment of six operators, one radio maintenance man, and one clerk has been stationed at Mackay to operate the station.

Intelligence

The activities of this section consisted of keeping posted a set of Australian Aeronautical Maps covering the progress of the war in this theater of operations both the Northeastern and Northwestern Area being posted. A set of strategic maps (4 miles to the inch) was also put up covering the immediate area of our operations and on these maps was posted the ground forces action, and location of enemy, particularly in relation to forward airports and drop zones. In addition, special maps for areas of interest at certain times were posted and maps for the other theaters of war were kept up to date from the news point of view. The sources of information on this posting activity were reports of Fifth Air Force Advance Echelon, Fifth Bomber Reports, Fifth Fighter Reports, Directorate of Intelligence Bi-weekly Summaries and tho\rough personal contact with the Australian forces. These maps were used to keep the organization itself abreast of developments and besides as a model for the Squadron Intelligence Sections, which served to keep the pilots acquainted with the dangers of the territory into which they were flying and also certain sections on the route to be avoided when possible.

The Intelligence Section also undertook to acquaint flying personnel with native customs, areas inhabited by head hunter natives, and the simple principles and rudiments of escape from the jungle should they crash land. This was accomplished by arranging lectures by old residents of New Guinea for the flying personnel, distributing booklets on the subject and individual discussions.

In many instances of assignments of missions to new dropping areas and aerodromes to which pilots had never flown, the intelligence section assembled all available photographs, aerial photo graphs of the region, maps, diagrams and information that would be of assistance in locating the place and advising the pilots of the airport or dropping area situation. In some instances this required talking to several special sources of information some of which had to be hunted down. From this activity was born the idea for a Troop Carrier Pilots Map, which was printed and since has been distributed to all troop carrier groups and squadrons serving in New Guinea.

In addition, the Intelligence Sections have maintained close surveillance of all censorship violations and conduct of a subversive nature. It has been the good fortune of this group that no major incidents have occurred; routine censorship violations have been dealt with by reprimands and punishment under AW 104.

The Combat Intelligence Section of this group, upon its transfer to APO 922, continued in some measure the work being down in the forward area such as posting situation maps and watching developments and the progress of the war in all theaters.

In addition to this activity, the task of republishing and making over the Route Guides in process of assembling by the 317th Troop Carrier Group when it was replaced by the 374th. Approximately fifty-five copies of the Route Guide were transferred to this organization and immediately all sources of information on airports were sought out, contacted, and arrangements made for the amendments, additions, and corrections in airports in Australia and the Northern Islands to be sent regularly to the group. In turn the information so received was passed on to the squadrons and each squadron was instructed and assisted in the development of a system for making the additions and corrections in each copy of the Route Guide assigned to them. Well over one thousand entries have been made by the Squadron Intelligence Sections in each copy of the Route Guides they maintain.

A shortage in the number of copies existed from the very start of our operations due to the increased number of planes flown by each squadron so the task of making thirty additional copies was undertaken, using newer, more up-to-date aerodrome maps in black and white. The survey of aerodromes made by the R.A.A.F. in the northeastern area was utilized as the source for the new maps. As the making of the thirty new Route Guides progressed the original guides were entirely re-edited so that all guides resulted in being completely uniform. During this conversion every available complete guide was kept in use and assigned to a plane for the pilot's use. The former loose leaf binders were discarded and a contact binder put in use - which is the standard Technical Order Binder of the Army Air Force.

In addition to the Route Guides the work of supplying maps was undertaken and a special accordion folder was designed to hold the sections of the Australian Aeronautical Maps included in the bag containing the Route Guide. On these maps has been drawn the courses, distances, and radio beams.

The object of this section has been to furnish to each plane upon departure a kit containing all the information possible for the completion of the mission; in the Route Guide information on over seven hundred airports in Australia and the Northern Islands; the kit of maps showing terrain, courses, distances, and radio beams for the territory to be covered in reaching the airport assigned.

The Health of the Group

During the months of October, November, December, 1942 and January, 1943, while the crews of the 6th, 21st, 22nd and 33rd Squadrons were billeted and rationed at Arcadia, medical facilities were inadequate. Medical supplies were non-available in that area, the nearest facilities being at the 10th Evacuation Hospital, a distance of six miles. The latrines did not comply with Army Regulations. Water supply was inadequate both as to quantity and quality. It was frequently impossible to shower, either because the

Natives at Bena Bena carry the wing flown in under the belly of another C-47 for installation on the damaged "Flamingo".

water tanks were empty or because the water was too hot for comfort having run through pipes exposed to the sun. Food consisted mainly of bully beef and hash.

During the 10 days the 6th Squadron stayed at Arcadia in October, 1942, it is reported that meals were served but twice a day and that within three days of arrival epidemic diarrhea was evident, affecting at one time or another fifty percent of the personnel. Patients hitch-hiked to the 10th Evacuation Hospital where they were given sulfaguanidine powder. Because of lack of transportation, flying personnel had to hitch-hike from Arcadia to the strip three miles distant.

On November 13, 1942, the flying personnel of the 6th Squadron moved its organizational equipment to newly selected camp site at Wards Drome. Sleep was interrupted during this period at least one out of five nights by enemy bombing raids. After planes and crews had completed their last missions for the day, personnel, including pilot officers, pitched their tents and dug slit trenches. Medical attention in the 6th Squadron in those early days in New Guinea consisted of a detachment of four enlisted men with meager first aid equipment. Epidemic diarrhea continued. Sanitary measures were deplorable and the first latrine was not in use until 20 November, 1942. Water supply was still a problem because of lack of transportation and the necessity for hauling all the water. Between 13 November, 1942, and 1 December, 1942, an open mess tent was pitched and showers were constructed. Water transportation was improved so that water was available 74% of the time.

On 1 December, 1942, the ground echelon of the 6th Squadron arrived in New Guinea and the squadron began to function as a unit once more. At this time sanitary conditions were unsatisfactory, there being but one latrine, poor garbage disposal, an unworkable soakage pit, and a mess tent too small to accommodate the troops. Water was also being improperly chlorinated. By requisition medical supplies were made available and with proper recommendations from the Medical Department improvements began at once. During the month of December, the water problem was gradually solved by obtaining transportation facilities. The food supply improved in quality but there was still a lack of fresh meat, fresh and canned fruits, fresh vegetables and milk. Preventative medicine was limited to vaccination of personnel, supervision of sanitation projects, moss inspection, tested chlorination of water, and mosquito elimination measures. Disturbance of sleep through bombing raids still continued during the month of December, 1942.

Upon the arrival of the ground echelon of the 33rd Squadron in New Guinea, on 28 December, 1942, construction of necessary camp facilities, including a First Aid Station was started at once. The food and water supply situation of the 33rd Squadron was comparable during this period to that of the 6th Squadron.

In the Group Quarterly Medical Report submitted on 1 January, 1943, the Medical Department reported three types of dermatitis prevalent. The most prevalent was the common heat rash. Another was a papule pustular dermatitis caused by secondary infection of the heat rash. The third was a localized urticarial dermatitis which follows the bite of an insect. Malaria was also reported as a serious problem despite attempts at suppressive treatment. Even as early as December, 1942, after a stay of two months, there was an incidence of 3% with the possibility that this figure would rise with the rainy season. The dysentery and diarrhea were prevalent, nearly all personnel becoming subject to them at one time or another. Paregoric, Kaopectate, and sulfaguanidine controlled most cases, but it was necessary to hospitalize about 10%, a large number of the hospitalized cases being of the Shiga type.

During January and February, 1943, Group Headquarters, 21st and 22nd Squadrons arrived in New Guinea, establishing camp sites at Wards Drome. Group Headquarters messed with the 33rd Squadron. The 21st and 22nd Squadrons built screened mess halls with concrete floors and put in grease traps to care for kitchen wastes. Concrete inclined plane incinerators were built for garbage disposal and regulation latrines were established as soon as possible. Both squadrons obtained piped water from a large tank located on a hill in their area. By March, 1943, all four squadrons as well as Group Headquarters had the advantage of piped water for bathing purposes. Drinking water was delivered by truck to conveniently located Lister bags and was then chlorinated.

By April, 1943, supplementary rations from the mainland having become available, the food situation was satisfactory both as to quality and quantity of food.

Mosquito control continued to be an disturbing problem during the period January, 1943, to April, 1943. Respiratory diseases were infrequent; even the common cold was seldom encountered. The venereal rate was also very low. As of 1 April, 1943, there were two cases of syphilis in the 22nd Squadron, one having been under treatment for several months and the other a "new" case developed from contact on the mainland.

From 21 December, 1942, to 20 March, 1943, the group had 2.1% days lost due to illness and 2.5% days lost due to all causes including illness. Hospital cases were cared for by the 10th Evacuation Hospital and the 171st Station Hospital at Koko Mission.

A group dentist was assigned 18 March, 1943. One surgeon, already replaced, was relieved from duty to return to the United States for training at the School of Aviation Medicine.

During the period April, 1943, to July, 1943, the 6th Squadron constructed a new dispensary. It was raised five feet above the ground, completely screened, and was provided with running water. Two pyramidal tents joined together constituted its roof. The 33rd Squadron lined its dispensary with celotex. Each of the squadrons during this period had set up an adequate and smoothly functioning dispensary. Also during this period one incinerator was constructed for the use of the group, dispensing with the four smaller ones.

Malaria control measures were also continued during the same quarter. High grass was cut and burned over all camp sites. Drainage ditches were dug where necessary and all stagnant water in the area was oiled repeatedly. The regulation requiring the wearing of long shirt sleeves and full length trousers was rigidly enforced.

In May and June, 1943, there was a marked increase in nasopharyngitis cases. This was attributed mainly to colds and infections resulting from leaves and furloughs to the mainland. Of a total of 207 man days lost due to naso-pharyngitis during this period, 140 were lost in June.

Since 26 March, 1943, the group had 24 hospital admissions for malaria, primary and recurrent cases included. A total of 540 days were lost due to malaria, and of this total 312 days were lost in June. During this period there was a slight improvement over the last quarter in percentage man days lost due to illness. 2% of the man days were lost due to all illnesses from 26 March, 1943, to 20 June, 1943, as compared with 2.1% man days lost in the preceding period. Fungus infection of the feet and groin remained at a high incidence, in spite of all medical treatment. The venereal rate was negligible, although two new cases of gonorrhea contracted on the mainland were reported.

Recommendations from the Squadron Surgeons through the Group Surgeon were made to the Group Commander for the evacuation of several of our personnel who were considered medically unfit for further duty in the combat area. These cases were severe psycho neurotics showing a tendency to complete breakdown, or malaria cases with one or more relapses. One case of aero-otitis was also recommended for evacuation.

During the period April, 1943, to July, 1943, the medical department notes many of our pilots and other personnel were beginning to show signs of fatigue and irritability because of long, continuous service in the theater. In May, 1943, all group planes were checked for TBA first aid equipment, shortages having been requisitioned and replaced. Folding and basket type litters were also placed on requisition to bring plane equipment up to TBA allowances. During this period one medical enlisted man was detailed to the Australian School for Malaria Control. Six of our medical officers took turns on detached service in forward areas occasioned by a dearth of medical officer personnel in New Guinea.

During the period July, 1943, to October, 1943, trouble with the group incinerator was experienced. The concrete cracked and the walls caved in after one month of operation. A non-commissioned officer and a detail of men were assigned to the care and maintenance of the incinerator and trash pile. During the period there was a reduction in man days lost on account of malaria, from 540 man days during the previous period to 353. The percentage of man days lost due to all illnesses for the period was 2%. The venereal disease rate remained negligible. Toward the end of the period, 13 officers and 20 enlisted men were evacuated to the United States upon the recommendation of the Group Commander. These men had served an average of 22 months overseas and had accumulated an average of 585 combat hours and 204 combat missions. An ambulance with one medical officer and two enlisted men was maintained daily at Wards Drome during this period. At night a medical officer was on call. This duty was rotated among the four squadrons.

During the first week of October, 1943, the 6th, 22nd, and 33rd Squadrons, as well as Group Headquarters, moved to APO 922, taking over the camp area previously occupied by the 317th Troop Carrier Group. The camp area is located approximately one mile east of Garbutt Field and two miles west of the city of Townsville. the area is flat, treeless, and dusty. Some of the men are housed in wooden buildings; others are living in unscreened pyramidal tents with wooden floors. Each squadron maintains its own dispensary in a wooden building in or near squadron headquarters. Water supply and sewage disposal is furnished by the City of Townsville. All drinking water is chlorinated before use. Food is obtained through the Base Section 2 Quartermaster. All three squadrons, both officer and enlisted personnel, have deemed it desirable to supplement their rations from individual contributions.

Medical supplies are easily obtained from Base Section 2 Medical Supply Depot, and from the 12th and 13th Station Hospital pharmacies. Hospital cases are sent to the 12th Station Hospital located in the City of Townsville, or to the 13th Station Hospital located approximately three miles southeast of the city. The 44th General Hospital replaced the 12th Station Hospital in February, 1944.

A small emergency first-aid station is maintained in the hangar at Garbutt Field for first-aid treatment to those on duty at the airdrome. An ambulance with a driver and first-aid man is present at the drome 24 hours daily. The group medical officer of the day is rotated among the squadron medical officers. He is present at the field during duty hours, and remains on call in the camp area at night after 1800, emergency calls are cared for in the 22nd Squadron dispensary.

During the period October, 1943, and January, 1944, 11 of the pilots and crew members with long overseas service and combat time were returned to the United States because of flying fatigue. The 11 men had an average of 808 hours flying time in the Southwest Pacific area of which 641.6 hours were combat time. They also had an average of 245 combat missions.

Man days lost due to malaria increased during this period as a result of recurrences of old cases following discontinuance of routine Atabrine ministration. Venereal disease also increased, especially among the officers, since moving to this area. With the marked reduction in days lost due to diarrhea, however, the total man days lost due to all diseases and injuries remained at 2%.

Although the flying hours of pilots and crew members are longer at this station, there is not the usual hazard of enemy interception that was encountered at APO 929. Weather hazards are greater however, and this together with long over-water flights causes manifestations of flying fatigue to appear almost as frequently as in New Guinea.

At Archer Field, 21st Squadron maintains its medical section in conjunction with Headquarters and Headquarters Squadron, Fifth Air Force. Captain Arthur V. Simmang, flight surgeon of the 21st Squadron and 5 enlisted men use the equipment and dispensary of Headquarters and Headquarters Squadron, as well as to help operate the dispensary. The dispensary is well equipped to handle all routine cases and also minor emergencies; if the necessity should arrive, twenty patients could be bedded in two wards, which are at present not utilized. Hospital patients are usually sent either to the 105th General Hospital or the 42th General Hospital, both at APO 923.

In addition to the routine medical duties, the medical detachment shares with Headquarters and Headquarters Squadron the responsibility of handling the arrival and disposition to hospitals of air evacuation patients.

RELIGION

Prior to March, 1943, there were no organized religious services for the group. While the 21st and 22nd Squadrons were stationed on the mainland at Archer Field and Essendon Drome respectively, personnel usually attended services at churches in neighboring communities. From October, 1942, to February, 1943, personnel had access to the chapel at Garbutt Field. In the early days in New Guinea, Catholic personnel usually attended services at the 27th Air Depot Group. Protestant personnel would journey to Port Moresby.

The first religious services for the group were held in New Guinea, 18 March, 1943. By arrangement with Colonel Paul H. Prentiss, the Group Commander and Major Fred M. Adams, the commanding officer of the 21st Squadron, the Mess Hall of the 21st Squadron was designated as the temporary Group Church. Chaplain John R. A. Maguire, then of the 27th Air Depot Group, conducted the first Catholic mass at 7:30 p.m. 18 March, 1943. Chaplain William Beebe of the 90th Bomb Group, conducted the first Protestant services the same day at 6:15 p.m.. Thereafter, until the end of June, 1943, services were held each Sunday at the 21st Squadron under the supervision of Chaplains Maguire and Beebe.

On 18 June, 1943, Chaplain John R. A. Maguire was assigned to the group. Shortly thereafter, the Catholic services were conducted in the 22nd Squadron Mess Hall at approximately the same time as the Protestant services. Chaplain Beebe continued to conduct Protestant services in the 21st Squadron Mess Hall.

A survey of denominations represented in the group reveals the following approximate breakdown: Protestant - 60%; Catholic - 35%; Jewish and others - 5%.

During the month of July, 1943, in Chaplain Beebe's absence on leave, Protestant services were held by Chaplain Monroe of the 871st Airborne Engineers and Chaplain Ray of the 872nd Airborne Engineers.

During July, August and September, 1943, while the 375th Troop Carrier Group, the 65th and 66th Squadrons of the 403rd Troop Carrier Group, and the 433rd Troop Carrier Group, were successively attached to the 374th, the Group Chaplain, assisted by Chaplain Beebe, also administered to the spiritual needs of their personnel.

Throughout the month of August, 1943, the Group Chaplain made weekly flights to the 2nd Air Task Force at Tsilli Tsilli; saying masses and hearing confessions, not only of American units of the task force, but also for detachments of Australian infantry and anti-aircraft personnel. On 16 August, 1943, Chaplain Maguire, together with Chaplain Shaw of the 35th Fighter Group, officiated at the funeral of 1st Lts. James F. Miles and Enoch P. Burley, T/Sgt. Edward R. Berringer and Pvt. John Knoka, Jr., all of whom had been killed in action the day before. It may rightly be said that the 374th not only brought to the troops in the forward areas the necessities for preserving their material life, but also brought them spiritual aid.

Upon arrival of the 6th, 22nd and 33rd Squadrons at Garbutt Field, in October, 1943, the Chaplain was able to conduct services for those Squadrons and Group Headquarters personnel at the Chapel of St. Theresa the Little Flower, Patroness of Fliers, for Catholic worship. Services for the Protestant personnel were conducted by Chaplain Jewett of the 45th Service Group in the Post Exchange. The Protestant services were held at 9 a.m.; Catholic masses were said at 9 a.m. and 6:30 p.m. on Sundays.

In November, 1943, due to the absence of the Group Chaplain on temporary duty Champlain Charles Quest of the 4th Air Depot said mass and the Reverend Frank Rush of the Staff of the Sacred Heart Cathedral, Townsville, said another mass.

About the 11th of December, 1943, Pfc. Louis Hillenbrand was assigned as the Chaplain's assistant and about a week later work was started on an office for the Chaplain. A portion of the Group Supply Building was partitioned off, making an inner an outer office.

On the 26th of December, 1943, the Chaplain paid an official visit to the 21st Troop Carrier Squadron at Archer Field and was able to talk personably with the majority of the officers and men. He found that the religious services were being conducted at a very inconvenient hour and suggested to the Chaplain of the Fifth Air Force that evening services be held to enable both the flying personnel and ground personnel to attend. During the Chaplain's absence in Brisbane, Chaplains Kropheski and Cavanaugh, casual officers awaiting assignment, said a mass each on New Years Day and the Sunday following.

Up until the end of January, 1944, the chaplain was without his "outfit" due to the fact that the 317th Troop Carrier Group had taken the items with them. A new "outfit" was issued so that on Sunday the 30th January, hymns were sung for the first time since our arrival on the mainland at the nine o'clock mass.

SPECIAL SERVICES

While the 21st Squadron was stationed at Archer Field and the 22nd Squadron at Essendon Drome and Garbutt Field, there was no organized Special Service program. The squadron special services officer equipped day rooms with books, magazines, pianos, radios and ping pong tables; athletic equipment was requisitioned and made available to personnel upon request.

During the first months after their movement to New Guinea, little or no attention was given by the 6th and 33rd Squadrons to an organized recreational program. Most of the daylight hours were devoted to hard intensive work, and at night lack of lighting facilities discouraged further diversional activity.

In the last months of 1942, there were several old broken down movie projectors in the Moresby area. The 6th Squadron occasionally loaded a truck with men and ventured through dust and mud for miles until they located a camp where a picture was being shown.

Especially deserving of mention was "Guinea Gold", the publication which passed from hand to hand among the men. It began to be distributed among the units in the Moresby area during November, 1942. In tribute, it can be said that the "Guinea Gold" achieved a reputation for accuracy and reliability among highly skeptical men.

The first squadron to show movies was the 33rd; its first movie was projected on a screen inside the squadron mess hall early in March, 1943. Immediately thereafter, a permanent screen was built alongside the Mess Hall from native logs. The projection booth was built from dunnage, native logs and sheet iron.

During March, 1943, the 33rd Squadron built a day room at the end of the Mess Hall from scraps of lumber obtained from the Fifth Air Force lumber yard. The 6th, 21st and 22nd Squadrons used their Mess Halls as day rooms, equipping them with radios and phonographs.

The 22nd Squadron obtained a projector the latter part of March, 1943, and began showing films three times each week. In June, 1943, the 6th Squadron began to show films three nights during the week.

The officers of the four squadrons pooled their efforts and resources and constructed commodious, airy grass huts which they used as clubs. The 6th Squadron had completed its club during January, 1943. The club was also used as an officers' mess. The 21st and 22nd Squadrons opened their clubs during the latter part of March, 1943. The 33rd Squadron had its gala opening a week or ten days after the great air raid of April 12, 1943. The Group Headquarters Mess Hall served as an Officers' Club after March, 1943. These clubs were invaluable as the only recreational facilities for the flying officers of the group.

A Group Headquarters Day Room in the form of a grass hut 40 feet by 10 feet was constructed by means of native labor for headquarters enlisted personnel the latter part of July, 1943. At the same time, the Group Theater was completed on a site adjacent to the day room. The 22nd Squadron discontinued its open air theater, lending its projector to Group Headquarters. The Group Theater was considered one of the best in New Guinea. Much credit for its construction must be given to Captain Marvin M. Scott who planned, supervised and improvised its many details. Its stage was 40 feet by 20 feet and was constructed of hardwood. The front curtain was a draw curtain made of burlap and another burlap curtain covered the motion picture screen located at the back of the stage. The stage was amply provided with footlights, top lights, and floodlights. Some of the personages and shows to appear on the stage were:

17 July, 1943 - Joe E. Lewis

5 August, 1943 - U.S.O. Unit #61. Harry Ross, The Heis Brothers, and S. Gustofson.

9 August, 1943 - Ray Bolger and Little Jack Little

11 August, 1943 - 857th Colored Engineers Jive Bank

15 August, 1943 - Lansing Hatfield and Edwin MacArthur

13 August, 1943 - 5th Special Service Unit Show

Crowds estimated at from 1,000 to 3,000 attended these stage shows. The theater was an open air installation, and no seats were provided for the audience. The projection booth was built 9 feet off the ground, and was 78 feet from the screen, which was 18 feet by 20 feet in size. The latest films and pictures were shown on Sunday, Wednesday, and Friday nights. Cpl. Stamler (Group Headquarters) and Cpl. Costello (33rd Squadron) were the operators. The motion picture projector was placed in operation May, 1943, and was still functioning when the Group moved south the early part of October, 1943. After arriving at APO 922, the projector was loaned to the 45th Service Group.

The group entered the 33rd Troop Carrier Squadron softball team in the Port Moresby Special Service Softball tournament. After winning the KOKI League championship, they won seven straight games, and were scheduled to play for the finals in the New Guinea softball tournament when the schedule was interrupted by our troop movement orders.

August, 1943, the group entered seven volleyball teams in the Air League of the Special Services volleyball tournament. The 21st Troop Carrier Squadron enlisted men's team won the league. They were awarded a silver trophy.

September 1943, a group Ping Pong tournament was held, Each squadron arranged an elimination contest to select its representatives in the Group play-offs. The final winner in the Enlisted Men's section played off with the best player in the Officer's Division. A Headquarters Officer was declared the Ping Pong Champion in the group. The play-off took place in the Headquarters Enlisted Men's day room. Red Cross girls served refreshment to an appreciative audience.

In October, 1943, the group moved down to the Australian mainland. Volleyball courts, a baseball field, horseshoe pitching areas were laid out, and the sports indulged in. Base Section #2, ran a tennis tournament; the group had 24 entries, and Cpl. Thompson of Group Headquarters reached the semi-finals. The 374th also entered some men in the Inter-Allied Track Meet held at the Townsville Sports Ground. None of group entrants reached the finals.

A group horseshoe pitching tournament was canceled because of the rainy season. Major Pearson coached the basketball team which entered the Base Section #2 tournament. This team finished second in its league, and thus was qualified to enter into the championship playoffs. It was defeated early in the tournament by th team that eventually won the championship.

Captain Simpson coached the group baseball team, which incidently was probably the first army baseball team to fly to play a game. In December, 1943, the team was flown to Charters Towers (90 miles) to meet the local Air Corps team there. The baseball team won the title in its league, and met the 44th General Hospital team in the finals. The play-off on 16 April, 1944, resulted in a defeat for the Group Team.

The Group day room at Garbutt Field was located in Barracks #96. The group barber and dentist also occupied sections of the same building. The day room had a very good library, a ping pong table, phonograph, and ample writing desks and chairs, also a number of lounge chairs. The day room was also used for various squadron meetings, and special service meetings. In one corner of the day room there was an equipment room. This building was adjacent to the 22nd Troop Carrier Squadron Area, but was used by all squadrons.

The 21st Squadron, since its return to the mainland conducted a day room for enlisted men at Archer Field. It was equipped with a piano, radio and a substantial library. A Post Theater provides motion pictures three nights each week.

New Guinea natives in ceremonial jungle war gear.

CHAPTER IV

1944 - 1945

Narrative of Events

February, 1944

On 20 February, 1944, the 21st Troop Carrier Squadron instituted its "Daily Night Courier" run of one ship from APO 923 to APO 929.

During the month a Group Post Exchange was placed in operation with 1st Lt. A. K. Faller as Post Exchange Officer. The availability of Coca Cola, chocolate candies and fruit juices has made the Post Exchange a daily stopping place for personnel of the Group.

The 33rd Troop Carrier Squadron sustained its first loss of personnel since 12 May, 1943, when on 2 February, 1944, VHCJM, "Shack Trooper", was missing on a flight to Milne Bay.

A number of Group planes and crews engaged in paratroop maneuvers at APO 923 and at Cairns, Queensland.

March, 1944

At Garbutt Field on 15, 16 and 17 March, 1944, Brigadier General Paul H. Prentiss made presentations of awards and decorations to 26 officers and 109 enlisted men of the 6th, 22nd and 33rd Squadrons.

During the month, group planes participated in Secret hauling missions in Western Australia and Northern Territory.

On 28 March, 1944, the Townsville area was swept by a violent 24 hour gale and rainstorm of unprecedented fury. The rain was blown into buildings and a number of tents fell. Garbutt Field was closed out for the day.

Group planes continued to engage in paratroop maneuvers.

```
           HEADQUARTERS
         ADVANCE ECHELON
          FIFTH AIR FORCE
          APO 713 UNIT #I
```
AG 201.22   2 April, 1944.
SUBJECT: Commendation.
TO   :   All Fifth Air Force Units, New Guinea Area.

1. The following commendation received from the Commanding General, 6th Army, in regards to the recent operations, is published for the Information of all concerned, and is to be posted on all command, wing, group and squadron bulletin boards:
TO: CG ADVON FIVE
FROM: ADV CP 6TH ARMY
CITE: WF 124
MY HEARTY CONGRATULATIONS AND THANKS TO YOU AND THE OFFICERS AND MEN OF YOUR COMMAND FOR A SUPERB PERFORMANCE IN SUPPORT OF THE OPERATIONS AGAINST MOMOTE COMMA LORENGAU AND THE SEADLER HARBOR PD THE GALLANTRY AND INDOMITABLE SPIRIT DISPLAYED BY ALL RANKS MERIT THE HIGHEST PRAISE PD THE CONDUCT OF ALL WHO PARTICIPATED IS IN KEEPING WITH THE FINEST TRADITIONS OF OUR ARMY PD   SGD KRUEGER"

1. The undersigned desires to convey to all concerned his heartiest congratulations for their part in these aggressive attacks against the enemy.

/s/ Ennis C. Whitehead
/t/ ENNIS C. WHITEHEAD,
Major General, United States Army,
Deputy Air Force Commander.

April, 1944

The movement by air of the 33rd Troop Carrier Squadron from APO 922 to APO 929 was accomplished during the period 14 April through 16 April, 1944. Except for one officer and three enlisted men who were left at APO 922, as a rear echelon, all squadron personnel, their baggage and personnel equipment, vehicles and organizational equipment weighing 45,415 pounds, were transported without mishap by the squadrons own planes. There still remains at APO 922, 181,580 pounds of squadron equipment, of which 24,600 pounds will be shipped by air and the remaining 57,980 pounds will be moved by boat.

On 14 April, at APO 929, a taxying plane assigned to the 33rd Troop Carrier Squadron collided with another plane belonging to the same organization, severely damaging both aircraft. The cause of the accident was a failure of the hydraulic system while engines were being run up. Both aircraft were transferred to the 478th Service Squadron.

On 25 April, Private Irdle V. Reece, was accidentally shot and fatally wounded by Corporal Vilmar A. Wicklund while both men were playing with their sidearms and jokingly threatening each other. Both men were members of the 22nd Troop Carrier Squadron.

On 25 April the Group Post Exchange was moved from its location across the street from Group Headquarters to a position within the area occupied by the enlisted men of the two squadrons remaining at Garbutt Field.

The final game of the Base Section II Baseball League was played at Bertrandias Field, Sunday 16 April, 1944, for the championship of the Base Section. The 374th Troop Carrier Group team lost to the 44th General Hospital by a score of 9 to 8.

Since the 374th Troop Carrier Group has been located at APO 922 it has been considered as a pool for plane replacements for the 54th Troop Carrier Wing. However, all planes assigned to the Group have been reassigned to the Squadrons. On 8 April a group pool was formed upon the receipt of 16 C-47A airplanes from the Fifth Air Force Reception Center, APO 922. During the remainder of the month the number of planes maintained by this pool fluctuated widely. Garbutt Field could not provide parking space for all the planes assigned to the group and on 13 April, 1944, the planes in the Group Pool were removed to the Ross River Strip. A constant guard was maintained over these planes. Headquarters furnished men for this guard from 14 April to 19 April inclusive. On 22 April, all C-47A aircraft in the pool were transferred to the Fifth Air Force Service Command for modification, and the use of the Ross River Strip was discontinued.

May, 1944

On 1 May, 1944, the 6th Squadron detachment at Mackay, Queensland was relieved by a detachment of the 22nd Squadron.

On 5 May, 1944, the 6th and 22nd Squadrons, together with Group Headquarters, sent detachments, together with all serviceable aircraft to operate out of APO 713 where they transported men and supplies to Hollandia, Tadji, Wakde, and other points. The 21st Squadron sent detachment to APO 929 from 5 May, 1944, to 16 May, 1944.

From 5 May to 31 May, 1944, the Squadrons hauled the following amounts of freight: 6th: 5,169,394 pounds; 22nd: 5,003,469 pounds; 33rd: 1,093,395 pounds. Total: 11,266,258 pounds. The

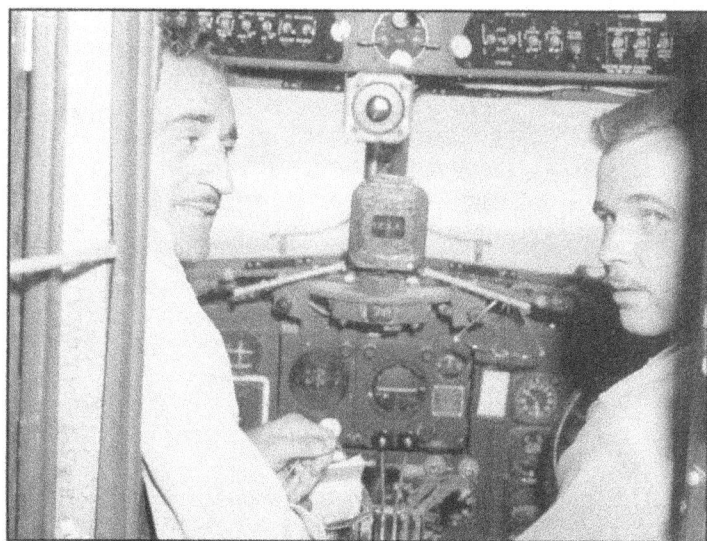

Col. Ed Imparato and Maj. Philip Hallem flying between Leyte and Manila, April, 1945.

largest amount of freight was hauled on 7 May, 1944, when the 6th carried 501,860 pounds and the 22nd carried 513,320 pounds, a total of 1,015,180 pounds. On 27 May 1944, the greatest number of trips was accomplished, 160 trips by 29 aircraft. The greatest number of aircraft in operation in a single day were 35 on 20 May, 1944 and 35 on 31 May, 1944.

During the month of May, 1944, the Group broke its all-time hauling record, having carried 18,339,207 pounds and having flown 1,289,513 miles. The 33rd Squadron alone had hauled 6,951,103 pounds.

On 13 May, 1944, Headquarters, Fifth Air Force, under authority of W. D. letter AG 322, dated 4 April, 1944, subject "Reorganization and Authorization of Combat Crews for certain Army Air Forces Units" authorized each Troop Carrier Squadron a total of 32 Combat Crews with an increased allowance for promotions to higher grades of both Officers and enlisted men, in proportion to the increment of combat personnel as assigned.

By authority of par 5 and 6 letter 31 May, 1944, Headquarters, Fifth Air Force, the previous allowance of 52 aircraft for the group was increased to 64 in number, with 6 additional aircraft allowed as a reserve.

On 3 May, 1944, official notification was received by the group that status of Lt. Richard B. Stanton, listed as missing from the 6th Squadron on 2 September, 1943, was changed to killed as of 2 September, 1943.

On 16 May, 1944, the 33rd Squadron transferred operations from Wards Drome to Jackson Drome.

The 374th Troop Carrier Group was commended by the Commanding General of the Fifth Air Force and by the Commanding General of the 54th Troop Carrier Wing for operations performed in New Guinea during the month of May. A copy of the commendation follows:

21 May 1944

From Wewak, a principal Japanese stronghold on the spine of New Guinea's Owen Stanley range, MacArthur bypassed Aitape which was 100 miles west of Wewak on the north coast of New Guinea. Aitape was lightly defended. MacArthur next executed a massive air attack and amphibious assault on Hollandia at Homboldt Bay and cleaned the last major Japanese force from New Guinea. There remained only the small but well-defended island of Wakde and the island of Biak to clear New Guinea of all active defending Japanese forces. Wakde was leveled by naval bombardment and artillery from battleships and cruisers. Biak Island had two airfields in fair condition and beautiful beaches. It is truly an island paradise.

As soon as Biak was cleared, the 374th moved its headquarters there. No sooner did we get established on Biak when a call from the Air Force commander of all forces in Biak, Major General Clement Mullens, summoned the group commander to his headquarters. He was informed the 374th was being assigned responsibility for Sorida Air Field on Biak. The 374th operation in support of the Hollandia operation resulted in a commendation for the group. The citation is as follows:

HEADQUARTERS
ADVANCE ECHELON
FIFTH AIR FORCE
APR 713, UNIT 1

AG 201.11   21 May, 1944.

SUBJECT: Commendation.

TO : Commanding General, 54th Troop Carrier Wing, AOT 713, Unit 1. (Copy to: Commanding General, Fifth Air Force, APO 925 for transmittal to 374th Troop Carrier Group.)

1. At the close of operations on 20 May, troop carrier efforts in New Guinea, reinforced by part of the 374th Troop Carrier Group, had delivered 2,000 plane loads of men, fuel, ammunition, and other supplies into the HOLLANDIA area during the first twenty (20) days of May. During the major portion of these operations from NADZAB, FINSCHAFER, and RADJI the combat crews had bad flying weather and extremely poor airdrome facilities at TADJI and HOLLANDIA. Despite these operating handicaps, the loss of personnel and equipment has been negligible.

2. The above superior performance of the troop carrier units engaged indicates a high state of training and a superior will to "go through" and complete the job. This headquarters desires to commend you and all the units of your Wing for making possible by the air supply of HOLLANDIA, the capture of another forward airdrome on WAKDE ISLAND.

3. It is requested that the above be brought to the attention of all subordinate units and noted by you and returned to this headquarters for inclusion in your 201 file.

s/ Ennis C. Whitehead
t/ ENNIS C. WHITEHEAD,
Major General, USA,
Deputy Command,
Fifth Air Force.

201.11   1st Ind.
HEADQUARTERS, 54TH TROOP CARRIER WING, APO 713, Unit #1, 24 May 1944

TO: Commanding Officer, 374 Troop Carrier Group, APO 713.

1. It is desired that this commendation be brought to the attention of every member of your command.

2. The commanding General, 54th Troop Carrier Wing, desires to add his personal commendation and appreciation for the excellent work accomplished.

3. The commendation from the Deputy Commander, Fifth Air Force, brings out very clearly how essential the operations of

this organization are to the war effort. It is hoped that every member of this command will realize the importance of his efforts and take just pride in the work that he is performing which is so necessary to the fulfillment of the mission of the command as a whole.

s/ Warren R. Carter
t/ WARREN R. CARTER,
Brig Gen, USA,
Commanding

June, 1944

On 10 June a new air route was pioneered over Dutch New Guinea. Major Myron C. Grimes of the 21st Squadron piloted the exploring ship over what is probably the largest unexplored territory in the world. Three passable air routes were discovered through the towering, snow-capped Oranjo Mountains from Merauke to Hollandia and other advanced Allied bases. On 26 June several planes and extra crews from this group were placed on detached service at Cairns, Queensland, to fly between Cairns and Hollandia via Nerauke over the newly discovered routes. These planes returned from detached service on 28 and 29 June.

The group detachment at APO 713 completed its mission with the 54th Troop Carrier Wing and returned to this station on 11 June. During the period 5 May through 11 June planes of the 374th Troop Carrier Group on detached service with the 54th Troop Carrier Wing carried 13,562,959 pounds of freight and personnel and flew 897,620 miles.

Per General order No. 7, Headquarters, Far East Air Forces (P), APO 925, dated 15 June, 1944, Headquarters, 374th Troop Carrier Group, 6th, 21st, 22nd and 33rd Troop Carrier Squadrons were relieved from assignment to the Fifth Air Force and assigned to the Far East Air Forces (P).

On 25 June, five planes from the 6th Squadron and three planes from the 22nd Squadron were ordered to Guadalcanal in the Solomons. Until the end of the month they performed flights between Guadalcanal and advanced bases in New Guinea.

On 27 June a plane assigned to the 6th Squadron plunged into the sea shortly after taking off from Lae, New Guinea. The copilot, 2nd Lt. Glenn M. Butler, who could not swim, was drowned after safely escaping from the sinking plane.

HEADQUARTERS
ADVANCE ECHELON
FIFTH AIR FORCE
APO 713 UNIT 1

14 June, 1944.

AG 201.22
SUBJECT: Commendation.

1. The following paraphrased message has been received by the Commander-in-Chief, Southwest Pacific Area, from General Marshall and Forwarded to this headquarters from Commanding General, Fifth Air Force:

PLEASE PASS ON MY THANKS AND CONGRATULATIONS TO KENNEY, KRUEGER, KINKAID, EICHELBERGER, AND THE DIVISION AND SEPARATE UNIT COMMANDERS CONCERNED. WITH THE CAPTURE OF MOKMER AIRFIELD I SEND YOU MY PERSONAL CONGRATULATIONS ON THE AITAPE-HOLLANDIA-MAFFIN BAY-BIAK CAMPAIGN WHICH HAS COMPLETELY DISORGANIZED THE ENEMY PLANS FOR THE SECURITY OF EASTERN MALAYSIA AND HAS ADVANCED THE SCHEDULE OF OPERATIONS BY MANY WEEKS. THE SUCCESSION OF SURPRISES EFFECTED AND THE SMALL LOSSES SUFFERED, THE GREAT EXTENT OF TERRITORY CONQUERED AND THE CASUALTIES INFLICTED ON THE ENEMY, TOGETHER WITH THE LARGE JAPANESE FORCES WHICH HAVE BEEN ISOLATED, ALL COMBINE TO MAKE YOUR OPERATIONS OF THE PAST ONE AND A HALF MONTHS MODELS OF STRATEGICAL AND TACTICAL MANEUVERS.

MARSHALL

1. The Deputy Commander wishes to further convey his appreciation to all units for their splendid performance which made these victories possible.

By command of Major General WHITEHEAD:
/s/ Merian C. Cooper
/t/ MERIAN C. COOPER,
Colonel, Air Corps,
Chief of Staff.

July, 1944

On 2 July a detachment from this group was sent on detached service to APO 713 to operate under the control of the 54th Troop Carrier Wing. The 21st Squadron was stationed at Nadzab and the 6th and 22nd Squadrons were stationed at Lae. The 22nd Squadron was to maintain ten planes and fly seven daily, the 6th and 21st to maintain fifteen planes and fly eleven. During the month of July these three Squadrons maintained a daily average of forty one aircraft, transported 3,099.28 tons of personnel and freight and flew 325,306 miles. Flights were made to all advanced bases, including the following places: The Admiralty Islands, Aitape, Hollandia, Owi, Biak and Neemfoor.

HEADQUARTERS
FIFTH AIR FORCE
APO 710

AG 201.22   11 July, 1944.
SUBJECT: Commendation.
TO : All Fifth Air Force Unit Commanders.

1. The following radiograms are published for the information of all concerned and are to be posted on all command, wing, group and squadron bulletin boards:

TO COMAF FIVE CMA COMAF THIRTEEN FROM KENNEY CITE ABLE XRAY THREE SEVEN EIGHT THREE NINE FOLLOWING MESSAGE RECEIVED QUOTE MY HEARTIEST CONGRATULATIONS TO THE FAR EASTERN AIR FORCES FOR THE SPLENDID EXECUTION OF THE NOEMFOOR OPERATION PD IT UPHELD THE BEST AIR TRADITION PD

MACARTHUR

TO COMMANDING GENERAL FIFTH AIR FORCE
FROM CG ALAMO FORCE OUR MSG NR WILLIAM TWO SIX FIVE SIX

MY SINCERE CONGRATULATIONS AND THANKS TO YOU AND THE OFFICERS AND MEN OF YOUR COMMAND FOR A SPLENDID PERFORMANCE IN SUPPORT OF OPERATIONS AGAINST NOEMFOOR PD AS IN THE PAST THE FIFTH AIR FORCE DISPLAYED A HIGH DEGREE OF SKILL CMA AND RESOURCEFULNESS PD PLEASE EXPRESS MY APPRECIATION TO ALL CONCERNED

2. In addition to the above, the undersigned desires to convey his heartiest congratulations to all ranks for the continued success in destroying the enemy.

/s/ Paul B. Wurtsmith
/t/ PAUL B. WURTSMITH,
Brigadier General, United States Army,
Deputy Commander.

Headhunters in the Lost Valley and Lt. Talman and the Cannibals

By M/Sgt. Glenn D. McMurray
from the book Moresby to Manila Via Troop Carrier

When the Army's main supply base moved to Hollandia, it was necessary to find a shorter route to the mainland of Australia. Leave personnel and special missions had to fly each day to Australia from Morotai, Biak, and the big base of Hollandia.

The logical route called for a straight flight to Merauke, Dutch New Guinea, and from there to Australia. But this route was dangerous. There were no apparent emergency landing grounds. Most of the route was over wild, unexplored country inhabited by cannibals. The Australian New Guinea Administration came to the rescue. They found a man, Squadron Leader O'Dea, who had flown a Ford trimotor plane into a 20-mile valley on this route five years ago. The valley was on a plateau 5500 feet above sea level about in the center of the proposed route and located near the headwaters of the Sepik River. In fact, Squadron Leader O'Dea had taken a native boy with him. The plan called for the boy to be flown into the valley. This would insure friendly reception by the cannibals.

Lt. Col. Joseph Anderson, executive officer of the 433rd Group, led a flight of four gliders, which were under the direction of Lt. Col. A. Felix DuPont, Jr. These gliders contained food, ammunition and heavy equipment sufficient to start a strip. Flying in and out of 12,000-foot mountain peaks with gliders is not easy. But the landing was made successfully on 17 October. The valley was found to be a regular paradise, untouched by any civilized human except O'Dea. The natives are all cannibals.

They rushed to the gliders, stopped in amazement as anybody would, then retreated. When they saw the native boy, they recognized him. (They thought he had been eaten by white men long ago.) Soon the whole village came out to welcome him. The Americans, 20 armed Papuan natives (who had been brought along as a precaution), Squadron Leader Leahy, a U.S. radio operator and an Air Force public relations officer, were well received. The natives, who had special adornments on both head and lower part of their body, put on a show for the men - dances and tribal rituals. Suddenly there was a shout and a neighboring cannibal tribe appeared for "war". But the sight of the gliders and the white men so frightened the neighboring tribe that an armistice apparently was declared.

Later two additional gliders were towed from Tadji to the valley. They contained an additional bulldozer and scraper. With this engineering equipment, a 3000-foot strip was constructed. It serves as an emergency strip in the route to Australia. The glider pilots, who were the first into the valley, were Lt. Benton V. Cornett, Flight Officer Bert C. Christiansen, Lt. Daniel T. Box, Jr., and Lt. Billy E. Powers.

The natives worked on the strip, receiving for their day's wages a teaspoon of salt which they valued much more than any other practical thing. Food was dropped to the Americans and Australians by Troop Carriers. Natives supplied pigs for fresh meat. Houses for the visitors were constructed of bamboo. Although no civilization had touched this valley, the people were found to have a set of laws designating right from wrong. set of laws designating right from wrong. Survival of the strongest was the prevailing law.

Five months before this, two other members of Troop Carriers - Lt. Ralph G. Talman, pilot, and Capt. J. Nixon-Smith, A.E.F., spent 15 days in unexplored headhunter country after being forced down in their plane. The plane crashed in native gardens at Mt. Michael near Aiyura, Papua. Natives, all dressed in wild, savage attire, finally were induced to right the overturned plane. They

Sgt. Klatt, 6th Squadron Line Chief.

thought it was a white man's god - one of the reasons why Lt. Talman and Capt. Nixon-Smith are alive today. Aided by natives, both men walked through the jungle for days. A section of Lt. Talman's diary, dated 31 May, describes in part his trip:

"Natives brought us a treat - ripe bananas.... Most of the time we are traveling through Kunai grass 10 feet tall. Stopped at 1030 hours, put up a shelter. Pitched chute (taken from plane) for protection against rain.... Lit a fire. We can now light a fire by using a stick and bamboo shoot with dry moss wood from the sago tree. Natives continually pawing over our stuff and have the 'gimmes'. Cannot understand our white skin and one old bastard seems to want to eat Capt. Smith.....Raining as usual, expect to be cold tonight, estimate we are 7000 feet high.... Slept in a cloud last night, with our hands on our guns as there is a definite war on between the various native villages along the route.

"At one time there were 16 natives and ourselves in one half-moon tent. One old boy had a human finger tied around his neck. Hope they are not getting any funny ideas.... Natives abandoned us at 1200 hours on 2 June. We tried to find our way but got lost even with compasses.... Very much lost today, waded through water up to our necks. The grass, ferns, jungle and cane so thick at times we could not see five feet ahead."

Lt. Talman and Capt. Smith finally walked to Port Romilly, where A.N.G.A.U. officers and men took them in and arranged for their rescue by a Catalina boat.

Life at Biak

By M/Sgt. Glenn D. McMurray
from his book Moresby to Manila Via Troop Carrier

Life at Biak was a study in contrasts. It started rough, remained rough for quite a while, and then ended in a real Hollywood-style "tropical island paradise".

Troop Carriers needed a base nearer the Philippines, the next objective. Biak was chosen. It is a coral island, about 52 miles by 36 miles, located about 75 miles from the equator in the Schouten Islands Group of the Netherlands East Indies.

Biak had been one of the more bitterly contested islands to be captured by the 41st Infantry Division. Japs had sneaked in reinforcements and had hidden them behind the ridges which line the shore for a mile back. The Nips waited until our infantry was ashore and then poured devastating fire into our ranks. Almost pushing us out. But a counter-attack, supported by air power, gave

374th Troop Carrier Group Headquarters, Biak Island, New Guinea, 1944. Group Commander Col. Edward T. Imparato on far left.

us another foothold and the infantry pushed in to take the western coastline, just opposite Owi Island, which was four miles away.

In fact the fighting was so bitter and the need for an airstrip so great that a landing was made on the tiny island, Owi. Here a strip, with two runways, was constructed and used until the infantry could make Biak secure. After being pushed from the coastline, the Japs scurried back into the hills and came out at night to raid our camps, kill stragglers, and make night patrolling a "must". When the Troop Carriers arrived, the Japs had been pushed along the coast where a defense perimeter had been set up to keep them from infiltrating the airstrips. General Warren R. Carter, commanding general at that time, selected a camp site just outside of the northern end of the defense perimeter.

There were no trails leading to the selected spot. An abandoned native village, which was to be torn down, marked the spot on the coastline. Its only entrance was by water. This village was situated at the bottom of a 75-foot ridge in the midst of a small clump of coconut trees, and the native houses were built out into the water on top of a coral-sandy beach.

This beach was to become a real "swimming hole", protected from sharks by a natural coral reef, about 300 yards from shore.

The main camp site was to be on top of this ridge, which was in the form of a plateau. Airplane observation showed that this particular spot was covered with heavy brush, but very few trees. An advance detail was sent to this spot to build a camp. Maj. Frederick Howard, assistant A-3, was in charge.

All camp material had been gathered by Capt. Maurice Sherman, who was Wing A-4 at that time. It was transported to the airstrip at Biak and stored there. The first step taken by the advance detail was to get a bulldozer and push, with the help of the area engineers, a road through virgin jungle to the camp site area.

Our very first night at the camp site brought the Japs. Our men killed several. A road block and a defense perimeter were set up. Guards were placed at outposts, while men worked. Maj. Arthur Roberts, air engineer assigned at this time to the Wing, was sent to the camp site and took charge. Working under extreme difficulties of jungle, brush, enemy fire, the work detail hacked and bulldozed a camp site, set up the main headquarters building, which was as large as that at Nadzab.

Using the headquarters building as living quarters, the men built the preliminary set-up of the camp. At this time an infantry platoon was assigned to protect the advance work detail. The remainder of headquarters personnel arrived. Everybody pitched into the work; enlisted men's quarters were made, officers' quarters built, more roads bulldozed from the jungle.

As if by magic, the camp site changed. It became a beautiful spot. The coral made wonderful roads; a large athletic field was cleared; a motion picture theater was built in a natural hollow, officers' and enlisted men's quarters were constructed with wooden or coral floors (logging operations produced sufficient lumber); water pipes were laid from a semi-salt-water well for showers; and electricity was wired to all parts of the camp. Large diesel engine generators provided the power.

The beach, which was the main recreational attraction, was next to receive attention. A bulldozer cleared away rough coral to make a path to a sand bar which was located about 50 feet from shore. This created a smooth path over the usually rough coral bottom and made a delightful swimming beach.

A raft of heavy timbers was constructed and placed on gasoline drums. Driftwood on the beach was cleared away by natives. The beach - the only usable one on Biak - became the Mecca not only of Troop Carriers but of many other units.

Weather in Biak is worthy of mention. Although the afternoons and late mornings were hot - so hot that the perspiration just poured off - the early evenings and nights were cool. Swimming served as a relief valve to the pressure of the heat. Food, at first, was better than usual as many American ships docked directly at the island. Many food items, including fresh meat, could be procured from these ships. But later, as the drive to capture the Philippines started, food became scarce.

Motion pictures, also came direct from the States to Biak. For the first time, the men were able to view some of the latest pictures, instead of two-year-old ones. This helped a great deal.

Caption William J. O'Shea took over command of Headquarters Squadron at Biak. Under his command, the enlisted men's section was equipped with concrete showers, a large concrete-floor mess hall, and a special Post Exchange, which boasted Coca-Cola and ice cream machines was constructed. Illuminated night basketball was introduced to overcome the exertion of playing in the daytime heat.

Remaining Troop Carrier groups, 375th, 433rd, 374th, and 21st Service Group, were located on Biak, with the latter group the nearest to the Wing. They, also, constructed their camps in similar style. In fact all camps on the island were above the ordinary.

A month after Wing had settled the infantry platoon which had been assigned to guard the area against raiding Japs was relieved. Guard duty was taken over by Wing men. The total score to date of writing has been: 105 Japs killed and 35 captured in this area by Wing personnel.

Effective 20 July 1944, the four squadrons of this group were reorganized in accordance with Table of Organization and Equipment 1-317, dated 12 May 1944 (a copy follows). Sixteen airplanes and thirty-two complete combat crews are authorized to place eighty men on duty requiring participation in regular and frequent aerial flights.

```
GENERAL ORDERS )              HEADQUARTERS
               )         FAR EAST AIR FORCES (P)
     No 77     )         APO 925 - 18 July 1944
```

REORGANIZATION OF TROOP CARRIER SQUADRONS

1. The following units will be reorganized, effective 20 July 1944, in accordance with Table of Organization and Equipment 1-317, 12 May 1944, without change of station of assignment:

TROOP CARRIER SQUADRONS
```
     6th     22nd
     21st    33rd
```

2. The above listed units will be reorganized in accordance with Table of Organization and Equipment quoted, less columns 15 and 26(Glider Flights) plus one (1) column 30 (Combat Crews). Authorized strength of each unit will be eighty-six (86) officers, one (1) warrant officer and two hundred fifty-eight (258) enlisted men. Officer and enlisted grades are authorized accordingly.

3. No personnel will be reduced in grade as a result of this action.

4. Overages in personnel will be absorbed by normal attrition. Equipment rendered excess will be absorbed in local stocks.

5. Report confirming reorganization will be radioed to this Headquarters without delay.

By command of Lieutenant General Kenney:

```
                         R. E. BEEBE,
                         Brigadier General, U.S. Army
OFFICIAL;                Chief of Air Staff

/s/ Perry C, Ragan,
    PERRY C. RAGAN,
    Colonel, A.G.D.,
    Air Adjutant General.
```

```
DISTRIBUTION
   " f "                    S E C R E T
A TRUE COPY:

    /s/ Elmer L. Tuck
        ELMER L. TUCK,
        Captain, Air Corps.
```

July, 1944

Lieutenant Colonel Edward T. Imparato assumed command of the 374th Troop Carrier Group. He succeeded Lieutenant Colonel Fred M. Adams who was relieved from his assignment and returned to the United States. Colonel Imparato has made no drastic changes in policy or administration.

Acting under the verbal orders of the Commanding General, Far East Air Forces and the Commanding General, 54th Troop Carrier Wing, the group commander on 20 August instructed the 6th, 21st and 22nd Squadrons to make immediate preparations for movement. Group Headquarters, the 6th and 21st Squadrons were to be stationed at Nadzab, New Guinea, APO 713, Unit 1, and the 22nd and 33rd Squadrons were to proceed to Finschhafen, APO 322, Unit 1 in conformity with Troop Movement Directive Number 108, Headquarters, Allied Air Forces, SWPA, dated 23 June 1944. All equipment and supplies that could be transported by C-47 aircraft was to be moved by the planes assigned to the group. The remaining equipment was to be left in the care of a rear echelon and shipped on the first available boat. On 21 August the Commanding General, FEAF ordered the movement of the 33rd Squadron postponed until further notice. Between the 26th and 30th of the month, the units concerned had sufficiently completed their movement by air to begin limited operations. The 6th, 21st and 22nd Squadrons were removed from the operational control of the Directorate of Air Transport and placed under the operational control of the 54th Troop Carrier Wing. As no written orders had been issued concerning this movement, the group remained assigned directly to the Far East Air Forces.

At the end of the month all units were operating from temporary offices set up in tents. Plans had been drawn up for the construction of permanent administrative buildings, a consolidated mess hall, a central water supply system, a power plant and other needed installations.

Effective 1 August, leaves and furloughs of ground personnel to Sydney, Australia were prohibited by FEAF; effective 31 August all leaves and furloughs for personnel stationed in New Guinea were discontinued. Last ground leave was given to group personnel on 15 August.

September, 1944

During the early part of the month Group Headquarters, the 6th Troop Carrier Squadron, and the 21st Troop Carrier Squadron completed the air movement from the mainland of Australia to their present location at APO 713 Unit #1, Nadzab, New Guinea. Practically all vehicles, equipment and supplies were transported by air. Only the heavy vehicles and a small amount of other bulky equipment were to be moved by water. This was left in the care of a small number of personnel comprising the rear echelon. The total weight moved by air for these three units was 527,500 pounds. The planes used in the movement flew 875:10 hours and a total distance of 131,280 miles.

Rapid progress was made on the construction of administration buildings, mess halls, showers, a power plant, and other camp installations. The manpower shortage for construction work and other details was solved by the timely arrival of fifty-seven enlisted men from the 91st Replacement Battalion on 1 September. Within a period of ten days the whole camp was functioning nor-

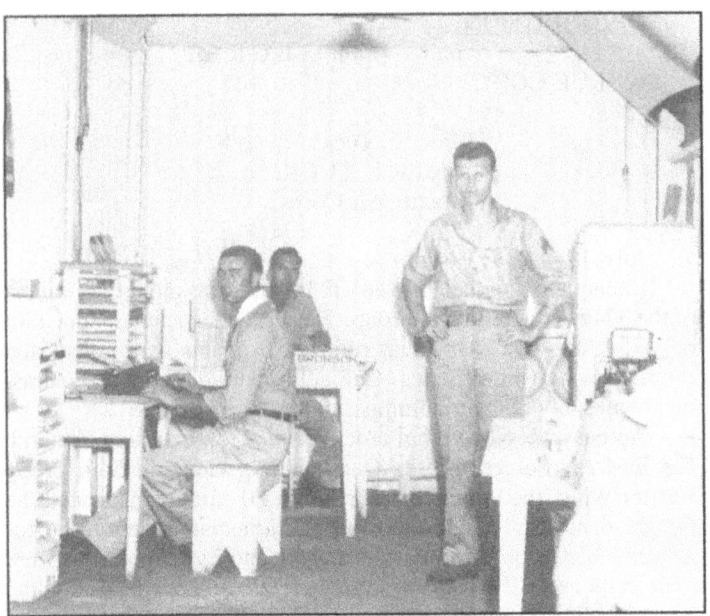
Captain Bronson and intelligence staff.

mally. Large airy buildings were erected for the use of Group Headquarters and for the squadron's orderly rooms. A sanitary, screened-in mess hall was constructed for the use of the enlisted men. A separate mess was maintained for the officers. The group utilities section, under the direction of Captain Marvin M. Scott, set up an efficient power plant and water system for the camp area. Adequate showers and an area for washing clothes were provided for all personnel. Later in the month, several enterprising enlisted men purchased a secondhand, home-made washing machine and established "The New Guinea White Wash Laundry". Prices were reasonable and business has been very good. The Special Services Section has been very active and has been presenting four movies each week. A Post Exchange has been put into operation and provides most necessities and a few luxuries. The cold Coca Cola sold at noon and late in the afternoon has been greatly appreciated by all personnel.

Effective 17 September, 1944, the 22nd Squadron was removed from the operational control of the 54th Troop Carrier Wing and placed under the operational control of the Directorate of Air Transport. The Squadron continued to maintain a detachment of five airplanes with crews and ground maintenance men at Mackay, Queensland, Australia, for the purpose of transporting leave personnel to and from the forward areas of New Guinea.

October, 1944

Effective 3 October, 1944, the 5298th Troop Carrier Wing (Prov) was activated per General Orders Number 232, Headquarters, Far East Air Forces, APO 925. Colonel Ray T. Elsmore was designated as commanding Officer. Paragraph III of the above order relieved Group Headquarters, 6th Squadron, 21st Squadron, 22nd Squadron, and 33rd Squadron of the 374th Troop Carrier Group from assignment to the Far East Air Forces and assigned these units to the 5298th Troop Carrier Wing (Prov). The 22nd and 33rd Squadrons were to be under the operational control of the new wing and Group Headquarters, the 6th and 21st Squadrons were to continue under the operational control of the 54th Troop Carrier Wing. The 5298th Troop Carrier Wing (Prov) was organized from the disbanded Directorate of Air Transport, Allied Air Forces. All officers, and enlisted men formerly on duty with the directorate of Air Transport and whose units are now assigned to the 5298th Troop Carrier Wing (Prov) were directed to remain in the same assignment and position at the station or stations where they were then located and perform the same general functions as they were performing with the Directorate of Air Transport.

Troop Movement directive Number 117, Headquarters, Allied Air Forces, Southwest Pacific Area, dated 18 September, 1944, was received in Group Headquarters in October. This directive ordered a change of station for the 374th Group Headquarters, and the 6th Squadron from Callous (Townsville, Queensland, APO 922) to Horlicks (Biak, APO 920) and a change of station for the 21st Squadron from Amatory (Brisbane, APO 923) to Horlicks (Biak, APO 920). These units had arrived at Automobile (Nadzab, APO 713, Unit 1) under verbal orders only.

On 7 October, 1944, the group commander was verbally instructed to prepare Group Headquarters, the 6th and 21st Squadrons for immediate movement by air to Biak. Movement Order Number 674, Headquarters, Fifth Air Force, APO 713 was cut on 9 October but was not received until after the move was completed. Preparations for movement were begun immediately and on 8 October an advance echelon was dispatched to Biak for the purpose of clearing an area and setting up a camp. The actual movement began on 11 October and was virtually complete by 21 October. A total of one hundred and thirty-four plane loads of personnel, personal baggage, vehicles, and organizational supplies and equipment were moved. Thirty planes were required to move Group Headquarters, fifty-two to move the 6th Squadron, and fifty-two to move the 21st Squadron. No unusual problems were encountered and no accidents occurred during the move. There was a certain amount of confusion and some delays, but because of the lack of time for advance planning this was to be expected.

Effective 14 October, Lt. Col. Edward T. Imparato, Group Commander, was designated as Base Commander of Sorido Air Base by the commanding general of the 54th Troop Carrier Wing. Consequently, the Group Operations assumed the functions of Base Operations.

After having been alerted for two months the 33rd Squadron was at last ordered to proceed to Hollandia, Dutch New Guinea, APO 565. The move was accomplished during the period 15 October through 18 October. The new camp site was located at the base of Cyclops Mountain Range. The squadron's planes are to operate from Sentani Strip.

CHRISTMAS EVE FOR A 33RD SQUADRON COMMANDER BILL SAMUELS AND CREW
LATE 1944

"It was Christmas eve day and I was flying a C-47 to Leyte in the Philippines. There was no fighter escort and we had to fly a couple of hundred miles out to sea past Halmahera which was occupied by Japanese. We had a navigator aboard who occasionally had us fly close to the surface so he could drop a smoke bomb to check the wind direction. I never did think this was a very accurate way to determine the wind direction at five thousand feet. This whole thing was a pretty hairy operation because we had no radio aids and hoped that when we made a left turn it would take us to Leyte Bay. There were no alternate fields and fierce fighting was going on in the immediate area. As I recall the airplane was loaded with hand grenades.

"Fortunately, through mostly luck, we did hit Leyte Bay about dusk and received landing instructions from a controller in a jeep. We landed on the metal strip and were told to clear the runway immediately as the field was about to come under an air raid attack. We parked and the four of us jumped off the plane and were directed to a series of holes among some trees close to the runway. We had one metal helmet so the last one in the hole got to wear the helmet. The air raid was light with only a couple small bombs landing nowhere near us but the sky was ablaze with anti-aircraft fire. The all-clear soon sounded.

"No mess hall had been set up. Our only meal was a can of grapefruit for supper. I went to check the airplane and found that a large crew was quickly unloading it. An operations officer told me we were scheduled to leave for New Guinea at four a.m. He stressed that strict radio silence was in effect and that a large American fleet filled Leyte Bay. I and my crew slept, what was left of the night, in the airplane.

"It was pitch dark as we followed a jeep to the end of the runway and were soon given a green light for takeoff. At about a thousand feet I noticed that the left engine oil temperature was rapidly going up and pegged out at the top. I had no choice but to shut down the engine and feather the propeller. I couldn't use the radio and I was concerned that if I turned around to go back the navy would think we were an enemy airplane. I turned on all the navigation and landing lights and lowered the landing gear, We were immediately inundated with a bunch of searchlights from ships down below. They must have recognized us because they didn't shoot. I landed back on the metal strip. We discovered that a piece of wood had jammed the oil radiator closed. The flight engineer removed it, we ran up the engine and found it okay. We took off again and had a long uneventful flight back to Hollandia. It was a memorable Christmas eve and morning."

The gap between life and death is very narrow. This is especially true in time of war and always critical in actual combat. The action, reaction, constant vigil and alertness may save a life.

Such a situation faced Bill Samuels, commanding officer of the 33rd Squadron on a flight out of Hollandia, New Guinea, in the fall of 1944. Here is his story:

"One early morning after taking off in a C-47 from Hollandia, New Guinea, I was climbing west through the rather narrow valley to get above the surrounding hills. In case of trouble like an engine failure or some other dire circumstance there was not enough room to make a one eighty to return to the field, therefore, it was necessary to climb straight ahead to approximately 4000 feet before having sufficient space to turn around.

"Suddenly my copilot and I saw an airplane approaching down the canyon headed straight for us. We had studied enough models and profiles of Japanese planes to instantly recognize the approaching twin engine plane as a "Betty" bomber. Our only armament beside our 45 caliber pistols was a Thompson sub machine gun, which, for all practical purposes, was utterly useless as an air-to-air weapon. As a matter of fact, none of us, including the flight engineer, had ever fired one.

"I edged over to the right and told the crew that it looked like about the only thing we could do would be to try to dive under the bomber. We couldn't turn around and I thought that if I tried to climb over him he would have a good shot at us. The time for decision was rapidly approaching when the flight engineer suddenly yelled, "He's got U.S. Air Corps markings."

"We found out later that the 'enemy' bomber had been captured intact, painted in American colors and was being flown into Hollandia for shipment to the states."

The 374th Troop Carrier Group Headquarters and the 33rd Troop Carrier Squadron were bivouacked in a rice paddy on the outskirts of Manila in the spring and summer of 1945. The group commander wrote a letter to the family explaining the most unusual incident. Here is the 33rd squadron commander's comments on the misfortune.

"One evening a sergeant due to be rotated home from the Philippines after long overseas service reached under his cot into a box for a can of beer. He felt something bite him on the finger. It hurt enough to make him think that it must have been a mouse or a rat.

"Within a very few minutes his hand had swollen and his entire arm, he said, felt like it was on fire. His tent mates sent for the flight surgeon and while waiting they discovered that the sergeant had been bitten by a small snake which they killed. When the doctor arrived the victim was in great difficulty and was immediately taken to the hospital about a half mile away. At the hospital his tongue had swollen to the point where he couldn't talk and thirty minutes later he was dead.

"This terrible incident caused an immediate investigation. It turned out that the snake, which the natives called rice snakes, was a species of deadly cobra. A search of all the squadron tents, latrines, etc. found a good number of the snakes including snake eggs in shoes, under boxes and under the bamboo tent floors.

"All of us were very frightened by this and some went so far as to refuse to sleep in their cots, preferring to spend the nights in the airplanes. Our doctor had no anti-venom but soon got some. It proved to be worthless because a few days later a man in another outfit was bitten, anti-venom was injected and he too died.

"While the rainy season lasted we were all very careful, watching where we walked and put our hands. When the rains ended and the area turned into a dust bowl the snakes disappeared."

Kelley, Hallam, and Soular.

Ben Maidenburg

A description written by Capt. Ben Maidenburg, a public relations officer of the 433rd Group, on the first trip from Biak to Mindoro tells what had by the end of the year, become a "routine Day's work" for Brigadier General Paul H. Prentiss' Troop Carrier Command. His account follows:

"They called down to this C-47 outfit late at night and said to get three planes ready to go on a secret mission.

"At 4 o'clock in the morning crews were rustled out of bed, hurried through a breakfast of G.I. coffee flavored by a faint taste of the G.I. can, dehydrated eggs and toast. Then to the briefing.

"The operations and intelligence officers sleepily spread maps and pointed to a general area on Mindoro Island. The infantry had landed there only five days before, and the route lay right through the middle of the Visayan Sea - which the Japs have been calling their own.

"The exact location of the strip? Well, it wasn't known. The engineers had rushed it through and it was in pretty fair shape, but that's all they knew about it.

"A quick look at the map showed the strip to be less than 200 miles from Manila. Another look at the map showed all the Jap-held islands in the book laying athwart the route.

"Soon the briefing was ended, and trucks rolled the crews out to the strip. In the gray dawn of this tiny coral island in the Netherlands East Indies, the troop-and-supply-carrying transports looked insignificant indeed when it came to flying right through the middle of Jap land in the Philippines.

"Off roared the transports to another tiny island a half-hour away where the loads were to be picked up. And shortly the C-47's were lumbering through the skies at 150 miles per hour, loaded from cockpit to tail with high-priority materiel and personnel, needed badly for General MacArthur's advance on Manila. A few hours, a few hundred miles later the transports sat down on another coral strip to refuel. The crews were told they'd remain overnight, which meant sleeping on litters or cots under the wings of the plane, and making the best of K-rations or C-rations.

"This 'R.O.N.' island was at Palau, a Jap base not so long ago, and it is still littered with huge concrete pillboxes. At night one is awakened often because Jap stragglers have a habit of trying to sneak through to the airstrip and do some damage, and the infantry fires off star shells which light up the heavens like midday. When the shells aren't going off, there are myriads of tiny flying bugs which bite like thunder, and land crabs which are big enough to steal the very blanket off you.

"Long before dawn the following morning, the transports were in the air again, and a little less than five hours later were landing at a big airstrip on Leyte Island.

"Half-hour of briefing, refueling an they were off again. Weaving in and out of islands - trying to keep over water all the time, and keeping a wary eye open for stray Nips. It was a 'buzz' job all the way, with the altimeter rarely showing more than 75 feet above sea level.

"A flight of P-38's overhead gave everyone a welcome relief. Some two and one half hours later the south tip of Mindoro Island came into sight. Ships laying off-shore were the identifying mark. Mindoro looked peaceful enough. Rice paddies here and there, and well-kept Filipino farms.

"And there, stretching in dusty relief, lay the strip - 'A' strip it was called. Five days before, Japs had lived in this area and now American troops were lolling around only 160 miles to the south of Manila.

"In a few minutes, amid gigantic clouds of dust, the transports had landed, and were being unloaded. All the Troop Carrier Command had done on this day was to extend its combat 'air lines' to more than 1300 miles. After today Mindoro would become a regular stop, and troops and supplies would pour in in an endless stream.

"Suddenly, without warning, there was a terrific concussion. A stick of bombs hit not more than 75 yards from where the three planes were parked. Earth and sticks flew all over.

"And then a brittle chatter in the sky overhead. Pilots and crews took off as fast as their feet would carry them. Over a low mound of earth all sped, and started hugging the ground as though it was home itself.

"A glance into the sky told the story. Some 20 or 30 Jap planes had sneaked in at high altitude, and the heavens resounded with the chatter of machine guns, an the roar of engines, as American Fighters attacked the Nips.

"Over the east end of the strip one plane started smoking, and burst into flame. It dove to earth like a rock, but not fast enough to hide the red ball that marks the Jap. To the north another plane was coming down in flames, and to the south still another. All in all, six Nip planes bit the dust in half an hour, and when it was over the C-47's wound up their engines and started hedgehopping back.

"They halted at another Leyte Island airdrome for the night. Right in the middle of K-rations, a Betty bomber came in for a try, and sweeping right across the transports, drew a sheet of ack-ack fire that, had it been 10 feet lower, would have wiped out the whole bunch.

"The crews slept on pins and needles that night. Early in the morning an officer came around. He had 30 or 40 wounded infantrymen to be flown back. So

Photo journalist on a mission.

the transports lifted up and landed at another strip, loaded the wounded, and started back to their original base.

"As the reports read, it was just another routine day for the Fifth Air Force's Troop Carrier Command."

Manila remained the prime object of General MacArthur's drive. And Manila was Luzon- an island still to be attacked and conquered. *Maptalk*, an Information and Education publication of the U.S.A.F.F.E., tells of the campaign to take Manila:

"The invasion, for which every S.W.P.A. operation since Buna has been a necessary preparatory step, was made at Lingayen Gulf, 100 miles northwest of Manila, and took place on Tuesday, 9 January, 82 days after the landing of Leyte.

"'The enemy evidently had not prepared for a landing in the Lingayen sector,' reported the communique, ' and as a result of this strategic surprise his forces were insignificant to oppose our landing. We are now in his rear. His main reinforcement and supply lines to the Philippines are cut and his ground fight for Luzon will have to be made with such resources as he now possesses. The back door is closed.'

"Only rank optimists would have dared predict the rapidity of gains made during the first week on Luzon.

"The initial 15-mile beachhead was stretched to embrace 44 miles of coastline along Lingayen Gulf; in five days more than 400 square miles of territory were seized; astride three highways to Manila armored spearheads were moving as fast as supply carriers could keep pace. As General MacArthur's communique summed it up: 'The enemy is as yet either unable to unwilling to seriously challenge our offensive drive into the central plains.'"

One week after its capture, Lingayen airfield had been extended from its original 4000-feet runway and was ready to receive fighters and transport planes. From it and other bases in the Philippines, General Kenney's planes took off to provide continued direct support to ground troops.

Troop Carriers immediately brought in fighter and bomber groups, as well as high-priority radio equipment. Lingayen airfield became a regular Troop Carrier stop. The effectiveness of quick transportation of air power to support ground forces was shown in the *Maptalk* release:

"Liberators blasted Bamban regularly, while Bostons and Mitchells smashed hard at Bicol Peninsula, destroying in one attack seven locomotives, plus a number of freight cars and motor vehicles. Lightnings struck the Baguio-Aparri road through the Benguet Mountains to the north, while Thunderbolts pressed home low-level attacks on Balete Pass, the enemy's lifeline from San Jose on the eastern side of Luzon plain, to Cagayen Valley, in the island's northeast corner.

"Escorted mediums caught 61 Jap planes aground on Clark Field, summarily wrecking them all. Repeated attacks at Japanese communications centers yielded the destruction of at least half the railroad stock on Luzon."

By January 23, U.S. troops had forged ahead to a point less than 60 miles from Manila and 10 miles from Clark Field, capturing Tarlac, city of 55,000 persons, and arriving at Bamban where they could see thick smoke curling from Clark Field. This field was to be one of the main Troop Carrier bases in the Philippines.

Seizure of Clark Field came early Thursday morning, January 25, and followed a steady drive that had carried troops of the XIV Corps through the towns of Bamban and Mabalacat and across the Bamban River. Nearby Fort Stotsenburg fell at the same time. Scarcely pausing for breath, forces then fanned out through the surrounding hills in pursuit of the Jap garrison, estimated to number 5000 strong.

6th Transport Squadron, 1944. Lt. P.M. Dobbins, Capt. Loder, and Capt. Kelley.

First U.S. troops to enter the area found no fixed defenses, few Japs, but plenty of land mines and booby traps. Their first impression of an easy victory was a false one.

Clark Field is really a misnomer. It is no single airdrome but a network of 13 or more strips flanking the main highway for a distance of about 10 miles between Bamban and Angeles.

Engineers quickly put the runways of several fields in Clark Field into shape and soon hundreds of paratroopers were moved by Troop Carrier into this area. Wounded were also quickly removed from the battle zone. The paratroopers were to play an important role in a later attack on Corregidor.

In February, the 317th Group led by Col. Lackey, group commander, (former 6th Squadron Commander) dropped paratroopers of the 11th Airborne Division to seize the 2000-foot Tagaytay ridge which commands five highways leading into Manila and Cavite Naval Base, 32 miles south. Cavite itself was captured on February 13.

Manila was entered by U.S. troops on February 3 - three years, one month and two days after its surrender to the Japs. Much of Manila was in ruins and fighting raged through its rubble-filled streets as the Japs set fire to virtually everything along the Pasig River north bank, exploded gasoline drums beneath office buildings, mined all the streets and mounted artillery pieces atop city skyscrapers. *Maptalk* again describes the situation:

"Fires were still burning throughout Manila, particularly in the old Intramuros District, where the Japs had set off fresh demolition charges. Shattered steel and fire-blackened walls were all that remained of much of the capital's show places. Hotels, theaters, banks, and department stores were razed as well as almost half of Chinatown. Although every effort was being made to rush adequate supplies by Troop Carrier, the food situation was critical. Filipino and Chinese residents, impoverished by systematic Japanese looting, were reported dying from hunger at the rate of several hundred a day."

Air supply of food and other critical items became a necessity as Manila harbor could not be used at first. Hundreds of sunken ships littered the harbor; wharf facilities were lacking. Air ech-

Hollandia after USAF Raids, 1944.

elons of Troop Carriers were sent to Clark Field and a regular shuttle system was inaugurated to bring food, ammunition, gasoline and priority radio equipment from other Philippine landing places, where docking and unloading facilities were better. As in the early days in New Guinea, Troop Carriers again made hundreds of daily trips to cover an emergency situation.

Bataan, where a broken force of Filipino-Americans fought a gallant but losing battle against the Japs three years ago, fell on February 15. One day later (Friday), a dual landing from the sea and air brought the capture of Corregidor, the island fortress four miles southeast of Bataan which guards the entrance to Manila Bay.

Waves of Parachutists from the 503rd Airborne Regiment (the unit that closed the circle at Lae in September, 1943) were dropped by Troop Carriers on the island's crest at 0830, while elements of the 24th Division, crossing from Bataan, hit the south beach. The air landing completely surprised the Japs, and paratroops quickly seized Corregidor's rocky plateau. Some 55 minutes after the landing the forces had linked up. All the island's decisive points were seized.

The air assault was planned by Col. Lackey and led by him personally. To make sure that the drop would be timed and completed exactly to schedule, General Prentiss and Col. Lackey piloted a command ship over Corregidor for nearly two and one-half hours, directing by radio just where and when each plane was to drop its paratroopers. The result was what General MacArthur termed a "great military success".

During the preliminary bombardment of Corregidor more than 2000 tons of bombs and shells rained on enemy defenses in three days. Just before the paratroops alighted, Liberators and Bostons were over the fortified areas, while a protective screen of fighters circled overhead and a swift-moving fleet of PT boats went close in shore. So effective was the early bombardment that Corregidor's once formidable shore guns were silenced several days before the invasion.

The part played by the 317th Troop Carrier Group in this assault may best be described in an article appearing in the *Sydney Morning Herald*:

"Bataan, Sunday. - General MacArthur's sense of the dramatic was demonstrated in the assault on Corregidor, whence he had left for Australia in March 1942. He made it the scene of the greatest parachute operation in the Southwest Pacific - a means of approach as militarily necessary as it was spectacular.

"The Troop Carriers of the 317th Group came in to drop men on the rock after it had been bombarded from the sea and air, with many times the power the Japanese had brought to bear on him in the tunnels three years ago.

"Corregidor was shaken terrifically by the concentrated fire of the ships guns.

"So much dust was raised by explosions that U.S. Signal Corps cameramen detailed to record the operation had sand flying in their eyes as they rode in tiny Piper Cubs at 700 feet, and the little planes rocked so violently that for a long time the men were unable to use their cameras.

"Throughout the earlier part of Friday Troop Carrier after Troop Carrier flew in and men parachuted on to the buildings on Corregidor and to the top of the rock itself.

"Most of the 'chutes blossomed white, carrying troops, but there were others, red, green, and yellow, bearing in ammunition and supplies for men faced with a desperate hand-to-hand fight.

"As the morning went on the hastily discarded parachutes draped the top of the rock or flew on to surrounding bushes, like washing left to dry in the sun.

"Dickson Brown, of the London *News Chronicle*, who landed on Corregidor with the sea-borne troops, thus describes the scene from the U.S. flagship, which stood close in as the paratroops landed:

"'As far as the eye could see from this flagship were transport planes, stretching for miles in line ahead formation. A strong north-easterly wind fortunately cleared Corregidor of the smoke and dust created by the bombing and shelling. Against a background of large, fleecy clouds, the first Troop Carriers sailed in low, and parachutists were soon seen floating down majestically where only a few minutes before bombs had rained.

"'Surrounding us are invasion landing craft of all descriptions, while forming a protective screen farther out are cruisers, destroyers and mine-sweepers. Standing out conspicuously are two smaller vessels, from which the White Ensign flutters.

"'Bostons are flying low to strafe the eastern side of the island to cut it in two and prevent the Japanese from rushing troops up to the high ground on the western extremity where the paratroops are descending. In am near enough to see their guns open up as they dive low and then turn and swoop up.

"' Some of the paratroops appear perilously near to falling into the sea. Actually some strike the steep, barren cliffs and are seen to scurry or slide down to the beach. Watchful P.T.'s are there to take care of them.'"

General MacArthur called the Corregidor paratroop mission one of the greatest military attacks in history.

While the Japs in Manila were being eliminated, liberation forces were rescuing 2146 prisoners from Los Banos, 25 miles inside enemy-held territory at the southern end of Laguna de Bay's western shores. The rescue was accomplished in co-ordinated attacks by Filipino guerrillas and 11th Airborne troops, who were dropped on to the prison camp by the Troop Carriers. While the guerrillas penetrated to the camp by land, the 11th made a jump directly on the camp site. The surprised Japs were overwhelmed, the internees were taken to waiting amphibious craft and evacuated to our lines. It was the fourth prison camp rescue since our January 9 landing at Lingayen Gulf, two of which the Troop Carriers made possible.

The Associated Press describes the Los Banos rescue in the following article:

LOS BANOS, Feb. 25 (A.A.P.). - By a daring and skillful raid United States troops on Friday rescued 2146 prisoners from Los Banos camp in the hills above Laguna de Bay, a large lake east of Manila.

"They included hundreds of Americans, British, Australians, Canadians, and Dutch.

"A selected detachment of the 511th Parachute Regiment jumped directly on the prison camp. Elements of the 11th Division on the night before the attack crossed Laguna de Bay in amphibious craft, and when the parachutists landed, these troops attacked, ,supported by guerrillas, who had been infiltrating for several nights previously.

"The Japanese guards were completely surprised. The commander, his staff, and the entire garrison of 243 were killed. American casualties were two killed and two wounded.

"A long line of people clutching little bags of clothing, and hugging children, came pouring from the buildings, yelling greetings.

"Jack Burnell, a tobacco firm executive, said: 'It's been a long time we've waited for just such Hollywood American Stuff.'

"The released prisoners were taken to safety in amphibious craft, and the covering force withdrew to our lines.

"General MacArthur, in his announcement of the rescue, said: 'Nothing can be more gratifying to a soldier's heart than this rescue. God certainly has been with us this day.'"

Again the mobility of the Troop Carrier combined with its versatility in landing in spots where no other airplane could, should be retold at this place. In hours' notice, ground crews of fighter squadrons and bomber outfits were hustled and placed on fields where they could function more effectively as air support for the infantry and artillery. Marines with their dive bombers were carried from as far as Green Island and Bougainville - thousands of miles away - to take part in the fray - to bring all the United States armed forces together as a single powerful force against the Jap. And again it was done in record time, across water and terrain which the Japs did not think it possible to cross.

In the early fighting - like that in Clark Field - Troop Carriers landed in rice paddies or fields, where only small donkey carts had driven - landed at night in many cases guided only by jeep headlights or the flash of artillery shells from Jap positions in the nearby hills - landed many times with shells forming a pattern not very far away.

Pilots and crews guarded their valuable planes against Jap infiltration - sometimes successfully, sometimes not so - while being unloaded. Yet the loads came in - precious loads of ammunition, medical supplies, food and radio equipment - at the rate of nearly a million pounds a day, making the huge Clark Field base operational almost overnight. Tired crews, knowing the need for their planes, kept shuttle runs going from bases in Mindoro and Leyte until they couldn't land any more - always evacuating wounded on their return trips.

The story of a guerrilla field - a field 150 miles behind the strong Jap lines in northern Luzon - is an accurate story of Troop Carrier work in the Philippines. Guerrillas captured a grass field - where once a small civilian strip was located - and several hours later G.H.Q. notified the Fifth Air Force to send 27 plane loads of radio equipment, key personnel, and other materiel needed to make the strip operational. Nobody knew of the field's existence until the order came to go. Within three hours the planes were loaded and two hours later were landing on a highly camouflaged strip.

Now this field functions as an advanced fighter base, adding more than 200 extra miles to our fighters, allowing them to roam just so much farther over the sea, cutting Jap communication lines and protecting our bombers farther on their way to Formosa and China coast.

The story of the guerrillas is still another side of the Troop Carriers' tale. Secret until March, 1945, the full story of these brave men's aid to our forces can now be told. Troop Carriers landed at night in secret island hideouts with ammunition, jeeps, food, and guns. They dropped supplies in inaccessible places where guerrillas were hammering away at Jap communication lines. Finally regularly scheduled freight runs were made to guerrilla fields. These fields were short, muddy, and in localities where heavy fighting was only a few miles distant. Jap rifle fire frequently clattered around the Troop Carrier planes as they flew low on their approach to make their difficult landings.

Troop Carriers for the first time in their history became actual "bombers" to help out in guerrilla warfare. Our new secret weapon, jelly fire-bombs, set up in gasoline drums and fused to explode on contact, were accurately dropped on Jap positions in the same manner as supplies were generally dropped from airplanes. The liquid fire spread over the Jap positions like a blanket, enabling the guerrillas and our infantry to penetrate defenses, up to then, impregnable to small forces.

All of this is a vital part of the full guerrilla story, a story which wouldn't have been so full if the Troop Carriers hadn't been there.

Before the story of the Troop Carriers' work in the Philippines is brought to a close, the men of this organization justifiably can again claim a great deal of credit for making possible - as before in New Guinea and the Dutch Netherlands - the advances of our great infantry as well as the other two tactical arms of the Fifth Air Force - the greatest air force in the world and the fightingest, backingest air force that any infantry ever had.

In reality it is just the dawn of a more glorious chapter in Troop Carrier history as General MacArthur, after fulfilling his promise to return to the Philippines, pushes on towards Japan proper.

And again thousands of infantrymen, lying in their foxholes, will look up and cheer as the Troop Carrier swings low to drop them the means of beating the enemy. And again hundreds of wounded men will know the value of swift transportation back to hospitals - transportation during which the hand of a woman gently ministers to their wants - when they walk again on the streets of the United States.

And so Troop Carriers have lived up to General Kenney's boast and have more than lived up to the original Troop Carrier motto - "Vincit Qui Primum Gerit" - the Latin phrase of old General Nathan Bedford Forrest: "Git thar fustest with the mostest."

ROYAL ARCH GUNNISON

Royal Arch Gunnison, writer of the 450-newspaper-syndicate, North American Newspaper Alliance, described the effective work of the Troop Carriers after he participated in one of the dropping missions:

"A trip in a 'Biscuit Bomber' is not a tea party - at least not this one. A G.I. outfit had been cut off for

Inevitable construction, 33rd Squadron, Hollandia, 1944.

five days inside the Jap lines and not only had their food run out, but they were rapidly firing away the last of their mortar and machine-gun ammunition. The Japs were moving up on them. Something has to be done - and done quickly.

"At the same time I was sitting on a box table that served as an office for a supply transport colonel at Lieutenant General Walter Kreuger's Sixth Army jungle headquarters when the telephone buzzed. The story came in rapidly from field headquarters.

"'O.K...O.K....we'll make the first drop in about three hours....Think they'll be all right until then?...O.K....O.K....Roger....Over and out.'

"'Hey, Joe!' the colonel yelled at a tall, lean captain who was striding through the sand across to a camouflaged bamboo hut. 'Here's your first job.'

"And that's how I happened to go on the first emergency supply drop made in the Philippines. Joe turned out to be Capt. Joe Turner, former Texas A. & M. football star and rancher from Marfa, Texas. As we bumped up the winding single-track road to the shoestring airstrip, Joe said, 'There's our ship,' and pointed out a grasshopper-like C-47 with a big brown camouflaged Jap truck backed up to the wide-open side door.

"I glanced inside the C-47. Its broad board floor clear up to the pilot and radio cabin was covered with a double layer of three-foot-long wooden crates wrapped with heavy rope. Each crate had a chubby parachute case on top. This was the 5500-pound load of ammunition and food that shortly would be reinforcing those G.I.'s dug in on a narrow ridge 50 miles across the island from us.

"Capt. Turner pulled his long legs into the plane ahead of me just as the starboard engine coughed and roared out. The black-haired Texan turned to his three drop sergeants. 'How many bundles?' he asked. 'Thirty-one, sir.' 'That means about eight runs over the target.' He shook his head and turned to me, 'Still want to go along?'

"Above the roar of the engines I shouted, 'Let's go!' We headed north up the San Juanico Straits and curved off across the low ridge that drops down into the rice-paddied American-occupied Leyte valley. Our chubby, shirtless radioman, headphones over his ears, peered out of the cabin door and shouted, 'Capt. Turner, base air control says to tell you the fighters that were flying cover for us on this mission have been diverted to intercept some bogies.'

"'That's just dandy - O.K., tell 'em to forget it,' said Turner. 'This isn't the first time we've gone in without help,' and Joe went back to join his two ex-cowhands and farmer in fitting the tin drop slide into the open door.

"'We usually make a free drop (no parachute) with food from about 100 feet.' Joe explained to me. 'If the pilots are good they'll almost stall the plane over the target and the stuff doesn't get badly broken. We figure anywhere from 85 to 95 per cent of the stuff is recovered, and we dropped as much as 500,000 pounds of ammo at Cape Gloucester last Christmastime in six days.'

"They put the 'chutes on the ammo and the plan was to drop it from 150 to 300 feet with or without a stall over the target. Ours would be the first to drop -

LTC Fred Adams, Group CO June 1943 - July 1944.

but before nightfall this and two other planes would have made two trips each to leave the marooned G.I.'s with about 30,000 pounds of equipment with which to hang on.

"Since we had no air cover - and with Jap planes known to be in the area - we hugged the tops of the palm trees, depending on our camouflage for protection. There's nothing fliers would rather shoot up than a clumsy transport. The foothills of the Leyte range were just off our left wingtip now. Now Carigara was behind us. Co-pilot Lt. Bob Milwee, of Dallas, who was going to fly the ship for the drop, came back for a last word with Capt. Turner.

"'We'll swing out over the bay the first time and come in counterclockwise on the Jap side of the ridge,' he outlined. 'Then we should be almost level with the tip of the ridge and can see the guys who need the stuff....'

"That was the plan, and Bob Milwee flew it just that way. We approached at about 400 feet - weaved up the narrow gorge. As we neared the top of the ridge a bright purple flare caught for a few seconds, burned as vividly as an acetylene torch - then smothered into a gray smoke smudge.

"This was it. We were to make the drop in the middle of a bomb-singed, high-grass meadow. But we had committed ourselves. Before we dropped anything we still had to make the circle over Jap positions on the far side of the ridge and over the Ormoc valley. The narrow muddy road was perhaps 500 feet below us as the valley opened up. It was spotted with Jap vehicles. A number of Jap soldiers with sprigs of bamboo in their helmet nets gaped up at us. We had come over the ridge so quickly we had surprised them. Not a shot was fired at us. And we had nothing with which to fire at them.

"I looked for Joe and the two cowboys and farmer to see whether they had noticed the Japs. They didn't have time. They were poised around the drop slide, awaiting the pilot's signal to 'Let 'er go!'

"We were now back on what we thought was the safe side of the ridge when white puffs from the ground showed the Japs on the other side of the Americans were firing at us. My first thought was, 'And here I am sitting on top of a plane full of mortar shells and machine-gun bullets.'

"But that was all the time I had for that kind of thinking. Co-pilot Bob Milwee had us down within 200 feet of the ridge. We were coming back. You could see the bomb-pocked ridge crest where Jap planes and mortar shells had been plastering these G.I.'s in and around their foxholes. You could see the boys turn over in their foxholes and stare up at us - then wave furiously or give a welcoming salute.

"This was the first sign of help they had seen in five days. The Biscuit Bomber was in. I was kneeling at the gaping entrance. Suddenly the buzzer jazzed in my ear. A couple of deft movements and the three bundles in the slide were out in the open air. I stuck my head out the door. The force of wind almost flew off my glasses. But I saw the bright red and two blue chutes open and the roped bundles swing three or four times before they dropped exactly in the middle of the grassy burned spot, not more than 50 yards behind what appeared to be the American headquarters dugout.

"By this time we were up on one wing and off toward the bay again. Capt. Turner and his men had three more bundles quickly packed into the slide before we had even made the turn to start back for the second run.

"'Ask Bob to come in a little lower and a little slower this time,' said Turner. 'This is awfully hard country to make a recovery in.'

"I climbed up the pilots' compartment and gave Lt. Milwee the message, and he said, 'Watch this one from here.' I stood just behind the two pilots' seats. The skipper, Lt. Johnny Clote, sat with his hand on the red 'bailout' button and watched the ground. Suddenly white puffs of smoke burst all along the ridge just under us and ahead of our right wing.

"'Whee-ee!' shouted the skipper, 'Jap mortar!' and he flipped the little red key. Milwee asked rather unconcernedly, 'Want to see the 'chutes open?' and he tipped the heavy transport up on its side as a fighter pilot would.

"There were four bundles dropped this time: two yellow and two blue 'chutes - yellow usually means ordnance, but today any color went. One of the blue 'chutes didn't open completely. The crated mortar shells tumbled out on the ground. I watched the jungle-suited G.I.'s jump from out of their foxholes, crouch over, and race for the parachutes which they quickly bundled up. This was to keep them from becoming air targets and, second, the 'chutes make good, soft mattresses inside a foxhole.

"After that it became routine - this parachute bombing of our own forces with what it was going to take to get them out of there . . .the Japs rising up out of their slit trenches, climbing on top of their pillboxes and shooting but somehow missing us at 300 feet . . . the G.I.'s waving and running for the yellow, red and blue 'chutes as the lumbering transport was gunned and climbed back over the indistinct Jap line of encirclement to the comparative safety of Carigara Bay.

"'You know,' Capt. Turner turned to me and said, 'I've had guys like those down there today tell me that the sight of these Biscuit Bombers dropping food and supplies to them gives them a bigger boost than mail call. That gives you a pretty good reason for keeping at it.'"

The Japs continued to bring in reinforcements and the battle for Leyte continued in the early part of December in unabated fierceness. On 7 December the Japs attempted an airborne operation. In the early morning hours, Jap transports unloaded paratroopers in the vicinity of Barauen where the 40th Troop Carrier Squadron of the 317th Group was erecting a camp. The paratroopers surrounded the camp and attacked. Our men fought bravely and some succeeded in escaping the ring of Japanese. The attack was soon broken when infantry came to the rescue. All the Jap paratroopers were mopped up. We lost 13 men and 4 wounded.

Seven days later infantry landed on Mindoro Island. Wading ashore during the early hours of Friday morning, 15 December, troops under command of Brigadier General William C. Dunckel quickly established strong beachheads at three separate points on Mindoro's southern plain. They ran into no organized shore resistance and quick seizure of high ground secured the positions against any possible local counter-attacks. When no counter-attacks came, infantrymen fanned out toward the foothills, while tanks, bulldozers, and the thousands of supply items followed on to the beaches.

San Jose village and its nearby airfield were occupied less than 24 hours later after troops had pushed five miles up the Bugsanga River. U.S. Engineers and R.A.A.F. construction crews immediately went to work

Award ceremony, New Guinea, 1943.

374th TC Group provided special fox holes for visiting Hollywood celebrities, 1944.

converting the small strip to Allied use. Within four hours after the strip had been completed a Troop Carrier plane of the 375th Group landed. Two days later our planes were landing after flying from bases as far away as Biak.

The need for more and more airborne supplies and movement of bomber and fighter personnel to the front lines was answered when the Second Combat Cargo Group went into action in the latter part of December and January with their huge freight-carrying C-46's - Curtis Commandos. This outfit - the first C-46 Group to ever cross the Pacific and the first such organization in this theater of operations - soon were helping Troop Carriers to set new records in tons hauled and ton miles flown. Their pot-bellied planes could carry loads up to 10,000 pounds (twice the C-47) and as many as 40 passengers. These planes arrived at a needed time and, after a bit of "breaking-in", lived up to the Troop Carrier tradition, even to the extent of taking their share of work in dropping supplies to the infantry. Once the Second Combat Cargo Group had found its feet, C-46's began slowly to replace the old workhorse of the air - the Douglas C-47 - in the other Groups and tonnage records continued to fall.

With the landing in Mindoro the S.W.P.A. spearhead reached close to Manila, capital city of the Philippines. From the southernmost part of Mindoro, the distance to Manila is only 175 miles; from the northern towns of Paluan and Calapan only 95 miles. A similar distance separates Mindoro from Bataan.

Mindoro itself is a small, mountainous island, roughly 100 miles long and 60 miles in width, some areas of which are yet to be explored. There is a fairly extensive coastal plain along the eastern fringe of the island and a much smaller one in the southwest where we landed. Rainfall here is much lighter than on Leyte.

Mindoro lies northwest of Leyte, the nearest town on the east coast, Bongabong, being 240 distant. The distance between Paluan on the extreme northwest tip and Ormoc, recent Jap stronghold on Leyte's west coast, is 325 miles. From a navigation standpoint Mindoro is sadly lacking in good harbors. There is only one noteworthy anchorage - Paluan Bay on the northwest coast.

In relative distances up the Philippine ladder, Leyte is approximately one third of the way up the archipelago, while Mindoro is about two-thirds of the way. The distance from Mindoro to the northernmost tip of the Philippine islands is only 350 miles. The direct approach from Leyte to Mindoro lies across the Visayan and Sibuyan seas, and through the narrow Jintotola channel between Masbate and Panay islands. This Jintotola channel at the narrowest point closes to a width of about 20 miles.

Thus with poor harbors at Mindoro, and shipping across the Visayan and Sibuyan seas in danger of attack, Troop Carriers again brought the needed items to the front lines.

Engineering office and Personnel.

Major Hayes, maintenance 54th wing.

Damaged Japanese aircraft at Hollandia, 1945.

General Warren Carter, New Guinea, 1944.

CHAPTER V

1945

JANUARY, 1945

Under the provisions of Paragraph I, General Order Number 39, Headquarters Far East Air Forces, dated 6 January, 1945, Group Headquarters, 6th Squadron, 21st Squadron, 22nd Squadron, and 33rd Squadron of the 374th Group Carrier Group, formerly assigned to the 5298th Troop Carrier Wing (Provisional), were assigned to the 322nd Troop Carrier Wing, effective 30 December, 1944. Paragraph III of the above General Order relieved the 322nd Troop Carrier Wing from assignment to Far East Air Forces and assigned it to Far East Air Service Command. Paragraph IV relieved Group Headquarters, 6th Troop Carrier Squadron and 21st Troop Carrier Squadron of the 374th Troop Carrier Group from the operational control of the 54th Troop Carrier Wing, 5th Air Force, and placed them under the operational control of the commanding officer 322nd Troop Carrier Wing, effective 6 January, 1945.

The Commanding Officer of the 374th Troop Carrier Group was relieved of immediate command of Sorido Air Strip by General Order Number 5, Headquarters, Air Base, APO 920, dated 21 January, 1945.

General Orders Number 18, Headquarters, United States Army Forces in the Far East, dated 24 January, 1945, announces that the 374th Troop Carrier Group is entitled to battle honors for participation in the New Guinea Campaign during the period 24 January 1943, to 24 January, 1945.

PERSONNEL

Captain Edward P. Langebartel assumed command of the 22nd Squadron 31 January, 1945 after Captain Joseph B. Kelley was reassigned to Group Headquarters. On 28 January, 1945, Major Robert E. Carlson, Commanding Officer of the 33rd Squadron was transferred to the 11th Replacement Bn., for return to the United States and Captain William J. Samuels was designated the new squadron commander.

General Orders Number 1, Headquarters, 374th Troop Carrier Group, dated 11 January, 1945, awarded the Good conduct Medal to 108 enlisted personnel of the group.

Destruction in Manila after recapture from the Japanese, April 1945.

Fourteen officer and five enlisted men of the 6th Squadron received the Air Medal per General order Number 5, Headquarters, Far East Air Forces, dated 1 January, 1945. From the 21st Squadron two officers were awarded the Oak Leaf Cluster to the Air Medal per General Orders Number 52, Headquarters, Far East Air Forces, dated 8 January, 1945, three enlisted men were awarded the Oak Leaf Cluster to the Air Medal per General Orders Number 60, Headquarters, Far East Air Forces, dated 9 January, 1945, and one enlisted man was awarded the Oak Leaf Cluster to the Air Medal per General Orders, Number 64, Headquarters Far East Air Forces, dated 10 January, 1945.

OPERATIONS

On 5 January, Group Headquarters, 6th Squadron, and 21st Squadron ceased operating for the 54th Troop Carrier Wing and on 6 January began operating for the 322nd Troop Carrier Wing. Because of the change of operational control relatively few flights were made into the Philippine Islands during the month. The 33rd Squadron continued to operate a courier plane to Leyte.

Normal operations were carried out on New Guinea, between New Guinea and the Australian mainland, and between New Guinea and adjacent islands. The 22nd and 33rd Squadrons continued to carry leave personnel to Mackay, Queensland, and to operate their usual courier runs.

ENEMY ACTIVITY

Aircraft of the group continue to fly over and adjacent to enemy held territory in the Philippines and in the Halmahara Islands but no enemy interception or activity against our aircraft was experienced.

ENGINEERING

With the increase in flying time per aircraft there have been increased demands on the engineering maintenance sections. All squadrons have begun or are making preparations to begin night maintenance. Proper lighting facilities are being requisitioned and installed.

Great difficulty has been experienced in obtaining engines and hydraulic fluid. Engines have become so critical that the group engineering officer has taken control of all engines available and allocates them to the squadron which needs them most. Quite frequently aircraft remain out of commission many days while awaiting engines.

COMMUNICATIONS

Usual operations were engaged in by Group Communications and by the Squadron communications. Several new radar mechanics were assigned during the month. The radio mechanics who were received during December continued receiving training in this theater and are gradually replacing the present combat crew members.

Traffic on the Group Radio Net showed some increase over the previous month. The net is not operating on a 24 hour basis as the volume of traffic does not indicate a necessity for this. There have been a few minor breakdowns, but generally the equipment has been operating satisfactorily.

Inspections of maintenance being performed on IFF and other airborne radar apparatus in the aircraft of the squadrons have been continued. IFF maintenance continues to be stressed with the view of having this important equipment in first class operating condition. A complete IFF inspection has been recommended with each 25 hour engineering inspection. It is expected that this will result in reducing the number of IFF breakdowns in flight as well as the number of IFF discrepancy reports.

INTELLIGENCE

Normal operations were carried out in the Intelligence sections. The greater part of intelligence departments work for the month consisted of the preparation of maps, their daily distribution, and collection.

MEDICAL

The health of the group continues to be very good. No unusual difficulties were encountered during the month. The number of days lost in quarters and hospital was 136 per 250 men. This was a substantial decrease over the two previous months. The average number of days lost to flying per man was 25.4. This was a slight increase over the two previous months.

SPECIAL SERVICES

Three stage shows and twelve pictures were shown to group personnel. Night lights for volleyball and badminton courts were constructed. Athletic activities consisted mainly of inter-squadron softball and volleyball games plus informal participation on horseshoes, badminton and swimming. Base "H" Special Service has been very cooperative in all phases of Special Service work.

The volume of business for the Post Exchange was $6364.80.

The Group Canteen encountered a sudden increase in the price of Coca Cola syrup and ice cream mix. This caused the canteen to operate temporarily at a loss. During the month 11,418 individual canteen cups of Coca Cola were dispensed.

PUBLIC RELATIONS, INFORMATION AND EDUCATION

The Group Newspaper was added to the subscription list of Camp Newspaper Service. This service has done much to improve the appearance and contents of the paper. Copies of the publication have been placed in the permanent files of the Army War college.

Additional press releases on 374th Troop Carrier Group personnel were submitted to FEAF Public Relations Officer for distribution to home town newspapers of the men concerned.

During the month a considerable number of men subscribed to the Armed Forces Institute and College Extension Courses.

A small number of men have been attending classes and forums conducted by Base "H" Information and Education Section.

FEBRUARY, 1945

Throughout the month of February Group Headquarters and the four squadrons carried on normal operations at their assigned stations.

Acting under verbal orders from the commanding General, Far East Air Service Command, Group Headquarters on 22 February ordered the 6th Squadron to move to the Philippine Islands. The all air movement was to begin 24 February using planes allotted by the 322nd Troop Carrier Wing. The movement was not actually begun until the 27th when two planes were dispatched to

Co-Pilot Hunter with a skull found in a cave at Atsugi, 29 August, 1945.

Leyte with an advanced detail to lay out a camp area and arrange for supplies and equipment.

Near the end of the month all detached service to the Mackay Rest Area was discontinued for ground personnel and leaves and furloughs for flying personnel suspended until further notice.

After turning in all squadron equipment which was scheduled to be transported by water, the squadron detachments at Brisbane and at Townsville returned to their parent organizations. With the closing of the Mackay Rest Area, operations at that station ceased and the 33rd Squadron detachment was ordered to return to Hollandia.

PERSONNEL

The following awards and decorations have been received by members of the 374th Troop Carrier Group:
6th Squadron: 1st Lt. Billy A. Davis, OLC to AM, 18 February, 1945
22nd Squadron: T/Sgt. Clarence E. Maham, OLC to DFC, 24 February, 1945.

OPERATIONS

During the month Group Operations discontinued the practice of receiving loads and destinations from the 322nd Troop Carrier Wing. Wing Operations began operating directly with the squadrons' operations. This has proved to be more satisfactory to all concerned.

All squadrons flew every available ship during the month. This put an increased burden on the Engineering Section but was instrumental in producing more satisfactory results.

Group Operations began making plans to open a Navigational Training Program for all pilots in the group. All pilots will be required to undergo this course of instruction.

Japanese prisoners from the Philippines - 1945.

Many pilots in the group flew a considerable number of combat hours while flying to newly captured airfields in the Philippines.

Effective 1 February, Group Operations acting on instructions received from the Commanding General, Far East Air Service Command, instituted a new method of recording the status of all assigned aircraft. By using an intricate set of forms, the status of every aircraft is recorded every fifteen minutes. A considerable amount of work is involved in preparing and consolidating these various forms. Numerous unforeseen questions and problems concerning the method of reporting unusual conditions arose during the month, but on the whole the reports from the squadrons were satisfactorily prepared. Instructions pertaining to this report and all the forms used are attached.

ENEMY ACTIVITY

No enemy planes were encountered during the month's operations. One aircraft assigned to the 33rd Squadron was hit by enemy antiaircraft fire on 16 February when flying over the North Coast of Mindoro. The right aileron was almost completely shot off and a large hole shot in the right wing. Both wing and aileron had to be replaced. No personnel casualties were sustained.

ENGINEERING

Airplane engines of the R-1830-900 and R-1830-92 Series continued critical in this area. The maintenance record of all squadrons were noticeably lowered because of the inability to get engines promptly. In all cases engines are being flown a greater number of hours before being removed for overhaul than ever before in the history of the group. The average time on all engines changed during the month was almost seven hundred hours. In some instances engines were flown over one thousand hours before being changed.

COMMUNICATIONS

A readjustment in the Group Communication teletype circuit was necessary when the 374th was relieved of base operations. The direct teletype circuit to AACS was discontinued, but arrangements were made with them to receive Notices to Airmen, and other important information in their possession which could be utilized by this headquarters. Toward the end of the month, a further change in teletype circuits was made. The Group Teletype was cut in on Base "H" Switchboard instead of that of 54th Troop Carrier Wing which has now ceased operations at this base. Service has not been impaired however, since communication with any organization at this base which has a teletype installation can still be made.

The Radio Net continued operating satisfactorily. There were no delays caused by breakdown of equipment during the month and operations were impaired only occasionally by atmospheric disturbances. The amount of traffic handled by the net is of interest. During the month of December, 1944, when the net began operating, only 166 messages of a total of 6619 groups were transmitted. During the following two months an average of 700 messages of approximately 18,000 groups were handled each month. These figures indicate that full utilization is being made by units of this group.

Progress was made during the month on development of some of the newer types of specialized aircraft radio equipment. Army Airways Communication System commenced the installation of SCS-51 Blind Landing Equipment at this base. Group Communications, acting on previous directives, had arranged for installation of RC-103 equipment in aircraft not already so equipped. This set gives the horizontal component of the blind landing receiving equipment. The ground installation is incomplete, as no guide path indicator is set up. Aircraft are not equipped with the receiver for this, as the item is unobtainable in this theater. The current set up, however, when operating, will allow with marker beacons a reliable method of blind approach until normal contact can be made, and should be a valuable aid to aircraft landing at this base in bad weather.

IFF program was continued during the current month. Extensive application of our test procedure proved the fact that available test equipment was not satisfactory for checking IFF with a degree of fool proof reliability, particularly with respect to detecting incipient breakdowns. It was determined after considerable research, that the only way that improper functioning IFF could be determined 100%, was by testing the equipment in flight, in the same manner as Flight Control Sector Air Warning Systems, namely by interrogating aircraft in flight. In view of this, correspondence was initiated with the object of procuring Radar Interrogator Set SCB-729. It is the intention of Group Communications to locate this at the Control Tower, where voice communication with aircraft will permit immediate steps to be taken to order the return of aircraft when IFF is not operating satisfactorily.

During the month 16 Radar Mechanics were assigned to this group. One was retained by Group Communications and the remainder were assigned to the squadrons. These technicians are a much needed addition to the radio sections of the squadrons and they will enable radar apparatus to be maintained in an efficient condition. A number of radio mechanics were also assigned and distributed among the squadrons as needed. They will serve as replacements, particularly in the 21st and 22nd Squadrons, to relieve men being returned to the United States on rotation.

INTELLIGENCE

A change of code grid coordinates on the fighter grid maps became effective 15 February. The previously installed system was repeated. The code for each day of the month was determined by the Group Headquarters Intelligence Section and sufficient copies were mimeographed for the squadrons to enable them to provide all planes going on Detached Service with an advanced supply of the daily code. Intelligence officers of the 433rd Troop Carrier Group and the 2nd Combat Cargo Squadron have familiarized themselves with this system and have initiated the same system throughout their own units.

Group Intelligence instructed the squadron Intelligence Officers in the use of the group code in recording on the pilots flight maps, the location of allied, guerrilla, and enemy held airfields in the Philippine Islands. Cloth maps of the Philippine Islands, southeast China, North Borneo and adjoining islands were placed in parachute emergency kits.

MEDICAL

No unusual problems were encountered in the Medical Department during the month. A total of 757 man days were lost by personnel being confined to quarters or to the hospital.

MARCH, 1945

The movement of the 6th Squadron from Sorido Strip, Biak, NEI to Tacloban, Leyte, Philippine Islands was completed on 12 March. A total of 73 plane loads of personnel and equipment was moved to the new station. The squadron camp area is located between two rice paddies about four miles from Tacloban. At the end of the month the construction of necessary installations of a more permanent nature was progressing satisfactorily.

Acting on the verbal instructions of the Commanding Officer of the 322nd Troop Carrier wing, APO 923, Colonel Imparato, the Group Commander, alerted the 33rd Squadron on 15 March to move to an unnamed station in the Philippine Islands.

PERSONNEL

During the month of March Change 3 of Troop Carrier Group T/O & E 1-312, dated 17 November, 1944, was received. This change authorized an addition of one major, to be "Group Air Inspector", and one captain, to be "Assistant Group Air Inspector". The position which was formerly designated as "Group Air Inspector" was redesignated as "Deputy Group Commander". Changes in Special Service personnel authorized one captain as "Information-Education Officer" and one 1st Lieutenant as "Physical Fitness Officer", one corporal as "Writer, Military Subjects" and one corporal as "Athletic Instructor".

A revision of squadron personnel resulted form Change 1 to Troop Carrier Squadron T/O & E 1-317, dated 4 October, 1944, which was received during the month. Troop Carrier Squadron Navigators were changed from "Navigators, 1034" to Navigators, radar, 1039". Two staff sergeants and two sergeants, radar mechanics, navigation, authorized in lieu of four privates, who were as follows: one clerk, 044; one clerk-typist, 405; and two messengers, 590.

Per General orders No. 32, Sq., Far East Air Service Command, APO 323, 27 March, 1945, the four squadrons were each authorized an addition of twelve navigators in the grades of one first Lieutenant and eleven 2nd Lieutenants. Each squadron is now authorized a total of twenty navigators.

Captain G. Conrad A. Rowland assumed command of the 21st Squadron on 5 March, relieving Major Joseph H. Moore who will be returned to the United States.

The following named officers received direct commissions as 2nd Lieutenants from the status of Flight Officers:
6th Squadron: 2nd Lt. Paul F. Schrepple;
21st Squadron: 2nd Lt. Saul T. Kysor, Jr.
21st Squadron: 2nd Lt. Donald R. Mitchell
21st Squadron: 2nd Lt. Salvatore J. Porrello
33rd Squadron: 2nd Lt. John P. Wunder

An outstanding example of courage, resourcefulness and good judgement was exhibited by 1st Lt. Frederick F. Gregory of the 6th Squadron on 26 March. A P-51 collided with the C-47 aircraft which he was piloting, shearing off approximately 35 feet of the left wing. The plane began losing altitude rapidly but by his coolness in the emergency and expert piloting, Lt. Gregory kept the aircraft under control by using full right rudder and right aileron. The aircraft was crash landed in a swampy rice field at a speed of 140 miles per hour and the landing was so expertly made that none of the crew suffered even minor injuries. For this outstanding accomplishment Lt. Gregory has been recommended to receive the Distinguished Flying Cross.

OPERATIONS

Under the direction of the Group Navigator, 1st Lt. Kenneth A. Euart, a Navigation Training Program for Pilots has been estab lished in the 374th Troop Carrier Group. While awaiting the arrival of the Air Navigation Manuals which have been requisitioned, a booklet on theoretical and practical navigational material has been drawn up, mimeographed, and a copy distributed to each pilot in the group. This booklet was designed to furnish a lecture outline for the navigator instructor and to furnish the pilot with a simplified text in which only the required subject matter is presented. Each squadron is required to present a minimum of four lectures each week. This requirement was established with the purpose of accelerating the completion of the course and thus prevent it from becoming a long, drawn-out, uninteresting affair. Twenty Navigational Kits authorized under the Basic Table of Allowances have been requisitioned for each squadron. These kits are necessary for giving adequate classroom instruction and for practice problems. Upon the completion of the course these kits should be placed in assigned aircraft and thus be available for the pilots to use in flight. It will enable them to practice what they have learned during the course and to become more proficient in Navigation.

A new policy of the group requires that co-pilots have a minimum of 500 hours of C-47 type aircraft before being checked out as first pilots. It is believed that a number of recent accidents were partially due to inexperience on the part of the pilot and could have been avoided if the pilots had been required to have more C-47 time.

The practice of flying every available aircraft has resulted in a much greater amount of weight being transported for the month of March than in recent previous months. There was an increase of two and half million pounds over the previous month. Weight hauled by the squadrons were as follows:

Philippine Village, 1945.

6th: 3,069,000 lbs; 21st: 1,640,60 lbs; 22nd: 2,546,600 lbs; 33rd: 2,558,800; Group Total: 10,015,000 lbs.

The 33rd Squadron set an all time record for aircraft flying time for a squadron of this group. This squadron topped the previous highest record by approximately 700 hours. The number of miles flown was also far in excess of that ever flown by any squadron in the group.

Enemy Activity

At 2100 o'clock, 23 March, a single twin-engine Jap bomber raided Sorido Strip and vicinity, dropping four 50 and four 100 pound fragmentation bombs. Cpl. David A. Morgan, Jr. of the 21st Squadron, visiting in the A.T.C. Camp Area, was the only casualty of this group. He suffered severe shock and was hospitalized. One bomb fell in close proximity to the group operations, communications, and engineering sections, but fortunately all personnel escaped injury. Slight damage to engineering equipment resulted. No group aircraft sustained damage.

Two planes assigned to the 22nd Squadron were subjected to enemy anti-aircraft fire while on an operational flight over Mindanao on 1 March. No damage resulted. While on a flight from Biak to Darwin an aircraft assigned to the 33rd Squadron encountered ineffective anti-aircraft fire over the Aroe Islands.

Planes of this group remaining overnight at Lingayen and other fields in Northern Luzon have experienced air raids by Japanese bombers. No casualties were sustained and there was no damage to any group aircraft.

Engineering

During the early part of the month a number of planes were kept out of commission because no engines were available. During the month the local depot received a new consignment of engines which were made available to the units at Biak and also to those at other stations.

Communications

The activities of Group Communications were mainly of a routine nature. Some damage was caused to communications installations in the Group Communications and Operations building by the explosion of Japanese bombs on the night of 22 March. All telephone lines to this building were destroyed and the antenna masts of the group radio station were blown down. All damages were repaired within 24 hours.

The radio net continued to operate successfully. The 6th Squadron at Leyte set up their radio station and began operating on 24 March. Despite the distance, transmission between that station and Biak has been very successful. After the initial contact, Group Headquarters has been in one hundred percent communication with the new station. All units of the Group continue to make full utilization of the facilities of the radio net. The 322nd Troop Carrier Wing also used it almost exclusively during the current month in communicating with this headquarters.

During the month an SCR 729 Radar Interrogator was secured with the intention of installing it at Sorido, for the purpose of checking aircraft IFF in flight to provide an infallible check on actual operation in the air. Installation was delayed pending the securing of an adequate power supply. The IFF test program was continued. A technical publication was secured from the Thirteenth Air Force outlining the modification of existing test equipment for IFF, which so far has not proved adequate for convenient IFF testing. It is believed that this modified test equipment will solve the problem of measuring the actual power radiated by IFF so that they may be adjusted to maximum efficiency. Steps have been taken to procure training files showing the importance of proper operations of IFF to prevent false air raid alarms. Since no such material is available at this base, films have been requisitioned by the local film exchange.

In anticipation of the impending move of Group Headquarters to the Philippines a complete new SCR 499 radio station was obtained as well as other shortages of signal equipment. The present SCR 399 will be turned in at this base before moving, as it has been found that the shelter in which it is located is not suitable for tropical operation. An additional SCR 499 will be obtained, and in this way a spare set of operating components will be provided to eliminate closing down the station due to the failure of any elements of the equipment. A duplicate installation of essential components is contemplated at the new station.

A total of eight radar mechanics was sent to the Loran Navigation School conducted by FEAF's CR & TC., to receive training in the maintenance of the new radar navigation equipment which will be standard equipment in all new aircraft assigned to Troop Carrier Units. The course is for a period of one month.

The localizer component of the air borne blind landing equipment has been installed in all squadron planes. All new C-47B and C-46 aircraft received in this area now arrive with complete blind landing equipment but at the present time glide path receiving equipment is not available for installation in the older aircraft assigned to the group.

Intelligence

On Tuesday, 13 March, representatives of the Counter Intelligence Corps presented a lecture to personnel of Group Headquarters and the 21st Squadron on security measures in the Philippines. This talk was both interesting and informative and impressed the troops with the necessity of exercising extreme caution when conversing with anyone in the Philippine Islands.

Group commander's airplane and two crew members: Sgt. Harry Baron (left) and Sgt. Donald W. Gellosch, 1945.

The Group Intelligence Officer has been instrumental in initiating a pre-flight briefing period in each squadron. Although in practice only a short time, it has already proved to be of great value to flying personnel. Subjects discussed during these briefings are: (a) The latest information available on allied guerrilla, and enemy held air strips. (b) Map displays showing the disposition of enemy troops and methods of evading capture. (c) Experiences and advise of pilots who have crash landed on the Philippine Islands. (d) Latest data from daily intelligence summaries. (e) Courses and distances of the daily flights. Pilots are cautioned against loose talk, particularly in their dealings with the Filipinos. Emphasis is placed on security measures regarding classified documents and maps. They are constantly reminded that these must be destroyed in the event of a crash landing or when being forced to abandon their ship.

The morale of the group flying personnel appears to be very good at the present time. This can be attributed mainly to the fact that practically all the old combat crew members have been returned to the United States and in the future, flying personnel can expect to be relieved from this theater before they have served as much as two years. Many of the older men who now have three years in this theater have become very discouraged at the poor prospects of being rotated. This failure of the ground rotation has also affected the morale of the great number of men who now have almost two and half years of overseas service.

Medical

No unusual problems were encountered in the Medical Department and the health of all personnel was found to be very good. All squadrons are completing the immunization of their personnel. No cases of venereal diseases were treated during the month. This is attributed to the fact that leaves and furloughs to the mainland of Australia have been discontinued.

Information and Education

A considerable number of press releases on group personnel was sent to FEAF Public Relations during the month. A press release publicizing the past achievements of the 374th Troop Carrier Group is being prepared.

Much interest in AFI Courses and College and University Extension Courses is still being exhibited and a number of subscriptions were received during the month.

Religion

After the departure of the 6th Squadron from Sorido air base their officers club was converted into a group chapel. This building has proved to be very satisfactory as a chapel in all respects. Services are held in the morning and in the evening of each Sunday.

Chaplain Lee has made several trips to the squadrons located at other stations to administer to the spiritual needs of the personnel.

April, 1945

In the 6th Squadron at Leyte, construction work on administrative buildings and other camp installations continued. Operations, Engineering, and other departments were assigned permanent locations and were able to begin normal operations again.

In compliance with Movement Directive Number 1, Headquarters, 322nd Troop Carrier wing, dated 6 April, 1945, the 33rd Squadron began its planned movement from Hollandia, Dutch New Guinea, APO 565 to Nielson Field, Manila, Philippine Islands, APO 75. A plane carrying an advance echelon left for the new station on 7 April and the actual movement began on 8 April. The squadron had never been definitely assigned to an area and even after some of the planes had arrived and unloaded the situation was still confused. This lack of previous planning by officials in charge necessitated an additional move after work had been started on one area. In spite of the numerous difficulties that were encountered during the initial period the work on the camp area progressed satisfactorily and at the month's end the squadron was fairly well organized and was able to turn more attention to its assigned task of transporting freight and personnel.

The movement of the 33rd Squadron necessitated the use of 72 planes. The total personnel weight moved by air was 95,026 lbs., and the freight weight was 323,189 lbs. Some heavy equipment and building material was left behind with a rear echelon of seven men to be sent up by boat.

Major General McMullen, Commanding General, Far East Air Service Command, commented favorably on the appearance of the group camp area after making an inspection on 25 April, 1945.

Personnel

The present shortage of enlisted personnel, together with the poor prospects of receiving additional replacements, gives every indication of developing into an acute problem. In addition to being far below T/O strength, the group has a considerable number of personnel on TDY in the U.S. at this time. In spite of these grave shortages the 374th Troop Carrier Group has assigned over twenty planes per squadron (T/O Strength, 16 planes) and is operating every plane that can be kept in commission. With the assignment of the new C-46 type aircraft which requires a greater amount of maintenance work than the old C-47, the strain on the engineering sections has become quite acute.

The rotation quota was drastically reduced for the month of May. The quota for enlisted men was reduced approximately fifty percent and eliminated altogether for officers.

Per SO 60, Sq., 374th Troop Carrier Group, Captain Jesse A. Webb was designated as Group S-1 and Administrative Inspector vice Major Gerald O. Wentworth relieved.

M/Sgt. Harry Friedman, former line chief of the 33rd Squadron, received a direct commission as 2nd Lt. F/O J. R. Shoemaker, 6th Squadron, also received a commission as 2nd Lt.

Operations

The Navigation Training program progressed satisfactorily in all squadrons except the 33rd Squadron which was moving during the period. With only a few exceptions all pilots in the other three squadrons have completed the first part of the course. Test problems are given after detailed instruction to determine if additional instruction is necessary. Most pilots are exhibiting more interest as the program proceeds.

Operations were begun on Nielson Field, Manila on 18 April by the 33rd Squadron and Group Operations assumed the responsibility of Base Operations on 19 April. In spite of the fact that operations is the only section of Group Headquarters operating at Nielson Field activities are being carried on with a minimum amount of confusion and loss of efficiency.

Group Operations has prepared a consolidated report on let down procedure on all fields used by the 374th Troop Carrier Group. This information was forwarded to the 322nd Troop Carrier Wing and to the Far East Air Service Command.

For several months there has been a preponderance of co-pilots over first pilots. During April a considerable number of co-pilots were reclassified as first pilots thus bringing about a more satisfactory condition. The equality will allow all pilots to put in an equal amount of flying time.

The assignment of C-46 type aircraft has presented many new problems to operations as well as to other departments. Unfamiliarity with the plane has been the most challenging problem. Pilots are being given transition flying and checked out as they become familiar with the plane. The C-46's have not been put into regular operational flying but are being used almost exclusively for transition.

Because of its short hauls the 6th Squadron carried a much greater amount of weight than any other squadron. The one way move of the 33rd Squadron and the fact that after the move was completed, flying was kept at a minimum while the camp area was being constructed accounted for the small amount of weight carried by that squadron. The great number of empty trips back from the Philippines kept the weight carried from reaching greater proportions. The weights carried by each squadron and by the Group were:

Headquarters: 88,000 lbs; 6th: 4,112,600 lbs; 21st: 2,313,400 lbs; 22nd: 2,453,600 lbs; 33rd: 1,673,600 lbs; Group Total: 10,641,200.

ENEMY ACTIVITY

No personnel were injured and no aircraft assigned to the group were damaged by enemy action. Enemy activity was encountered on 8 April when a plane assigned to the 21st Squadron was fired upon by a heavy machine gun while dropping food supplies to Filipino Guerillas in Northern Luzon. No hits were sustained by the plane. On 26 April a plane assigned to the 22nd Squadron was ineffectively fired upon by light caliber enemy anti-aircraft fire between Girgil and Awar, New Guinea.

ENGINEERING

The squadron engineering sections are finding it increasingly difficult to meet all maintenance requirements for the following reasons: (1) shortage of personnel (2) assignment of more aircraft than is authorized by existing T/O & E (3) flying every aircraft in commission (4) assignment of C-46 type aircraft with which group personnel are totally unfamiliar and which requires more maintenance than the C-47.

Aircraft engines remain critically short and a number of planes have been grounded while awaiting engines. This has materially affected the percentage of aircraft in commission.

At the end of the month the group had in its possession thirteen C-46 type aircraft recently assigned. This is the first time that the 374th Troop Carrier Group has come in contact with this type plane. Consequently the engineering personnel and pilots are totally inexperienced in the maintenance and operation of this plane. Inspections and other maintenance proceed at an extremely slow pace and will continue that way until actual experience is obtained. Pilots are being checked out slowly but satisfactorily. Maintenance has been further hampered by the lack of special tools which were sent by water and which have not yet arrived in this area.

In spite of the above difficulties, the fine record of the group did not suffer during the period. In fact, the percentage of aircraft out of commission was not below the average and more aircraft hours were flown than for any month in the history of the group.

During the month six enlisted men were returned to the United States to attend schools in the maintenance of C-46 type aircraft, IV ASAC at APO 920 conducted classes of instruction on the new plane, and factory representatives assisted both maintenance personnel and pilots to become acquainted with the ship.

374th TC Group at Manila, 1945, full Headquarters staff. Group commander Imparato at far right.

COMMUNICATIONS

The Group Communications Section was engaged in normal activities until 21 April, at which time the group radio station left the air preparatory to moving to Manila. The old group station was turned in to the depot and new equipment was drawn. The two new and more powerful SCB-449's were sent to Manila and installed by the Group Communications Officer.

The 21st Squadron took over control of the group net until such time as the new Group Radio Station could be set up at APO 75. A new 350 watt SCR-499 transmitter was put into operation and performed very efficiently. Due to the frequencies assigned and the skip distance involved, direct contact cannot be made with APO 75 from APO 920. Messages are relayed through the 6th Squadron at Leyte, APO 72.

A telephone switchboard, telephones, and all necessary equipment were sent to APO 75 so that an adequate communications system could be established prior to the movement of Group Headquarters. The administrative personnel of communications remained at APO 920.

INTELLIGENCE

No outstanding events of historical importance occurred in the Intelligence Section. Normal activities were engaged in. Maps and information on new fields recently captured were obtained and passed on to all pilots in the group. Squadrons continued to brief all pilots before scheduled flights.

All units in the group are being educated in positive security measures by posters and frequent lectures. Personnel in the 6th and 33rd Squadrons have been especially warned against loose talk, fraternizing with unknown natives, and of the danger of sabotage by pro-Japanese Filipinos.

Morale in Group Headquarters can be considered good at this time. This can be attributed mainly to the contemplated move to Manila.

Because of an improvement in the food, adequate PX supplies, and luxuries, ice cream, Coca Cola and comfortable living conditions, the morale in the 21st Squadron is reported to be better than usual.

The 22nd Squadron reports that morale is somewhat impaired due to poor food and long working hours, but on the whole is still very good.

The recent move of the 33rd Squadron to Manila has brought its personnel in contact with civilization again and has been a great factor in improving morale. The poor location of the camp area, many new difficulties and much hard work incident to the move caused much griping, but was not considered detrimental to morale.

Certain factors have influenced different types of personnel. The speeded up rotation for flying personnel has resulted in most of the old men being returned to the States and has improved the morale of all flying personnel. The greatly reduced quota for ground personnel for the month of May has greatly reduced the morale of the men with long periods of overseas service. The unavailability of leaves and furloughs has somewhat affected morale. The continued successes in Europe and prospects of an early victory have been the basis for hopes that replacements will soon be coming to this theater and that rotation will be speeded up.

MEDICAL

The health of the Group was exceptionally good during the month. On one occasion a number of enlisted men in the 22nd Squadron were hospitalized because of Ptomaine poisoning. Personnel of the 6th and 33rd Squadrons experienced a number of cases of diarrhea, probably contracted from local fresh fruits and vegetables, water supplies, and local unsanitary conditions. No cases on venereal disease were reported.

The first American flag to fly over the Japanese Empire - August 28, 1945.

SPECIAL SERVICES

Special ServiceS presented sixteen movies and two USO Stage Shows during the month. Facilities for volleyball, badminton, softball and horseshoes were provided.

At the present time each unit in the group has either a Coca Cola machine or an ice cream machine or both. New machines have been ordered in Australia so that every squadron will have a Coca Cola and an ice cream machine. These services are considered very important to the morale of all personnel.

MAY, 1945

During the month the 33rd Squadron continued construction of necessary installations in their new camp area at APO 75. Tin buildings with cement floors were constructed for all departments. Showers, latrines, a water system, and a power plant were all operating efficiently early in the month. Before the end of May such great progress had been made that the officers and men were able to turn their attention toward improving their own living quarters.

In compliance with VOCG, Sq. FEASC, 28 May and Movement Order Number 2, Headquarters, 322nd Troop Carrier Wing, the Group Headquarters of the 374th Troop Carrier Group moved from its station at Biak, APO 920, to Nielson Field, Manila, Philippine Islands, APO 75. Per verbal orders, 322nd Troop Carrier Wing, the main movement began 23 May and was completed 30 May. The official change of station was effective 0700/I, 28 May. All personnel, equipment and supplies arrived at APO 75 without accident.

The Group Headquarters area, adjacent to the 33rd Squadron area, is located approximately one half mile east of Nielson Field from which the Group and 33rd Squadron planes will operate. All Group departments, including operations, are located within the camp area, rather than at the field itself. The utilities section of the advance echelon had erected most of the departmental buildings and as a result the various sections were able to begin operating with a minimum amount of delay and confusion after arriving.

THE SHANGRI-LA SAGA

While still headquartered in Biak, our commander was constantly flying the route from Biak to Port Moresby to oversee the functioning of 374th Squadrons. On one such flight, while returning to Biak, an overnight stop was made at Hollandia to confer with MacArthur's headquarters and our wing commander, Col. Ray T. Elsmore who was stationed there. By a strange coincidence, a few days before a crash had occurred in the mountain south of Hollandia that cost the lives of 21 officers, airmen and Wacs. Their flight mission was purely recreational. The immediate search of the crash area from the air discovered three survivors, two men and a Wac (Women's Army Corp). Medical supplies, food and a portable radio were dropped to the survivors immediately. At this point, wing commanding officer, Col. Ray T. Elsmore, requested assistance from the group to fly to the site, make an appraisal of the situation, and try to determine a rescue plan for the survivors. The following clipping described the events that followed the first flight into the crash site.

374TH TROOP CARRIER TOPICS

Volume 3 Number 7 Philippine Islands   10 June 1945

A.P. AND RADIO GET VALLEY STORY
COLONEL FLIES HIDDEN VALLEY MERCY SHIP

All indications were of a routine flight, that morning not so long ago, when Col. Edward T. Imparato, Group Commander, Lt. Chester Hunter, and their C-47 crew, Sergeant Donald Gellasch and Cpl. Harry Baron took off for a run south into New Guinea. But before the day was out one of the most exciting missions every undertaken by any members of the Group was to materialize - for they were to journey into the forbidden "Hidden Valley."

The Hidden Valley of New Guinea has a unique history which dates back to the early days of the war, when a constant search was in progress for new and safer air routes to the far-flung Allied bases. Colonel Ray T. Elsmore, now commanding the 322nd Troop Carrier Wing, and Major Myron Grimes, former CO of the 21st Squadron, were on such a mission when accidentally blown off course, they burst out over a tremendous valley, about 25 miles long, 5100 feet above sea level and surrounded by inaccessible mountains through which the lowest pass stood at 9,500 feet. This was new territory, never before charted on maps, and which possessed unbelievable agricultural developments.

Although pictures were taken of the Valley, and attempts were made to discover some history of its inhabitants, it did not remain long in the military eye, for the war was moving away from the vicinity and air routes skirted the Valley by many miles. Col. Elsmore, however, did not forget the Valley and continued his research as somewhat of a hobby.

The organization that raised the flag over Japan and its commander, Major A.C. Jordan.

Due to the inaccessibility of the mountains, and the small knowledge of the native inhabitants, flights over the Valley were subsequently prohibited; but there was still danger in becoming lost in the Valley. Not so long ago, a transport, loaded with passengers suffered just such a fate. But to some unknown cause, the ill-fated aircraft crashed into the densely wooded mountainside of the Valley. Search planes scoured the Valley floor and sides for a trace of the accident and in a short time noted three persons, the only survivors, standing on the mountainside.

It was just about this time that the 374th plane and crew were flying to NewGuinea, and the authorities called on Colonel Imparato, long experienced in drop missions, to bring his ship and crew into the rescue. Because of the scarcity of knowledge of the natives, paratroops were to be dropped to protect the survivors, Lt., T/Sgt and a Wac enlisted woman. Supplies had to be dropped to sustain them until plans could be formed for bringing the party out of the Valley.

Col. Imparato and his crew flew into the Valley, from which no white men had returned, and flying at the incredible slow speed of 75 miles an hour 20 feet off the ground, dropped weapons, medical supplies and ammunition to the paratroops dropped on the first run, from normal conditions. Walkie-talkie communications were established between ground and the plane and in a short time everything was going as planned.

Thus far, the survivors met natives only once and then nothing occurred. However, from the fact that natives shot arrows and threw spears at the low-flying aircraft, it would be assumed that they are not friendly. And yet from all appearances, the natives are semi-civilized. The Valley floor is well-farmed, modern methods of irrigation are in practice, and many villagers with livestock, dotting the river bank, show them to be gregarious people.

The survivors of the crash and rescue party wait now, until some means of escape can be arranged. It would be impossible to walk out of the Valley - an estimated three months trek. As for going down river, one end is blanked by a two to three hundred foot waterfall, and the other way leads into Jap held territory. Only two plausible possibilities remain. One, flying in small aircraft and bringing them out one by one, or building a strip in the Valley to accommodate transport aircraft.

So there it stands, one more mystery of New Guinea's jungle mazes - and one more exploit to chalk up in the 374th record of achievement.

STOP PRESS: Yesterday morning, Saturday, the Radio and Associated Press carried the "Hidden Valley" story for release to the United States

The 374th Troop Carrier "*Topics*" article was just the beginning of a long stream of stories and articles about the rescue operation. According to Burrell's Press Clipping Bureau, this event received more national and international coverage than any other happening in recent history. It was even a feature on the popular radio program of the time called "the March of Time."

This rather strange yet unusual wartime event is recorded here to emphasize a few important phenomenon of human life and especially the American mystique.

1. In the middle of a desperate war where limited resources are available and men and women are critical to the current military need, that the Commanding General, General Douglas MacArthur, will consent to giving up some of his limited resources to save a few lives - three to be exact. And at the same time give up, at least for a time, the 100 officers and men, aircraft and equipment to support the mercy mission. The complete operation consumed 47 days.

2. The airborne part of the mission proved the viability and flexibility of air drop of supplies and parachutist in otherwise in-

accessible places in deep jungle and mountainous terrain at high altitude.

3. The deep compassion we hold for our fellow man is in some cases beyond belief and unclear.

4. Tasks which seem impossible bring out the best in us. The imagination and ingenuity of the military man is boundless.

5. The sanctity of our life is held dear to us while we kill the enemy with impunity.

6. This unusual rescue operation so gripped the nation that it seemed to overshadow the news of military operations both in Europe and the Far East.

May 13, 1945

Sometime the exigencies of the military services are pushed aside and non military, but humanitarian causes, take top priority. Such was the case when a devastating air plane crash occurred in the deepest jungle of New Guinea. Of the 24 persons aboard a C-47 on a recreational flight, only three survived the crash. The delicate task of finding the survivors, caring for them in their long ordeal in the jungle and eventually effecting the rescue, fell largely to the 374th Troop Carrier Group. All four groups of troop carrier in the theater eventually became involved.

The Shangri La episode began on May 13, 1945. It was at this time that MacArthur's forces were well established in the Philippines. The 374th was preparing to move its operation to Manila and massive attacks by Navy, Army and Air Forces of the Allied powers were hammering Okinawa into submission. MacArthur's staff was working diligently on the ultimate strategic plan for the assault on the Japanese mainland.

With all the feverish military action under way, it was MacArthur's great compassion for human life that he permitted a large element of his meager forces to be used in the rescue of the survivors. In all, hundreds of men and scores of airplanes were used in the rescue. Thousands of pounds of food, equipment and supplies were flown into the crash site and base camp daily. And the rescue operation took 47 days.

The 374th group commander has written a book on the rescue operation.[1] Australian historian and author Robert Piper has provided in his book *"The Hidden Chapters"*, a well researched and documented overview and with his permission it is sighted here:

Col. Hutchison thanking Group Commander Imparato for the flight.

"Concealed within the towering mountains of Irian Jaya (former Dutch New Guinea) lies a rich and pleasant valley whose official name is Baliem, and through which meanders a large river of the same name. A place of mystery and legend, the valley is cooled by altitude and protected by 13,000 foot peaks on all sides. World headlines were created in mid-1945 with the unique rescue of two men and a woman, the sole survivors of an aircraft crash, by a tug plane and glider. The news media of the time were quick to dub this place Shangri La after the mythical hidden valley of Tibet in James Hilton's famous novel Lost Horizon. Hollywood was later to produce movies on both that novel and the New Guinea rescue story.

"By May of 1945 the war against Japan had reached her very doorstep and Hollandia (now Djaypura) was a large sleepy base in the backwaters of Dutch New Guinea. On Sunday, the 13th of that month, a joy flight and navigation exercise was organised by Colonel Peter J. Prosson of the Far East Service Command (FEASC), then stationed there. Prosson was to pilot the aircraft accompanied by eight servicewomen and 15 servicemen, all members of the U.S. Army, on a planned flight over what was known as Hidden Valley.

"The hot tropical coastline and Sentani airstrip were soon left far behind as the Douglas C-47 transport (no 41-23952 and Australian civil registration VH-CHG), which departed at 1410 hours, droned steadily upwards to cooler skies. For those who might be superstitious, the aircraft's nose art designated it Gremlin Special and its tail number was "13", coincidentally, the same day of the month as its fateful last flight. All aboard Gremlin Special were naturally excited. Rumours and stories abounded about the Hidden Valley among the personnel back at Hollandia. They told of tall, light-skinned people who farmed complex irrigation systems that could provide only one answer to their origin - a lost civilisation!

"First Lieutenant John S. McCollom, one of only two men to survive the subsequent crash, was later to record what happened that day:

"*'We flew at approximately 7000 feet all the way. I checked the altitude and airspeed once, just for the heck of it. We never reached Hidden Valley, our course was 224 degrees and the plane must have been about 15 air miles from the place when we crashed.*

"*'Our aircraft had been flying about an hour when it entered a canyon. The floor of this pass must have been about 6500 feet and the peaks on both sides were about 11,000 feet. Weather was clear and visibility good, but there were clouds around the tops of the mountains.*

---

[1] The complete story of this jungle saga is recorded in a book written by Group Commander Edward T. Imparato. *Rescue From Shangri-La*© published by Turner Publishing Company, P.O. Box 3101, Paducah, KY 42002-3101. 1997. See Appendix 'GG'

"'Just prior to the crash I noticed that the door to the pilot's compartment was open. Sgt. Helen Kent was sitting in the pilot's seat and Major Nicholson was flying the plane from the co-pilot's position. Colonel Prossen, our pilot, was standing in the radio room looking towards the front of the transport. Prior to that, and during most of the trip, he was in the main cabin talking to personnel.

"'I noticed that Major Nicholson saw white clouds ahead, applied power and started to climb. We started going through the clouds and you could see the ground occasionally, but it was definitely instrument flying.

"'Just before we hit you could see the treetops below. I turned to Corporal Margaret Hastings and said: "This is going to be darnn close but I think we can get over it." Just then we hit. I was thrown from the left hand side to the right hand side of the aircraft, turning somersaults in the process. Landed on my hands and knees about halfway up the cabin. Flames were all around me. Saw a white spot to the rear and crawled towards it. Scrambled out a hole where the tail end of the plane had torn loose from the fuselage. Corporal Hastings crawled out through the same opening.

"'After I had returned to the aircraft and rescued Sgt. Laura Besley and Private Eleanor Hanna, Sgt. Decker came walking around from the front of the plane on the right hand side. He seemed to be dazed and in a state of shock, didn't know what he was doing or what was going on. All five survivors owed their lives, at this stage, to the fact that they had been seated in the very rear of the aircraft, away from the main impact point.'

"As the intensity of the fire increased, it was to continue spasmodically until the afternoon of the following day, when the party retreated to a ledge some 30 feet away, with McCollom carrying Private Hanna. The regular afternoon rain then began falling, adding to their discomfort.

"McCollom made repeated trips back to the crash site, recovering two containers of water, hard sweets called Charms, yellow tarpaulins and a signal kit from emergency life rafts. Not once did he make mention that his twin brother, 1st Lieutenant Robert E. McCollom, was somewhere back inside the broken, smouldering fuselage.

"As night approached the four swathed themselves and the badly injured Eleanor Hanna in tarpaulins to endure the long, cold night. They were at nearly 9000 feet and temperatures would drop close to the zero mark. With Dawn it was found that Eleanor Hanna had died from her severe burns and she was carefully wrapped in one of the canvas squares and laid beside a nearby tree.

"That morning, 14 May, the first search plane flew over. There were 24 sent out and although the group signaled with a mirror, they were not seen. Ken Decker was to dryly comment that the previous day had been his 36th birthday and he wasn't impressed with what he had received! All felt relieved, though, that they were missed and a search had begun. In the afternoon Laura Besley died, probably from internal injuries, as she couldn't keep water down, and was placed with Eleanor Hanna.

"At daylight on Tuesday (the 15th) the three survivors began a slow trek down the mountain using a compass from one of the life rafts to maintain direction. In this way they hoped to find a village or open ground where searchers could more easily spot them. Following fast-flowing mountain streams, passing waterfalls and wading they eventually reached a clearing, on an embankment, at midday on Wednesday.

"During the mountain descent Margaret's long hair had repeatedly become entangled in bushes until, in desperation, she asked McCollom to cut it short with his penknife. Decker, who back in Hollandia had been refused a date by Margaret, never lost an opportunity to remind her in the days that followed.

"The three survivors, lying in a small sunlit clearing to warm up, again heard the engines of a large aircraft heading their way. Yellow tarpaulins were hurriedly laid out but the four-engined Flying Fortress continued on its way. However, early in the afternoon it returned and this time they were seen. The pilot momentarily cut his engines and rocked the wings as a signal to those below that they had been sighted.

"A large group of timid natives visited the small, grassy knoll later that day. They chatted in their own language and smoked mountain tobacco as they relaxed with the white strangers. Their obvious friendliness and humour was a welcome relief.

"On Thursday a radio was dropped by parachute. Decker and McCollom quickly rigged it up and contact was clearly established with the circling aircraft overhead. The names of survivors were relayed and brief details of the tragedy told. Food, jungle kits, medicine, bandages and jungle knives were located with other chutes nearby.

"Another aircraft returned the following day and this time dropped two paratroopers further down the valley, in more hospitable country. Both were Filipinos and trained medical orderlies. One, Corporal Rammy Ramirez, injured his ankle but despite this both

Colonel D.M. Dunne with crew under the wing of C-46-7769.

Relaxing at the control tower, (from left) Sgt. Barin, Lt. Hunter, Maj. Langbartel, and Maj. Lieberman at Atsugi, August, 1945.

he and Sgt Ben Bulatao soon arrived at the camp and set to work. Fires were lit and hot food and drinks performed wonders for the three survivors.

"Ken Decker's right elbow was badly sprained, there was a deep gash on his forehead as well as burns on both legs and buttocks. Margaret was burnt about the ankles, left foot and right hand with blisters on the left side of her face. Lt. John McCollom had burnt hands, a little hair singed off but was otherwise uninjured.

"On Sunday May 20 a transport aircraft dropped Captain Earl Walters and 10 paratroopers into the main Baliem Valley, some 45 miles further south. Two of these men remained behind to set up camp and build a glider strip while the rest set out to link up with the survivors. They arrived five days later.

"Captain Walters and a burial party then proceeded back up the mountain to the crash site with 20 crosses and a Star of David. These were erected over the graves and identity tags draped on each. Later, an aircraft circled overhead with a funeral service being read over its radio by Catholic, Protestant and Jewish representatives. The survivors below, at the grassy knoll, listened in on their radio.

"Decker, McCollom, and Margaret Hastings felt fit enough to talk out on 15 June. It was time for them and the paratroop party to head for the main valley and glider strip. For the three a long, slow and painful journey. They arrived to be greeted by a surprisingly comfortable accommodation consisting of large partitioned tents and even makeshift tables and a bath.

"Assorted shells had been especially flown in to be used for bartering with the locals, especially to purchase local pigs for food.

On Thursday 28 June a C-46 Curtiss Commando released a Waco glider, named 'Fanless Faggot', over the Shangri La camp. Piloted by Lt. Henry E. Palmer the glider swooped silently down to a perfect landing on the 300-foot strip. Meanwhile, a Douglas C-47, 'Leaking Louise', which had also flown in, flew in slow circles overhead. On radio request she was to be the glider's tug for the return trip. The initial load for the glider consisted of Lt. Paver, the pilot, the three survivors and two Filipino paratroopers. Preparations were quickly completed and on a radio call the lightly laden transport, with Major Samuels at the controls, swept down low in a shallow dive. Samuel's first attempt was successful, his tow hook snatched the line between the two posts, and he roared off down the valley to pick up speed with Leaking Louise in a gentle climb.

"However, at this critical stage tragedy nearly overtook the party again. As the glider slithered down the strip it snagged an old supply parachute on its skid, which luckily didn't re-open but created some additional drag as it trailed behind. Leaking Louise clawed for altitude in the thin air, her speed dropped to 105 mph, and some trees were skimmed before she finally began to climb. Major Samuels continued to circle the area for some time until the sufficient height was gained to clear the mountains, then swung north with his glider obediently bobbing behind.

"The return trip was also not without its problems as the dragging chute, buffeted by the slipstream, continually slapped the thin wooden fuselage of the glider. A two foot hole was torn in the plywood floor and gave the nervous passengers an uninterrupted view of the jungle passing below.

"After a 90-minute flight the glider was released over the coast and settled gently down for a welcome landing back at Hollandia. As the waiting media snapped photos and bombarded Margaret, John and Ken with questions the three remained understandably quiet. Although it was a tremendous relief to finally be back after 46 days their thoughts continually returned to their 21 friends who were still back on the mountain.

"In October 1958 Dutch officials, exploring the Pas Valley for the wreckage of a Short Sealand missionary aircraft that crashed in 1955, chanced upon the wreckage of Gremlin's Special at a height of 7200 feet. A United States search and recovery team from Hawaii made the necessary arrangements to visit the site and arrived in Hollandia on 18 November 1958. A week later, at the Netherlands Government Station in the Baliem Valley, Dutch officers briefed the team on the terrain and climatic conditions they would encounter. Especially noteworthy was the temperature variation which dropped from 80 degrees Fahrenheit during the day to only 45 degrees as night approached. High winds and heavy rains usually accompanied this sudden change in temperature. Meanwhile, members of a Dutch patrol returning from Pas Valley reported being attacked by previously friendly natives. Despite this, a party of 31 men, armed for protection, departed for the crash site on 4 December. The team successfully accomplished their mission and the remains of those left behind 13 years earlier were recovered and returned to the U.S.

"Unbeknown or forgotten to the U.S. Army and world media in 1946 was the fact that the Baliem Valley area had in fact been visited in 1938. Much of the area had been examined by the Archbold Expedition of more than 100 outsiders. A combined scientific research group of Dutch and Americans with Dyak carriers. This group, with soldiers and scientists in their ranks, operated with the then new Catalina flying boat.

"Superbly equipped, the expedition with their aircraft, named Guba II, landed on both the Baliem River and nearby Lake Habbema, the latter an amazing 10,500 feet altitude. Over 100,000 specimens were collected by the party in a little more than a year. The entire project had been supported by an aircraft that was itself to become a legend within a few years, during World War II.

"Post war, John McCollom married and became a civilian project engineer for the U.S. Air Force at the Wright Patterson air force base in Ohio. Kenneth Decker went to the engineering department of the Boeing Aircraft Corporation in Washington. Margaret Hastings married, had a daughter and was last heard of in New York.

"The Baliem Valley area is still an extremely dangerous area to fly, even in modern aircraft. In 1977 the Australian air force lost an Iroquois helicopter when it crashed while negotiating the Pas Valley in poor weather conditions. The captain was killed and four of the other five on board were injured. At the time the Indonesian authorities were being assisted with the mapping of Irian Jaya. An accompanying helicopter witnessed the accident and quickly re-located the site with signals transmitted from a latter day activated survival beacon."

On 20 May, Colonel Imparato Group Commander, began the initial operations of a plan to rescue three Army Air Force personnel from the deep impenetrable jungle in New Guinea. Shortly before this date a plane loaded with personnel had crashed in "Hidden Valley" deep in the interior of New Guinea. This rich valley, inhabited by an unknown type of native, had never been visited by a white man. Major Myron Grimes, formerly of the 21st Squadron, was a co- discoverer of this inaccessible valley, now receiving widespread attention. It is 5100 feet above sea level and is surrounded by impassable mountains in which the lowest pass is 9500 feet. It was considered impossible to affect a rescue of the three survivors of the crash except by air. Since there is no area within the valley suitable for use as a landing strip, it was decided to drop supplies and paratroops into the valley to protect the survivors from possible savage natives until a feasible rescue plan could be formulated.

Colonel Imparato volunteered for the mission, and accompanied by Lt. Chester Hunter, Co-pilot, Sgt. Donald Gellasch, Crew Chief, and Cpl. Harry Baron, Radio Operator, dropped Filipino and American paratroops with necessary supplies and equipment into the valley to sustain them. Radio contact was established with the rescuers on the ground within fifteen minutes. And thus ended the first phase of a rescue operation which will further prove that the United States Army will allow no obstacles, no matter how forbidding, to stand in the way of saving human life. The paratroopers dropped into the valley were instructed to walk out of the valley to the crash site, tend the injured survivors and on their recovery return to the valley for rescue.

Personnel

Under General Orders Number 15, Hq., 322nd Troop Carrier Wing, APO 323, dated 11 May, Captain Donald K. Hartley O-675431, was appointed Commanding Officer of the 6th Squadron, relieving Major Isaac W. Smith who is to be returned to the United States. The effective date of the change of command was 15 May.

Per special orders Number 69, Hq., 374th Troop Carrier Group, dated 18 May, Captain William J. Samuels O-353311, Commanding Officer of the 33rd Squadron, was relieved from assignment to that organization and reassigned to Group Headquarters as Deputy Group Commander.

Captain Robert T. Best O-803731 was appointed Commanding Officer of the 33rd Troop Carrier Squadron per General Orders Number 16, dated 19 May, Hq., 322nd Troop Carrier Wing, APO 323 vice Captain William J. Samuels relieved.

Sgt. Cecil E. Batte was killed on Peleiu Island 5 May when the landing gear of the airplane on which he was crew chief collapsed pinning him in the landing gear well.

Shortly after R-Day, 12 May, information on the Army's Readjustment Program was received, and work was immediately begun compiling the points of all Group Personnel. The film "Two Down and One To Go" was presented to all personnel to explain the point system and how it would affect service personnel in this theater. Considerable confusion arose in determining what battle stars were authorized. The situation was not alleviated by the conflicting opinions emanating from higher headquarters concerning the Group's eligibility for certain campaign participations.

Operations

Under the provisions of Operations Memorandum Number 17, Hq., 374th Troop Carrier Group, dated 21 May, each squadron will be assigned 16 operational aircraft of which 75%, or 12 planes, are to be operated daily for the 322nd Troop Carrier Wing. In addition, each squadron will be assigned and will maintain two C-47's for the squadron pool and two C-47's for the group pool, making a total of 20 aircraft per squadron. These four extra aircraft will be used to maintain twelve aircraft in operational flight. The squadrons were informed that they may fly more than twelve planes per day for the purpose of increasing pilots flying time, provided that it does not inflict an unnecessary burden on the Engineering Section.

In order to reduce the excessive number of avoidable accidents all squadron commanders have been ordered to reclassify to co-pilot status immediately any pilot who has a taxying accident. A complete investigation will be made immediately by the Operations Officer and a report forwarded to the Accident Investigation

Maj. Gen. Joe Swing on right and his Chief of Staff Brig. Gen. Pearson.

Board within three days. If it is the decision of the Board that the accident was not due to pilot error the officer concerned will be reclassified first pilot.

A gratifying number of co-pilots were reclassified to first pilots status during the month. The transition program in the C-46 aircraft was progressing satisfactorily. Per Group Operations Memorandum Number 16, all pilots must meet the following requirements before being checked out a first pilots in C-46 type aircraft: (a) Pilots who have been checked out as first pilots in C-47 type aircraft and have 1000 hours or more C-47 time will be required to have a minimum of 50 hours in C-46 type aircraft before being checked out as first pilots and going on operational missions as first pilots in C-46 type aircraft. (B) Pilots who have been checked out as first pilots in C-47 type aircraft and have less than 1000 hours, minimum 500 hours, C-47 time will be required to have a minimum of 75 hours in C-46 type aircraft before being checked out as first pilot and going on operational missions as first pilot in C-46 type aircraft. (c) Pilots must have a minimum of three hours hood instrument time in C-46's.

Group Operations continued in the capacity of Base Operations at Nielson Field until 1 June, at which time the 93rd Airdrome Squadron assumed the responsibility of Base Operations.

The weights carried by each squadron and by the group for the month were: 6th: 1711.3 tons; 21st: 1489.7 tons; 22nd: 989.9 tons; 33rd 1183.3 tons; Group Total: 5075.1 tons.

ENEMY ACTIVITY

No enemy activity was encountered by any group planes or personnel during the month.

ENGINEERING

No unusual difficulties were encountered in the engineering sections during the month. Maintenance personnel became more familiar with the C-46 through actual experience in pulling maintenance on them.

COMMUNICATIONS

The Communications Section carried on normal operations at APO 920 while the advance echelon was busy at APO 75 making preparations for telephone, teletype, and radio service.

On 5 May, a group of officers from the 21st Squadron and Group Headquarters participated in a series of blind landing equipment tests undertaken by the 403rd Troop Carrier Group. The two systems being compared were the SCS 51 System and the Radar GCA System. It was found that considerable time and care were necessary for proper installation of the SCS 51 System, while the GCA System housed in two trucks, could be placed in operation almost immediately at any given location. The flying accuracy of the two systems were about equal. It was recommended by the 403rd in their formal report to higher headquarters that GCA System be used initially at newly acquired strips until the permanent SCS 51 System could be properly installed and calibrated. Neither system necessarily excludes the other, but there is definite value in one complimenting the other. At present all new C-46 aircraft being received by this group are completely equipped with SCS 51 airborne components, and all C-47 aircraft have the localizer unit installed.

The movement of the communications Section was completed on 25 May. Prior to this date the old SCR 399 which had been used as the group radio station was turned in to the signal depot. The SCR 499 which the 21st Squadron began operating at APO 920 has been very satisfactory.

Col. Charles T. Tench, commander of the advance party of 150 on the day of arrival of the 11 Airborne Division, 29 August, 1945.

Adequate storage and administrative housing facilities were ready to receive the section upon its arrival. Space and facilities for the maintenance and repair of radios, telephone installations, etc., were allotted.

The signal equipment on hand very nearly complies with the allowances set forth in T/O & E 1-312.

INTELLIGENCE

Normal activities were engaged in by the Intelligence Section. Briefing pilots, preparing and keeping up to date various maps, and presenting the news were the chief accomplishments.

The announcement of the Army's contemplated demobilization plan caused an unprecedented boost of morale. However, the film "Two Down and One to Go" somewhat curbed these high spirits. However, most of the personnel feel that their chances for being returned to the United States are much better than they have been at any time in the past. Unnumerable rumors concerning the replacement plan have been circulating through the group. No definite information as to how the plan will work has bee announced by higher headquarters and until such time as those facts are presented it is anticipated that speculation will run rampant.

MEDICAL

No unusual problems were met by the Medical Department. From the 2039 assigned and attached personnel the daily average sick call was 66.67 per day, or 3.3%. The total man days lost in hospital and quarters was 1345 or 2.14%. A total of 661 flying personnel lost 715 days or 3.5%. No cases of venereal disease were reported during the month.

UTILITIES

The Utilities Section was sorely pressed to meet the requirements demanded of it. The new camp area had to be prepared and all necessary installations constructed and made ready for occupancy by the end of the month. Building materials were extremely hard to procure but this problem was met by moving nine portable buildings from New Guinea. Grading equipment and concrete mixers were lacking and it was only through the courtesy of neighboring organizations that these necessary machines were obtained. Ten Filipino carpenters were obtained and assisted greatly in the construction of the camp. The 33rd Squadron shared its electrical power and water with Group Headquarters.

INFORMATION AND EDUCATION

Within thirty-five minutes after the end of the war in Europe was announced, an extra edition of the Group newspaper, "Topics" went to press. On the morning of VE Day the group personnel had the unusual experience of being provided with a newspaper at the breakfast table of an Army mess hall.

Applications for Army Institute Courses continued to be received. These educational courses appear to be arousing more interest at the present time than at any period in the past.

In addition to the large number of routine press releases, several feature stories were submitted to FEAF Public Relations.

JUNE, 1945

During the month of June Group Headquarters and the four squadrons were engaged in normal activities. The Group Headquarters area was further improved and more permanent installations were erected. All buildings, barracks, and tents were properly wired by the Utilities Section. The water system throughout the camp area was further improved and extended. A single barracks was constructed for the headquarter's officers and the enlisted men were encouraged to construct wooden floors for their tents and otherwise improve their living quarters.

On 28 June, a C-47 piloted by Major William J. Samuels, Jr., of Group Headquarters, picked up a glider from the floor of Hidden Valley in New Guinea and thereby completed the rescue of the survivors of the tragic crash mentioned in the May installment of the Group History. Other crew members on this outstanding flight were as follows: Co-pilot, Captain W. G. McKenzie, 33rd Troop Carrier Squadron; aerial engineer, Sgt. Donald W. Gellasch, Headquarters; and radio operator, S/Sgt. Bert Goodwin, 21st Troop Carrier Squadron.

Major Samuels and his crew had practiced for several days on pickups in preparation for the difficult feat of picking up a glider from an altitude of over 5,000 feet and then rising to almost 11,000 feet to clear the surrounding mountains. On one dry run the wench controlling the two cable broke and the cable snapped back through the ship wounding Sgt. Harry Baron, the regular radio operator, and thus preventing him from going into the valley on the actual rescue mission.

The glider was picked up on the first pass. The plane which was making approximately 137 miles an hour was slowed down to 105 miles per hour when it hit the glider stanchion. Major Samuels pulled up to about 10,000 feet but couldn't hold that altitude and so dropped to about 8,000 feet. The remainder of the trip was uneventful, although the glider kept shedding fabric on the way back to Hollandia because of tears sustained on the take off.

After undergoing the strains and stresses of the several glider pick-ups the plane used was practically ready for the salvage dump by the time the rescue had been made.

All the major press services were witness to the above feat and newsreel cameras were grinding continuously. One newsreel man was dropped by parachute into the valley to be brought out in a later glider pickup. The rescue crew was photographed, questioned, and even made recordings for future broadcasts.

Major Samuels has been recommended for the D.F.C. while the other crew members have been recommended for the Air Medal.

As an aftermath of the above operations, the following crew members of the 21st Troop Carrier Squadron towed two more gliders into the valley and picked them up again, bringing out the paratroopers and other personnel who remained behind: 1st Lt. Robert W. Fitzgerald, Co-Pilot; Pfc. Tigh, aerial engineer, and Pfc. Laboch, radio operator.

Lt. General George Kenney, Commander Far East Air Forces, strides briskly to his meeting with MacArthur at Atsugi, August 30, 1945. General Kenney arrived about one-half hour after MacArthur.

Personnel

Captain Jesse A. Webb Group Personnel Staff Officer and Captain Elmer L. Tuck, Group Statistical Control Officer, attended the Personnel and Statistical Conference held in Manila by the Far East Air Forces, on 27 and 28 June. Much valuable information was obtained and many questions were answered during the course of the meeting. Full information on the readjustment program was obtained and disseminated to all group personnel. The facts as obtained denoted that the plan would be applied conservatively for several months. There is no reason for optimism among the members of this group even though almost fifty percent of ground personnel have an adjusted service rating score above the critical score.

The following named officers occupied the positions indicated at the end of the period covered: Commanding Col. Edward T. Imparato; S-1 Capt. Jesse A. Webb; S-2 Maj. Lamont N. Rennels; S-3 Maj. William J. Samuels, Jr.; S-4 Capt. Marvin M. Scott; Adjutant Maj. Gerald O. Wentworth; Statistical Control Capt. Elmer L. Tuck; Air Inspector Capt. Stephen S. Geatches; Communications Officer Maj. Alexander Lieberman; Engineering Officer Capt. Marvin M. Scott; Group Flight Surgeon Maj. Charles E. Hellweg

The following named personnel are missing on operational flights and are considered killed: 1st Lt. Odis B. Torbett, Pilot; 2nd Lt. Melvin L. Pruett, Co-Pilot; S/Sgt. Arnold M. Ross, Crew Chief; and Sgt. John A. Morgan, Radio Operator, all of the 6th Squadron, and 2nd Lt. T. V. Lair, Pilot; 2nd Lt. C. V. Ludwig, Co-Pilot; Sgt. W. O. Waldrop, Crew Chief; Sgt. E. F. Wummer, Radio Operator, and S/Sgt. John P. Skodis, passenger, 21st Squadron.

Operations

Only normal operations were engaged in by Group Headquarters and by the squadrons.

The weights carried by the squadrons and by the group as a whole are listed here: 6th: 1529.8 tons; 21st: 1063.1 tons; 22nd: 887.5 tons; 33rd: 1517.6 tons; Group Total: 4998.0 tons.

Enemy Activity

No enemy activity was encountered by any group plane or personnel during the month.

Engineering

Aircraft engines of the 1830-92 series were critical during the month. There was an increase of AGP's in C-46 type planes because of a scarcity of certain parts, especially brakes and struts. However, there now appears to be adequate supplies available.

A C-47B type aircraft assigned to the 6th Squadron, Serial No. 43-49762 has been missing since 20 June. 1st Lt. Odis B. Torbett was piloting the plane on a routine operational mission. The C-47B, 43-19762, assigned to the 21st Squadron, has been missing since 24 June. The plane piloted by 2nd Lt. Talbert B. Lair, left Merauke for Biak and was not heard from again.

Communications

On 6 June the new "Tracer" switchboard located in the rear of the group operations building went into operation, taking over the former "Tracer" board operated by the 33rd Squadron. Trunk lines to the central switchboards were secured, giving the 374th Troop Carrier Group a complete coverage on the Manila and adjacent areas.

On 4 June the group radio station KS11, went on the air taking over net control which was handled by the 21st Squadron Station, HYH2, during the period of the group's move from Biak to Manila. A new SCR-499 transmitter with an output of 350 watts has been installed to take the place of the SCR-188 transmitter which had been used by the 33rd Squadron.

The Signal Message Center also started operations on 4 June in conjunction with the radio station. All incoming and outgoing messages are thoroughly checked for paraphrasing and stereotyping in order to conform with existing security regulations of the Far East Air Forces.

On 20 June an EE-97 teletypewriter was installed in the Signal Message Center with a direct line to the central switchboard of FEAF located at Fort McKinley. This hook-up enables the signal message center teletype section to contact any headquarters having a teletype in the Manila and Clark Field area. Arrangements having been made with the Army Airways Communications System, they are now sending to this Headquarters all Notams (notices to airmen) in regards to radio facility changes in the south and southwest Pacific areas. These changes are sent to the four squadrons daily in a communications information letter so that they may have the latest information available.

On 9 and 10 June an inspection of the 6th Squadron communications section at APO 72 was made by the Group Communications Officer. The section was found to be in good order except for a few minor discrepancies. The squadron communications officer was advised of the changes to be made in each section so that his department would be operating in accordance with current regulations, circulars, and memorandums.

A course in the use of Loran Navigation equipment has been in the process of compilation and will be ready for issue by 15 July. It consists of printed matter and illustrations designed to provide a self-contained course of instructions for radio operators and pilots. A similar training course is being set up for the GCA (Ground Control Approach) and SCS 51 Blink Landing Systems. This course is primarily intended to familiarize pilots with the use of the systems in case of an emergency. The course will be conducted in conjunction with the S-3 section and will include checking out individual pilots on the system.

Intelligence

The Group Headquarters Intelligence Section in a new route guide which contains the latest information on airstrips in the Philippines and Okinawa, and the courses and distances between these strips. Master copies were distributed to the squadron intelligence officers so that the required number of copies could be prepared for their needs. Sufficient Navigational Charts covering these areas were also distributed to the squadrons. At a recent meeting of the group staff officers, the group intelligence officer presented a thorough explanation regarding the contents and need for entering all current information in the new route guides.

Through contact with the office of the Assistant Chief of Air Staff, A-3, FEAF, the Group has received initial copies of "The Airdrome Guide to Southwest Pacific Area". This guide, still in the process of being developed by the above headquarters, will contain the location of airstrips, surrounding terrain, landmarks, and available facilities at airstrips in Australia, New Guinea, and adjacent islands, and the Philippines. Future amendments will include Okinawa and additional territory captured from the enemy. These guides will be very constructive when briefing pilots and especially the newly arrived replacement.

The Daily Air-Sea Rescue Facilities are now being received via teletype.

Rumors were numerous in Group Headquarters and in all the squadrons. Most of the rumors were concerned with the readjustment program. They were practically eliminated at the end of the month by the dissemination of all available facts on the readjustment plan through the medium of the Group newspaper. The two day conference held by FEAF was instrumental in answering most of the questions which had been brought up by group personnel. However, the one question asked by every individual with an adjusted rating score above the critical score, "When am I going Home", could not be answered.

The morale of flying personnel continues to be excellent. This can be attributed to better than average flying conditions under which the men usually operate, and to the fact that rotation for combat crew members is definite after a reasonable number of flying hours in this theater. The morale of the ground personnel appears to be in an unsettled state due to the uncertainty of the new readjustment plan. The first quota was very disappointing but the hope for better future quotas kept morale from dropping drastically. The morale of most of the older men is definitely on the decline and in many cases this has decided effect on the men who have less overseas service.

MEDICAL

Diarrhea was the greatest cause of loss of time during June. There were sharp increases in venereal disease, respiratory disease, and skin disease in the units stationed at Manila. Efforts at control have consisted of chlorination of all water regardless of point of origin, testing for chlorine content three times daily, fly control measures, feces examination of Filipino food handlers, and showing of training films.

Daily sick call for 1824 men averaged 34.48 men per day or 2%. Man days lost in hospital and quarters were 1132 or 2.1%. A total of 658 flying personnel lost a total of 749 flying days of 3.3% of total flying days.

Nine new cases of venereal disease was reported. Eight of these were acquired in Manila. During June, 1945, the number of cases per thousand men per year was 45.

SPECIAL SERVICES

The Group Post Exchange located in the 33rd Squadron area began operating during the month. The Coca Cola machine was installed and kept in operations seven days a week. Installation of the 33rd ice cream machine was completed but a lack of ice cream mix prohibited production.

The area south of Group Headquarters area was acquired for use by the special Service Section. A screen and projection booth was built for the presentation of movies to the personnel of Headquarters and the 33rd Squadron. Bad weather and shortage of construction equipment limited work on the athletic program but, nevertheless, a softball diamond was constructed and put in use before the month's end.

The 33rd Squadron baseball team, the only team representing the Air Corps in the Manila area, has made an impressive beginning in the Monday Special Service League at Rizal Stadium. Out of the five games played there were no losses.

Group personnel have been kept notified of all Base "X" Special Service activities and provided with transportation to and from all sports events.

Lt. Gerald A. Schrom was assigned to the department as Assistant Special Service Officer.

INFORMATION AND EDUCATION

To the 22nd Squadron went the distinction of being the first squadron to publish its own newspaper "Deuces Wild" made its first appearance on 23 June.

A series of weekly discussions was inaugurated at APO 75 by the Group Headquarters and 33rd Squadron I and E sections. The first topic was "Amateur Photography" and the attendance was very satisfactory. The 22nd Squadron also started a weekly discussion program.

Several men from Group Headquarters and from the 33rd Squadron have enrolled at the Philippine Institute Classes which are conducted in the Manila High School by Army instructors. A large number of courses are offered and it is hoped that more personnel will take advantage of this opportunity of furthering their education.

JULY, 1945

PERSONNEL

The unusually large readjustment quota of 81 enlisted men and three officers was received with much enthusiasm by all group personnel. The squadrons lost many valuable key men. The 6th Squadron was especially hard hit, losing 31 of its long serving personnel. But the operating efficiency of the squadrons was not materially affected. Approximately 100 replacements for enlisted ground personnel were received during the month. Although they were new and inexperienced in the squadrons, they helped to soften the blow of the large number of men lost to readjustment.

OPERATIONS

During the month the 374th Group accepted 36 C-46 type aircraft. Upon receipt of five more C-47's all squadrons will have its full strength of 16 of the new type aircraft. It is planned that each squadron have assigned to it 16 C-46's for operational purposes, and two C-47's for administrative purposes.

During the month the Group received three B-25 type aircraft to be used for administrative purposes, and five BT-13 type aircraft to be used primarily for training in instrument flying.

Aircraft Accident Boards have been set up in each of the squadrons to meet and make prompt recommendations on accidents involving pilots or planes of that squadron.

MacArthur and staff pose for photographers and newsreel cameramen. MacArthur stayed in this general posture for one half hour to give the photographers their fill of photos, August 30, 1945.

Co-pilots are now required to be checked out in C-46 type aircraft before being classified as first pilots.

Two new courier runs were added during the month. A night courier from Manila to Hollandia was established and a day courier from Manila to Okinawa went into effect.

The Operations Section of the 21st and 22nd Squadrons were inspected and found to be very satisfactory.

The weight carried by each of the squadrons and by the group as a whole were: 6th: 1896.9 tons; 21st: 1001.9 tons; 22nd: 843.3 tons; 33rd 1345.4 tons; Group Total: 5087.5 tons.

ENEMY ACTIVITY

No enemy activity was encountered during the month.

ENGINEERING

The maintenance sections of all the squadrons have performed their duties very satisfactorily during the period of transition from C-47's to C-46's and the efficiency of the organization has not suffered.

COMMUNICATIONS

Extension of the radio net facilities was accomplished with the installation of an SCR-188 radio station at the 322nd Troop Carrier Wing Headquarters in Hollandia. Messages for Manila can now be relayed through the station at Biak with greater speed than AACS could ever provide. This installation was made primarily to facilitate the impending FEASC move.

Additional security is now afforded radio transmission over the group net by use of two different ciphers, one for operational messages and one for administrative traffic. Simplification of monthly traffic security reports was made possible by elimination of reports on violations by the individual stations. A central Radio Intelligence Station in Manila now monitors all frequencies and makes its own reports to higher headquarters on security violations. All radio operators of the ground stations have been cautioned again regarding security regulations in transmitting messages by radio. So far no infractions have been reported on the Group Net by higher headquarters.

Several tests were made in the use of blind landing aids by Group pilots. The purpose was to evaluate the reliability of the system and estimate how much training would qualify a pilot for its use. After several runs the SCS-51 system was abandoned because it was found to be unreliable and would involve a great amount of training. Available information indicates that the GCA system which will be installed shortly will offer reliable approach facilities and will involve a minimum amount of training.

A Loran Training Course for pilots and radio operators, consisting of a course outline and syllabus has been drawn up and distributed to the squadrons. The course requires eight hours of instruction to radio operators and four hours to pilots. The course is being conducted by the Squadron Navigators and will enable position fixes to be made by pilot or radio operators using the Loran equipment which is standard on all C-46 aircraft.

Air-sea rescue information addressed to Group Intelligence Officer now comes in regularly over the teletype system and is immediately dispatched by the message center clerks. After 2100 hours, when communications personnel leave for the night, the CQ stays in the Communications office and takes care of any late messages coming in by telephone or teletype, in addition to his other duties.

Carl A. Spaatz, George Kenney, and Douglas MacArthur at Atsugi air base, Japan, for the surrender ceremonies.

INTELLIGENCE

In view of the fact that Group aircraft are now making daily flights into Okinawa the Group Intelligence Section has arranged to have the Daily Air-Seas Rescue Intent sent direct to the 374th Troop Carrier Group via teletype. It is then passed on to the 33rd Intelligence Officer who briefs the pilots on the Air-Sea Rescue facilities available for the following day.

The Airdrome Guide to the southwest Pacific area, prepared by Far East Air Forces and mentioned in the June history, was received and distributed to the four squadrons to be included in the 374th Troop Carrier Route Guide.

Navigation charts covering the Philippine Islands, French Indo-China, China, Formosa, Okinawa, and South Japan were prepared and prominently displayed. Enemy concentrations, allied bomber strikes, the Daily Air-Seas Rescue Intent, and the combat line of 18 April, 1945, are clearly defined on these maps.

The photographic section of the Group Intelligence completed the taking of identification pictures of the officers of Group Headquarters and the 33rd Squadron.

Security posters are still considered very important and are prominently displayed in all departments and on all bulletin boards.

The submission of monthly intelligence summaries is no longer required by higher headquarters. However, the squadron intelligence officers are required to keep a log of all important events occurring during each month.

In spite of the fact that an unusually large readjustment quota was received by the group during the month of July the morale of the group as a whole was not materially raised. Because of a new interpretation on the requirements for being eligible for battle participation, personnel of the 6th Squadron and 33rd Squadron had their adjusted service rating score reduced by ten points and personnel of Headquarters, 21st and 22nd Squadron had their scores reduced by fifteen points. This left relatively few individuals in the entire group with an adjusted service rating score about 85.

Many men who have 33 or more months of overseas service are becoming increasingly bitter because there is no provision for returning them to the United States. This bitterness and consequent lowering of morale, can not much longer be checked with excuses and indefinite promises.

MEDICAL

No epidemics or unusual problems were encountered in the Medical Department during the month of July. Respiratory diseases were the greatest cause of loss of time, there being an increase of fifty cases per one thousand men per year over the month of June. There was a substantial decrease in fever undetermined origin, diarrhea, and venereal diseases.

The daily sick call for 2243 men averaged 77.74 men pr day or 3.5%. May days lost in the hospital and in quarters for the same number of men were 1023, or 1.47% of all man days. 663 men lost 593 flying man days over a 28 day period or 3.2% of all flying man days.

Information on venereal diseases per 100 men per year is as follows:
Group average for year 1944: 26.2
Group average for July 1944: 30.0
Group average for July 1945: 25.6

PUBLIC RELATIONS, INFORMATION AND EDUCATION

With the publication of the 8 July issue, the Group Newspaper was renamed the "Hashmark", a significant title symbolizing the group's more than three years service in the Pacific. At the same time Camp Newspaper Service congratulated the publication on its progress since the first issue thirty seven weeks ago.

A supply of the latest mimeographing materials has been received from the United States and in quality it is far better than any previously received in this theater. The new materials will contribute materially to the appearance of the newspaper and will also prove invaluable in printing I & E posters and bulletins.

Due to the large number of men returning to the United States, many new replacements being assigned to the group, and the great number of promotions received by group personnel, the number of press releases for the month was very high.

AUGUST, 1945

PERSONNEL

During the month of August men were returned to the United States for discharge under a new policy. The numerical monthly quota based on points was changed to a plan based on individual eligibility. Under this revised policy the group prepared to release all men with a critical score of 85 points or more. However, during the month only a handful of personnel were placed on orders. It is expected that the plan will reach its peak during the coming month. The Combat Crew Replacement Plan was continued for flying personnel and under it an average number of men were returned to the United States. During the month the group also dropped from its rolls under the authority of a War Department radiogram. T/Sgt. Robert DeShazer and S/Sgt. Dale Rife, who were on TDY in the United States.

By direction of the President the group was cited in FEAF GO 1744 for outstanding performance of duty during the Wau Campaign (a copy follows). At the time strong enemy forces had penetrated into the Wau-Bulolo Valley, New Guinea, in an effort to capture the valuable Wau Airdrome. Along with planes from another organization, unarmed aircraft of the group carried on a series of air movements under enemy fire to save the drome.

For aerial participation in the Luzon, Philippine Islands Campaign and the Bismarck Archipelago Campaign the group was given battle credit in GO 118 and GO 138, GHQ, AFPAC (copies follow). The additional Adjusted Service Rating points authorized by these battle participations enabled several of our personnel to accumulate sufficient points to put them over the critical score.

Sgt. Norman D. Morden 36417057 of Headquarters, a veteran of 33 months overseas, died as a result of a poisonous snake bite on the 7 August, 1945. The entire group mourned the passing of Sgt. Morden and full military honors were accorded him at funeral services the next day. In tribute to Sgt. Morden's athletic skill and fine sportsmanship, the group baseball diamond has been named MORDEN MEMORIAL FIELD.

OKINAWA - 1945

By Harris B. "Stew" Stewart

It all happened just 50 years ago, but I am still haunted by it. Is is possible? Could it have been he?

The two Pratt and Whitney 2400s at my left and right hummed reassuringly as my C-47 transport plane crossed high above the smell green Babuyan Islands off the north coast of Luzon. It was 1945, and the silver-gray sea far below looked like polished pewter. The war seemed far away, and my co-pilot and I talked of the States and our homes. Okinawa was still over two hours away. We were carrying ammunition, medical supplies, mail and Yank Magazines to the soldiers and marines mopping up on that war ravaged island.

The steady purring of those engines had a soporific effect, and my co-pilot went aft to take a cat-nap on one of the litters we used when evacuating wounded. I was happy in the cockpit. The C-47 is a comfortable plane to fly, and I loved flying. We had no navigator, but I knew the course to Okinawa. There was no electronic navigation equipment, no LORAN, no ground-controlled approach systems at the airstrips. It was strictly seat-of-the-pants navigation.

We evidently had a crosswind from the east, for I first spotted Okinawa far ahead but somewhat off to the right. We passed over the strips at Naha and Kadena and headed for Machinato where we were to unload. There was no tower to call for landing instructions. Technology had not caught up with the speed of the war's advance. I dragged the stript at 100 feet looking for holes in the runway and pulled up in a climbing right turn onto my downwind leg. The airstrip below seemed deserted. No hangar, no tower, just one small Quonset hut beside the runway. On our approach leg, we skimmed over shattered trees and a few burned-out dwellings to touch down on the crushed rock runway. We rolled to a stop at the far end, and I gunned the right engine to turn us around and shut down. The propellers slowly - almost reluctantly - stopped turning, and the world became quiet. An Army 6-by-6 with two tired and bored GIs showed up, and we were unceremoniously unloaded.

Tomorrow they would bring a dozen or so wounded to be flown back to Manila, so we were stuck there for the night. It was time for our late lunch of c-rations. Our "stove" was a number ten can full of gravel with a wire grill. There was a draincock on the plane's fuel tank that allowed the condensed water to be drawn off. But once the gas had no more water bubbles, we were getting pure gasoline, and it made a great fuel for our little stove.

Our Spam and powdered coffee were heating when a jeep roared up and came to a dust-throwing stop under the plane's wing. In it were two marines from Carlson's Raiders. They were unshaven and looked battle-weary. They were also hungry. They climbed out of their jeep and came over to our "dinner table". I invited them to share our lunch, and they quickly accepted. I recovered my last two cans of baked beans from the good box in the plane and added them to the menu. Once the beans were heated up on our gasoline-fired grill, the two marines devoured them.

Although they enjoyed their meal, those two also enjoyed needling us fly boys". The Marine Corps and the Army Air Corps were not overly friendly in the Southwest Pacific in 1945.

"You guys don't know what the war is really like. Come with us, and we'll show you fly boys."

My co-pilot elected to stay with our plane, but I agreed to go with them. I was 22, and they both seemed about my age or maybe even younger. Kids fight wars. Kids become men in wars, and I was about to see what they called "the real war", the one that is fought on the ground.

Climbing the metal ladder into the plane to collect my helmet and our only armament - a .45 pistol - I wondered what I had gotten into. I felt that the honor of the Air Corps was at stake, and I couldn't back out. The marines sat in front, I in the back. The jeep went fast, avoiding shell holes and bumping over mounds of dirt and the debris of war. After what must have been two, maybe three, miles of dust and shattered landscapes, we came to an abrupt stop at a barricade of big logs lying across the dirt road and below a long steep cliff to our right.

"Now we'll show you 'throttle-jockey' what this war is all about."

One of the marines took what appeared to be a knapsack from the back seat and started to scramble up the backside of the cliff. He soon appeared at the top directly above what looked like the entrance to a cave, but I was told that it was one of several tombs along the face of the cliff.

"Here, take his rifle and watch."

Not knowing what to expect, I crouched down behind the barricade next to the other marine and rested the barrel of the rifle across the top log and waited. The marine on the cliff lowered a line with the knapsack on the end until it was even with the tomb entrance. It was hauled back up, the satchel-charge was ignited and thrown out in a wide arc to enter the tomb just as it exploded.

Crouched behind the barricade, I heard the muffled blast of the explosion and saw the cloud of dust and smoke that billowed out of the entrance. Three Japanese soldiers, crouched over and coughing, staggered out through the smoke a mere 20 yards in front of me.

"Shoot, fly boy, get yourself a Jap." Then, "Goddammit, shoot!", he shouted.

I couldn't do it. Maybe it was the human counterpart to buck fever, and I could not shoot. But the marine did. He dropped two of them, and the third one ran out of range along the base of the cliff.

Our return ride was quiet. I was eager for the rela-

General Douglas MacArthur signing the Japanese surrender documents on the Battleship Missouri, September 2, 1945.

tive peace and safety of my C-47. Back at Machinato, my co-pilot was waiting for us. He had broken out his cherished bottle of Johnny Walker Red. Each of the marines had a shot, and we talked briefly there under the wing.

"I certainly don't want to fight the war your way", I said, "And now that I've seen it, I know why."

"Fly boy", one of them replied, "My way is better. You couldn't get me into that Gooney Bird of yours. That's a damn dangerous way to travel around here."

Then the other one added, "De gustibus non disputandem."

I knew from my boarding school days that this was Latin for 'No Dispute Concerning Taste', but it seemed strangely out of character for a burly marine. I wondered where he had learned it, but I never found out, for after a second shot of scotch, they climbed into their dusty jeep and left. Only after they were gone did I realize I had never asked their names, nor they mine. We were just an Air Corps pilot and two marines that met and shared a few moments together in the midst of a dirty war.

Some forty years later, as a widower, I married Louise Conant from ST. Louis. It was several months after our wedding that she first told me about her brother. His name was Judson, but he was called Judd. In 1943, he had been accepted for the class of 1948 at Princeton but had enlisted in the Marine Corps instead. In 1945 as a member of Carlson's Raiders, Judd was killed on Okinawa. He was only 19.

Was Judd one of those two marines I met long ago on the far-away Pacific island? We will never know, but we often wonder.

OPERATIONS

During the month of August, group aircraft participated in the FEASC move with excellent results. The move, scheduled for 10 days, was completed in 7 days with a schedule of 18 aircraft per day. One ship, number 7937, crashed on take-off and was a total loss with no injury to passengers or crew.

The 6th and 21st Squadrons were on D.S. at Florida Blanca from 12 - 31 August for 54th Troop Carrier Wing moving. The first three days all ships available operated in moving the 11th Airborne Division from Lipa to Okinawa for the occupation of Japan.

One ship, number 8454, was lost at Naha on the 13th August with all the crew and passengers aboard being killed. The passengers aboard the ship were American-Japanese interpreters. Captain Geatches, Captain Hunter, Sgt. Springer, and Sgt. Stamler were Headquarters representatives for ten days D.S. at Florida Blanca.

The 22nd Squadron is nearing completion of an area directly behind the 33rd Squadron Operations and Engineering at Nielson Field. As yet no Operations and Engineering buildings have been erected, but work upon them is slated to begin in the near future.

The group had two C-46's and one C-47 taken over by AACS for the installation of communications equipment which consisted of GHQ teletype transmitter and receiver and was flown to Atsugi Field, Japan on the 28th of August by 374th Group pilots including all Headquarters flying personnel. On the trip to Japan, ships were stationed every 110 miles with homing for aircraft as a navigational aid. No difficulties were encountered as an exceptionally good landing field was the destination. Arriving two days before General Douglas MacArthur, the crews RONed three nights at Atsugi Airdrome, left the communication plane and returned on an ATC C-54 to Okinawa.

One C-46 belonging to the 33rd Squadron has been missing since the 30th August. The plane, Number 8352, cleared from Morotai for Manila. An organized search has failed to uncover any evidence as to its location.

The 33rd and 6th Squadrons have three planes equipped with cabin tanks to haul gasoline into Tokyo, but as Japan now has fuel facilities, the tanks will be removed.

The weights carried by each of the squadrons and by the group as a whole were: 6th: 1381.6 tons; 21st: 8907 tons; 22nd: 1170.1 tons; 33rd: 1082.5 tons; Group Total: 4524.9 tons.

Enemy Activity

No enemy activity was encountered during the month.

Engineering

The maintenance sections of all squadrons have become completely orientated to work on C-46 type aircraft and the transition from C-47's to C-46's has been carried out smoothly.

Two operational aircraft were lost by accident during the month. On 8 August a C-46D was lost due to fire and on 14 August a C-46D was lost in a crash at Okinawa.

Communications

During the month of August activities of the Communications Section were limited to routine operations and maintenance. Additional telephone lines and a teletype line to FEASC were made operative. Two teletype circuits are now available, one to FEAF switchboard and a direct line to 322nd Troop Carrier Wing.

Radio net operation was satisfactory, although some difficulty was experienced in maintaining contact with the 22nd Squadron who experienced several breakdowns toward the end of the month.

Arrangements were made with FEASC to send four Radio Mechanics to V ASAC Radio School to take a two week course in radio set AN/ART-13 maintenance. This new set, replacing the old SCR-274, is new to the squadrons and a training program is necessary.

With heavy traffic to Okinawa, necessitating long over water flights, responsibilities of the radio operators was increased. Special information for their guidance was distributed, including air-sea rescue facilities, radio facilities, Loran maps, and blind flying and landing facilities.

Increased ground traffic at Nielson Field showed need for two-

Colonel D.M. Dunne with Edward Imparato, immediately after landing at Atsugi, August 28, 1945.

way radio communications between tower and 33rd Squadron Operations jeep. Two transceivers were obtained from the signal Depot and this service was found practicable.

Movement of the 22nd Squadron Advance Echelon into their new area began toward the end of the month and two telephone linemen, excess in this section, were transferred to help establish a telephone system. Several telephones and four miles of field wire were loaned the 22nd Squadron for this purpose, no such equipment having arrived with the advanced echelon.

Intelligence

In view of future flights by group aircraft into Allied-controlled airstrips into Japan, Intelligence Section made up new map folders of AAP Aeronautical Charts covering all the areas of Japan. One each will be added to the present group of Flight Folders, maintained for the flying officers of Headquarters. During the latter part of August, a special set of maps, with courses and distances, were made up for group planes which flew to Atsugi Strip in the Tokyo area of Japan to prepare the way for the major occupational forces which were to be landed upon Japan's formal surrender.

AAP Aeronautical Charts covering the areas of the northern Philippines, Formosa, Okinawa, Korea, Japan, and the Kuriles were acquired during last month and sufficient quantities were distributed to the squadrons for their operational requirements. All pertinent data regarding new airfields were also forwarded to them, as well as Allied bulletins, magazines, and other publications.

The Daily Air-Sea Rescue Intent was received with greater punctuality throughout the month via teletype. This information is immediately forwarded to the 33rd and 22nd Squadron Intelligence Departments for briefing of pilots on the Air-Sea rescue facilities for the following day.

With the assistance and cooperation of the 33rd Intelligence Officer, all data available on "Traffic Control, Okinawa to Tokyo" was obtained, and sufficient copies were mimeographed for distribution to all squadrons to be inserted in all Flight Folders for use by the pilots.

The 374th Troop Carrier Group Route Guide was maintained and kept up to date; all additional information on old strips was copied into each of the six Route Guides used by Headquarter's pilots, and new sheets were made up on airfields which have recently opened. Principal additions to the Route Guide were strips on Okinawa. A new section - Airstrips on Japan - is being added to the route guide and facilities sheets will be compiled and entered as soon as the information is received by Intelligence. Group Intelligence is also keeping up Colonel Elsmore's (322nd Troop Carrier Wing) flight folder, and brings it up to date periodically.

A monthly log of matters pertaining to intelligence is being kept up by the department now that the Monthly Intelligence Summary has been discontinued. All important data is entered into the log should there be any need for the information in the future.

The photographic lab, which has been under the jurisdiction of group intelligence, is now being turned over to the 33rd Troop Carrier Squadron.

The department lost its two oldest and most capable enlisted men during the month, when both T/Sgt. Teegardin and Sgt. Stamler left for the United States for discharge under the point system. Cpl. Jerome Trapp has been transferred into the section from Communications and was trained in all the duties of an Intelligence Clerk.

MEDICAL

No epidemics or unusual problems were encountered in the Medical Department during the month of August.

Sick call attendance and man days lost for the entire group:
Daily sick call for 1257 men averaged 38.8 men per day - 3%
Man days lost in Hospital and Quarters for 1257 men were 492 - 1.25%

Venereal Disease: cases per 1000 men per year:
Group average for year 1944: 26.2
Group average for August 1944: 21
Group average for August 1945: 12

SPECIAL SERVICE

With the war's end the need for recreational equipment to fill off-time hours increased greatly and the department has made every effort to procure additional sporting facilities and reading material.

A great effort was put forth to acquire lumber for the building of a stage in conjunction with the Group Theater, however, in the meantime, personnel have been notified of all Base Special Services activities and transportation is arranged for them, making attendance possible.

The Post Exchange operated efficiently during the month with ice-cream and Coca Cola being made available to all personnel. Additional supplies were requisitioned for the 22nd Squadron and as soon as their entire organization arrives, they plan to open a Branch Post Exchange of their own.

PUBLIC RELATIONS, INFORMATION AND EDUCATION

The first issue of the group newspaper, the "Hashmark" produced by photo-offset printing methods was released 19 August, when the front page carried pictures of the "Miss Troop Carrier" contest winners. The beauty contest provoked a great deal of interest throughout the entire group.

The group's third Distinguished Unit Citation was the subject of a Stateside press release submitted to FEAF. The story recalled the past two Citations and included a brief history of the organization during the Papuan and Wau campaigns.

A large supply of materials dealing with the post-war opportunities of servicemen has been received and distribution to the squadrons was carried out early in the month.
HEADQUARTERS

374TH TROOP CARRIER GROUP
APO x

4 October 1945.

MEMORANDUM:

TO: All Personnel, 374th Troop Carrier Group

For the past many months it has been my good fortune to command the most outstanding Troop Carrier Group. During this time more records and accomplishments have been recorded so that the 374th Troop Carrier Group is now the most decorated of all Army Air Force units anywhere in the world.

It is with sincere regret that I leave the organization and untie the strings of affection that has bound me to you in the accomplishment of great and difficult tasks. Many of you I will meet again in more pleasant tasks and surroundings, but it will not be as we have been together building and erecting a record of achievement that we all can justifiably be proud.

My sincere wish in saying "Goodbye" is that each and everyone as a member of the 374th Troop Carrier Group knows that our record belongs to all and not to any single person or group of persons, and for this spirit of mutuality all are to be congratulated.

/s/ Edward T. Imparato
EDWARD T. IMPARATO,
Colonel, Air Corps,
Commanding

George Kenney, who ran the "air show" in MacArthur's section of the Pacific.

CHAPTER VI
FINAL PHASE

The 374th Troop Carrier Group received its most challenging and significant assignment from General MacArthur's headquarters on August 20, 1945. The Japanese had given signs of capitulation at a conference with Allied Forces Commander General Douglas MacArthur at Manila on August 15, 1945. Immediate steps were taken to confirm their resolve to terminate hostilities. The Commanding General dispatched requests to the Commander, 374th Troop Carrier Group to prepare to fly a group of selected high-level negotiators to Atsugi, Japan, to arrange for the security of Atsugi with the assistance of the 111th Airborne Division until the arrival of MacArthur with the support of Eichelberger's 9th Army and Nemitz' massive Navy. The initial contingent to consist of members of support services to provide for base essential services at Atsugi for air craft traffic control and refueling and maintenance support to air field engineering and maintenance. The total of the 150 man contingent included a specific mission for the 374th. The Commander of the 374th was directed to fly to Motoba Airfield on Okinawa on the 20th of August.

On arrival there he was approached by a group of technicians with instructions to install a ground radio station in his aircraft - a C-46 Curtiss Commando. The installed radio would be the primary contact with Manila and MacArthur's Headquarters. In addition the Commander was given the manifest for his assigned flight to Atsugi.

On August 28, 1945 the C-46 took off from Motoba Airfield, Okinawa, at 4:00 a.m. - destination Atsugi. The flight terminated at Atsugi at about 8:00 a.m. on the 28th of August. Though the flight was routine there was a great deal of apprehension about what the initial contingent would discover at Atsugi. The Japanese were known to have 2.5 million men and women armed and prepared to defend the homeland against invasion. The Kamikaze training base at Atsugi housed the Kamikaze pilots and the surrounding area was their bedroom community. They gave notice to the Emperor and his royal and loyal supporters of their intent to frustrate the arriving troops from the Allied Powers. It was this apparent delicate situation that faced the 374th Commander and his 28 passengers and crew. The mission was completed successfully and the 374th C-46 was the first enemy of Japan ever to set foot on Japanese soil while Japan was still in a state of war.

A detailed description of the flight and the gradual chain of events which led to this most important flight can be found in the Group Commander's book 'MacArthur, Melbourne to Tokyo" published by White Mane Publishing Company, Shippensburg, Pa. 1997.

The following photos were taken at Atsugi after the arrival of the 374th at that base.

Col. C.R. Hutchison GSC U.S.A. directing his men to assemble.

S/Sgt. Gellash prepares lunch under the horizontal stablizer of a C-46, August 28, 1945.

C-46 Curtis Commando being readied for the removal of the wings. Crew chief is being assisted by Japanese mechanics.

Ready for the last roll to the designated area – Lt. Hunter (relief pilot, left), and Capt. Getches (co-pilot, right) August 28, 1945.

APPENDIX 'A'

CHARTER ROSTER - 374TH TROOP CARRIER GROUP

HEADQUARTERS

The 374th Troop Carrier Group Charter Members were assigned essentially from selected individuals originally assigned to the squadrons of the group. The activation date was 21st November, 1942.

Col. Prestiss, Paul
Lt. Col. Nichols, Erickson S.
Maj. Adams, Fred M.
Maj. Beebe, Robert C.
Maj. Hampton, Edgar Wade
Maj. Imparato, Edward T.
Maj. Jackson, Eugene R.
Maj. Jacobs, John F.
Maj. Jennings, William P.
Capt. Beck, Abe J.
Capt. Foster, George R.
Capt. Lichter, Carl J.
Capt. Pearson, John D.
Capt. Simpson, Harold B.
Capt. Vandiver, Raymond
1st Lt. Rennels, Lamont N.
1st Lt. Soular, Fred M.
2nd Lt. White, Lacy W., Jr.

6TH TROOP CARRIER SQUADRON

Capt. Fredrickson, John C.
Capt. Jacobs, John F.
Capt. Lackey, John J., Jr.
Capt. Lieberman, Alexander
Capt. Smith, Frank W.
1st Lt. Best, Robert T.
1st Lt. Church, Frank C.
1st Lt. Dial, Irwin W.
1st Lt. McCluney, John H.
1st Lt. Mentzer, Fred R.
1st Lt. Peterson, William A.
1st Lt. Rowland, Conrad A.
1st Lt. Stanton, Richard B.
1st Lt. Tossier, Henri W.
1st Lt. Wells, William D.
2nd Lt. Burleigh, Albert H.
2nd Lt. Bates, James W.
2nd Lt. Beaver, George W.
2nd Lt. Benesh, Albert J.
2nd Lt. Bronson, Hubert S.
2nd Lt. Cater, Wilson C.
2nd Lt. Corsa, Victor A.
2nd Lt. Echard, Rexford W.
2nd Lt. Evans, Delbert T.
2nd Lt. Evans, Robert W.
2nd Lt. Fairey, John P.
2nd Lt. Ford, Ernest C.
2nd Lt. Gaylor, Don G.

2nd Lt. Gilbertson, Gillman W.
2nd Lt. Gittis, Morris
2nd Lt. Goldstein, Sidney B.
2nd Lt. Goodwin, Edwin G.
2nd Lt. Grassi, Amerigo
2nd Lt. Hackett, Wilbur M.
2nd Lt. Hagerty, Joseph A.
2nd Lt. Halper, Charles
2nd Lt. Halye, Roy O.
2nd Lt. Harris, Clarence S.
2nd Lt. Heasley, Lyle E.
2nd Lt. Houston, Cortez E.
2nd Lt. Kerr, Robert R.
2nd Lt. Korthals, Albert H.
2nd Lt. Knight, Robert S.
2nd Lt. Lambert, Albert L.
2nd Lt. Large, Shadrack J.
2nd Lt. Lattaer, Earl B.
2nd Lt. Libuse, Frank C.
2nd Lt. Loder, Robert W.
2nd Lt. Luetzow, William E.
2nd Lt. Majure, Harold B.
2nd Lt. Malmstrone, Blesch
2nd Lt. Manger, Billy E.
2nd Lt. McFarland, Orland W.
2nd Lt. McWilliams, Joseph W.
2nd Lt. Meeks, John R., Jr.
2nd Lt. Neal, Jasper F.
2nd Lt. Noggle, Willis A.
2nd Lt. Parker, Chester P.
2nd Lt. Parker, John W.
2nd Lt. Pearce, George M., Jr.
2nd Lt. Portman, Vernon F.
2nd Lt. Rodgers, Jaffus M.
2nd Lt. Rothman, Jay C.
2nd Lt. Silsby, Edward M.
2nd Lt. Simpson, Jerome L.
2nd Lt. Staun, Philip J.
2nd Lt. Thompson, Thomas G.
2nd Lt. Triol, Raymond H.
2nd Lt. Vaughter, David C.
2nd Lt. Wagoner, Kenneth G.
2nd Lt. Watson, Frederick S.
2nd Lt. Weaver, James W.
2nd Lt. Webb, Glenn E.
2nd Lt. Weedin, Wilbur H.
2nd Lt. Zartman, Rufus H.
1st Sgt. Chain, Charles H.A., Jr.
M/Sgt. Kullich, Michael
M/Sgt. Mackey, Donald A.
T/Sgt. Bramer, Delmer C.
T/Sgt. Hawley, Joseph C.
T/Sgt. Ilse, Ward C.
T/Sgt. Janavich, Vincent J.
T/Sgt. Kepke, Casimir J.
T/Sgt. McGregor, Ralph B.
T/Sgt. Mills, Robert J., Jr.
T/Sgt. Paul, Joseph E.

T/Sgt. Palmer, Gerald L.
T/Sgt. Proctor, William E.
T/Sgt. Purring, Alexander J.
T/Sgt. Shandor, Frank J.
T/Sgt. Shireman, Paul
T/Sgt. Stephens, Clifford D.
T/Sgt. Stefecik, John M., Jr.
T/Sgt. Thompson, Lee B., Jr.
Sgt. Acord, Lawrence L.
Sgt. Armstrong, Terry M., Jr.
Sgt. Banner, Eugene B.
Sgt. Bartels, Melvin W.
Sgt. Believe, Arthur
Sgt. Beville, Roy F., Jr.
Sgt. Bliss, Edgar J.
Sgt. Bunke, Harvey C.
Sgt. Clayton, Clay D.
Sgt. Craycraft, William C.
Sgt. Daniel, James W.
Sgt. Deardorff, Richard S.
Sgt. Deonier, Jack J.
Sgt. Ferguson, James A.
Sgt. Finkbeiner, Clarence H.
Sgt. Fundum, Walter H.
Sgt. Garton, Kvan K.
Sgt. Garton, Warren L.
Sgt. Gillentine, Lloyd A.
Sgt. Goyette, Frank R.
Sgt. Gregg, John C.
Sgt Haber, Vincent A.
Sgt. Hanson, Paul M.
Sgt. Hibner, William G.
Sgt. Hoffman, William
Sgt. Hudson, John A.
Sgt. Kempf, Joseph L.
Sgt. Kewin, Kenneth J.
Sgt. Klar, Wesley W.
Sgt. Knauss, Charles I.
Sgt. Ludlow, Chester M.
Sgt. Maber, Vincent A.
Sgt. Magill, Hugh R., Jr.
Sgt. Mahaffey, Joseph H.
Sgt. Maul, Walter E.
Sgt. McMann, Lyle G.
Sgt. Milisci, Ferdinand
Sgt. Mills, Curtis T.
Sgt. Moore, John B.
Sgt. Nelson, Carl I.
Sgt. Parrish, Harvey R.
Sgt. Perez, Joseph T.
Sgt. Peterson, Garrett V.
Sgt. Philpot, Louie E.
Sgt. Pineno, James
Sgt. Proffitt, Arthur
Sgt. Putzman, John E.
Sgt. Ramzy, James R.
Sgt. Reinhardt, Walter A.
Sgt. Richardson, Warren E.

Sgt. Roberts, Roye K.
Sgt. Rodgers, Thurman W.
Sgt. Rosenthal, Herman
Sgt. Rutko, John A.
Sgt. Samalis, Edward A.
Sgt. Scarsella, Antonio
Sgt. Scouten, Claude A.
Sgt. Sidorowicz, Stanley J.
Sgt. Smith, Herbert G.
Sgt. Stanton, Stanley J.
Sgt. Stolarski, Walter M.
Sgt. Varner, Pershing W.
Sgt. Venditto, Angelo
Sgt. Wagner, Karl V.
Sgt. Wooten, Ernest C., Jr.
Sgt. Yonker, Merle F.
Sgt. Zimmerman, Norman F.
Cpl. Awtrey, Elmer F.
Cpl. Bahr, Alfred W.
Cpl. Baker, Eugene C.
Cpl. Batson, Oscar J.
Cpl. Beehrle, Louis E.
Cpl. Berryman, Lester C.
Cpl. Billmaier, Lawrence P.
Cpl. Blake, Clarence W.
Cpl. Blumenkrantz, Jacob
Cpl. Bogacki, Gerald J.
Cpl. Bokshan, Louis D.
Cpl. Bonito, Frank L.
Cpl. Boyd, William H.
Cpl. Boyle, Edward J.
Cpl. Caputo, Anthony
Cpl. Carter, Henry C.
Cpl. Castle, Floyd, Jr.
Cpl. Coleman, Janes L.
Cpl. Crooks, George H.
Cpl. Cullender, Bascom C.
Cpl. Davis, Marvin
Cpl. DeGeorge, Pasquale A.
Cpl. Eads, Gilbert
Cpl. Fidler, Walter
Cpl. Flatt, Armel L.
Cpl. Forrest, Robert R.
Cpl. Fraser, Robert
Cpl. Geidel, Keith C.
Cpl. Glanzer, Joseph P.
Cpl. Goldthwait, Edward L.
Cpl. Hill, Horace V.
Cpl. Hubbard, Jessie H.
Cpl. Kerr, Robert L.
Cpl. Krigsvold, Ralph C.
Cpl. Laitas, Walter
Cpl. Lincoln, Wayne E.
Cpl. Logan, George M.
Cpl. Manas, Bernard
Cpl. Manes, Vincent W.
Cpl. Martinson, Raymond W.
Cpl. McWilliams, Earl T.
Cpl. Metzger, Marlin D.
Cpl. Middleton, Marvin D.
Cpl. Miles, Cecil S.
Cpl. Mooney, Sidney C.
Cpl. Nance, Floyd D.
Cpl. O'Brien, Thomas F.
Cpl. Osborn, Francis R.

Cpl. Prince, Arthur F.
Cpl. Redding, Daniel W.
Cpl. Retzger, Marlin D.
Cpl. Reynolds, Adam
Cpl. Rickers, Erwin M.
Cpl. Robbins, Wilbur G.
Cpl. Robutka, Peter J.
Cpl. Runnels, Gilbert L.
Cpl. Rusina, Milton P.
Cpl. Salerno, Louis R.
Cpl. Schreiner, John Z.
Cpl. Shea, Daniel P.
Cpl. Sobierzj, Bernard J.
Cpl. Spieerto, Pasquale
Cpl. Sterrett, Jack H.
Cpl. Templin, Frank A.
Cpl. Thompson, Samuel R.
Cpl. Tudor, Neal
Cpl. Vancio, John
Cpl. Wurtz, Camillus J.
Cpl. Zakrzewski, Norbert B.
Pfc. Affronte, Samuel J.
Pfc. Arnzon, Cyril H.
Pfc. Augustyn, Leo J.
Pfc. Ballantine, John V.
Pfc. Brabec, Sidney J.
Pfc. Byers, James E.
Pfc. David, Eldon F.
Pfc. Doyle, Patrick L.
Pfc. Gurnean, Lawrence T.
Pfc. Kopelson, Sidney
Pfc. Kostelecky, Lloyd E.
Pfc. Lawrence, Kenneth L.
Pfc. Lloyd, Wallace G.
Pfc. Lowry, Russell
Pfc. McGowan, James J.
Pfc. Meli, Jerome S.
Pfc. Milbereger, Carl L.
Pfc. Miller, Emanuel W.
Pfc. Opello, Louis E.
Pfc. Penska, Frank S.
Pfc. Ross, Arnold M.
Pfc. Sampson, Olaf
Pfc. Schwartz, Walter C.
Pfc. Sharrett, Charles W.
Pfc. Sisson, Edward I.
Pfc. Sullivan, James E.
Pfc. Sullivan John L.
Pfc. Sutton, Raymond
Pfc. Thayer, Herbert H.
Pfc. Vroman, Robert L.
Pvt. Mullally, John F.
Pvt. Severino, Anthony J.

21st Troop Carrier Squadron

Capt. Adams, Fred M.
Capt. Gunn, Paul I.
Capt. Hampton, Edgar W.
1st Lt. Andrews, Robert G.
1st Lt. Anglin, Raymond E.
1st Lt. Arts, Henry F.
1st Lt. Bidwell, Herbert L.
1st Lt. Boyd, Richard G.
1st Lt. Burley, Enoch P.

1st Lt. Campbell, James E.
1st Lt. Carroll, Frank W.
1st Lt. Cathcart, Charles O.
1st Lt. Clinkscales, Robert S.
1st Lt. Crook, Thomas E., Jr
1st Lt. Dunn, Thomas S.
1st Lt. Eken, Joseph S.
1st Lt. Eliot, Harold D.
1st Lt. Ferry, William J.
1st Lt. Flaherty, Wayne
1st Lt. Fleming, Forrest
1st Lt. Fortin, Floyd F.
1st Lt. Foster, George
1st Lt. Gibson, Jim
1st Lt. Gibson, Victor N.
1st Lt. Gerrero, Arthur
1st Lt. Henry, Fred G.
1st Lt. Holcomb, Westley O.
1st Lt. Holeman, Harry G.
1st Lt. Hurd, Walter L., Jr.
1st Lt. Imparato, Edward T.
1st Lt. Kominis, George J.
1st Lt. Levine, Arnold F.
1st Lt. Marcus, John
1st Lt. McCullough, James A.
1st Lt. Miles, James F.
1st Lt. Moore, Allen D.
1st Lt. Nellor, Joseph G.
1st Lt. Penn, Perry H.
1st Lt. Stroup, John F.
1st Lt. Turk, James M., Jr.
1st Lt. Wilde, Norman (Aust)
1st Lt. Wyman, Frederick J.
2nd Lt. Baer, Charles R.
2nd Lt. Boyd, Benjamin M.
2nd Lt. Callison, Russell L.
2nd Lt. Cederholm, Bernard
2nd Lt. Corkrum, Uriah F.
2nd Lt. Crandell, John A., Jr.
2nd Lt. Davidson, George M.
2nd Lt. Driver, Harry E.
2nd Lt. Dunn, Willard B.
2nd Lt. Eckberg, Phillip M.

2nd Lt. Fiest, Robert D.
2nd Lt. Franklin, Charles F.
2nd Lt. Forry, Harry P.
2nd Lt. Gerling, Robert J.
2nd Lt. Gollnik, Arden K.
2nd Lt. Graham, H. Allen
2nd Lt. Grimes, Myron J.
2nd Lt. Hallmark, William T.
2nd Lt. Ingram, James W.
2nd Lt. Johnson, Robert G.
2nd Lt. Kennedy, Joseph W.
2nd Lt. King, Hall
2nd Lt. Lenhardt, Edward J.
2nd Lt. Lewis, Melvin C.
2nd Lt. Marsh, Russell A.
2nd Lt. Morrison, William J.
2nd Lt. Murphy, Daniel J.
2nd Lt. O'Neill, William A.
2nd Lt. Patterson, Jack Q.
2nd Lt. Perdival, Edward L.
2nd Lt. Reitman, Michael L.
2nd Lt. Stearns, Willard R.
2nd Lt. Stewart, Eugene L.
2nd Lt. Stover, George E.
2nd Lt. Thomas, Arthur D.
2nd Lt. Vandiver, Ray
2nd Lt. Williams, John L.
2nd Lt. Wingard, Walton C.
2nd Lt. Wise, John W.
2nd Lt. Yuska, Victor A.
2nd Lt. Walker, Talmadge E.
F/O Hamilton, Darwin R.
M/Sgt. Daddario, Frank R.
M/Sgt. Flick, Corb L.
M/Sgt. Gibbons, Jay W.
M/Sgt. Kellett, Thomas J.
M/Sgt. Rensberger, Franklin D.
M/Sgt. Sahs, Elwood R.
M/Sgt. Smith, Floyd F.
M/Sgt. Summers, Frank W.
T/Sgt. Beringer, Edward R.
T/Sgt. Bryman, Julius
T/Sgt. Burton, William H.

T/Sgt. Davis, Jack A.
T/Sgt. Lenander, Albin F.
T/Sgt. Moorman, Arthur W.
T/Sgt. Morris, Ralph T.
T/Sgt. Pitaro, Alfred
T/Sgt. Rechlin, Frank H.
T/Sgt. Safranek, William C.
T/Sgt. Tilton, Merle E.
T/Sgt. Valdez, Israel
T/Sgt. Watkins, Harvey O., Jr.
T/Sgt. Watson, Osborn J.
T/Sgt. Whitehead, Charles D.
S/Sgt. Ahmann, Everett L.
S/Sgt. Brady, Lester M.
S/Sgt. Burns, Wilbert R.
S/Sgt. Culver, David H.
S/Sgt. Fabianich, Victor
S/Sgt. Gingno, John F.
S/Sgt. Gower, Lorenzo R.
S/Sgt. Hardgrove, William E.
S/Sgt. Lawrence, Harry F.
S/Sgt. Liberti, Joseph P.
S/Sgt. Lodge, Darold D.
S/Sgt. Millard, Theodore S.
S/Sgt. Miller, Leland F.
S/Sgt. Morris, Robert F.
S/Sgt. Potts, Robinett A.
S/Sgt. Roudebush, Barrett A.
S/Sgt. Scharp, Melvin C.
S/Sgt. Sell, Ramon C.
S/Sgt. Shafer, Paul V.
S/Sgt. Vantrease, James F.
Sgt. Bahr, Roger
Sgt. Baumstein, Harold L.
Sgt. Ewas, Michael
Sgt. Firchau, Carl H.
Sgt. Hosey, Lawrence F.
Sgt. Latteman, William C.
Sgt. LeBlanc, Alfred J.
Sgt. Norgan, Leroy M.
Sgt. Pylant, James H.
Sgt. Ropenski, Frank J.
Sgt. Slocki, Theodore
Sgt. Thall, Edward
Sgt. Tucker, George A.
Sgt. Vail, Raymond M.
Sgt. Vonk, William J.
Sgt. Williamson, Milton C.
Cpl. Ahlers, Robert H.
Cpl. Allen, Ned (RAAF)
Cpl. Boutross, Ferris T.
Cpl. Cox, John D.
Cpl. Fetzer, William H.
Cpl. Hickman, James G.
Cpl. Prince, Nathan D.
Cpl. Verdi, Dominic P.
Cpl. Yarosh, John S.
Pfc. Donovan, Carleton C.
Pfc. Frederick, Harry R.
Pfc. Gallagher, Joe S.
Pfc. Hutchinson, Donald M.
Pfc. Juhl, George F.
Pfc. Lambert, Milford W.
Pfc. Lundy, Robert G.
Pvt. King, James, Jr.

Pvt. Kvaka, John, Jr.
Pvt. Larrimore, Doyt T.
Pvt. Law, Marvin J.
Pvt. Smith, Rolfe M.
Pvt. Walsh, James F.
Brewer, Maurice
Brogden, Paul
Brown, Charles C.
Cape, Wesley
Gloss, Ellon C.
Green, James
Happerle, Kay C.
Hayden, Harold R.
Holder, Herbert
Jones, Wilfred B.
Klatt, Fred W.
Kott, Edward
Ley, Bob
Marshall, Allan
Martin, Lee
McFarland, Don
McNutt, Don M.
Miller, Charles J.
Nakishir, Fred
Ogden, R. D.
Olcott, Carlyle
Oliver, Richard E.
Olney, Richard B.
Pantos, Manuel
Revezzo, Frank
Samuel, Wilbur
Smallwood, John W.
Stillwell, Howard
Stoeser, Ben J.
Urban, George R.
Watts, F. R.
Williams, Emmons C.

22ND TROOP CARRIER SQUADRON

Maj. Bradford, William L.
Capt. Beebe, Robert C.
Capt. Feeney, Francis R.
Capt. Gary, Willis J.
Capt. Jacques, Pierre D.
Capt. Linn, John R.
Capt. Strong, William D.
Capt. Swenson, Raymond T.
Capt. Winn, Roger E.
1st Lt. Alverson, Leo C.
1st Lt. Bailey, Boyce S.
1st Lt. Baker, Leonidas
1st Lt. Borne, Irvin J.
1st Lt. Burr, Albert H.
1st Lt. Carlson, William H.
1st Lt. Clack, Melvin W.
1st Lt. Cobb, James O.
1st Lt. Culp, William K.
1st Lt. Dawson, Paul E.
1st Lt. Dixon, Robert
1st Lt. Doyle, Richard W.
1st Lt. Dreigen, David H.
1st Lt. Gillette, George
1st Lt. Glassburn, Kenneth L.
1st Lt. Greene, Theodore S.

1st Lt. Harper, James T.
1st Lt. Kendall, Delvin E., Jr.
1st Lt. Krebs, William W.
1st Lt. Lakin, Clarence A.
1st Lt. Langebartel, Edward P.
1st Lt. Lighter, Carl J.
1st Lt. Little, Loyd F.
1st Lt. Martin, James H., Jr.
1st Lt. McClure, John M.
1st Lt. Notestine, Ronald E.
1st Lt. Peterson, Malcolm E.
1st Lt. Rehrer, Harvey E.
1st Lt. Schumacher, Roman T.
1st Lt. Sigman, Leslie B.
1st Lt. Slingsby, Harold G.
1st Lt. Soular, Mike
1st Lt. Starr, Stephen A.
1st Lt. Thompson, Francis R.
1st Lt. Turk, Hugh L., Jr.
1st Lt. Uhrig, Charles E., Jr.
1st Lt. Whittington, Robert G.
2nd Lt. Adamczyk, Theodore S.
2nd Lt. Adelberger, Richard G.
2nd Lt. Berkovitz, Samuel
2nd Lt. Boise, Louis A.
2nd Lt. Byrne, Thomas I.
2nd Lt. Carroll, Frank W.
2nd Lt. Coile, Henry G., Jr.
2nd Lt. Cooper, Dowd L.
2nd Lt. Cornette, Charles M.
2nd Lt. Crecilius, William R.
2nd Lt. Crowley, Elmer C.
2nd Lt. Davis, Robert L.
2nd Lt. Dingman, Harry D.
2nd Lt. Forry, Harry P.
2nd Lt. Grams, Clair L.
2nd Lt. Gregg, James L.
2nd Lt. Hawley, Robert E.
2nd Lt. Maxwell, Neil D.
2nd Lt. McIlvain, Joseph T.
2nd Lt. McLean, Bruce E.
2nd Lt. Means, Russell E.
2nd Lt. Monson, Robert S.
2nd Lt. Moran, Louis A.
2nd Lt. Mumford, Robert A.
2nd Lt. Otten, Harold R.
2nd Lt. Pond, Philip R.
2nd Lt. Premo, Harold L.
2nd Lt. Rowell, John R.
2nd Lt. Shaw, Donald N.
2nd Lt. Sherman, Morris I
M/Sgt. Andreas, Nicholas J.
M/Sgt. Andreucci, Lewis F.
M/Sgt. Clark, Lawrence R.
M/Sgt. Gostage, Russell D.
M/Sgt. Lindley, Harold O.R.
M/Sgt. McMurray, Glenn D.
M/Sgt. Palma, Benjamin
T/Sgt. Applegate, Rex A.
T/Sgt. Bigham, James H.
T/Sgt. Dobson, Dorsey T.
T/Sgt. Feramisco, James
T/Sgt. Matutis, Nick
T/Sgt. McClard, Bert G.

T/Sgt. Shupe, John L.
T/Sgt. Smith, Ronald D.
T/Sgt. Soular, Theodore F.
T/Sgt. Tedzak, Harry B.
T/Sgt. Zubritsky, Michael
S/Sgt. Dorsett, Jack H.
S/Sgt. Glenn, Jack O.
Sgt. Boettger, Eugene
Sgt. Fazio, Robert S.
Sgt. Freshour, Donald J.
Sgt. Green, Walter R.
Sgt. Greening, Glen F.
Sgt. Kelley, Charles A.
Sgt. Shrader, John W.
Sgt. Simons, Ralph R.
Sgt. Swenson, John M.
Sgt. Whelchal, Frank E.
Cpl. Coury, Charles L.
Cpl. Reed, Lawrence E.
Cpl. Brown, Lawrence R.
Cpl. Murray, Dennis
Cpl. Peaff, John J.
Cpl. Rogers, Roy J.
Cpl. Williams, Clifford
Pfc. Meike, Albert A.
Pfc. Strazdas, Vito F.
Pfc. Tate, Eugene W.
Pfc. Trach, Leon M.
Pvt. Lawson, Henry T.
Douglas, Jack
Enloc, Steve
Glasscock, David
Glover, Allan B.
Greenleaf, Robert C.
Greilling, Bill
Hughes, Richard
Lukasevich, Nicholas P.
Lyle, William
Mageie, Harold
Shingleton, Jack
Temple, Harold
Watson, Robert
Wedow, Lawrence

33rd Troop Carrier Squadron

Capt. Jackson, Eugene R.
Capt. Kackley, Desmond D.
Capt. Pearson, Eric E.
Capt. Ross, William R.
Capt. Smith, Charles P.
Capt. Ward, Robert L.
1st Lt. Alexander, Jesse, Jr.
1st Lt. Dodge, James M.
1st Lt. Kimball, George C.
1st Lt. LaRoche, James N.
1st Lt. LaSalle, Leonard E.
1st Lt. McBreen, Donald R.
1st Lt. Miller, Ned K.
1st Lt. Phillips, E. R.
1st Lt. Quinn, William H.
1st Lt. Roth, Oliver N., Jr.
1st Lt. Vanek, Robert W.
1st Lt. Wentworth, Gerald O.

2nd Lt. Adams, Ira A.
2nd Lt. Ashley, Burl S.
2nd Lt. Banges, Robert
2nd Lt. Biggin, Richard M.
2nd Lt. Brandt, Marvin L.
2nd Lt. Bruce, Forrest D.
2nd Lt. Carlson, Robert E.
2nd Lt. Carson, Robert J.
2nd Lt. Cartwright, Philip E.
2nd Lt. Cornette, Charles M.
2nd Lt. Conquet, John D.
2nd Lt. Coveney, Ray M.
2nd Lt. Crawford, George
2nd Lt. Doyle, Richard W.
2nd Lt. Foltz, John W.
2nd Lt. Gardener, Allen W.
2nd Lt. Glotzbach, Gene R.
2nd Lt. Graves, Andrew J.
2nd Lt. Harrington, Elmer E.
2nd Lt. Holden, Preston
2nd Lt. Johnson, Robert G.
2nd Lt. Krolik, Richard
2nd Lt. Maxwell, Neil D.
2nd Lt. Nabors, Jack
2nd Lt. Otten, Harold R.
2nd Lt. Patterson, Claude W.
2nd Lt. Rennels, Lamont N.
2nd Lt. Reucker, Quentin C.
2nd Lt. Ridley, Paul R.
2nd Lt. Schnieders, George A.
2nd Lt. Schwensen, Robert H.
2nd Lt. Sexton, Robert L.
2nd Lt. Shea, Vernon L.
2nd Lt. Sherman, Henry W.
2nd Lt. Smith, Bryce V.
2nd Lt. Thompson, Robert J.
2nd Lt. Thompson, Walter B.
2nd Lt. Vanderevort, George W.
2nd Lt. Wamsley, George W.
2nd Lt. Watson, James C.
2nd Lt. Wylie, Johnston H.
T/Sgt. Anderson, Alf L.
T/Sgt. Banack, Stanley F.
T/Sgt. Bukovitch, Joe
T/Sgt. Check, Willis
T/Sgt. Dorland, Robert J.
T/Sgt. Kirsch, A. F.
T/Sgt. Lande, Albert
T/Sgt. Loy, Darrell D.
T/Sgt. Payton, Dalton C.
T/Sgt. Scalise, Raymond F.

T/Sgt. Sullivan, John J.
T/Sgt. Terchin, Harold
S/Sgt. Bloodsworth, Robert E.
S/Sgt. Chamberlain, Arthur C.
S/Sgt. Dillman, Robert L.
S/Sgt. Domigan, Harry
S/Sgt. Fisher, Kensel S.
S/Sgt. Garrett, Robert L.
S/Sgt. Gerrity, John J.
S/Sgt. Grabner, Carl A.
S/Sgt. Hager, J. W.
S/Sgt. Hensman, R. V.
S/Sgt. Horn, Robert M.
S/Sgt. Kopperud, Konrad H.
S/Sgt. Metzer, Leon W.
S/Sgt. Monson, Robert S.
S/Sgt. Mortenson, Benjamin F.
S/Sgt. Moseley, Harry T.
S/Sgt. Pennell, George E., Jr.
S/Sgt. Rau, Leander J.
S/Sgt. Rice, Charles D.
S/Sgt. Rosemarin, Jerome
S/Sgt. Swenson, Marvin D.
S/Sgt. Tarver, William L.
S/Sgt. Thompson, John
S/Sgt. Weitz, Arthur
S/Sgt. Wolf, Francis W.
Sgt. Archanbaul, Joseph
Sgt. Baltascavage, Joseph G.
Sgt. Brassell, Bobby G.
Sgt. Busch, Francis L.
Sgt. Carlson, Elwood C.
Sgt. Fitch, Steven J.
Sgt. Fitzwater, John L.
Sgt. Gardiner, Louis D.
Sgt. Glogowski, Sylvester J.
Sgt. Holland, Thomas E.
Sgt. Kershner, George R.
Sgt. Kleinberger, Sidney G.
Sgt. Kohler, Earl R., Jr.
Sgt. Kraft, Robert E.
Sgt. Lampe, Marcellus A.
Sgt. LanFranchi, Louis C.
Sgt. Mamalakis, Manuel
Sgt. Olson, Orwin S.
Sgt. Platt, Wilmer E.
Sgt. Stein, Edward G.
Sgt. Taylor, Joe R.
Sgt. Thompson, Marvin J.
Sgt. Wallace, Robert R.
Sgt. Wolfsberger, Elwood H.
Sgt. Zorbach, George E.
Cpl. Bement, Barry W.
Cpl. Borchert, Robert E.
Cpl. Christofferson, Lester D.
Cpl. Conte, Antonio
Cpl. Conway, William E.
Cpl. Delaney, Edwin
Cpl. Ericson, Emil W.
Cpl. Evans, Evan C.
Cpl. Heidt, Nicholas A.
Cpl. King, Benjamin F.
Cpl. Kovelesky, S. L.
Cpl. Lamar, James O.
Cpl. Marley, William P.
Cpl. Pastor, Florentino P.
Cpl. Teasdale, George E.
Pfc. Boggs, Charles C.
Pfc. Bradley, William B.
Pfc. Bryan, Hugh M.
Pfc. Edict, Fred S.
Pfc. Schweickhard, Paul A.
Pfc. Smith, Lloyd G.
Pfc. Stadterman, George L.
Pfc. Pickertowski, Edward G.
Pvt. Clark, Frank
Pvt. Fawn, Clifford J.
Pvt. Myers, W. C.
Aisenson, David
Arnold, John
Barwick, Ray C.
Bashore, Harold
Beachy, William B.
Beimel, Harry
Berg, Alvin
Bernard, Marwin A.
Bittner, James
Bona, Julius
Bozlinski, Joe
Bray, Adolphus T.
Call, Fredrick R.
Callahan, Carl G.
Channell, Elmer
Chasteen, Wilton O.
Cihak, Lawrence A.
Clark, Lester
Clemmens, Al D.
Colberg, Donald R.
Coleman, Robert G.
Coutts, James M.
D'Orazio (navigator)
Dales, E. Scott
Dart, Tom
Davis, Harold
DeMonaco, Salvatore
Dinardi, Demetrio A.
Douglass, Donald
Eckardt, Arnell
Falls, Robert P.
Fonfara, Frank
Force, Ralph E.
Freedman, Joe
Gligora, Nick
Grabin, Dan
Gramorossa, Steve
Gregory, Kenneth
Harmon, Ralph
Headley, Donald
Helgeson, Alvin C.
Herb, Bruce
Hesse, Herbert G.
Hill, Bill A.
Icke, Donald A.
James, Willie B.
Jones, Robert L.
Judson, Anthony
Kellander, Robert
Klopek, Albert
Kobrzycki, Edward
Komm, Albert
Lidel, Roland P.
Longman, John
Lorentz (navigator)
Lovorn, Cell Roane
Macis, Joe
Marion, Emmett H.
Marvin, (Navigator)
McCullough, Hugh
Mead, Charles R.
Meixell, Boyd
Miller, Lawrence
Mitrzak, John R.
Mittag, Conrad
Myers, Harry Lee
Myers, Benjamin T.
Neil, Ben
Nicolette, (Navigator)
Nowak, Jack
O'Bannon, James
O'Reilly, Robert
Oliver, Albert
Parrott, John
Paynter, Paul R.
Pencille, John W.
Pendleton, D. F., Jr.
Pickens, Charles D.
Plog, Buford J.
Redd (Navigator)
Ridloff, Solomon
Roberts, Eugene H.
Ryon, Maurice G.
Samuels, William J.
Sanborn, Dick
Sazer, Bernard
Schnaufer, John
Shank, Clifford
Skubal, Alan V.
Snapp, Richard W.
Snow, Ray E.
Speros, Harry
Stanley, Richard
Starek, George
Stewart, Harris B.
Stone, Charles A.
Teegardin, Boyd
Tippen (navigator)
VanZile, Walter
Varley, Charles R.
Vasquez, David
Veatch, John
Venturo, Attilio S.
Weese, Brice F.
Weinroth, Jack
Wilson, Sam K.
Worsham, James M.
Wowk, Mike
Young, Paul R.
Zabawa, Bernard J.
Zable, Harvey J.
Zarn, Fred

APPENDIX 'B'

HEADQUARTERS
ADVANCED ECHELON
FIFTH AIR FORCE
A.P.O.

31 January, 1943

Subject: Commendation
To: Commanding Officer, 374th Troop Carrier Group, APO 929.

    1. All of our Armed Forces in the Southwest Pacific are grateful for the fine piece of work which the 374th Troop Carrier Group performed on January 29, 30 and 31st, 1943. Only the efficiency of your organization and the bravery and the skill of your flying personnel in moving combat troops, artillery, ammunition and food saved the valuable airdrome area of the Bulolo Valley, from capture by the enemy. History is replete with historical illustrations of dramatic arrival of reinforcements on the field of battle. The operations of your group into Wau carrying men and guns while enemy mortar fire and small arms fire was reaching the landing strip adds another epic illustration in the history of the war. Your group has again proven the great striking power of a properly organized and co-ordinated Troop Carrier Effort.

    2. It is requested that the above be brought to the attention of every organization in your group.

/s/ ENNIS C. WHITEHEAD,
Brigadier General, AUS,

APPENDIX 'C'

HEADQUARTERS
54TH TROOP CARRIER WING
APO 929

24 September, 1943.

TO THE OFFICERS AND MEN OF THE 374TH TROOP CARRIER GROUP:

It is with real regret that I realize that the close association with you over a period of almost a year in New Guinea is about to terminate. It has been an honor and a pleasure to have commanded such an organization.

I believe I am correct in saying that the personnel of your group have received more decorations than any other organization of similar size in our services and it is rightly so as the records of deeds done will testify. You can leave here for your new assignment knowing that your work was well done, and that you have brought comfort, supplies, and aid to thousands of our own troops and to those of our Allied and much discomfort to our enemies.

I feel sure that you will continue your brilliant record and hope that the relief from the strain of combat flying and air raids and with some of the comforts of civilization available, that those of you who are war weary will soon regain your former good health.

The friendships and associations made here will always be a pleasurable recollection and I hope that those of you who fly up here from time to time will make it a point to come by and see us and give us all the good news from down below.

So long, good luck, and happy landings,

                                                          s/Paul H. Prentiss
                                                          t/PAUL H. PRENTISS,
                                                          Colonel, Air Corps,
                                                          Commanding.

<u>A CERTIFIED TRUE COPY</u>:

    s/John D. Pearson
    t/JOHN D. PEARSON
     Major, Air Corps,
     Adjutant,
     374th Tr Carrier Gp.

APPENDIX 'D'

6TH TROOP CARRIER

LINEAGE. Constituted 6th Transport Squadron on 1 Oct 1933. Activated on 14 Oct 1939. Redesignated: 6th Troop Carrier Squadron on 4 Jul 1942; 6th Troop Carrier Squadron (Heavy) on 21 May 1948.

ASSIGNMENTS. 10th Transport Group, 14 Oct 1939; 60th Transport Group, 1 Dec 1940; 61st Transport Group, 19 May 1941; 315th Transport Group, Mar 1942; 63rd Transport (later Troop Carrier) Group, Jun 1942; 374th Troop Carrier Group, 12 Nov 1942; 403rd Troop Carrier Group, 15 May 1946; 374th Troop Carrier Group, 15 Oct 1946; 1503rd Air Transport Wing, 18 Nov 1958 -.

STATIONS. Olmsted Field, Pa, 14 Oct 1939; Camp Williams, Wis, 23 Mar 1942; Dodd Field, Tex, 16-23 Sept 1942; Port Moresby, New Guinea, 13 Oct 1942; Garbutt Field, Australia, 2 Oct 1943; Nadzab, New Guinea, c. 26 Aug 1944; Biak, c. 20 Oct 1944; Tacloban, Leyte, 12 Mar 1945; Nielson Field, Luzon, 1 Jan 1946; Nichols Field, Luzon, 10 May 1946; Okinawa, 10 Jun 1946; Tachikawa, Japan, 13 Apr 1947; Harmon Field, Guam, 1 Dec 1947; Tachikawa, Japan, 5 Mar 1949 -.

AIRCRAFT. Included C-33, C-39, and C-53 in period 1940 - 1942; C-47, 1942 - 1945; C-46, 1945 - 1947; C-54, 1947 - 1952; C-124, 1952 -.

OPERATIONS. Aerial transportation in South, Southwest, and Western Pacific during World War II, and in Far East during Korean War.

SERVICE STREAMERS. None

CAMPAIGNS. World War II: Air Offensive, Japan; Papua; New Guinea; Northern Solomons; Bismarck Archipelago; Western Pacific; Leyte; Luzon; Southern Philippines. Korean War: UN Defensive; UN Offensive; CCF Intervention; First UN Counteroffensive; CCF Spring Offensive; UN Summer-Fall Offensive; Second Korean Winter; Korea Summer-Fall, 1952; Third Korean Winter; Korea Summer-Fall, 1953.

DECORATIONS. Distinguished Unit Citations: Papua, (Oct) 1942 - 23 Jan 1943; Papua, 12 Nov - 22 Dec 1942; Wau, New Guinea, 30 Jan - 1 Feb 1943; Korea, 27 Jun - 15 Sep 1950. Air Force Outstanding Unit Award: 1 Jan - 31 Dec 1961. Philippine Presidential Unit Citation: 1 Jul 1951 - 27 Jul 1953.

EMBLEM. On a disc blue, narrow bordered black, over a representation of a tin "Bully Beef" white, edged red, caricatured bull's head front face brown, mouth and horns yellow, beard black, eyeballs white, pupils black, nose red and with a fighting mad expression and snorting detail white from nose. (Approved 1 Dec 1952.)

Left to right: Maj. Rehrer, Lt. Pearce, and 1st Sgt. Chain.

APPENDIX 'E'

21st Troop Carrier

LINEAGE. Constituted 21st Transport Squadron on 7 Mar 1942. Activated on 3 Apr 1942. Redesignated 21st Troop Carrier Squad ron on 5 Jul 1942. Inactivated on 31 Jan 1946. Activated on 15 Oct 1946. Redesignated: 21st Troop Carrier Squadron (Heavy) on 21 May 1948; 21st Troop Carrier Squadron (Med ium) on 2 Feb 1951; 21st Troop Carrier Squad ron (Heavy) on 1 Dec 1952; 21st Troop Carrier Squadron (Medium) on 18 Sep 194\56.

ASSIGNMENTS. Air Transport Command, US Army Forces in Australia (later Air Carrier Service, Air Service Command, Fifth Air Force), 3 Apr 1942; 374th Troop Carrier Group, 12 Nov 1942 - 31 Jan 1946. 374th Troop Carrier Group, 15 Oct 1946; 483rd Troop Carrier Group, 18 Sep 1956; 483rd Troop Carrier Wing, 8 Dec 1958; 315th Air Division, 25 Jun 1960 -.

STATIONS. Archerfield, Australia, 3 Apr 1942; Port Moresby, New Guinea, 18 Feb 1943; Archerfield, Australia, 28 Sep 1943; Nadzab, New Guinea, 26 Aug 1944; Biak, 14 Oct 1944; Atsugi, Japan, 20 Sep 1945; Manila, Luzon, Dec 1945 - 31 Jan 1946. Harmon Field, Guam, 15 Oct 1946; Clark AFB, Luzon, 27 Jan 1950; Tachikawa, Japan, 29 Jun 1950; Ashiya, Japan, 21 Jul 1950; Brady AB, Japan, 3 Sep 1950; Itzauke, Japan, 24 Oct 1950; Tachikawa, Japan, 25 Jan 1951; Ashiya, Japan, 26 Jul 1951; Tachikawa, Japan, 18 Oct 1951; Ashiya, Japan, 28 Mar 1952; Tachikawa, Japan, 1 Dec 1952; Naha, Okinawa, 15 Nov 1958 -.

AIRCRAFT. Included DC-2, DC-3, C-39, C-40, C-49, C-50, C-53, C-56, C-60, B-17, B-18, and LB-30 during 1942; C-47, 1942 - 1946; C-46, 1945 - 1946; C-46, 1946 - 1949, 1950; C-47, 1950 - 1952; C-54, 1946 - 1950, 1952 - 1956; C-119, 1956 - 1959; C-130, 1958 -.

OPERATIONS. Included paratroop drops at Nadzab, New Guinea, in Sep 1942 and airborne assault on Sukchon/Sunchon, Korea, in Oct 1950, as well as aerial transportation in South and Southwest Pacific during World War II and in Far East during Korean War.

SERVICE STREAMERS. None

CAMPAIGNS. World War II: Papua; New Guinea; Northern Solomons; Bismarck Archipelago; Western Pacific; Leyte; Luzon; Southern Philippines. Korean War: UN Defensive; UN Offensive; CCF Intervention; First UN Counteroffensive; CCF Spring Offensive; UN Summer-Fall Offensive; Second Korean Winter; Korea Summer-Fall, 1952; Third Korean Winter; Korea Summer-Fall, 1953.

DECORATIONS: Distinguished Unit Citations: Papua 23 Jul 1942 - 23 Jan 1943; Papua, 12 Nov - 22 Dec 1942; Wau, New Guinea, 30 Jan - 1 Feb 1943; Korea, 27 Jun - 15 Sep 1950; Korean, 28 Nov - 10 Dec 1950. Philippine Presidential Unit Citation. Republic of Korea Presidential Unit Citation: 1 Jul 1951 - 27 Jul 1953.

EMBLEM. On a white disc bordered light golden brown, a stylized delta-winged bee, his head, body and upper wings light golden brown; eyes, lower wings, and stripes on body, red; encircling the upper part of the disc and surmounting the border a stylized stringer wreath, red. *Motto*: Superimposed over the border and wreath at the top of the emblem, "BEE liners," inscribed white. (Approved 31 Jul 1959.)

Capt. Phil Eckberg as Squadron CO.

APPENDIX 'F'

22D TROOP CARRIER

LINEAGE. 22d Transport Squadron activated on 3 Apr 1942 prior to constitution on 4 Apr 1942. Redesignated 22d Troop Carrier Squadron on 5 Jul 1942. Inactivated on 31 Jan 1946. Activated on 15 Oct 1946. Redesignated 22d Troop Carrier Squadron (Heavy) on 21 May 1948.

ASSIGNMENTS. Air Transport Command, US Army Forces in Australia (later Air Carrier Service, Air Service Command, Fifth Air Force), 3 Apr 1942; 376th Troop Carrier Group, 12 Nov 1942 - 31 Jan 1946. 374th Troop Carrier Group, 15 Oct 1946; 1503d Air Transport Wing, 18 Nov 1958 -.

STATIONS. Essendon Airdrome, Australia, 3 Apr 1942; Garbutt Field, Australia, 11 Oct 1942; Port Moresby, New Guinea, 24 Jan 1943; Finschhafen, New Guinea, 29 Aug 1944; Nielson Field, Luzon, Aug 1945 - 31 Jan 1946. Nichols Field, Luzon, 15 Oct 1946; Clark Field, Luzon, 23 Apr 1947 (detachment operated from Wiesbaden Germany, 3 Oct - 16 Nov 1948); Tachikawa, Japan, 16 Nov 1948 -.

AIRCRAFT. Included DC-2, DC-3, C-39, C-49, C-53, C-56, C-60, B-17, and B-18 durign 1942; C-47, 1942 - 1945; C-46, 1945 - 1946. C-46, 1946 - 1949; C-54, 1946 - 1948, 1949 - 1952; C-124, 1952 - 1957, 1959 -.

OPERATIONS. Included paratroop crop on Nadzab, New Guinea, as well as aerial transportation in South, Southwest, and West ern Pacific, during World War II. Berlin Airlift. Aerial transportation in Far East during Korean War. Not operational, Jun 1957 - Apr 1959.

SERVICE STREAMERS. None

CAMPAIGNS. World War II: Air Offensive, Japan; Papua; New Guinea; Northern Solomons; Bismarck Archipelago; Western Pacific; Leyte; Luzon; Southern Philippines. Korean War: UN Defensive; UN Offensive; CCF Intervention; First UN Counteroffensive; CCF Spring Offensive; UN Summer-Fall Offensive; Second Korean Winter; Korea Summer-Fall, 1952; Third Korean Winter; Korea Summer-Fall, 1953.

DECORATIONS. Distinguished Unit Citations: Papua, 23 Jul 1942 - 23 Jan 1943; Papua, 12 Nov - 22 Dec 1942; Wau, New Guinea, 30 Jan - 1 Feb 1943; Korea, 27 Jun - 15 Sep 1950. Air Force Outstanding Unit Award: 1 Jan - 31 Dec 1961. Philippine Presidential Unit Citation. Republic of Korea Presidential Unit Citation: 1 Jul 1951 - 27 Jun 1953.

EMBLEM. On a medium blue disc, wide border light red, a caricatured, light gray donkey, trimmed white and black, having large, light red pack, outlined black, strapped about the middle by heavy, black bond climbing hilly terrain light brown, shaded dark brown. (Approved 17 Jun 1944.)

Major John D. Pearson and his personnel staff at Townsville, Australia, 1943.

APPENDIX 'G'

33D TROOP CARRIER

LINEAGE. Constituted 33d Transport Squadron on 2 Feb 1942. Activated on 14 Feb 1942. Redesignated 33d Troop Carrier Squadron on 4 Jul 1942. Inactivated on 15 Feb 1946.

ASSIGNMENTS. 315th Transport (later Troop Carrier) Group, 14 Feb 1942; 374th Troop Carrier Group, 12 Nov 1942 - 15 Feb 1946.

STATIONS. Olmsted Field, Pa, 14 Feb 1942; Bowman Field, Ky, 17 Jun 1942; Florence, SC, 3 Aug - 30 Sep 1942 (detachments operated from New Caledonia, 25 Oct - 29 Nov 1942, and Cairns, Australia, c. 1 Nov - 10 Dec 1942); Brisbane, Australia, 1 Dec 1942; Port Moresby, New Guinea, 28 Dec 1942; Garbutt Field, Australia, 5 Oct 1943; Port Moresby, New Guinea, Apr 1944; Hollandia, New Guinea, 15 Oct 1944; Nielson Field, Luzon, 8 Apr 1945 - 15 Feb 1946.

AIRCRAFT. C-47, 1942 - 1946; C-46, 1945 - 1946.

OPERATIONS. Aerial transportation in South and Southwest Pacific during World War II.

SERVICE STREAMERS. None

CAMPAIGNS. Papua; New Guinea; Guadalcanal; Northern Solomons; Bismarck Archipelago; Western Pacific; Leyte; Luzon; Southern Philippines.

DECORATIONS. Distinguished Unit Citations: Papua, (Nov) 1942 - 23 Jan 1943; Papua, 12 Nov - 22 Dec 1942; Wau, New Guinea, 30 Jan - 1 Feb 1943. Philippine Presidential Unit Citation.

EMBLEM. See below.

33rd Group Carrier Squadron, left to right: Major George Wamsley, Captain Gerald Wentworth, Captain Robert Carlson, and 1st Sgt. Art Merman.

APPENDIX 'H'

374TH TROOP CARRIER GROUP

Constituted as 374th Troop Carrier Group on 7 Nov 1942 and *activated* in Australia on 12 Nov. Assigned to Fifth AF. Transported men and materiel in the theater from Nov 1942 until after the war, operating from Australia, New Guinea, Biak, and the Philippines. Used war-weary and worn-out aircraft, including B-18's, C-39's, C-49's, C-56's, C-60's, DC-3's, and DC-5's, until equipped with C-47's in Feb 1943. Engaged in supplying Allied forces in the Papuan Campaign, receiving one DUC for these missions, and being awarded another DUC for transporting troops and equipment to Papua and evacuating casualties to rear areas, Nov - Dec 1942. Received third DUC for transporting men and supplies over the Owen Stanley Range, 30 Jan - 1 Feb 1943, to aid the small force defending the airdrome at Wau, New Guinea. Participated in the first airborne operation in the Southwest Pacific on 5 Sep 1943, dropping paratroops at Nadzab, New Guinea, to seize enemy bases and cut inland supply routes. Other operations included evacuating wounded personnel, flying courier routes, making passenger flights, and helping to move the 11th Division from Luzon to Oki nawa in Aug 1945 for staging to Japan. From Sep 1945 to May 1946 hauled cargo to the occupation army in Japan and flew courier routes from the Philippines to Japan. *Inacti vated* on Luzon on 15 May 1946.

Activated in the Philippines on 15 Oct 1946. Assigned to Far East Air Forces. Transferred, without personnel and equipment, to Guam on 1 Apr 1947. Remanned and equipped with C-46 and C-47 aircraft. Flew courier, passenger, and cargo routes in the western Pacific. *Redesignated* 374th Troop Carrier Group (Heavy) in May 1948. Began converting to C-54's. Moved to Japan in Mar 1949. Began operations in the Korea War in Jun 1950, using C-47 and C-54 aircraft, the C-47's being replaced with C-124's in 1952. Transported men and cargo to Korea and evacuated wounded personnel on return flights. Remained in Japan after the war.

SQUADRONS. *6th:* 1942 - 1946; 1946 -. *19th:* 1946 - 1948. *21st:* 1942 - 1946; 1946 -. *22nd:* 1942 - 1946; 1946 -. *33d:* 1942 - 1946.

STATIONS. Brisbane, Australia, 12 Nov 1942; Port Moresby, New Guinea, Dec 1942; Townsville, Australia, 7 Oct 1943; Hadzab, New Guinea, c. 1 Sep 1944; Biak, c. 14 Oct 1944; Nielson Field, Luzon, 28 May 1945 - 15 May 1946. Nichols Field, Luzon, 15 Oct 1946; Harmon Field, Guam, 1 Apr 1947; Tachikawa, Japan, 5 Mar 1949 -.

COMMANDERS. Lt Col Erickson S Nichols, 12 Nov 1942; Maj Edgar H Hampton, 14 Dec 1942; Col Paul H Prentiss, 17 Dec 1942; Maj Fred M Adams, 22 May 1943; Lt Col Edgar H Hampton, 12 Jul 1943; Lt Col Fred M Adams, 2 Aug 1943; Col Edward T Imparato, c. 3 Aug 1944; Col John L Sullivan, Oct 1945 - unkn; Lt Col Forrest P Coons, 1947 - unkn; Col Troy W Crawford, 1949; Lt Col Benjamin T Tarver Jr, Aug 1949; Col Herbert A Bott, 22 Jul 1950; Col Charles W Howe, Jul 1951; Col Edward H Nigro, Sep 1951; Lt Col James F Hogan, Apr 1952; Col Edward H Nigro, 11 Aug 1952; Lt Col Frederick C Johnson, 11 Sep 1952; Col Francis W Williams, 24 Apr 1953; Col Hollis B Tara, 15 Jun 1954 -.

CAMPAIGNS. *World War II:* Air Offen sive, Japan; Papua; New Guinea; Northern Solomons; Bismarck Archipelago; Western Pacific; Leyte; Luzon. *Korean War:* UN Defensive; UN Offensive; CCF Intervention; 1st UN Counteroffensive; CCF Spring Offen sive; UN Summer-Fall Offensive; Second Korean Winter; Korea Summer-Fall, 1952; Third Korean Winter; Korea Summer-Fall, 1953.

DECORATIONS. Distinguished Unit Citations: Papua (Nov) 1942 - 23 Jan 1943; Papua, 12 Nov - 22 Dec 1942; Wau, New Guinea, 30 Jan - 1 Feb 1943; Korea, 27 Jun - 15 Sep 1950. Philippine Presidential Unit Citation. Republic of Korea Presidential Unit Citation: 1 Jul 1951 - 27 Jul 1953.

INSIGNE: *Shield:* Per bend azure and or, in chief a hand coupled in armour, holding a dagger, point upward, issuing from its handle an arrow and a wheat stalk or, in base a winged foot azure. *Motto:* CELERITER PUGNARE - Swiftly to Fight. (Approved 3 Jul 1951.)

APPENDIX 'I'

54TH TROOP CARRIER WING

Constituted as 54th Troop Carrier Wing on 26 Feb 1943. *Activated* in Australia on 13 Mar 1943. Assigned to Fifth AF. Engaged in troop carrier and transport operations from May 1943 until after the end of the war. *Inactivated* in the Philippines on 31 May 1946.

Redesignated 54th Fighter Wing. Allotted to ANG (Ga) on 1 Jun 1946. Extended federal recognition on 2 Oct 1946. Called to active service on 10 Oct 1950. *Inactivated* On 11 Oct 1950.

GROUPS. *2d* Combat Cargo: 1944 - 1946. *317th* Troop Carrier: 1943 - 1946. *374th* Troop Carrier: 1943 - 1946. *433d* Troop Carrier: 1943 - 1946.

STATIONS. Brisbane, Australia, 13 Mar 1943; Port Moresby, New Guinea, 3 May 1943; Nadzab, New Guinea, 18 Apr 1944; Biak, 5 Oct 1944; Leyte, 14 Feb 1945; Clark Field, Luzon, Jun 1945; Tachikawa, Japan, Sep 1945; Manila, Luzon, Jan - 31 May 1946.

COMMANDERS. Brig Gen Paul H Prentiss, 20 May 1943; Brig Gen Warren R Carter, 30 Mar 1944; Brig Gen Paul H Prentiss, 19 Nov 1944; Brig Gen William D Old, c. Oct 1945 - unkn.

CAMPAIGNS. Air Offensive, Japan; New Guinea; Bismarck Archipelago; Western Pacific; Leyte; Luzon; Southern Philippines; Ryukyus.

DECORATIONS. Philippine Presidential Unit Citation.

INSIGNE. None.

APPENDIX 'J'

Fifth Air Force

Constituted as Philippine Department AF on 16 Aug 1941. *Activated* in the Philippines on 20 Sep 1941. *Redesignated* Far East AF in Oct 1941, and Fifth AF in Feb 1942. This air force lost most of its men and equipment in the defense of the Philippines after 7 Dec 1941. Later in Dec 1941 headquarters and some crews and planes moved to Australia, and in Jan 1942 they were sent to Java to help delay Japanese advances in the Netherlands Indies. The Fifth did not function as an air force for some time after Feb 1942 (the AAF organizations in the Southwest Pacific being under the control of American-British-Dutch-Australian Command and later Allied Air Forces). Headquarters was remanned in Sep 1942 and assumed control of AAF organizations in Australia and New Guinea. The Fifth participated in operations that stopped the Japanese drive in Papua, recovered New Guinea, neutralized islands in the Bismarck Archipelago and the Netherlands East Indies, and liberated the Philippines. When the war ended in Aug 1945 elements of the Fifth were moving to the Ryukyus for the invasion of Japan. After the war the Fifth, a component of Far East Air Forces, remained in the theater, and from Jun 1950 to Jul 1953 it was engated in the Korean War.

COMMANDS. V Bomber: 1941 - 1946. V Fighter: 1942 - 1946.

STATIONS. Nichols Field, Luzon, 20 Sep 1941; Darwin Australia, Dec 1941; Java, Jan - Feb 1942; Brisbane, Australia, 3 Sep 1942; Nadzab, New Guinea, 15 Jun 1944; Owi, Schouten Islands, 10 Aug 1944; Leyte, c. 20 Nov 1944; Mindoro, Jan 1945; Clark Field, Luzon, Apr 1945; Okinawa, Jul 1945; Irumagawa, Japan, c. 25 Sep 1945; Tokyo, Japan, 13 Jan 1946; Nagoya, Japan, 20 May 1946; Seoul, Korea, 1 Dec 1950; Taegu, Korea, 22 Dec 1950; Seoul, Korea, 15 Jun 1951; Osan-Ni, Korea, 25 Jan 1954; Nagoya, Japan, 1 Sep 1954 -.

COMMANDERS. Brig Gen Henry B Clagett, 20 Sep 1941; Maj Gen Lewis H Brereton, Oct 1941 - Feb 1942; Lt Gen George C Kenney, 3 Sep 1942; Lt Gen Ennis C Whitehead, 15 Jun 1944; Maj Gen Kenneth B Wolfe, 4 Oct 1945; Maj Gen Thomas D White, 16 Jan 1948; Lt Gen Earle E Partridge, 6 Oct 1948; Maj Gen Edward J Timberlake, 21 May 1951; Maj Gen Frank F Everest, 1 Jun 1951; Lt Gen Glenn O Barcus, 30 May 1952; Lt Gen Samuel E Anderson, 31 May 1953; Lt Gen Roger M Ramey, 1 Jun 1954 -.

CAMPAIGNS. *World War II:* Philippine Islands; East Indies; Air Offensive, Japan; China Defensive; Papua; New Guinea; Northern Solomons; Bismarck Archipelago; Western Pacific; Leyte; Luzon; Southern Philippines; China Offensive. *Korean War:* UN Defensive; UN Offensive; CCF Intervention; 1st UN Counteroffensive; CCF Spring Offensive; UN Summer-Fall Offensive; Second Korean Winter; Korea Summer-Fall, 1952; Third Korean Winter; Korea Summer-Fall, 1953.

DECORATIONS. Distinguished Unit
Citations: Philippine Islands, 8 - 22 Dec 1941; Philippine Islands, 7 Dec 1941 - 10 May 1942; Papua, (Sep) 1942 - 23 Jan 1943. Philippine Presidential Unit Citation.

INSIGNE. On an ultramarine blue disc, the Southern Cross consisting of five stars in white between a flaming comet, the head consisting of a white five pointed star, charged with a red roundel, within a blue disc outlined in white, its tail consisting of three white streamers; all surmounted by an Arabic numbers "5", golden orange. (Approved 25 Mar 1943.)

APPENDIX 'K'

Battles and Campaigns

A number of the personnel assigned to Air Transport Command and later to the 21st and 22nd Transport Squadrons had participated in the Philippine Islands and East Indies Campaigns.

The entire group participated in the Papuan and New Guinea Campaigns.

It should also be noted that seven of the planes and crews and a complement of ground personnel of the 33rd Squadron actually participated in the Guadalcanal Campaign from October 25, 1942 to November 29, 1942. Whether personnel thus engaged are entitled to wear a star for the campaign depends upon an interpretation of Army Regulations.

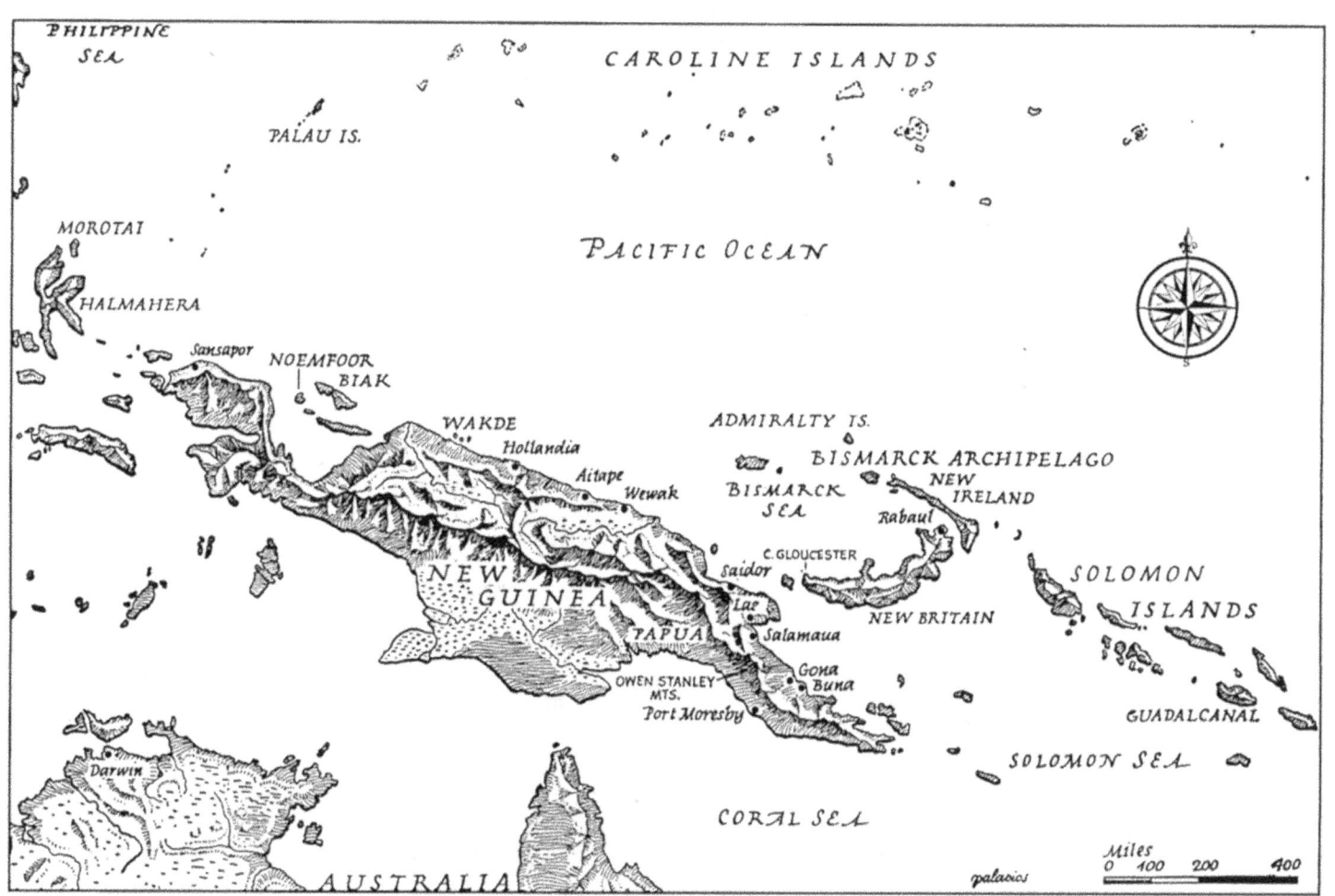

APPENDIX 'L'

OPERATIONS

Aircraft - Assignment of Aircraft

The original Air Transport Command began its operations with 8 aircraft, consisting of five Douglas C-53s, two B-18s, and one C-39. In March, 1942, the organization received three L-14s, 8 Lockheed C-56s, three Douglas DC-5s, two Douglas DC-3s, and two Douglas DC-2s, all former Netherlands East Indies K.N.I.L.M. aircraft. In April, 1942, two new C-47s and three old C-39s were added. As of April 24, 1942, in a memorandum to General Brett, Group Captain Harold Gatty reported four C-39s, two C-47s, one B-17, two C-53s , eleven C-56s (purchased from Dutch Army), and two C-40s (purchased from Dutch Army) in operation by Air Transport Command. In a report to General Brett, dated 16 May, 1942, Captain Gatty disclosed the following planes assigned to Air Transport command: four C-39s, two C-47s, two C-53s, eleven C-56s, one B-17, one B-18, two DC-2s, two DC-3s, three DC-5s and three Lockheed 14s.

Operations Order No. 20, dated 20 May, 1942, Air Transport Command Headquarters, showed the following assignment of aircraft to the 21st Transport Squadron: one B-18, two C-39s, two C-53s, one C-47, two DC-2s, two DC-3s, three DC-5s, and 2 Lockheed 14s.

Operations Order No. 21, dated 21 May 1942, Hq., Air Transport Command, showed the following assignment of aircraft to the 22nd Transport Squadron: one B-17, eleven C-56s, two C-39s, one C-47, and one Lockheed 14. Temporarily assigned to the 22nd were a B-18 and a C-53.

Late in August, 1942, eight C-49s and three C-50s were assigned to the 21st Troop Carrier Squadron. Thirteen Lockheed C-60s arrived early in September and were flown for two weeks by the 21st Squadron before being turned over to the 22nd. Late in September, all former K.N.I.L.M. planes were turned over to the Airlines of Australia.

In October, 1942, the air echelon of the 6th Troop Carrier Squadron had begun to operate in the Southwest Pacific theater with thirteen C-47s. Late in November, 1942, the 33rd Troop Carrier Squadron had begun to operate its eleven C-47s in the Southwest Pacific Theater.

Memorandum issuing out of Headquarters, Air Carrier Service, dated 2 November, 1942, showed the following assignment of aircraft:

6th Troop Carrier Squadron:	12 C-47s	
21st Troop Carrier Squadron:	1 C-47	6 C-49s
	3 C-50s	3 C-53s
	2 LR-30s	1 Tiger Moth
22nd Troop Carrier Squadron:	3 C-39s	10 C-60s
	1 B-17c	1 R-17e
	3 LC-1s	
33rd Troop Carrier Squadron:	6 C-47s (5 additional ships arrived later)	

As of 5 December, 1942, the Group showed the following assignments of aircraft:

6th Troop Carrier Squadron:	13 C-47s (Including 4 total losses)	
21st Troop Carrier Squadron:	6 C-49s	
	3 C-50s (Including 1 lost at sea)	
	3 C-53s	1 C-47
	2 LB-30s	1 Tiger Moth
22nd Troop Carrier Squadron:	3 C-39s	10 C-60s
	1 B-17c	1 B-17e
	3 LC-1s (all three crashed)	
33rd Troop Carrier Squadron:	13 C-47s (including 4 total losses)	

In January, 1943, the 374th was completely equipped with the new C-47s of the 317th Troop Carrier Group by an exchange of all aircraft. After January, 1943, the group began to operate C-47 type aircraft exclusively.

APPENDIX 'M'

APPENDIX 'N'

Aircraft Losses - 374th Troop Carrier Group - By Squadron

1942 - 1945

6th Squadron

DATE	TYPE	LOCATION	CAUSE	DISPOSITION	REMARKS
Oct 16/42	C-47	Efogi Area	Miss in act	Comp. Loss	Crashed dropping freight
Nov 4/42	C-47	Poppendetta	Crashed into side of hill	Comp. Loss	Crashed into hill
Nov 13/42	C-47	Pongani	Crashed into side of hill	Rebuilt	Collision caused by another C-47
Nov 26/42	C-47	Dobodura	Enemy action	Comp. Loss	Shot down in flames 5 miles south of Dobodura
Dec 3/42	C-47	Poppendetta	Pilot error	Comp. Loss	Crashed and burned
Jan 27/43	C-47	Bena Bena	Pilot error	Rebuilt	Ground collision
Mar 8/43	C-47	Bulolo	Pilot error	Salvaged	Overshot field
Mar 27/43	C-47	Dobodura	Pilot error	Rebuilt	Scraped tree tops believing enemy in area
Apr 12/43	C-47	Wards Drome	Enemy action	Rebuilt	Enemy bomb action
Apr 12/43	C-47	Wards Drome	Enemy action	Rebuilt	Enemy bomb action
Jul 30/43	C-47	Wards Drome	Loading	Rebuilt	Door sill damaged by Jeep: fell off loading ramp
Aug 19/43	C-47	Pulpit	Dust caused poor vision	Rebuilt	Ran into another plane
Oct 19/43	C-47	Cloncurry	Unknown	Comp. Loss	Crashed; bad weather
Nov 13/43	C-47	Cloncurry	Collision	Rebuilt	Hit by B-24 on ground
May 14/44	C-47	Hollandia			
May 27/44	C-47	Gussap			
Jun 11/44	C-47A	Cooktown			
Jun 27/44	C-47A	Lae			
Sep 6/44	C-47A	Boroke	Taxying Collision		Tfrd for repairs
Sep 6/44	C-47A	Boroke	"		"
Nov 1/44	C-47A	Dobodura	Fire	Poss Salv	Burning gas truck
Nov 1/44	C-47A	Dobodura	Collision	Repaired	Formation flying
Nov 26/44	C-47A	Anguar	Ground Collision	Repaired	Struck by bulldozer

DATE	TYPE	LOCATION	CAUSE	DISPOSITION	REMARKS
Nov 27/44	C-47A	Leyte	Taxying collision	Repaired	
Dec 8/44	C-47A			Salvage	Acid spill on floor & control cables
Dec 2/44	C-47A	Finschhafen		Salvage	Acid leak
Dec 23/44	C-47A	Leyte Collision	Taxying	Salvage	nose section damaged
Dec 24/44	C-47A	Leyte	Taxying collision	Repaired	Left wing tip damaged
Jan /45		?	Mid-air collision	Salvaged	
Jan /45		?	Landing accident		Trfd for repairs
Feb /45		Leyte		Salvage	brakes failed on landing
Feb /45			Mechanical failure		Ran into revetment
Feb /45					C-46 struck plane
Feb /45					Weapons carrier struck plane
Feb /45			Taxying		
Mar /45				Salvage	Ground looped
Mar /45			Collision	Salvage	Crash landed & burned
Mar /45			Pilot error	Repaired	Clipped a tree top
Mar /45			Taxying	Repaired	
Apr /45				Salvaged	Landing gear collapsed
Apr/45					Damaged on landing
Apr /45			Taxying (3)		
May /45			Taxying (2)	repaired	
May /45			Loading		
Jun /45	C-47B		Missing in action		
Jun /45					Damaged by truck
Jul /45			Taxying	Repaired	
Jul /45			Loading	Repaired	
Jul /45			Landing	Repaired	
Aug /45			Taxying	Repaired	
Aug /45			Loading	Repaired	
Aug /45			Taxying	Repaired	

DATE	TYPE	LOCATION	CAUSE	DISPOSITION	REMARKS
Aug /45			Unloading	Repaired	
Aug /45		Okinawa	Crashed		28 passengers & crew killed

21st Squadron

DATE	TYPE	LOCATION	CAUSE	DISPOSITION	REMARKS
Feb 4/42	C-53	Bathurst Is.	Enemy action	Salvaged	
Feb 28/42	C-53	Drysdale Mission	Forced down	Comp. Loss	
May 25/42	C-39	Alice Springs	Unknown	Comp. Loss	
Jun 23/42	DC-2	Charters Towers	Unknown	Comp. Loss	
Aug 17/42	DC-3	New Guinea	Enemy action	Rebuilt	Enemy bomb action
Oct 11/42	C-56	Archer Field	Unknown	Rebuilt	
Nov 15/42	C-50C	Buna - Coral Sea	Enemy action	Salvaged	A.A. at Buna - Failed in flight to Cairns
Nov 20/42	C-49	Poppendetta	Mech. failure	Salvaged	Landing gear failure
Jan 15/43	C-49	Wards Drome	Mech. failure	Rebuilt	Landing gear failure
Jan 30/43	C-47	Wau	Ground crash	Salvaged	Another plane overshot field and crashed into it
Jan 30/43	C-47	Wau	Pilot error	Salvaged	Overshot field; crashed into 2 planes: operated by 317th Group
Jan 30/43	C-47	Wau	Ground crash	Rebuilt	Another plane overshot field and crashed into it
Jan 31/43	C-47	Wards Drome	Mech. failure	Rebuilt	Hydraulic failure
May 12/43	C-47	Dobodura	Unknown	Comp. loss	Missing in action
Jun 13/43	C-47	Selebob	Carelessness	Rebuilt	Hit by box of supplies dropped by another plane in same flight
Aug 15/43	C-47	Pulpit	Enemy action	Comp. loss	Shot down
Aug 15/43	C-47	Pulpit	Enemy action	Comp. loss	Shot down
Nov 16/43	C-47	Springsure, Queensland	See remarks	Comp. loss	Disintegrated in heavy storm
Nov 19/43	C-47A	Cairns	Pilot error	Salvaged	Undercarriage damaged while landing
Dec 1/43	C-47A	Townsville	Mech. failure	Salvaged	Landing gear failure
Dec 1/43	C-47A	Townsville	See remarks	Salvaged	Struck by plane
Dec 1/43	C-47A	Townsville	See remarks	Rebuilt	Struck by plane
Dec 15/43	C-47A	Brisbane	See remarks	Rebuilt	Damaged in storm

DATE	TYPE	LOCATION	CAUSE	DISPOSITION	REMARKS
Jul 20/44	C-47A	Wadke			
Sep 8/44	C-47A		Taxying collision		For repairs
Sep 14/44	C-47	Nadzab	Nosed over	Repaired	
Sep 15/44	C-47A	Nadzab	Ground collision		For repairs
Nov 1/44	C-47A	Tadji	Crash	Demolished	All prsnl killed
Nov 6/44	C-47A	Sorido	Ground collision	Repaired	Unknown ground vehicle
Nov 21/44	C-47A	Sorido	Ground collision	Repaired	Vehicle
Nov 22/44	C-47A	Peleliu	Pilot error	Repaired	Left propellor hit runway
Nov 24/44	C-47A	Peleliu	Ground crew	Repaired	Small stove ignited
Nov 26/44	C-47A	Owi	Ground collision	Salvaged	Struck by B-24
Dec 12/44	C-47A	?			Missing in action
Dec 10/44	C-47A	Finschhafen	Acid spill		
Dec 12/44	C-47A	Sorido	Ground collision	Repaired	Struck by another plane
Dec 12/44	C-47A	Sorido	Ground collision	Repaired	Struck another plane
Dec 12/44	C-47A	?			Missing in action
Dec 14/44	C-47A	En route Moratai	Rough weather		Structure weakened
Dec 14/44	C-47A	Sorido	Taxying	Repaired	Struck by taxying aircraft
Dec 15/44	C-47A	Finschhafen	Acid spill	Repaired	
Dec 24/44	C-47A	Sorido	Taxying	Repaired	
Jan /45			Fire	Salvaged	
Feb /45					Prop wash of Navy F4U
Feb /45					Taxying
Feb /45					Unknown
Mar /45			Engine failure	Salvaged	On take-off
Mar /45			Acid spill	Repaired	
Mar /45			Taxying		
Apr /45		Luzon			Overshot field
Apr /45			Taxying		

DATE	TYPE	LOCATION	CAUSE	DISPOSITION	REMARKS
Apr /45			Taxying		
May /45			Landing		Trfd for repairs
May /45			?		Landing gear washed out on takeoff
May /45			Ground collision		
Jun /45	C-47B		Missing in action		
Jun /45			Acid spill		Trfd for repair
Jun /45			Fire	Salvage	
Jun /45			Taxying		Trfd for repair
Jun /45			Taxying	Repaired	
Jul /45			Ground collision	Repaired	
Jul /45			Landing	Repaired	
Jul /45			Collision	Repaired	
Jul /45			Truck	Repaired	
Aug /45			Vehicle	Repaired	
Aug /45			Taxying	Repaired	

22ND SQUADRON

DATE	TYPE	LOCATION	CAUSE	DISPOSITION	REMARKS
?	L-14	?	Unknown	Rebuilt	No date or location given
?	C-56	?	Unknown	Rebuilt	No date or location given
Jul 14/42	C-56	At sea	See remarks	Comp loss	Missing in action
Aug 17/42	C-56	New Guinea	Enemy action	Comp. loss	Enemy bomb action
Aug 17/42	C-56	New Guinea	Enemy action	Comp. loss	Enemy bomb action
Aug 17/42	C-56	New Guinea	Enemy action	Comp. loss	Enemy bomb action
Aug 29/42	C-47	Batchelor	Unknown	Rebuilt	
Sep 23/42	DC-2	Cocktown	Unknown	Rebuilt	
Oct 8/42	L-14	Rockhampton	Unknown	Comp. loss	Plane destroyed by fire
Oct 8/42	L-14	Cocktown	Unknown	Comp. loss	Given away
Oct 22/42	C-60	Wards Drome	Pilot error	Rebuilt	Ground looped on take off
Oct 29/42	C-56	Cocktown	Pilot error	Rebuilt	Belly landing
Nov 12/42	C-60	Townsville	Pilot error	Rebuilt	Belly landing
Dec 3/42	C-60	Wards Drome	Pilot error	Salvaged	Crashed on landing

DATE	TYPE	LOCATION	CAUSE	DISPOSITION	REMARKS
Jan 15/43	C-60	Wards Drome	Pilot error	Rebuilt	Nosed over taxying
Jan 7/43	C-60	Dobodura	Pilot error	Comp. loss	Crashed on take off
Feb 8/43	C-47	Wards Drome	Pilot error	Salvaged	Retracted landing gear too soon
Feb 14/43	C-47	Wards Drome	Collision	Rebuilt	Hit by B-24 while parked
Mar 11/43	C-47	Skindawai	Unknown	Comp. loss	Dropping mission
Mar 27/43	C-47	Wau	Collision	Rebuilt	Ground collision
Mar 27/43	C-47	Wau	Pilot error	Rebuilt	Crashed into another 22nd plane by rolling
Apr 12/43	C-47	Wards Drome	Enemy action	Rebuilt	Enemy bomb action
Apr 12/43	C-47	Wards Drome	Enemy action	Rebuilt	Enemy bomb action
Apr 12/43	C-47	Wards Drome	Enemy action	Rebuilt	Enemy bomb action
May 15/43	C-47	Wards Drome	Pilot error	Rebuilt	Taxied off runway into ditch
May 16/43	C-47	Wards Drome	Pilot error	Rebuilt	Taxying
Jun 27/43	C-47	Wards Drome	See remarks	Rebuilt	Hit by truck while parked
Jul 11/43	C-47	Wards Drome	Unknown	Comp. loss	Crashed in June one-half mile from Poppendetta
Oct 28/43	C-47	Wards Drome	Pilot error	Rebuilt	Wheels retracted too soon
Dec 19/43	C-47A	Rockhampton	Unknown	Comp. loss	Bad weather
Jan 14/44	C-47	Dutch New Guinea	Mech. failure	Salvaged	Bad weather
Sep 26/44	C-47A	Finschhafen	Pilot error		Ran over an empty gas drum
Sep 27/44	C-47A	Finschhafen	Ground crew		Fire caused by lighted match
Nov 15/55	C-47A	Finschhafen	Ground coll.	Repaired	Hit crew chief stand
Nov 17/44	C-47A	Kainantu	Soft runway	Abandoned	landing nose over
Nov 21/44	C-47A	Moratai	Jap bomb	Salvaged?	
Dec 3/44	C-47A	Salium	Crashed		All personnel killed
Dec 10/44	C-47A	Finschhafen	Co-pilot error	Trfd out	Raised landing gear
Dec 22/44	C-47A	Moratai	Taxying	Repaired	Struck by taxying C-46
Jan /45			Mechanical failure		
Mar /45			Taxying		
Mar /45			Taxying		
Mar /45			Taxying		
Mar /45			Brake failure		

DATE	TYPE	LOCATION	CAUSE	DISPOSITION	REMARKS
Apr /45			Taxying (2)		
Apr /45					Jeep ran into plane
Apr /45					Buzzing a boat
May /45			Human error		Landing gear collapsed Safety pins removed
Jun /45			Pilot error	Repaired	
Jun /45			Truck collision	Repaired	
Jul /45			Truck collision	Repaired	
Jul /45			Truck collision	Repaired	
Aug /45			Pilot error		
Aug /45			Mechanical fail.	Complete loss	

33rd Squadron

DATE	TYPE	LOCATION	CAUSE	DISPOSITION	REMARKS
Nov 8/42	C-47	Solomon Is.	Enemy action	Comp. loss	Shot down in action
Nov 24/42	C-47	Solomon Is.	Pilot error	Comp. loss	Crashed into truck on take off
Nov 10/42	C-47	Dobodura	Unknown	Comp. loss	Crashed into hill
Nov 26/42	C-47	Dobodura	Enemy action	Comp. loss	Shot down in action
Jan 8/43	C-47	Townsville	Pilot error	Rebuilt	Crashed on take off; retracted landing gear too soon
Jan 14/43	C-47	Wards Drome	Pilot error	Salvaged	Same as above
Jan 25/43	C-47	Jacksons Drome	Enemy action	Comp. loss	Enemy bomb action
Feb 7/43	C-47	Wau	Enemy action	Comp. loss	Missing with Zeros in vicinity
Mar 19/43	C-47	Wau	Collision	Rebuilt	Hit concrete roller in tall grass on runway
May 12/43	C-47	Dobodura	See remarks	Comp. loss	Believed crashed in pass
Jun 15/43	C-47	Wards Drome	Mech. failure	Rebuilt	Tire blew out on take off
Jun 29/43	C-47	Wards Drome	Mech. failure	Rebuilt	Forced into ditch by strong wind
Sep 16/43	C-47	Kaipit	Mech. failure	Salvaged	Landing gear collapsed; rough field
Dec 12/43	C-47A	Mackay	Mech. failure	Salvaged	Landing gear and engine failure
Feb 3/44	C-47A	En route Fall River	Unknown	Comp. loss	Missing over Coral Sea

DATE	TYPE	LOCATION	CAUSE	DISPOSITION	REMARKS
	C-47	Tadji			
Sep /44	C-47	Middleburg Island	Taxying		To depot for repairs
Sep 27/44	C-47A	Moresby	Formation Collision	Repaired	Rt Aileron & Wing tip replaced
Sep 27/44	C-47A	Moresby	"		Lt. Elevator & tail wheel damaged
Sep 27/44	C-47A	Finschhafen			Aileron & wing tip damaged
Nov 7/44	C-47A		Wing tip	Repaired	
Nov 22/44	C-47A	Hollandia	Pilot error	Repaired	
Jan /45			Taxying collision	Repaired	Struck by a B-24
Feb /45		Phil.	Japanese antiaircraft		
Feb /45			Taxying		
Mar /45			Taxying		
Mar /45			Taxying		
Apr /45			Taxying (4)		
Apr /45					Truck backed into plane
May /45			Taxying		
May /45			Ground collision		
Jun /45			Taxying		Trfd for repairs
Jun /45			Truck collision	Repaired	
Jul /45			Loading	Repaired	
Jul /45			Truck	Repaired	
Jul /45			Truck	Repaired	
Aug /45			Fork-lift		
Aug /45			Collision		
Aug /45			Fork-lift		
Aug /45			Taxying		
Aug /45			Loading		
Aug /45			Collision		

DECORATIONS AND AWARDS OF THE
U. S. ARMY
TO THE
54TH TROOP CARRIER WING UNITS

> The means of recognizing valor in the United States Army is through an award or a decoration. These material factors represent all the bitterness and pain, the dirt and squalor, and the indomitable heroic spirit of the individual in war.
>
> The Troop Carriers have earned their share of awards and decorations in the battle to free the Philippines. Units of the Wing have received a total of 6593 awards and one group has been cited twice in General Orders.

DISTINGUISHED SERVICE CROSS

... who distinguish themselves by extraordinary heroism in connection with military operations against the enemy ... must perform an act of heroism so notable and involving a risk of life so extraordinary as to set him apart from his comrades.

374TH TROOP CARRIER GROUP
One Award

LEGION OF MERIT

... who distinguish themselves by exceptionally meritorious conduct in the performance of outstanding services.

374TH TROOP CARRIER GROUP
Four Awards

H.Q. SQUADRON WING
One Award

SILVER STAR

... who distinguish themselves by gallantry in action not warranting the award of the Medal of Honor or the Distinguished Service Cross.

374TH TROOP CARRIER GROUP
23 Awards

H.Q. SQUADRON WING
Two Awards

DISTINGUISHED FLYING CROSS

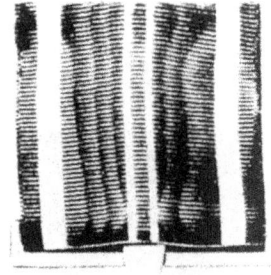

... who distinguish themselves by heroism or extraordinary achievement while participating in aerial flight ... evidenced by voluntary action in the face of great danger above and beyond the line of duty. For extraordinary achievement the results accomplished must be so exceptional and outstanding as clearly to set him aside from his comrades.

374TH TROOP CARRIER GROUP
528 Awards

433RD TROOP CARRIER GROUP
(SIX SQUADRONS)
546 Awards

317TH TROOP CARRIER GROUP
279 Awards

375TH TROOP CARRIER GROUP
317 Awards

H.Q. SQUADRON WING
Nine Awards

BRONZE OAK-LEAF CLUSTER
TO DISTINGUISHED FLYING CROSS

... for each succeeding award of a Distinguished Flying Cross decoration already received.

374TH TROOP CARRIER GROUP
573 Awards

317TH TROOP CARRIER GROUP
Six Awards

375TH TROOP CARRIER GROUP
11 Awards

433RD TROOP CARRIER GROUP
(SIX SQUADRONS)
374 Awards

H.Q. SQUADRON WING
Six Awards

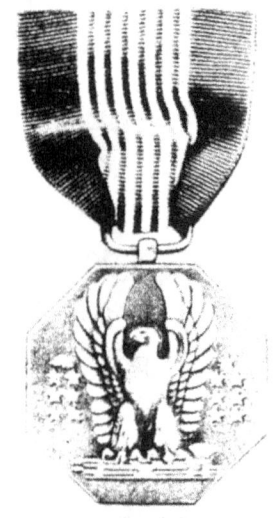

SOLDIER'S MEDAL

... who distinguish themselves by heroism not involving actual conflict with the enemy ... for the performance of an act of heroism involving voluntary risk of life under conditions other than those of conflict with the enemy.

374TH TROOP CARRIER GROUP
Four Awards

317TH TROOP CARRIER GROUP
Two Awards

PURPLE HEART

... who are wounded in action against an enemy of the United States, or as a direct result of an act of such enemy, provided such wound necessitates treatment by a medical officer.

374TH TROOP CARRIER GROUP
57 Awards

433RD TROOP CARRIER GROUP
(SIX SQUADRONS)
Four Awards

H.Q. SQUADRON WING
One Award

AIR MEDAL

... who distinguish themselves by meritorious achievement while participating in aerial flight and must be accomplished with distinction above that normally expected ... to recognize single actions of merit or sustained operational activities against the enemy.

374TH TROOP CARRIER GROUP
519 Awards

317TH TROOP CARRIER GROUP
472 Awards

375TH TROOP CARRIER GROUP
425 Awards

433RD TROOP CARRIER GROUP
(SIX SQUADRONS)
624 Awards

H.Q. SQUADRON WING
12 Awards

804TH M.A.E.S.
52 Awards

BRONZE OAK-LEAF CLUSTER
TO AIR MEDAL

For each succeeding award of an Air Medal decoration already received.

374TH TROOP CARRIER GROUP
357 Awards

317TH TROOP CARRIER GROUP
373 Awards

375TH TROOP CARRIER GROUP
490 Awards

433RD TROOP CARRIER GROUP
(SIX SQUADRONS)
500 Awards

H.Q. SQUADRON WING
Eight Awards

804TH M.A.E.S.
13 Awards

DISTINGUISHED MERIT BADGE

... Worn by members of organizations cited for outstanding performance of duty in action on or after December 7, 1941.

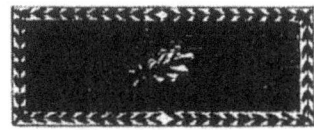

374th TROOP CARRIER GROUP
Cited Three Times

APPENDIX 'P'

DISTINGUISHED UNIT BADGE

It was in the hell of Salerno that the Third Battalion, 141st Infantry, won the Army's Distinguished Unit Badge. Formerly a Texas National Guard unit, the Third Battalion landed in assault waves on the Paestum beaches. They were met with terrific fire from fortified Nazi positions. But the Texans hung on - and advanced.

Two fierce counterattacks, with tank support, were driven back. But by this time the Third's position seemed hopeless. Their support unit on the right was pinned to the ground by machine gunfire. Their expected left support unit was delayed in landing. Though many knew they were going to certain death, the men of the Third doggedly pushed on against the concerted fury of German frontal and flanking attacks. The objective was attained, but only through the heroic sacrifice of this now famous battalion.

Other famous wearers of the Presidential Citation Badge include men of the 374th Troop Carrier Group and Battery C, 17th Field Artillery Battalion. During the Japanese attack on Papua, the 374th Troop Carrier Group flew unarmed transport planes through the battle area, carrying several thousand troops, artillery and supplies and evacuating wounded on their return. Battery C won its citation in a brief but bloody fight near Tebourba, Tunisia, when 10 Messerschmitts suddenly dived on the battery position, strafing and bombing, while 30 Nazi tanks simultaneously struck in front and on the flanks, with infantry support. The furious resistance of Battery C enabled another battery to reach the scene, driving off the Nazis.

Authorized by Executive Order in February 1942, the Distinguished Unit Badge, companion award to the Navy's Presidential Unit Citation, is given only to units selected after extreme heroism in overcoming unusually hazardous conditions. The gold-framed blue ribbon of the citation is worn on the right breast above the pocket, whereas all other decorations of the United States services are worn on the left breast. For regiments, groups and units entitled to individual flags or colors, the citation is indicated by a blue streamer with the name of the action embroidered in white.

The Distinguished Unit Badge was first awarded on March 9, 1942, to 14 heroic Philippine defense units. Since then, Army units in every theater have been cited.

One of the best-known actions to result in unit citations was the daring attack on the Ploesti oil fields by Army Bombardment Groups 44, 93, 98, 376 and 389.

A more recent citation has focused attention on the all but incredible achievements of the men of the Air Transport Command who fly the aerial "Burma Road" across the Himalayas, carrying vital supplies to China. Their operations are carried out in unarmed transports, through areas patrolled by Japanese fighters, through violent storms and vicious air currents, with peaks often hidden by snow or clouds.

In December, the month for which the India-China Wing was cited, the weather was literally impossible, yet the India-China Wing not only carried its scheduled load but exceeded it.

For repeated acts of heroism, units of the Army may be cited again by the President, a Bronze Oak Leaf Cluster being added to the ribbon. To date, the most famous recipient of the Distinguished Unit Badge is the historic 19th Bombardment Group, cited four times for outstanding action in the Philippines, the Netherlands East Indies, and later action in the South Pacific.

APPENDIX 'Q'

AWARDS AND DECORATIONS - 374TH TROOP CARRIER GROUP

GROUP HEADQUARTERS

OCTOBER 1942 - AUGUST 1945

NAME	DFC	OLC TO DFC	AM	OLC TO AM	SOLDIERS MEDAL	SILVER STAR	LEGION OF MERIT	PURPLE HEART
Brig Gen Prentiss, Paul H.	x					x		
Colonel Hampton, Edgar W.	x	x				x		x
Lt. Col Imparato, Edward T.	x		x	x			x	
Major Vandiver, Ray	x	x	x	x				
Major Beck, Abe J.	x		x	x				
Major Foster, George M.	x						x	
Major Hayes Harry M.					x	x		x
Major Waatson, James C.				2				
Capt. Eurat, Kenneth A.				2				
Capt. Soular, Fred M.			x					
Capt. White, Lacy W., Jr.					x			

6TH TROOP CARRIER SQUADRON

OCTOBER 1942 - AUGUST 1945

NAME	DFC	OLC TO DFC	AM	OLC TO AM	SOLDIERS MEDAL	SILVER STAR	LEGION OF MERIT	PURPLE HEART
Lt Col Lackey, John H. Jr	x					x		
Major Smith, Isaac W.	x	2	x	2				
Major Wells, William D.	x	2	x	2				
Capt. Burleigh, Albert H.	x	3	x	1				
Capt. Church, Frank C.	x	2	x	1				
Capt. Fairey, John P.	x	3	x	2				
Capt. Fredrickson, John C.	x		x					
Capt. Gaylor, Don G.	x	3	x	2				
Capt. Grisbeck, Wilbur J.	x		x	2				
Capt. Hallam, Philip G.	x	1	x					
Capt. Hurley, Russell D.			x					
Capt. Johnson, William H.			x					
Capt. Libuse, Frank C.	x	3	x	2				
Capt. Malmstone, Blesch	x	2	x	1				
Capt. McWilliams, Francis X.	x		x	1				
Capt. Meder, Joseph F.				1				
Capt. Peterson, Wm. A.	x	2	x	2				
Capt. Ridley, Thomas M.	x	2	x					
Capt. Rodgers, Jaffus M.	x	4	x	1				
Capt. Rowland, Conrad A.	x	3	x	2				
Capt. Sample, Earl K.				1				
1st Lt. Anderson, Kenneth A.			x					
1st Lt. Beaver, George W.	x	2	x	1				
1st Lt. Best, Robert T.			x					
1st Lt. Bledsoe, Jack E.			x					
1st Lt. Boettcher, Wendell D.	x	2	x	2				
1st Lt. Bronson, Hubert S.	x	2	x	2				
1st Lt. Cox, Arthur W., Jr.			x					
1st Lt. Davis, Billy A.			x	1				
1st Lt. Devin, Gerald			x					
1st Lt. Dial, Irwin W.	x	4	x	1				
1st Lt. Elder, Alan W.			x					

NAME	DFC	OLC TO DFC	AM	OLC TO AM	SOLDIERS MEDAL	SILVER STAR	LEGION OF MERIT	PURPLE HEART
1st Lt. Fitzgerald, William E.			x					
1st Lt. Ford, Ernest C.	x	4	x	1				
1st Lt. Hardee, Norman T.	x	2	x	1				
1st Lt. Houston, Cortez E.	x	3	x	2				
1st Lt. Jones, Norman A.			x					
1st Lt. Kelley, Joseph B.	x		x					
1st Lt. Knight, Robert S.	x	3	x	2				
1st Lt. Lawson, William V.				1				
1st Lt. Martin, William W.	x	1	x					
1st Lt. McCluney, John H.	x		x	1				
1st Lt. McFarland, Orland W.	x	4	x	1				
1st Lt. McWilliams, Joseph W.	x	3	x	1				
1st Lt. Meeks, John R., Jr.	x	3	x	1				
1st Lt. Miller, Helmick R.				1				
1st Lt. Pearce, George M., Jr	x	2	x	1				
1st Lt. Remitz, Henry W.			x					
1st Lt. Rogers, Eugene M.	x	1	x					
1st Lt. Ryburn, Samuel S.			x					
1st Lt. Ruhl, Robert A.				1				
1st Lt. Scheffey, Merl H.	x							
1st Lt. Silsby, Edward M.	x	3	x	1				
1st Lt. Smith, Ned F.			x					
1st Lt. Thompson, Thomas G.	x	3	x	1				
1st Lt. Vaughter, David C	x	4	x	2				
1st Lt. Wagoner, Lee K.			x					
1st Lt. Warren, Norman D.				1				
1st Lt. Weedin, Wilbur H.	x	3	x	1				
1st Lt. Williams, Dean H., Jr.				1				
2nd Lt. Bolton, William E.			x					
2nd Lt. Hackett, Wilbur M.	x	2	x	1				
2nd Lt. Lehrman, Abraham			x					
2nd Lt. Mentzer, Fred R.	x		x					
2nd Lt. Schrepple, Paul F.				1				
2nd Lt. Simpson, Jerome L.	x							
F/O Cooper, Dowl L.	x							
M/Sgt. Bramer, Delmer C.	x	1	x					
M/Sgt. Janavich, Vincent J.	x		x					
M/Sgt. Korthals, Albert H.	x							
M/Sgt. Kullich, Michael	x						x	
M/Sgt. Shandor, Frank J.	x							
T/Sgt. Evans, Delbert T.	x	1	x	1				
T/Sgt. Grassi, Amerige	x	2	x	1				
T/Sgt. Hawley, Joseph C.			x					
T/Sgt. Ilse, Ward C.	x	1	x	1				
T/Sgt. Klotz, George					x			
T/Sgt. Kepke, Casimir J.	x	3	x	1				
T/Sgt. Large, Shadrack J.	x	3	x	1				
T/Sgt. Palmer, Gerald L.	x	2	x	1				
T/Sgt. Reinhardt, Walter A.	x	1	x	2				
T/Sgt. Shireman, Paul	x		x					
T/Sgt. Stofocik, John M. Jr	x	1	x	1				
T/Sgt. Weyant, Robert	x	1	x					
S/Sgt. Affronte, Samuel J.	x		x	1				
S/Sgt. Augustyn, Leo J.	x	1	x	1				
S/Sgt. Ballantine, John V.	x	2	x	2				
S/Sgt. Bogacki, Gerald J.	x	2	x	2				
S/Sgt. Clayton, Clay D.	x	1	x	1				
S/Sgt. Crane, John A.	x	1	x	2				
S/Sgt. Dugan, Frank G.			x					
S/Sgt. Fears, Claude E.			x					

NAME	DFC	OLC TO DFC	AM	OLC TO AM	SOLDIERS MEDAL	SILVER STAR	LEGION OF MERIT	PURPLE HEART
S/Sgt. Fundum, Walter H.			x					
S/Sgt. Gilbertson, Gillman W	x	2	x	1				
S/Sgt. Gregg, John C.	x	2	x	1				
S/Sgt. Kerr, Robert R.	x	1	x					
S/Sgt. Lincoln, Wayne E.	x		x	1				
S/Sgt. Manger, Billy E.	x		x					
S/Sgt. Mills, Curtis T.	x	2	x	3				
S/Sgt. Neal, Jasper F.	x	3	x	1				
S/Sgt. Noggle, Willis A.	x	2	x	1				
S/Sgt. O'Brien, Thomas E.	x		x	2				
S/Sgt. Parker, John W.	x	2	x	1				
S/Sgt. Philpot, Louie E.	x	2	x	2				
S/Sgt. Pineno, James	x	1	x	2				
S/Sgt. Portman, Vernon F.	x							
S/Sgt. Putzman, John E.	x	2	x					
S/Sgt. Rickers, Erwin M.	x	1	x	2				
S/Sgt. Scouten, Claude A.	x	1	x	3				
S/Sgt. Trowbridge, Nolon L.				2				
S/Sgt. Wagoner, Kenneth G.	x	2	x	1				
S/Sgt. Weaver, James W.	x							
Sgt. Autrey, Elmer F.	x	1	x	2				
Sgt. Barton, Ivan K.	x	2	x	1				
Sgt. Bates, James W.	x	2	x	1				
Sgt. Billmaier, Lawrence P	x	2	x	1				
Sgt. Bonito, Frank L.	x	2	x	1				
Sgt. Bunke, Harvey C.	x	3	x	1				
Sgt. Kerr, Robert L.	x	1	x					
Sgt. Klar, Wesley W.	x	3	x	1				
Sgt. McMann, Lyle G.	x	2	x	1				
Sgt. Milisci, Ferdinand	x	2	x	1				
Sgt. Moore, John B.	x	2	x	1				
Sgt. Perez, Joseph T.	x	2	x	2				
Sgt. Ramey, James R.	x	1	x					
Sgt. Rogers, Thurman			x					
Sgt. Spencer, Wesley F.				2				
Sgt. Sterrett, Jack H.			x					
Sgt. Stolarski, Walter			x					
Sgt. Wooten, Ernest C. Jr	x	2	x	1				
Cpl. Berryman, Lester C.	x	2	x	1				
Cpl. Boyd, William H.	x		x					
Cpl. Byers, James E.			x					
Cpl. Epling, Raymond			x					
Cpl. Hubbard, Jessie H.	x	1	x	1				
Cpl. Krigsvold, Ralph C.	x	1	x					
Cpl. Logan, George M.	x		x					
Cpl. Martinson, Raymond W.	x	2	x	1				
Cpl. Middleton, Marvin D	x	1	x					
Cpl. Osborn, Francis R.	x		x					
Cpl. Redding, Daniel W.	x							
Cpl. Runnels, Gilbert L.	x	2	x					
Cpl. Smith, Herbert G.	x	1	x	1				
Cpl. Tudor, Neal	x							
Cpl. Zakrzewski, Norbert B	x	1	x					
Pfc. Arnzon, Cyril H.	x	2	x	1				
Pfc. Lawrence, Kenneth L.	x		x					
Pfc. Milberger, Carl L.	x	1	x	1				
Pvt. Mullally, John F.	x							

21st Squadron

October 1942 - August 1945

NAME	DFC	OLC TO DFC	AM	OLC TO AM	SOLDIERS MEDAL	SILVER STAR	LEGION OF MERIT	PURPLE HEART
Major Baer, Charles R.	x	1	x	1				
Major Corkrum, Uriah F.	x	3	x	2				
Major Eckberg, Philip M.	x	1	x	2				
Major Grimes, Myron J.	x	2	x	2				
Major Henry, Fred G.	x	1	x					
Major Lewis, Melvin C.	x		x	2				
Major McCullough, James A.	x	1	x	1				
Major Moore, Alan D.	x	1	x					
Major Penn, Perry H.	x	2	x	1				
Major Stearns, Willard R.	x	1	x	2				
Major Stover, George E.	x	1	x	1				
Major Thomas, Arthur D.	x	3	x	2				
Major Wise, John W.	x	1	x					
Capt. Andrews, Robert G.			X					
Capt. Bidwell, Herbert L.			x					
Capt. Boyd, Richard G.	x	2	x	2				
Capt. Campbell, James E.	x		x					
Capt. Cederholm, Bernard	x	1	x	1				
Capt. Crandell, John A., Jr.	x	1	x	2				
Capt. Fortin, Floyd F.				2				
Capt. Franklin, Charles F.	x		x					
Capt. Gerling, Robert J.	x	1	x	2				
Capt. Gerrero, Arthur				1				
Capt. Glassburn, Kenneth L.	x	2	x	1				
Capt. Holeman, Harry G.				1				
Capt. Hurd, Walter L., Jr.	x	2	x	3				
Capt. Ingram, James W.	x	1	x	1				
Capt. Kominis, George J.				1				
Capt. Martin, William W.	x	1	x	2				
Capt. Martin, Wilmer H.				1				
Capt. Rahrer, Harvey E.	x	2	x	2				
Capt. Rogers, Eugene M.	X	2	x	1				
Capt. Strong, John F.	x	1	x	2				
Capt. Turk, Hugh L.	x	1	x	2				
Capt. Turk, James M.	x	1	x	2				
Capt. Woods, Richard L.				1				
Capt. Yuska, Victor A.	x	2	x	1				
1st Lt. Anglin, Raymond E.	x	1	x		(Deceased)			
1st Lt. Arts, Henry F., Jr.	x	3	x	2				
1st Lt. Boyd, Benjamin M.	x	2	x	3				
1st Lt. Burley, Enoch P.	x		x		(Deceased)			
1st Lt. Cathcart, Charles O.	x		x		(Missing in action)			
1st Lt. Davis, William H.	x		x	1				
1st Lt. Dingley, Dana C.	x							
1st Lt. Eken, Joseph S.			x					
1st Lt. Fewell, Milton L.				2				
1st Lt. Gibson, Victor N.	x	2	x	1	(Missing on Operational Flig)			
1st Lt. Hart, John M.	x	1	x	2				
1st Lt. Kelley, Arthell	x		x					
1st Lt. Kominis, George J.	x		x					
1st Lt. Lenhardt, Edward J.	x	3	x	2				
1st Lt. Marsh, Russell A.	x	3	x	1				
1st Lt. Miles, James F.	x				(Deceased)			
1st Lt. Modelevsky, Hyman			x					
1st Lt. Morrison, William J.	x	2	x	3				
1st Lt. Murphy, Daniel J.	x	3	x	1				
1st Lt. Palms, Cyril S.	x	2	x					

NAME	DFC	OLC TO DFC	AM	OLC TO AM	SOLDIERS MEDAL	SILVER STAR	LEGION OF MERIT	PURPLE HEART
1st Lt. Petterson, John N.				1				
1st Lt. Scott, Roy W.	x							
1st Lt. Stearns, Hayden E.	x		x					
1st Lt. Tennies, William B.			x					
1st Lt. Thomas, Charles J.	x		x	1				
1st Lt. Walker, Talmadge E.	x	1	x	1				
2nd Lt. Eliot, Harold D.	x	1	x					
2nd Lt. Evans, Erskine	x							
2nd Lt. Hoag, Stanley G.	x		x					
2nd Lt. Nellor, Joseph G.	x		x	1				
2nd Lt. Reitman, Michael L.	x	1	x	2	(Missing on Operational Flig)			
2nd Lt. Williams, Raymond T.	x		x					
2nd Lt. Wingard, Walton C.	x	1	x					
F/O Hamilton, Darwin R.	x		x		(Missing in action)			
F/O Root, Paul H.	x		x					
W/O Brady, Lester M.			x					
M/Sgt. Burton, William H.	x							
M/Sgt. Gibbons, Jay W.	x							
M/Sgt. Hardgrove, William F.			x					
M/Sgt. Kellett, Thomas J.	x		x	1				
M/Sgt. Lambert, Milford W.	x		x		x			
M/Sgt. Lundy, Robert G.	x		x					
M/Sgt. Smith, Floyd F.			x					
M/Sgt. Summers, Frank W.	x		x	1				
T/Sgt. Barry, Robert H.	x							
T/Sgt. Beringer, Edward R.	x				(Deceased)			
T/Sgt. Brynan, Julius	x		x					
T/Sgt. Davis, Jack A.	x	1	x					
T/Sgt. Garnand, Daniel E.			x					
T/Sgt. Lenander, Albin F.	x		x					
T/Sgt. Malligo, Edward J.	x		x					
T/Sgt. Mitchell, Fred E.			x					
T/Sgt. Moorman, Arthur W.	x		x					
T/Sgt. Morris, Ralph T.	x	3	x	1				
T/Sgt. Norgan, LeRoy M.	x		x	1				
T/Sgt. Rechlin, Frank H.	x	3	x	2				
T/Sgt. Safranek, William C.	x		x	1				
T/Sgt. Whitehead, Charles D.	x	2	x					
S/Sgt. Ahmann, Everett L.	x				(Missing on Operational Flig)			
S/Sgt. Burns, Wilbert R.	x	1	x	2	(Also DSC)			x
S/Sgt. Cox, John D.	x	1	x					
S/Sgt. Culver, David H.	x	2	x					
S/Sgt. Dry, James E.			x					
S/Sgt. Eudman, Robert			x					
S/Sgt. Fichthorn, Andrew R.	x	2	x	2				
S/Sgt. Frederick, Harry R.	x	2	x	2				
S/Sgt-Pilot Gower, Lorenzo R.	x		x	1	(Missing in action)			
S/Sgt. Higgins, Clarence G.	x	1	x	1				
S/Sgt. Horton, Charles M.	x	2	x	1				
S/Sgt. Lavender, Edward C.			x					
S/Sgt. Lawrence, Harry F.	x	4	x	2				
S/Sgt. Lodge, Darold D.	x	1	x					
S/Sgt. Morris, Robert F.	x	3	x	1				
S/Sgt. Prince, Nathan D.	x		x	1				
S/Sgt. Raley, Lawrence E.	x	1	x	2				
S/Sgt. Roudebush, Barrett A.	x	1	x					
S/Sgt. Scharp, Melvin C.	x	2	x	2				
S/Sgt. Sell, Ramon C.	x	3	x	1				
S/Sgt. Walsh, James F.	DFC		x	1				
S/Sgt. Watkins, Harvey O.	x	1	x					
S/Sgt. Wiggins, Harry A., Jr.	x	1	x	1				

NAME	DFC	OLC TO DFC	AM	OLC TO AM	SOLDIERS MEDAL	SILVER STAR	LEGION OF MERIT	PURPLE HEART
S/Sgt. Wilk, Frank E.	x		x	1				
Sgt. Barrett, Dale L.			x					
Sgt. Chrisco, William C.	x	3	x	1				
Sgt. Cinquegrana, Vincent E Jr	x		x					
Sgt. Eastus, Wardin M.	x	1	x					
Sgt. Evonnk, Eugene	x	1	x	2				
Sgt. Firehau, Carl H.	x	1	x	1				
Sgt. Hansen, Milton T.	x							
Sgt. Kleinhens, John D.	x							
Sgt. Koeiunas, Stanley J.	x	1	x	2				
Sgt. Larimore, Doyt T.	x	2	x	1				
Sgt. Letteman, William C.	x	1	x					
Sgt. Lee, Robert E.	x		x					
Sgt. Pylant, James H,	x	2	x	3				
Sgt. Scolari, Santino	x		x	1				
Sgt. Serracino, James L.	x		x					
Sgt. Slocki, Theodore	x		x		(Missing in action)			
Sgt. Steward, Edward C.	x	1	x	1				
Sgt. Terrett, Thomas L.	x	2	x	1				
Sgt. Thall, Edward	x	2	x	1				
Sgt. Vail, Raymond M.	x	1	x	1				
Sgt. VanSickle, Burns J.	x	2	x	2				
Sgt. Vonk, William J.	x	2	x	1				
Sgt. Watson, Osborn J.	x	1	x					
Sgt. Webb, Carlton E.	x							
Sgt. Winslow, Hammond A.			x					
Cpl. Ahlers, Robert H.			x					
Cpl. Boutress, Ferris T.	x							
Cpl. Dempsey, Joseph J.			x					
Cpl. Fetzer, William H.	x	2	x	1				
Cpl. Giugno, John F.	x				(Missing on Operational Flig)			
Cpl. Goodrich, Judson J.	x		x	1				
Cpl. Hickman, James G.	x		x		(Missing in action)			
Cpl. Kelley, James E.	x		x					
Cpl. Millhouser, Donald R.	x							
Cpl. Smith, Richard N.			x					
Cpl. Verdi, Dominic P.	x				(Missing in action)			
Pfc. Bousquet, Donald H.	x							
Pfc. Dunbar, Willis J.			x					
Pfc. Williams, Boyd F.	x	1	x					
Pvt. Odneal, Wallace E.	x							
Pvt. Taylor, Frank B.	x		x					

Awards Made to Personnel While Attached to 21st troop Carrier Squadron

2nd Lt. Nollkamper, James L.			x					
F/O Thompson, Harold C.			x					
F/O Zindler, Heaman J.			x					
Cpl. Jostad, Clinton L.			x					

22nd Squadron

October 1942 - August 1945

Major Baker, Leonidas	x	1	x					
Major Beebe, Robert C.	x	1	x	1				
Major Feeney, Francis R.	x							
Major Jacques, Pierre D.	x		x	1				
Capt. Alverson, Leo C.	x	2	x	1				
Capt. Berne, Irvin J.	x	1	x	1				

NAME	DFC	OLC TO DFC	AM	OLC TO AM	SOLDIERS MEDAL	SILVER STAR	LEGION OF MERIT	PURPLE HEART
Capt. Burr, Albert H.	x	2	x	2				
Capt. Carlson, William H.	x	1	x	3				
Capt. Cobb, James O.	x							
Capt. Dawson, James P.			x	1				
Capt. Gary, Willis J.	x		x					
Capt. Gillenwater, Ray V.				1				
Capt. Gilreath, Hugh J.				1				
Capt. Greene, Theodore S.	x	1	x					
Capt. Hickey, Donald L.			x					
Capt. Holcomb, Leslie C.	x	1	x	1				
Capt. Lakin, Clarence A.	x	3	x	2				
Capt. Langebartel, Edward P.			x					
Capt. Lighter, Carl J.	x		x	1				
Capt. McConnell, Robert L.D.			X					
Capt. Perry, Robert L.	x	1	x	1				
Capt. Rehrer, Harvey E.				2				
Capt. Schumacher, Boman T.	x	1	x	1				
Capt. Strong, William D.	x	1	x	1				
Capt. Thompson, Francis R.	x	1	x	1				
Capt. Whittington, Robert G.	x	1	x	2				
Capt. Winn, Roger E.	x	2	x	2				
1st Lt. Anderson, Kenneth M.	x		x					
1st Lt. Bailey, Boyce S.	x	1	x	2				
1st Lt. Cooper, Dowd L.	x	1	x	1				
1st Lt. Cornette, Charles M.	x	2	x	3				
1st Lt. Crowe, Charles M.	x	1	x	1				
1st Lt. Decker, William J.			x					
1st Lt. Doyle, Richard W.	x	3	x	2				
1st Lt. Euart, Kenneth A.			x	1				
1st Lt. Gasper, Joseph S.			x					
1st Lt. Gillette, George	x	2	x	2				
1st Lt. Grams, Claire L.	x	1	x	2				
1st Lt. Hawley, Robert E.	x	1	x					
1st Lt. Hench, Robert C.			x					
1st Lt. Holmes, Carlton F.			x					
1st Lt. Jarman, Logan S.	x							
1st Lt. Kendell, Delvin E.	x		x	1				
1st Lt. Krebs, William W.				1				
1st Lt. Kurtz, Glen M.			x					
1st Lt. Layton, Clyde G.				1				
1st Lt. Malcomb, Austin N. Jr	x		x					
1st Lt. Martin, James H. Jr	x	2	x	1				
1st Lt. Maxwell, Neil D.	x	2	x	1				
1st Lt. McClure, John M.	x		x					
1st Lt. McNair, James H.	x	1	x					
1st Lt. Means, Russell E.	x	2	x	2				
1st Lt. Moran, Louis A.	x	1	x	1				
1st Lt. Notestine, Ronald E.			x					
1st Lt. Osborn, Ralph P.	x	1	x	1				
1st Lt. Otten, Harold R.	x	3	x	2				
1st Lt. Premo, Harold L.	x		x					
1st Lt. Quenon, Augustyn			x					
1st Lt. Ryan, Thomas N. Jr	x		x					
1st Lt. Shaw, Donald N.	x	1	x	1				
1st Lt. Sigman, Leslie B.	x		x					
1st Lt. Steiner, Albert A.	x	2	x	1				
1st Lt. Uhrig, Charles E. Jr	x	3	x	2				
1st Lt. Vincent, Arnold W.			x					
2nd Lt. Berkovitz, Samuel			x					
2nd Lt. Coile, Henry G. Jr	x		x	1				
2nd Lt. Crecelius, William R.	x	1	x	1	(post)			

NAME	DFC	OLC TO DFC	AM	OLC TO AM	SOLDIERS MEDAL	SILVER STAR	LEGION OF MERIT	PURPLE HEART
2nd Lt. Granucci, Robert F.			x					
2nd Lt. Kurtz, Glenn M.	x							
2nd Lt. Oakley, Thomas D.			x					
2nd Lt. Reed, Bertram S.	x							
2nd Lt. Templin, Ronald R.	x	1	x	1				
F/O Clifton, Roy M.			x					
F/O Hastings, Richard K.	x	1	x	1				
F/O Rogers, William H.	x				(Atchd 317)			
M/Sgt. Andreucci, Lewis F.	x		x					
M/Sgt. Berquist, Jesse D.	x	1	x	1				
M/Sgt. Drevyanko, M. G.			x					
M/Sgt. Gostage, Russell D.	x		x					
M/Sgt. Greening, Glenn F.	x							
M/Sgt. Hendrickson, Gordon				1				
M/Sgt. Lindley, Harold O.R.	x	1	x	1				
M/Sgt. Painter, Pascal P., Jr.				1				
M/Sgt. Palma, Benjamin	x				(post)			
M/Sgt. Smith, William C.	x		x	1				
M/Sgt. Warren, John M.			x	1				
M/Sgt. Watson, Roy E.			x					
T/Sgt. Adams, Forrest M.	x	1	x	1				
T/Sgt. Andreas, Nicholas J.	x		x					
T/Sgt. Barney, Charles H.	x	2	x	1				
T/Sgt. Biondo, Nunsie E.			x					
T/Sgt. Bloodworth, Robert E.			x	1				
T/Sgt. Boddie, William P.			x					
T/Sgt. Boffa, William E.	x	1	x	1				
T/Sgt. Brynan, Julius	x		x					
T/Sgt. Burkey, Jack C.	x	2	x	1				
T/Sgt. Byrne, Thomas I.	x	1	x	2				
T/Sgt. Clark, Lawrence R.	x	1	x	1				
T/Sgt. Compton, Ruben C.	x		x	1				
T/Sgt. Creasey, Elmer C.			x					
T/Sgt. Dempsey, Thomas M.	x	1	x	1				
T/Sgt. Doan, Donald F.	x		x					
T/Sgt. Feramisco, James	x	2	x	1				
T/Sgt. Hallmark, DeBaze	x							
T/Sgt. Johnson, William E., Jr.				1				
T/Sgt. Maham, Clarence E.	x	2	x	2				
T/Sgt. Manuel, Vernon C.	x		x	1				
T/Sgt. Matulis, Nick	x	1	x	1				
T/Sgt. McBride, Dorsey T.	x							
T/Sgt. McGrath, Thomas R.	x	1	x					
T/Sgt. Smith, Elmer L.	x		x					
T/Sgt. Snyder, Delmer S.	x	1	x	1				
T/Sgt. Tedzak, Harry B.	x	1	x	1				
T/Sgt. Trentacosta, Frank				2				
T/Sgt. Ulissi, Dominick	x	1	x					
T/Sgt. White, Errol A.	x		x	2				
S/Sgt. Adamczyk, Theodore S.	x	1	x	1				
S/Sgt. Aldridge, Leroy A.	x	1	x					
S/Sgt. Applegate, Rex A.	x	2	x	1				
S/Sgt. Bigham, James E.	x		x	1				
S/Sgt. Caskey, Martin D.	x							
S/Sgt. Clack, Melvin W.	x	1	x	1				
S/Sgt. Crane, Gordon R.	x		x	1				
S/Sgt-Pilot Crowley, Elmer C.	x	1	x	1	(all post.)			
S/Sgt. Dobson, Dorsey T.	x	2	x	3				
S/Sgt. Freund, Isidore			x					
S/Sgt. Glenn, Jack O.	x	2	x	2				
S/Sgt. Gregg, James L.	x		x					

NAME	DFC	OLC TO DFC	AM	OLC TO AM	SOLDIERS MEDAL	SILVER STAR	LEGION OF MERIT	PURPLE HEART
S/Sgt. Hall, Elbert W.	x		x	1				
S/Sgt. Hancock, Kenneth E.			x					
S/Sgt. Heckman, Jay W.			x					
S/Sgt. Kiernan, Paul H., Jr.				1				
S/Sgt. Lasater, Milton K.			x					
S/Sgt. Lucas, Charles E.	x	1	x	3				
S/Sgt. Lucewicz, Casimer J.	x	1	x	3				
S/Sgt. Mader, Robert W.	x		x					
S/Sgt. Mumford, Robert A.	x		x					
S/Sgt. McHattie, Robert G.	x		x					
S/Sgt. Parsons, Levi E., Jr.	x	1	x					
S/Sgt. Phillips, Alvin S.	x	1	x					
S/Sgt. Porter, William W.	x		x					
S/Sgt. Seaver, William H.	x	1	x	1				
S/Sgt. Shippey, Jack D.			x					
S/Sgt. Shore, Norman	x		x	2				
S/Sgt. Shupe, John L.	x	2	x	1				
S/Sgt. Starr, Harold J.	x	1	x	2				
S/Sgt. Stevens, Ellis R.	x		x	1				
S/Sgt. Stipech, Frank R.	x		x	1				
S/Sgt. Sullivan, William A.				2				
S/Sgt. Tymchak, William A.				2				
S/Sgt. Wooten, Ralph M.				2				
Sgt. August, George E., Jr.	x	2	x	2				
Sgt. Baker, Howard D.	x							
Sgt. Behrens, George H.	x							
Sgt. Creasey, Elmer W.	x							
Sgt. Deyarmond, Jacob J.		1		1				
Sgt. Drawdy, Dall C.	x	1	x					
Sgt. Goodrich, George B., Jr.	x		x	1				
Sgt. Green, Walter R.	x	1	x	2				
Sgt. Greiling, William R.	x	1	x					
Sgt. Henley, William O.	x	1	x	1				
Sgt. Jones, Oscar D.	x		x					
Sgt. Kelley, Charles A.	x					(post)		
Sgt. Kelley, James E.	x							
Sgt. Kirby, Sherwood W.	x	1	x					
Sgt. Lansalaca, Nich R.	x	1	x					
Sgt. Lowder, Guy M.	x	2	x	2				
Sgt. Moore, Walter A.	x		x					
Sgt. McIlvain, Joseph T.	x	2	x	2				
Sgt. McLean, Bruce E.	x	1	x					
Sgt. Saylor, Camden T.	x	1	x					
Sgt. Simons, Ralph R.	x	1	x	2				
Sgt. Swenson, John M.	x	1	x	2				
Sgt. Webster, John H.	x		x					
Sgt. Williams, Clarence	x							
Cpl. Brown, Lawrence R.	x		x					
Cpl. Coffman, Robert F.	x							
Cpl. Kerns, Russell R.			x	1				
Cpl. King, Bland			x					
Cpl. Lee, Robert E.	x		x					
Cpl. McGowan, James R.			x					
Cpl. Prodan, Nicholas M.			x					
Cpl. Proffitt, Arthur	x	1	x	3				
Cpl. Shephard, Clant E.	x		x					
Cpl. Shephard, Royce L.	x	1	x	2				
Cpl. Smith, Richard N.			x					
Cpl. Tenhoff, Richard W.	DFC		AM					
Cpl. White, Roy E.	x	1	x					
Pfc. Dilbeck, Boyd W.	x							
Pfc. Gray, George H.	x							

NAME	DFC	OLC TO DFC	AM	OLC TO AM	SOLDIERS MEDAL	SILVER STAR	LEGION OF MERIT	PURPLE HEART
Pfc. Knight, Ralph C.			x					
Pfc. Lattner, Edward J.			x					
Pfc. Maiurano, Joseph J.	x							
Pfc. Piecoro, Arson A.			x					
Pfc. Robinson, Floyd I.	x	1	x	2				
Pfc. Thurston, John E.	x		x					
Pfc. Trach, Leon M.			x		(post.)			
Pvt. Hamilton, Loren E.	x							
Pvt. Rutland, Henry R.			x					
Pvt. Weinshank, Robert D.			x	1				

33rd Squadron

October 1942 - August 1945

NAME	DFC	OLC TO DFC	AM	OLC TO AM	SOLDIERS MEDAL	SILVER STAR	LEGION OF MERIT	PURPLE HEART
Major Jackson, Eugene R.	x		x	1		x		
Capt. Carlson, Robert E.	x	5	x					
Capt. Cartwright, Philip E.	x	2	x			x		
Capt. Clapper, John W.	x	1	x					
Capt. Gardener, Allen W.	x	5	x	1				
Capt. Glotzbach, Gene R.	x	3	x	1		x		
Capt. Krupski, Charles A.				1				
Capt. Martin, Richard F.				1				
Capt. McGovern, Albert S.				1				
Capt. McKenzie, William G.				1				
Capt. Miller, Frank R.				1				
Capt. Pearson, Eric E.				1				
Capt. Ridley, Paul R.	x	4	x	1				
Capt. Ross, William R.	x	3	x					
Capt. Schnieder, Francis L.	x	5	x					
Capt. Schnieders, George A.	x	5	x	1				
Capt. Shea, Verner L.	x	4	x					
Capt. Smith, Bryce V.	x	4	x	1				
Capt. Smith, Charles P.				1				
Capt. Wamsley, George W., Jr.	x	4	x					
Capt. Warrick, Thomas J.	x	1	x					
Capt. Watson, James C.	x	3	x					
Capt. Wood, William D., Jr.	x		x					
1st Lt. Adler, Monroe A.	x	3	x	1				
1st Lt. Alexandeer, Jesse, Jr.			x					
1st Lt. Allen, John R., Jr.	x							
1st Lt. Ashley, Burl S.	x	4	x	1				
1st Lt. Dean, Zach. W.	x							
1st Lt. Dodge, James M.			x					
1st Lt. Donovan, John D.	x	1	x					
1st Lt. Foltz, John W.	x	1	x					
1st Lt. Gibson, Victor N.	x	1	x					
1st Lt. Greer, William S. Jr.	x		x	1				
1st Lt. Grooms, Harry B.				1				
1st Lt. Hauer, Eddy G., Jr.	x		x					
1st Lt. Holden, Preston (NMI)	x	3	x	1				
1st Lt. Jordan, Elwyn P.				1				
1st Lt. LaSalle, Leonard E.				1				
1st Lt. Nabors, Jack (NMI)	x	1	x	1				
1st Lt. Patterson, Claude W.	x	4	x					
1st Lt. Ready, William D.				1				
1st Lt. Skalski, Joseph (NMI)	x		x					
1st Lt. Spears, LeRoy C.	x	3	x					
1st Lt. Stearns, Hayden E.	x							
1st Lt. Thompson, Robert J.				1				

NAME	DFC	OLC TO DFC	AM	OLC TO AM	SOLDIERS MEDAL	SILVER STAR	LEGION OF MERIT	PURPLE HEART
1st Lt. Thompson, Walter B.	x	1	x			x (deceased)		
1st Lt. Wester, George H.				1				
1st Lt. Williams, Wm. E., Jr	x		x					
2nd Lt. Adams, Ira A.	x	5	x					
2nd Lt. Crawford, George H.	x	3	x	1				
2nd Lt. Harrington, Elmer E.	x	3	x	1				
2nd Lt. Johnston, Robert G.	x	4	x	1				
2nd Lt. Reitman, Michael L.	x	1	x					
2nd Lt. Sherman, Henry W.	x				(deceased)			
2nd Lt. Schwensen, Robert H.	x		x		(deceased)			
2nd Lt. Wylie, Johnston H.	x	4	x	1				
W/O Sexton, Robert L.	x		x					
F/O Bruce, Forrest D.	x	2	x					
F/O Kanaske, Henry G.	x		x					
F/O Gerrity, John J.	x	2	x					
M/Sgt. Banack, Staneley F.	x							
M/Sgt. Payton, Dalton C.			x					
M/Sgt. Wolf, Francis W.	x	2	x	1		x		
T/Sgt. Anderson, Alf L.	x	4	x					
T/Sgt. Bloodsworth, Robert E.	x		x	2				
T/Sgt. Check, Willis (NMI)	x	1	x		(deceased)			
T/Sgt. Dorland, Robert J.	x		x					
T/Sgt. Loy, Darrell D.	x				(deceased)			
T/Sgt. Crabner, Carl A.	x	1	x					
T/Sgt. Christofferson Lester O	x	2	x	1				
T/Sgt. Enkovich, Joseph (NMI)	x							
T/Sgt. Fisher, Kensel S.	x							
T/Sgt. Lande, Albert (NMI)	x							
T/Sgt. Moseley, Harry T.	x		x					
T/Sgt. Scolise, Raymond P.	x							
T/Sgt. Terchin, Harold				2				
T/Sgt. Thompson, Roy C.	x	1	x	1				
T/Sgt. Wycheck, John (NMI)	x	2	x					
T/Sgt. Zoll, Richard L.	x		x					
T/Sgt. Zorbach, George E.	x	2	x					
S/Sgt. Arneth, John P.	x	2	x					
S/Sgt. Bement, Barry W.	x	2	x	1				
S/Sgt. Borchert, Robert F.	x	1	x					
S/Sgt. Bradley, William B.	x	1	x	1				
S/Sgt. Clark, Fred M.	x	1	x					
S/Sgt. Edwards, Victori L.	x	1	x	1		x		
S/Sgt. Hager, J. W.	x		x					
S/Sgt. Hawley, John P.				1				
S/Sgt. Horn, Robert M.	x	1	x	1				
S/Sgt. King, Benjamin F.	x	3	x					
S/Sgt. Kopperud, Konrad H.	x	1	x	1				
S/Sgt. Mortenson, Benjamin F.	x	2	x					
S/Sgt. Ottwork, H.				1				
S/Sgt. Page, Russell L.	x		x	1				
S/Sgt. Poole, Stanley (NMI)	x	1	x	1				
S/Sgt. Rice, Charles D.	x	1	x					
S/Sgt. Rogers, Clarence				1				
S/Sgt. Rosemarin, Jerome	x		x	1				
S/Sgt. Sarver, William L.	x	1	x	1				
S/Sgt. Simonson, Jack A.	x			2				
S/Sgt. Swenson, Marvin D.	x	2	x	1				
S/Sgt. Tarchin, Harold (NMI)			x					
S/Sgt. Thompson, John (NMI)	x	1	x					
S/Sgt. Thompson, Marvin J.	x	1	x					
S/Sgt. Vokoun, Jerome (NMI)	x	1	x	2				
S/Sgt. Wallace, Robert R.	x		x					

NAME	DFC	OLC TO DFC	AM	OLC TO AM	SOLDIERS MEDAL	SILVER STAR	LEGION OF MERIT	PURPLE HEART
S/Sgt. Weitz, Arthur (NMI)	x	1	x			x		
S/Sgt. Whatley, Edmund W.	x	1	x					
S/Sgt. Wiesen, Francis X.				2				
Sgt. Brassell, Bobby G.	x							
Sgt. Busch, Francis H.	x		x					
Sgt. Chapman, James A.	x							
Sgt. Fitzwater, John L.	x	1	x					
Sgt. Gardiner, Louis D.	x	1	x	1				
Sgt. Glenn, Ralph E.	x		x	1				
Sgt. Glogowski, Sylvester J.	x		x	1			x	
Sgt. Halstead, Alva E.	x	2	x					
Sgt. Hawley, John P.	x	2	x					
Sgt. Holland, Thomas E.	x							
Sgt. Houck, Kenneth W.	x		x					
Sgt. Jubik, John W.	x		x					
Sgt. Kershner, George R.	x	1	x					
Sgt. Kleinberger, Sidney G.	x	2	x	1				
Sgt. Kohler, Earl R., Jr.	x							
Sgt. Lampe, Marcallus A.	x		x	1		x		
Sgt. McDevitt, Thomas E.	x		x	1				
Sgt. Murray, John V.	x							
Sgt. Olson, Orwin S.	x		x					
Sgt. Paulman, William K.	x	2	x					
Sgt. Platt, Wilmer E.	x	1	x	1				
Sgt. Polson, Cleveland, Jr.	x	1	x	1				
Sgt. Rogers, Clarence (NMI)	x	1	x					
Sgt. Rose, Ernest L.	x							
Sgt. Stein, Edward G.	x	2	x					
Sgt. Taylor, Joe R.	x		x	1				
Sgt. Till, William B.	x		x					
Sgt. Wright, Matthew C.	x		x					
Sgt. Zipay, Michael (NMI)	x		x					
Cpl. Erickson, Emil W.			x		(deceased)			
Cpl. Eurchard, James (NMI)	x		x					
Cpl. Haessner, William (NMI)	x		x					
Cpl. Myers, William G.	x	3	x			x		
Cpl. Nakisher, Fred (NMI)	x	1	x	1				
Cpl. Ottwork, Henry J.	x		x					
Pfc. Gallagher, Joe S.	x		x					
Pfc. Mehring, Harold A.			x					
Pfc. Turgeon, Clair T.	x	1	x					
Pvt. Fawn, Clifford J.			x		(deceased)			

Cemetery in New Guinea, 1943.

APPENDIX 'R'

374TH TROOP CARRIER GROUP

ENLISTED MEN, WARRANT OFFICERS, AND FLIGHT OFFICERS RECEIVING DIRECT COMMISSIONS

JANUARY 1943 - AUGUST 1945

NAME	DATE OF APPOINTMENT AS SECOND LIEUTENANT	NAME	DATE OF APPOINTMENT AS SECOND LIEUTENANT
GROUP HEADQUARTERS		F/O Philo H. Rhynehart	May 1944
		F/O Paul H. Root	May 1944
M/Sgt Harry M. Hayes*	1 January 1943	F/O Saul T. Kysor, Jr.	3 February 1945
M/Sgt Corb Flick*	1 January 1943	F/O Donald R. Mitchell	9 February 1945
M/Sgt Lacy W. White, Jr.	1 January 1943	F/O Salvatore J. Perrello	March 1945
M/Sgt Fred M. Soular	26 January 1943		
		22ND SQUADRON	
*Appointed 1st Lt's		F/O Boyce S. Bailey	30 September 1943
		F/O Henry G. Coile, Jr.	16 November 1943
6TH SQUADRON		F/O Dowd L. Cooper	25 October 1943
S/Sgt. Pilot George M. Beaver	8 April 1943	S/Sgt. Pilot Charles M. Cornette	8 April 1943
S/Sgt. Pilot Hubert S. Bronson	8 April 1943	F/O William R. Crecilius	28 September 1943
S/Sgt. Pilot Erwin W. Dial	8 April 1943	S/Sgt. Pilot Richard W. Doyle	8 April 1943
S/Sgt. Pilot John F. Fairey	8 April 1943	F/O Claire L. Grams	20 September 1943
S/Sgt. Pilot Ernest C. Ford	8 April 1943	F/O Robert N. Hawley	20 September 1943
S/Sgt. Pilot Cortez E. Houston	8 April 1943	S/Sgt. Pilot Neil D. Maxwell	8 April 1943
S/Sgt. Pilot Robert S. Knight	8 April 1943	S/Sgt. Pilot Russell E. Means	13 April 1943
S/Sgt. Pilot Orland W. McFarland	8 April 1943	F/O Louis A. Moran	20 September 1943
S/Sgt. Pilot Joseph W. McWilliams	8 April 1943	S/Sgt. Pilot Harold R. Otten	8 April 1943
S/Sgt. Pilot John R. Mecks, Jr.	8 April 1943	F/O Harold L. Premo	20 September 1943
S/Sgt. Pilot Edward M. Silsby	8 April 1943	F/O Donald N. Shaw'	20 December 1943
S/Sgt. Pilot Thomas G. Thompson	8 April 1943	F/O Charles E. Uhrig	8 April 1943
S/Sgt. Pilot David C. Vaughter	8 April 1943	CW/O Samuel (NMI) Barkovitz	16 October 1943
S/Sgt. Pilot Wilbur H. Weedin	8 April 1943	S/Sgt. Pilot George (NMI) Gillette	13 April 1943
F/O George M. Pearce, Jr.	20 September 1943	F/O Ronald R. Templin	29 February 1944
F/O Wilbur M. Hackett	20 September 1943		
F/O William E. Bolton	May 1944	*33RD SQUADRON*	
F/O Earl S. Smith	May 1944		
F/O Francis E. Baker	May 1944	F/O Ira A. Adams	29 October 1943
F/O William T. Sampson	May 1944	F/O Burl S. Ashley	20 September 1943
F/O Paul F. Schrepple	2 February 1945	F/O Forrest D. Bruce	
F/O J. R. Shoemaker	April 1945	F/O George H. Crawford	20 September 1943
		F/O Elmer E. Harrington	29 October 1943
21ST SQUADRON		F/O Robert G. Johnson	20 September 1943
		F/O Claude W. Patterson	20 September 1943
S/Sgt. Pilot Henry F. Arts, Jr.	13 May 1943	F/O Johnston H. Wylie	20 September 1943
S/Sgt. Pilot Benjamin M. Boyd	8 April 1943	F/O Jack (NMI) Nabors	20 September 1943
S/Sgt. Pilot Edward J. Lenhardt	8 April 1943	CW/O Robert L. Sexton	16 October 1943
S/Sgt. Pilot Russell A. Marsh	13 May 1943	F/O Forrest D. Bruce	7 April 1944
S/Sgt. Pilot William J. Morrison	8 April 1943	F/O Henry G. Kanaska	16 April 1944
S/Sgt. Pilot Daniel J. Murphey	8 April 1943	F/O Harry C. Russell	May 1944
F/O Harold D. Eliot	26 November 1943	F/O Stacy Salisbury	May 1944
F/O Joseph G. Neller	26 November 1943	F/O Roy M. Clifton	12 October 1944
F/O Raymond (NMI) Williams	23 November 1943	F/O John P. Wunder	March 1945
F/O Walton C. Wingard	26 November 1943	M/Sgt. Harry Friedman	April 1945
F/O Charles E. Renaud	May 1944		

APPENDIX 'S'

374TH TROOP CARRIER GROUP

RETURN OF PERSONNEL TO THE UNITED STATES

GROUP HEADQUARTERS

NAME OF OFFICER	DATE OF RETURN TO U.S.	REMARKS
Lt. Col. Edgar W. Hampton	26 April 1943	EWH - Returned to organization on 12 July 1943
Major Carl J. Lichter	26 April 1943	
Major William D. Strong	26 April 1943	
Major Ray Vandiver	30 May 1943	
Major Charles R. Baer	4 October 1943	
Lt. Col. Edward T. Imparato	29 November 1943	Leave of absence. Returned to organization 21 January 1944.
Major Eugene R. Jackson	February 1944	(on flying status)
Sgt. Allen C. Conrad	February 1944	rotation plan
Sgt. John L. Tucker	February 1944	rotation plan
Sgt. Raymond G. VanAbel	February 1944	rotation plan
Cpl. John H. Hunt	February 1944	rotation plan
Major George M. Foster	20 March 1944	flying fatigue
T/Sgt Edwin E. Eard	8 May, 1944	
Sgt. Robert L. Heaven	8 May 1944	
Sgt. Thomas E. Oliver	8 May 1944	
Sgt. Arthur J. Pastor	8 May 1944	
Sgt. Lavern T. McKinny	13 May, 1944	
Major Robert C. Beebe	3 June 1944	flying fatigue
Major Robert J. Gerling	12 June 1944	flying fatigue
T/Sgt Norman Braun	30 June 1944	rotation plan
T/Sgt Robert E. Frank	30 June 1944	rotation plan
S/Sgt Harold L. Fogel	30 June 1944	rotation plan
S/Sgt Carl J. Horvath	30 June 1944	rotation plan
S/Sgt George E. Teasdale	30 June, 1944	rotation plan
Sgt Billy E. Atkinson	30 June, 1944	rotation plan
Lt. Col. Fred M. Adams	3 August, 1944	combat replacement
Capt. Harold B. Simpson	24 August, 1944	rotation plan
Sgt. Leroy C. Johnson	24 August, 1944	rotation plan
Pfc. Alfred G. Moss	24 August, 1944	rotation plan
Maj. Emmett E. Rhoades	16 September 1944	rotation plan
T/Sgt. Jacob G. Ferenz	16 September 1944	rotation plan
S/Sgt. Franklin E. Longacre	16 September 1944	rotation plan
Cpl. August Diliberti	16 September 1944	rotation plan
Capt. Harold R. Otten	16 September 1944	rotation plan
Maj. Philip E. Cartwright	9 October 1944	combat replacement
Maj. John D. Pearson	18 October 1944	rotation plan
Cpl. Patrick E. Moore	18 October, 1944	rotation plan
Cpl. Rickie C. Martinez	19 October, 1944	rotation plan
Sgt. Clyde B. Suterland	23 November, 1944	rotation plan
Cpl. Charles H. Nix	23 November, 1944	rotation plan
S/Sgt. Joseph F. Swontkoski	12 December, 1944	rotation plan
Capt. William D. Wood, Jr.	January, 1945	combat replacement
Capt. Albert A. Steiner, Jr.	January, 1945	combat replacement
M/Sgt. Arthur W. Moorman	January, 1945	combat replacement
M/Sgt. William C. Safranek	January, 1945	combat replacement
T/Sgt. Edward J. Malligo	January, 1945	combat replacement
Sgt. Thomas Lantz	January, 1945	rotation plan
Pvt. Edward J. Peterson	January, 1945	rotation plan
Maj. James C. Watson	February, 1945	combat replacement
Maj. Philip G. Hallam	February, 1945	combat replacement
M/Sgt. Glenn F. Greening	February, 1945	combat replacement
Capt. Fred M. Soular	February, 1945	rotation plan

NAME OF OFFICER	DATE OF RETURN TO U.S.	REMARKS
T/Sgt. Jack L. Terry	February, 1945	rotation plan
S/Sgt. Melvin J. Littig	February, 1945	rotation plan
Sgt. Edward E. McIntyre	February, 1945	rotation plan
Maj. Joseph H. Moore	March, 1945	combat replacement
Capt. George J. Kominis	March, 1945	combat replacement
Sgt. Alexander Legres, Jr.	April, 1945	rotation plan
Maj. Joseph B. Kelley	May, 1945	combat replacement
Pfc. Harry N. Speropulos	June, 1945	compassionate rotation
Cpl. John A. Simone	June, 1945	over age
Sgt. Gilbert Eads	June, 1945	readjustment
Capt. William E. Thompson	July, 1945	combat replacement
Maj. Andrew J. Graves	July, 1945	readjustment
1st Lt. William P. Veeck	July, 1945	readjustment
M/Sgt. Lee B. Hammond	July, 1945	readjustment
T/Sgt. William M. McKenney	July, 1945	readjustment
Sgt. Frank J. Sevic	July, 1945	readjustment
Sgt. Edward J. Boyle	July, 1945	readjustment
Sgt. Charles J. Schroeder	July, 1945	readjustment
Capt. Marvin M. Scott	August, 1945	readjustment
Capt. Kenneth A. Euart	August, 1945	combat replacement
M/Sgt. Dalton C. Payton	August, 1945	combat replacement
M/Sgt. William P. Boddie	August, 1945	combat replacement

6TH TROOP CARRIER SQUADRON

NAME OF OFFICER	DATE OF RETURN TO U.S.	REMARKS
S/Sgt. Robert R. Kerr	17 July 1943	Aviation Cadet
1st Lt. Wendell D. Boettcher	27 August 1943	
Major William D. Wells	30 November 1943	
Capt. Jaffus M. Rodgers	25 January 1944	
1st Lt. Ernest C. Ford	10 January 1944	
T/Sgt. Casimir J. Kopko	10 January 1944	
Capt. John H. McCluney	18 January 1944	
T/Sgt. Jasper F. Neal	January 1944	
Capt. William A. Peterson	February 1944	
1st Lt. Thomas G. Thompson	February 1944	on flying status
1st Lt. Norman T. Hardee	28 March 1944	flying fatigue
T/Sgt. Willis A. Noggle	28 March 1944	flying fatigue
T/Sgt Shadrack J. Large	28 March 1944	flying fatigue
Capt. Albert H. Burleigh	24 April 1944	flying fatigue
Capt. Don C. Caylor	24 April 1944	flying fatigue
M/Sgt John M. Stofocik, Jr.	24 April 1944	flying fatigue
T/Sgt Gerald L. Palmer	24 April 1944	flying fatigue
Cpl Eldon F. David	8 May 1944	rotation plan
2nd Lt. William E. Bolton	6 May 1944	recall of glider pilots
2nd Lt. Earl S. Smith	16 May 1944	recall of glider pilots
2nd Lt. Frances E. Baker	16 May 1944	recall of glider pilots
2nd Lt. William T. Sampson II	16 May 1944	recall of glider pilots
Capt. Orland W. McFarland	12 June, 1944	flying fatigue
1st Lt. Robert S. Knight	12 June, 1944	flying fatigue
M/Sgt. Delmar C. Bramer	12 June, 1944	flying fatigue
S/Sgt Harvey C. Bunke	12 June, 1944	flying fatigue
1st Lt. Joseph W. McWilliam	28 June, 1944	flying fatigue
1st Lt. Edward M. Silsby	28 June, 1944	flying fatigue
1st Lt. John R. Meeks	30 June 1944	flying fatigue
1st Lt. Wilbur H. Weedin	30 June, 1944	flying fatigue
Pfc Kenneth L. Lawrence	28 June, 1944	rotation plan
S/Sgt. John W. Parker	9 July, 1944	combat replacement
Sgt. John B. Moore	9 July, 1944	combat replacement
Capt. Frank C. Libuse	27 July, 1944	combat replacement
Capt. Conrad A. Roland	27 July, 1944	combat replacement
1st Lt. Joseph Sanzo	29 July, 1944	medical
Capt. Paul E. Krupko	August, 1944	Aviation Med. School

NAME OF OFFICER	DATE OF RETURN TO U.S.	REMARKS
Pfc. Wallace G. Lloyd	15 Sept., 1944	combat replacement
Maj. Harvey E. Rehrer	15 Sept., 1944	combat replacement
Capt. David C. Vaughter	15 Sept., 1944	combat replacement
Capt. Irwin W. Dial	15 Sept., 1944	combat replacement
T/Sgt. James W. Bates	15 Sept., 1944	combat replacement
T/Sgt. Kenneth G. Wagoner	5 Sept., 1944	combat replacement
S/Sgt. John E. Putzman	15 Sept., 1944	combat replacement
Sgt. Frank L. Bonito	15 Sept., 1944	combat replacement
Sgt. Ferdinand Milisci	15 Sept., 1944	combat replacement
Capt. Cortez E. Houston	4 October, 1944	combat replacement
1st Lt. Hubert Bronson	4 October, 1944	combat replacement
S/Sgt. Ivan K. Barton	4 October, 1944	combat replacement
S/Sgt. Wesley W. Klar	4 October, 1944	combat replacement
S/Sgt. Claude E. Scouten	29 October, 1944	combat replacement
1st Lt. George M. Pearce	19 November, 1944	combat replacement
Capt. John P. Fairey	January, 1945	combat replacement
Capt. Raymond C. Hosback	January, 1945	combat replacement
Capt. Wilbur J. Grisbeck	January, 1945	combat replacement
1st Lt. Billy A. Davis	January, 1945	combat replacement
1st Lt. Helmick R. Miller	January, 1945	combat replacement
1st Lt. Lee K. Wagoner	January, 1945	combat replacement
T/Sgt. Gillman W. Gilbertson	January, 1945	combat replacement
T/Sgt. Amerigo Grassi	January, 1945	combat replacement
S/Sgt. James R. Ramsy	January, 1945	combat replacement
S/Sgt. Gilbert L. Runnels	January, 1945	combat replacement
Sgt. Elmer F. Awtrey	January, 1945	combat replacement
Sgt. Francis R. Osborn	January, 1945	combat replacement
Sgt. Edwin M. Rickers	January, 1945	combat replacement
Sgt. Norbert B. Zakrerewski	January, 1945	combat replacement
S/Sgt. Cyril H. Arnzen	January, 1945	combat replacement
S/Sgt. Lawrence P. Billmaier	January, 1945	combat replacement
S/Sgt John C. Gregg	January, 1945	combat replacement
S/Sgt. Raymond W. Martinson	January, 1945	combat replacement
S/Sgt. Curtis T. Mills	January, 1945	combat replacement
S/Sgt. Louie E. Philpot	January, 1945	combat replacement
Sgt. Carl L. Milberger	January, 1945	combat replacement
Sgt. Thomas F. O'Brien	January, 1945	combat replacement
Sgt. Jack H. Sterrett	January, 1945	combat replacement
Capt. Wilbur M. Hackett	February, 1945	combat replacement
1st Lt. Samuel S. Ryburn	February, 1945	combat replacement
1st Lt. Carl A. Norton	February, 1945	combat replacement
M/Sgt. Ward C. Isle	February, 1945	combat replacement
M/Sgt. Frank J. Shandor	February, 1945	combat replacement
T/Sgt. Billy E. Manger	February, 1945	combat replacement
T/Sgt. Herbert Weyant	February, 1945	combat replacement
S/Sgt. Daniel W. Redding	February, 1945	combat replacement
S/Sgt. William H. Boyd	February, 1945	combat replacement
S/Sgt. Wayne E. Lincoln	February, 1945	combat replacement
S/Sgt. John V. Ballentine	February, 1945	combat replacement
S/Sgt. Jessie H. Hubbard	February, 1945	combat replacement
S/Sgt. Lyle G. McMann	February, 1945	combat replacement
Sgt. Joseph T. Perez	February, 1945	combat replacement
1st Lt. Patman M. Dobbins	March, 1945	rotation plan
T/Sgt. Delbert T. Evans	March, 1945	combat replacement
T/Sgt. Walter A. Reinhardt	March, 1945	combat replacement
S/Sgt. John A. Crane	March, 1945	combat replacement
S/Sgt. Samuel J. Affronte	March, 1945	combat replacement
S/Sgt. Gerald J. Bogacki	March, 1945	combat replacement
S/Sgt. Leo J. Augustyn	March, 1945	combat replacement
S/Sgt. Thurman W. Rodgers	March, 1945	combat replacement
Capt. Russell D. Hurley	March, 1945	combat replacement
1st Lt. Earl W. Ascher	March, 1945	combat replacement

NAME OF OFFICER	DATE OF RETURN TO U.S.	REMARKS
1st Lt. Ned F. Smith	March, 1945	combat replacement
T/Sgt. Vernon F. Portman	March, 1945	combat replacement
S/Sgt. Lester C. Berryman	March, 1945	combat replacement
S/Sgt. James Pineno	March, 1945	combat replacement
T/Sgt. Charles I. Knauss	March, 1945	combat replacement
S/Sgt. Warren L. Garton	March, 1945	combat replacement
S/Sgt. Paul M. Hanson	March, 1945	combat replacement
S/Sgt. Ralph C. Kringsvold	March, 1945	combat replacement
S/Sgt. Earl T. McWilliams	March, 1945	combat replacement
Sgt. James E. Byers	March, 1945	combat replacement
Sgt. Samuel Peltz	March, 1945	combat replacement
1st Lt. Walter M. Jurgensmier	March, 1945	combat replacement
1st Lt. Dale D. Madison	March, 1945	combat replacement
Capt. F. X. McWilliams	April, 1945	combat replacement
Capt. W. H. Johnson, Jr.	April, 1945	combat replacement
1st Lt. A. W. Elder	April, 1945	combat replacement
M/Sgt. V. J. Janavich	April, 1945	combat replacement
M/Sgt. A. H. Korthals	April, 1945	combat replacement
M/Sgt. Paul Shireman	April, 1945	combat replacement
S/Sgt. W. C. Craycraft	April, 1945	combat replacement
S/Sgt. E. C. Goodwin	April, 1945	combat replacement
Maj. Isaac W. Smith	May, 1945	combat replacement
1st Lt. William A. Bolton	May, 1945	combat replacement
S/Sgt. James L. Colemen	May, 1945	combat replacement
Cpl. Roger A. Coil	May, 1945	rotation plan
S/Sgt. Sidney J. Brabec	June, 1945	combat replacement
S/Sgt. John F. Mullally	June, 1945	combat replacement
T/Sgt. Walter H. Fundum	June, 1945	combat replacement
1st Lt. Sebastian Spina	June, 1945	combat replacement
Capt. Earl K. Sample	June, 1945	combat replacement
1st Lt William C. Thomas, Jr.	June, 1945	combat replacement
Capt. Norman A. Jones	June, 1945	combat replacement
M/Sgt. William E. Proctor	June, 1945	readjustment
T/Sgt. Clay D. Clayton	June, 1945	readjustment
T/Sgt. Lyle E. Heasley	June, 1945	readjustment
T/Sgt. Earl S. Seifried	June, 1945	readjustment
S/Sgt. Terry M. Armstrong, Jr.	June, 1945	readjustment
S/Sgt. James A. Ferguson	June, 1945	readjustment
S/Sgt. Lloyd A. Gillentine	June, 1945	readjustment
S/Sgt. Morris Gittis	June, 1945	readjustment
Sgt. Frank R. Gayette	June, 1945	readjustment
Sgt. Merle F. Yonker	June, 1945	readjustment
Sgt. John Vancio	June, 1945	readjustment
Pvt. Samuel D. Cammisa	June, 1945	readjustment
1 Officer & 14 enlisted men	July, 1945	combat replacement
1 Officer & 31 enlisted men	July, 1945	readjustment
14 enlisted men	August, 1945	combat replacement
1 Officer	August, 1945	emergency leave

21st Troop Carrier Squadron

Capt. Charles F. Franklin	24 April 1943	
1st Lt. Talmadge F. Walker	24 April 1943	
Capt. George E. Stover	28 May 1943	
Capt. John W. Wise	30 May 1943	
Capt. John A. Crandell, Jr.	30 May 1943	
S/Sgt. James F. Walsh	15 June 1943	Aviation Cadet
Capt. James E. Campbell	20 June 1943	
Capt. James W. Ingram	8 July 1943	
Capt. James M. Turk	8 July 1943	
Capt. Bernard Cedarholm	12 July 1943	

NAME OF OFFICER	DATE OF RETURN TO U.S.	REMARKS
Capt. Victor A. Yuska	12 July 1943	
S/Sgt. John D. Cox	13 July 1943	
S/Sgt. Nathan D. Prince	13 July 1943	
T/Sgt. Harvey O. Watkins, Jr.	17 July 1943	Aviation Cadet
W/O Lester M. Brady	31 July 1943	
Major Arthur D. Thomas	16 September 1943	
Capt. Uriah F. Corkrum	24 September 1943	
Major Philip M. Eckberg	24 September 1943	
Major Melvin C. Lewis	24 September 1943	
Major Willard R. Stearnes	24 September 1943	
T/Sgt. Frank H. Rechlin	26 September 1943	
Sgt. Doyt T. Larimore	26 September 1943	
S/Sgt. Wilbert R. Burns	27 September 1943	
T/Sgt. Albin F. Lenander	27 September 1943	
S/Sgt. Harry R. Frederick	27 September 1943	
S/Sgt. Ramon C. Sell	27 September 1943	
Capt. Richard G. Boyd	3 October 1943	
S/Sgt. Robert F. Morris	3 October 1943	
S/Sgt. Melvin C. Scharp	3 October 1943	
S/Sgt. David H. Culver	3 October 1943	
S/Sgt. Robert F. Morris	3 October 1943	
Capt. John F. Strong	3 October 1943	
Pfc Carleton C. Donovan	5 October 1943	over age (Trfd to ERC)
T/Sgt. William H. Burton	30 November 1943	
M/Sgt. William F. Hardgrove	1 December 1943	
M/Sgt. Frank W. Summers	11 December 1943	
M/Sgt. Milford W. Lambert	4 January 1944	
T/Sgt. Jack A. Davis	4 January 1944	
T/Sgt. Ralph T. Morris	4 January 1944	
T/Sgt. Julius Bryman	18 January 1944	
T/Sgt. Leroy M. Norgan	18 January 1944	
T/Sgt. Charles D. Whitehead	18 January 1944	
Capt. Edward J. Lenhardt	February 1944	
Capt. Russell A. Marsh	February 1944	
T/Sgt. Andres R. Richthorn	February 1944	
S/Sgt. William A. Chrisco	February 1944	
Sgt. Boyd F. Williams	February 1944	on flying status
S/Sgt. Anthony J. Allaria	February 1944	
Cpl Ben Karch	February 1944	rotation plan
Capt. Henry F. Arts	15 March 1944	flying fatigue
Capt. Benjamin M. Boyd	15 March 1944	flying fatigue
Capt. Daniel J. Murphy	20 March 1944	flying fatigue
2nd Lt. Robert L. Cooper	20 March 1944	medical
Captain John M. Hart	4 April 1944	medical
2nd Lt. Charles E. Renaud	May 1944	recall of glider pilots
2nd Lt. Phile M. Rhynehart	May 1944	recall of glider pilots
2nd Lt. Paul H. Root	May 1944	recall of glider pilots
F/O Noel J. Rood	May 1944	recall of glider pilots
T/Sgt Robinett A. Pette	May 1944	rotation plan
S/Sgt Billy E. O'Neil	May 1944	rotation plan
Cpl Vincent T. Hayman	May 1944	rotation plan
Capt. William W. Martin	5 June, 1944	flying fatigue
1ST Lt. Roy W. Scott	27 June, 1944	flying fatigue
M/Sgt Franklin J. Rensberger	30 June 1944	flying fatigue
T/Sgt Daniel E. Garnand	30 June, 1944	rotation plan
Cpl James F. Rogers	30 June, 1944	rotation plan
Maj. Myron J. Grimes	13 July, 1944	medical
Capt. William J. Morrison	30 July, 1944	combat replacement
Capt. Thomas M. Ridley	13 July, 1944	medical
M/Sgt. Jay W. Gibbons	13 July, 1944	combat replacement
S/Sgt. James L. Serracino	23 July, 1944	combat replacement
S/Sgt. Edward Thall	23 July, 1944	combat replacement

NAME OF OFFICER	DATE OF RETURN TO U.S.	REMARKS
S/Sgt. Burns J. VanSickle	6 July, 1944	combat replacement
S/Sgt. Harry A. Wiggins, Jr.	6 July, 1944	combat replacement
Pvt. Roscoe F. Posey	July, 1944	medical
Sgt. James B. Phillips	24 August, 1944	rotation plan
Corp. Frank L. Moses	24 August, 1944	rotation plan
Pvt. Marcus E. Bragg	24 August, 1944	rotation plan
M/Sgt. Frank R. Daddario	16 Sept., 1944	rotation plan
T/Sgt. Israel Valdez	16 Sept., 1944	rotation plan
S/Sgt. Harold H. Hale	20 Sept., 1944	rotation plan
Sgt. Jacob Blumenkrantz	20 Sept., 1944	rotation plan
Sgt. Earl H. Doherty	20 Sept., 1944	rotation plan
Cpl. Marvin Davis	16 Sept., 1944	rotation plan
Pfc. Joe L. Marcos	16 Sept., 1944	rotation plan
M/Sgt. George F. Juhl	26 Sept., 1944	combat replacement
M/Sgt. Floyd F. Smith	16 Sept., 1944	combat replacement
T/Sgt. Eugene Evonuk	26 Sept., 1944	combat replacement
S/Sgt. Santino M. Scolari	16 Sept., 1944	combat replacement
T.Sgt. Edward C. Stewart	26 Sept., 1944	combat replacement
Capt. John Marcus		combat replacement
Capt. Cyril S. Palms	9 October, 1944	combat replacement
Capt. Eugene M. Rogers	9 October, 1944	combat replacement
1st Lt. Arthel Kelley	30 October, 1944	combat replacement
T/Sgt. Barrett A. Roudebush	7 October, 1944	combat replacement
T/Sgt. Thomas L. Terrett	30 October, 1944	combat replacement
S/Sgt. Warden M. Eastus	7 October, 1944	combat replacement
T/Sgt. Stanley Federsky	20 October, 1944	rotation plan
S/Sgt. Junior E. Maxwell	20 October, 1944	rotation plan
Sgt. Robert D. VanSlyke	20 October, 1944	rotation plan
2nd Lt. Joseph R. Hogsett	23 November, 1944	rotation plan
M/Sgt. Jonathan A. Bugger	23 November, 1944	rotation plan
Sgt. Duard D. Franklin	23 November, 1944	rotation plan
Cpl. George E. Laudenslager	23 November, 1944	rotation plan
Pfc. Michael C. Adamski	23 November, 1944	rotation plan
S/Sgt. Wade Faircloth	12 December, 1944	rotation plan
S/Sgt. Joseph P. Liberti	12 December, 1944	rotation plan
S/Sgt. Alvin J. Truxille	12 December, 1944	rotation plan
Capt. William H. Davis	January, 1945	combat replacement
Capt. Dana E. Dingley	January, 1945	combat replacement
Capt. Harold D. Eliot	January, 1945	combat replacement
1st Lt. Walton C. Wingard	January, 1945	combat replacement
T/Sgt. Judson J. Goodrich	January, 1945	combat replacement
T/Sgt. Harry F. Lawrence	January, 1945	combat replacement
T/Sgt. Donald A. Lodge	January, 1945	combat replacement
T/Sgt. Raymond M. Vail	January, 1945	combat replacement
T/Sgt. Osborn J. Watson	January, 1945	combat replacement
T/Sgt. Frank E. Wilk	January, 1945	combat replacement
S/Sgt. Robert H. Ahlers	January, 1945	combat replacement
S/Sgt. James J. Dry	January, 1945	combat replacement
S/Sgt. Charles M. Horton	January, 1945	combat replacement
S/Sgt. Frank L. Jones	January, 1945	combat replacement
S/Sgt. Stanley J. Kociunus	January, 1945	combat replacement
S/Sgt. Robert E. Lee	January, 1945	combat replacement
S/Sgt. Donald R. Millhouser	January, 1945	combat replacement
S/Sgt. William C. Meyers	January, 1945	combat replacement
S/Sgt. James H. Pylant	January, 1945	combat replacement
S/Sgt. Lawrence E. Raley	January, 1945	combat replacement
S/Sgt. William J. Vonk	January, 1945	combat replacement
Sgt. Milton T. Hassen	January, 1945	combat replacement
Sgt. Lawrence F. Hosey	January, 1945	combat replacement
Sgt. Earl G. McNew	January, 1945	combat replacement
Cpl. John Doss	January, 1945	combat replacement
S/Sgt. Edward C. Lavender	January, 1945	rotation plan

NAME OF OFFICER	DATE OF RETURN TO U.S.	REMARKS
S/Sgt. Brunnin J. Lindsey	January, 1945	rotation plan
Sgt. Aaron H. Ledbetter	January, 1945	rotation plan
Cpl. Charles V. Lance	January, 1945	rotation plan
Cpl. John R. Tudgay	January, 1945	rotation plan
Pvt. Edd B. Owen	January, 1945	for discharge
Capt. William B. Tennies	February, 1945	combat replacement
1st Lt. John N. Petterson	February, 1945	combat replacement
1st Lt. Fredrick J. Wyman	February, 1945	combat replacement
T/Sgt. William C. Latteman	February, 1945	combat replacement
S/Sgt. Jack N. Greer	February, 1945	combat replacement
S/Sgt. Paul V. Shafer	February, 1945	combat replacement
Sgt. Alfred J. Leblanc	February, 1945	combat replacement
Cpl. Joseph J. Dempsey	February, 1945	combat replacement
1st Lt. Claudie R. Copeland	February, 1945	rotation plan
1st Sgt. Daniel G. Lacey, Jr.	February, 1945	rotation plan
S/Sgt. Oscar J. Lewis	February, 1945	rotation plan
S/Sgt. Hubert E. Little	February, 1945	rotation plan
S/Sgt. Johnnie J. Spearman	February, 1945	rotation plan
S/Sgt. Carleton E. Webb	February, 1945	rotation plan
Cpl. John J. Bolda	February, 1945	rotation plan
Sgt. Hammond A. Winslow	February, 1945	medical
Pfc. Richard I. Kassnoff	February, 1945	medical
T/Sgt. William L. Heath	March, 1945	rotation plan
T/Sgt. Robert C. Mendell	March, 1945	rotation plan
T/Sgt. Borge Nielsen	March, 1945	rotation plan
S/Sgt. Raymond Frederick	March, 1945	rotation plan
Sgt. John J. Alansky	March, 1945	rotation plan
Sgt. George A. Tucker	March, 1945	rotation plan
Sgt. Marvin C. Williams	March, 1945	rotation plan
S/Sgt. Ferris T. Boutross	March, 1945	combat replacement
S/Sgt. Vincent E. Cinquegrana	March, 1945	combat replacement
Sgt. Donald H. Bosquet	March, 1945	combat replacement
S/Sgt. John Parkalop	March, 1945	combat replacement
S/Sgt. Elmer R. Redinger	March, 1945	medical
Capt. A. F. Levine	April, 1945	rotation plan
M/Sgt. E. R. Sahs	April, 1945	rotation plan
T/Sgt. F. R. Margoluis	April, 1945	rotation plan
T/Sgt. M. E. Tilton	April, 1945	rotation plan
S/Sgt. J. F. Vantrease	April, 1945	rotation plan
S/Sgt. V. Fabrianich	April, 1945	rotation plan
Sgt. R. R. Kanney	April, 1945	medical
Capt. H. L. Bidwell	April, 1945	combat replacement
Capt. S. D. Hoag	April, 1945	combat replacement
1st Lt. W. V. Abell	April, 1945	combat replacement
1st Lt. R. G. Andrews	April, 1945	combat replacement
1st Lt. M. L. Fewell	April, 1945	combat replacement
1st Lt. W. H. Martin	April, 1945	combat replacement
1st Lt. C. W. Wilde	April, 1945	combat replacement
T/Sgt. F. E. Mitchell	April, 1945	combat replacement
S/Sgt. R. Budman	April, 1945	combat replacement
S/Sgt. C. F. McCullough, Jr.	April, 1945	combat replacement
S/Sgt. F. D. McKendall	April, 1945	combat replacement
1st Lt. T. E. Crook, Jr.	April, 1945	combat replacement
1st Lt. Rufus W. Oldham	May, 1945	combat replacement
1st Lt. Henry J. Plennert	May, 1945	combat replacement
1st Lt. Robert P. Walsh	May, 1945	combat replacement
S/Sgt. Robert W. McGowan	May, 1945	medical
T/Sgt. Trent D. Siple	May, 1945	rotation plan
S/Sgt. Ralph J. Janek	May, 1945	rotation plan
Sgt. Joseph W. Andros	May, 1945	rotation plan
Capt. Harry G. Holeman	June, 1945	combat replacement
Capt. Joseph G. Nellor	June, 1945	combat replacement

NAME OF OFFICER	DATE OF RETURN TO U.S.	REMARKS
Capt. Charles J. Thomas	June, 1945	combat replacement
1st Lt. Eugene P. Horton	June, 1945	combat replacement
2nd Lt. Saul T. Kysor	June, 1945	combat replacement
S/Sgt. Donald E. Devore	June, 1945	combat replacement
S/Sgt. Joseph P. Hunter	June, 1945	combat replacement
S/Sgt. Harry Sloszewski	June, 1945	combat replacement
S/Sgt. Samuel Sternhell	June, 1945	combat replacement
S/Sgt. Kenneth L. Thornton	June, 1945	combat replacement
T/Sgt. Sherwood A. Cleveland	June, 1945	rotation plan
S/Sgt. Charles E. Klett	June, 1945	rotation plan
Sgt. David S. Hershey	June, 1945	rotation plan
Sgt. Edward I. Hessler	June, 1945	rotation plan
Sgt. John A. Holland	June, 1945	rotation plan
Sgt. Peter Keysock	June, 1945	rotation plan
Cpl. Braden A. Hummel	June, 1945	rotation plan
T/Sgt. Forest L. Fast	June, 1945	medical
S/Sgt. Richard M. Carmen	June, 1945	medical
Sgt. Andrew Summerville	June, 1945	medical
3 Officers & 9 enlisted men	July, 1945	combat replacement
14 enlisted men	July, 1945	readjustment
2 enlisted men	July, 1945	medical
1 enlisted man	July, 1945	over age
6 Officers & 5 enlisted men	August, 1945	combat replacement

22ND TROOP CARRIER SQUADRON

Capt. Harold G. Slingsey	22 March 1943	
Capt. David H. Dreigen (MC)	22 March 1943	
Capt. Frank W. Carroll	24 April 1943	
Capt. James O. Cobb	24 April 1943	
1st Lt. William K. Culp	24 April 1943	
Capt. Paul E. Dawson	24 April 1943	
Major Francis R. Feeney	24 April 1943	
Capt. Willis J. Gary	24 April 1943	
1st Lt. Delvin E. Kendall, Jr.	24 April 1943	
Capt. Roman T. Schumacher	24 April 1943	
1st Lt. Leslie B. Sigman	24 April 1943	
Major Pearre D. Jacques	2 May 1943	
Capt. Francis R. Thompson	2 May 1943	
Capt. Theodore S. Greene	9 May 1943	
Major Fred G. Henry	30 May 1943	
Capt. James A. McCullough	30 May 1943	
Capt. Alan D. Moore	30 May 1943	
Capt. Robert G. Whittington	30 May 1943	
Capt. Kenneth L. Glassburn	8 July 1943	
Capt. Walter L. Hurd, Jr.	8 July 1943	
Capt. Clarence A. Lakin	8 July 1943	
Capt. Hugh L. Turk, Jr.	8 July 1943	
1st Lt. Leo C. Alverson	8 July 1943	
1st Lt. Russell E. Means	30 July 1943	
Major Perry H. Penn	24 September 1943	
Capt. Albert H. Burr	24 September 1943	
Capt. Roger E. Winn	24 September 1943	
Capt. James H. Martin, Jr.	24 September 1943	
Capt. William E. Carlson	24 September 1943	
S/Sgt. Theodore S. Adamczyk	27 September 1943	
T/Sgt. Nick Matutis	27 September 1943	
Capt. Irvin J. Borne	27 September 1943	
Pfc Albert A. Meike	5 October 1943	over age (Trfd. To ERC)
S/Sgt. Thomas I. Byrne	26 November 1943	
T/Sgt. Harry B. Tedzak	26 November 1943	

NAME OF OFFICER	DATE OF RETURN TO U.S.	REMARKS
1st Lt. Richard W. Doyle	26 November 1943	
1st Lt. Charles E. Uhrig, Jr.	26 November 1943	
T/Sgt. Dorsey T. Dobson	7 December 1943	
M/Sgt. Harold O. R. Lindley	7 December 1943	
1st Lt. George Gillette	7 December 1943	
1st Lt. Russell E. Means	7 December 1943	
1st Lt. Charles M. Cornette	6 January 1944	
M/Sgt. Nicholas J. Andreas	6 January 1944	
T/Sgt. James Feramisco	6 January 1944	
M/Sgt. Lewis F. Andreucci	10 January 1944	
S/Sgt. Jack O. Glenn	21 January 1944	
M/Sgt. Lawrence R. Clark	January 1944	
T/Sgt. Melvin W. Clack	January 1944	
M/Sgt Russell D. Gostage	February, 1944	
T/Sgt. Rex A. Applegate	February, 1944	
T/Sgt James H. Bigham	February, 1944	
T/Sgt Coleman A. Robinson	February, 1944	
S/Sgt George E. August	February, 1944	on flying status
S/Sgt William C. Henson	February, 1944	
S/Sgt Milton K. Lasater	February, 1944	rotation plan
S/Sgt. Nick R. Lanzalaca	8 March, 1944	flying fatigue
Capt. Robert L. D. McConnell	12 April 1944	flying fatigue
S/Sgt. Bruce McLean	17 April, 1944	flying fatigue
Capt. Neil D. Maxwell	May 1944	flying fatigue
M/Sgt Thomas R. McGrath	May 1944	flying fatigue
2nd Lt. Stanley E. Allen	May 1944	recall of glider pilots
F/O Howard M. Allred	May 1944	recall of glider pilots
F/O Marion J. Glasgow	May 1944	recall of glider pilots
S/Sgt. John R. Dahl	May 1944	rotation plan
Cpl Thomas Mooney	May 1944	rotation plan
Cpl Henry T. Rutland	May 1944	rotation plan
Cpl Charles Zake	May 1944	rotation plan
T/Sgt Charles H. Barney	11 June, 1944	flying fatigue
S/Sgt Joseph T. McIlvain	11 June, 1944	flying fatigue
S/Sgt. Martin D. Caskey	1 July, 1944	ground rotation plan
Cpl. Lawrence R. Brown	1 July, 1944	ground rotation plan
Cpl. Arron A. Piecaro	21 July, 1944	combat replacement
Capt. Stephen A. Starr	28 July, 1944	combat replacement
T/Sgt. William E. Boffa	13 July, 1944	combat replacement
T/Sgt. Clarence G. Higgins	1 July, 1944	combat replacement
S/Sgt. James L. Gregg	9 July, 1944	combat replacement
S/Sgt. Harold J. Staff	11 July, 1944	combat replacement
1st Lt. W. T. Porter	3 August, 1944	combat replacement
T/Sgt. R. A. Aldridge	12 August, 1944	combat replacement
T/Sgt. D. S. Snyder	22 August, 1944	combat replacement
Corp. C. Williams	1 August, 1944	combat replacement
M/Sgt. E. L. Smith	24 August, 1944	rotation plan
Corp. W. F. Hinde	24 August, 1944	rotation plan
Pvt. L. E. McQueen	24 August, 1944	rotation plan
1st Lt. Samuel Berkovitz	16 Sept., 1944	rotation plan
T/Sgt. Gene A. Gilbert	16 Sept., 1944	rotation plan
T.Sgt. Charles M. Prater	16 Sept., 1944	rotation plan
Sgt. Wayne H. Harber	16 Sept., 1944	rotation plan
Sgt. Giles L. Harris	16 Sept., 1944	rotation plan
Sgt. John W. Harrison	16 Sept., 1944	rotation plan
Sgt. James R. McGowan	16 Sept., 1944	rotation plan
Sgt. Lushion N. Pool	16 Sept., 1944	rotation plan
Sgt. Ray V. Stoner	16 Sept., 1944	rotation plan
T/Sgt. Alvin L. Phillips	16 Sept., 1944	combat replacement
S/Sgt. William O. Henley	16 Sept., 1944	combat replacement
Capt. Ralph P. Osborn	30 October, 1944	combat replacement
1st Lt. Boyce S. Bailey	30 October, 1944	combat replacement

NAME OF OFFICER	DATE OF RETURN TO U.S.	REMARKS
M/Sgt. Jesse D. Berquist	7 October, 1944	combat replacement
T/Sgt. Thomas M. Dempsey	7 October, 1944	combat replacement
T/Sgt. Errol A. White	4 October, 1944	combat replacement
S/Sgt. Dell C. Drawdy	7 October, 1944	combat replacement
S/Sgt. Guy Lowder	4 October, 1944	combat replacement
T/Sgt. Thomas O. Green	20 October, 1944	rotation plan
S/Sgt. David E. McLernon	20 October, 1944	rotation plan
S/Sgt. Wayne W. DeCamp	20 October, 1944	rotation plan
Sgt. Emery Escoe	20 October, 1944	rotation plan
Sgt. Lloyd W. Moore	20 October, 1944	rotation plan
Sgt. H. P. Sanchez	20 October, 1944	rotation plan
T/Sgt. Gerald Coleman	23 November, 1944	rotation plan
S/Sgt. Welherne R. Francis	23 November, 1944	rotation plan
S/Sgt. Carl H. Templeton	23 November, 1944	rotation plan
T/Sgt. John T. Treanor	23 November, 1944	rotation plan
Sgt. Donald J. Freshour	12 December, 1944	rotation plan
Sgt. Wayne H. Galloway	12 December, 1944	rotation plan
Cpl. Marvin D. Cox	12 December, 1944	rotation plan
T/Sgt. George B. Goodrich		combat replacement
1st Lt. Austin N. Malcombe, Jr.	January, 1945	combat replacement
1st Lt. Henry G. Coile, Jr.	January, 1945	combat replacement
1st Lt. Dowd L. Cooper	January, 1945	combat replacement
Capt. Thomas N. Ryan, Jr.	January, 1945	combat replacement
Capt. Charles H. Crowe	January, 1945	combat replacement
1st Lt. Donald N. Shaw	January, 1945	combat replacement
1st Lt. Louis A. Meran	January, 1945	combat replacement
F/O George M. Matteson	January, 1945	combat replacement
T/Sgt. Jack C. Burkey	January, 1945	combat replacement
S/Sgt. Camden T. Saylor	January, 1945	combat replacement
Sgt. Boyd W. Dilbeck	January, 1945	combat replacement
M/Sgt. Forrest M. Adams	January, 1945	combat replacement
M/Sgt. Dorsey B. McBride	January, 1945	combat replacement
M/Sgt. William G. Smith	January, 1945	combat replacement
S/Sgt. Clifford W. Tenhoff	January, 1945	combat replacement
S/Sgt. Roy C. White	January, 1945	combat replacement
Pfc. John H. Webster	January, 1945	combat replacement
T/Sgt. Gordon R. Crane	January, 1945	combat replacement
T/Sgt. Cassiner J. Lucewicz	January, 1945	combat replacement
T/Sgt. Robert A. Mumford	January, 1945	combat replacement
T/Sgt. Clarence E. Maham	January, 1945	combat replacement
S/Sgt. John M. Swensen	January, 1945	combat replacement
S/Sgt. Nicholas M. Prodan	January, 1945	combat replacement
Capt. Louis A. Boise	January, 1945	rotation plan
M/Sgt. Earl T. Erlandson	January, 1945	rotation plan
Cpl. Frederick A. Moulton	January, 1945	rotation plan
Pvt. Bland King	January, 1945	rotation plan
1st Lt. Paul R. Savage	February, 1945	combat replacement
1st Lt. Ronald R. Templin	February, 1945	combat replacement
T/Sgt. Levi E. Parsons, Jr.	February, 1945	combat replacement
S/Sgt. Jacob J. Dayarmond	February, 1945	combat replacement
S/Sgt. John E. Thurston	February, 1945	combat replacement
T/Sgt. Bert G. McClard	February, 1945	rotation plan
T/Sgt. Theodore F. Soular	February, 1945	rotation plan
S/Sgt. Howard D. Baker	February, 1945	rotation plan
Cpl. Sol Hariton	February, 1945	rotation plan
Pfc. Joseph Piccolantenie	February, 1945	rotation plan
S/Sgt. Norbert E. Bernard	March, 1945	rotation plan
Sgt. Albert R. Conwell	March, 1945	rotation plan
Sgt. Louis H. Difiere	March, 1945	rotation plan
Cpl. Ralph Jernigan	March, 1945	rotation plan
Cpl. Marzie D. Thomas	March, 1945	rotation plan
Cpl. Alexander Zdunczyk	March, 1945	rotation plan

NAME OF OFFICER	DATE OF RETURN TO U.S.	REMARKS
Pfc. Ray T. Hatem	March, 1945	rotation plan
Pfc. William W. Shunk	March, 1945	rotation plan
1st Lt. Glenn M. Kurtz	March, 1945	combat replacement
T/Sgt. Robert F. Coffman	March, 1945	combat replacement
T/Sgt. Elmer C. Creasey	March, 1945	combat replacement
S/Sgt. Ellis R. Stevens	March, 1945	combat replacement
T/Sgt. DeBaze Hallmark	March, 1945	combat replacement
S/Sgt. Elbert W. Hall	March, 1945	combat replacement
1st Lt. William J. Decker	March, 1945	combat replacement
M/Sgt. Walter A. Moore	March, 1945	combat replacement
T/Sgt. Robert E. Bloodsworth	March, 1945	combat replacement
S/Sgt. Charles E. Lucas	March, 1945	combat replacement
S/Sgt. Norman Shore	March, 1945	combat replacement
Capt. Kenneth M. Anderson	March, 1945	combat replacement
1st Lt. Daniel K. Barton	March, 1945	combat replacement
1st Lt. James T. Harper	March, 1945	combat replacement
1st Lt. Carleton F. Holmes	March, 1945	combat replacement
M/Sgt. Robert W. Mader	March, 1945	combat replacement
S/Sgt. Clant E. Shepherd, Jr.	March, 1945	combat replacement
S/Sgt. R. C. Haskins	April, 1945	rotation plan
Sgt. C. H. Flanagan	April, 1945	rotation plan
Sgt. R. A. Lawson	April, 1945	rotation plan
Sgt. C. C. Riley	April, 1945	rotation plan
Sgt. A. Rosalanka	April, 1945	rotation plan
Sgt. W. M. Ward	April, 1945	rotation plan
Cpl. B. E. Warehulski	April, 1945	rotation plan
1st Lt. V. H. Landgraf	April, 1945	combat replacement
2nd Lt. E. R. Nalle	April, 1945	combat replacement
T/Sgt. M. G. Drevyanke	April, 1945	combat replacement
Sgt. G. H. Gray	April, 1945	combat replacement
Sgt. Grady L. Jones	April, 1945	combat replacement
1st Lt. W. C. Hood	May, 1945	combat replacement
1st Lt. William M. Spence	May, 1945	combat replacement
Sgt. Grady L. Jones	May, 1945	combat replacement
S/Sgt. Donald J. Irwin	May, 1945	rotation plan
Sgt. John W. Berger	May, 1945	rotation plan
Cpl. Henry G. Dragun	May, 1945	rotation plan
T/Sgt. Carl E. Lenzrtz	June, 1945	combat replacement
Sgt. Edward J. Lattner	June, 1945	combat replacement
S/Sgt. Jack D. Shippey	June, 1945	combat replacement
2nd Lt. Charles B. Ingram	June, 1945	rotation plan
S/Sgt. Ara Darpinian	June, 1945	rotation plan
S/Sgt. Arthur L. Helms	June, 1945	rotation plan
S/Sgt. Joseph S. Jackson	June, 1945	rotation plan
S/Sgt. Nick Pulcinello	June, 1945	rotation plan
Sgt. Charles L. Beckley	June, 1945	rotation plan
Sgt. Jimmie V. Knowles	June, 1945	rotation plan
Cpl. Robert J. Raymond	June, 1945	rotation plan
Cpl. Harold W. Sutterfield	June, 1945	rotation plan
Cpl. Herbert E. Elmquist	June, 1945	readjustment
3 Officers and 19 enlisted men	July, 1945	combat replacement
18 enlisted men	July, 1945	readjustment
2 Officers & 11 enlisted men	August, 1945	combat replacement
2 enlisted men	August, 1945	readjustment

33RD TROOP CARRIER SQUADRON

Capt. Robert L. Ward	3 May 1943	
Cpl. Edwin Delaney	5 August 1943	under age
T/Sgt. John J. Sullivan	1 September 1943	
Cpl. William E. Conway	1 September 1943	over age (Trfd to ERC)

NAME OF OFFICER	DATE OF RETURN TO U.S.	REMARKS
Cpl. Evan C. Evans	1 September 1943	over age (Trfd to ERC)
Cpl. Nicholas A. Heidt	1 September 1943	over age (Trfd to ERC)
Cpl. William P. Marley	1 September 1943	over age (Trfd to ERC)
Pfc. Charles C. Boggs	1 September 1943	over age (Trfd to ERC)
Pfc. Fred S. Edick	1 September 1943	over age (Trfd to ERC)
Pfc. Paul A. Schweickhard	1 September 1943	over age (Trfd to ERC)
Pfc. George L. Stadterman	1 September 1943	over age (Trfd to ERC)
Pvt. Frank Clark	1 September 1943	over age (Trfd to ERC)
S/Sgt. Harry Domigan	20 September 1943	
Cpl. Florentino P. Pastor	20 September 1943	
Capt. William R. Ross	24 September 1943	
T/Sgt. Alf L. Anderson	8 December 1943	
Capt. George A. Schnieders	8 December 1943	
1st Lt. John W. Foltz	18 January 1944	
Cpl. Antonio Conte	16 January 1944	
Capt. Bryce V. Smith	18 January 1944	
S/Sgt. Marvin D. Swenson	18 January 1944	
Capt. Leroy C. Spears	15 March 1944	flying fatigue
Cpl. Joe S. Gallagher	15 March 1944	flying fatigue
Capt. Vernon L. Shea	10 April 1944	flying fatigue
1st Lt. Johnston H. Wylie	10 April 1944	flying fatigue
M/Sgt. Roy C. Thompson	10 April 1944	flying fatigue
M/Sgt Lester D. Christofferson	10 April 1944	flying fatigue
S/Sgt. William L. Tarver	10 April 1944	flying fatigue
M/Sgt George E. Zorback	May 1944	flying fatigue
2nd Lt. Harry C. Russell	May 1944	recall of glider pilots
2nd Lt. Stacey Salisbury	May 1944	recall of glider pilots
Capt. Paul R. Ridley	6 June, 1944	flying fatigue
M/Sgt Raymond W. Vaughn	6 June, 1944	flying fatigue
Capt. Allen W. Gardener, Jr.	23 June, 1944	flying fatigue
Capt. Francis L. Schneiders	23 June, 1944	flying fatigue
1st Lt. Robert G. Johnson	15 July, 1944	combat replacement
Maj. George W. Wamsley, Jr.	17 July, 1944	combat replacement
Capt. Gene R. Glotzback	25 July, 1944	combat replacement
S/Sgt. John W. Shroder	24 August, 1944	rotation plan
Corp. Thomas E. Smith	24 August, 1944	rotation plan
Cpl. Francesco Verrengia	16 Sept., 1944	rotation plan
Pfc. Louis C. Hillenbrand	16 Sept., 1944	rotation plan
Pfc. Lloyd B. Locke	16 Sept., 1944	rotation plan
Capt. Preston Holden	26 Sept., 1944	combat replacement
1st Lt. Elmer E. Harrington	26 Sept., 1944	combat replacement
Capt. Monroe A. Adler	6 October, 1944	combat replacement
1st Lt. George H. Crawford	6 October, 1944	combat replacement
S/Sgt. B. F. King	30 October, 1944	combat replacement
S/Sgt. E. G. Stein	30 October, 1944	combat replacement
S/Sgt. Barry W. Bement	6 October, 1944	combat replacement
Sgt. Paul Lujan	23 October, 1944	rotation plan
Pvt. John E. Carrothers	23 October, 1944	rotation plan
Sgt. Lenial E. Carter	23 November, 1944	rotation plan
Pvt. James D. McAnich	27 November, 1944	rotation plan
Sgt. Floyd H. Tripe	3 December, 1944	medical
Pfc. Shelton Ainsworth	29 December, 1944	medical
Capt. George Bladen	31 December, 1944	Aviation Medical Sch.
Sgt. Robert H. Berry	11 December, 1944	rotation plan
Capt. Burl S. Ashley	23 December, 1944	combat replacement
Capt. Claude W. Patterson	23 December, 1944	combat replacement
Pvt. James B. Kelley	27 December, 1944	combat replacement
1st Lt. John P. Allen	January, 1945	combat replacement
Capt. William E. Williams, Jr.	January, 1945	combat replacement
1st Lt. Henry T. Howard	January, 1945	combat replacement
1st Lt. Donald R. McBreen	January, 1945	combat replacement
2nd Lt. Roy M. Clifton	January, 1945	combat replacement

NAME OF OFFICER	DATE OF RETURN TO U.S.	REMARKS
1st Lt. William S. Greer, Jr.	January, 1945	combat replacement
Capt. Jack Nabors	January, 1945	combat replacement
2nd Lt. Forrest D. Bruce	January, 1945	combat replacement
Maj. Robert E. Carlson	January, 1945	combat replacement
S/Sgt. Charles D. Rice	January, 1945	combat replacement
M/Sgt. Francis W. Wolf	January, 1945	combat replacement
Sgt. Clair T. Turgeon	January, 1945	combat replacement
T/Sgt. Edmund W. Whatley	January, 1945	combat replacement
T/Sgt. John Wycheck	January, 1945	combat replacement
T/Sgt. Victor A. Edwards	January, 1945	combat replacement
T/Sgt. Carl A. Grabner	January, 1945	combat replacement
T/Sgt. Stanley Poole	January, 1945	combat replacement
S/Sgt. William B. Bradley	January, 1945	combat replacement
Pvt. Willard M. Mitchell	January, 1945	rotation plan
1st Lt. James M. Malley	February, 1945	combat replacement
T/Sgt. Arthur Weitz	February, 1945	combat replacement
Sgt. Kenneth W. Houck	February, 1945	combat replacement
S/Sgt. Alva E. Halstead	February, 1945	combat replacement
S/Sgt. Clarence Rogers	February, 1945	combat replacement
T/Sgt. John Thompson, Jr.	February, 1945	combat replacement
T/Sgt. Marvin J. Thompson	February, 1945	combat replacement
S/Sgt. Robert M. Horn	February, 1945	combat replacement
S/Sgt. Sidney G. Kleinberger	February, 1945	combat replacement
S/Sgt. Wilmer E. Platt	February, 1945	combat replacement
1st Lt. Oran D. Williams	March, 1945	rotation plan
1st Lt. Richard F. Martin	March, 1945	combat replacement
1st Lt. William D. Ready	March, 1945	combat replacement
1st Lt. Elwyn P. Jordan	March, 1945	combat replacement
1st Lt. Robert W. Vanek	March, 1945	combat replacement
T/Sgt. Thomas E. Holland	March, 1945	combat replacement
S/Sgt. Jonn P. Arneth	March, 1945	combat replacement
S/Sgt. James Burchard	March, 1945	combat replacement
S/Sgt. John L. Fitzwater	March, 1945	combat replacement
S/Sgt. Louis D. Gardiner	March, 1945	combat replacement
S/Sgt. Ralph E. Glenn	March, 1945	combat replacement
S/Sgt. J. W. Hager	March, 1945	combat replacement
S/Sgt. Konrad H. Kopperud	March, 1945	combat replacement
S/Sgt. Thomas E. McDevitt	March, 1945	combat replacement
S/Sgt. William K. Paulman	March, 1945	combat replacement
S/Sgt. Jack A. Simonson	March, 1945	combat replacement
S/Sgt. Joe R. Taylor	March, 1945	combat replacement
T/Sgt. Kensel S. Fisher	March, 1945	combat replacement
S/Sgt. Jerome Vokoun	March, 1945	combat replacement
T/Sgt. Harold Terchin	March, 1945	combat replacement
S/Sgt. William Haessner	March, 1945	combat replacement
S/Sgt. Ernest L. Rose	March, 1945	combat replacement
T/Sgt. James A. Chapman	March, 1945	combat replacement
T/Sgt. John W. Jubik	March, 1945	combat replacement
T/Sgt. Robert R. Wallace	March, 1945	combat replacement
S/Sgt. Leon I. Burt	March, 1945	combat replacement
S/Sgt. Bobby G. Brasswell	March, 1945	combat replacement
1st Lt. Emory H. Phillips	March, 1945	combat replacement
S/Sgt. Matthew C. Wright	March, 1945	combat replacement
1st Lt. G. R. Irwin	April, 1945	rotation plan
1st Lt. E. R. Phillips	April, 1945	combat replacement
1st Lt. G. H. Wester	April, 1945	combat replacement
1st Lt. H. G. Kanaska	April, 1945	combat replacement
S/Sgt. M. C. Wright	April, 1945	combat replacement
S/Sgt H. J. Ottwork	April, 1945	combat replacement
S/Sgt. J. Rosemarin	April, 1945	combat replacement
S/Sgt. L. W. Metzer	April, 1945	medical
Cpl. G. H. Anderson	April, 1945	medical

NAME OF OFFICER	DATE OF RETURN TO U.S.	REMARKS
Capt. Joseph Skalski	May, 1945	combat replacement
1st Lt. Harry B. Grooms	May, 1945	combat replacement
1st Lt. James D. Vinson	May, 1945	combat replacement
1st Lt. Ned K. Miller	May, 1945	combat replacement
T/Sgt. Sylvester J. Glogowski	May, 1945	combat replacement
T/Sgt. Richard L. Zoll	May, 1945	combat replacement
T/Sgt. Russel L. Page	May, 1945	combat replacement
S/Sgt. John P. Hawley	May, 1945	combat replacement
S/Sgt. Benjamin F. Mortenson	May, 1945	combat replacement
S/Sgt. Harold A. Nehring	May, 1945	combat replacement
S/Sgt. Marcellus A. Lampe	June, 1945	combat replacement
Capt. Eric E. Pearson	June, 1945	combat replacement
T/Sgt. Francis L. Busch	June, 1945	combat replacement
S/Sgt. Arthur C. Chamberlain	June, 1945	combat replacement
S/Sgt. Earl R. Kohler, Jr.	June, 1945	combat replacement
S/Sgt. George E. Pennell, Jr.	June, 1945	combat replacement
Capt. Eddie G. Hauer, Jr.	June, 1945	combat replacement
S/Sgt. Edward A. Burton	June, 1945	combat replacement
1st Lt. Samuel Deines	June, 1945	combat replacement
S/Sgt. Preston H. Yawn	June, 1945	readjustment
Sgt. Wallace F. Costello	June, 1945	readjustment
S/Sgt. James J. Murphy	June, 1945	over age
Cpl. Francis H. Emmerich	June, 1945	over age
Pfc. Orville A. Griffith	June, 1945	over age
6 Officers and 16 enlisted men	July, 1945	combat replacement
13 enlisted men	July, 1945	readjustment
1 enlisted man	July, 1945	medical
4 Officers & 6 enlisted men	August, 1945	combat replacement
1 enlisted man	August, 1945	emergency furlough

On our way to victory.

APPENDIX 'T'

*374TH TROOP CARRIER GROUP PERSONNEL TRANSFERRED TO 54TH TROOP CARRIER WING**

Name	Transferred from (Organization)	Date
Officers		
Colonel Paul H. Prentiss	Hqrs.	20 May 1943
Major William F. Jennings	Hqrs.	20 May 1943
Major John H. Lackey, Jr.	6th T.C.Sq.	20 May 1943
Major Ray Vandiver	Hqrs.	20 May 1943
Captain Leonidas Baker	22nd T.C.Sq.	20 May 1943
Captain Harry M. Hayes	Hqrs.	20 May 1943
Captain Frank W. Smith	6th T.C.Sq.	20 May 1943
1st Lt. Lacy W. White, Jr.	Hqrs.	28 May 1943
2nd Lt. Morris I. Sherman	22nd T.C.Sq.	5 July 1943
1st Lt. William H. Quinn	33rd T.C.Sq.	30 June 1943
1st Lt. Curtis H. King	Hqrs.	8 July 1943
1st Lt. James N. LaRoche	33rd T.C.Sq.	9 July 1943
2nd Lt. Richard Krolik	Hqrs.	13 July 1943
Major Abe J. Beck	Hqrs.	23 July 1943
Captain Alexander Lieberman	6th T.C.Sq.	30 July 1943
Lt. Colonel Edgar W. Hampton	Hqrs.	1 August 1943
Major John F. Jacobs	Hqrs.	4 August 1943
Major Devitt L. Gordon	Hqrs.	8 August 1943
Lt. Norman R. Wilde (Aust)	Hqrs.	8 August 1943
1st Lt. Blesch Malmstrone	6th T.C.Sq.	11 August 1943
1st Lt. Elmer F. Iverson, Jr.	Hqrs.	27 August 1943
2nd Lt. Royal F. Hibblen	Hqrs.	27 August 1943
F/O Frank G. Matthieu	Hqrs.	27 August 1943
Captain Desmond D. Kackley	33rd T.C.Sq.	28 August 1943
Enlisted Men		
S/Sgt. Jay W. Heckman	Hqrs.	8 June 1943
S/Sgt. Ernest E. Newton	Hqrs.	8 June 1943
Sgt. Lyle W. Albrecht	Hqrs.	8 June 1943
Sgt. Louis C. Lanfranchi	33rd T.C.Sq.	8 June 1943
Sgt. Laurence R. Lanier	Hqrs.	8 June 1943
Sgt. William L. Lockman	Hqrs.	8 June 1943
Sgt. John W. Shrader	22nd T.C.Sq.	8 June 1943
Cpl. George E. Teasdale	33rd T.C.Sq.	8 June 1943
Cpl. John S. Yarosh	21st T.C.Sq.	8 June 1943
Pvt. James King, Jr.	21st T.C.Sq.	8 June 1943
Cpl. Roy J. Rogers	22nd T.C.Sq.	12 June 1943
Cpl. Clarence E. Shelnut	6th T.C.Sq.	12 June 1943
Cpl. Lawrence E. Reed	22nd T.C.Sq.	12 June 1943
Pfc Roland J. Ross	6th T.C.Sq.	12 June 1943
Pfc Vito F. Strazdas	22nd T.C.Sq.	12 June 1943
Pvt. Henry T. Lawson	22nd T.C.Sq.	12 June 1943
Pvt. Joseph R. Linderman	Hqrs.	12 June 1943
T/Sgt. Michael Zubritsky	22nd T.C.Sq.	13 June 1943
S/Sgt. Robert L. Garrett	33rd T.C.Sq.	18 June 1943
1st Sgt. John W. Drahos	Hqrs.	18 June 1943
Cpl. Robert R. Maywhere	Hqrs.	27 June 1943
S/Sgt. Edward P. Cosgriff	Hqrs.	28 June 1943
Sgt. Earl Q. Melton	Hqrs.	2 July 1943
Sgt. Carl H. Firchau	21st T.C.Sq.	11 July 1943
Sgt. Manuel Mamalakis	33rd T.C.Sq.	11 July 1943
T/Sgt. Ronald D. Smith	22nd T.C.Sq.	11 July 1943
S/Sgt. Glenn D. McMurray	Hqrs.	15 July 1943
Pfc. Lloyd G. Smith	33rd T.C.Sq.	28 July 1943
T/Sgt. Raymond F. Scalise	33rd T.C.Sq.	1 August 1943
S/Sgt. George R. Kershner	Hqrs.	6 August 1943
Pvt. Thomas I. Varney	Hqrs.	6 August 1943
Sgt. Robert E. Kraft	33rd T.C.Sq.	8 August 1943
Pfc. Eugene W. Tate	22nd T.C.Sq.	12 August 1943
Cpl. Preston J. Dabbs	Hqrs.	12 August 1943
Cpl. Glenn A. Lym	Hqrs.	27 August 1943
Cpl. Seymour Mark	Hqrs.	27 August 1943
Cpl. Gordon T. Berger	Hqrs.	30 August 1943
Sgt. Eugene Boettger	22nd T.C.Sq.	27 September 1943

Col. Edgar Wade Hampton.

---

* This Appendix lists the transfer of officers and enlisted men from the 374th Troop Carrier Group that supplied the talent and skills for the initial organization of the 54th Troop Carrier Wing.

APPENDIX 'U'

OFFICER STAFFING - 374TH TROOP CARRIER GROUP

GROUP HEADQUARTERS

1942 - 1944

EXECUTIVE OFFICERS

Lt.Col. Erickson S. Nichols	from	12 Nov/42	to	14 Dec/42
Maj. Edgar W. Hampton	from	14 Dec/42	to	17 Dec/42
Col. Paul H. Prentiss	from	17 Dec/42	to	22 May/43
Maj. Fred M. Adams	from	22 May/43	to	1 Aug/43
Maj. Edward T. Imparato	from	1 Aug/43	to	1 Oct/45

ADJUTANT

2ND Lt. Curtis H. King	from	17 Dec/42	to	2 Jan/43
2nd Lt. Lacy W. White, Jr.	from	2 Jan/43	to	28 May/43
Capt. John D. Pearson	from	28 May/43	to	

INTELLIGENCE OFFICER

Maj. William P. Jennings	from	17 Dec/42	to	20 May/43
Maj. John F. Jacobs	from	20 May/43	to	4 Aug/43
1st Lt. Lamont N. Rennels	from	4 Aug/43	to	20 Feb/44
Capt. Harold B. Simpson	from	20 Feb/44	to	

OPERATIONS OFFICER

Capt. Abe J. Beck	from	17 Dec/42	to	23 Feb/43
Capt. Carl J. Lichter	from	23 Feb/43	to	25 Apr/43
Capt. Roy Vandiver	from	25 Apr/43	to	20 May/43
Capt. Abe J. Beck	from	20 May/43	to	23 Jul/43
Capt. George M. Foster	from	23 Jul/43	to	15 Oct/43
Maj. Eugene R. Jackson	from	15 Oct/43	to	24 Feb/44
Maj. Robert C. Beebe	from	24 Feb/44	to	

ENGINEERING OFFICER   (See Materiel Officer)

SUPPLY OFFICER   (See Materiel Officer)

MATERIEL OFFICER   (Supply and Engineering)

Capt. Edward T. Imparato	from	12 Dec/42	to	1 Aug/43
1st Lt. Fred M. Soular	from	1 Aug/43	to	

(Upon adoption of new T/O about 1 Aug/43, Captain Soular became Engineering Officer and Captain Andrew J. Graves became Supply Officer)

6TH TROOP CARRIER SQUADRON

1942 - 1944

COMMANDING

1st Lt. John H. Lackey, Jr.	from	17 Feb/42	to	22 May/43
Capt. Frank W. Smith (acting-ground echelon)	from	23 Sep/42	to	1 Dec/42
Capt. William D. Wells	from	22 May/43	to	3 Dec/43
Capt. William A. Peterson	from	3 Dec/43	to	

Adjutant

2ND Lt. Robert W. Loder	from	22 Aug/42	to

Intelligence Officer

1st Lt. Henri W. Tessier	from	27 Sep/42	to	2 Oct/42
Capt. John F. Jacobs	from	2 Oct/42	to	8 Mar/43
1st Lt. Henri W. Tessler	from	8 Mar/43	to	

Operating Officer

2nd Lt. William D. Wells	from	1 Jul/42	to	20 Nov/42
1st Lt. Frank C. Church	from	20 Nov/42	to	31 Aug/43
Capt. William A. Peterson	from	31 Aug/43	to	28 Sep/43
Capt. Jaffus M. Rodgers	from	28 Sep/43	to	12 Dec/43
Capt. Albert H. Burleigh	from	12 Dec/43	to	2 Feb/44
Capt. Don G. Gaylor	from	2 Feb/44	to	

Engineering Officer

2nd Lt. Rexford W. Echard	from	2 Aug/42	to

Supply Officer

Administrative Supply:

2nd Lt. Frederick S. Watson	from	22 Aug/42	to

Technical Supply:

1st Lt. Conrad A. Rowland	from	31 Aug/43	to	30 Nov/43
1st Lt. John H. McCluney	from	30 Nov/43	to	25 Jan/44
1st Lt. Irwin W. Dial	from	25 Jan/44	to	2 Feb/44
1st Lt. Frederick S. Watson	from	2 Feb/44	to	

21st Troop Carrier Squadron

1942 - 1943

Commanding

Maj. Edgar W. Hampton	from		to	12 Oct/42
Maj. Fred M. Adams	from	12 Oct/42	to	23 May/43
Capt. Philip N. Eckberg	from	23 May/43	to	23 Sep/43
Maj. Myron J. Grimes	from	23 Sep/43		

Adjutant

1st Lt. Fred M. Adams	from	20 Feb/42	to	12 Oct/42
2nd Lt. James W. Ingram	from	12 Oct/42	to	10 Mar/43
2nd Lt. Eugene L. Stewart	from	10 Mar/43	to	14 May/43
2nd Lt. Jack Q. Patterson	from	14 May/43	to	

Intelligence Officer

2nd Lt. Jack Q. Patterson	from	16 Mar/43	to	14 May/43
2nd Lt. Willard B. Dunn	from	14 May/43	to	

Operations Officer

2nd Lt. Melvin C. Lewis	from	23 Mar/42	to	25 Nov/42
1st Lt. Perry H. Penn	from	25 Nov/42	to	5 Jun/43
1st Lt. Melvin C. Lewis	from	5 Jun/43	to	13 Oct/43
1st Lt. Henry F. Arts, Jr.	from	13 Oct/43	to	

ENGINEERING OFFICER

1st Lt. Edward T. Imparato	from 20 Feb/42	to	11 Dec/42
1st Lt. Fred G. Henry	from 11 Dec/42	to	3 May/43
1st Lt. Willard R. Stearns	from 3 May/43	to	5 Oct/43
1st Lt. William J. Perry	from 5 Oct/43	to	

SUPPLY OFFICER

2nd Lt. Charles R. Baer	from 20 Feb/42	to	4 Apr/42
2nd Lt. Uriah F. Corkrum	from 4 Apr/42	to	16 Mar/43
2nd Lt. Edward L. Perdival	from 16 Mar/43	to	

22ND TROOP CARRIER SQUADRON

1942 - 1944

COMMANDING

1st Lt. Francis R. Feeney	from 3 Apr/42	to	2 May/42
Capt. Raymond T. Swenson	from 2 May/42	to	21 May/42
Maj. William L. Bradford	from 21 May/42	to	22 Jul/42
Maj. Francis R. Feeney	from 22 Jul/42	to	6 Apr/43
Capt. Pearre D. Jacques	from 6 Apr/43	to	30 Apr/43
Capt. Fred G. Henry	from 30 Apr/43	to	30 May/43
Capt. Perry H. Penn	from 30 May/43	to	26 Sep/43
Maj. Robert C. Beebe	from 26/Sep/43	to	

ADJUTANT

None assigned	from 3 Apr/42	to	1 May/42
1st Lt. Robert C. Beebe	from 1 May/42	to	2 Mar/43
2nd Lt. Philip R. Pond	from 2 Mar/43	to	10 Aug/43
2nd Lt. Louis A. Boise	from 10 Aug/43	to	

INTELLIGENCE OFFICER

None assigned	from 3 Apr/42	to	10 Jun/42
Capt. Raymond T. Swenson	from 10 Jun/42	to	1 Oct/42
None assigned	from 1 Oct/42	to	17 Oct/42
1st Lt. Leonidas Baker	from 17 Oct/42	to	21 Feb/43
2nd Lt. Daniel Lipsky	from 21 Feb/43	to	

OPERATIONS OFFICER

1st Lt. Francis R. Feeney	from 3 Apr/42	to	12 Aug/42
Capt. William D. Strong	from 12 Aug/42	to	17 Oct/42
Capt. Pearre D. Jacques	from 17 Oct/42	to	28 Mar/43
Capt. Francis R. Thompson	from 28 Mar/43	to	4 May/43
Capt. Alan D. Moore	from 4 May/43	to	31 May/43
1st Lt. Wesley C. Holcombe	from 31 May/43	to	25 Jun/43
1st Lt. James H. Martin, Jr.	from 25 Jun/43	to	3 Oct/43
Capt. James C. Watson	from 3 Oct/43	to	7 Feb/44
1st Lt. John N. Ryan, Jr.	from 7 Feb/44	to	

ENGINEERING OFFICER

None assigned	from 3 Apr/42	to	27 Apr/42
2nd Lt. Richard G. Adelberger	from 27 Apr/42	to	10 Jun/42
1st Lt. Carl J. Lichter	from 10 Jun/42	to	22 Feb/43
Capt. James O. Cobb	from 22 Feb/43	to	4 May/43
Capt. Robert G. Whittington	from 4 May/43	to	31 May/43
Capt. William E. Carlson	from 31 May/43	to	3 Oct/43
1st Lt. Lloyd F. Little	from 3 Oct/43	to	

Supply Officer

2nd Lt. Roger E. Winn	from	3 Apr/42	to	15 Jun/42
2nd Lt. Wesley C. Holcombe	from	15 Jun/42	to	12 Aug/42
1st Lt. Leonidas Baker	from	12 Aug/42	to	31 Oct/42
1st Lt. Roger E. Winn	from	31 Oct/42	to	22 Feb/43
2nd Lt. Harold R. Newman	from	22 Feb/43	to	1 Jul/43
2nd Lt. Louise A. Boise	from	1 Jul/43	to	22 Jul/43
1st Lt. Harold R. Newman	from	22 Jul/43	to	22 Aug/43
1st Lt. Robert Dixon	from	22 Aug/43	to	

Technical Supply Officer

2nd Lt. Willis J. Gary	from	3 Apr/42	to	22 Feb/43
W/O Samuel Berkovitz	from	22 Feb/43	to	

33rd Troop Carrier Squadron

1942 - 1943

Commanding

1st Lt. Elmer F. Estrumse	from	17 Feb/42	to	1 Sep/42
1st Lt. Campbell M. Smith	from	1 Sep/42	to	28 Dec/42
Capt. George C. Kimball (acting -ground echelon)	from	30 Sep/42	to	7 Oct/42
Capt. Robert L. Ward (acting -ground echelon)	from	7 Oct/42	to	11 Oct/42
Capt. Eugene E. Jackson (acting -ground echelon)	from	11 Oct/42	to	28 Dec/42
Capt. Eugene E. Jackson	from	28 Dec/42	to	15 Oct/43
Capt. George W. Wamsley, Jr.	from	15 Oct/43		

Adjutant

2nd Lt. Phillip E. Cartwright	from	3 Jul/42	to	30 Sep/42
2nd Lt. Lamont N. Rennels	from	30 Sep/42	to	5 Oct/42
2nd Lt. Oliver N. Roth, Jr.	from	5 Oct/42	to	8 Dec/42
2nd Lt. James N. LaRoche	from	8 Dec/42	to	14 May/43
1st Lt. Gerald O. Wentworth	from	14 May/43	to	

Supply Officer

2nd Lt. Phillip E. Cartwright	from	3 Jul/42	to	16 Jul/42
2nd Lt. John D. Conquest	from	16 Jul/42	to	1 Oct/42
2nd Lt. Andrew J. Graves	from	1 Oct/42	to	28 Jul/43
1st Lt. Oliver N. Roth, Jr.	from	28 Jul/43	to	

Intelligence Officer

2nd Lt. Phillip E. Cartwright	from	3 Jul/42	to	12 Aug/42
1st Lt. George C. Kimball	from	12 Aug/42	to	1 Oct/42
1st Lt. William H. Quinn	from	1 Oct/42	to	1 Jul/43
1st Lt. Lamont N. Rennels	from	1 Jul/43	to	4 Aug/43
2nd Lt. Robert J. Carson	from	4 Aug/43	to	

Operations Officer

2nd Lt. Phillip M. Cartwright	from	3 Jul/42	to	4 Jul/43
1st Lt. Gene R. Glotzbach	from	4 Jul/43	to	

Engineering Officer

2nd Lt. Phillip E. Cartwright	from	3 Jul/42	to	9 Sep/42
2nd Lt. Richard M. Bigger	from	9 Sep/42	to	

APPENDIX 'V'

Newspaper unknown, c. 1988

WWII Plane Found in New Guinea

PORT MORESBY, Papua New Guinea (AP) - A U.S. transport plane shot down by Japanese fighters during World War II has been found in dense jungle along with remains of the five crewmen, an Australian mining company said today.

The company, CRA, said the wreckage was discovered two months ago in rugged terrain near Wau, where the company is prospecting for gold. Wau is about 185 miles north of Port Moresby, the capital.

Word of the find was delayed while the geologist who stumbled upon the wreck researched the plane's history, the company said.

Papua New Guinea, just north of Australia, was the scene of bitter fighting during the Pacific war.

In his report, made available to The Associated Press in Sydney, Australia, geologist Grant Malensek identified the aircraft as number 1-38658 of the 33rd Troop Carrier Squadron of the 374 Troop Carrier Group, U.S. 5th Air Force.

The crew reported missing were: Pilot 1st Lt. Robert H. Schwensen, co-pilot 1st Lt. Henry Sherman, engineer Cpl. Emil Errickson, radio operator Pvt. Clifford Fawn and trainee gunner Edward Piekutowski. Their hometowns were not available. Malensek said only Errickson's dog tag was clearly identifiable.

CRA's report could not be immediately confirmed independently.

A U.S. recovery team arrived at the crash site Wednesday and will remain there until all the remains are recovered, Malensk said.

"There's not much left," a CRA official said. "It obviously nose-dived into the side of a hill. Only the tail is sticking out of the ground. In all probability the rest was covered by later landslides."

Malensek said in his report that the plane was probably shot down by Japanese Zero fighters on Feb. 7, 1943.

He said it was one of three U.S. transport planes that had taken off from Jackson's Field in Port Moresby and was probably carrying foodstuffs and supplies. The other two planes survived and reported the crash.

The National Museum in Port Moresby confirmed that the plane had been shot down while the Battle of Wau was in its last stages with the Japanese being pushed back over the mountains to Salamaua.

He said the file on the plane was closed in 1949 with the five men classified as missing, presumed dead.

Other wreckages found in the area include another DC-3 and a B-17 Flying Fortress, according to CRA, a major gold explorer in Papua New Guinea.

Major Charles Hellweg, 374th Flight Surgeon viewing destroyed aircraft at Hollandia, 1944.

APPENDIX 'W'

GENERAL ORDERS)   HEADQUARTERS
:   FAR EAST AIR FORCES
No. 1744)   APO 925 - 2 August 1945

UNIT CITATION

By direction of the President, under the provisions of Executive Order No. 9396 (Section I, Bulletin 22, WD, 1943), superseding Executive Order No. 9075 (Section III, Bulletin 2, WD, 1942), and of Section IV, Circular No. 333, WD, 1943, the following units are cited by the Commanding General, Far East Air Forces.

***   ***   ***

374TH TROOP CARRIER GROUP

For outstanding performance of duty in action of 30 and 31 January and 1 February 1943. At that time strong enemy ground forces had penetrated into the Wau-Bulolo Valley, New Guinea, in an effort to capture the valuable Wau Airdrome, which was garrisoned by a token Allied force too small to repulse the invaders. Along with planes from another organization, the 374th Troop Carrier Group made an unprecedented series of air movements to save the drome. For three days the unarmed transport planes of the two groups carried Allied troops, ammunition, light artillery and supplies over the hazardous Owen-Stanley Mountains until late in the afternoon, when treacherous weather would ordinarily have stopped aerial operations. As soon as the planes had rolled to a stop on the up-hill landing strip, which was under the lobbing fire of enemy mortars, Allied infantry jumped out of the transports and immediately opened fire on the enemy. On 30 January, 40 planes made 66 trips; on 31 January, 35 planes delivered 71 loads; and on 1 February, 40 aircraft transported 53 5000-pound cargoes. By this time the Japanese had been killed or driven off, and Wau Airdrome, later to be used as a staging base for Allied air attacks on Lae and Salamaua, had been saved. With the loss of only 3 aircraft, these troop carrier groups flew a total of 948,000 pounds of personnel and materiel into Wau. The courage and skill of the aircrews in flying over a highly hazardous route subject to enemy interception and in landing under fire, as well as the tireless efforts of the ground echelon in keeping the aircraft in constant operation, were a vital factor in the success of the Allied counter-offensive against the Japanese forces which had pushed down into southeastern New Guinea. The achievements of the 374th Troop Carrier Group uphold the highest traditions of the armed forces of the United States.

***   ***   ***

/s/ George C. Kenney
/t/ GEORGE C. KENNEY,
General, United States Army,
Commanding.

TRUE EXTRACT COPY:

/s/ G. O. Wentworth
/t/ G. O. WENTWORTH
Major, Air Corps

APPENDIX 'X'

GENERAL HEADQUARTERS
UNITED STATES ARMY FORCES, PACIFIC

GENERAL ORDERS)   APO 500
:   19 August 1945
NO. . . . . 118)

BATTLE PARTICIPATION CREDIT - LUZON CAMPAIGN

   1. Pursuant to AR 260-10, 25 October 1944, and General Orders 33, War Department, 1945, the following Air Force units are entitled to battle honors for participation in the Luzon Campaign.

                                    *   *   *

374 Troop Carrier Group

                                    *   *   *

1st Air Cargo Control Squadron (Special)

                                    *   *   *

6th Air Cargo Resupply Squadron

                                    *   *   *

   2. The awarding of battle honors in paragraph 1 above, does not of itself entitle members of units listed therein to wear the Bronze Service Star on the Asiatic-Pacific Theater ribbon. Unit commanders will cause the necessary entries to be made in the personnel records of members of their organization who are eligible to wear the Bronze Service Star under the provisions of War Department Circular 62, 1944, as amended by War Department Circulars 195,1944; 90, 1945; and 142, 1945.

                                    *   *   *

AG-PA 200.6

   By command of General MacARTHUR:

                                                            R. K. SUTHERLAND,
                                          Lieutenant General, United States Army
                                                        Chief of Staff

OFFICIAL:

     /s/ B. M. Fitch
     B. M. FITCH,
  Brigadier General, U. S. Army,
     Adjutant General.

                                                         A TRUE EXTRACT COPY:

                                                         /s/ Paul E. Maloney
                                                         PAUL E. MALONEY
                                                         1st Lt., Air Corps.

APPENDIX 'Y'

GENERAL HEADQUARTERS
UNITED STATES ARMY FORCES, PACIFIC

GENERAL ORDERS)   APO 500
:   28 August 1945
NO. . . . . 138)
           <u>Section</u>

***   ***   ***

BATTLE PARTICIPATION CREDIT - BISMARCK ARCHIPELAGO CAMP...III

***   ***   ***

III. BATTLE PARTICIPATION CREDIT-BISMARCK ARCHIPELAGO CAMPAIGN.

     2. In addition to units listed in General Orders 100, Headquarters United States Army Forces in the Far East, 28 Apr 45, as amended by General Orders 101, this headquarters, 8 Aug 45, and pursuant to AR 260-10, 25 October 1944, and General Orders 33, War Department, 1945, the following named units are entitled to battle participation credit for the Bismarck Archipelago Campaign:

      **   **   **

     374th Troop Carrier Group

      **   **   **

     By command of General MacARTHUR:

                                        R. K. SUTHERLAND
                                    Lieutenant General, U. S. Army
                                           Chief of Staff

OFFICIAL:

     /s/ B. M. Fitch
     /t/ B. M. FITCH
  Brigadier General, U. S. Army
      Adjutant General

A CERTIFIED TRUE EXTRACT COPY:

     /s/ Paul E. Maloney
     /t/ PAUL E. MALONEY
      1st Lt., Air Corps

APPENDIX 'Z'

Deceased, Missing in Action and Missiing Personnel

Group Headquarters.

No personnel assigned to group headquarters was deceased, missing in action, or missing as of 31 January, 1944.

6th Troop Carrier Squadron.

The first member of the squadron to lose his life was 2nd Lt. William E. Luetzow. He was killed on 26 December 1941, while riding as a passenger in a non-squadron plane when it crashed 3 miles north of Slain, Pennsylvania.

On 5 March, 1942, Sgt. John A. Rutko was killed in a non-squadron aircraft crash, 35 miles north of West Palm Beach, Florida.

The squadron lost its first plane and crew on 16 October, 1942, on a combat mission in the Efogi area while dropping freight. The deceased crew members were: 2nd Lt. Wilson C. Cater, S/Sgt. Pilot Glenn E. Webb, and M/Sgt. Donald A. Mackey.

On 5 November, 1942, another plane crashed on a combat mission near Poppendetta, New Guinea. Apparently, a parachute shroud used in dropping supplies became wrapped around the tail of the plane. Crew members killed were 2nd Lt. Harold B. Mejure, T/Sgt. Clifford D. Stephens, and Sgt. Jack J. Deonier.

On 26 November, 1942, another of the squadron's ships was shot down in flames by Zeros near Dobodura, New Guinea. Crew members killed were 2nd Lt. Earl B. Lattaer, T/Sgt. Joseph E. Paul, and Sgt. Arthur Believe.

On the evening of 24 December, 1942, 2nd Lts. Jerome L. Simpson and Edwin R. Hayboer were fatally injured in a jeep accident on Ward's Airdrome, New Guinea.

On 14 June, 1943, Cpl. Marlin D. Metzger and Pfc. Frank S. Penska were killed at Mackay, Queensland, when the leave ship crashed on the take-off.

On 2 September, 1943, 1st Lt. Richard B. Stanton was reported missing when a B-24 of the 90th Bomb Group upon which he was a passenger, failed to return from a test flight.

The first loss sustained by the squadron since its return to the mainland of Australia, occurred on 19 October, 1943, when a plane crashed at Cloncurry, Queensland, apparently due to bad weather. Crew members killed were Captain John C. Fredrickson, 1st Lt. Fred R. Mentzer, M/Sgt. Michael Kullich, Sgt. Robert L. Kerr and Cpl. Marvin D. Middleton.

21st Troop Carrier Squadron.

On 25 May, 1942, a C-39 crashed near Alice Springs, Northern Territory, Australia, while on a combat mission, killing its crew consisting of 2nd Lts. Russell L. Callison and William A. O'Neill, and Pvts. Marlin J. Law and Rolfe M. Smith.

On 13 November, 1942, 2nd Lt. Harry E. Driver and Pfc. Donald M. Hutchinson were killed near Loganlea, Queensland, Australia, when their Tiger Moth plane struck a high tension wire and plunged into a creek.

On 12 May, 1943, a plane and its crew, consisting of S/Sgt. Pilot Lorenzo R. Gower, and Cpls. James G. Hickman and Dominic F. Verdi, failed to return from a combat mission near Oro Bay, New Guinea, and as of 1 January, 1944, were listed as "missing in action".

On 15 August, 1943, two planes were swarmed upon by Zeros at Tsilli Tsilli, New Guinea. The one plane crashed, killing its crew consisting of 1st Lts. Enoch F. Burley and James F. Miles, T/Sgt. Edward R. Beringer, and Pvt. John Kvaka, Jr. The other plane has never been located. Its crew, consisting of 1st Lt. Charles O. Cathcart, F/O Darwin R. Hamilton, Sgt. Theodore Slocki, and Cpl. William H. Fetzer, are listed as "missing in action".

The squadron sustained its first loss after its return to Australia when on 16 November, 1943, one of its planes disintegrated in the air, near Springsure, Queensland, Australia, killing its crew consisting of 1st Lt. Raymond E. Anglia, 2nd Lt. Joseph W. Kennedy, Sgt. Frank J. Ropinski and Sgt. Harold L. Brumstein.

On 21 November, 1943, a plane disappeared in the vicinity of Rockhampton, Queensland, Australia. Its crew, consisting of 1st Lt. Victor N. Gibson, 2nd Lt. Michael L. Reitman, S/Sgt. Everett L. Ahmann, and Cpl. John F. Giugno, are listed as "missing".

22ND TROOP CARRIER SQUADRON.

The squadron sustained its first losses on 14 July, 1942, when a plane was missing after take-off at Essendon Drome, Melbourne, Victoria, Australia. Its crew consisting of 2nd Lts. Robert L. Davis, Harry P. Forry, and S/Sgt Jack H Dorsett, are listed as "missing".

On 31 December, 1942, Captain John R. Linn and 1st Lt. Malcolm E. Peterson lost their lives in the crash of a B-25 somewhere between Townsville and Charters Towers, Queensland, Australia.

On 11 March, 1943, a plane crashed on a dropping mission at Skindawai, New Guinea, killing its crew of S/Sgt. Pilot Elmer C. Crowley, M/Sgt. Benjamin Palma, Sgt. Charles A. Kelley, Cpl. John J. Peaff, and Pfc. Leon M. Trach.

On 2 May, 1943, 1st Lt. John M. McClure died in his sleep of heart disease at his station at Ward's Drome, Port Moresby, New Guinea.

On 14 June, 1943, S/Sgt Frank E. Whelchel lost his life when the Mackay leave ship crashed on take-off at Mackay, Queensland, Australia.

On 11 July, 1943, 2nd Lt. Harry D. Dingman, Cpl. Charles L. Coury and Cpl. Dennis Murray were killed when their plane crashed while on a combat mission near Poppendetta, New Guinea.

On 19 December, 1943, a plane proceeding south from Townsville, Queensland, Australia, disintegrated in the air near Rockhampton, Queensland, killing all persons aboard. Its crew consisted of 2nd Lt. William R. Crecelius, 2nd Lt. John R. Rowell, T/Sgt John L. Shupe and Sgt. Robert S. Fazio.

33RD TROOP CARRIER SQUADRON.

The squadron sustained its first loss of personnel when Sgt. Joseph Archambault died on 29 August, 1942, at Florence, S.C., as a result of injuries sustained in a motor vehicle accident.

On 5 November, 1942, one of the squadron planes held at New Caledonia was struck by enemy fire on taking off at Henderson Field, Guadalcanal Island. It burst into flames and crashed, killing its crew consisting of S/Sgt Pilots Ray V. Hensman and Robert L. Dillman, Sgt. Elwood C. Carlson, and Cpl. James O. Lamar.

On 10 November, 1942, a plane loaded with 20 Australian Infantry troops crashed in the Owen Stanley Mountains near Dobodura, New Guinea. 2nd Lt. George W. Vandervort and Sgt. Steven J. Pitch were killed, while Sgt. George R. Kershner, radio operator, was miraculously spared. Sgt. Kershner wandered through the New Guinea jungles for 38 days before he was rescued and taken to the 10th Evacuation Hospital at Port Moresby, New Guinea.

On 26 November, 1942, a squadron plane was shot down by Japanese fighters near Dobodura, New Guinea, killing its crew consisting of S/Sgt. Pilots Marvin L. Brandt and Quentin C. Reucker, Sgt. Joseph G. Baltascavage and Pfc. Hugh M. Bryan. Listed as "missing in action" are 2nd Lts. Robert H. Schwensen and Henry W. Sherman, Cpl. Emil W. Ericson, Pfc. Edward G. Piekertowski, and Pvt. Clifford J. Fawn, the crew of a plane which was last seen on 6 February, 1943, going over a mountain with Zeros in pursuit near Wau, New Guinea.

On 12 May, 1943, a ship of the 33rd crashed in the mountains near Dobodura, New Guinea, killing its crew consisting of 1st Lt. Walter B. Thompson, F/O Robert Ranges, T/Sgt. Willis Check, T/Sgt. Darrell D. Loy and Sgt. Elwood H. Wolfsberger.

APPENDIX 'AA'

WHOLE DIVISIONS MOVED BY AIR IN ROUT OF JAPS

By H. E. Patterson
(Accredited War Correspondent)
With the Troop Carrier, Command, Southwest Pacific

—America has created two machines without which the allies would not be able to run this war - one is the jeep and the other is the Douglas C-47 airplane.

The man who made that flat declaration is Lt. Col. Edward T. Imparato, executive officer of the first Troop Carrier Command unit organized in the Southwest Pacific, the gang who flew 5,000,000 miles carrying troops and supplies in the first six months of the war, the gang whose exploits make even the most fantastic Hollywood air war pictures look silly.

Back in 1942, a year before we finally captured Salamaua, this outfit flew 200 Australian Commando troops into an old gold strip at Wau. The commandos were to try to capture, or at least harass the Japs at Salamaua. The strip at Wau is short, 3,300 feet, and runs uphill with a 7,000-foot mountain at the end of it.

DOES JOB IN HURRY

"We flew in, six ships at a time, landed on the strip, slowed down just enough for the troops to leap out, turned around and took off without a stop," said Captain Harvey Rehrer of Reading, Pa., one of the squadron leaders. "The landing was very tricky. You are climbing when you land. One of the boys cracked up because he could not figure the approach right."

Back in March, 1942, when the Japs were bombing Darwin, the Troop Carrier unit flew an entire battalion of anti-aircraft troops, complete with their guns and ammunition, 1,800 miles across Australia to Darwin.

"We loaded them so that each plane carried a gun, ammunition and crew, ready to jump out, set up and start shooting," said Colonel Imparato. "The Japs had a big surprise the day when they came over."

WHOLE DIVISION BY AIR

In September, 1942, the unit moved an entire division of men from Australia and landed them southeast of Buna. They were landed on a strip surrounded by impassable jungle, were supplied by air all the time they were driving the Japs back from their big push on Port Moresby - and were moved out again by C-47s in January, 1943.

The saving of the Wau airdrome back in January, 1943, was one of the unit's proudest - and most rugged - operations.

"The Japs made a push from Salamaua and Lae to capture the strip at Wau and we flew in 700 troops a day for four days to stop the drive," sand Captain James Watson, of Dallas, Texas.

"To make our approach up the valley we had to fly over the Jap lines, over ack-ack and mortar fire. The Japs killed a number of troops at one end of the runway while one of our ships was turning around and getting off again.

WIND IS SMALL WORRY

"Snipers were shooting at us as we made our turn and we had to take off and fly out over the Jap lines again. But the takeoff was down hill and we got away from there fast. We paid no attention to wind direction, just banged in, dropped the troops, spun around and gunned out again."

Back in October, 1942, part of the outfit flew supplies to our troops on Guadalcanal, landed at Henderson Field when the Japs were only 1,000 yards away.

"Jap snipers used to kill our men while they were putting gas into the ship," said Lieut. Burl Ashley, of Tetark Falls, Ohio. "We flew in ammunition and took out wounded. We always carry stretchers in the airplane and in all our operations where we carry in supplies we haul out wounded. A man can be shot in New Guinea and in a few hours be resting in a general hospital in Australia."

THIS IS A REST

The unit has now been pulled out of front line action and are now "resting" - hauling supplies and men along an 1,800 mile airline from Australia to New Guinea. They are flying C-47 airplanes with 5,000 pound payloads in all kinds of weather.

All C-47 airplanes used in this theater now are flown to Australia from the west coast of America.

"There were 13 planes that took off," said Captain Conrad Rowland of Ezel, Ky., who made such a flight. "We flew down here in six hops and never lost a plane. When we landed in Australia we had flown more than 7,000 miles over open ocean in 54 hours flying time."

This is the gang that flew two and a half ton trucks into Wau - they even hauled mules.

THEY FLY EVERYTHING

"I think that mule hauling deal was an experiment to determine if we could haul whole artillery units," said Major George Foster, of Wellesley, Mass. "We rigged up special stalls and catwalks and put three mules in the C-47. They took off and flew around a couple of times to see if it could be done. We have hauled about everything else you can mention."

They mentioned a few: planes loaded with bread, with bombs, with grenades, with troops, lumber, pipe, bulldozers, caterpillar tractors. They even hauled a complete radio station up to Darwin in the early days of the fighting - cut the big radio tower in sections and loaded it in.

"You know that steel runway at Doboura - we hauled every one of those mats across the mountains," said Capt. Robert G. Whittington of Dallas. "We lugged 7,000,000 pounds of steel mats over to Doboura for the runways."

The mats are eight by two and a half feet and weight 69 pounds. They carried 80 mats per trip.

- Wings For Invasion -

APPENDIX 'BB'

G.I. DIARY

THE THOUGHTS OF A SOLDIER OVERSEAS 1942-1944

By M/Sgt. Glenn D. McMurray
from the book Morseby to Manila Via Troop Carrier

1942

Tuesday, 1 September. Left Camp Stone man, San Francisco, at 6:30 p.m. We unloaded from the train about 10:30 p.m. and were finally loaded into the ship about midnight. We are just in front of the engine room in the hold above the water line. It is a Dutch ship. Dutch officers and Japanese help. The bunks are strung between two pipes and eight bunks to each group. Twenty-four inches between each bunk. Groups are end to end and aisles of about 30 inches in width. There is a preserver on each bunk. The bunks are canvas tied in by 3/8-inch rope. The floors in the center are removable so they can load the bottom of the ship. The cranes are all electric. The ship was built in 1939 and was a cargo passenger ship.

Wednesday, 2 September. Had boiled eggs for breakfast. At about 9:30 a.m. we shoved off and left American soil. We pulled away and it was really a beautiful sight. San Francisco bridge and the Golden Gate in full view. We stopped out in the harbor to wait for the convoy. Laved up in the latrine in the front of the boat - cold salt water - ouch. Volunteered to do some typing. While working the boat started to move and was under the Oakland bridge. Then we passed under the Golden Gate bridge. It was a beautiful sight. The city of San Francisco all outlined on the side of the mountains. The two bridges spanning the water. A Navy blimp zig-zagging around overhead. Coastguard cutters all around. This was about 4:30, and then out into the Pacific Ocean. At 6:00 p.m., I saw my last of America. How grateful I will be when I see it again.

Thursday, 3 September. Set clocks back 1 hour. Read. Slightly dizzy. The ocean is the most beautiful blue you ever saw.

Friday, 4 September. Time chanted another hour. Worked in the library a while. Gun practice this afternoon. Had a community sing on deck.

Saturday, 5 September. Set clocks back _ hour. Formed a glee club to sing in the lounge each evening.

Sunday, 6 September. Set clocks back _ hour. Very impressive church service this morning. We all felt pretty reverent today.

Monday, 7 September. Set clocks back _ hour. School starts at home. Kinda like to be back teaching. Saw first flying fish. It seemed they were in droves. Slept on deck.

Wednesday, 9 September. Set clocks back _ hour. Had fire drill. Made up some song sheets.

Thursday, 10 September. They initi ated the officers for King Neptune at dinner.

Friday, 11 September. Set time back _ hour. Crossed the equator today. Officers and sergeants got the works. Stripped to shorts and then faced charges against them that were of course ridiculous. They smeared garbage on them, faces and all, and then threw them into a large vat of water. After that they proceeded to turn the hose on the privates standing around. Sang my new song, "Freedom Forever, this evening. They liked it.

Sunday, 13 September. Church again. Met Link, the ship's purser. Quite a guy. Haircut. Talk of shore leave, so that means land.

Monday, 14 September. Supposed to dock sometime tomorrow night. Fiji Islands we think. Presented two new songs, "Stars in the Night" and "Blue Mists".

Tuesday, 15 September. Set time back _ hour. Land-ho. Wonder if we land?

Thursday, 17 September. Interna tional date line. One day went into thin air.

Sunday, 20 September. Shore Leave today. This place is called Suva. Some place Fiji. More like the St. Louis Zoo. Had good dinner.

Monday, 21 September. Shore leave. Big meal at Grand Pacific Hotel.

Tuesday, 22 September. Shore leave again. Suva is seeing quite a bit of us. Saw a man who had both arms taken off by a shark when he dived into the water after money that was thrown overboard by tourists. Ugh.

Wednesday, 23 September. Shore leave again but were told that we were leaving. We were pretty well ready to leave at 3 p.m. The glee club had their pictures taken while in Suva. We're off.

Thursday, 24 September. Saw my first albatross. It landed on the mast. Good omen.

Saturday, 26 September. Sick today. Ugh.

Tuesday, 29 September. Exciting day. We are supposed to dock sometime today. We did too, at 4 o'clock. Where - Brisbane, Queensland, Australia. At Camp Dooben. Visited Brisbane - some place.

Friday, 9 October. Got first mail from home.

Tuesday, 13 October. Moved from Ascot park to Camp Muckley. Close to Archer Field.

Friday, 27 November. Big brawl in Brisbane last night. Aussies and the Yanks got into it. Just letting off steam.

Saturday, 28 November. French Fleet scuttled. Running movies now. Working in orderly room.

Wednesday, 23 December. Found out I am leaving for an assignment. Good.

Thursday, 24 December. Lt. King is going with me. We have been assigned to the 374th Troop Transport, with the Ad vance Echelon at Port Moresby. In a B-24. Christmas evening in Townsville. Hot as sin.

Christmas Day, 25 December. Flying again, landed at Iron Range and had dinner. Bully beef, tomatoes, corn and peas. Very flat but food. This is quite a place. Cut right out of the jungle. Landed at Moresby about 4 p.m. Chow at 5 o'clock over at Arcadia. Spent Christmas night in a slit trench. Ugh.

Saturday, 26 December. They are picking out a camp for us. It looks like it will be on the side of a large hill on an old ack-ack installation. There is a ship in the harbor that was sunk five or six years ago. They use it for bombing practice.

Monday, 28 December. Things are kinda rough. 33rd Squadron came in today.

Tuesday, 29 December. Saw my first wallaby today. Staying in a grass hut. It leaks too.

Thursday, 31 December. Last day of year. Eventful too. Cpl. Lockman and I are alone here in a tent. The Japs are trying to hit this place. At one time it caused them quite some trouble they say.

1943

Friday, 1 January. Made a few little private resolutions today. Sgt. Cosgriff will move in tomorrow. One other guy by the name of Roberts.

Sunday, 3 January. Sgt. White got his commission. He is a 2nd Lt. now. Boy is he tickled.

Wednesday, 6 January. Evening paper is encouraging. It says the war will be over in 1943 for sure. Hope so. Paper is called "The Guinea Gold". Owen Stanleys are beautiful this morning. Wish I had a camera. Natives are going to build a grass hut for an office. Boy do those natives stink. Ugh.

Sunday, 10 January. Air raid. One of my first this moon. Colonel Prentiss coming back from Brisbane. Things will snap now.

Wednesday, 13 January. Lockman cracked a rib somehow. He is laid up. Soriano supposed to come in a few days.

Thursday, 14 January. Had a darn good raid tonight. They are coming pretty regular nowadays. Gee those Japs are bum shots.

Friday, 15 January. Not much work. Hope I can sleep tonight. Sleep? I should say not. I did for a while and the shots were fired. I had to go to the latrine and between the G.I.'s and the bombs I was in a dither. I made it *back* to the slit trench in nothing flat. Was I ever scared. I've never been scared like that before.

Saturday, 16 January. Another good raid tonight. When are we going to get some sleep? Issue of cigs and things tomorrow.

Saturday, 23 January. Captured Sanananda. Raids and more raids. The Buna campaign is now over.

Sunday, 24 January. Raid again. Boy, I'm hitting the trench every time. It is good life insurance. They got lucky tonight and got planes in their sights. Been cutting hair here of late. Lt. King, Major Imparato, Luckman, Hampton, White and McCartney. Should see the scissors and comb I use. Ha.

Tuesday, 26 January. Lt. White wanted to cut my hair in exchange today and it took Lockman about an hour to get it fixed up. Several raids again tonight. They got some of the boys over near Ward's.

Saturday, 30 January. Pushing the Japs back at Wau now. Good. Cut Col. Prentiss' hair. Talked a streak all the while. Got a new niece.

Saturday, 7 February. Caught a parrot today. He bit h— out of my hand.

Tuesday, 9 February. Wish they would get the mess hall done. Get tired standing up to eat. Major Hampton is a colonel now, as of 31 Jan. Played hearts a while. Air raids still coming.

Sunday, 14 February. Got our special service phonograph today. Boy, was that music ever good. Lots of work now. Typed 43 endorsements, 10 full letters and several stencils. Raids are beginning to come during the day now. Several alerts.

Thursday, 25 February. Finally getting acquainted with Sgt. Drahos. Saw a Jap motorcycle. Rugged, trying to drive on the wrong side of the road here.

Monday, 1 March. Lt. King is now a 1st Lt. Big raid on Rabaul and Lae this morning. Lights for the first time. They are still writing of the big Bismarck Sea battle. There is talk about furloughs. Wonder where. Typed over 30 stencils today. I went to bed pronto this morning.

7 April. Had a 100 plane raid today. That was the last straw. They did plenty of damage too. I hope they don't do that very often. The raids are getting fewer and fewer lately. This was a dilly though.

1 July. Made staff sergeant today.

2 September. One year has passed since coming overseas. I am still in New Guinea. I am now in the 54th Troop Carrier Wing. Have had two leaves to Mackay. I am in good health. Have floor in tent now. Playing volleyball. Seen first gliders - parachutes. Saw a plane explode in the air. Varney all tanked up. Cosgriff lost front teeth. Got hit in mouth by washing machine crank. Made me a ring out of a florin.

5 September. Saw large-scale airborne operations. Saw first glimpse of General MacArthur. Col. Prentiss led the flight. Got up at five to watch it. Took a trip to native village today too.

26 October. Group went to the main land. Prentiss is a brigadier general now.

1 December. Went with Maj. Jacobs on a trip to Nadzab, Gusap and back to Dobodura. Saw a lot of interesting things. Lucky I did not get mixed up in a raid. Went swimming in a fresh-water river. O.C.S. staring me in the face. Don't really care to go though.

27 December. Am a T/Sgt. Now. Got to go on furlough to Sydney for 15 days.

1944

15 March. Rotation started. Drahos, Barney and Warren gone on 28 Feb. My buddie Kuhn dead from B-19 crash over England. Col. Lackey going to Staff School at Ft. Leavenworth. Mom got Darlene a string of pearls for Xmas.

20 March. New rotation setup now. It will go by points. Three for New Guinea, one for Australia. I have quite a figure. I wonder if that will hold up?

31 March. General Prentiss, Capt. White and Lt. Malmquist all gone to Brisbane, V AFSC. Maj. Beck to Advance Echelon, Fifth Air Force. Col. Hampton was thinking about going too but did not.

18 April. Moved to Nadzab. We had the move all over in one day and had one of the best dinners I've eaten. We are situated in a beautiful coconut grove.

1 May. Made a nice trip to Wakde and saw real dead Japs. It was D plus 5. Took a trip into a native village through the jungles. It was an interesting trip. I will never forget it. The natives are really a lazy dirty bunch.

6 June. Invasion of France. What we have really been waiting for.

4 August. Rain. Troop Carrier Command in process now. Everything going good. Folks are fine and so am I. War going good; collapse on all fronts.

16 August. My birthday. I'm 27. Left for Mackay on leave, via food ship. Lockman went with me. Had to sleep in recreation hall the first night. Got to stay there 20 days because the transportation setup was bad.

4 September. Arrived back at Moresby. Boy what a deserted place. When I finally got back to Nadzab, I found out that I had been promoted to Master. Was I ever surprised. That was on the 28th of August. I am very happy.

15 September. Invasion of Palau. Maj. Smith is due to go home on a medical.

16 September. Rotation quotas show that I haven't a chance. Ugh.

20 September. Bought a Parker 51.

4 October. Packing up to move. Loading in a C-46, my first. Must have on 10,000 pounds.

5 October. Off at 7 a.m. Swell take-off. Arrived at 11 a.m. Some place this. Hot, etc. Office is all set up so we just moved in.

6 October. In business at 9:30 a.m. Swimming good on beach. Lt. Washburn and Capt. Iverson are out of the squadron now.

12 October. Tent about up. Michael J. Stosic, Lockman and myself so far. Rocco next. Alert on 10th but nothing happened. No Japs as yet. A negro boy was killed in an auto accident the other day. Crushed his skull. Col. Hurst new A-1 reported. He is an all right guy too.

20 October. Another friend, Warren Smothers, killed in France. Too bad. Philippines attacked. Leyte. Had 25 men for T.D. to States for November. Have been hunting cat eyes. Swimming fine. Palms, sea, etc. very beautiful.

27 October. "Jap hunting" spree became too realistic with one fatality to our side and four to theirs.

10 November. General Prentiss coming back. Surprise. Having a Christmas choir. Had 15 the first night. Played hostess to one of 6 U.S.O. girls. Had cake and coffee after the show. One, Nan Shannon, gave me some music. Nice of her.

17 November. Have about 15 rolls of film. Also one roll of color.

29 November. General Prentiss is back about a week now. Malmquist and White too. Capt. White is home on T.D. right now. Rain. Am an uncle again now. That's two I've missed. Had Thanksgiving dinner and all the boys got G.I.'s over the meat. What a night. Me too.

12 December. Japs slapped a bunch of the 317th boys at Leyte. Bad. Cpl. Kruch got burned badly. In hospital. One of the cooks got a couple of fingers blown off when playing with a cap. Loach and Scott left for T.D. Having ice cream now. That is swell.

25 December. Choir gave concert this evening. It all went fine. It was the best singing I've heard since being out of college. They did swell. War in Europe not so good. Been going backward lately. Terrible losses. Swell Xmas dinner.

31 December. Last day of a year. Oh me. Just looking over my old diary. Some stuff. Hot today. Rotation a joke. Saving quite a wad of money.

Color Guard, 1943.

Nadzab 374th TCG Campsite, 1944.

APPENDIX 'CC'

LIFE IN NADZAB

By M/Sgt. Glenn D. McMurray
from his book Moresby to Manila Via troop Carrier

Nadzab - as almost everybody in the Wing knows - is situated about 25 miles northwest of Lae. And as everybody in the Wind - virtually everybody but the 317th Group - learned it was one of the finest places we ever had to set up camp. All the other Wing units were there - the 375th, the 433rd Group, the 21st Service Group, the 804th and 820th Medical Air Evacuation Squadrons, and the 333rd Signal Company.

The Markham Valley at Nadzab was flat and dusty. Judicious selection placed the Troop Carrier units in excellent locations. Wing headquarters area was the finest of all. Quarters of both officers and enlisted men were situated in a coconut grove whose lofty trees offered just the right degree of shade. A cool, invigorating wind blew through the camp almost regularly at 3 p.m. Two streams, one on each side of the camp site, provided water for showers and laundry.

Enlisted men had their own laundry set-up - G.I. operated. The officers' laundry was taken care of by native boys, provided by the New Guinea Administration and paid for from the officers' mess fund. Quarters, both for officers and enlisted men, had wooden floor tents, raised from the ground and screened in.

A coconut-lined road separated the enlisted men's area from the officers' section. Behind the officers' section, in another coconut grove, was located the 333rd Signal Company's quarters. There was an athletic field behind the Signal Company's section. Volleyball and badminton courts were set up in the officers' and enlisted men's sections.

Directly in front of the camp was "Hollywood Mountain" - named because its kunai-grass-covered surface made it look unreal - a phoney in plain language.

A few miles away from the camp site was some of the world's finest scenery, a setting of tropical splendor which could only be obtained in normal times via an expensive travel tour. It was all ours for the asking.

The Groups were located near the various strips at Nadzab. All had nearly a similar set-up - providing the mot comfort that Troop Carriers had had up to April 1944. As one G.I. put it, "We were more than lucky to find a camp in such a swell spot, from which we could also work so effectively in pushing back the Jap."

Wing headquarters building was a virtual "corporation structure" for New Guinea. It was a huge I-shaped building with a double roof to keep it cool. There was plenty of room in which to work and very few mosquitoes. An electric ice-water cooler was the envy of all outsiders. What more could we ask for? Nothing - and that is what we did. For once everybody seemed satisfied.

The officers' club was situated across from the headquarters building. It was a concrete-floor L-shaped building, which served as a combination mess all and social club. The enlisted men's dayroom, with its ice-cold Coca-Cola dispensing unit, was across the road from the main headquarters building. A short distance away was the open air motion picture theater and stage - a ramshackle affair, but serving its purpose admirably, rainy nights included.

Moonlight nights, which turned the area into almost daylight brilliance, found many affairs at both the enlisted
men's and officers' clubs. There were no women at these affairs (except nurses at officers' functions) but the gatherings were a lot of fun, just like reunions. As tonnage record after record continued to be broken and as Troop Carriers hauled more and more supplies out of this valley northwards, the shadows of forthcoming events were cast on this valley garden spot. When Hollandia was captured, we knew our days in this ideal camp site were numbered.

When our time came to move - from June on - the men reminisced, talking about how tough it was when the 433rd Group came to Nadzab in September 1943 - the countless raids, the dusty roads, the lack of food, the continual drive to do our work from daylight to late at night. Yes, everything wasn't so wonderful at Nadzab as it was finally in April 1944.

In 1943 men lived right beside their airplanes for the first few months. Some men were killed by Jap bombs. Others were injured when planes were strafed b Nips as they flew down the valley.

So nobody begrudged the Troop Carriers their so-called few luxurious months in 1944 - April through June - when, by their own effort and skill, they created a camp typically American - every comfort possible so that the men could do a better job. And a better job they did, as the record shows.

33rd Squadron, Nadzab, 1944.

APPENDIX 'DD'

SKYTRAINS

THIS IS THE STORY OF A REMARKABLE SAFETY RECORD

By M/Sgt. Glenn D. McMurray
from his book Moresby to Manila Via Troop Carrier

The 41st Troop Carrier Squadron of the 317th Group completed one of the greatest safety and delivery records believed ever achieved by any single unit of its size anywhere in the world.

This unit did not lose a single airplane or have a single fatal accident or injury to crew members in 25 months. This time period included 14 months of flying hazardous trips throughout northern Australia and combat flying in New Guinea.

During the 14 months overseas, the unit flew more than 2,800,000 miles, carried 22,000,000 pounds of freight, 47,500 passengers, hauled and dropped thousands of paratroopers, and accumulated 21,000 flying hours, all without marring its record. In its 11 months in the United States, the unit flew over 1,000,000 miles in which it participated in paratroop maneuvers, tried out new ideas in carrying airborne infantry and artillery, and maintained a regular freight run from Stout Field, Indianapolis, to Pope Field, Fort Bragg, N.C.; Bowman Field, Louisville, Ky,; and Lawson Field, Fort Benning, Ga.

In its overseas flying, this unit had to evade Jap bombing and strafing in flights to Darwin and in New Guinea, pioneer new and unfamiliar landing fields in northern Australia, cross the dangerous 700-mile Coral Sea hundreds of times and battle what is called the worst flying weather in the world. One pilot said the downpour of rain sometimes encountered in this area "reaches astronomical feroc ity, literally forcing the plane to lose altitude by the sheer weight of water".

In its New Guinea flights, the pilots and crews of the 41st Squadron brought needed supplies to Lae, Nadzab, Finschhafen, Saidor, Arawe and Cape Gloucester, led the first paratroop drop in the Markham Valley, and were the first Troop Carrier planes to land on Kiriwina and Goodenough Islands after its capture.

Col. Ray T. Elsmore; commanding officer of the Directorate of Air Transportation, under which the 41st Squadron served while in Australia, said in a letter of commendation, *"When we consider the fact that your pilots, young in age and experience, came into an entirely new theater where terrain and weather were new, aids to navigation few, and emergency landing fields scarce, the record becomes outstanding and exceeds our fondest hopes.*

"We who have the responsibility of dispatching your aircraft and flight crews into inclement weather and often across long stretches of water, desire to express our sincere appreciation, not only to flight personnel, but to every officer in your group."

All planes of this unit have been named after famous railroad trains. Pilots have had many varied and interesting experiences, which many times came close to breaking its safety record.

Lt. James Fay of Scottsbluff, Nebr., tells of a humorous one, which was nearly fatal. "Did you ever hear of a pilot having his goose almost cooked by a roast duck?" he said. "We had taken off with a full load of personnel just before dawn from Townsville, (Queensland) Australia. We were about 100 to 300 feet in the air when we ran into a flock of ducks. I could hear them splattering against the plane. Our left engine started acting up. We circled the field several times, testing the engine and then decided to continue our journey,. After landing we inspected the plane. And I know it is difficult to believe, but we found a duck difficult to believe, but we found a duck wedged between the cylinders of the left engine, done to a crisp."

Another close call was when Lt. Robert Wilson of Scottsbluff, Nebr., and Capt. Emerson J. Watson of Sevierville, Tenn., were piloting a plane load of paratroopers on a special practice maneuver at Cairns, Queensland. The plane was about a mile offshore. The maneuver called for the plane to skim the water, about 20 feet above the waves and make for a target area on shore. Capt. Watson suddenly felt the plane jerk to the left. He looked out and saw the left propeller and gear housing had fallen off. He "slapped" on the power of the right engine, managed to gain 400 feet of altitude and make an emergency landing on a taxiway.

Just two examples of close calls which almost ruined this Troop Carrier Squadron's record, a record of which the Wing is proud.

Departing Japanese troops late in the day at Atsugi Airfield, August 28, 1945.

APPENDIX 'EE'

```
            HEADQUARTERS                              PHP/gdm
         54TH TROOP CARRIER WING
       OFFICE OF THE COMMANDING GENERAL
                APO 929
                                                18 February, 1944.
```

SUBJECT: Commendation.

TO :   MAJOR HERBERT WALDMAN, Commanding Officer, 41st Troop Carrier Squadron, 317th Troop Carrier Group, APO 929 (THRU: Commanding Officer, 317th Troop Carrier Group, APO 929).

    1. It is my understanding that this date marks a very unique anniversary in your squadron's history; namely, the completion of two (2) years of flying operations without a fatal accident to passengers or members of the crew and also without the loss of an airplane.

2. This record is particularly outstanding in view of the valuable contribution which your squadron and others of the 317th Group have made to the war in the Southwest Pacific, first on the mainland and later in New Guinea. Flying to Wau in January of last year, dropping paratroopers at Nadzab in September, and carrying the daily loads to the Markham Valley and north have not been the safest assignments for your C-47's, and it is to the everlasting credit of your pilots, crews, maintenance personnel, and yourself that no serious accidents have been sustained throughout the thirteen months of foreign duty.

3. I wish to take this opportunity to extend my appreciation to every officer and enlisted man in your squadron, and to express the hope that next year will see the record unchanged - and all of us a lot nearer to the successful end of the war.

```
                              PAUL H. PRENTISS,
                              Brig Gen, U.S.A.,
                              Commanding.
```

APPENDIX 'FF'

Synopsis

*Into Darkness: A Pilot's Journey Through Headhunter Territory**

By Edward T. Imparato

A True Story

In 1943 a B-24 crashed mysteriously in a remote region of New Guinea. The Fifth Air Force commander desperately wanted to find out why, because they suspected engineering flaws were at fault and might compromise further lives and missions in air battles with the Axis powers around the world.

The problem was that the crucial evidence was in an unknown location somewhere in the remote, mountainous and uncharted jungles of this vast island where white men had never set foot. Further compounding the dilemma was that this area was known to be inhabited by cannibals and headhunters.

The task of resolving the mystery in the face of these dangers fell to a young Air Force Major. This is the story of that dangerous mission into primitive territory. Unprepared for challenges of this kind of mission, the Major was forced to improvise and organize a way to get to and find the crucial answers on which untold future lives might depend. The initial planning took place at the command Headquarters at Port Moresby, New Guinea.

Chief among the tasks was determining who and what might be needed for the task. It might be likened to looking for a needle in a haystack while you faced danger at any moment from poisoned arrows in the back. Jungles are forbidding enough places, but 10,000 foot mountains blanketed by dense jungle makes the journey many times more arduous and dangerous.

This is the story of an assorted team of American Airmen, Australians and native aborigines, thrown together in a desperate mission with scant experience, little knowledge of each other, and barriers to communication that further intensified the dangers they were to face.

The Americans and Australians had a common language but beyond that the differences were many. But it was the Australians familiarity with the natives and the territory that were to make the Aussies indispensable to the Major. Navigating the dense and forbidding jungles called for a rare experience, capability and courage.

If the differences between the Americans and Australians were large, those between the English speaking members of the party and the natives were lake a gaping chasm. Their primitive language, customs, work habits and fears presented the Major with a formidable challenge in his efforts to get the search party launched into uncharted terrain.

It is in part One that we understand the difficulty of melding this collection of vastly different people into a team with the common goal of finding and reporting back on the downed plane. Part One ends with the search party on its way and headed into headhunter territory.

Fear is a constant companion on Part Two. It is not long before an attack by hostile natives shatters the deceptive calm of the jungle region. Confusion resigns before an uncertain truce is achieved after the brutal clash of wills.

That such brutality could be followed by a "sing-sing" celebration with the entire tribe is one of those strange events that seem to occur amongst these unusual people. We see a people capable of fierce combat and alternatively gentle, playful behavior. Their similarities to the airmen's ideas of civilization were notable yet in other ways their behavior left the American English speaking party dumbfounded.

Throughout the journey thus far, the Europeans had come to rely on their friendly native porters and come to respect their industriousness if still somewhat bemused by their habits and fears. The Major had seen in his "boy" a certain spark of life and enjoyment that engendered a real fondness.

Further into uncharted territory, the terrain became more impossible. And then a second attack, this time from headhunters with poisoned arrows shook the party. Again there was panic and confusion and much yelling and screaming. As before, the attaching headhunters were eventually subdued after a brutal confrontation, but not before the Major's "boy" was killed by an arrow through the side of his head. We can feel the remorse as he hands over for burial this boy of eight who had barely begun to live.

And finally high in the mountains of deepest New Guinea, the party's efforts bear fruit with the location of the downed plane. And just when success is within their grasp, a third attack by hostile natives embroils them in a fight for survival. This time one of the American officers takes a poisoned arrow and later succumbs despite the search party's superiority in fire power then a speedy return to Port Moresby where another tragedy, with sad and odd turns took place for the young Major and his teams missions very end.

It was with careful and meticulous searching that they locate the crucial tail section of the plane and recover from the rudder area the tell-tale sheared bolts that were to prove conclusively in later tests to be the culprits in the mysterious crash.

No one can tell what would have happened had not this valiant group of men had the courage and stamina to complete this dangerous mission and provided valuable knowledge that helped to keep the bombers in the air all over the world. This is the story of personal heroism in a primitive and uncharted world.

---

*©1995 Edward T. Imparato. Published by Howell Press, Inc., 1147 River Road, Suite 2, Charlottesville, Virginia 22901.

APPENDIX 'GG'

SYNOPSIS

*RESCUE FROM SHANGRI-LA**

By Edward T. Imparato

A TRUE STORY

In shock and intense pain, Maggie Hastings stumbled clear of the wreckage of the flaming C-47 in which 24 passengers and crew had set off earlier from Hollandia, New Guinea for a weekend holiday. The odor of burning flesh permeated the air and she could still hear the moans and screams of the others just minutes before the plane had plowed into the mountainside in a desolate, unreachable, dense jungle of Central New Guinea. Maggie, one of only five survivors — two of whom would succumb within 24 hours — was badly burned. It was the beginning of a nightmare, one of the most dramatic and fascinating incidents in World War II. The story of this lovely young WAC and her two surviving companions' ordeal in headhunter territory and the details of their amazing rescue fascinated the world and filled the headlines in the spring of 1945.

The day was May 13, 1945 at Hollandia, New Guinea. MacArthur's forces along with Admiral Nimitz's massive navy were heavily engaged in softening Japanese defenses on the island surrounding the approaches to Japan and Okinawa. Okinawa was under heavy siege by Nimitz's forces. Okinawa was the last bastion of Japanese strength short of Japan itself. Then a tragedy gripped the United States like no other incident in World War II. A tiny young woman lay seriously injured on a distant jungle mountainside, the result of an airplane crash at the approach to Hidden Valley, New Guinea. The location was 140 miles southeast of MacArthur's Headquarters at Hollandia, which is on the north coast of New Guinea.

The morning was one of eager anticipation for the young woman — the opportunity to see a civilization of stone-age people that few in this world have ever seen. The day was going to be filled with excitement — a day to remember. Maggie dressed hurriedly. There were things to do at the office before making it to the airplane. The take-off was set for one-o'clock — right after lunch. Maggie thought constantly about the afternoon's mission to fly over Hidden Valley, the Shangri-la of central New Guinea. Even the name Shangri-la was intriguing — the name given to the mysterious and mythical, lush valley in James Hilton's story *Lost Horizon* (New York: Morrow, 1936).

All 24 passengers and crew, off on an R & R weekend, filled with anticipation as the C-47 took off from Santani Air Field at Hollandia, New Guinea that spring Sunday afternoon. As the aircraft ascended to flight altitude of 7,000 feet and leveled off, the pilot, Col. Peter Prossen, left the cockpit and entered the cabin to orient the passengers on the sights and scenes passing below. Everything was serene for more than half an hour and then the pilot advanced power to the engines to initiate a climb to over-fly the lower mountain range that guarded the high pass at Hidden Valley.

Suddenly one of the passengers with considerable flying experience was heard yelling at the top of his lungs, "Pull up, pull up." Lt. John McCollom, an engineer by training, could see through the gathering mist and forming clouds, the ground coming up to meet the plane. Then screams and moans of despair as the aircraft crashed into the mountainside.

For reasons that to this day remain a mystery, the aircraft did not clear the 8,000-foot high barrier mountain ridges guarding the entrance to the pass at Hidden Valley. Of the five survivors of the crash, two were dead within 24 hours. Then there were only three — Margaret Hastings, a WAC corporal, Technical Sergeant Kenneth Decker and 1st Lieutenant John McCollom.

Perhaps it was because of Maggie that this saga received the greatest amount of coverage, both newspapers and radio, than any other single episode of World War II, according to Burrell's Press Clipping Bureau.

Maggie did not notice her scorched legs or the pain. All she knew at that moment was that someone else was alive and he was running toward her. McCollom was his name and he looked like a knight in shining armor to her. Miraculously, McCollom had no injuries. In a moment, Kenneth Decker, barely alive, staggering, wobbly, confused and seriously injured, slowly approached from the front of the still-burning airplane.

The survivors gathered on a small clearing a short distance from the aircraft and McCollom reentered the plane a number of times to carry out two still-living WAC's and all the supplies he could find, such as tarpaulin, aid kits, water and candy.

It was certainly a miracle that the three survived. Now the second miracle occurred. A short 25 yards away was a gully leading to a stream. It was the margin of survival that would sustain them for a period of time.

The dense jungle at and surrounding the crash site would prohibit searching aircraft from discovering the survivors at their present location so as soon as the three injured survivors were settled on tarpaulin and doctored from the aid kits, McCollom, Boy Scout trained, decided to climb a nearby tree to search for a large clearing for easier visibility from the air. He discovered such a clearing about a mile down the mountainside and decided to make the effort to reach it the next day.

McCollom buried the two WAC's at the crash site. He marked the location and then assembled the material gathered from the aircraft and set out for the clearing with the two injured survivors.

The second day, Army Air Force aircraft were heard approaching the area of the crash site giving some encouragement to the survivors. McCollom, using a small hand mirror from the aid kit, tried to get the attention of the aircraft searching the area but failed.

After the difficult and treacherous struggle down the gully to the clearing, the group spread the brightly colored tarps and prayed for discovery. About noon, Wednesday, three days after the crash, an Air Force B-17, circling the area in its search for survivors, spotted the bright orange tarps and the survivors jumping up and down screaming, knowing they could not be heard. The B-17 circled them three times to establish their precise position, dipped its wings in recognition of their discovery, and flew away to Hollandia to begin the rescue effort.

---

*©1997 Edward T. Imparato. Published by Turner Publishing Company, P.O. Box 3101, Paducah, KY 42002- 3101. 1997.

The following day a C-47 flew to the crash site and stopped food, medical supplies and radio equipment. Only one tenth of the supplies were recovered by McCollom.

On the next day, Friday, two Filipino jungle fighters, who were medical aid technicians, were dropped by parachute at the crash site. Radio contact was established with the survivors and the rescue operation began.

Looking into the jungle, Maggie broke into tears at the sight of the two medical technicians who had parachuted into the tangled underbrush two miles away. The medics were concerned at the sight of the survivors who looked emaciated from their five days without real food, yet h ighly animated and joyful for the first sign of the rescue effort.

Meanwhile, back at Hollandia, discussions were underway to try to find a way to bring the survivors out of the jungle. Consultation with Dutch and Australian authorities produced no constructive solutions. The U.S. Navy was called on to survey the feasibility of landing a seaplane on the Belim River which flowed through the Hidden Valley. Their survey proved unsuccessful. Engineers and jungle-wise Australian and Dutch authorities on interior New Guinea advised against attempting to organize a safari to trek into and out of the crash sight as too dangerous. Dense jungle, dangerous, fast-flowing streams and, above all, hostile headhunting cannibals would impede any effort to penetrate their territory.

But one thing was certain. The survivors would have to be brought into Hidden Valley to a location which could easily be supplied by air and secured; an area where medical facilities could be established to care for the injured until a rescue could be arranged.

That a rescue was eventually successful is a testament to the determination, tenacity and courage of the people who made it happen. Even the unique method that was used to finally extricate all the injured and the medical team out of that dense, impenetrable jungle is one of amazing resourcefulness. The daring final stages of the rescue makes the ending of this heroic tale as fascinating as the beginning.

Lt. McCollom with the first native he met.

Natives help turn glider around for pick-up.

APPENDIX 'HH'

SYNOPSIS

MACARTHUR - MELBOURNE TO TOKYO*

By Edward T. Imparato

A TRUE STORY

"One of the greatest gambles in history"
- General Douglas MacArthur

Prophetic words expressed by General Douglas MacArthur to a group of his advisors about the dispatch of a small group of 150 Americans to Tokyo's Atsugi Airfield on August 28, 1945 to test the Emperor's resolve to end hostilities with the allied powers in World War II. MacArthur did not know what was going to happen, nor did the Japanese, and neither did anyone else.

Here are the true facts about the events leading up to the Japanese surrender, the stress and trauma of the actual first flight into Tokyo and the dramatic events after the first flight.

Written by the pilot of the history making flight of Army Air Corps Aircraft C-46 Curtis commando Air Corp Number 7769 into Atsugi, this was the first military contingent to land on Japanese soil by an enemy of Japan in all Japanese history.

This true story tells of the dramatic events that resulted in the original contact with the Emperor on August 15, 1945 - eight days after the Atom Bomb dropped on Hiroshima; the gathering of 14 members of the Japanese high command at MacArthur headquarters in Manila; and the flight itself carrying Col. Charles T. Tench, Chief of MacArthur's negotiating team to Atsugi.

Mac Arthur arrival at Atsugi at 2 p.m., August 30, 1945, aboard a C-54 from Okinawa.

---

*©1997 Edward T. Imparato. Published by White Mane Publishing Company, Inc., P.O. Box 152, Shippensburg, PA 17257

APPENDIX "II"

Final Roster

374th Troop Carrier Group

21st Troop Carrier Squadron Roster of Enlisted Men
1 June 1945

	Name	ASN	Department / Duty	Duty Code
			Master Sergeants	
1.	Barnum, James F.	39011934	Eng-Ap & Eng Mech	747
2.	Bodine, Richard W.	13048602	Eng-Line Chief	2750
3.	Jorgens, William E.	17001023	Eng-Flight Chief	750
4.	Mahoney, John J.	20620324	HQ-1st Sgt, Grnd Safe NCO	502
5.	Morell, Carter P.	34143479	TDY-USA	750
6.	Ptak, Eugene S.	36043095	TDY-USA	750
			Tech Sergeants	
7.	Barrett, Dale L.	17031690	Comm-Comm Chief	542
8.	Barto, Albert J.	13048306	Eng-Parachute Rprman	620
9.	Baum, Charles D.	17019644	Eng-Ap Elec Mech	685
10.	Brookey, Bill E.	18049761	Eng-Ap & Eng Mech	747
11.	Cleveland, Sherwood A.	11029365	Eng-Ap & Elec Mech	685
12.	Davis, Leroy	36054526	Comm-Radar Mech, TC, Sq IFF Inspector	849
13.	Davis, William G., Jr.	6576953	Comm-Radio Opr & Mech	2756
14.	Dusenberry, Donald L.	37130368	Eng-Flt Chief	750
15.	Fast, Forrest L.	18050749	Eng-Ap & Eng Mech	747
16.	Gass, Ford A.	17056304	Opns-Clerk, typist	405
17.	Haverfield, Vincent C.	17034905	Eng-Flt Chief	750
18.	Heywood, Joseph B.	19056632	Eng-AP Inst Mech	686
19.	Holtzclaw, Ray L.	37038246	Eng-Ap Maint Tech	2750
20.	Magyar, Joseph D.	17027423	Eng-Ap Maint Tech	2750
21.	Mattison, Howard E.	32100745	HQ-Adm Spec	502
22.	Spencer, Herbert T.	15062120	Eng-Ap Maint Tech	2750
23.	Stusse, Alvin R.	37019710	Eng-TDY Australia	750
			Staff Sergeants	
24.	Amendola, Joseph F.	33056595	Eng-Ap & Eng Mech	747
25.	Arnold, Henry W.	36121116	Eng-Ap & Eng Mech	747
26.	Aupperle, Kay C.	18069806	Eng-Sheet Metal Worker	555
27.	Baker, Paul C.	13027299	Opns-Clerk, typist	405
28.	Barton, Charles W.	19055862	Eng-Ap & Eng Mech	747
29.	Bien, Robert	16144729	Eng-Ap & Eng Mech	747
30.	Boyce, Ray L.	18038756	Eng-Ap & Eng Mech	747
31.	Brown, William B.	34168987	Eng-Ap & Eng Mech	747
32.	Carman, Richard M.	32536424	Eng-Ap & Eng Mech	2750
33.	Clapp, John P.	19067781	Trans-Truckmaster	014
34.	Clary, Thomas N.	33096490	Eng-Ap & Eng Mech	747
35.	Covington, Robert E., Jr.	38150775	Eng-Ap & Eng Mech	2750
36.	Culligan, James J.	32910460	Eng-Ap & Eng Mech	2750
37.	Devore, Donald E.	32433651	Comm-Radio Opr & Mech	2756
38.	Egle, Harry L.	34152170	Eng-Ap & Eng Mech	747
39.	Harris, Donald A.	17017775	TDY-USA	821
40.	Holder, Herbert E.	13041299	Eng-Ap & Eng Mech	747
41.	Hunter, Joseph P.	37199503	Eng-Ap Inspector	2750
42.	James, David O.	37348656	Comm-T & T Lineman	238
43.	Klein, John E.	32287335	HQ-Stat Clerk	405
44.	Klett, Charles E.	37048663	Eng-Welder, Combination	256
45.	Lumry, Willis M.	20838405	Eng-Ap & Eng Mech	747
46.	McKay, Richard A.	34169715	Comm-Radio Opr & Mech	2756
47.	Odell, Charles E.	37111271	Eng-Ap & Eng Mech	747
48.	Ogden, Robert D.	12066468	Intel-Intel Clerk	631
49.	Olcott, Carlyle G.	36126307	Eng-Ap Dope & Fabric Wkr	548
50.	Perrin, Ronald R.	36177826	Eng-TDY USA	747
51.	Pilkington, William F.	10641081	Comm-Radio Opr & Mech	2756
52.	Pricer, Robert B.	33283234	Eng-Ap & Eng Mech	747
53.	Rea, Billy A.	38433219	Comm-Radio Opr & Mech	2756
54.	Reisch, Daniel E.	32375135	Opns-Adm Spec	502
55.	Skodis, John P.	33231947	Mess-Mess Sergeant	824
56.	Sloszewski, Harry	36531845	Comm-Radio Opr & Mech	2756
57.	Sternhell, Samuel	32436450	Comm-Radio Opr & Mech	2756
58.	Thornton, Kenneth L.	19004499	Eng-Ap Maint Tech	2750
59.	Tourkin, Richard B.	33375603	Comm-Radio Opr & Mech	2756
60.	Upchurch, Henry T.	18209386	Eng-Ap Maint Tech	2750
61.	Walters, James M.	38410865	Tech Supply-AAF Sup Tech	826

Sergeants

#	Name	Serial	Assignment	Code
62.	Baker, Robert C.	34700193	Eng-Ap Maint Tech	2750
63.	Barker, Owen	17014447	Eng-Parachute Rprman	620
64.	Beecher, Donald A.	12034271	Eng-Ap Eng. Tech	747
65.	Bemb, John E.	36580533	Comm-Radio Opr & Mech	2756
66.	Beville, Roy F., Jr.	6953241	HQ-Barber	590
67.	Bliss, Edgar J.	17016416	Comm-Telephone Opr	650
68.	Brown, Everton A.	19088460	Eng-Ap Prop Mech	687
69.	Cain, William C.	16144258	Eng-Ap Maint Tech	2750
70.	Carbone, Leo F.	36044583	Mess-Cook	060
71.	Courtney, Robert W.	15340476	Eng-Ap Maint Tech	2750
72.	Cross, Herbert W.	37261032	Comm-Radar Mechanic	849
73.	Duffy, Otto C.	15016696	Medical Corpsman	657
74.	Eads, John N.	37132948	TDY-USA	590
75.	Felts, Walker L.	38444077	Med-Adm Spec	673
76.	Foreman, Stanley M.	39041931	Eng-Ap Maint Tech	2750
77.	Gainer, Jack W.	15089266	Trans-Chauffeur	345
78.	Giles, Eugene R.	35106610	Sq Supply-Supply Clk	835
79.	Godwin, Bert A.	19175493	Comm-Radio Opr & Mech	2756
80.	Graham, Andrew C.	33207290	Mess-Cook	060
81.	Greene, James D.	34188119	Eng-Ap & Eng Mech	747
82.	Hansen, Raymond L.	37263334	Eng-Ap Maint Tech	2750
83.	Harper, James D.	34187982	Opns-Clerk, Typist	405
84.	Heavin, Harvey E.	39262813	Eng-Ap Elec Mech	685
85.	Hershey, David S.	13048267	Mess-Cook	060
86.	Hessler, Edward I.	13048386	Eng-Ap & Eng Mech	747
87.	Hill, David C.	18118955	Comm-Radio Opr & Mech	2756
88.	Hoggard, Joseph C.	34117304	Eng-Ap & Eng Mech	747
89.	Hojnacki, John J.	36503222	Trans-Auto Equip Mech	014
90.	Holland, John A.	13052469	Eng-Parachute Rprman	620
91.	Hooper, Alvis C.	38435388	Comm-Radio Opr & Mech	2756
92.	Jones, John D.	15383185	Comm-Radio Opr & Mech	2756
93.	Kelley, Jack L.	12031310	Trans-Chauffeur	345
94.	Ketchem, Charles E.	37086831	Mess-Cook	060
95.	Keysock, Peter	13052603	Mess-Cook	060
96.	King, James Jr.	36503459	HQ-Duty NCO	566
97.	Kodatt, Joseph	34402013	Comm-Radio Mechanic	754
98.	Koester, Duane C.	37275158	HQ-File Clerk	055
99.	Lamb, Fred E.	33601801	Comm-Radio Opr & Mech	2756
100.	McDaniel, John W.	34168926	DS Enroute to Join	824
101.	McGraw, Donald P.	32316436	Eng-AP Armorer	511
102.	Mikus, John T.	12173814	Comm-Radio Opr & Mech	2756
103.	Morello, James G.	32334001	HQ-Carpenter, general	050
104.	Olson, Donlin C.	37426913	Comm-Radio Mechanic	754
105.	Olson, Richard J.	39317346	Trans-Auto Equip Mech	014
106.	Price, William M.	34643757	Comm-Radio Mechanic	754
107.	Radziewicz, Bruno J.	36519731	Eng-Ap & Eng Mech	747
108.	Rinn, Edmond V., Jr.	38183903	Tech-Supply-Stock Clk	835
109.	Roberts, Harold E.	18209595	Eng-Ap Maint Tech	2750
110.	Rothman, Morris	32303208	Sq Supply-Supply Clerk	835
111.	Schmidt, Merlin	38107455	Comm-Radio Opr & Mech	2756
112.	Schwartz, Herman	32801543	Comm-Radio Opr & Mech	2756
113.	Smith, Lloyd S.	33248478	Eng-Ap Maint Tech	2750
114.	Smith, Lyle S.	16009262	Eng-Ap Maint Tech	2750
115.	Summerville, Andrew	19149135	HQ-PX Steward	055
116.	Townsend, Dallas W.	15320076	Comm-Teletype Opr	237
117.	Urban, Robert J.	13092347	Comm-Radio Mechanic	754
118.	Ushock, Alfred J.	33623950	Comm-Radio Opr & Mech	2756
119.	Van Winkle, Kenneth G.	37477612	Comm-Radio Opr & Mech	2756
120.	Weintraub, Bernard	13152120	Eng-Ap & Eng Mech	747
121.	Weitzen, Julius	31170764	Comm-Radio Mechanic	754
122.	Wexler, Seymour	39393682	Comm-Radar Mech, TC	849
123.	Wilbon, John B.	33643271	Eng-Ap Maint Tech	2750
124.	Williams, Odell F.	33634608	Eng-Ap Maint Tech	2750
125.	Wummer, Edwin F.	13125117	Comm-Radio Opr & Mech	2756

Corporals

#	Name	Serial	Assignment	Code
126.	Baalson, Arnold B.	37176562	Eng-Ap & Eng Mech	747
127.	Barker, Basil H.	35329956	Trans-Dispatcher	055
128.	Bartell, Alfred A.	32465470	Sq Supply-Supply Clerk	835
129.	Betts, John M.	12209140	Eng-Ap & Eng Mech	747
130.	Bormolini, William A.	13179880	Eng-Ap Maint Tech	2750
131.	Cassell, Alfonzo	33534775	Mess-Cook	060
132.	Cassell, Alonzo	33534780	Mess-Cook	060
133.	Colucci, Vito V.	32854264	Eng-Ap Inst Mech	686
134.	Curr, Vernon F.	39682761	Eng-Ap & Eng Mech	747
135.	Cyphers, Howard C.	17113766	Eng-Ap Maint Tech	2750
136.	Dickens, Raymond E.	18118628	Eng-Clerk, Typist	405
137.	Dorsa, Anthony J.	32778900	Eng-Ap Maint Tech	2750
138.	Douglas, Frederick E.	33509456	Eng-Ap Maint Tech	2750

139.	Farlow, Marshall W.	34303352	HQ-Duty Soldier	590
140.	Gates, Neal P.	13048293	TDY-Australia	055
141.	Gibson, James L.	39416603	Comm-Radio Opr & Mech	2756
142.	Giovannelli, Nicholas	33691690	Eng-Ap Maint Tech	2750
143.	Gosch, Louis F.	31332910	Comm-Radio Opr & Mech	2756
144.	Gracia, Ernest G.	39853796	Trans-Auto Equip Mech	014
145.	Griswold, Elvin J., Jr.	18217311	Intel-Clerk, General	055
146.	Hayden, Harold R.	35634749	Eng-Ap Maint Tech	2750
147.	Heckner, Charles D.	36818484	Comm-Radio Opr & Mech	2756
148.	Hill, Mack E., Jr.	34607650	Mess-Cook	060
149.	Hjelm, Carl F.	17114115	Comm-Radio Opr & Mech	2756
150.	Holmes, Edwin B., II	31427522	Eng-Ap Maint Tech	2750
151.	Hover, James V.	35589165	Eng-Ap Eng Mech	747
152.	Hummell, Braden A.	13048279	Mess-Cook's Helper	590
153.	Hunter, Charles W.	19170874	Comm-Radio Opr & Mech	2756
154.	Hyatt, Sargent A.	32926819	Eng-Ap & Eng Mech	747
155.	Keleher, John L., Jr.	32930666	Eng-Ap Maint Tech	2750
156.	Kelleher, Cornelius J.	31085745	Trans-Auto Equip Opr	345
157.	Krasovec, Albert J.	16138794	Eng-Ap & Eng Mech	747
158.	Kysela, Paul F.	35532649	HQ-Clerk, Typist	405
159.	Labate, Frank E.	12190695	Comm-Radio Opr & Mech	2756
160.	Lyon, Everett W.	19143973	Comm-Radio Opr & Mech	2756
161.	Maloney, John C.	36598509	Eng-Ap Maint Tech	2750
162.	Mathews, William E.	35141572	Eng-Ap Maint Tech	2750
163.	Meyer, George	15130502	Comm-Radio Opr & Mech	2756
164.	Morgan, David A., Jr.	13086143	Comm-Cryptograph Tech	805
165.	Morgan, Paul K.	17005893	Comm-Radio Opr & Mech	2756
166.	Neelis, Melvin W.	36182300	Trans-Chauffeur	345
167.	Nolan, Hugh P.	32140699	TDY-USA	055
168.	Norman, William J.	17063512	Comm-Radio Opr & Mech	2756
169.	O'Malley, Coleman C.	12075936	Comm-Radio Opr & Mech	2756
170.	Perovich, George	19021239	Comm-Radio Opr & Mech	2756
171.	Pruss, Norbert J.	36591756	Eng-Ap & Mech	747
172.	Rae, James	35798002	Eng-Ap Maint Tech	2750
173.	Raspet, Harry F.	37349138	Eng-Ap & Eng Mech	747
174.	Rosen, Bernard S.	13055231	Comm-Telephone Opr	650
175.	Ross, Harvey D., Jr.	35803896	Comm-Radio Opr & Mech	2756
176.	Sampson, Tillman R.	37097849	Trans-Auto Equip Opr	345
177.	Schuch, Elverton E.	36590782	Eng-Ap Inst Mech	686
178.	Sherrell, Forney E.	34802390	Eng-Ap Maint Tech	2750
179.	Shope, Lawrence C.	15075319	Trans-Auto Equip Mech	014
180.	Shy, Gerald E.	39528672	HQ-Unit Mail Clerk	055
181.	Spisak, Frank A.	12144820	Eng-AP Maint Tech	2750
182.	Stanford, Arthur W.	6955963	HQ-Clerk, Typist	405
183.	Stevens, Wallace E.	39700204	Eng-Ap Prop Mech	687
184.	Stoeser, Benjamin J.	37557230	Eng-Ap Maint Tech	2750
185.	Strebeck, Andrew E., Jr.	33717676	Comm-Radio Opr & Mech	2756
186.	Surber, Herman E.	15328987	Comm-Radar Mech, Nav	853
187.	Tagliaferri, George J.	32325404	Mess-Cook	060
188.	Vuletich, Nicholas	33672790	Eng-Ap Maint Tech	2750
189.	Walczak, Walter E.	35053058	Eng-Ap Maint Tech	2750
190.	Waldrop, William O.	34659483	Eng-Ap Maint Tech	2750
191.	Watson, George L.	39610972	Eng-Ap Maint Tech	2750
192.	Wells, Cecil L.	37199609	Med-Ambulance Chauffeur	345
193.	Werner, Henry J.	13126845	Eng-Ap Maint Tech	2750
194.	Whitten, Jerome	13152276	Comm-Radio Opr & Mech	2756
195.	Wilke, Gottlieb R.	18190987	Eng-Sheet Metal Worker	555
196.	Wilson, John A.	16030383	Eng-Ap & Eng Mech	747
197.	Wood, Arthur E., Jr.	19160597	Comm-Radar Mech, Nav	853
198.	Yost, Russell H.	33830538	Comm-Radar Mech, Nav	853
199.	Young, Clyde E.	18118416	Eng-Welder, combination	256
200.	Young, Robert B., Jr.	15305727	Eng-Ap Maint Tech	2750
201.	Zierke, Robert R.	36246203	Eng-Ap & Eng Mech	747
202.	Ziyacz, George	33360414	Eng-Ap & Eng Mech	747
			Privates First Class	
203.	Alvis, Clifford B.	37444143	Medical Corpsman	657
204.	Anderson, Albert G.	19143431	HQ-Basic	590
205.	Anderson, Ervin A.	37274485	HQ-Basic	590
206.	Belford, Charles E.	32900922	Trans-Auto Equip Opr	345
207.	Bielitsky, Raphael	33789746	Comm-Radio Opr & Mech	2756
208.	Collman, Robert L.	19170183	Trans-Auto Equip Opr	345
209.	Contreras, Robert H.	19039417	Mess-Baker	060
210.	Curtsinger, Foster M.	35701175	Eng-Ap Maint Tech	2750
211.	Damon, Gerald C.	17069413	Eng-Parachute Rprman	620
212.	Fredricksen, Fred	39031341	HQ-Basic	590
213.	Laboch, Leon	12169907	Comm-Radio Opr & Mech	2756
214.	Mitchell, High T., Jr.	38510653	Tech Supply-Stock Clk	835
215.	Pallas, Nicholas C.	32891439	Eng-Ap Maint Tech	2750
216.	Pantos, Manuel	32707804	Eng-Ap & Eng Mech	747

#	Name	ASN	Duty	Code
217.	Samuel, Wilbur E.	18209683	HQ-Power Plant Opr	590
218.	Schneider, Elwood F.	33387596	Mess-Cook	060
219.	Staich, Stephen	13114110	Eng-Ap Maint Tech	2750
220.	Tighe, James J.	32915311	Eng-Ap Maint Tech	2750
221.	Woodman, Robert C.	14044646	Eng-Ap Maint Tech	2750

Privates

#	Name	ASN	Duty	Code
222.	Fratti, Nello J.	33356034	Eng-Clerk, Typist	405
223.	Martinez, Henry A.	39280335	Mess-Cook	060
224.	McClendon, William H., Jr.	14140593	Mess-Cook	060
225.	McFadin, Floyd P., Jr.	39041604	Eng-Ap & Eng Mech	747
226.	Olsen, Robert H.	39020831	Comm-Telephone Opr	650
227.	Rock, Rue C.	38089360	HQ-Power Plant Opr	590
228.	Schnoop, Leon F.	32852654	Trans-Auto Equip Opr	345

21st Troop Carrier Squadron Roster of Officers

#	Name	ASN	Flying Status	Duty	Duty Code
	Captains				
1.	Rowland, Conrad A.	0-790039	P	Commanding	1051
2.	Copeland, Bert F.	0-683409	P	Test Pilot; Asst Eng O	1051
3.	Ferry, William J.	0-856455	NP	Engineering Officer	4823
4.	Flaherty, Wayne E.	0-679064	P	Check Pilot	1051
5.	Fortin, Floyd F.	0-737758	P	Asst Flt Ldr, Flt A, Check Pilot	1051
6.	Grossman, Herbert D.	0-649056	NP	Intel O, Censor, Sq Historical O	9300
7.	Guerrero, Arthur	0-745887	P	Flt Ldr, Flt A, Check Pilot	1051
8.	Holeman, Harry G.	0-727466	P	Check Pilot	1051
9.	Holstein, Elmer M.	0-792992	P	Pilot, Exec O, Sq Council, Sum Court O	1051
10.	Kott, Edward G.	0-856069	NP	Comm O, Unit Crypt Security Officer	0200
11.	Nellor, Joseph G.	0-888773	P	Pilot (TDY T'ville)	1051
12.	Percival, Edward L.	0-564009	NP	Supply O, Armament O, Squadron Council	4000
13.	Thomas, Charles J.	0-669632	P	Check Pilot	1051
	1st Lieutenants				
14.	Brogden, Paul M.	0-753188	P	Flt Ldr, Flt F	1051
15.	Chambers, William J.	0-387513	N	Navigator	1034
16.	Dawson, William R.	0-1313383	P	Pilot, Asst Adjutant	1051
17.	Eken, Joseph S.	0-798267	P	Flt Lder, Flt H	1051
18.	Falkinburg, Timothy W., Jr.	0-833669	P	Pilot, Asst Mess O, Asst Flt Ldr, Flt E	1051
19.	Fitzgerald, Robert W.	0-721682	P	Asst Opns O, Asst Flt Ldr, Flt D	1051
20.	Glass, Edward T.	0-810864	P	Copilot, Asst Opns O, Wts and Bal Officer	1051
21.	Glasscock, David G.	0-2058779	P	Flt Ldr, Flt B	1051
22.	Graebner, Paul N.	0-2058786	P	Asst Flt Ldr, Flt H	1051
23.	Hale, Ralph B.	0-821699	P	Pilot	1051
24.	Horton, Eugene P.	0-677008	P	Pilot	1051
25.	Hunt, Philip W.	0-2036772	NP	Adj, Stat Cont O, Pers O, War Bond O, Insur O, Squadron Council	2110
26.	Johnston, Robert R.	0-464166	P	Flt Ldr, Flt C	1051
27.	Miller, Charles Jr.	0-780674	P	Flt Ldr, Flt D, Asst Eng Officer	1051
28.	Modelevsky, Hyman	0-805095	P	Flt Ldr, Flt E	1051
29.	Olney, Richard B.	0-395752	P	Opns O, Unit Gas O, Air Move Control O	2161
30.	Sanders, Clarence	0-831278	P	Asst Flt Ldr, Flt G	1051
31.	Taylor, Robert L.	0-769592	P	Pilot	1051
32.	Weiss, Alan B.	0-820380	P	Asst Flt Ldr, Flt C	1051
33.	Woods, Richard L.	0-675017	P	Flt Ldr, Flt G	1051
	2nd Lieutenants				
34.	Aldrich, Robert C.	0-857339	P	Pilot, Asst Comm O, IFF O, Utilities O	1051
35.	Arthur, David R., Jr.	0-836552	P	Copilot	1051
36.	Brown, Douglas K.	0-720073	P	Pilot, PX Officer	1051
37.	Buckingham, Mervin B.	0-771287	P	Copilot	1051
38.	Cederberg, Dallas W.	0-774537	P	Pilot, Asst Supply O	1051
39.	Cowell, Theodore C.	0-775809	P	Copilot, Pub Rel O, Range Officer	1051
40.	Cullen, Thomas D.	0-765937	P	Copilot, Asst Opns O	1051
41.	Danner, Dillon E.	0-1030648	P	Copilot, Mess O	1051
42.	Doane, Byron L.	0-774577	P	Pilot, Asst Supply O	1051
43.	Dudley, Orie L.	0-765943	P	Pilot, Trans O	1051
44.	Ellwood, William L.	0-2071565	N	Navigator	1034
45.	Enloe, Steven L.	0-769407	P	Pilot, Asst Comm O	1051
46.	Fleming, Forrest	0-769413	P	Pilot, Asst Intel O	1051
47.	Goodliffe, Junior L.	0-769422	P	Pilot; Asst Eng O	1051
48.	Graff, James R.	0-831155	P	Pilot	1051
49.	Ilgen, Luther P., Jr.	0-780608	P	Copilot, Fire Marshall	1051
50.	Johnson, Jay B.	0-769458	P	Copilot	1051
51.	Johnson, Joseph S.	0-721105	P	Copilot, Asst PX O	1051
52.	Kaufman, Albert A.	0-779153	P	Copilot	1051
53.	Kirchhoff, Donald E.	0-835219	P	Pilot, Spec Serv O	1051
54.	Kysor, Saul T., Jr.	0-2007379	P	Pilot	1051

55.	Lair, Thelbert V.	O-720525	P	Pilot, Asst Supply O		1051
56.	Leatherman, David S.	O-776346	P	Pilot, Asst Pub Rel O		1051
57.	Lowrance, Frank S.	O-836620	P	Pilot, Asst unit Gas O		1051
58.	Ludwig, Christian J.	O-778520	P	Copilot, Asst Sq Historical Officer		1051
59.	Magee, Harold J.	O-720305	P	Copilot, Asst Comm O		1051
60.	Marshall, Allen R.	O-778869	P	Copilot, Asst Adj		1051
61.	Martin, Lee M.J.	O-697152	P	Copilot, Asst Mess O		1051
62.	Mitchell, Donald R.	O-2007415	P	Pilot		1051
63.	Olker, Robert D.	O-836629	P	Pilot, Asst Trans O		1051
64.	Paternostro, Emanuel	O-782612	P	Pilot, Pers Equip O		1051
65.	Peach, Homer E.	O-769543	P	Asst Flt Ldr, Flt F		1051
66.	Peterson, Alvin L.	O-769544	P	Pilot, Asst Trans O.		1051
67.	Plank, Dale L.	O-721857	P	Copilot		1051
68.	Porrello, Salvatore J.	O-2007372	P	Asst Flt Ldr, Flt B		1051
69.	Root, Owen N.	O-720347	P	Pilot, Ground Safety O		1051
70.	Sampsel, Donald E.	O-2059122	P	Copilot		1051
71.	Sedgewick, Richard D.	O-835544	P	Copilot		1051
72.	Severyn, Henry J.	O-777844	P	Copilot		1051
73.	Shaw, Billy L.	O-780742	P	Pilot, Recognition O		1051
74.	Showalter, Jack F.	O-1312724	P	Pilot, Asst Intel O		1051
75.	Simon, LeRoy J.	O-2071724	N	Navigator, Asst Intel O		1034
76.	Taylor, Ralph J.	O-696609	P	Pilot, I & E O		1051
77.	Taylor, Thomas R., Jr.	O-818974	P	Copilot, Asst Eng O		1051
78.	Weller, Richard R.	O-781476	P	Copilot, Asst Sup O		1051
79.	Williams, Clayton R.	O-833460	P	Copilot		1051
80.	Wood, James R.	O-2058906	P	Copilot, Asst Pers Equip O		1051
81.	Bell, John D., Jr.	T-4176	P	Copilot		1051
82.	Ehrne, Richard J.	T-2907	P	Pilot		1051
83.	Gleason, James E.	T-3484	P	Pilot, Asst Pers Equip O		1051
84.	Linvall, Allen R., Jr.	T-3626	P	Copilot		1051
85.	Manley, Charles L.	T-4205	P	Copilot, Asst Spec Svc O		1051
86.	Minvielle, Damon P.	T-4212	P	Copilot		1051
87.	Rash, Eugene H.	T-133922	N	Navigator, Asst Intel O		1034
88.	Smith, Edward K.	T-3637	P	Copilot, Asst Arm O		1051
89.	Spellman, Harry M.	T-4478	P	Copilot		1051

NOTE: P Pilot   NP Non-Pilot   N Navigator

22nd Troop Carrier Squadron Roster of Enlisted Men

	Name	ASN	Department / Duty	Duty Code
			1st Sergeant	
1.	Busby, Fred L.	6925342	HQ-1st Sgt	502
			Master Sergeants	
2.	Green, Victor V.	19023450	Eng-Maint Chief	750
3.	Hendrickson, Gordon	15117883	Eng-Flight Chief	2750
4.	Meeks, Charles R.	15329644	Eng-Flight Chief	2750
5.	Painter, Pascal P., Jr.	14071120	Eng-Line Chief	2750
6.	Quinn, Charles D.	37069296	Eng-Tech Insp	750
7.	Stutler, Isaac W., Jr.	35279191	Eng-Flight Chief	2750
			Tech Sergeants	
8.	Arkell, Edward M.	36505197	Eng-Crew Chief	2750
9.	Behrens, George H.	36343904	Comm-Radar Mech TC	849
10.	Biondo, Nunzio E.	12006010	Eng-Crew Chief DS US	2750
11.	Brynan, Julius	6907925	Eng-Crew Chief	2750
12.	Feather, Francis W.	13021599	Eng-Crew Chief	2750
13.	Gaffney, Thomas R.	32316193	Eng-Crew Chief	2750
14.	Gunningham, James G.	19056715	Eng-Crew Chief	2750
15.	Hancock, Kenneth E.	37575801	Eng-Crew Chief	2750
16.	Hengen, Lester W.	19148253	Eng-Crew Chief	2750
17.	Hodges, Carroll R.	6268263	Eng-Crew Chief	2750
18.	Huntington, Glen E.	36164567	Eng-Crew Chief	2750
19.	Johnson, William E., Jr.	14082000	Eng-Crew Chief	2750
20.	Jones, Oscar D.	34186501	Eng-Crew Chief	2750
21.	Lenartz, Carlton E.	36155120	Eng-Crew Chief	2750
22.	Litke, Albert F.	16020585	HQ-Clerk	055
23.	McCarthy, Daniel T., Jr.	33087795	HQ-Clerk	055
24.	Parrish, Conrad C.	15332667	Eng-Crew Chief	2750
25.	Senseney, Max W.	15085604	Intel-Intel Spec	631
26.	Trentacosta, Frank T.	32617997	Comm-Rad Opr	2756
27.	Watson, Elton V.	6261027	Opns-Parachute Rig	620
			Staff Sergeants	
28.	Avants, Alvin	19049180	Mess-Baker	017
29.	Clayton, Charles W.	39383462	HQ-Carpenter	050
30.	Darpiniae, Ara	19065302	Trans-Auto Equip Mech	014
31.	DeCorleto, Arthur P.	11073531	Eng-Crew Chief	2750

#	Name	Serial	Role	Code
32.	Edwards, Robert A.	31208916	Comm-Rad Opr	2756
33.	Ellis, Joe B.	14072010	HQ-Adm NCO TDY US	502
34.	Forrest, Robert R.	34205736	Opns-Parachute Rig	620
35.	Freund, Isidore	12156436	Comm-Rad Opr	2756
36.	Fruauff, Robert H.	12141396	Eng-Crew Chief	2750
37.	Garrison, Frederick C.	32075430	Eng-Machinist	114
38.	Green, Walter R.	39601781	Comm-Rad Opr	2756
39.	Harter, Max E.	16148586	Eng-Crew Chief	2750
40.	Helms, Arthur L.	18062100	HQ-Clerk	055
41.	Jackson, Joseph S.	6830288	Eng-Adm NCO	502
42.	Kalness, Donald L.	19077979	Trans-Trans NCO	014
43.	Kiernan, Paul H.	12096709	Comm-Rad Opr	2756
44.	Lauver, Abram B., Jr.	13157532	Opns-Adm NCO	502
45.	Marks, Thomas J.	15334651	Eng-Crew Chief	2750
46.	Maslak, John J.	15377056	Comm-Rad Opr	2756
47.	Power, Clayton E.	35403283	Eng-Crew Chief	750
48.	Petersen, Rex B.	19072650	Eng-Crew Chief	750
49.	Price, Eugene M.	38183454	Eng-Crew Chief	2750
50.	Pulcinello, Nick	13048258	Sq Supply-Clerk	835
51.	Rogers, William R.	38425530	Eng-Crew Chief	2750
52.	Shippey, Jack D.	36408528	Comm-Rad Opr	2756
53.	Steeves, Gerald O.	31316992	Comm-Rad Opr	2756
54.	Stiltz, Harry L.	13051213	Comm-Rad Opr	2756
55.	Stonerock, Ermil E.	35270617	Eng-Crew Chief	2750
56.	Stoner, Ray W., Jr.	39253348	Eng-Crew Chief	2750
57.	Storey, Rufus K.	38426868	Eng-Crew Chief	2750
58.	Sullivan, William A.	11033541	Eng-Crew Chief	2750
59.	Surplus, Laverne J.	39088119	Mess-Mess Sgt	824
60.	Taylor, Frank B.	6744385	Eng-Asst Tech Insp	750
61.	Thran, Hermann J.	37277925	Medics-Med Adm Spec	673
62.	Tucker, William B.	17164197	Comm-Radar Mech TC	849
63.	Tymchak, William A.	15376965	Comm-Rad Opr	2756
64.	Wheeler, William A.	34110940	Eng-Crew Chief	750
65.	White, James M.	34107737	Eng-Crew Chief	750
66.	Wicklund, Vimar A.	37313664	Comm-Rad Opr	2756
67.	Wilgus, Carl A.	15070778	Comm-Rad Opr	2756
68.	Wooten, Ralph M.	37230397	Comm-Rad Opr	2756

Sergeants

#	Name	Serial	Role	Code
69.	Altamiran, Julian P.	19062576	Comm-Clerk	055
70.	Ashcraft, George V.	35274571	Trans-Auto Equip Opr	345
71.	Beam, Max E.	35099292	Comm-Rad Opr	2756
72.	Beckley, Charles L.	15089365	Eng-Electrical Spec	685
73.	Boardman, Carl G., Jr.	11068098	Eng-Crew Chief	2750
74.	Boyd, William	15115124	Comm-Rad Opr	2756
75.	Brite, Charles E.	32819319	Comm-Rad Opr	2756
76.	Cohen, Benjamin	11101172	Eng-Sheet Metal Worker	555
77.	Cordtz, Raymond B.	35537059	Comm-Cryptographer	805
78.	Davis, John W.	14174759	Eng-Prop Speck	687
79.	Dickens, Frank	18178538	Eng-Crew Chief	2750
80.	Duke, Joseph B.	38350630	Eng-Crew Chief	2750
81.	Eskenazi, David S.	32716066	Comm-Rad Opr	2756
82.	Fible, Harold J.	15300377	Comm-Rad Opr	2756
83.	Gentile, Carmelo P.	32519614	Eng-Armorer	511
84.	Glover, Allan B., Jr.	35560136	Comm-Rad Opr	2756
85.	Halutick, Charles	13048421	Eng-Crew Chief	2750
86.	Hamill, Martin	32877003	Eng-Crew Chief	2750
87.	Harvey, Edwin R.	35499563	Comm-Rad Opr	2756
88.	Heltsley, Harry S.	35354864	Comm-Rad Opr	2756
89.	Holeman, Cecil C.	34289935	Comm-Rad Opr	2756
90.	Kasunic, Joe D.	35285745	Eng-Ap Mech	747
91.	Klinar, Martin C.	33256592	Comm-Rad Opr	2756
92.	Knowles, Jimmie V.	35255157	Mess-Cook	060
93.	Lamberson, Floyd E.	15081704	Eng-Electrical Spec	685
94.	Lattner, Edward J.	13060915	Eng-Crew Chief	2750
95.	Liebert, Charles L.	35476020	Comm-Radar Mech TC	849
96.	Maaser, Otto H.	37236559	Mess-Cook	060
97.	Martin, Dan	33210753	Eng-AP Mech	747
98.	McCall, James W., Jr.	34762017	Eng-Crew Chief	2750
99.	McCown, Jerry C.	36073091	Opns-Clerk Typist	405
100.	McNiven, William D.	39508077	Opns-Tech Supply Clerk	835
101.	Metzger, Robert C.	33634987	Comm-Rad Opr	2756
102.	Middleton, Archie C.	32755487	Eng-Clerk	055
103.	Milak, Stephen C.	15074664	Comm-Rad Mech TDY US	754
104.	Mosby, Travis H.	36330662	Eng-Ap Mech	747
105.	Nichols, Richard V., Jr.	32755639	Eng-Instrument Spec	686
106.	Nickelson, Jack J.	38072903	Trans-Auto Equip Opr	345
107.	Payne, Warren H.	34313346	Eng-Fabric & Dope Worker	548
108.	Peoples, Jesse E.	14069872	Mess-Cook TDY US	060
109.	Perry, Wilton W.	17063300	Comm-Rad Opr	2756

#	Name	Serial	Role	Code
110.	Phelps, Warren G.	38183854	HQ-Clerk	055
111.	Pirtz, Joseph	36243990	Eng-Elec Spec	685
112.	Pulice, Frank J.	36148833	Eng-Ap Mech	747
113.	Richards, Thomas J.	13055632	Mess-Cook	060
114.	Rogers, Jack D.	34811022	Eng-Crew Chief	2750
115.	Seddon, Norman A.	36502067	HQ-File Clerk TDY US	055
116.	Serotta, Seymour	39258408	Eng-Ap Mech	747
117.	Skalmoski, Joseph D.	16092169	Intel-Clerk	055
118.	Smith, John F.	12182060	Eng-Crew Chief	2750
119.	Tiffany, William H.	34782432	Comm-Rad Opr	2756
120.	Tilden, Don W.	37412699	Comm-Teletype Mech	239
121.	Viton, Leonard A.	35060203	Comm-Rad Opr	2756
122.	Ward, Verley R.	18085564	Eng-Crew Chief	2750
123.	Wedow, Lawrence C.	15085686	Supply-Clerk	055
124.	Whitesell, Harold J.	36054576	HQ-Duty NCO	590
125.	Wright, Orville C.	35798964	Eng-Crew Chief	2750
126.	Wuchina, Thomas E.	33671441	Comm-Rad Opr	2756

Corporals

#	Name	Serial	Role	Code
127.	Alms, Robert	33691266	Eng-Crew Chief	2750
128.	Ames, Earl E.	33787975	Intel-Clerk	055
129.	Baer, Sidney	32435367	Comm-Rad Opr	2756
130.	Bollinger, Clarence A.	32767890	Mess-Cook	060
131.	Buchner, Joe E.	17143360	Eng-Crew Chief	2750
132.	Casteen, Edgar J.	34675536	Eng-Crew Chief	2750
133.	Cieslewicz, Raymond	32844321	Comm-Rad Opr	2756
134.	Clark, James E.	33759966	Comm-Rad Opr	2756
135.	Clark, Lewis C.	34700889	Trans-Auto Equip Opr	345
136.	Conway, Gerard T.	12181913	Comm-Rad Opr	756
137.	Danielak, Michael C.	31332926	Eng-Crew Chief	2750
138.	Divito, Vincent	42000310	Eng-Crew Chief	2750
139.	Duschinski, David D.	35647180	Comm-Rad Opr	2756
140.	Elkins, Warren J.	38209785	Trans-Auto Equip Mech	014
141.	Elliott, Arkley B.	34736323	Eng-Crew Chief	2750
142.	Elmquist, Herbert E.	16067117	Trans-Auto Equip Opr	345
143.	Farnquist, Donald K.	37262568	Tech Supply-Clerk	835
144.	Fitzgerald, Richard S.	37703420	Supply-Clerk Typist	405
145.	Fullerton, Rex A.	38554904	Opns-Clerk Typist	405
146.	Gamp, Paul A.	35139365	Opns-Parachute Rigger	620
147.	Gehrke, Henry A.	35057424	Eng-Crew Chief	2750
148.	Giovanetti, Joseph W.	31360364	Eng-Crew Chief	2750
149.	Glenzer, Milton W.	32431902	Comm-Rad Opr	2756
150.	Goldstein, Sidney B.	33071587	Comm-Rad Opr	2756
151.	Golyar, Mike F.	36159014	Eng-Welder	256
152.	Gregory, Charles H.	39551751	Trans-Auto Equip Opr	345
153.	Grubbs, Otis W.	13036736	Tech Supply Duty Soldier	590
154.	Hall, Jo A.	16030344	Comm-Rad Opr	2756
155.	Herrick, Robert N.	35394614	Eng-Crew Chief	2750
156.	Hurst, Forrest J.	36480700	Comm-Rad Opr	2756
157.	Jarrett, Wyatt D.	14152598	Eng-Crew Chief	2750
158.	Jones, Donald P.	32446499	Eng-Crew Chief	2750
159.	Knat, Andrew J.	37394331	Eng-Crew Chief	2750
160.	Kosola, Paul	37282123	HQ-Carpenter	050
161.	Lapczynski, Benislaus F.	36170166	Mess-Cook	060
162.	Leckie, Andrew F., Jr.	35223383	Eng-Crew Chief	2750
163.	Lindsey, J.W. (io), Jr.	18078207	HQ-Duty Soldier	590
164.	McIntosh, James W.	39384196	Trans-Auto Equip Mech	014
165.	Melchiorre, Thomas	33827853	Eng-Crew Chief	2750
166.	Meyer, Kinch E.	18189382	Eng-Ap Mech	747
167.	Meyer, Robert A.	16006461	Mess-Cook	060
168.	Moran, Blaine E.	33759942	Eng-Crew Chief	2750
169.	Nally, David A.	19175878	Eng-Ap Mech	747
170.	Obsta, Edgar L.	38458954	Comm-Rad Opr	2756
171.	Orihuela, Henry	12082971	Comm-Rad Opr	2756
172.	Patterson, Fred L.	38105712	Eng-Ap Mech	747
173.	Pearcy, Fred W.	36503402	Mess-Duty Soldier	590
174.	Pearson, James E.	14060064	Eng-Crew Chief	2750
175.	Petri, Charles	32890817	Eng-Crew Chief	2750
176.	Phelps, Robert C.	32140416	Trans-Auto Equip Opr	345
177.	Pietzch, Paul J., Jr.	18117665	Eng-Ap Mech	747
178.	Platt, Otto	18117826	Eng-Ap Mech	747
179.	Pyle, John W.	17015097	Supply-Clerk TDY US	055
180.	Radick, Nicholas	33689462	Comm-Rad Opr	2756
181.	Rawiszer, Henry R.	32973558	Eng-Crew Chief	2750
182.	Raymond, Robert J.	39018508	Mess-Duty Soldier	590
183.	Robinson, Floyd I.	39609913	Trans-Auto Equip Opr	345
184.	Rosen, Laurence S.	34809568	Eng-Crew Chief	2750
185.	Rubolina, Joseph R.	13124978	Eng-Crew Chief	2750
186.	Schultz, Harold G.	34472778	Eng-Crew Chief	2750
187.	Slater, Daniel B.	35392013	Eng-Crew Chief	2750

188.	Sokol, Stephen R., Jr.	15377246	Comm-Rad Opr	2756	
189.	Spiridondes, Themo	31269446	Eng-Crew Chief	2750	
190.	Stamper, Marion J.	35746551	Trans-Auto Equip Opr	345	
191.	Stepnik, Zigmund J.	36503369	Medics-Med Corpsman	657	
192.	Stjern, Orville N.	17084516	Comm-Radar Mech TC	849	
193.	Sutterfield, Harold W.	17044748	Supply-Clerk	055	
194.	Taylor, Douglas L.	33181603	Eng-Instrument Spec	686	
195.	Tomasetti, Mario A.	33592456	Comm-Radar Mech TC	849	
196.	Weekley, Grover S.	37112280	Tech Supply-Clerk	835	

Privates First Class

197.	Barr, Bird M.	39331291	HQ-Duty Soldier	590	
198.	Campos, Paul	18230848	Mess-Duty Soldier	590	
199.	Escobar, Antonio A.	38554563	Mess-Duty Soldier	590	
200.	Foss, Vernon A.	39615695	Comm-Rad Opr	2756	
201.	Gardner, Clifford S.	38089537	Eng-Ap Mech	747	
202.	King, Harold	35438433	Trnas-Auto Equip Opr	345	
203.	Lawrence, Vernon D.	34329688	Medics-Med Corpsman	657	
204.	Marsh, Howard N.	36762724	Eng-Ap Mech	747	
205.	McCarthy, John J., Jr.	31146988	Eng-Crew Chief	2750	
206.	Miller, Franklin H.	32988151	Comm-Rad Mech	754	
207.	Parham, Lloyd, Jr.	38507180	Eng-Duty Soldier	590	
208.	Parolin, Pio P.	32938397	Eng-Ap Mech	747	
209.	Seegull, Robert	12143125	Comm-Rad Opr	2756	
210.	Silvaggio, Frank J.	35058734	Eng-Crew Chief	2750	
211.	Stone, William J.	12180776	Eng-Armorer	511	
212.	Tabler, John D.	15328005	Eng-Crew Chief	2750	
213.	Waters, John A.	35368109	Eng-Crew Chief	2750	
214.	Zoldi, Julius	39571281	Eng-Crew Chief	2750	

Privates

215.	Anderson, Raynold V.	17153871	Eng-Ap Mech	747	
216.	Belmont, Richard L.	19081888	Mess-Duty Soldier	590	
217.	Carmichael, Donaldeen	37477419	Comm-Rad Opr	2756	
218.	Flournoy, George T., Jr.	18216782	HQ-Duty Soldier	590	
219.	Little-Light, Frank	19070481	Comm-Switchboard Opr	650	

22nd Troop Carrier Squadron Roster of Officers
31 May 1945

	Name	ASN	Flying Status	Duty	Duty Code
	Captains				
1.	Langebartel, Edward P.	0 754434	Pilot	Commanding	1051
2.	Dixon, Robert	0 562874	Non-Pilot	Intel O	9300
3.	Feigus, Samuel J.	0 562980	Non-Pilot	Exec O-Adm Insp	2120
4.	Foltz, Robert G.	0 673347	Pilot	"B" Flt Comdr	1051
5.	Garber, Jacob S.	0 1689514	Flt Surg	Sq Surgeon	3162
6.	Gasper, Joseph S.	0 806429	Pilot	"C" Flt Comdr	1051
7.	Gillenwater, Ray V.	0 747251	Pilot	"H" Flt Comdr	1051
8.	Horr, Stanley F.	0 854497	Non-Pilot	Comm O-Crypt O	0200
9.	Lepsky, Daniel	0 363623	Non-Pilot	Supply O	4000
10.	Little, Lloyd F.	0 563651	Non-Pilot	Eng O	4823
11.	Premo, Harold L.	0 888637	Pilot	"F" Flt Comdr	1051
12.	Quenon, August O.	0 810025	Pilot	"D" Flt Comdr	1051
13.	Seeple, Robert C.	0 680091	Pilot	Pilot	1051
14.	Thomas, James E.	0 564464	Non-Pilot	Adj-Stat Cont O	2110
15.	Vincent, Arnold W.	0 680124	Pilot	Pilot	1051
	1st Lieutenants				
16.	Beecroft, Melvin T.	0 810400	Pilot	"G" Flt Comdr-Arm O	1051
17.	Buckelew, Morris T.	0 1635638	Pilot	Co-Pilot	1051
18.	Deleski, Edwin J.	0 802262	Pilot	Pilot	1051
19.	Gilreath, Hugh J.	0 812803	Pilot	Pilot-Wt & Bal O	1051
20.	Granucci, Robert F.	0 809946	Pilot	"A" Flt Comdr	1051
21.	Grayson, Robert C.	0 720247	Pilot	Pilot	1051
22.	Green, Clarence E.	0 769426	Pilot	Pilot-Tech Insp-Asst Eng O	1051
23.	Hargreaves, Robert H.	0 681584	Pilot	Pilot	1051
24.	Krebs, William W.	0 820514	Pilot	Pilot	1051
25.	Moore, John H., Jr.	0 800024	Pilot	Pilot	1051
26.	Murdock, Thomas B.	0 426917	Pilot	Pilot	1051
27.	Prior, James C.	0 769552	Pilot	Pilot	1051
28.	Schotta, Richard E.	0 831314	Pilot	Pilot	1051
29.	Shawver, Kenneth R.	0 832257	Pilot	Pilot	1051
30.	Temple, Harold E.	0 831295	Pilot	Pilot	1051
31.	Thompson, Francis C.	0 828256	Pilot	Pilot	1051
32.	Towne, Gerald L.	0 801916	Pilot	Opns O-Oxy O	2161
33.	Twardzik, John F.	0 831621	Pilot	Pilot-Asst Ops O	1051
34.	Ungerbuehler, Alvin R.	0 832290	Pilot	Pilot	1051

#	Name	ASN		Duty	
35.	Wells, Albert S., Jr.	O 826331	Pilot	Pilot	1051
36.	White, Donald P.	O 721273	Pilot	Pilot	1051
37.	White, Joseph L.	O 831869	Pilot	Pilot	1051
38.	Yost, Merle K.	O 707756	Pilot	"E" Flt Comdr	1051

2nd Lieutenants

#	Name	ASN		Duty	
39.	Andrews, Donald K.	O 775736	Pilot	Copilot	1051
40.	Burns, Eugene F.	O 780119	Pilot	Copilot-Asst Transp O	1051
41.	Conard, William F.	O 779100	Pilot	Copilot	
42.	Flora, Edward B.	O 2027103	Pilot	Pilot	1051
43.	Gent, George A.	O 2007617	Pilot	Pilot-Fire Marsh	1051
44.	Gilbert, Dean W.	O 772345	Pilot	Copilot	1051
45.	Gunter, Lyle W.	O 783544	Pilot	Pilot-Asst Comm O	1051
46.	Hood, Jack M.	O 2058073	Pilot	Copilot-Asst Pro	1051
47.	Horn, Ralph R.	O 765983	Pilot	Copilot	
48.	Hurley, William G.	O 720258	Pilot	Pilot-I & E O	1051
49.	Ingram, Charles B.	O 2037337	Non-Pilot	Trans O-Censor O-Pub Rel O	0600
50.	Johnson, Henry, Jr.	O 720396	Pilot	Copilot	1051
51.	Kelly, Robert D.	O 2058204	Pilot	Copilot-Gnd Safety O	1051
52.	Kincheloe, Robert S.	O 718508	Pilot	Pilot-Asst Opns O Air Movement O	1051
53.	Koncelik, Alvin J.	O 2057318	Pilot	Copilot	1051
54.	Layton, Clyde G.	O 2068694	Navigator	Pers Equip O-Asst Intel O	1042
55.	Lillis, Dale J.	O 721134	Pilot	Copilot	1051
56.	Linford, Amasa M.	O 779167	Pilot	Copilot-PX O	1051
57.	McCay, Howard W.	O 780122	Pilot	Copilot-Hist O	1051
58.	Mills, Homer O., Jr.	O 780676	Pilot	Pilot	1051
59.	Newsom, Francis A.	O 774736	Pilot	Copilot	1051
60.	Parker, Carroll H.	O 781651	Pilot	Copilot	1051
61.	Plass, Vernon R.	O 687150	Pilot	Pilot	1051
62.	Pruitt, Victor C.	O 780717	Pilot	Pilot	1051
63.	Rector, James D.	O 779220	Pilot	Copilot	1051
64.	Remus, Edward D.	O 769554	Pilot	Copilot-Util O	1051
65.	Robert, William A.	O 836640	Pilot	Copilot	1051
66.	Sexton, Gerald K.	O 780741	Pilot	Copilot	1051
67.	Shingleton, John D.	O 835262	Pilot	Pilot-Spec Ser O	1051
68.	Smith, Arthur A.	O 830998	Pilot	Copilot	1051
69.	Tarr, Eason	O 780765	Pilot	Copilot	1051
70.	Watson, Robert W.	O 832298	Pilot	Pilot	1051
71.	Winningham, Donald A.	O 2027104	Pilot	Pilot	1051

F/O

#	Name	ASN		Duty	
72.	Abraham, Donald L.	T 125899	Pilot	Pilot	1051
73.	Corn, Allen L.	T 125924	Pilot	Pilot-Asst Util O	1051
74.	Hunt, William I.	T 2916	Pilot	Pilot-Asst Sup O	1051
75.	Lyle, William C.	T 123303	Pilot	Pilot	1051
76.	Muncaster, William L.	T 4445	Pilot	CoPilot-Asst Pers Equip O	1051
77.	Stowell, Raymond J., Jr.	T 3505	Pilot	Copilot-Mess O	1051
78.	Valerio, Samuel J.	T 3644	Pilot	Copilot	1051
79.	Weil, Shael J.	T 3673	Pilot	Copilot-Chem Warfare O	1051
80.	Williams, Arthur R.	T 4307	Pilot	Copilot	1051
81.	Williams, Clyde B.	T 65583	Pilot	Pilot-Asst Intel O-Recognition O	1051

33rd Troop Carrier Squadron Roster of Officers
31 May 1945

	Name	ASN	Duty Code	Duty

Captains

#	Name	ASN	Duty Code	Duty
1.	Best, Robert T.	0803731	1051	Commanding Officer
2.	Adams, Ira A.	0888710	1051	"A" Flight Leader
3.	Bigger, Richard M.	0854951	4823	Engineering Officer
4.	Carson, Robert J.	02035181	9300	Intell. O., Censor
5.	Falls, Robert P.	02036170	2110	Adjutant, War Bond Officer, Ins/Stat O
6.	Hauer, Eddy G., Jr.	0669576	1051	Pilot
7.	Krupski, Charles A.	0754017	1051	"D" Flight Leader
8.	MacGuire, William B., Jr.	0479009	3162	Flight Surgeon
9.	McKenzie, William G.	0809982	1051	"C" Flight Leader
10.	Miller, Frank R.	0810193	2161	Operations Officer
11.	Pearson, Eric E.	0448050	1034	Navigator
12.	Rantze, George F., Jr.	0564102	0200	Comm O, Cryptographic Sec O
13.	Roth, Oliver N., Jr.	0564177	4113	Supply, Transportation, Unit Gas O
14.	Smith, Charles P.	0810240	1051	"B" Flight Leader

1st Lieutenants

#	Name	ASN	Duty Code	Duty
15.	Aurand, Orville H.	02058953	1051	Pilot
16.	Barganier, James A.	0581741	4823	Asst Engineering O
17.	Barwick, Raymond C.	0812356	1051	Pilot, Utilities O
18.	Bernards, Marwin A.	02059940	1051	Pilot
19.	Bledsoe, Richard M.	0809087	1051	Pilot
20.	Brush, Douglas H.	0805695	1051	Pilot

21.	Campbell, Clarendon, Jr.	0813335	1051	Pilot
22.	Deines, Samuel	0812388	1051	Pilot
23.	Dodge, James M.	0521251	1051	"F" Flt Ldr, Asst Eng O
24.	Harris, Edgar L.	02060011	1051	Pilot
25.	Hasty, Wilton H.	02059035	1051	Pilot
26.	Haynes, William S.	02036769	2120	Asst Adjutant
27.	Headley, Donald G.	0806842	1051	"H" Flight Leader
28.	Herb, Bruce E.	02059045	1051	Pilot, Asst Opns O
29.	Hixson, Kenneth H.	0827340	1051	Pilot
30.	McCullough, Hugh F., Jr.	0808298	1051	"G" Flight Leader
31.	McGovern, Albert S.	0745149	1051	"E" Flight Leader, Asst Eng O
32.	Osborne, Philip W.	0693229	1051	Exec O
33.	Rendler, Thomas F.	0809287	1034	Navigator
34.	Rich, Arthur H.	0462002	1051	Pilot
35.	Thompson, Robert J.	0827320	2161	Asst Opns O
36.	Van Ness, William D.	0818466	1051	Pilot, Personal Equip, Wts & Bal O
37.	White, Robert L.	01166209	1051	Copilot, Tech Supply O

2nd Lieutenants

38.	Adams, Clifford P.	02058945	1051	Copilot
39.	Alexander, Jesse E., Jr.	02071503	1034	Navigator, Asst Trans O
40.	Arkebauer, Byron T., Jr.	01298005	1051	Mess Officer
41.	Arnold, John H.	0776213	1051	Pilot
42.	Bittner, Edward J.	02057107	1051	Pilot
43.	Bitterle, Douglas R.	0721021	1051	Copilot
44.	Bozlinski, Joseph	0778707	1051	Copilot
45.	Burrell, Harry S.	0815068	1051	Copilot
46.	Byrns, John W.	0721639	1051	Pilot, Fire Marshall
47.	Call, Frederick R.	0720435	1051	Copilot
48.	Callahan, Carl G., Jr.	02059973	1051	Copilot
49.	Carden, Harvey H.	0775697	1051	Pilot
50.	Christenson, Charles R.	0777587	1051	Copilot, Acft Recog O
51.	Clemmens, Alfred D.	0776236	1051	Copilot
52.	Coleman, Robert G.	0815840	1051	Copilot, Ground Safety O
53.	Crandall, Channing L.	0778417	1051	Copilot
54.	Dales, Edward S.	02058922	1051	Pilot, Sp Svc O
55.	Dykes, Clarence J.	0829956	1051	Copilot, Asst Supply O
56.	Eldridge, William R.	02059015	1051	Pilot
57.	Gligora, Nick, Jr.	0718612	1051	Copilot
58.	Gomer, Frederick L., Jr.	0720669	1051	Pilot
59.	Hamann, Melvin J.	0720996	1051	Copilot
60.	Haddock, Albert J.	0819912	1051	Pilot
61.	Hastings, Walter D.	0769435	1051	Pilot, Asst Ops O
62.	Lovorn, Cell R., Jr.	0713825	1051	Copilot
63.	Myers, Benjamin T.	0721177	1051	Pilot
64.	Parker, Robert F.	0831987	1051	Copilot
65.	Parker, Roland W.	0769539	1051	Pilot, Asst Tech Supply O
66.	Parrott, John H., Jr.	0816566	1051	Copilot, Asst Comm O IFF Officer
67.	Pope, Joseph A.	0692917	1051	Pilot, Air Movement O
68.	Richmond, Charles C., Jr.	0776050	1051	Copilot, Asst Intel O
69.	Ryon, Maurice G.	0713556	1051	Copilot
70.	Schleif, Wayne W.	0782377	1051	Copilot
71.	Scott, Wallace W., Jr.	0834034	1051	Pilot
72.	Smith, Herbert W.	0495614	1051	Copilot
73.	Smith, James J.	0833609	1051	Pilot, Athletic O
74.	Stewart, Harris B., Jr.	0827533	1051	Copilot, I&E O
75.	Solomon, Arnold M.	0769577	1051	Pilot, Pub Relations O
76.	Tillotson, Robert L.	0833629	1051	Copilot (DS)
77.	Weinroth, Jack L.	0770039	1051	Copilot
78.	Weiss, Herbert B.	0833643	1051	Copilot, Asst Sp Svc
79.	White, Milton R.	02007378	1051	Pilot
80.	Wirts, George L.	0824814	1051	Copilot
81.	Wunder, John P.	02007387	1051	Pilot
82.	Young, Elden J.	0384086	1051	Copilot, Asst Exec O

F/Os

83.	Berg, Alvin O., Jr.	T-4384	1051	Copilot, Armament O
84.	Greber, Charles E.	T-62246	1051	Pilot
85.	Krikorian, Anthony	T-4428	1051	Copilot
86.	Lidel, Roland P.	T-4204	1051	Copilot
87.	O'Bannon, James R.	T-3961	1051	Copilot
88.	Pendleton, Dorse F., Jr.	T-4219	1051	Copilot
89.	Potter, John K.	T-2558	1051	Pilot, Asst Mess O
90.	Rade, Raymond H.	T-2923	1051	Pilot, Historical O
91.	Rushford, Lou M.	T-4463	1051	Copilot
92.	Trexler, William C.	T-3986	1051	Copilot

Attached
1st Lieutenant

1.	Vandell, Norman H.	01583786	4805	

33rd Troop Carrier Squadron Roster of Enlisted Men
1 June 1945

	Name	ASN	Duty Code	Duty
	1st Sergeants			
1.	Mermelstein, Arthur A.	33088464	502	1st Sgt-Ground Safety NCO
	Master Sergeants			
2.	Banack, Stanley F.	6895587	750	Maintenance Chief
3.	Bukovich, Joseph	13017876	750	Line Chief
4.	Carbone, Michael	32222003	754	Comm Chief-RO Mech
5.	Dorband, Robert J.	7033189	2750	Asst. Line Chief
6.	Kiser, Kenneth W.	35172355	750	Airplane Mech
7.	Lande, Albert	13007018	2750	Crew Chief
	Tech Sergeants			
8.	Beachy, William B.	33206204	2750	Crew Chief
9.	Busch, Francis L.	37096794	2750	Flight Chief
10.	Forto, Nicholas S.	13003259	747	Airplane Mech
11.	Hesse, Herbert G.	19004190	2750	Crew Chief
12.	King, Hobart T.	31081045	750	Flight Chief
13.	Lloyd, Robert M.	14120346	405	Operations Clerk
14.	Longman, John H.	16037895	2750	Crew Chief
15.	Melnick, Frank	7021293	687	Prop Specialist
16.	Myers, Harry L., Jr.	13032264	826	Tech Supply Clerk
17.	Stanley, Davie L.	34188949	502	Personnel Clerk
18.	Stephens, Carl L.	36054812	405	Orderly Room Clerk
19.	Stone, Charles A.	34187460	502	Engineering Clerk
20.	Till, William B.	34199162	750	Flight Chief
21.	Wilcox, William H.	15040709	2750	Crew Chief
22.	Williams, Clifford	6668845	055	Operations Clerk
	Staff Sergeants			
23.	Bray, Adolphus T.	14128742	631	Intel Spec
24.	Burton, Edward A.	34205272	2750	Crew Chief
25.	Chamberlain, Arthur C.	15117100	2756	Radio Operator
26.	Channell, Elmer R.	15107922	685	Elec Spec
27.	Church, Robert	19142118	2750	Crew Chief
28.	Dart, Thomas L.	12143081	2756	Radio Operator
29.	Glosenger, Rex G.	33179996	405	Opns Clerk-TDY US
30.	Grabin, Daniel	33350598	2750	Crew Chief
31.	Grosso, Harry R.	33346675	2756	Radio Operator
32.	Harmon, Ralph	16052749	756	Ground Sta RO
33.	Hoiland, Kermit T.	37283787	345	Truck Driver
34.	Icke, Donald A.	35310754	2750	Crew Chief
35.	Kellander, Robert A.	13145808	2756	Radio Operator
36.	King, Laurel G.	35455093	590	Duty NCO
37.	Kohler, Earl R., Jr.	35269646	2750	Crew Chief
38.	Kovalesky, Stanley L.	33170122	756	Ground Sta RO
39.	Kramer, Harry L.	33018053	747	Airplane Mech
40.	Lanfranchi, Louis C.	32358653	821	Adm Supply Sgt
41.	Langbecker, William L.	16009105	620	Parachute Rigger
42.	Mathes, Philip D.	11041180	747	Airplane Mech
43.	McCleskey, John C.	34351322	405	Engineering Clk
44.	McLees, David C.	39268549	2756	Radio Operator
45.	McPheron, Herschel J.	16053453	2750	Crew Chief
46.	Mead, Charles R., Jr.	37210696	555	Sheet Metal Wkr
47.	Miller, Lawrence E.	36074753	345	Transportation NCO
48.	Miller, Robert A.	35133547	657	Medical NCO
49.	Murphy, James J.	32075877	747	Airplane Mech
50.	Pencille, John W.	39251162	2750	Crew Chief
51.	Pennell, George E., Jr.	35412510	2756	Radio Operator
52.	Quillopo, Tommy B.	32408269	060	Cook
53.	Ridloff, Solomon	32329950	620	Parachute Rigger
54.	Sanborn, Richard C.	31108812	405	Personnel Clerk
55.	Scollan, Edward J.	32587441	2756	Radio Operator
56.	Southwick, Murl W.	17016497	824	Mess Sgt
57.	Spooner, Curtis O.	31072251	747	Airplane Mech
58.	Staton, Theodore R.	38326347	555	Sheet Metal Wkr
59.	Stevenson, William E.	38426887	2750	Crew Chief
60.	Stringer, Jackson R.	14139058	2756	Radio Operator
61.	Upton, Sydney Y.	31091725	055	Intelligence Clerk
62.	Varley, Charles R.	17068581	238	Wire Tech
63.	Wiesen, Francis X.	16176145	2756	Radio Operator
64.	Worsham, James M.	38171245	835	Tech Supply Clerk
65.	Yamber, Joe	33079830	747	Airplane Mech
66.	Yawn, Preston H.	34350867	754	Radio Mechanic
67.	Young, Paul R.	35455537	405	Chief Comm Clerk
68.	Zwiegel, John W., Jr.	38239676	685	Elec Spec

Sergeants

#	Name	Serial	Code	Role
69.	Bona, Julius F.	35329852	060	Cook
70.	Boyd, Lawrence P.	13107370	014	Auto Mechanic
71.	Canut, Alex	33263392	590	Duty Soldier
72.	Carbo, Joe B.	35429237	055	Dispatcher
73.	Cardinelli, John J.	32358360	055	Mail Clerk
74.	Castro, Willie G.	38156656	2750	Crew Chief
75.	Chasteen, Wilton O.	34121500	055	Adm Supply Clerk
76.	Clark, Lester A.	15331353	2750	Crew Chief
77.	Costello, Wallace F.	17108600	590	Sp Service NCO
78.	Danielson, Delmar P.	37285933	060	Cook
79.	Denny, James L.	37342552	060	Cook
80.	Freedman, Joseph	32377442	835	Tech Supply Clerk
81.	Gehrke, Hilbert F.	37273260	932	Heavy Equip Opr
82.	Gregory, Kenneth C.	37150027	747	Airplane Mech
83.	Jobe, Willie B.	6271278	835	Adm Supply Clerk
84.	Karp, Felix H.	33349212	050	Carpenter
85.	Klopek, Albert	18154947	2750	Crew Chief
86.	Koziel, William J.	33281656	037	Butcher
87.	Kramarz, Edward G.	35310769	2750	Crew Chief
88.	Lenmark, Jacques E.	36290271	673	Medical Adm Tech
89.	Manganello, John J.	36328246	2750	Crew Chief
90.	Marion, Emmett H.	34602812	055	Orderly Room Clerk
91.	Mc Isaac, John E.	11054842	650	Switchboard Opr
92.	Mc Kee, Wilfred C.	37236703	050	Carpenter
93.	Mink, Warder O., Jr.	15107682	2750	Crew Chief
94.	Mitchelson, John L.	36585195	853	Radar Mechanic
95.	Mitrzak, John R.	32385230	835	Adm Supply Clerk
96.	Mittag, Conrad E.	37116428	014	Auto Mechanic
97.	Munden, Gordon B.	37304183	2750	Crew Chief
98.	Murray, John V.	17056862	2750	Sq Inspector
99.	Nelson, Charles R.	32017523	548	Dope & Fabric Wkr
100.	Niel, Benjamin F.	37379656	754	Radio Mech
101.	Nowak, Florian I.	16111545	2750	Crew Chief
102.	Oliver, Albert W.	38095975	835	Adm Supply Clerk
103.	Palmer, Donald C.	20931461	805	Cryptographic Tech
104.	Pentland, George	35250619	686	AP Inst Mech
105.	Rau, Leander J.	37543112	747	Airplane Mech
106.	Scholtz, Arlo A.	16092842	747	Airplane Mech
107.	Shank, Clifford E.	13020418	055	Comm-Clerk
108.	Snow, Ray E.	17126836	2756	Radio Operator
109.	Starek, George R.	33282141	060	Cook
110.	Swisher, Robert C., Jr.	13038830	2750	Crew Chief
111.	Tobey, Rodney N.	32253809	747	Airplane Mech
112.	Venturo, Attilio S.	32778094	2750	Crew Chief
113.	Warshawsky, Louis	32411694	055	PX Clerk
114.	Wolfe, Charles H.	35406147	060	Cook
115.	Zabawa, Bernard J.	36427003	060	Cook
116.	Zipay, Michael	13047087	2750	Crew Chief
117.	Albino, John	12045141	2756	Radio Operator
118.	Alosi, Peter	39393813	2756	Radio Operator
119.	Averman, John H.	33735649	2756	Radio Operator
120.	Baldridge, Virgil E.	38237312	060	Cook
121.	Barnett, Joseph W., Jr.	6982490	747	Airplane Mech
122.	Barrick, William C.	35496924	060	Cook
123.	Bochnovich, Paul S.	33748375	2750	Crew Chief
124.	Bodian, Morris L.	32864492	622	Personnel Clerk
125.	Boss, Duane E.	16159444	2750	Crew Chief
126.	Boyette, Richard L.	33851591	2750	Crew Chief
127.	Cihak, Lawrence A.	37473497	932	Heavy Equip Opr
128.	Clark, Bernard H.	34330047	345	Truck Driver
129.	Colberg, Donald R.	17109836	345	Truck Driver
130.	Costine, Maurice P.	11110729	747	Airplane Mech
131.	Creighton, Allen E.	19105896	2756	Radio Operator
132.	D'Augereau, Rene J.	38484986	2756	Radio Operator
133.	Davis, Howard M.	16055922	657	Medical Corpsman
134.	Dinardi, Demetria A.	13145722	2756	Radio Operator
135.	Dukowski, Raymond F.	35514821	060	Cook
136.	Emmerich, Francis H.	37207737	345	Truck Driver
137.	Ferguson, Francis R.	34783311	2750	Crew Chief
138.	Force, Ralph E.	33572143	2756	Radio Operator
139.	Garcia, Juan G.	38103084	345	Truck Driver
140.	Grey, Geoffrey H.	10641080	405	Intell-Clerk
141.	Head, H.T., Jr.	18119120	747	Airplane Mech
142.	Hill, Billy A.	18208748	2750	Crew Chief
143.	Holsoapple Robert	33249082	932	Heavy Equip Opr
144.	Jones, Robert L.	15117198	345	Truck Driver
145.	Juchniewicz, Anthony J.	36867895	2756	Radio Operator
146.	Kneller, Lloyd M.	37088690	932	Heavy Equip Opr
147	Komm, Albert E.	31144604	511	Armorer

148.	Lebo, Richard K.	33828563	2750	Crew Chief
149.	Macis, Joseph E.	35746390	2756	Radio Operator
150.	Magnuson, Roland T.	36177984	345	Truck Driver
151.	Malkiewicz, John F.	32393853	590	Duty Soldier
152.	Mathis, Homer V.	37226190	747	Airplane Mech
153.	Monson, Robert S.	36670846	750	Airplane Mech
154.	Nasi, John H.	37304483	747	Airplane Mech
155.	Olivero, Alfred P.	12025660	2756	Radio Operator
156.	Plog, Buford J.	36426789	345	Truck Driver
157.	Roberts, Elwood S.	32662718	055	Operations Clerk
158.	Rutkowski, Alexander T.	13060946	590	Duty Soldier
159.	Sazer, Bernard	36597552	2750	Crew Chief
160.	Sheets, William H.	18219312	055	Operations Clerk
161.	Snapp, Richard W.	35138540	2756	Radio Operator
162.	Stanislawski, Richard C.	36607907	2750	Crew Chief
163.	Turk, George	31353950	2750	Crew Chief
164.	Turner, Raymond H.	13089125	754	Radio Mechanic
165.	Ubaldini, Bernard	31383436	747	Airplane Mech
166.	VanZile, Walter H.	39855217	2750	Crew Chief
167.	Vasquez, David F.	39134421	2756	Radio Operator
168.	Vosbury, Alfred H.	35412395	345	Amb Driver
169.	Warner, William H.	13143070	2756	Radio Operator
170.	Washington, Kenneth	39036467	2756	Radio Operator
171.	Weddle, Harvey E.	33648289	747	Airplane Mechanic
172.	Whitehead, Frank E.	31312379	853	Radar Mechanic
173.	Williams, Dee C.	18039696	750	Airplane Mechanic
174.	Wilson, Samuel K.	36694329	853	Radar Mechanic
175.	Wise, George A.	35068770	853	Radar Mechanic
176.	Wood, John T.	38377543	2750	Crew Chief
177.	Wraight, Harry E.	35141299	2750	Crew Chief
178.	Young, Robert E.	38519085	2756	Radio Operator
179.	Zabel, Harvey J.	17120220	055	Engineering Clerk

Privates First Class

180.	Baradine, Edward S.	31332440	590	Duty Soldier
181.	Barnhart, Robert E.	36458503	345	Truck Driver
182.	Behrens, Elliott B.	19147232	2756	Radio Operator
183.	Boone, Duard M.	17136000	754	Radio Mechanic
184.	Chatelain, Herman J.	18139056	754	Radio Mechanic
185.	Clift, Ernest E.	18132556	620	Parachute Rigger
186.	Cooper, Arthur L.	14105254	345	Truck Driver
187.	Cooper, Elza H.	35466936	747	Airplane Mechanic
188.	Coutts, James M.	16146084	835	Tech Supply Clerk
189.	DiPietrantonio, Tony	31295343	2750	Crew Chief
190.	Doolin, Willie	33215485	050	Carpenter
191.	Dragonetti, Anthony	32969694	747	Airplane Mechanic
192.	Ferguson, Walter A.	18216813	747	Airplane Mechanic
193.	Frasik, Bernard S., Jr.	16057912	756	Comm Ground Sta RO
194.	Gramarosso, Stephen R.	32887293	687	Prop Specialist
195.	Helgesen, Alvin C.	36818398	2750	Crew Chief
196.	Kastner, Arthur F.	37565139	2750	Crew Chief
197.	Johnson, Raymond E.	11110846	2756	Radio Operator
198.	Lawler, Leon E.	37723020	686	Instrument Spec
199.	Mathias, Robert P.	35546661	2756	Radio Operator
200.	Mulholland, James R.	35229262	2756	Radio Operator
201.	Nunes, Ferdinand P.	31119981	345	Truck Driver
202.	Olson, Orwin S.	19067683	650	Switchboard Opr
203.	Paradiso, Lawrence	32882425	2750	Crew Chief
204.	Paynter, Paul R.	37678807	2750	Crew Chief
205.	Pickens, Charles D.	35390019	345	Truck Driver
206.	Pruet, J.P.	38396440	345	Truck Driver
207.	Rosen, Stanley J.	32896686	2750	Crew Chief
208.	Schiro, Joseph	32886903	2750	Crew Chief
209.	Serab, James	7021188	2750	Crew Chief
210.	Spradley, Richard N.	38364855	2756	Radio Operator
211.	Stout, James B.	36519654	345	Truck Driver
212.	Tonsman, Horace	34729185	747	Airplane Mechanic
213.	Veatch, John C.	16104228	2756	Radio Operator
214.	Walsh, William F.	12124879	345	Truck Driver

Privates

215.	Bashore, Harold C.	36166149	2756	Radio Operator
216.	Cook, James B.	34332461	055	Dispatcher
217.	Dudka, Alvin J.	16064993	345	Truck Driver
218.	Dyer, Douglas B.	19175996	747	Airplane Mechanic
219.	Espinosa, Pablo V.	38250323	620	Parachute Rigger
220.	Fonfara, Frank	33459747	2756	Radio Operator
221.	Griffith, Orville G.	38189187	590	Duty Soldier
222.	Heffner, Robert L.	15196780	620	Parachute Rigger
223.	James, Willie B.	38175860	590	Duty Soldier

#	Name	ASN	Duty	Duty Code
224.	Jacquez, Raul	18120631	590	Duty Soldier
225.	Jones, Harold R.	35726874	747	Airplane Mechanic
226.	Norris, Sam P.	35389903	590	Duty Soldier
227.	Parrish, Henry A.	34313017	256	Welder
228.	Scholz, Frank M.	14058060	747	Airplane Mechanic
229.	Weiss, Charles H.	12177882	2756	Radio Operator
230.	White, Andrew J.	14161058	511	Armorer

Headquarters Roster of Enlisted Men

#	Name	ASN	Duty	Duty Code
			Master Sergeants	
1.	Adair, Charles J.	6295781	Eng-Inspector (DS 33rd Sq)	2750
2.	Boddie, William P.	36046865	Eng-Inspector (TDY USA)	2750
3.	Hammond, Lee B.	14070844	HQ-Chief Clerk	502
4.	Payton, Dalton C.	17010345	Eng-Inspector	2750
			Tech Sergeants	
5.	De Shazer, Robert F.	13033969	HQ-Clerk (TDY USA)	502
6.	Gilliatt, Robert L.	35258891	Comm-Communications Chief	542
7.	McKenney, William M.	33126238	Tech Supply-Tech Supply Clk	826
8.	Ressinger, Raymond D.	35439348	HQ-Medical NCO	673
9.	Stehl, John W.	13069224	HQ-Duty Sergeant	502
			Staff Sergeants	
10.	Appling, Frank N., Jr.	15319053	HQ-Clerk	405
11.	Cohen, Leonard	32542709	HQ-Clerk	502
12.	Cotton, Clarence E.	38413025	Trans Chief-Auto Mechanic	014
13.	De Witt, Carl F.	35410674	HQ-Stat Clerk	405
14.	Jackish, Mike M.	33281063	Supply-Supply Clerk	835
15.	Larson, Leslie N.	36182167	Oper-Clerk	055
16.	Mackrell, William S.	17051951	Mess-Mess Sgt	824
17.	Magill, Hugh R., Jr.	31066046	Eng-Clerk	405
18.	Murrah, Warren S.	37222017	Oper-Clerk	405
19.	Rife, Dale E.	13092572	HQ-Personnel NCO (TDY USA)	502
20.	Seward, Edward S.	6950438	HQ-Personnel NCO	405
21.	Sherrill, Walter H.	6390929	Mess-Cook	060
22.	Teegardin, Boyd E.	15110442	Intelligence Specialist	631
23.	Yoseph, David E.	32270308	Comm-Diesel Mechanic	013
			Sergeants	
24.	Boulden, John F.	32270393	HQ-File Clerk	055
25.	Boyette, James A.	34788338	Supply-Supply Clerk	835
26.	Boyle, Edward J.	33085052	Trans-Driver	345
27.	Derricks, Robert W.	36214185	Mess-Cook	060
28.	Eads, Gilbert	37188974	Trans-Driver	345
29.	Gage, Lyle O.	38566119	HQ-Clerk	405
30.	Gellasch, Donald W.	16065407	Eng-Aerial Eng	2750
31.	Hedger, Frank E.	36070776	Util-Utilities Tech	822
32.	Hennings, Robert H.	39101103	Comm-Cryptographic Tech	805
33.	Joe, Ernest S.	34612724	Mess-Cook	060
34.	Kirchenbauer, Charles J.	38427983	Util-Carpenter	050
35.	Kirkpatrick, Hillis O.	37186423	Mess-Cook	060
36.	Lambert, Jesse A.	38427775	P Ex-Clerk	055
37.	Morden, Norman D.	36417057	Trans-Clerk	405
38.	Nelson, John W.	17063270	Util-Carpenter	050
39.	Pettus, Albert C.	18182879	Util-Electrician	078
40.	Rusch, Clifford	36292033	Comm-Radio Operator	756
41.	Scharer, Ernest J.	32469246	HQ-Mail Clerk	056
42.	Schroeder, Charles J.	16162680	HQ-Med Corpsman-Dental Tech	657
43.	Severson, Cameron R.	6819121	Trans-Driver & Dispatcher	345
44.	Sevic, Frank J.	33163002	HQ-Clerk	405
45.	Smith, Leon C.	38181504	Comm-Tel&Tel Linesman	238
46.	Stamler, Charles	32330382	Intelligence-Clerk	405
47.	Traue, Otto F., Jr.	32178173	Mess-Cook	060
48.	Valvano, Salvatore C.	12162849	Radio Mechanic, AAF	754
			Corporals	
49.	Baron, Harry	32540621	Comm-Radio Operator & Mech	2756
50.	Blevins, Elmer G.	6289540	Parachute Rigger & Rep	620
51.	Campbell, William H., Jr.	18181449	Trans-Driver	345
52.	Cushwa, John M.	36354052	Util-Carpenter	050
53.	Eckwahl, Roland J.	32829569	Comm-Radio Operator	756
54.	Keene, Emery R.	16062389	Trans-Driver	345
55.	Kemerer, Paul R.	33690013	Trans-Driver	345
56.	Kimbrell, Alvin D., Jr.	14184760	Trans-Driver	343
57.	Lebarton, Rowland G.	33696084	Comm-Teletype Operator	237
58.	Lopin, Stanley J.	32442895	Util-Painter	144
59.	McDermott, Bernard G.	37480575	Trans-Driver	345

60.	Meyer, Leonard A.	34823415	I&E Public Relations Spec	274	
61.	Nelson, Robert R.	37303992	Trans-Driver & Dispatcher	345	
62.	Rowekamp, Richard J.	35681745	Intell-Clerk	405	
63.	Schwartz, Walter C.	32217672	HQ-Medical Corpsman	657	
64.	Sharpe, Charles F.	36574360	HQ-Sanitary Technician	196	
65.	Soutar, David A., Jr.	36718320	Comm-Teletype Mechanic	239	
66.	Springer, Ralph B., Jr.	34547006	Oper-Clerk	155	
67.	Sterhens, Eldon S.	37500338	Supply-Supply Clerk	835	
68.	Sullivan, John L.	31073075	HQ-Duty Soldier (Orderly)	590	
69.	Sylvester, Phillip	12091968	Trans-Driver	345	
70.	Trapp, Jerome A.	16117685	Comm-Radar Mechanic	853	
71.	Wagner, Walter H.	33347853	P Ex-Clerk	055	

Privates First Class

72.	Assel, William J.	33696788	Comm-Telephone Switch-Opr	650
73.	Croy, Cecil L.	33652179	Comm-Telephone Switch-Opr	650
74.	Doehring, Kerwin S.	32553381	HQ-Draftsman	070
75.	Gentry, Wayne H.	34606116	Oper-Clerk	055
76.	Goudsward, John J.	32771836	Comm-Teletype Mechanic	239
77.	Hansen, Arthur G.	36694954	Supply-Clerk	055
78.	Hixson, Norman G.	19175317	Trans-Driver	345
79.	Mahon, John L.	12165165	Comm-Teletype Operator	237
80.	Page, Lewis J.	34367506	HQ-Personnel Clerk	405
81.	Pierce, Richard C.	33538284	Comm-Teletype Mechanic	239
82.	Schroeder, Ralph H.	36119404	HQ-Duty Soldier	590
83.	Van Damme, Lawrence T.	36524118	HQ-File Clerk	405-1
84.	Wickersham, Clifford H.	37287016	Medical Technician	409
85.	Wyss, Delmar W.	37494395	Medical Technician	409

Privates

86.	Green, John L.	13096006	Trans-Driver	345
87.	Wilson, Virgil L.	15320045	Util-Duty Soldier	590

Attached
Tech Sergeant

1.	Seifried, Earl	7201524	Utilities Technician	822

Headquarters Roster of Officers
31 May 1945

	Name	ASN	Flying Status	Duty Code	Duty

Colonels

1.	Imparato, Edward T.	0 376 554 AC	Sr Pilot	1024	Gp Commander

Majors

2.	Graves, Andrew J.	0 913 566 AC	Non-Pilot	4902	Liaison Officer
3.	Hellweg, Charles E.	0 328 868 MC	Non-Pilot	3161	Flight Surgeon
4.	Lieberman, Alexander	0 911 872 AC	Non-Pilot	0200	Communications O, Cryptographic O
5.	Rennels, Lamont N.	0 913 703 AC	Non-Pilot	9307	S-2, Summary Court, Claims Officer
6.	Wentworth, Gerald O.	0 913 857 AC	Non-Pilot	2110	Adjutant, Ground Safety Officer

Captains

7.	Dunn, Willard B.	0 562 906 AC	Non-Pilot	1042	Personal Equipment O, Assistant S-3
8.	Echard, Rexford B.	0 854 702 AC	Non-Pilot	—	TDY - USA
9.	Emery, Walter A.	0 482 899 DC	Non-Pilot	3170	Group Dentist
10.	Euart, Kenneth A.	0 811 597 AC	Navigator	1034	Asst S-2, Asst S-3, Recognition O
11.	Faller, Andrew K.	0 562 968 AC	Non-Pilot	5004	I&E Officer, HQ Mess Officer
12.	Geatches, Stephen S.	O 677 709 AC	Pilot	2166	Air Inspector
13.	Johnston, Mark G., Jr.	0 801 764 AC	Pilot	2166	S-3, Tactical Insp
14.	Ketchman, Sam H.	0 352 005 AC	Non-Pilot	5000	Special Service O., (Athl & Rec) Asst S-2
15.	Lee, Russell K.	0 503 974 ChC	Non-Pilot	5310	Group Chaplain
16.	McCullen, William J., Jr.	0 809 397 AC	Navigator	1034	Nav Asst S-3
17.	Samuels, William J.	0 355 311 AC	Pilot	1051	Dpy Gp Commander
18.	Scott, Marvin M.	0 194 343 AC	Non-Pilot	4902	S-4, Utilities O
19.	Thompson, William E.	0 803 906 AC	Pilot	2140	Air Liaison Staff O Assistant S-3
20.	Tuck, Elmer L.	0 560 423 AC	Non-Pilot	6402	Stat Control Officer Gp Historical O
21.	Webb, Jesse A.	0 462 323 AC	Non-Pilot	2121	S-1, War Bond O, Ins Officer, Adm Insp

First Lieutenants

22.	Brown, Robert S.	0 492 498 AC	Non-Pilot	0141	Asst S-4, IFF, Asst Comm O, Asst Crypt
23.	Hunter, Chester H.	0 684 663 AC	Pilot	2161	Asst S-3, Weight & Balnce Officer
24.	Vandall, Norman B.	01 583 786 Ord	Non-Pilot	4530	Gp Ord Officer, HQ Trans Officer
25.	Veeck, William P.	0 564 529 AC	Non-Pilot	5000	Censor, Fire Marshall Asst Spcl Service
26.	Vogler, Harry G., Jr.	0 580 281 AC	Non-Pilot	6402	Asst Stat Control O

6th Troop Carrier Squadron Roster of Officers
31 May 1945

	Name and Rank	ASN	Flying Status	Duty	Duty Code
			Captains		
1.	Hartley, Donald K.	0-675431	Pilot	Commanding	1051
2.	Burmester, Frederick F.	0-685924	Navigator	Asst Intell O, Asst Censor	1034
3.	Fitzgerald, Willian E.	0-677252	Pilot	C-47 Check Pilot	1051
4.	Jones, Norman A.	0-740445	Pilot	C-47 Check Pilot	1051
5.	Loder, Robert W.	0-560053	Non-Pilot	Ex O, Sol Voting O, Hist O, I&E O, Asst Intell O	2120
6.	Patterson, Jack Q.	0-566387	Non-Pilot	Adjutant, Censor, Stat O, Life Ins O, War Bond O	2110
7.	Sample, Earl K.	0-803283	Pilot	C-47 Check Pilot	1051
8.	Tessier, Henri W.	0-902441	Non-Pilot	Intelligence O	9300
9.	Watson, Frederick S.	0-560450	Non-Pilot	Supply O	4000
10.	Willis, Frank L., Jr.	0-560483	Non-Pilot	Comm O, Crypto O, Security O, IFF O, Asst Intell O	0200
			First Lieutenants		
11.	Anderson, Kenneth K.	0-803532	Pilot	C-47 Check Pilot, Liaison O	1051
12.	Baker, Joseph D.	0-818477	Pilot	Operations O	2161
13.	Bledsoe, Jack E	0-802240	Pilot	Flt "D" Comdr	1051
14.	Cox, Arthur W., Jr.	0-827171	Pilot		1051
15.	Dezendorf, Burton E.	0-677994	Pilot	Flt "A" Comdr	1051
16.	Frew, James M.	0-806427	Pilot	Flt "H" Comdr	1051
17.	Geesey, Frederick M.	0-824465	Pilot		1051
18.	Green, John L.	0-577745	Non-Pilot	Asst Engineering O	4823
19.	Gregory, Fredrick F.	0-801854	Pilot		1051
20.	Holbrook, Robert B.	0-782288	Pilot	Engineering O	4823
21.	Jenkins, Charles D.	0-1174331	Pilot		1051
22.	Lackey, William A.	0-821906	Pilot	Flt "G" Comdr	1051
23.	Lawson, William V., II	0-815511	Pilot	Flt "E" Comdr	1051
24.	Lewis, Elroy M.	0-822211	Pilot		1051
25.	Martino, Armanto J.	0-817988	Pilot		1051
26.	McDonough, Thomas J.	0-769711	Pilot	Flt "F" Comdr	1051
27.	Meder, Joseph F.	0-803095	Pilot	Flt "B" Comdr	1051
28.	Moos, Earl W.	0-1290287	Pilot	Arm O	1051
29.	Remitz, Henry W.	0-805673	Pilot	Flt "C" Comdr	1051
30.	Robinson, Robert E.	0-804040	Co-Pilot	Pers Equip O, T-Supply O, Asst Eng O, Asst W&B O	1051
31.	Ruhl, Robert A.	0-809197	Pilot		1051
32.	Shenk, Clarence S., Jr.	0-2036129	Non-Pilot	Trans O, Mess O, Summary Court O, Asst Comm O, Asst Supply O	4113
33.	Spina, Sebastian	0-692220	Pilot		1051
34.	Thomas, William C., Jr.	0-689919	Pilot		1051
35.	Torbett, Odis B.	0-782410	Pilot	Asst Operation O	1051
36.	Whitsitt, Robert D.	0-768774	Pilot		1051
37.	Williams, Dean H., Jr.	0-739212	Pilot		1051
38.	Zuker, Charles J.	0-2036236	Non-Pilot	(TDY U.S.)	4823
			Second Lieutenants		
39.	Adkins, Gerald D.	0-806600	Pilot		1051
40.	Betts, William A.	0-714621	Co-Pilot	Asst PX O	1051
41.	Bulin, James L.	0-720161	Co-Pilot		1051
42.	Bussert, Jack F.	0-826095	Pilot		1051
43.	Butler, Stanley L.	0-777577	Co-Pilot		1051
44.	Cotterill, Wray P.	0-719569	Pilot		1051
45.	Culver, Julian H.	0-774959	Co-Pilot		1051
46.	Cunningham, John G., Jr.	0-720448	Pilot		1051
47.	Dickson, Jackson C.	0-774574	Co-Pilot		1051
48.	Dresslar, Frank A., Jr.	0-778752	Co-Pilot		1051
49.	Ellingson, Erling O.	0-774590	Co-Pilot		1051
50.	Ellis, Stephen W.	0-778755	Co-Pilot		1051
51.	Flud, Cecil W.	0-718604	Co-Pilot	Asst Trans O	1051
52.	Gary, Edward E.	0-824463	Pilot		1051
53.	Greer, Buford D.	0-778784	Co-Pilot		1051
54.	Harper, Robert M.	0-765973	Pilot	Athletic O.	1051
55.	Harral, William R., Jr.	0-831700	Co-Pilot	Asst PX O	1051
56.	Hathaway, Frank C.	0-769436	Pilot	Asst Eng O	1051
57.	Hession, Harold J.	0-782281	Co-Pilot	Asst Pers Equip O	1051
58.	Hicks, Earl G., Jr	0-769446	Co-Pilot	Public Relations O	1051
59.	Hubbard, Robert A.	0-2071605	Navigator		1034
60.	Jacobsen, Thomas F.	0-765990	Co-Pilot	Asst Mess O	1051
61.	Jones, Kenneth V.	0-719678	Co-Pilot		1051
62.	Keep, Donald L.	0-721774	Co-Pilot		1051
63.	Lehrman, Abraham	0-2071812	Navigator		1034

#	Name	ASN	Role	Duty	Code
64.	Michaels, George	O-834467	Pilot	Asst Supply O.	1051
65.	Miller, Robert K.	O-696946	Co-Pilot	Asst Ins O, Asst War Bond O	1051
66.	Pethke, Clarence M.	O-834490	Pilot	Asst Supply O	1051
67.	Quilici, Ray A.	O-719736	Co-Pilot		1051
68.	Richards, Daniel W.	O-822811	Co-Pilot	Asst Eng O, Asst Comm O	1051
69.	Schrepple, Paul F.	O-2007315	Pilot	Ground Safety O	1051
70.	Scott, Ruford D.	O-831820	Co-Pilot	Post Ex O Asst Comm O	1051
71.	Shaver, Monson W.	O-769356	Co-Pilot	W & BO	1051
72.	Shoemaker, J.R.	O-2007616	Pilot		1051
73.	Siegle, Richard W.	O-680075	Co-Pilot		1051
74.	Snyder, Rudolph D.	O-2060122	Co-Pilot		1051
75.	Southgate, Douglas D.	O-833838	Co-Pilot	Asst T-Supply O	1051
76.	Summer, Charles E., Jr.	O-720363	Co-Pilot	Asst Intell O	1051
77.	Tatum, Charles M.	O-819212	Co-Pilot	Asst Adj, Asst Operation O	1051
78.	Vittum, Calvin H.	O-835301	Pilot		1051
79.	Warren, Norman D.	O-689830	Pilot		1051
80.	Welton, Tom, Jr.	O-766976	Co-Pilot		1051
81.	West, Virgil W., Jr.	O-837585	Co-Pilot	Special Serv O	1051

Flight Officers

#	Name	ASN	Role	Duty	Code
82.	Brashear, Sam O.	T-125905	Pilot		1051
83.	Delong, James M.	T-3653	Co-Pilot		1051
84.	Hebbel, Donald D.	T-2914	Pilot	Fire Marshall	1051
85.	Hoxie, William E.	T-3487	Co-Pilot		1051
86.	Kramer, Wayne M.	T-125790	Pilot		1051
87.	Larosa, Frank C.	T-2917	Pilot		1051
88.	Loudin, Blaine H.	T-124117	Co-Pilot		1051
89.	Murphy, Joseph D.	T-3958	Co-Pilot	Asst W & BO	1051
90.	Tveit, Orvin A.	T-4241	Co-Pilot		1051
91.	Wheeler, Ray A.	T-124906	Pilot		1051
92.	Zagata, John L.	T-65832	Co-Pilot		1051
93.	Zarkos, Arthur J.	T-4495	Co-Pilot	Recognition O, Asst Intell O	1051

Officers Attached

Captain

#	Name	ASN	Role	Duty	Code
94.	Simmang, Arthur V.	O-39888		Flight Surgeon	3161

6th Troop Carrier Squadron Roster of Enlisted Men

	Name	ASN	Department/Duty	Duty Code

1st Sergeants

1.	Chain, Charles H.A., Jr.	33082151	Orderly Room-1st Sgt	502

Master Sergeants

2.	McGregor, Ralph B.	15017315	Eng-Electrical Spec	685
3.	Proctor, William E.	6903782	Comm-Section Chief	542
4.	Russell, George A.	17018675	Eng-Crew Chief	750
5.	Weaver, James W.	17014371	Eng-Line Chief	750

Tech Sergeants

6.	Acord, Lawrence L.	19005107	Eng-Inspector	2750
7.	Arehart, Weldon B.	7020850	T Supply-T Supply NCO (TDY US)	826
8.	Canaday, Charley C.	6549933	Trans-Motor NCO (TDY US)	014
9.	Clayton, Clay D.	17025186	Eng-A/C Maint Tech	747
10.	Evans, Robert W.	39163683	Eng-Carpenter	050
11.	Finkbeiner, Clarence H.	33071699	Comm-Tel & Tel Lineman	238
12.	Fundum, Walter H.	17021119	Eng-Crew Chief	2750
13.	Gilzow, Sim H.	17008560	Eng-Crew Chief	2750
14.	Grose, Leo R.	15017599	Eng-Crew Chief	2750
15.	Halper, Charles	12008932	Eng-Instrument Spec	686
16.	Harris, Clarence S.	33077893	Trans-Mechanic	014
17.	Hawley, Joseph O.	17025223	Eng-Flight Chief	2750
18.	Heasley, Lyle E.	13009159	Eng-Adm NCO	502
19.	Hoffman, William	15074914	Eng-Elec Spec	685
20.	Kiger, Burl H.	15019646	Eng-A/C Maint Tech	747
21.	Lambert, Albert L., Jr.	33082161	Orderly Room-Chief Clerk (TDY US)	502
22.	Lindgren, Loel C.	37307012	Orderly Room-Adm NCO	502
23.	Purring, Alexander J.	20330513	Opns-Parachute Shop Chief (TDYUS)	620
24.	Seifried, Earl S.	7021524	SD-374th TC Gp, Util Tech	822
25.	Smith, Herbert G.	38089483	Eng-A/C Maint Tech (TDY US)	747
26.	Staun, Philip J.	33088393	Eng-Welder	256
27.	Thompson, Lee B., Jr.	13017927	Adm Supply-Adm Supply NCO	821
28.	Van Winkle, Albert E.	15045504	Eng-Crew Chief	750
29.	Zartman, Rufus H.	33078277	Comm-Radar Mech	849

Staff Sergeants

#	Name	Serial	Role	Code
30.	Armstrong, Terry M., Jr.	17008729	Comm-Radio Mech	754
31.	Banner, Eugene B.	33088531	Trans-Mechanic	014
32.	Benesh, Albert J.	33088643	Mess-Actg Mess Sgt	824
33.	Brabec, Sidney J.	37168468	Comm-Radio Oper & Mech	2756
34.	Castle, Floyd, Jr.	35266245	Comm-Radio Mech	754
35.	Clukey, Joseph A.	31147358	Comm-Radio Mech	754
36.	Corsa, Victor A.	33078231	Eng-Carpenter (TDY US)	050
37.	Deardorff, Richard S.	33078202	Eng-Elec Spec (TDY US)	685
38.	Dugan, Frank G.	12137044	Eng-Crew Chief	2750
39.	Epling, Raymond	35508187	Comm-Radio Oper & Mech	2756
40.	Fears, Claude E.	16073461	Comm-Radio Oper & Mech	2756
41.	Ferguson, James A.	17027446	Mess Sgt	824
42.	Fusaro, Anthony P.	32561026	Comm-Radio Oper & Mech	2756
43.	Gillentine, Lloyd A.	38089345	Orderly Room-Mail Clerk	055
44.	Gittis, Morris	33071609	Adm Supply-Clerk	835
45.	Goldthwait, Edward L.	31073270	Eng A/C Maint Tech	747
46.	Hagerty, Joseph A.	33071589	Operations-Parachute	620
47.	Halye, Roy O.	13007232	Operations-Adm NCO	502
48.	Helton, Albert P.	37151446	Eng-Crew Chief	2750
49.	Hibner, William G.	15081058	T Supply Clerk	835
50.	Klotz, George	7022722	Operations	502
51.	Kopp, Wilbur W.	36324520	Mess-Asst Mess Sgt	824
52.	Logan, George M.	38102879	Eng-Crew Chief	2750
53.	Maher, Vincent A.	33013955	Comm-Radio Mech	754
54.	Mullally, John F.	37145461	Eng-Crew Chief	2750
55.	Neighbors, James D.	35696678	Comm-Radio Oper & Mech	2756
56.	Nelson, Carl I.	37144972	Eng-Crew Chief	2750
57.	Parker, Chester P.	16062805	Eng-Crew Chief	2750
58.	Petersen, Garrett V.	37145308	Eng-Crew Chief	2750
59.	Richardson, Warren E.	17002880	Eng-Crew Chief	2750
60.	Robbins, Wilbur G.	37097079	Eng-Crew Chief	2750

Staff Sergeants

#	Name	Serial	Role	Code
61.	Roberts, Foye K.	18065977	Eng-Crew Chief	2750
62.	Rosenthal, Herman	32334538	Eng-A/C Maint Tech	747
63.	Ross, Arnold M.	37162406	Eng-Crew Chief	2750
64.	Rothman, Jay C.	33071632	Eng-Instr. Spec.	686
65.	Sidorowicz, Stanley J.	36110223	Comm-Clerk Typist	805
66.	Stanton, Stanley J.	32419490	Intell-Intell Spec	631
67.	Stolarski, Walter M.	12080363	Eng-Crew Chief	2750
68.	Terkel, Charles	32320476	Operations Clerk	055
69.	Triol, Raymond H.	33085305	T-Supply Clerk Typist	405
70.	Wilson, Walter R.	38438053	Eng-Crew Chief	2750
71.	SgtsBaker, Eugene C.	33118407	Intell-Clerk	055
72.	Bargainnier, Malcolm M., Jr.	34088504	Eng-Crew Chief	2750
73.	Bartels, Melvin W.	17018641	Mess-Asst Mess Sgt	824
74.	Batson, Oscar J.	18085973	HQ-Duty Soldier	590
75.	Bokshan, Louis D.	16062802	Eng-Crew Chief	2750
76.	Brooks, Guy M.	33089327	Eng-A/C Maint Tech	747
77.	Caputo, Anthony	33139900	Eng-A/C Maint Tech	747
78.	Carter, Henry C.	31036999	Eng-Clerk Typist	405
79.	Cissell, William R.	38293427	Eng-Inst Spec	686
80.	Cooper, Joseph F.	33162852	Eng-A/C Maint Tech	747
81.	Crooks, George H.	31037023	HQ-Carpenter	050
82.	Cullender, Bascom C.	38089386	Eng-Carpenter	050
83.	Daniel, James W.	35210794	Mess-Cook	060
84.	DeGeorge, Pasquale A.	32235433	Mess-Cook	060
85.	Droz, Theodore J.	36328197	Eng-A/C Maint Tech	747
86.	Filler, Stephen J.	33603486	Operations-Parachute	620
87.	Fidler, Walter	16045939	Adm Supply-Stock Rec Clerk	835
88.	Fischmann, Herschel W.	36326247	Eng-Crew Chief	2750
89.	Flatt, Armel L.	18097020	Trans-Truck Driver	345
90.	Fraser, Robert	33173889	Mess-Cook	060
91.	Geidel, Keith C.	33163188	Eng-A/C Maint Tech	747
92.	Goyette, Frank R.	17016442	Trans-Mech	014
93.	Hammond, Dean F.	17055162	Comm-Radio Oper & Mech	2756
94.	Herr, Charles L.	39255579	Eng-A/C Maint Tech	747
95.	Hill, Horace V.	34201855	Comm-Clerk	055
96.	Hudson, John A.	38086699	Eng-Clerk Typist	405
97.	Johns, Ross N.	36880816	Comm-Radio Oper & Mech	2756
98.	Jury, Maurice E.	18075731	Eng-Crew Chief	2750
99.	Kempf, Joseph L.	17021073	Trans-Spec Vehicle Oper	932
100.	Kewin, Kenneth J.	36232983	Trans-Truck Driver	345
101.	Kiefer, Clifford E.	12077522	Comm-Radio Oper	756
102.	Kohn, Morris L.	31134752	Comm-Radio Oper & Mech	2756
103.	Kopelson, Sidney	35285866	Eng-A/C Maint Tech	747
104.	Ludlow, Chester M.	35350425	Adm Supply-Clerk Typist	405
105.	Manes, Vincent W.	32410027	Eng-Crew Chief	2750
106.	Maul, Walter E.	32293240	Eng-Welder	256

#	Name	Serial	Duty	Code
107.	Meli, Jerome S.	32282514	Eng-Crew Chief	2750
108.	Miles, Cecil S.	37181555	Operations-Clerk Typist	405
109.	Mooney, Sidney C.	39019207	Eng-A/C Maint Tech	747
110.	Morgan, John A.	34240940	Comm-Radio Oper & Mech	2756
111.	Nance, Floyd D.	38089102	Eng-A/C Maint Tech	747
112.	Nelson, Paul L., Jr.	34828475	Comm-Radio Oper & Mech	2756
113.	Parrish, Harvey R.	17012702	Trans-Spec Vehicle Oper	932
114.	Prince, Arthur F.	35134482	Eng-A/C Maint Tech	747
115.	Reynolds, Adam	32282707	Eng-Crew Chief	2750
116.	Salerno, Louis R.	32139777	Eng-Sheet Metal Worker	555
117.	Samalis, Edward A.	36502245	Mess-Cook	060
118.	Scarsella, Antonio	39389840	Mess-Cook	060
119.	Serritella, Vincent F.	32451462	Comm-Radio Oper & Mech	756
120.	Sharrett, Charles W.	35617027	Orderly Room-Personnel Clerk	405
121.	Shea, Daniel P.	32419963	Operations-Clerk	055
122.	Sobieraj, Bernard J.	33173821	Eng-Inst Spec	686
123.	Spierto, Pasquale	31139029	Comm-Clerk	055
124.	Thompson, Samuel R.	32139569	Eng-Dope & Fabric Worker	548
125.	Tootsey, Louis	15097583	Comm-Radio Oper & Mech	2756
126.	Trowbridge, Nolen L.	15333710	Eng-Crew Chief	2750

Sergeants

#	Name	Serial	Duty	Code
127.	Tudor, Neal	38102894	Eng-Elec Spec	685
128.	Vancio, John	20225174	Eng-A/C Maint Tech	747
129.	Varner, Pershing W.	39600983	Eng-Armament	511
130.	Wilhelm, Russell E.	33618128	Comm-Radio Oper & Mech	2750
131.	Wurtz, Camillus J.	18136813	Eng-Crew Chief	2750
132.	Yonker, Merle F.	17012129	Trans-Truck Driver	345

Corporals

#	Name	Serial	Duty	Code
133.	Alagood, Oscar L.	38563145	Comm-Radio Oper & Mech	2756
134.	Babachicos, James C.	31127480	Comm-Radio Oper & Mech	2756
135.	Bahr, Alfred W.	33078337	Trans-Truck Driver	345
136.	Beehrle, Louis E.	37167316	Eng-Painter	144
137.	Blake, Clarence W.	37166902	Eng-Armament	511
138.	Blalack, Raymond A.	38529962	Comm-Radio Oper & Mech	2756
139.	Bloise, Frank S.	42041908	Eng-Crew Chief	2750
140.	Borowski, Bernard F.	36502433	Mess-Cook	060
141.	Brady, Johnny H.	35651593	Eng-Crew Chief	2750
142.	Busse, Carl	35048400	Eng-Crew Chief	2750
143.	Canavan, Robert J.	32868785	Eng-Crew Chief	2750
144.	Carroll, Loren H.	38530712	Comm-Radio Oper & Mech	2756
145.	Casteline, Peter	32778081	Eng-Crew Chief	2750
146.	Clark, Albert	33694526	Eng-A/C Maint Tech	747
147.	Clayton, Daniel M.	35459808	Trans-Truck Driver	345
148.	Collins, Sherman D.	32779005	Eng-Crew Chief	2750
149.	Connolly, Henry F.	12147809	Eng-Crew Chief	2750
150.	Corn, Hyman	32982358	Eng-Crew Chief	2750
151.	Davidson, Ernest H.	34490555	Comm-Radio Oper & Mech	2756
152.	Donovan, Joseph D.	37737457	Eng-Crew Chief	2750
153.	Doyle, Patrick L.	31085740	T-Supply-Clerk	835
154.	Elliott, Herbert	38462080	Comm Radio Oper & Mech	2756
155.	Ferguson, Robert E.	14060671	Eng-A/C Maint Tech	747
156.	Fetterman, Francis J.	33014552	Eng-A/C Maint Tech	747
157.	Figert, Earl E.	35584882	Operations-Parachute	620
158.	Fikso, Adam, Jr.	19187977	Comm-Radio Oper & Mech	2756
159.	Fitchitt, Thomas E.	19146669	Comm-Radio Oper & Mech	2756
160.	Fuchs, August E.	36531785	Comm-Radio Oper & Mech	2756
161.	Gallagher, Robert H.	32779056	Eng-Crew Chief	2750
162.	Giovanangelo, Leo D.	11062711	Eng-A/C Maint Tech	747
163.	Glanzer, Joseph P.	39091119	Trans-Truck Driver	345
164.	Goldberg, Samuel	39271901	Comm-Radio Oper & Mech	2756
165.	Gronek, Adolph J.	32934418	Comm-Radio Oper & Mech	2756
166.	Gunderson, Walter H.	32800410	Comm-Radio Oper & Mech	2756
167.	Guzzetta, John	36649446	Comm-Radio Oper & Mech	2756
168.	Jones, Calvin C.	38230267	Eng-Crew Chief	2750
169.	Kost, Robert E.	37563605	Comm-Radio Oper & Mech	2756
170.	Labow, Robert G.	16147565	Orderly Room-Clerk Typist	405
171.	Manas, Bernard	32419879	Trans-Speck Vehicle Oper	932
172.	McCabe, Edward L.	12089598	Comm-Radio Oper & Mech	2756
173.	McGowan, James J.	32417316	Mess-Duty Soldier	590
174.	Moffett, Herbert L.	35793116	Comm-Radio Oper & Mech	2756
175.	Nauenburg, Harold M.	17122736	Operations-Clerk Typist	405
176.	Opello, Louis E.	33142042	Trans-Truck Driver	345
177.	Peters, Keith L.	37346579	Eng-Crew Chief	2750
178.	Pierce, Carl F.	17070929	Eng-Crew Chief	2750
179.	Rayon, Louis C., Jr.	38240468	Eng-A/C Maint Tech	747
180.	Roloff, Oscar	35066217	Eng-Crew Chief	2750
181.	Ruddy, George	13108918	Eng-Asst Inspection	2750
182.	Schreiner, John Z.	12073547	Comm-Radio Oper & Mech	2756

183.	Sisson, Edward L.	37141186	Mess-Cook	060
184.	Snyder, Carl E.	17128587	Eng-A/C Maint Tech	747
185.	Stephenson, George B.	19115907	Comm-Radar Mech	849
186.	Sullivan, James E.	31073288	T Supply-Stock Clerk	835
187.	Sutton, Raymond	37371770	Trans-Speck Vehicle Oper	932
188.	Thaler, Joseph	11069730	Comm-Radio Oper & Mech	2756
189.	Thayer, Herbert H.	32379292	Trans-Truck Driver	345
190.	Thompson, Creighton E.	18086252	Orderly Room-Clerk Typist	405
191.	Vandyke, Claude H.	33647078	Comm-Radar Mech	849
192.	Volkart, Kenneth L.	33564580	Comm-Radio Oper & Mech	2756

Corporals

193.	Vroman, Robert L.	16035784	Mess-Duty Soldier	590
194.	Williams, Charles R.	36594227	Eng-Crew Chief	2750
195.	Winters, Alan M.	17084521	Comm-Radar Mechanic	849
196.	Wilson, Kenneth D.	38517079	Comm-Radar Mechanic	849

Privates First Class

197.	Alley, James B.	6966208	Comm-Radio Oper & Mech	2756
198.	Ashley, Carl R.	14140174	Mess-Cook	060
199.	Black, Hermus L.	35805436	Eng-Crew Chief	2750
200.	Bobber, Raymond G.	36246603	Eng-A/C Maint Tech	747
201.	Cohen, Jerome L.	32875908	Eng-A/C Maint Tech	747
202.	Crowley, Eugene A.	32472765	Comm-Radio Oper & Mech	2756
203.	David, Roy L.	37505057	Trans-Truck Driver	345
204.	Eames, Douglas A.	12084352	Comm-Radio Oper & Mech	2756
205.	Frair, Warren H.	38338297	Mess-Butcher	037
206.	Garvey, Ross W.	17151498	Eng-Crew Chief	2750
207.	Gurneau, Lawrence T.	37166906	HQ-Duty Soldier	590
208.	Hanes, Leroy	38343595	Eng-Crew Chief	2750
209.	Hanna, Robert B., Jr.	38385564	Eng-Crew Chief	2750
210.	Hill, Rolland E.	18161490	Trans-Duty Soldier	590
211.	Humphrey, Willie H.	39457192	Trans-Truck Driver	345
212.	Kelley, Joe H.	17112132	Eng-A/C Maint Tech	747
213.	Kostelecky, Lloyd E.	38444566	Eng-Crew Chief	2750
214.	Laszewski, Chester S.	32913592	Eng-Crew Chief	2750
215.	Marrs, Oscar D.	36742830	Comm-Radio Oper & Mech	2756
216.	Miller, Emanuel W.	37141231	Trans-Truck Driver	345
217.	Mitchell, Elmer E.	20367095	Eng-Crew Chief	2750
218.	Neely, Joseph S.	32486199	T Supply-Clerk Typist	405
219.	Nostrand, Fred R.	32888541	Eng-Crew Chief	2750
220.	Sadler, Robert W.	20913205	Comm-Radio Mech	754
221.	Sampson, Olaf	37166630	Eng-Duty Soldier	590
222.	Taylor, Henry F.	6927207	Trans-Mechanic	014
223.	Wooten, William G.	34722934	Eng-A/C Maint Tech	747

Privates

224.	Cammisa, Samuel D.	6948832	Eng-Duty Soldier	590
225.	Denton, Robert A.	35805601	Adm. Supply-Duty Soldier	590
226.	Gordon, Eugene S.	37336125	HQ-Duty Soldier	590
227.	Karp, David	12027968	Comm-Radio Oper & Mech	2756
228.	McFadyen, William B.	18178289	Eng-A/C Maint Tech	747
229.	Severino, Anthony J.	32177125	Eng-Duty Soldier	590
230.	Spencer, Wesley F.	37503093	Comm-Radio Oper & Mech	2756

Medical Detachment Assigned

Staff Sergeants

231.	Venditto, Angelo	32178407	Medical-Medical NCO	673

Corporals

232.	Laitas, Walter	16053300	Medical-Medical Corpsman	657
233.	Lowry, Russell	35133531	Medical-Medical Corpsman	657
234.	Robutka, Peter J.	32250205	Medical-Medical Corpsman	657

Index

Editor's Note: This index does not include entries from Appendix 'A' through Appendix 'II', only the general history is indexed.

– A –

Abau Island 40
Absolom, John 41, 42
Adams, Fred 14, 15, 23, 36, 45, 46, 53, 63, 64, 82, 89, 97
Adelaide 73
Admiralty Islands 86
Aisenson, David 9
Aitape 85, 86
Aiyura 87
Alexishafen 68
Alice Springs 18, 73
Allen, Ned 20, 74
Amami 53
Amberley Field 10, 38
Anderson, Joseph 87
Appling, Sgt. 49
Arcadia 51, 76
Archer Field 16, 17, 18, 24, 26, 38, 49, 54
Arthur, Lt. 41
Ashcroft, Lucas J. 9
Ashley, Burl 31
Auckland 51
August, Floyd 40, 42
Australia 8, 20, 30, 31, 34, 38

– B –

Baer, Charles R. 9, 14, 15, 22, 24, 26, 46
Baker, Leonidas 63
Ballams 64
Barin, Sgt. 111
Baron, Harry 104, 108, 112, 114
Barron, Theodore W. 39, 42
Batchlor Air Field 19
Bates, Private 41
Bathurst Island 16, 48
Batte, Cecil E. 112
Bauer, Indian Joe 38
Baylor, Blair D. 78
Beaver, George 27
Beebe, Robert C. 46, 64
Beebe, William 82
Bell, William J. 62
Bellus, John 42
Bena Bena 22, 53, 57, 61, 62, 64, 71, 72
Berringer, Edward R. 82
Besley, Laura 110
Best, Robert T. 112
Biak 56, 68, 69, 85, 86, 87
Bill, Lieutenant 41
Bitoi Ridge 64
Blamey, General 65
Bobdubi Ridge 63, 64
Boddie, William P. 77
Bolger, Ray 52, 83
Booth, John 46
Bostrom, Frank 17
Bougainville 69, 96
Boulden, Sgt. 49
Bowman Field 49
Box, Daniel T. 87
Boyington, Pappy 38
Bradford, William L. 46
Brady, Lester M. 20
Brandon, Martin 42
Brereton, Lewis H. 4, 16
Brisbane 11, 16, 18, 23, 26, 27, 38, 45, 48, 49, 51, 54, 69, 71, 73, 82
Bronson, Captain 90

Broome 16, 48
Brown, Dickson 95
Bulatao, Ben 111
Bulkeley, John B. 17
Bulolo 11, 21, 22, 43, 53, 60, 64, 72
Buna 23, 30, 39, 63, 69
Burley, Enoch P. 82
Burma 45
Burnell, Jack 96
Butler, Duane 40, 42
Buttons 37

– C –

Cactus 37
Cagayen Valley 93
Cairns 51, 86
Camp Darley 16
Canberra 18
Canton Island 27, 34
Cape Cod 4
Cape Gloucester 97
Cape Hatteras 4
Carlson, Robert E. 51, 100
Carter, Warren 57, 86, 88, 99
Cartwright, Philip 63
Cavanaugh 82
Cederholm, Bernard 15
Charleville 26, 69
Cherry, Bill 33, 34
Chesapeake 6
Christiansen, Bert C. 87
Christmas Island 27, 33, 34
Church, Frank 23, 66
Clack, Mel 9
Clapper, Raymond 63
Cloncurry 19, 26, 69, 71
Clote, Johnny 98
Coile, Henry G. 62
Cooper, Merian C. 86
Corkrum, Uriah F. 15, 25
Cornett, Benton V. 87
Corregidor 17
Costello 83
Coutts, James M. 9
Crandell, John A. 9, 42
Crecelius, Randall 63
Cressey, George J. 46
Crete 6
Crossette 22
Crystal Creek Trail 64
Cuba 49
Curtin, John 67

– D –

Daly Waters 19, 45, 69, 73
Darwin 16, 17, 19, 24, 26, 30, 45, 64, 73
Davies, Ron 40, 42
Decker, Kenneth 110, 112
DeGarmo, James 9
Del Monte Air Field 17
DeMeza, Janice 9
DeShazer, Robert 49, 118
Dewitt, Sgt. 49
Dillman, Robert 36
Dobbins 93
Dobodura 11, 23, 53, 54, 60, 76
Doubilet, David 34
Dulag 69
Duncan Field 6

Dunckel, William C. 98
Dunn, John R. 46, 47
Dunne, D.M. 110, 120
DuPont, A. Felix 87

– E –

Echard, Rexford W. 77
Eckberg, Philip 9, 42, 46
Efate 37
Elsmore, Ray T. 90, 108
Erickson 60
Espíritu Santo 35
Essendon 49
Estrumse, Elmer F. 46, 47, 49
Ethell, "Paddy" 41
Euart, Kenneth A. 103

– F –

Fahey, W. J. C. 9
Failing, Carlos 40, 42
Fall River 54
Farr, Ned 9
Fawn 60
Feeney, Francis R. 46
Feigus, Capt. 49
Fenton 64
Fernow 39
Field, Henderson 51
Fiji Island 34
Finisterre Mountains 66, 67
Finschhafen 21, 54
Fitch 67
Fitzgerald, Robert W. 114
Floyd, Privates 40
Ford, Ernest C. 9, 27, 29
Formosa 120
Foss, Joe 38
Foster, George 31, 63, 74
Frank, Sam 74
Franklin, Charles F. 70
Frederick Howard 88
Friedman, Harry 105
Fryberger, Alan 38
Ft. Benning 6

– G –

Garbutt Field 49, 54, 76, 83
Garoke 53
Garrison Hills 64
Gatty, Harold 16, 48
Geatches, Stephen S. 115, 120
Gellasch, Donald 104, 108, 112, 114, 122
Gerling, Robert J. 9, 14, 15, 16, 30, 39
Gerry, William 9
Gibson, Charles A. 48, 70
Glotzback, Gene R. 52, 54, 60
Gona 60
Goodenough Island 54
Goodwin, Bert 114
Green Island 96
Greening, Glenn F. 77
Gregory, Frederick F. 103
Grimes, Lt. 22, 24, 26
Grimes, Myron 46, 86, 108, 112
Groote Island 64
Grove, Gerald 40, 42
Guadalcanal 23, 31, 35, 36, 37

Guile, Cecil B. 62
Gunn, Paul I. 16, 18, 47
Gusan 54
Gustofson, S. 83

– H –

Hackett, Major 9
Hackman, Jay 9
Haiti 49
Hallem, Philip 85, 91
Halmahara Islands 100
Halsey 34, 38
Hamilton Field 14, 31
Hammond, Sgt. 49
Hampton, Edgar W. 16, 21, 23, 24, 43, 45, 46, 51, 62, 66
Hanna, Eleanor 110
Harmon, General 51
Hartley, Donald K. 112
Hastings, Margaret 110, 111
Hatfield, Lansing 52, 83
Hayes, Harry M. 63
Hayes, Major 99
Hellweg, Charles E. 49, 64, 115
Henderson Field 31, 34, 36, 37
Henry 18
Henry, Fred G. 20, 46, 48
Hensman, Ray 36, 51
Herring, General 58, 65
Hickam Field 33
Hicks, Ed 40, 42
Higgins, Clarence G. 15
Hill Field 14, 15
Hillenbrand, Louis 82
Hilton, James 109
Hix, John 57
Holcomb, General 38
Hollandia 56, 69, 84, 85, 86, 108
Holleman, Ed 39, 40, 42
Holleman, Sergeant 40
Holt, Arthur E. 14
Homboldt 85
Honolulu 32
Horn Island 64
Horn, William 9
Horr, Stanley F. 78
Horst, Larry 50
Howe, John D. 15
Hunter 101, 108 111, 112, 120
Huon Peninsula 64
Hutchison 109, 122
Hyde Park 54

– I –

Imparato, Edward T. 7, 8, 11, 14, 15, 16, 18, 20, 25, 30, 33, 35, 40, 42, 46, 63, 76, 85, 88, 89, 90, 108, 109, 115, 120, 121
Imparato, Jean C. 9
Ingram, James W. 14, 20
Iron Bottom Bay 37
Islands, Babuyan 118

– J –

Jackson Airdrome 28
Jackson, Eugene 23, 47, 51
Jackson Strip 27
Jacobs, John F. 63
Jacques, Pearre D. 46, 78
Java 16, 48
Jeffries 41
Jennings, William P. 63
Jewett, Chaplain 82
Johnson, Sergeant 59

Johnston, George 22, 24
Jordan, A.C. 108
Jordan, J.B. 14, 15

– K –

Kadena 118
Kaiapit 66
Kavieng 69
Kelley, Joseph B. 91, 93, 100
Kenney, George 9, 18, 23, 57, 61, 114, 117, 121
Kent, Helen 110
Keough, John J. 46
Kershner, George 40, 42
Ketchman, Sam 50, 64
Kimball, George C. 47
King, Ben 32, 33
King, Curtis 63
Kirsch, Albert 36
Kirschner, Sergeant 37
Klatt, Sgt. 87
Knoka, John 82
Kokoda 21, 49, 60
Komiatum 63, 64
Kreuger, Walter 97
Krolik, Richard 63
Kropheski, Chaplains 82
Kuriles 120
Kysor, Saul T. 103

– L –

Lababia 64
Lackey, John 23, 27, 28, 46, 47, 53, 62, 93
Lae 11, 20, 21, 31, 53, 54, 56, 58, 60, 63, 64, 66, 69, 86
Lair, Talbert B. 115
Lakin, Clarence A. 9
Laloki River 52
Lamar, Jim 36
LaMay, Curtis 5
Langebartel, Edward P. 8, 100, 111
LaRoche, James N. 63
Lattier, Lt. 27
Lawson, Captain 5
Lawson Field 6
Lee, Bill 6
Lee, Chaplain 105
Leiberman, Capt. 49
Leron 66
Lewis, Joe 52, 83
Lewis, Melvin C. 16, 25, 30, 35
Leyte 56, 69, 90, 99
Lieberman, Alexander 78, 111, 115
Lingayen Gulf 93
Little, Little Jack 52, 83
Livingstone, Bob 9
Loder 93
Los Banos 96
Lownie, Captain 70
Ludwig, C. V. 115
Luzon 43, 56, 93

– M –

MacArthur, Douglas 4, 6, 8, 9, 15, 17, 18, 19, 20, 21, 34, 38, 62, 108, 117
Machinato 118
Mackay 54, 84
Madang 21, 68
Maguire, John R. A. 82
Maidenburg, Ben 92
Malmstone, Blesch 9, 63
Manila 62, 99, 109
Manning, Mr. 60
Manokwari 69

Markham-Ramu Valley 64, 65, 66, 67, 68
Marsh, David 40, 41
Marshall, G.C. 20, 21
Maxwell, Neil O. 49
McArthur, Edwin 52, 83
McCain, John 60
McCartney, David T. 78
McClelland, Hamish 46, 47
McCollom, John 109, 111, 112
McCollom, Robert E. 110
McCollough 18
McCullen, Lt. 49
McCullock 42
McCullough, James A. 48
McIlvain, Joe 9
McLean, Bruce 9
McMurray, Glenn 8, 9, 43, 65, 87
Means, Russell E. 9
Melbourne 6, 10, 17, 18, 49, 73
Menauri 72
Merauke 64
Merman, Arthur 51
Mihalos 22
Miles, James F. 82
Milne Bay 11, 23, 49, 58, 60
Milwee, Bob 97
Mindoro 43, 92
Mingoes, Howard 29
Mitchell, Billy 4, 5, 6
Mitchell, Donald R. 103
Moak, Vernon 42
Mobley, John 40, 42
Monroe, Chaplain 82
Monson, Robert S. 9
Montez, Antonio 42
Moore 18
Morden, Norman D. 118
Morgan, John A. 115
Morgan, David A. 104
Morotai Island 68, 69
Mt. Hagen 53
Mubo 63, 64
Mullens, Clement 85

– N –

Nadzab 20, 54, 56, 64, 65
Naha 118
Neemfoor 86
Nerauke 86
New Caledonia 23, 27, 34, 38
New Guinea 7, 18, 19, 20, 22, 23, 27, 28, 30, 31, 37, 38, 49, 51, 52, 56
New Hanover 68
New Hebrides 36
Newfoundland 49
Newton, Ted 9
Nichols, Erickson S. 11, 16, 24, 45, 48, 51
Nichols, Ruth 16
Nixon-Smith, J. 87
Noemfoor Island 68
Norgan, Leroy M. 14, 15
Notestine, Ronald E. 49

– O –

Okinawa 6, 20, 120
Olson, John E. 9
Oodnadatta 73
O'Shea, William J. 89
Owi 86, 88

– P –

Padilla, Margarito 42
Palau 56
Palmer, Henry E. 111

Palmyra Island 33
Panay islands 99
Paolillo, J. 41
Papua 19, 23, 52
Pasig River 93
Patrick, Robert 8
Patterson, H.E. 30
Patton, Marvin 40, 42
Payne, Samuel V. 62
Payton, Doggie 46
Pearce, George M., Jr. 9
Pearl Harbor 32
Pearson, John D. 20, 21, 63, 67, 79, 83, 112
Peleiu Island 69, 112
Pemberton 39
Penn, Perry 9, 27, 30, 33, 46, 53
Pershing, General 4
Perth 16, 48, 73
Peterson, Corporal 39
Peterson, Lawrence 42
Peterson, William A. 46
Philippines 17, 20, 43, 120
Piekutowski 60
Piper, Robert 7, 9, 39, 109
Pitaro 25
Pitch, Steven J. 40, 42
Pitts, Joel G. 62, 69
Pongani 23, 39, 60
Popondetta 23, 60
Porrello, Salvatore J. 103
Port Moresby 10, 11, 17, 18, 19, 20, 21, 22, 23, 24, 27, 30, 31, 37, 38, 39, 45, 49, 51, 54, 55, 56, 57, 58, 62, 66, 70, 71, 76
Port Romilly 87
Powers, Billy E. 87
Prentice, Paul P. 43
Prentiss, Paul H. 24, 45, 51, 53, 56, 61, 62, 67, 82, 84, 92
Prosson, Peter J. 109
Pruett, Melvin L. 115

– Q –

Queensland 10, 49, 51, 54
Quest, Charles 82
Quinn, William H. 63

– R –

Rabaul 69
Raddatiz, Charles 42
Radji 85
Ramirez, Rammy 110
Ramu River 66
Ray, Chaplain 82
Reece, Irdle V. 84
Rehrer, Harvey 30, 53
Rennels, Lamont N. 63, 115
Rennels, Pete 53
Ressenger, Sgt. 49
Rhoades, Emmett E. 78
Rhodes, Dusty 64
Rickenbacker, Eddie 33, 34, 51
Ridley, Captain 41
Rife, Dale 49, 118
Rigo 40
Roberts, Arthur 88
Roche, Hal J. 8
Rockhampton 54
Romero, Theodore 42
Roosevelt, President 20
Roses 37
Ross, Arnold M. 115
Ross, Harry 83

Rowland, Conrad 31, 103
Rush, Frank 82
Ruskin, John 7

– S –

Sador 21
Safia 41
Salamaua 11, 21, 30, 31, 60, 63, 69
Samar Islands 69
Samoa 27
Samuels, Bill 90, 91
Samuels, William 9, 90, 91, 100, 112, 114, 115
San Cristobal 36
San Francisco 15
Sansapor 69
Scanlon, General 48
Schaefer, Dick 9
Schaefer, Ellen 9
Scheer, Private 41
Schrepple, Paul F. 103
Schrom, Gerald A. 116
Schuster 25
Schwensen 60
Scott, Marvin M. 48, 49, 70, 83, 90, 115
Sell, Ramon C. 14, 15
Sevic, Sgt. 49
Sexton, Pappy 46
Shaw, Chaplain 82
Sherman 60
Sherman, Maurice 88
Sherman, Morris I. 63
Shine, Ed 46
Simmang, Arthur V. 81
Simons, Ralph R. 9
Simpson, Hal B. 49, 53, 64, 70, 83
Skindaiwa 64, 72
Skodis, John P. 115
Smith, Bryce 33
Smith, Campbell M. 47
Smith, Don W. 65
Smith, Frank W. 23, 46, 47, 63, 65
Smith, Isaac W. 112
Smith, Robert Barr 8
Smith, William 42
Snow, Major 52
Solomon Islands 23, 36, 38
Soular, Mile 55, 91
Spaatz, Carl A. 117
Springer, Sgt. 120
Stamler, Sgt. 83, 120, 121
Stanton, Richard B. 85
Staun, Philip J. 77
Stearns, Willard R. 15
Sterns, Bill 29
Stewart, Harris B. "Stew" 118
Stokes, Charles 42
Stover 18, 22
Summit 64
Sutherland 17, 67
Swenson, Raymond T. 46
Swing, Joe 112
Sydney 16, 54

– T –

Tacloban 69
Tadji 69, 84, 85, 87
Talman, Ralph G. 87
Teegardin, T/Sgt. 121
Tench, Charles T. 113
Thirty Mile 60
Thomas, Arthur 15, 16, 22, 53
Thomas, Frank 40, 42

Thompson 33, 83
Tokyo 6, 8, 56
Tokyo Rose 28
Tontouta 37, 38
Torbett, Odis B. 115
Townsville 11, 23, 27, 38, 45, 49, 54
Trobriand Islands 54
Tsilli Tsilli 29, 53, 64, 66, 82
Tuck, Elmer L. 89, 115
Turner, Joe 97

– U –

Ulio, J.A. 20, 21

– V –

Vandegrift, Alexander 37, 38
Vandervort, George 37, 39, 42
Vandiver, Ray 18, 23
Vaughter, David C. 9
Vaughter, Dick 26
Verstey, James 42
Vickers Ridge 64
Victoria 49

– W –

Wakde 69, 84, 85
Waldrop, W. O. 115
Walker, Talmadge E. 48
Wallace, G. 41
Walters, Earl 111
Wamsley, George 8, 9, 31, 34, 47, 51, 58
Wamsley, Gerorge 61
Wanegela 23
Ward, Robert L. 47
Warden, JoAnn 9
Warren, John 77
Washington, D.C. 4
Watson, James 31
Wau 11, 21, 22, 24, 29, 30, 31, 43, 52, 53, 56, 58, 59, 60, 61, 63, 64, 69, 71, 72
Webb, Jesse A. 105, 115
Weedin, Wilbur H. 9
Wells, William D. 46
Wentworth, Gerald 51, 52, 105, 115
Wewak 21, 68, 69
Wheeler, R. 41
Whiston, Lt. 70
White, Charles 41
White, Lacy W. 63
Whitehead, Ennis C. 38, 43, 52, 61, 65, 70, 84, 85
Whitmore, Earl T. 14
Whittington, Robert G. 31
Wicklund, Vilmar A. 84
Wilde, Norman 23
Wise 18
Wolfert, Ira 34
Wood, Herman C. 9
Woodlark Island 54
Wright Field 14
Wummer, E. F. 115
Wunder, John P. 103
Wurtsmith, Paul B. 86

– Y –

Yeisley, Keith P. 9
Young, Charles H. 9
Youngren, Earl L. 63
Yuska, Victor A. 15, 25

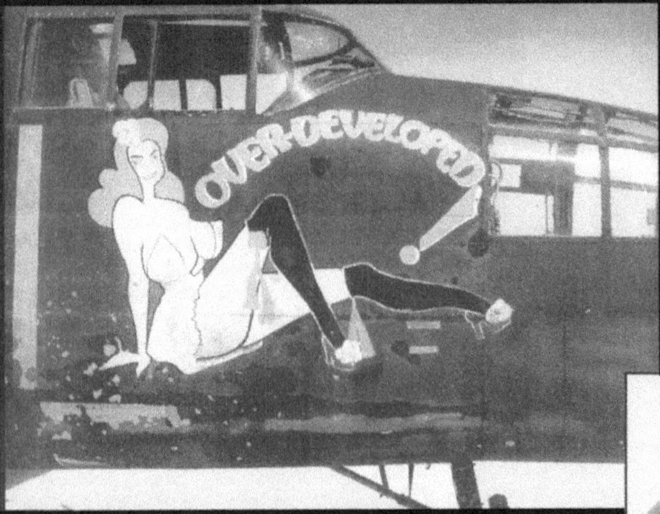
OVER-DEVELOPED

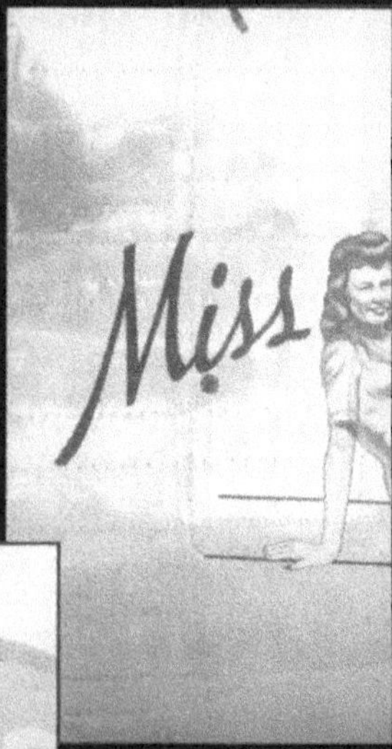
Miss

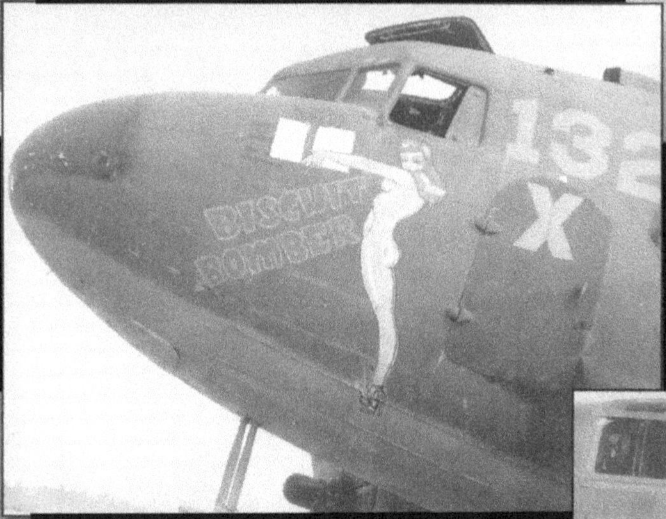
BISCUIT BOMBER
132
X

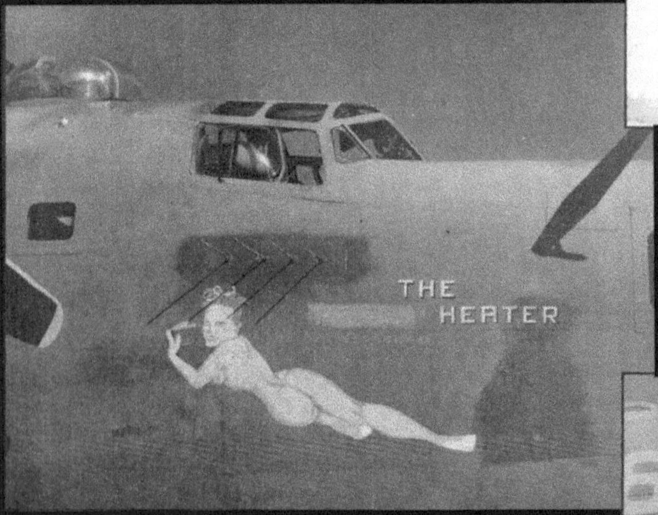
THE HEATER

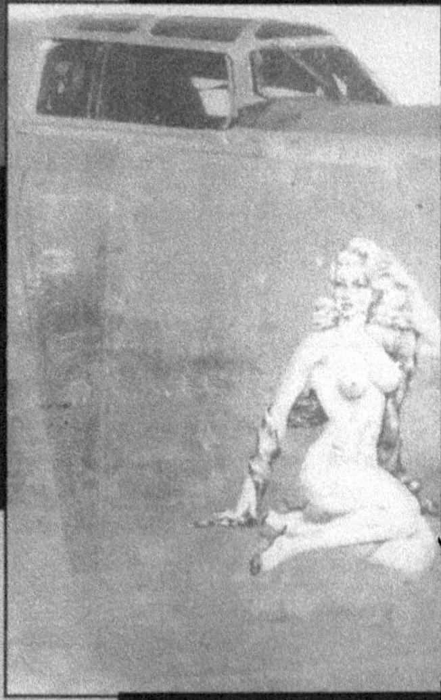

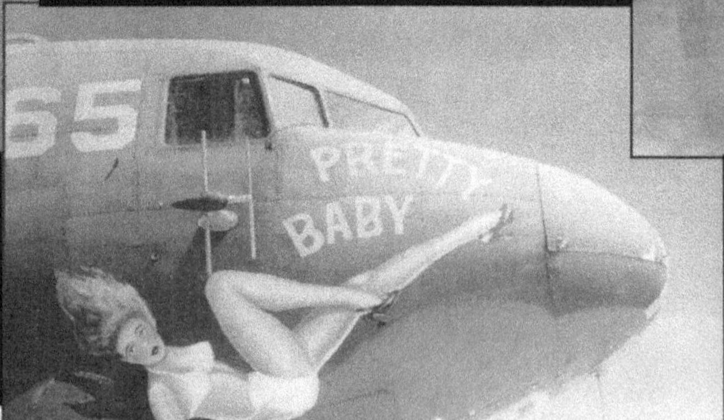
65
PRETTY BABY

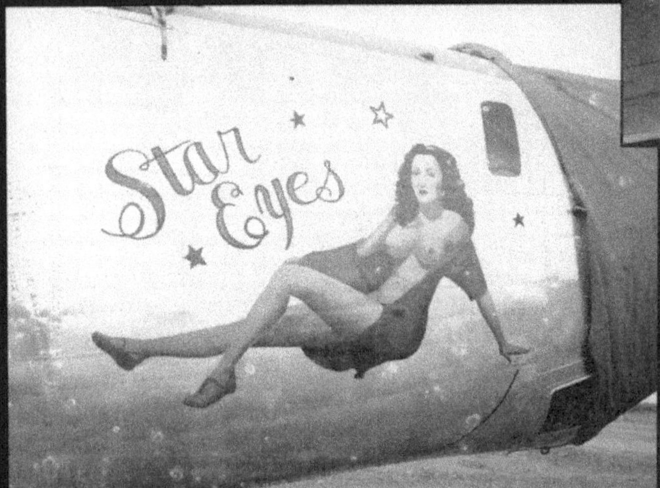
Star Eyes

SWEET THING

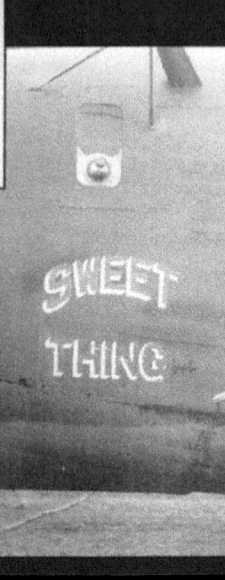

www.ingramcontent.com/pod-product-compliance
Lightning Source LLC
Chambersburg PA
CBHW081847170426
43199CB00018B/2840